EROS & GREEK ATHLETICS

EROS

& GREEK ATHLETICS

Thomas F. Scanlon

UNIVERSITY PRESS

2002

OXFORD
UNIVERSITY PRESS

Oxford   New York
Athens   Auckland   Bangkok   Bogotá   Buenos Aires   Cape Town
Chennai   Dar es Salaam   Delhi   Florence   Hong Kong   Istanbul   Karachi
Kolkata   Kuala Lumpur   Madrid   Melbourne   Mexico City   Mumbai   Nairobi
Paris   São Paulo   Shanghai   Singapore   Taipei   Tokyo   Toronto   Warsaw

with associated companies in
Berlin   Ibadan

Copyright © 2002 by Oxford University Press

Published by Oxford University Press, Inc.
198 Madison Avenue, New York, New York 10016

Oxford is a registered trademark of Oxford University Press

Library of Congress Cataloging-in-Publication Data

Scanlon, Thomas Francis.
    Eros and Greek athletics / Thomas F. Scanlon.
        p. cm.
    Includes bibliographical references and index.
    ISBN 0-19-513889-9; 0-19-514985-8 (pbk.)
        1. Athletics—Greece—History.   2. Sports—Greece—History.   I. Title.
GV21 .S32 2002
796'.09495—dc21   2001021492

9 8 7 6 5 4 3 2 1

Printed in the United States of America
on acid-free paper

L. J. S. *et* M. M. S.

parentibus carissimis

et

W. J. R.

coniugi amatissimae

PREFACE

When I first began teaching and researching in the area of Greek athletics twenty years ago, I immediately saw that it was both a rich area for innovative study and one of the most fascinating windows on the ancient world for students. This study took shape over the past decade, following naturally from a series of three studies I did on women in Greek athletics. A vase in the Getty Museum (figure 8-1) depicting Eros with an athlete first pointed me to the explicit connection of the god with the agonistic sphere. Further study of literary and artistic sources has filled in the abundant and complex associations. Athletics was for the Greeks less a field of dreams than one of desire, where Eros himself played a productive role in the formation of both male and female youths into adults and the establishment of social hierarchy by bestowing honor on victors.

I owe very much to friends and colleagues who have substantively influenced my thinking on Greek culture and athletics generally, and this work in particular: Nigel Crowther, Colin Edmonson, Donald Kyle, Mark Golden, David Larmour, Steve Lattimore, Hugh Lee, Stephen Miller, Harry Pleket, Michael Poliakoff, David Romano, and David Young. I am grateful to Robert Barney of the University of Western Ontario, David Larmour of Texas Tech University, and David Konstan of Brown University for the opportunity to present earlier versions of chapter 8 at their campuses; at each place the feedback of the audience was most appreciated.

I am indebted to dozens of individuals who were helpful in obtaining the photographs for the figures in this text, with particular thanks to the following: Nicoletta Mehrmand and Theda Shapiro of the University of California, Riverside; Jacklyn Burns and Marit Jentoft Nilsen of the J. Paul Getty Museum; Jane Cody of the University of Southern California; Ian McPhee of Latrobe University in Australia; Richard Keresey and Katherine N. Urban of Sotheby's, New York; Robert A. Bridges, Maria Pilali, and especially Marie and Craig Mauzy of the American School of Classical Studies in Athens. George Steinhauer, Director of the Piraeus Museum, Lydia Palaiokrassa of the University of Athens, and Lily Kahil all helped with access to the Arkteia vases in Attica. Faith Tilley, Linda Casteel, and Emily Papavero of the University of California, Riverside, were invaluable in their assistance in contacting rights holders, sending permission fees, and other tasks.

Portions of this work have been previously published in other venues and appear here with the permission of the rights holders, for which I am very grateful. Select portions, totaling 15 pages, from the introduction, and chapters 3, 8, and 10 appeared in my essay "Gymnikē Paideia: Greek Athletics and the Construction of Culture," *Classical Bulletin* 74.2 (1998) 143–57. Chapter 2 is a revised and updated version of my contribution, "The Ecumenical Olympics: The Games in the Roman Era," originally published as 37–64 in *The Olympic Games in Transition*, Jeffrey O. Segrave and Donald Chu, editors (Champaign, Illinois: Human Kinetics Books, 1988). Chapter 4 is a substantially revised and updated version of my article, "The Footrace of the Heraia at Olympia," *The Ancient World* 9 (1984) 77–90. Chapter 5 is a revised version of my contribution, "Virgineum Gymnasium: Spartan Females and Early Greek Athletics," 185–216 in *The Archeology of the Olympics*, W. Raschke, editor (Madison, Wisconsin: University of Wisconsin Press, 1988), reprinted by permission of The University of Wisconsin Press, ©1988. Chapter 6 is a revised version of my article, "Race or Chase at the Arkteia of Attica?" *Nikephoros: Zeitschrift für Kultur im Altertum* 3 (1990) 73–120.

All translations of the ancient Greek or Latin texts and of German, French, or Italian scholarship are my own, unless otherwise indicated. Single quotation marks are used to set off special usages of English terms. The Greek or Latin is quoted for some crucial words, phrases, and passages of ancient texts. Frequently used key terms from Greek, such as *agōn* or *aretē*, have been transliterated. Greek proper names commonly used in a Latinized form in English are given here in that form, for example "Hyacinthus" and "Lycurgus," not "Hyakinthos" and "Lykourgos"; less common Greek names are given in conventional transliteration, for example "Kaisareia."

I thank Candice Getten, my research assistant, for her careful help with the bibliography and copyediting. The Academic Senate and two deans of the College of Humanities, Arts and Social Sciences at the University of California, Riverside, Carlos Vélez-Ibáñez and Patricia O'Brien, have been generous in their funding of my research grants for this project. I am very grateful to Karen Leibowitz, Sunny Lee, Robert Milks, Elissa Morris, and others at the Oxford University Press for their very patient and enthusiastic support.

My deepest debt is to Wendy Raschke, whose contributions have enormously enriched this work through countless conversations, and whose inspiration to me otherwise goes beyond words.

CONTENTS

Introduction—Reconstructing Ancient Sport, 3

1. Greek Athletics and Religion, 25

2. The Ecumenical Olympics—The Games in the Roman Era, 40

3. Athletics, Initiation, and Pederasty, 64

4. Racing for Hera—A Girls' Contest at Olympia, 98

5. "Only We Produce Men"—Spartan Female Athletics and Eugenics, 121

6. Race or Chase of "the Bears" at Brauron? 139

7. Atalanta and Athletic Myths of Gender, 175

8. Eros and Greek Athletics, 199

9. Drama, Desire, and Death in Athletic Performance, 274

10. Conclusions—The Nexus of Athletics, Religion, Gender, and Eros, 323

Abbreviations, 335

Notes, 337

Select Bibliography, 435

Index, 449

EROS & GREEK ATHLETICS

INTRODUCTION—
RECONSTRUCTING ANCIENT SPORT

The last decades of the past century witnessed in many countries the literal and metaphorical unveiling of the body, a huge interest in sports both as a medium of personal fitness and as immensely profitable big business, fervid public discussion of sex and gender, and radical restructuring of conventional religious institutions. Academics concerned with ancient Greece and Rome, spurred on by these cultural dynamics, are asking new questions of ancient material, to some extent so that classical constructions of sex, gender, sports, and religion might open up new perspectives on analogous modern phenomena. Cultural relativity shows us alternative modes of thinking about individual behavior and societal institutions. By noting similarities and differences with the ancient civilizations on which European culture was based, and by recognizing the ways in which cultural constructions in general take place, the dialogue with the past continues to enlighten the present. In this work, explicit comparisons and contrasts with parallel modern phenomena will mostly be left to the readers; many parallels will be obvious from individual experiences of contemporary social contexts.

The primary concern of this study is to characterize Greek athletics and body culture in its connections with religion, sexuality, and rituals for bringing youths to adulthood. My own path to the project began years ago with research for an article on the unusual footrace for girls in the festival of Hera at Olympia, which in turn led to studies of Greek female athletic events in ritual contexts at Sparta and in Attica. Then, during a visit to the Getty Museum in Malibu, California, I came upon a Greek vase that showed two athletes practicing a javelin-throw on one side and a winged figure of the god Eros holding a strigil and facing a javelin-thrower on the other (figure 8–1a and 1b). Eros and the athlete, I discovered, constituted not only an image repeated on many vases but one that has broad connections with Greek sexuality, gender, and religious cults. This work is the result of my exploration of these connections by examination of the artistic and literary sources ranging from the time of Homer in the eighth century B.C. to the end of the ancient Olympics in the late fourth century A.D. This introductory chapter begins with a general outline of the topics I will pursue and with some fundamental observations about the characteristics and ideology of Greek athletics that differ markedly from our own sports.

Religion, Initiation, and Eros

Many questions arise in the attempt to make sense of a variety of ancient activities to which today we give the name 'sports'. What did the ancient Greeks consider to be 'sports'? Was their concept comparable to our own? How were the phenomena formalized in public settings, and how did those formal activities relate to other social institutions such as religion and military training? How did 'sports' transmit societal values, particularly the prescribed roles of each gender, to young Greek men and women? Why was Eros, the divinity of desire, worshipped as a primary god of the gymnasium? How can images in myth or legend illuminate the historical study of this topic? What differences existed from place to place? And how did Greek concepts of sports change over some thousand years from the first Olympics to the period of Roman domination in the early centuries A.D.? To understand Greek athletics without prejudice, we must abandon so far as possible our modern notions of what constitutes sports and what its function is in a society.

This study seeks to understand more clearly Greek athletics, with general reference to the formation and transmission of civic and cultural values which both reinforce and transform the social order. Such a study will, of course, be selective, and cannot include all social aspects of all athletic events for all periods of the ancient Greek world. For the most part, the economics and politics of athletics, about which others have written authoritatively and at length,[1] are of a real but secondary concern here to illuminate the wider social context of certain cultural phenomena. The more standard sports-historical questions, interesting and valuable in their own right, regarding how and why a particular athletic event was played, or how and why a particular city or region indulged in athletics, will be addressed only insofar as they shed light on the questions of cultural history that are the primary focus.[2]

The three broad, interrelated topics to be investigated here include the religious and ritual contexts of athletics, which invest the games with broader cultural and, from the Greek perspective, wider cosmic significance (chapters 1–2); athletic contests that serve as rites of passage to adulthood (chapters 3–7); and the construction of an 'athletic eros' which, in its most general sense, promotes bonds between individuals, groups, or even independent political units (chapter 8).[3] This notion of eros is finally explored as a broader phenomenon of desire in tension with death and risk in athletic contests (chapter 9). For the Greeks, athletics was more a field of desire than of dreams. These aspects of athletics are interrelated: a cultic context reflected humans' relation to divinities and gave authority to the games; athletic contests were attached at various times and places to myths and rituals of initiation to adulthood; and certain gods, including Eros, through their associations with athletic festivals or gymnasia, oversaw and fostered the appropriate roles of gender and sexuality. In short, the Greeks saw athletic phenomena, like much else in their society, as the interaction of divine and human strata within a cosmic hierarchy. The divine was accessible through religious cult and ritual, and gods may act in accord with or in reaction to human behavior. Public sacrifice at the great games or at initiatory rituals, private sacrifice by participants in athletic festivals or by those in gymnasia, and even the athletic competitions at sacred festivals are some of the more obvious instances where Greek athletics and religion overlap. And through a successful competition or a festival, the victorious athlete or producer of the games could win social honor and even power, socially endorsed in part because the success reflected divine favor. We should not assume that all expressions of religious power are mainly the products of practical, secular, political, or social forces, as has often been argued. "[P]ower is not an institution, a structure or a certain force with which certain people are endowed; it is the name given to a complex strategic situation in a given society," cautioned Foucault, and in social hierarchies, political power is not to be privileged above that of the power immanent in religious activities.[4] Athletic competition was, in short, not only bound up with political or economic power but a real manifestation of religious power as the Greeks saw it. All these forms of power are, from a certain viewpoint, culturally constructed and manipulated by members of society, though tradition itself in religion, politics, and so on, had an authority that even the manipulators had to respect in their representation of the construction. Athletics, religion, and sexuality are certainly all 'pawns' in this cultural game, but they carry the weight of received tradition. A careful reading of each cultural element can help us unravel the ways in which they relate to each other and to Greek society as a whole. It was the ritualized and symbolic aspect of the contests together with the Greek focus on the self as an active body that made athletics a particularly powerful vehicle for transmitting social mores, including the relation of the individual to the gods, the formation of gender roles, and the character of sexual relations.

Athenaeus (13.561d) explained the presence of the three gods whose shrines were most frequently found in the ancient gymnasium by positing that Hermes presided over eloquence (λόγος), Heracles over strength (ἀλή), and Eros over friendship (φιλία).[5] This late rationalization accurately reminds us of the historical presence of these cults in the gymnasium since at least the classical period. The three cults served complementary social functions and literally enshrined the ideals of physical strength, bodily beauty, and communication or transition. The first two of these, the domains of Heracles and Eros, are two primary concerns here, the agonistic and erotic spirits. The third god represents a third thematic concern with athletics as a medium of communication and of initiation to adulthood. Hermes, crucial in the narrowly conceived rhetorical and philosophical education of the gymnasium (not of direct concern here), is important as a deity of the transmission of social values, of 'education' very broadly conceived by the Greeks as *paideia*, more properly translated "formation" or "upbringing."[6]

The association of athletics with Greek religious festivals and cultic activities from the earliest historical periods, largely under the influence of the games at Olympia, will be discussed in chapter 1. Chapter 2 examines the attempts to reconcile disparate Roman and Greek interests in the latter centuries of the Olympics and shows how athletics was a tool of cultural unification. The relation between athletics, homosexuality, and rituals that marked the initiation of young males to adulthood is surveyed in chapter 3, with insight into the possible chronological intertwining of these three phenomena. Chapters 4 to 6 focus on initiatory contests for girls, specifically at Olympia, Sparta, and Brauron on the Greek mainland. By investigating the 'fringes' or margins of agonistic activity, specifically the smaller, local athletic festivals involving females, we can come to understand several unique and general characteristics of the Greek games, particularly the way in which they reflect gender roles and transmit cultural ideals. In this regard, the myth of the athletic heroine Atalanta also points to the contrasting, normative male virtues of the Greek athlete (chapter 7). In Chapter 8, a study of Eros, both the Greek god and the concept of "Desire" in relation to athletics reveals an essential and dynamic connection between that figure and *Agon*, the spirit and concept of "Contest." Not only does the competitive ideal underlie the Greek notion of Eros as a struggle, but the essential antagonism of Agon is mitigated or resolved by its association with desire. Athletes are desired and desire; athletes worship Eros; and Eros himself indulges in athletics, even against the ultimate opponent *Anteros*, "Reciprocal Desire." The final chapter (9) discusses the ways in which Greek athletics can be understood metaphorically as a performance in which the element of 'desire,' taken most broadly in the context of competition as a life-affirming impulse (see Lucian, *Anacharsis* 36, quoted later), is balanced against risk of harm, and ultimately against death. The conclusion surveys chronologically the relation of athletics to religion, gender, and sexuality; it investigates the ways in which Greek society has organized its athletics around some of the fundamental ideals of the culture, grafting social contexts and cults to athletics, and athletics to social institutions.

The balance of this introduction discusses, by way of orientation to the social context of Greek athletics, our definition of sports and sports history in relation to the Greeks, sketches Greek society as a 'contest system', and reviews the values that inform that system. In particular, I survey the views of two Greek authors of different periods, Pindar and Lucian, as illustrations of how those values were applied. Next, the story of one exceptional female Olympic victor, Cynisca, is investigated as a reflection of the differences between male and female values in athletics and society generally.

Defining Sport

It can be misleading to speak of a universal 'history of sports,' as if the similar activities have essentially the same function since they recur in various societies over time and can be traced diachronically.[7] While the physical actions may resemble one another, the meanings of those actions are very much the unique construction of the society in which they occur. A 'history' of these pursuits can therefore be meaningfully discussed only to the extent that the activities we call 'sports' in one society have evolved from, or somehow affected those pursuits in, another society. Often the causal links over time are difficult or impossible to detect. In many cases in which a society consciously and explicitly attempts to adopt or adapt the 'sporting' practices of another, the translation results in activities that resemble those of their antecedents in name only. In the example of the modern Olympic movement, which was modeled on the ancient Greek Olympics, the contemporary hybrid is a virtually complete distortion of the ancient reality.[8] So too the Romans completely transformed Greek athletic events into spectacles of entertainment when they grafted a few Greek events onto their public games.[9] One can, of course, attempt to trace a 'history' of wrestling, for example, simply by selecting all known examples from various periods and locales through the centuries, and arguing for direct cross-cultural influences where the evidence warrants. But there will be radical changes in the function of wrestling in, say, the bout between Gilgamesh and Enkidu, the Egyptian duels before the pharaoh, the match of Heracles and Antaeus, the contest at the end of the pentathlon at the ancient Greek festivals, and the exaggerated exhibitions of the World Wrestling Federation seen on American television. Identical techniques and holds may be employed in each, yet the cultural functions will differ radically. It is therefore necessary to explore first the common definitions of sport and to explain the fundamental approach adopted here.

The word "sport" has evolved in English from its earliest meaning of "pastime; diversion; recreation" to the narrower current definition of "a specific diversion, usually involving physical exercise and having a set form and body of rules" only in the past hundred or so years.[10] The sphere of activities covered by the current term is, like much human behavior, a construction of the society in which the activities are found. Almost every society has adopted or created a number of leisure activities, playful competitions, which are most commonly today assigned the name "sports," with appropriate linguistic variants in other languages.[11] Yet the cross-cultural term obscures or obliterates many important functions of these activities within their own cultural context. The precise events and rules vary; even phenomena that bear a superficial resemblance to one another may function in radically different ways from culture to culture. In short, each society invests its sporting activities with a particular set of cultural values preserved in and transmitted by those practices. While the modern term "sport" gives a false sense of the fixed categorization of certain kinds of activity, it also forestalls the better understanding of those activities free of anachronistic prejudice. The 'sport' of any one society can only be understood to the extent that the values, implicit or explicit, of such activity can be understood in their own proper and total historical and social contexts.

Sports are generally acknowledged to be a universal human activity, mutatis mutandis, found in almost all societies and in all eras; indeed they have been seen as an essential and unique trait of human society.[12] Hajo Bernett has defined sport generally as "spontaneous motor activity arising from a playful impulse which aims at measurable performance and regulated competition."[13] This definition differs from the dictionary one given earlier in not requiring the activity to have a "set form," and in omitting reference to "physical exercise," qualities that more accurately describe a popular understanding of the word "sport" but that are not perhaps broadly inclusive enough for all times and cultures. A useful taxonomy of "sport" proposed by Allen Guttmann describes it as a competitive variety of "games," which are in turn an organized form of "play."[14] In the sense that sporting activities are widespread and at least formally analogous in human society, but are not strictly essential for human survival, sports can resemble certain other formalized behavior such as religious ritual, seasonal holiday celebrations, and customs commemorating birth, death, and marriage.

The origins and development of 'sport' have also been studied by scholars for over a century. Guttmann has also offered a list of "seven characteristics of modern sport," namely secularism, equality of opportunity in participation and conditions, secularization of roles, rationalization, bureaucratic organization, quantification, and the quest for records.[15] He argues that each of these characteristics is something found widely in 'sports' of the last century or so and not prevalent in ancient or primitive cultures. While such a general synthesis is useful and thought-provoking, it does not do justice to the specific function of these activities in their own particular societal contexts. Apparent, formal similarities such as the existence or absence of records, the rational or irrational character of rules, and the presence of a bureaucracy are used to characterize phenomena in the broad categories of 'ancient' (or 'primitive') and 'modern' societies. Yet ancient Greece and Rome did exhibit in some form and to a greater or lesser extent all of these supposedly 'modern' characteristics as far back as the contests described by Homer.[16] The very categories of characterization are themselves protean and require much qualification. Another author, David Sansone, proceeding from the thesis that there is "no essential difference between modern sport and the sport of other and earlier societies," maintains that sport is "the ritual sacrifice of physical energy," an essentially human ethological phenomenon, and a relic of palaeolithic hunting cultures.[17] Diachronic studies of formal aspects, like that by Sansone, seek to demonstrate that something called 'sport' exists as an essential phenomenon of human behavior and that differences from one culture to the next are epiphenomenal matters whereby each culture gives different emphases to this essential impulse.

I will not argue that 'sport' is a universal phenomenon. It may or may not be universal and uniquely human. Intuition suggests that if it is, a comprehensive definition, which takes into account all eras, cultures, and varieties of behavior, would be either so complex or so reductive as to be either absurd or meaningless. Nor will I argue that human sports can be accounted for by a single explanation, as Sansone and others have suggested.[18] To do so, in my view, is to argue *obscurum per obscurius* and to be guilty of overstated monocausalism.[19] It is just as reasonable to argue that the limits of human physiology and psychological drives will produce a similar pattern of universal activity in habits of eating, dressing, sexual practices, sleeping, working, and playing, including forms of play currently grouped under the term "sport." Even if a single origin, like religious cult or primitive hunting ritual, could be isolated, it does not follow that origins are the key to all cultural interpretations. A monocausal theory of origins is not required to explain similarities across cultures; a careful social and historical study of sport within a given culture can, however, illuminate important cross-cultural differences.

My approach, then, is to accept the diversity of the phenomena of human cultural activities collected under the overly simple term "sports," to resist imposing a single explanation for these activities, and to investigate each manifestation wholly, as widely as possible in its diachronic and synchronic dimensions, and in its specific historical and cultural contexts. We can thereby judge clearly what those activities meant for those individuals at that period of time. The differences reveal the rich diversity of human experience and the complexity of a single polity.

The focus here is limited to the athletics of the Greeks, including selected topics relating to all periods from the Bronze Age to Roman times. I use the term "athletics" rather than "sports" consistently in this study since in its literal Greek sense "athletics" contains all the connotations the Greeks themselves conveyed in their related terms for "a contest for prizes," $\hat{\alpha}\theta\lambda\alpha$ (ἄεθλα) and $\hat{\alpha}\theta\lambda\sigma\varsigma$ (ἄεθλος), including both "gymnic" and "hippic" events, that is, track and field contests, forms of boxing and wrestling, and chariot- and horse-racing. The Greek phenomenon is in some senses of wider interest than that of other societies, in part because of the influential role of culture in the formation of modern Western notions of athletic competition, most obviously the Olympic Games, and in part because of the rich variety of literary and archaeological evidence, which permits a broad historical study of a culture in many ways foreign to our own in the twenty-first century. The establishment of the modern Olympics has led many to assume mistakenly that in our sports, as in many other aspects of our culture, "we are all Greeks," but the modern realities behind our sporting culture are radically different from its ancient counterparts.[20]

"Body Culture" and the Greek Contest System

The Heracles-Eros-Hermes triad in the gymnasium can, in a sense, stand for the physical, spiritual, and intellectual aspects of the individual which are fostered by the contest system. The *agōn* or "contest" is the unifying concept behind the themes of this work, and it is important to understand its social context. Jacob Burckhardt's influential thesis, which argues that the Greek *agōn* is unique and central to our understanding of ancient society, has rightly been criticized in detail, yet his main point remains true.[21] A. Gouldner, in a useful elaboration of the "Greek contest system," derives a number of chief themes in Greek culture from the agonal spirit.[22] Gouldner notes that the Greeks prized youth, health, and beauty, all objects with a "body locus," and that not so much the possession of these goods as fame itself, the more stable and enduring product of them, constituted the superior honor in that society. The ideology of the athlete in particular held physical beauty and strength as claims to fame, as Greek literature and honorary decrees frequently attest.[23] The proliferation in the archaic age of probably about twenty thousand *kouroi* statues, larger than life and idealized images of naked youths (or youthful divinities), testifies to the widespread idolization of the healthy male figure.[24] "Fame" (Greek *kleos*, *timē*, *eukleia*, etc.) is of course a very broad concept. To the bodily centered objects which, according to Gouldner, foster fame, we could add many others that promote a "good life," "happiness," and, ipso facto, fame in the Greek view. Lucian's Solon, in *Anacharsis* 15 quoted below, cites not only bodily health as a prime product of athletics, but also personal and civic freedom, enjoyment of ancestral festivals, security for the household, and even wealth.

These lists of the possessions that bestow fame raise several questions regarding the value of extrinsic objects ("wealth"), the personal-civic polarity, and the relation of self to society. Wealth is intrinsically neither good nor evil in Greek thought, nor is it, according to many such as Herodotus' Solon (1.32.), essential for happiness and fame.[25] So Gouldner is correct to stress the Greeks' "low object-attachment," or lack of attachment to extrinsic and ephemeral possessions, and to see their "basic locus of security in the embodied self." Possessions external to the self are not valued as ends in themselves, but as manifestations of personal honor. The self-seeking greediness and gluttony of "the race of athletes" in Euripides' *Autolycus* and of comic heroes in Aristophanes illustrate a kind of baseness which may have been common in social behavior but is used mainly as a negative exemplum.[26] The ideal of low object-attachment may also be evidenced in the absence of value prizes in Panhellenic athletic contests, while the reality of human acquisitiveness was served by lavish prizes from less prestigious local contests and by valuable compensation from one's own polis for the honor of a Panhellenic victory.

One common Greek term for "person" or "individual" is *sōma*, literally and originally meaning simply "body."[27] A focus on the "embodied self" does not imply that the individual is completely self-sufficient, but that he or she must attain honor through *personal* achievement while remaining a member in good standing of the polity. The Herodotean Solon, using that very term, in fact asserts that no individual/body (*sōma*) is self-sufficient in the personal struggle for happiness and honor.[28] It is clear that the fame of the individual member of the polis will redound upon the household and the community, particularly for athletes participating in public festivals. "Body locus" and "body culture" as discussed here, then, refer both to identification of "person" with "body" in Greek language and culture, and to the evaluation of fame by the actual achievements of the individual "body" in its civic context.

The contest system is further characterized by Gouldner as follows. Fame must be achieved by one's own, active efforts, usually recognized as *aretē* or "excellence." The social struggle to attain fame was a "zero-sum" contest, that is, one in which the glorification of one individual often entailed the diminution of others.[29] The total amount of glory is finite, and at any given time it cannot be spread thinly over large numbers of citizens. In a public contest, a few were proclaimed victors and most were left as anonymous "also-rans." The striving for glory often provoked envy and required the exercise of shame (*aidōs*) to guard against excess in effort (*hybris*).[30] Pindar, as we shall see, illustrates these values in reference to the athlete. Sexuality is, in Greece and many societies, a common arena in which honor is won, lost, or displayed. The contest system, Gouldner argues, benefited Greek society indirectly by leading to the establishment of alternatives that unify citizens despite the self-seeking impetus of competition, notably rationalism and homosexuality. This latter point will be discussed at length in chapter 8, where, we may add, heterosexual relations are also shown to be a factor in the contest system. By emphasizing individual achievement over incidental wealth, or what you are instead of what you own, the system encouraged a search for value in personal excellence. In particular it encouraged the high valuing of ideas that are freely available, such as "wisdom" and other demonstrations of rationalism most fully expounded by Plato and Aristotle. Though *mens sana in corpore sano*, "a healthy mind in a healthy body," is a Roman dictum, it expresses well the spirit espoused by Plato in his *Republic*. The schools of Plato, Aristotle, and the Cynics were, after all, founded in the settings of gymnasia.

The essential 'rule' of the contest system, then, was to win more fame than others. This form of rank-demonstration could be pursued by various means, including success in warfare, provision of honorific liturgies, verbal persuasion, and athletic competition before impartial judges. The amount of fame acquired depended upon the value of the stakes, the degree of risk ventured, the status of the opponent, and the degree of fame acquired in the past. As applied to athletics, the prestige of the contest, real or symbolic value of the prize, fierceness of the competition, and past record of victories all determined the qualification of fame. Thus Greek athletes, particularly in the Hellenistic and Roman eras, delighted in listing on victory inscriptions any special qualifications of their victories, namely winning by a "walkover" (*akoniti*), without drawing a bye, without a fall, as the first of one's countrymen, with multiple victories in different events on the same day, and so on.[31]

"The wreath or death" was more than a hyperbolic boast. The trainer of a competitor in pankration, a fierce combination of boxing, wrestling, and kick-boxing, wrote in praise to the boy's mother: "If you should hear that your son has died, believe it, but if you hear that he has been defeated, do not believe it."[32] Some primary modern ideals—health, sportsmanship or entertainment—were important, but clearly secondary to fame in the Greek athletic hierarchy.[33] Historically, Greek athletics almost always took place as a part of religious festivals, and one's performance in them was taken as a measure of status and honor. As such, athletics was pursued with deadly seriousness and with one eye on our human relation to the divine cosmos; winning was supremely important; almost all contests were competitions between individuals; and participation was open to all classes from an early period.[34]

Paideia and the Contest System

The contest system, both in everyday life and in athletics, had important corollary rules, however, which placed the competition for honor in its wider cultural and historical contexts. While contests, athletic and otherwise, were generally taken very seriously in all cities and in all periods of Greek culture, the qualification of fame and the means by which it was obtained varied. And the contest itself could be circumvented or mitigated in various important ways. If absolute detachment from the system was rare or impossible, degrees of self-sufficiency could still be asserted according to individual prejudices. In the field of athletic competition, individuals could eschew participation to avoid dishonor. Alcibiades in the late fifth century B.C. is said to have disdained gymnic contests in view of the low birth, village origins, and poor education of the competitors.[35] And Xenophanes ca. 525 B.C. criticized the custom of honoring the strength of the athlete above the wisdom of the philosopher.[36]

More frequently athletics was justified and its brutal ethic of "victory-or-death" was mitigated by appeal to the ameliorating social effects of public contests. Lucian and Pindar contribute extensively to this rationale, as we shall shortly see, and the cults of Heracles, Eros, and Hermes in the gymnasium are reminders of different aspects of the social benefits. One scholar has demonstrated how a variety of collective activities or "rituals of conviviality," including those of cult associations, informal political groups, cliques of friends, and gatherings of athletes contribute in various ways to the polis.[37] These group activities can provide socialization in political life, apprenticeship in civic values, and places for expressing social order—"the disparities of fortune, the hierarchies of power," as Schmitt-Pantel notes. Each activity is an instrument of *paideia*, of social formation.[38] The importance of these groups, it is argued, changes over time, so that while they fulfill the roles of civic institutions more widely in the archaic age, by the fourth century B.C. collective activities belong to the common domain and are not the sole possession of an élite political stratum. By the later period, political assemblies are less directly controlled by the aristocrats than they had been in earlier social organizations.

Greek *agōnes*, public contests, clearly epitomize the culture's contest system, both in the struggle of individuals for fame, and in the positive benefits of "rituals of conviviality." Athletics also intersects with a number of other crucial, collective activities, namely religious cults, erotic liaisons, politico-economic fraternities, symposia, and choral groups.[39] Athenaeus (14.629b), for example, illustrates the complexity of these intersections when he suggests that the movements of "ancient" (presumably classical or earlier) dance influenced the shapes of ancient statues, whose postures (*schēmata*) were in turn carried over to choral dance and then to palaestra exercises: "For by means of the music and the concern for their bodies [τῇ τῶν σωμάτων ἐπιμελείᾳ] they acquired courage and for movements in armor they exercised accompanied by song." However specious this aetiology of the third century A.D. writer may be, it demonstrates a very traditional association between several collective activities and social realia: dance, sculpture, choruses, music, song, and athletic exercise.[40] In particular, these bodily centered phenomena were thought to foster the valor of the heroic warrior. The Spartan educational system was renowned for its integration of competition into all aspects of adolescent life, as Xenophon writes with regard to the concerns of the legendary reformer, 'Lycurgus':

> Since he saw that those who had in them the strongest spirit of rivalry
> [φιλονεικία] produced choruses most worthy of hearing and athletic
> contests most worthy of seeing, he thought that, if he could join the
> youths in a struggle for excellence [ἀρετῆς], they would also in this
> way best arrive at a high degree of many nobility.
> (*Respublica Lacedaemoniorum* 4.1–2)

Aside from the vexed problem of the historicity of Lycurgus and his alleged reforms, this passage again reflects the traditional Greek obsession with a contest system that can be both validated and moderated by a program of collective activities such as choruses and athletics. My study investigates some of the broader cultural connections of the Greek contest system, centered ultimately on the embodied self and its *paideia* through group activities.

Historicizing Athletic Ideology

Like the social and political functions of other group activities of the polis, those of athletics changed over time. Equestrian contests remained consistently the domain of the powerful and wealthy who alone could finance participation. But the so-called gymnic events, today considered athletics proper, normally the running contests, the combat sports, and discus and javelin events as part of the pentathlon, were probably more the arena of the élite prior to the fifth century B.C. but saw the wider participation of all classes of citizens thereafter.[41] The change in social background of athletes in the fifth century coincides roughly with the general shift in control over collective activities out of the hands of the traditional aristocracy after the archaic age. This is not to suggest that athletics lost its informal political influence in the fifth and fourth centuries, as the importance of social liaisons in gymnasia and ephebic groups clearly attest, but that, like other group activities, the political ties of athletics probably became less necessary and less direct. To the extent that there was an increase in athletic participation by the non-élite in the fifth century, their ability to share in aristocratic ideology may indicate a less rigid and more democratic social hierarchy of that period. In any case, and more crucial to our main themes here, Pleket has argued that the ideology of the élite dominated the gymnic events throughout their history, and that this ideology is transmitted in literature from Homer, the 'Bible' of the Greeks, to Pindar, and to later authors like Lucian and Philostratus. Displays of the "manly and military values of sport," generally labelled *aretē* (excellence) but including *andreia* (courage), *ponos* (toil), *karteria* (endurance), and others, added to the honor of the athlete. While Pleket accurately notes the values and their line of transmission, the ideology is more accurately that of the good warrior than necessarily of a noble 'élite.'

Originally, Homeric *aretē* was the quality of the best fighters, and only tied to nobles since they happened to have served as the warrior class prior to the eighth century. The flowering of a hoplite system of warfare (heavily armed men with shields and spears in massed battle formations) in the seventh and sixth centuries B.C. displaced the aristocracy from their privileged position as the warriors of the city, and "deprived of significance in the military sphere, the *agōn* centered on sport."[42] While hoplites included both aristocrats and other citizens of moderate means who could afford the armor, athletes probably comprised a similar social admixture of all who had sufficient leisure and capital to train for the contest. This is not to say that athletic training served directly as military training. Tyrtaeus, the seventh-century poet of Spartan war songs contrasted athletic skill unfavorably with martial prowess (fr. 12.1–2, 10–14, West), and Euripides echoed the criticism (*Autolycus*, fr. 282).[43] The military benefits of gymnic exercises were mostly indirect. Yet the ethos of *aretē* was held in common; it permeated both the hoplite ranks and the realm of athletes and thereby united diverse strata of society in the archaic period. The use of hoplites waned in the fifth century, but an adherence to martial values persisted.

Thus, the array of moral virtues and sense of civic responsibility conveyed by athletics remained, in name at least, fairly constant despite sociological changes in the participants. Yet the precise interpretation of certain values could become politically charged. In the late archaic age, the theme of "envy of the successful or prominent man," as illustrated, for example, in Pindar, became more urgent when it was seen to be directed against the aristocracy in general by a more democratic society.[44] Plato criticizes the type of shame (*aidōs*) enforced in the educational system of timocratic societies like Sparta that emphasized athletic and physical education over a more balanced education in which musical and intellectual pursuits were combined with athletics in his ideal state (*Republic* 547d–548b).[45]

Lucian, Pindar, and the Ethos of Athletics

Ancient texts are our best sources for the ways in which athletics was thought to transmit social values, and thereby to mitigate or justify the overt antagonism of the contest system. I have chosen, for reasons of chronological diversity and richness of narrative, Lucian's *Anacharsis* and select passages of Pindar's *Odes* to illustrate what the values were and how they were thought to be communicated. Lucian's *Anacharsis* is an imaginary comic prose dialogue written ca. A.D. 170, but set in Athens of the sixth century B.C., between the Athenian lawgiver Solon and a visiting Scythian and famous sage after whom the work is named. Here we have a justification of athletics by the Greeks themselves to those from other cultures; Lucian, a native of Syria, was no doubt sensitive to the outsiders' puzzlement at Greek customs. The setting is the Lyceum, the famous gymnasium of Aristotle, where the foreign visitor wonders at athletic practices and questions their social value. Lucian invests this account with the humor of miscommunication between men of very different cultures, and Solon's defense of Greek agonistic culture is cliché-filled and rhetorically overdone.[46] Yet Lucian's fictional construction, written in the second century A.D., accurately reflects some of the widely shared values found in the Homeric epics, in Pindar, and in other literary and epigraphical testimonia.

It is not coincidental that Lucian's dialogue is set at a time before Greek athletics had become the common cultural coin of the Eastern Mediterranean region, as they were by the time of Lucian himself. This gives the author the opportunity to represent an anachronistic and non-Greek viewpoint, a view analogous to that of Herodotus' wonder at non-Greek customs or to that of a modern cultural anthropologist who wonders about behavior without parallel in his own land. Lucian's work is useful for us in this regard; it distances us, as it did his original audience, from the familiar events of Greek athletics. In the dialogue (6), Solon assures the visitor that athletics may seem to be an "insanity" or a display of "excessive violence" (μανία ... ἐφ᾽ ὕβρει), but it really has "a certain utility not without pleasure" (τινὰ χρείαν οὐκ ἀτερπῆ) and contributes a "healthy bloom" (ἀκμὴν) to the body. The type of "pleasure" here is Greek *terpsis*, the emotion of enjoyment associated with Greek games since Homer, the "delight" essential to competition, the "joy" of participation in the contest, even though the delight involves physical pain and effort.[47] The "bloom" or "prime" of the body is the glow of the peak of beauty that was axiomatic in Greek love poetry for an essential quality of sexual attractiveness.

The famous physician Galen, Lucian's contemporary, vehemently denied the alleged benefits of health and beauty from athletics (*Adhortatio ad artes* 11–12). Health, Galen contends, is impaired by excesses of overexertion and overeating, while beauty is even ruined by overfattening and becoming maimed in competition. Whatever the validity of Galen's complaints, which echo the overstatement of other elitist critics in antiquity, the remarks actually support the view expressed in Lucian's *Anacharsis* that health and beauty were commonly valued as by-products of the athletic life.

These are personal benefits. Following the general lines of Plato's arguments for inclusion of athletics in education in the ideal state (*Rep.* 3, 403c–404e, 410b–412b, 441e–442a), Lucian's Solon also defends the social good derived from the practice of athletics by the youth. Prizes are not the reason for the contests since very few are able to win; a greater good is sought for the entire polis:

> For a certain other contest is established in common for all good citizens and the crown is not of pine or laurel or wild celery, but one which includes human happiness, such as I might call freedom both of oneself individually and of the state in common, and wealth, fame, enjoyment of ancestral festivals, safety for one's household, and, in sum, the finest benefits which one might pray to receive from the gods. All these are bound up in the crown of which I speak and they arise from that contest to which these exercises and labors lead. (*Anacharsis* 15)

Lucian here draws upon a metaphorical sense of a spiritual "contest" and the "crowns" of freedom and happiness that are won by those who participate in athletics. He draws upon the imagery of Pericles' famous description of the liberal, democratic spirit of classical Athens (Thuc. 2.38, 46) but reappropriates the image to imply that freedom and happiness of the state are in some way directly a product of the practice of athletics. And it is noteworthy that these positive attributes that lead to fame are ultimately ascribed to the gods. The ways in which athletic contests promote civic and personal well-being are further indicated by Lucian's Solon at the end of his dialogue:

> [At athletic festivals, the spectator's] zeal for the athletic events is thereby increased if they see the best among the competitors honored and proclaimed as victors in the midst of the assembled Greeks. . . . The prizes then . . . are not small, namely praise from the spectators, to become most distinguished, and to be pointed out as one thought to be the best among equals. Therefore many of the spectators who are still of the age to participate in athletics will go away from such experiences with an inordinate desire for excellence and hard work. (*Anach.* 36)

Here the attractions of rank-demonstration are made explicit. Solon thus sees the public contests as a direct inducement, or rather a seduction provoking "inordinate eros" (οὐ μετρίως . . . ἐρασθέντες) whereby the desire of the observers as well as the participants will be aroused to excel and do one's best in all areas of life. In short, the games bestow not only health upon participants and delight for the athletes and spectators, but they ennoble all of society by inspiring real achievement. Athletes, in Lucian's dialogue and elsewhere in Greek literature, therefore see this activity as a symbolic one, a kind of *paideia* that can directly affect behavior in nonathletic endeavors.[48]

Despite Lucian's humorous, cross-cultural dialectic in the *Anacharsis*, we can observe a conventional defense of Greek athletics and the "human freedom" that they afford, a term summarizing all the particular benefits such as health and the delight in contests. Another rich literary source for understanding the symbolic value of athletics is, most obviously, Pindar. Pindar's victory ode "anticipates, or enacts, the re-incorporation of the returning athlete into his community; along with the praise of his achievements , and the comparisons with the greater, yet more ambivalent heroes of myth."[49] Thus the poems and the virtues they extol embrace in literal and figurative images both the struggle of the individual to achieve fame, and the civic benefits obtained from the collective activity.

The primary athletic virtue, like that of the heroic warrior, was *aretē* (ἀρετή), an untranslatable term, including notions of "manly excellence," "merit," "achievement," and "accomplishment."[50] The fact that *aretē* was so pervasive a concept in all aspects and in all eras of Greek culture does not dilute its importance in the sphere of athletics; it suggests that athletic *aretē* shared the essential qualities of the generalized notion of *aretē* and could therefore have widespread symbolic importance. In the traditional view of Pindar, *aretē* was something obtained by nature, improved by practice, and seen through to success with the assistance of the gods, as expressed in this ode to a victor in boys' boxing:

> Sharpening one who is naturally excellent [φύοντ' ἀρετᾷ],
> a man [as trainer], with the guiding hand of god, can rouse him to
>   enormous fame.
>
> (*Ol.* 10. 20–21)[51]

The chief purpose of *aretē* within the social contest system was "to win fame" (κῦδος [κλέος, εὖχος] ἀρέσθαι), to obtain a measure of immortality, and to do so in accordance with the prosperity of one's family and community.[52] The dictum of Laodamas to Odysseus in inviting him to compete in their contests is the locus classicus of this attitude:

> There is no greater fame [κλέος] for a man, so long as he lives,
> than that which he achieves by both his hands and his feet.
>
> (Homer, *Od.* 8. 147–48)

The sentiment is echoed in Pindar, where a father who was an Olympic victor lives to see his son win in the Pythian Games. Here the fame of the victor is redoubled by the achievement of his son:

... but blessed and worthy of the poet's song is the man
who by the power of his hands and the excellence (ἀρετᾷ) in his feet
takes by strength and daring the highest of prizes,
and then, while still alive, sees his young son
in due turn attain the Pythian crown.

(P. 10.22–26)

What matters is not only the honor that accrues to one victor, but the transmission of that spirit of excellence from one generation to another.[53] So the primary athletic values are excellent achievement and good reputation, which Pindar states in other terms at the end of an ode that can be taken to apply to all aspects of life:

To enjoy success is the first of prizes;
to be well spoken of is the second best fate; the man who
attains and holds both of these
receives the highest crown.

(P. 1.99–199b)

A complex of other athletic values in Pindar are found beside these primary ones, notable among them the positive preconditions for success, namely work (πόνος), expense (δαπάνα), risk (κίνδυνος), an attitude of respect (αἰδώς), and the aid of the gods:[54]

Work and expense always in the company of excellent accomplishments (ἀρεταῖσι) struggle for a deed, wrapped in risk. (Ol. 5. 16–17)

Excellent achievements without risk [ἀκίνδυνοι δ᾽ἀρεταὶ] are honored neither among men, nor in hollow ships; many remember if something fine is accomplished with toil [πονηθῇ]. (Ol. 6.9–11)

Expenditure of effort and resources, accompanied by innate excellence, are therefore required to attain victory and win fame. And it is essential that the task be characterized by risk to elevate the status of the deed. The accomplishment is ordinarily neither remembered nor honored if any of these vital components is absent. So Pelops, legendary founder of the Olympics, prays to Poseidon before the famous chariot race to win Hippodameia as his bride and there makes clear the incentive for any individual to face risks to avoid obscurity. He also illustrates the need for human and god to cooperate in the successful completion of the task. Obviously this athletic strategy has much broader implications for the social contest system generally:

Great risk does not attach itself to a man without [a display of] strength.
... Since men must die, why should anyone sit in darkness and

foolishly lead a life ending in an obscure old age without his allotted
portion of all good things? So this contest [ἄεθλος] is my lot, may you in
turn grant the fair deed. (*Ol.* 1.81–85)

The athletic value of *aidōs* has a range of meanings including "moderation,"
"restraint," "shame," or "respect," all of which indicate that the athlete's achievement needs to be tempered or checked in view of given realities of power, authority, or convention. Furthermore *aidōs* can be obtained from or fostered by the gods.
After listing an impressive string of athletic victories in one ode, Pindar prays, "Zeus,
god of accomplishment, grant restraint [αἰδῶ] and the sweet fortune of delight
[τερπνῶν]" (*Ol.* 13.115–115b).[55] The proper modesty is required to temper the pride
of achievement so that it will provoke envy in neither gods nor humans. Pindar
indicates that *aidōs*, and with it one's fame, can be eroded or erased by improper
demonstrations of desire for material gain: "*Aidōs* which brings fame is secretly stolen away by desire for gain" (*N.* 9.33–34).[56] Even though Greek ideology espoused
"low object-attachment," the reality was that competitors were sometimes (often?)
attracted to value prizes as ends in themselves. We may recall that, in later years,
at least one athlete was disqualified from the Olympics for dishonoring the games
by arriving late after collecting cash prizes at local contests en route.[57] It has also
been shown that the material rewards for competitors were great in Pindar's day
and earlier.[58]

Another aspect of the complex of athletic values is *hybris* (ὕβρις), the negative
characteristic, antithetical to *aidōs*, whereby one deliberately inflicts dishonor on
others to enhance one's own stature.[59] *Hybris* is a vice endemic to the Greek contest system, and one that all civic ideology disdains. The hybristic individual may
appear to challenge the gods, or to behave like an animal. Pindar in fact associates
hybris with the violent behavior typical of animals (*P.* 10.36; *N.* 1.50). And the poet,
in an ode for Diagoras the Rhodian boxer, combines the themes of aversion to *hybris*
with those of *aretē*, *aidōs*, and the need for divine assistance:

Honor, father Zeus, . . .
the man who has found excellence with his fist (πὺξ ἀρετὰν), grant him
    the favor of a respected reputation (αἰδοίαν χάριν)
among both fellow citizens and strangers. When he walks straight on
    the path hostile to insolent violence (ὕβριος),
you clearly illuminate the ways which the upright minds of his ances-
    tors used.

(*Ol.* 7. 87–92)

Diagoras has demonstrated his *aretē*, and Zeus is asked to bestow on him the favor-
able reputation characteristic of the boxer's own restraint. This *aidōs* is further
shown in the athlete's aversion to violence, which is in accordance with his ances-

tral character,[60] again a mark of natural *aretē*. If the poet's prayerful petition is fulfilled, the athlete will have respect in turn from his fellow citizens and from strangers (*xenoi*), that is, he will be properly reincorporated into the community and the wider world with a newly magnified status.

Lucian's Solon is quick to point out to the barbarian that the punching and tumbling of the athletes is not done out of *hybris* or insanity, but for a certain social utility (*Anach.* 6). Later in the same work, he points out that athletic training serves the state by diverting youthful wildness away from its inclination to insolent violence (ὑπ' ἀργίας εἰς ὕβριν τρεπομένοις, 30). We see in the two passages of Lucian the apparent paradox in Greek attitudes toward violent behavior. Physical force, commonly expressed by the Greek term *bia* ("bodily strength," "force"; "violence"), was sanctioned in the controlled environment of the stadium where an outsider might mistakenly call it *hybris*, "insolent violence" in our terms, that is, force taken too far. But similar acts of insolent dishonoring of others were censured when undertaken in public; *hybris* by definition implies that these acts were committed without acceptable justification.[61] Context and the apparent intention of the actor determine the social acceptability of the action.

Despite their separation by about six and a half centuries, Pindar and Lucian endorse essentially the same athletic ideology, centered on the *aretē* of the embodied self, reliant on the assistance of patron deities, requiring the restraint of *aidōs* against *hybris*, and valorizing the contributions of this ethos to the community at large. The collective activity of athletics incorporating the ethos of the heroic warrior, and perhaps of the earlier élite as well, arguably surpassed all other "rituals of conviviality" by enabling athletes and audience to reenact heroic-type contests. Athletic *aretē* thus not only embodied in microcosm the spirit of the ancestral contest system, it offered one way in which the rifts created by the system could be healed by the communal spirit of the athletic festival. Nonathletic religious rituals, other forms of *paideia* and initiation of children to adulthood, and the more or less formal bonds of sexual relations also served to mitigate antagonism in the struggle for personal fame. But athletics often overlapped with these spheres of social interaction and thus affords a unique and crucial perspective from which to view Greek society.

Women and the Contest System

In ancient Greek society, almost all public business was carried on by men, whereas women's duties and spheres of influence were restricted to the home.[62] Greek athletics and the contest system in general were, not surprisingly, almost exclusively part of the male domain and constituted a very strongly male, quasi-heroic ideal and served to reinforce patriarchal religious and social hierarchies. The few, important exceptions in early Greece, to be discussed later, were isolated athletic contests exclusively for girls in honor of deities who had power over important aspects of women's life. The complex of athletic values surrounding female competitions differed almost entirely from those of men. Thus, before we proceed further, we need to understand the place of the female in the system. In classical Greece, female *aretē* and reputation were in general very differently defined, most famously perhaps in the dictum of Thucydides' Pericles, who says that "[f]ame will be great for you not to fall short of your nature, such as it is, and for the woman whose reputation (κλέος) for excellence (ἀρετῆς) or blame is least known among males" (2.45.2).[63] In other words, women's fame and excellence were in this assessment reckoned almost exclusively in the private sphere, in the domain of the household, specifically in terms of being a good daughter, wife, and mother.[64]

Female *aidōs*, accordingly, normally referred to a kind of shame or decorum related to propriety or loyalty in the roles of daughter or wife and mother, most especially in sexual mores.[65] Although women competed in a contest system with different rules, their physical beauty could still contribute to their fame, and, as with men, their appearance had to be attended by virtues such as *aidōs* to win good repute. Thus, the saying of a Hellenistic philosopher:

> Neither in a male child, nor in maidens
> who win the gold (παρθέων τῶν χρυσοφόρων), nor in deep-bosomed
>   women
> is their appearance fair, unless it is by nature adorned.
> For modesty (αἰδὼς) is that which fertilizes the bloom.
>   (Clearchus, *FGH* 2.314 [4–3 c. B.C.], *ap.* Ath. 13.564b)

The reference to "maidens who win the gold" probably refers to girls such as those living in a city on the Alpheus River near Olympia, who, winning the prize in a beauty contest, were known by such an epithet (Ath. 13.609f). *Aidōs* is therefore particularly important for women of all ages, as it is for boys, since all of these are socially subordinate to adult males. Apart from the rare beauty contest, however, girls had far fewer opportunities to exhibit *aidōs* or other virtues in a public forum than did boys.

One exception that proves this rule as applied to the realm of athletics is the story of the most famous female victor, indeed an Olympic victor, Cynisca of Sparta.[66] Women were excluded from competing in the Olympics, except for the chariot- and horse-race events where, like today, the owner and not the jockey or driver were honored as victor. The first such female victor was Cynisca, who won in the four-horse chariot race at Olympia ca. 390 B.C. We are fortunate to have as sources indicating contemporary attitudes to this phenomenon the literary testimonia of Xenophon, Plutarch, Pausanias, and her victory epigram, preserved both in the *Palatine Anthology* and on an inscription found at Olympia:[67]

Σπάρτας μὲν βασιλῆες ἐμοὶ πατέρες καὶ ἀδελφοί·
ἅρματι δ᾽ ὠκυπόδων ἵππων νικῶσα Κυνίσκα
εἰκόνα τάνδ᾽ ἔστασα. μόναν δ᾽ ἐμέ φαμι γυναικῶν
Ἑλλάδος ἐκ πάσας τόνδε λαβεῖν στέφανον.

My fathers and brothers were kings of Sparta.
I, Cynisca, having won with a team of swift-footed horses,
dedicated this statue. I assert that I am the only woman
in all Greece to have taken this crown.

Victory boasts do ordinarily record "firsts" on "onlys" of the following sort: "first to win event *x* and *y* on the same day," or "first athlete from city *x* to win at *y* games," and so on.[68] But this epigram displays what is, so far as I am aware, the only athletic victory dedication claiming distinction on the basis of gender. A few other women did follow Cynisca as Olympic chariot victors, and most of these were also daughters of wealthy nobles or rulers.[69] Certainly these women won some political capital for the fatherland, but also the prospect of some visibility as women attracted them to the competition, as Cynisca's proud epigram attests.

Yet a very interesting anecdote told by Xenophon and Plutarch about Cynisca's entry into Olympic fame would seem to eclipse her pride in her sex: "[King Agesilaus] persuaded his sister Cynisca to breed horses for chariot-racing, and showed by her victory that this breed is not an example of manly valor (*andragathias*), but of wealth" (Xen., *Ages.* 9.6).[70] The assumption here is that, if a woman can accomplish this deed, it therefore reflects not *aretē*, but some other quality, namely, in this case, possession of wealth.[71] It was doubtless as true then as it is today that any individual, male or female, could raise prize-winning horses, since that requires only the money with which to feed, stable, hire trainers, own land for training, and so on. The fact that Agesilaus had to use a woman to make this point illustrates my point, that "excellent accomplishments" in public competition were considered a male prerogative, and that when or if a woman equaled a normally male achievement, the excellence of that achievement was at once called into question. As I said earlier, this anecdote would seem to be at odds with Cynisca's victory epigram.

The public inscription was written under a very impressive bronze sculpture by Apelles showing an almost life-sized team of horses, driver, and Cynisca herself. Such an impressive monument would of course not have been the place for Agesilaus to make his point about excellence versus wealth. That would have impugned the excellence not only of his sister, but of every Greek who ever won in the hippic events at Olympia! Yet Agesilaus must have been tempted to make his point once and for all in writing "to the Greeks" at Olympia, as the anecdote relates. Ironically, Cynisca herself became the most famous woman Olympic victor of all time (Paus. 3.8.1), and her epigram and monument at Olympia no doubt contributed to her fame. Even today a sourcebook on women in the ancient world records the victory epigram but omits the anecdote about Agesilaus.[72]

So Cynisca resides in that ambiguous middle ground between male and female athletic values, achieving and not achieving *aretē* and fame usually reserved for males. Perhaps Cynisca's problematic athletic fame is balanced by another, less well publicized monument that displays her concurrent devotion to a role that is clearly female. A small Doric capital with her name on it, apparently set up as a base for a dedication to Helen, was found at Sparta.[73] Cynisca was, therefore, a devotee of the heroine/goddess who was admired by Spartan girls gathered at their racecourse and had "the role of conducting Lacedaimonian adolescent girls to full sexual maturity."[74] To Cynisca we may compare another woman of the first century A.D., Damodica of Cyme in Asia Minor, whose epitaph states that she died "not without fame since she left a son and the glory of victory in a four-horse chariot."[75] Like Cynisca, Damodica obtained both traditional female and male types of fame.

The general exclusion from the public sphere not only kept women from competing against men at public athletic festivals, as one might expect on the basis of general differences in strength; it also kept them for the most part from competing against each other at established festivals, or from forming their own women's athletic festivals; the few notable examples will be examined in detail later.[76] Participation in those few games for women were restricted to unmarried girls, and the contests themselves were in all known instances footraces. That is, the games for women were not meant as demonstrations of the excellence of adult females, who were kept to the house,[77] but as celebrations by maidens of their transitional, prenuptial status between the 'wildness' of adolescence of the past and the 'tameness' to come with marriage. The restriction of the competition to footraces indicates, on one hand, that the games themselves were of the least violent sort and thus far removed from the elements of 'risk' and the need to avoid *hybris* of the physically violent sort which could characterize men's contests. But footraces also indicate that female contests literally reenacted, as we shall see, the abstract state of transition and eager orientation to a "goal," the natural *telos* of wife and mother according to Greek culture.[78] As we shall see in the chapters to follow, the cultic and ritual contexts of both men's and women's contests not only support the interpretation of athletic values outlined above, they add to it the dynamic aspect of performance which displays those values in action to both athletes and audience.

The customary exclusion of females from participation in athletic festivals is analogous to their exclusion from taking part in hunting, warfare, or any other of the public activities reserved for men. Only later under the Roman Empire, in the first century A.D., is there any evidence of young women personally competing in traditionally men's athletic festivals in such contests as chariot racing or footraces. But even here girls probably competed only against other girls.[79] Mention of girls personally entering athletic competitions at established festivals are few and late, suggesting exceptional social circumstances and perhaps the pressure of the Roman political system, which allowed the daughters of the wealthy to participate in men's festivals.[80]

The gendered contest system of Greek society, then, is not only reflected in its athletics; athletics itself is an intrinsic aspect of that society, at once defining and defined by religious, initiatory, and gender-related concerns. Female contest victors, like the male victors in Pindar's odes, were reincorporated into society with enhanced status. To paraphrase Lucian's Solon, both male and female youths contribute to the freedom of self and state by the public pursuit of their respective ideals. If Heracles, Hermes, and Eros were the chief patrons of male gymnasia and representatives of male *aretē*, Hera, Artemis, Dionysus, and other divinities oversaw the competitions of girls in rituals of female excellence. The central place of athletic festivals and gymnasium life in Greek culture is unique at least in Western culture. The complex athletic resolution of antagonism, of the individual's relation to gods through competitive rituals, of male and female roles, and of sexual tensions is a singular achievement of the Greeks. Alas, the resulting construction of a contest system has been influential in the modern world more through idealized misapprehensions of the spirit and reality of Greek athletics, especially of the Olympics, than through a careful appreciation of those aspects of culture at which this study aims.

1

GREEK ATHLETICS AND RELIGION

Despite the fact that the contemporary term "sport" (originally from Latin *deportare*, "to carry away") has largely different connotations from ancient terms for "contest," we share the notion of being "carried away" by such contests with the Greeks, who set aside special occasions for athletics. Perhaps the clearest difference between us and the Greeks is that in the Greek mind, at least by the seventh century B.C., games were closely connected with cult festivals to the gods. In the great Funeral Oration of Pericles, Thucydides tells us of the Athenian attitude:

> We have also provided for our minds very many sources of relief from labor, adopting as custom games and sacrifices throughout the year, and becoming accustomed to the beauty of our personal estates and possessions. The daily delight of these things banishes our distress. (Thuc. 2.38.1)

The historian naturally groups contests and sacrifices (ἀγῶσι μέν γε καὶ θυσίαις), and the Greeks had probably always related the two phenomena. This is not to say that every contest was accompanied by a festival proper (*panēguris, heortē*), as most were in the classical period, but that animal sacrifices to the gods, along with libations and feasting, were normal components of funeral games, wedding games, banquet games, and so on. It is also noteworthy that the "delight" (*terpsis*) of escape from daily cares, which is a hallmark of athletics in Homer and Pindar, is here extended to public religious sacrifices and even aesthetic pleasures of personal possessions.

The following is a history, in brief outline, of the relation between religion, that is, communal expressions of worship of gods and heroes, and athletics in early Greece in order to see how that relation may have begun and how it changed fundamentally over time.[1] This chapter along with chapter 2 will provide some necessary general background on the evolution of athletic festivals in religious contexts. Later chapters will then take up several cult-related functions of the games, specifically the initiation of young men and women into adulthood, and the fostering of eros. Since the religious aspect of Greek athletic festivals was closely bound to their initiatory and erotic functions, and since this aspect has been neglected in recent scholarship, this overview will provide a narrative 'core' for the present study. I begin with a survey of some of the various religious occasions for games in Greece in both the poetic and the historical record, and then focus on the cult history of the oldest and most influential of the Panhellenic festivals, the Olympic Games to Zeus.

Gods and Games in Early Poetry

Athletic contests in ancient Greece were the spontaneous expression of the native human urge to compete, and the competitive spark. "Always to do one's best and to surpass others" (*Il.* 6.208), was the heroic ethos, an ideal of Greek culture.[2] Epic heroes delighted in and valued prowess in boxing, the footrace, or discus-throw; displays of these abilities were no less valued for being impromptu. Athletic pastimes were deemed spectacles worthy of honoring the dead hero at his funeral, both in Greek legend and life.[3] So the three extensive passages describing games in Homer's eighth-century epics all report spontaneous occasions for games, including most prominently funeral games:[4] impromptu, after-dinner games are staged for the honored guest Odysseus on Phaeacia (*Od.* 8.97–384), Odysseus' boxing match with the beggar Iros is arranged on the spur of the moment (*Od.* 18.66–101), and Achilles hastily organizes funeral games for Patroclus (*Il.* 23.256–897). None of these could properly be called sacred "festivals" held in the context of particular "cults," yet on all occasions gods were not only present, but actively involved in the competitions. The mythical motif of divine intervention may have served for the Greeks of Homeric and later times as a rationalization of how gods are directly, but invisibly, involved in the competition. We may speculate that this epic concept of divine involvement at least fostered, if it did not in fact give rise to, the later, historical incorporation of contests into the more formal contexts of cult. Homer's Athena serves as a kind of umpire to proclaim Odysseus' stone-toss the best in the contest (*Od.* 8.193–98), and she puts strength into that hero's limbs before his boxing match with Iros (*Od.* 18.69–71, 133–34). During the chariot race of the funeral games, Apollo caused Diomedes to lose his whip, but Athena promptly gave it back (*Il.* 23.383–400); in the footrace Athena caused Ajax to slip and then made Odysseus' limbs light (*Il.* 23.770–76); and in the archery contest, Apollo helps Meriones to hit his mark and win the prize (*Il.* 23.872–73).[5] This is not to say that the contests are entirely determined by gods or beyond human control, but that, in the Homeric worldview, a god often worked with a human who had shown special favor to that god, and only the foolish would ignore the divine influence on their endeavors.

Another clear expression of the athlete's relation to the gods, as the Greeks saw it, is Pindar's tenth *Pythian Ode*, his earliest extant work, written about 498 B.C. There Hippocleas, a victor in the boys' *diaulos* or two-lap, 400-meter race at the

Pythian Games, is reminded by the poet of his debt to the patron god of the games, Apollo:

> Apollo, the goal and the start for mortals
> are made sweet when a god drives them on.
> By your design he performed it. . . .
> (Pythian 10.10–12)

The god "drives" the athlete (δαίμονος ὀρνύντος), in the sense of "spurs on," or "rouses" him. The competitor's entire efforts, from beginning to end, "are made sweet," with connotations from the Greek verb here (αὔξεται) that his performance "is strengthened" or "made greater," thanks to Apollo's encouragement. And the achievement is done in accord with the god's "design," here literally "counsels" or "plans" (μήδεσι). As in the scenes from the *Iliad*, divine help here takes on the form of personal favor shown by a divinity to the competitor. Here the god rouses the winner rather than hinders his opponents, and the outcome is seen to be in accord with the plans of the divinity. The precise reasons for the patronage are left obscure, although they presumably include the inherent worthiness of this youth whose father was an Olympic victor also in running events (ibid., lines 13–15). So, even in the fifth century, the Homeric notion of divine intervention in the contests persists alongside the by then well-established incorporation of athletic contests into periodic cult festivals.[6]

The earliest literary reference to an athletic festival performed specifically in honor of a god comes in the *Homeric Hymn to Apollo* 146ff., a passage dated to the seventh century B.C.[7]:

> But it is in Delos, O Phoibos, that your heart delights the most,
> for Ionians with trailing garments gather there
> in your honor with their children and modest wives.
> And with boxing matches, dancing and song,
> they delight you and remember you whenever they hold the contests.
> (Homeric Hymn to Apollo 146–50, A. Athanassakis, trans.)

Here the relation of the god to the human event is one of "delight," conveyed in two Greek words with the same root *terp-[8] (ἐπιτέρπεαι, 146; τέρπουσιν, 150): the god's heart takes joy and the Delians give him delight. It is also noteworthy that it is not only the competitor, but also the organizers, the audience composed of the entire community including women and children, who give joy to the deity by assembling in his honor. The *agōn*, the festival of competition, takes on its sacred character from the total gathering of audience and participants and from the sum of their actions.

Another early instance of athletics associated with a specific cult is found in Hesiod's recommendation that athletes show devotion to the powerful goddess Hecate:

> Good is [Hecate] also whenever men compete in a contest,
> for there too the goddess is present for them and gives them profit.
> He who wins with might and strength easily carries off
> a fine prize with delight, and brings fame to his parents.
>
> (*Theogony* 435–38)

It may be the magical powers of this deity which make her the patroness of contests depending much on good fortune. More important, she illustrates a principle of the relation of patron deities to athletes in competition in late-eighth-century Greece. The athlete's demonstration of his own strength and ability seems to be a necessary condition for victory, to which Hecate could contribute her favor and tip the balance for a pious competitor. The Hecate passage also shows that the valuable prize and "fame" (κῦδος) for one's kin were the desired results of devotion. This notion is entirely compatible with the role of the gods in the Homeric contests.

To return to Homeric athletics, the victor received both honor from the god and often a material reward from a mortal sponsor to symbolize his excellence, as in the honor paid to Achilles from the splendid prizes in the funeral games set by Thetis (*Od.* 24.80–94). Whether these legendary games more accurately reflect the practice and thinking of Homer's eighth century or the Bronze Age is a matter of controversy that will not be taken up here, though the well-developed forms of contests in the Patroclus games suggest a reflection of contemporary, eighth-century practice but probably also include some competitions that go back as early as the Bronze Age.[9] Homer has combined the traditional ethos of earlier times, partly as an accurate reflection of Bronze Age traditions, partly artificially archaized, with the complexity of an eighth-century program of events.

Although the games are not represented as a necessary accompaniment to the heroic funeral in Homer, funeral games did become an established tradition in myth and in historical practice. The Olympics, according to some traditions, were founded by Heracles in honor of the hero Pelops, or else by Pelops in honor of the local king Oenomaus. The other three great Panhellenic festivals also have legendary origins in funeral games. Nine of eleven contests famous in antiquity, as mentioned in a fragmentary list of Hyginus (*Fabulae* 273), were funeral games. There was clearly some association of cults of the dead with games in the conceptual world of the prehistoric Greeks, but this connection is obscured by Homer's time.[10] In fact, the activities of the participants are represented as a performance and a celebration of heroic daily life—the struggle for fame, honor, and material rewards. The magnitude of the prizes and the splendor of the games was clearly meant to redound to the glory and imperishable fame of the deceased (cf. *Od.* 24.85–94), but the funeral games had no fixed cult associations with patron gods in the heroic age as Homer relates it.

Another occasion for games which supplied a popular motif in Greek myth, marriage contests, also had little direct connection with a divine cult, although games might be held to a god in thanksgiving after the fact.[11] The mythical tradition of contests for a bride, which was not much practiced in historical times, included the footrace of Atalanta, the chariot race of Pelops and Oenomaus, the archery contest of Odysseus and the suitors, and the wrestling match between Peleus and Thetis. Similarly, contests to determine kingship were not in themselves sacred in nature, but games may have been held by the successor to give thanks to his patron, just as they were held by military victors to celebrate their victories in historical times.[12]

The Diffusion of the Athletic Festival

The large number and variety of Greek athletic festivals known in historical times prohibit a comprehensive list and a full litany of the gods and heroes with whom each festival was associated.[13] We may, however, note that since the traditional founding of the Olympic Games in 776 B.C. and the establishment of the other three Panhellenic games, namely the Pythia, Isthmia, and Nemea, between 586 and 573 B.C., there arose a popular tradition throughout the Greek world of including an agonistic element in the major local festivals of pre-established cults. In the epinician odes of Pindar (518–438 B.C.), there is mention of at least twenty, presumably regularly held, games in addition to the four Panhellenic festivals.[14] In a comprehensive study of inscriptional evidence for games of the Greek mainland (except Athens) and the Aegean Islands (except Euboea), one scholar has catalogued some 140 different games, about one-third of which are attested only in the Roman period.[15] By the Roman imperial era, another estimate has it, the agonistic market gained such popularity as to offer at least 270 athletic festivals to athletes, who were then better organized in professional unions.[16]

The Olympics represent the most influential early custom of combining athletic contests with a periodic cult festival, a practice that became the model for the other Panhellenic and local games. The subsequent popularity of the Panhellenic movement and of athletics in general resulted in a proliferation of games for personal status and profit. This proliferation also led to a formal distinction between the so-called stephanitic or "crown" games (agōnes stephanitai), the four sacred or Panhellenic games in which a crown was the only prize, and the "thematic games" (agōnes thematikoi), also called "prize" or "local" games, which were sometimes modeled on the crown games in their programs, but which always awarded valuable prizes. All games of both classes were, however, held in the context of religious festivals, naturally associated with the cult that was most popular at the site of the competition. Of the crown games, besides the Olympic Games for Zeus, there were the Pythian Games for Apollo at Delphi, the Isthmian for Poseidon at the Isthmus of Corinth, and the Nemean for Zeus at Nemea in the northeastern Peloponnese. Among the most important prize games were the Panathenaia for Athena in

Athens, the Asclepieia for Asclepius at Epidaurus and Cos, the Eleusinia for Demeter at Eleusis, and the Heraia for Hera at Argos. These festivals were sometimes named for the site of the sanctuary, for example, the Isthmia; sometimes for a mythical association, for example, the Pythia from the "Python," the serpent slain by Apollo at Delphi; and sometimes for an element in the ceremony, for example, the Hecatombaea at Argos alluding to the sacrifice of a hecatomb, a hundred oxen. In the Roman era, a number of games arose which were named Caesarea, Augustea, Neronea, and the like, in honor of the divine emperor and his cult.

Under the late Roman Republic and early Empire, the religious aspects of the festival were maintained, but the number of contests grew by accumulation. Despite a widespread imitation of games on the sacred Panhellenic models, the athletic program occupied the greater part of the festival activities while the cult ceremonies served as an important, but relatively reduced, ritual framework. A number of extrinsic causes, including religious, political, and cultural changes, as well as an increase in the sheer number of competitions, resulted in festivals with more athletics and less ritual activity. Yet each festival still retained a sacred character and a sacred 'core.'

In spite of this shift toward a more secularized festival, the Olympics themselves managed to maintain their sacred prestige due to ideological conservatism on the part of the Elean sponsors. The Pythia, Nemea, and Isthmia also preserved their religious character to a large extent, partly due to the competition among these festivals for enhanced status and hence larger audiences on the "circuit" (*periodos*) of the four major festivals.[17] But the Isthmia, perhaps owing to its commercially important location, became the most politicized of the Crown Games, serving as the rostrum from which Flamininus and later Nero proclaimed the freedom of the Greeks. In his report of this event, Livy describes the popularity and prestige of the Isthmian Games:

> This festival had always been well attended even on other occasions,
> not only because of the innate Greek interest in a spectacle in which
> contests of every type of skill of both strength and agility are witnessed,
> but also because of the convenience of the site. For by its useful position
> for supplying all things to all humankind over two seas, this commer-
> cial center was a gathering-place of Asia and Greece. (Livy 33.32)

The Isthmia also shifted its program to suit popular tastes with numerous competitions in music, poetry, drama, and even painting added to the athletic program by the Roman imperial period.[18] Dio Chrysostom paints a vivid picture of philosophers, poets, magicians, prophets, lawyers, and peddlers gathered for their own individual reasons at the time of the Isthmian Games:

> That was also the time to hear throngs of accursed sophists around the
> Temple of Poseidon shouting and insulting one other, and their so-

called students as they fought with one another, and many historians reading out their dull narratives, and flocks of poets reciting their poetry as they praise the work of other poets, and many magicians performing their tricks, many fortune-tellers telling fortunes, countless lawyers perverting justice, and not a few peddlers peddling whatever each happened to sell. (*Oratio* 7.9)

Athletics and Initiation

In addition to the more famous Panhellenic and local athletic festivals, there were a number of smaller, regional, cult festivals that were primarily religious but also had an athletic element, often functioning to ensure the prosperity of the state and its members, and/or to mark transitions of social status, as from youth to adulthood as part of a local ritual. We merely mention these at this point as examples of alternatives to the more common athletic festivals; they will be discussed more fully in chapters 3 to 6. The Spartan Carneia held in honor of Apollo Carneius, for instance, included a footrace of the "Grape Runners" (*Staphylodromoi*) and promoted both civic and individual prosperity, with elements of initiation into adulthood.[19] This was apparently a harvest festival in which a certain boy was pursued by the "Grape Runners" and, if they caught him, they obtained something good for the state. The Athenians had a similar festival, the Oschophoria or "Carrying of the Vine-branch," in which boys ran a 7-kilometer course from the temple of Dionysos in Athens to the sanctuary of Athena Sciras in the Piraeus.[20] The victor won the right to taste of a special drink. The Attic festival of the Arkteia held for Artemis at Brauron and at Munichion probably included a footrace for young girls and required their participation in this and other cult activities before they could marry. A girls' race to Dionysus Colonatas and an unnamed local hero at Sparta, also restricted to maidens, may have had an initiatory character. These and other similar local festivals were held regularly, either to reenact a local legend, to serve as a stage in the initiation of youths to adulthood, or to commemorate seasonal change.

Ritual contests attached to cult festivals differed markedly from the usual agonistic festivals in the absence of a well-developed athletic program. Scholars have long debated, without resolution, the question whether such ritual contests were the prototypes for the more purely athletic festivals like the Panhellenic and other local games, or whether the ritual contests developed independently. The latter alternative is more likely, with most 'initiatory' contests developing in the seventh century B.C. or later, as our study in later chapters will show. Yet prior to the formal athletic festivals that begin with the Olympics in the eighth century, athletic contests of the sort Homer describes probably existed for centuries, apart from local cult festivals without contests. For the most influential example of the linking of athletics with cult festival, we now turn to the early history of Olympia, where religious elements were deeply connected with the games from their earliest stages.

Cult and Contest at Olympia

The early cultic and athletic history of Olympia can be roughly divided into three periods: 2000–1100 B.C., including the Middle Bronze and Mycenaean Ages; 1100–800 B.C., including the so-called "Dorian Migration" and the Geometric period; and 800–476 B.C., the early Archaic and Classical periods. The first two periods and part of the third are most difficult to untangle due to a mass of conflicting legends and scattered, mostly nonathletic archaeological evidence. Contradictions in stories may be a result of alternate versions by the citizens of nearby Elis and Pisa who vied for the sponsorship of the games.[21] But contradictions concern us less than points of agreement between common tales and the archaeological monuments. Reference to ancient mythical chronology at least gives a sense of the relative sequence of events in the tradition, not, of course, in historical time.

Pindar (518–446 B.C.), our earliest surviving source for the origins of the Olympic Games in the first period, gives a masterfully succinct report of Heracles' founding of the games in the thirteenth century by ancient chronology,[22] as a thank offering to Zeus for his victory over the local King Augeas (Ol. 10.29–92). The five events in the games were the stade-length footrace, wrestling, boxing, javelin, and "stone" (discus?)-throwing. These took place near the site of Pelops' tomb, where Heracles is said to have also established a sanctuary to Zeus, called the "Altis." Strabo (63 B.C.–A.D. 21) attributes the games to the descendants of Heracles who first celebrated the games (by ancient chronology ca. 1150 B.C.; Geographica 8.3.30).[23] Phlegon (ca. A.D. 138, FGH 2 B 257, 1160 F) tells of a tradition in which the hero Pelops celebrated the games prior to Heracles (in ancient reckoning ca. 1270 B.C.) with funeral games for the local king, Oenomaus of Pisa.[24] Although Pelops is not mentioned as a founder of games by other key sources such as Strabo, Pausanias (5.1.7), and Pindar, his cult worship, his myth, and his sanctuary are very much involved with the Olympics in historical times. Numerous literary sources and archaeological evidence relate the story of Pelops' successful victory over Oenomaus in a chariot race and his winning of the king's daughter, Hippodameia, in marriage.[25] The sculpture of the east pediment of the Temple of Zeus at Olympia from the second quarter of the fifth century showed Pelops and his bride together on one side of the central figure, Zeus, the patron of the race. The suggestion of a chariot race in the Mycenaean period fits well with the historical picture of Mycenaean nobles, who relied on the chariot in warfare and probably held occasional races.[26] Though the "mound of Pelops" or Pelopion, the hero's supposed burial site, has been located in the sanctuary at Olympia just north of the Temple of Zeus, exactly where Pausanias had seen it in the second century A.D., its early history has been disputed.

The Pelopion as a shrine may go back as far as the second half of the second millennium B.C., which would accord with a mythological date in the thirteenth century, but its importance as a cult place in the Archaic period and later is much more certain.[27] The Pelopion remained a cult site until at least the second century A.D. Though modern historians continue the debate over the date of origins, what all these conflicting legends and the monumental reminders of them share is the belief in a tradition of Olympic Games prior to the traditional reorganization in the eighth century. The consensus on this point alone gives weight to the supposition that athletic contests did take place prior to the Panhellenic establishment of the festival, though they may have been much smaller and less regularly held, as Hugh Lee has argued.[28] Just how far before the eighth century these games and the cult to Zeus existed, and what form they took are matters of less certainty.

Some topographical orientation is necessary for an appreciation of other archaeological finds of this early period. Olympia was (and is) a marvelous playground and a rustic retreat, splendid in its natural setting and distant from any sizable polity. It is dominated by the imposing Hill of Cronus to the north of the sanctuary, the wide River Alpheus to the south, and the River Cladeus to the west. Its relatively neutral and 'marginal' strategic position resembled those of Delphi and Nemea and made it ideal as a forum for the interaction of the members of polities from all over Greece.[29] During the period 2000 to 1550 B.C., there were several apsidal houses within the later sanctuary area, three of which are oriented to the Hill of Cronus, a possible indication of their cultic function.[30] This earliest building style is copied in the only extant house in the area during the second period at Olympia, the Geometric period (1100–800 B.C.), namely a house near the Pelopion and possibly serving as a cult building for it. This geometric building is the only link between the apsidal (cult?) building of the Mycenaean age and the apsidal Bouleuterion of the sixth century, that is, the third period of the site. The Bouleuterion or council house is the earliest Olympic structure surviving into the historical period, and it served as the judges' residence during the games and the place where athletes and umpires took their oaths before the festival.[31]

The second period is most obscure in legend. Strabo (*Geog.* 8.3.30) reports that a 'Dorian migration' overran the area in the person of Oxylus and the Heracleidae or descendants of Heracles, and that they first established the Olympian Games to Zeus. Who the Dorians were and the date of their arrival are long-debated questions, but most hypotheses suggest that arrival ca. 1200 B.C. is likely.[32] Of course the Linear B tablets indicate that Zeus and many other Olympian gods were worshiped in Greece already in the Mycenaean Bronze Age, but it is possible that the legends refer to a Dorian introduction of the cult to Zeus, the Dorian god of the sky and of warfare, at the Peloponnesian site later known as Olympia. With the Dorians may have come the establishment at Olympia of other Olympian cults and the familiar names of Hera, Artemis, Gaia, and so on. But it is not clear to what extent these cults simply may have replaced or were syncretized with earlier ones at the site, nor is it clear whether games had been held at the site prior to the Dorian migration, as the traditions regarding Pelops and Heracles related by Pindar and Phlegon suggest. If there were earlier games, the lack of archaeological evidence in the sanctuary area suggests that they were either insignificant or held elsewhere nearby.[33] One hypothesis is that the hero cult for Oxylus and other prominent ancestors of the Eleans occupied a central place at or near the present site of the theater at Elis, where graves dating to the eleventh century B.C. have been found; dances and athletic contests may have formed part of the cults of ancestor worship.[34] In any case, the period from 1100 to the eighth century B.C. remains a dark era in Olympic history. Pausanias comments as follows (5.8.8):

> After the reign of Oxylus, who also celebrated the games, the Olympic festival was discontinued until the reign of Iphitus [king of Elis, ca. 776 B.C.]. When Iphitus . . . renewed the games, men had by this time forgotten the ancient tradition, the memory of which was revived bit by bit, and as it was, they made additions to the games.

The lack of archaeological evidence relating to the games during this period conforms with the silence of the literary sources. If the site still functioned as a cult center, its importance was relatively diminished. During this period an ash altar to Zeus may have been set up northwest of the Pelopion. And although evidence is slight, there may also have been several female cults in the sanctuary, and perhaps one to Cronus. Their greater antiquity is suggested in part by the location, in later times, of shrines to female deities at the foot of the "Hill of Cronus." There seems also to have been an oracle of the earth goddess Gaia, and evidence still remains of early shrines to Eileithyia, Hera, Themis, and Artemis.[35] It has even been argued on the basis of dedications at Olympia that prior to the early seventh century, the Olympic sanctuary was of greater interest as an oracular shrine than as a site of Panhellenic games.[36] The collection of cults at this site gave it the genuine character of the Olympic family, and this polytheistic aspect may have been an early feature of the sanctuary.

A formal reorganization of the Olympic Games in 776 B.C. marks the beginning of the third Olympic period, when a truce was agreed upon by the Peloponnesian rulers, Iphitus of Elis, Cleosthenes of Pisa, and Lycurgus of Sparta. This so-called Truce of Iphitus, inscribed on a discus like some later dedications, called for the establishment of quadrennial games to Zeus and a suspension of hostilities during the festival period.[37] The historicity of this tradition is less important here than the formal merger of political interests with religious and athletic custom that it makes evident. With this legendary treaty began a remarkable Greek tradition combining two strands of earlier tradition, one consisting of the aristocratic custom of athletic competition and the religious festival to Zeus at Olympia, the other, the revolutionary idea of inviting other Greek states to celebrate and compete under the protective sponsorship of a common Olympian deity.[38] According to legend, the Delphic oracle suggested the truce and other historical movements may be identified as catalysts for the event.

Now we come to the question of why a regular religious festival became joined with an athletic contest prior to the fusion of both of these with an interstate gathering. It was suggested above that the epic representation of divine intervention in contests implies a fundamental association of gods with athletic activity in the minds of the Greeks. The abnormal, unusual, or fortuitous occurrence during a contest was best ascribed to the gods' participation. The festival of a particular deity of regional importance might, we may infer, have served as an ideal occasion for holding contests in which the competitors and their supporters prayed and made offerings to the patron deity for victory in the games. Indeed, those attending the festival may have vied with one another in the very acts of prayer and sacrifice, making the religious activities themselves into forms of competition to secure favor in the athletic contests. In this way the patron gods became the prime benefactors of devotees who sought special favors, either for the immediate events, or for other esoteric reasons. The athletic events were, in their festival context, only an added incentive for displays of ritual piety. Athletes, like Hippocleas in the Pindaric ode discussed above, could feel that they were spurred on by the patron deity in the contest itself. A victor would afterward follow up with thanksgiving to the god, and the defeated had only their own inadequacies, physical or devotional or both, to blame.

Another possible reason that athletics was joined to cult festivals at Olympia was the specially appropriate ritual symbolism of the original contest, in this case a simple footrace, which may have been attached to the local cult ritual performed for Zeus before the games took on a Panhellenic importance. According to Philostratus (*Gymn.* 5), the footrace ended at or near Zeus' altar: "The runners were one stade away from the altar and there stood in front of it a priest with a torch acting as umpire." Scholarly controversy over the Philostratus account here requires discussion. Alfred Mallwitz found no archeological traces of an early stadium ending at Zeus' altar.[39] Yet, in support of Philostratus' testimony, a first stadium running up to the altar may well have been so rudimentary as to leave no discernible traces. The program consisting only of footraces from 776–712 B.C. required only the simplest of tracks, and the audience that was likely much smaller at those early, one-day games needed no wells for water nor embanked seats. Hence, we can also question Mallwitz's argument, based on the absence of traces of a stadium prior to the end of the eighth century, that the games were not founded until about 708 B.C. Even if Mallwitz's placement of the earliest stadium is correct, the altar need not have been exactly at the finish, but only in its vicinity, which accords with both Mallitz's plan and Philostratus' statement.

Philostratus continues that the footrace victor was given a symbolic prize and honored as a hero. So the preeminence of the deity among the Olympians was acknowledged in a manner analogous to that of the victor elevated among his mortal peers. In a more general way, the strength and vitality of the supreme victor were celebrated; the subordination of the defeated and others was made evident. The very symbolism of victory is an appropriate metaphor for the elevation of the patron god. Not only are such ritually symbolic athletic 'trials' found in many cults in later Hellenic culture, as mentioned earlier, but they are also known to have existed in Hittite and Egyptian practice of the second and third millennia B.C.[40] The latter parallels are mentioned more to demonstrate the widespread and early evidence for athletic rituals in the Bronze Age Mediterranean than to suggest that they served as models, a more remote possibility about which I will not speculate here. Rather let us turn to the later Hellenic examples that furnish much formal and functional parallels to what we know of the first historical Olympics.

For the first thirteen Olympiads, 776 to 728 B.C., the only event was the one-stade (stadion) footrace of ca. 200 meters. In the fourteenth Olympiad (724), the double-stade race or diaulos was added and in the fifteenth (720), the long race or dolichos. Until the pentathlon and wrestling were added in the eighteenth Olympiad (708), the only events were footraces (Paus. 5.8.5–7). The prestige of the stade race is also attested by the fact that each Olympiad was named after the victor of the stade race (Xenophanes, fr. 2.17f. Diehl). This enhanced status of the footrace in addition to the frequent occurrence of footraces in other later cult contexts, such as the Staphylodromoi or the Oschophoria mentioned before, suggests that the footrace may have been practiced long prior to the reorganization of the games. Chariot races, which, in view of the Pelops myth, one might expect to have had priority, were not a part of the Olympic program until the twenty-fifth Olympiad (680 B.C.).[41] Philostratus' account (Gymn. 5) of the stade victor's lighting the sacrifices on the altar of Zeus further underlines the cultic importance of the stade race. The victor, no doubt, like athletic victors in Homer's account, owed his success to the patron god, and, as thanks for his honor, led the sacrifice to Zeus. The stade victor became in a real sense immortalized by his fame and by his name, which became attached to a period of Greek history.

The earliest stadium at Olympia was, by all accounts, located partly within the Altis. In the fourth century the stadium moved farther east and out of the sanctuary, but it was still linked to the sacred precinct by a tunnel.[42] The tunnel was not only a ceremonial entrance way, it was a symbolic 'umbilicus' tying the stadium to its center. This direct physical link of the athletic space with the sacred space is also evidenced in the stadium tunnel at Epidaurus linking the racecourse to the sanctuary of Asclepius, and in the more recently excavated tunnel at Nemea, extending from the stadium toward the sanctuary of Zeus that lies several hundred yards away.[43] The fact that these tunnels were all constructed in the fourth or third centuries B.C. does not detract from the important point that the athletic site had to be tied as directly as possible with the sanctuary, even when practical consideration of seating forced the stadia to be moved some distance away. At sites like Isthmia and Delphi, where there are no tunnels, the stadia were linked directly to the main altar and temple area by paths. Of course, part of the motivation for the connection may have been a practical one of easing passage for all the festival pilgrims from the religious site to the competition place. And yet it appears, at least from the extensive graffiti by athletes at Nemea, that the tunnel was largely used as a ceremonial entrance or even a waiting area for competitors, and probably also for umpires, priests, and other officials. The tunnel was therefore an overt symbol of the religious-athletic connection.

By the end of the third period under discussion, that is, by 472 B.C., the Olympic program was fully developed with eighteen events spread over five days.[44] Despite changes in the athletic program, the religious ritual remained fixed. The regular time for the festival was every four years at the second full moon after the summer solstice.[45] The central act of worship during the festival, the sacrifice of one hundred oxen at the altar of Zeus, probably took place on the day after the full moon, originally just before the central contest, the stade race, as Philostratus relates it. During the evening before, there was an almost equally important sacrifice to the hero Pelops. While the program was small, the athletic events all took place on the same day as the sacrifice to Zeus, but as more events were added to comprise a five-day program, some were probably held during the first two days prior to the full moon, and others on the day after the central day of sacrifice, with the fifth day reserved for the awarding of prizes and a celebratory feast.[46] The evening sacrifice to Pelops and the daytime sacrifice to Zeus occupied the chronological center and were the religious foci of the festival.

Pelops and Zeus are antithetical, with altars east and west. Sacrifice of a black ram was made to Pelops in a pit, and of a multitude of oxen to Zeus on a twenty-two-feet high (in Pausanias' day) ash altar. To eat of the meat of Pelops' sacrificial ram caused exclusion from Zeus' sanctuary (Paus. 5.13.1–3). Pelops was essentially an old, local, chthonic hero tied to images of darkness, death, and the earth; Zeus, an Olympian sky-god associated with brightness, the heavens, and the imperishable fame of the victor. Zeus' games were naturally held in the bright light of day. The fire that the victor used to light the sacrifices of Zeus marked a transition from bloody slaughter to purifying fire, or as one scholar puts it, "from an encounter with death to a full sense of survival manifested in the power of the victor."[47] The transition from Pelops to Zeus, from night to day, from death of victims to a renewal of life in glorious victory is an artfully balanced antithesis preserved in the ritual sacrifices central to the games to which we will return in chapter 9. This aspect of renewal in the games is something preserved in festivals with contests at other sites, such as the Athenian Panathenaia and the Spartan Carneia, which occur near the beginning of their respective calendars.

Aside from this central antithesis of cults at Olympia, there existed numerous other religious elements of the festival which enforced the position of Zeus as overseer and divine patron. Prior to the festival, *spondophoroi* or "truce-bearing messengers" were sent out to all Greek cities to announce the sacred truce for the period of the games. In the region of Elis, according to the "Olympic Armistice" (ἐκεχειρία), often misnamed the "Olympic Peace," all hostilities were to be suspended, pilgrims were guaranteed safe passage, all legal disputes postponed, and no death penalties carried out. Participants were under the protection of Zeus, violators were under the threat of real punishment at the hands of the judges or Zeus.[48]

The Hellanodikai or "Greek Judges" were responsible for the organization of both the religious and the athletic aspects of the games. All athletes spent a period of either one month or ten (sources are conflicting) of rigorous training at Elis and were kept to a prescribed diet (cheese until at least the sixth century B.C., Paus. 6.7.10) before the festival began.[49] Just prior to the games, athletes, their fathers and brothers as well as their trainers, were made to swear an oath before the statue of Zeus in the Bouleuterion (Paus. 6.24.9–10) that all regulations for training had been followed. "This statue is of all images of Zeus most likely to strike terror into the hearts of sinners," Pausanias tells us. "He is surnamed *Horikos* [God of Oaths] and in each hand he holds a thunderbolt." Even judges must swear that they will decide fairly without taking bribes. Violators were subject to banishment from the games, whipping, or a monetary fine. Fines were used to finance the setting up of bronze statues of Zeus or *Zanes*, in the area just before the entrance to the stadium, serving as visual reminders of the sacred sanctions against cheating by competitors, bribery of officials, and other infractions.[50] The prize for victors during the first five Olympiads was an apple, but this was replaced by an olive crown at the command of the Delphic oracle (Phlegon, *FGH* II b 257 fr. 1). The crown, which may have been influenced by the customs of an earlier tree cult at the site, is an obvious symbol of the natural vitality which is the heritage of the victor.[51]

Zeus' games were games for men, strictly so as participants, and primarily so as spectators. Married women were prohibited from attending on penalty of death (Paus. 5.6.7, 6.7.2). The only exception was the priestess of Demeter Chamyne, who occupied a seat of honor at a marble altar opposite the seats of the umpires in the stadium. Maidens were apparently permitted into the games as spectators. The festival thus disrupted normal family bonds, and the segregation by gender seen here has been taken by some as an indication of initiatory traditions behind the games, since contests in tribal initiation segregate men from women in games and worship.[52] Yet it is more likely that the prohibition of married women was a conservative custom of the Elean organizers, and the Olympics were not initiatory in origin.

Women did practice their own cult duties and hold their own games at Olympia apart from the men, and these traditions may go back to the cults to a goddess which preceded the advent of Zeus at Olympia. Women held regular rites to Pelops' bride Hippodameia, and special games to Hera in gratitude for Hippodameia's marriage discussed fully in chapter 4. The Games to Hera, like those to Zeus, were structured with a procession, a contest, a sacrifice, the awarding of crowns of olive leaves, and a celebratory meal. The contest was a simple stade race for maidens divided into three age classes, another custom that may reflect original initiation rites. Women also attended special shrines to Eileithyia, goddess of childbirth, and the "Savior

God," Sosipolis, not far from Hera's temple (Paus. 6.20.2–5).[53] The females' role—with its emphasis on marriage and procreation—complemented the men's of blood sacrifice and victory in combat sports. The women's goddess, Hera, had a temple at Olympia which predates that of Zeus (ca. 600 vs. 556 B.C.), the probable reason being that women's social space was associated with a house, while men's was in the outdoors, the place of Zeus' altar.[54]

So the Olympics incorporated, from their origins, the Greek belief that gods somehow participated in and could influence contests as they did daily life; the festival was naturally suited to the elevation of the victorious hero and the patron god; and it was invested, perhaps from its beginning, with special importance for male valor distinct from that of the female. Certain characteristics at Olympia suggest to some scholars that early local games there may have had an initiatory function to introduce local youths to adulthood, but this theory lacks sufficient data, as will be argued in chapter 3. The ultimate reasons for the union of cult and games at Olympia have been obscured by its change to a more political, Panhellenic function in the eighth century. Whatever the origins of the Olympic Games, this brief survey has shown that there is a wide gap between the various uses of athletics in relation to cults, from the impromptu play of Homeric nobles devoid of cult ceremony, to the very ritualized contests of certain local cults, and the complex festival of Zeus at Olympia. It is also clear that the ancient Olympic festival became the single most influential athletic phenomenon of antiquity and was in many ways the model for hundreds of other athletic-religious festivals for about a millennium after its reorganization in the eighth century.

2

THE ECUMENICAL OLYMPICS—
THE GAMES IN THE ROMAN ERA

During their history of over a millennium, Olympia and the Olympics underwent a series of dynamic transformations, particularly during the period of Roman 'imperial' hegemony in the Eastern Mediterranean. The changes, most notably the general accommodation of Roman interests and the wider geographic spectrum of participants, in part evidence the vitality of the festival. The Olympic metamorphosis also illustrates, a fortiori, how athletic institutions in general reflected and influenced their contemporary society. As we shall see in subsequent chapters, even lesser, local festivals adopted and adapted athletics to serve the interests of the time and place, for example, in the initiation of its young citizens and in the fostering of communal values. Just as those from Rome and the far reaches of the Roman Empire could participate in the Olympics and be assimilated into the unique complex of Greek athletic values, so too the girls' Heraia Games at Olympia or the Games for Eros at Thespiae could offer to women or men of many cities a festival experience where common goals were forged. Athletic phenomena were, in short, the signifiers, the media for transmitting messages of collective importance and for reflecting the social contexts of their times.

Standard modern histories of the Olympics during the Roman era characterize the period as one of "the monopoly of professionals," "the general degradation of athletics," the exploitation by the "clever politics of Roman expansion," and finally, the victimization by "the all-conquering power of Christianity."[1] It is, according to these versions, a period when Greeks were forced to undergo the indignities of Roman affronts to Hellenic ideals to enjoy the financial security of the *pax Romana*; in short, a period "between farce and restoration," as the title of one treatment summarizes the condition.[2] For the most part, these historical overviews accurately present the facts of the years from 146 B.C. to A.D. 394 when Olympia was part of the Roman province of Greece, but the interpretation of Olympian development as a gradual decline or distancing from high classical ideals to profit-minded professionalism is essentially erroneous. David Young has very convincingly exposed the unhistorical view that an ideal period of amateurism preceded the late

Classical and Hellenistic 'decline' of professionalism. The professional Greek athletes of Roman times were carrying on fundamentally the same, if somewhat better organized, traditions of competing for money or for value prizes. This chapter attempts a more balanced and accurate view of Olympia's transformation from a center of Hellenic culture to one of 'ecumenical' or international culture. The 'farce' of Roman indignities were occasional and short-lived; the 'restoration' of the Olympics as they had been in Classical and pre-Classical Greece never occurred. Rather, the games underwent a gradual and permanent metamorphosis that scrupulously preserved most ancient religious and athletic traditions of the festival in its physical appearances but altered the character of the celebration by incorporating the Cult of the Emperor into the sanctuary and by playing host to a more cosmopolitan pool of competitors. The metamorphosis was a necessary one that met with remarkably little resistance from Elean organizers. It is a mistake to think of the resulting 'ecumenical Olympics' as a somehow debased or inferior version of the earlier festival. It was rather a surprisingly vigorous, new creation with some international flavoring, but a strong Hellenic essence that survived centuries of radical political, economic, and religious changes in the Mediterranean world of Rome.

In the analysis that follows, I have divided the Olympics in the Roman era into four somewhat arbitrary but usefully distinguishable periods: (1) the Late Republic, 146–40 B.C., that is, from the period when Rome annexed Greece as a province to the rise of the first emperor, Augustus; (2) the Julio-Claudian era, 36 B.C. to A.D. 67, encompassing the reigns of Augustus through Nero; (3) the middle Imperial period, A.D. 69 to 177, including Vespasian to Marcus Aurelius and the 'Olympic renaissance' of the second century; and (4) the late Imperial period, A.D. 181 to 383, from the emperors Commodus to Theodosius I, when the games showed great resilience against the political and financial deterioration of the Empire.

A survey of the significant political and cultural events of each period with reference to Olympia will be followed by a closer look at the games themselves and the ethnic origins of known Olympic victors for that period.

The Late Republic, 146–40 B.C.

Rome had aided Greece in the Second Macedonian War (200–197 B.C.) against Philip V of Macedon, who was finally defeated by Titus Quinctius Flamininus at Cynoskephalae in 197 B.C. At the Isthmian Games of 196, Flamininus in fact made a dramatic declaration of the freedom of the Greeks. After some initial resistance to Roman supremacy, Elis, the patron city of the Olympics, was forced to join the Achaean League, which became an instrument of Roman hegemony in Greece. During the Third Macedonian War (169–168 B.C.), the Achaeans fully supported the Roman general Quintus Marcius Philippus and erected an equestrian statue in his honor at Olympia.[3] After the defeat of King Perseus of Macedon at Pydna in 168, the Roman commander Lucius Aemilius Paulus visited Olympia, was deeply moved by Phidias' monumental statue of Zeus, and offered homage to the god (see Livy 28.5). The statue and the cult of the supreme Olympian continued to transfix visiting Romans for centuries to come.

But the Achaean League's open defiance of Rome in 146 B.C. precipitated the repressive campaign of the Roman general Mummius, culminating in his capture and sack of Corinth in 146 B.C. The Achaean League was dissolved, and Greece, losing its vestiges of independence, finally became a Roman province in 27 B.C. Thus Rome enacted her usual policy of political division of a country into smaller units that retained local government and customs but were ultimately accountable to the central authority of Rome. Although Mummius' soldiers were guilty of pillaging in Greece, the commander himself acted with restraint and respect, eventually "repairing the site in Isthmia and adorning the temples in Delphi and Olympia" (Polyb. 39.6.1). Mummius was in fact the first Roman on record to set up a dedication at a Greek sanctuary: "He dedicated a bronze Zeus at Olympia from the spoils of Achaea" (Pausanias 5.24.4). The Roman's legacy lived on, as we discover from the inscription on a monument one century later in honor of Mummius and the ten legates who administered Greece under him (*Die Inschriften von Olympia*, hereafter *I.Ol.* nos. 278, 281, 319). The commander was popular at Olympia and the Eleans were grateful for his respect. The historian Polybius may have even intervened on Olympia's behalf, since Elis also set up a statue of Polybius at Olympia.[4]

The greatest indignity perpetrated by the Romans against Olympia in this period and the only occasion in history when the sanctuary was plundered by a Roman occurred in 86 B.C., when Sulla took statues and other treasures from Olympia and other major Greek sanctuaries to pay for a successful campaign against Mithridates VI. The Roman commander assumed a dictatorship at Rome in 80 B.C., and, to celebrate the event, transferred the entire Olympic festival to Rome except for the boys' stade (200 meter) footrace.[5] "His excuse," Appian (*Bellum Ciuile* 1.99) tells us, "was that the masses needed a breathing spell and revitalization after their toils." Insult was added to injury in what seems to have been the only attempt in history to reestablish the games in another city. Sulla's animosity toward Olympic officials may have been exacerbated by the fact that they had previously dedicated an honorary statue to Sulla's Roman arch-foe, Marius (*I.Ol.* no. 326). The transfer, however, had no lasting effect, since Sulla died before the next Olympiad and the games returned home to stay.

One should not, however, put too much weight on the effects of the Sullan Olympics. Overall détente between Rome and Olympia was good in this period, as evidenced by the numerous honorary statues to Roman officials at Olympia in the late second to first centuries B.C.[6] Noteworthy among these were statues to Q. Fufius Calenus, Caesar's legate in central Greece, and possibly even to Caesar himself.[7] These statues were conspicuously placed alongside the Sacred Way running south of the Altis (Olympic sanctuary). The "decline of competition" after Sulla that

Gardiner alleges is simply inaccurate.[8] The relatively complete record of ten athletic and five hippic victors for the 72 B.C. games shows that, among athletic victors, four were from Asia Minor, one from Egypt, three from mainland Greece beyond the Olympic region of Elis, and two from Elis. All known hippic victors were local Eleans in the five Olympiads before Sulla's games. And Gardiner's claim that "corruption reappears" after Sulla is equally misleading, since the instance of bribery in 68 B.C. (Paus. 5.21.9) was an isolated case, and it was properly punished by officials.[9]

It is not to be denied that Olympia and Greece in general were suffering financially in the late Republic due to civil wars and petty boundary disputes in the new Roman province, for example, the disputes documented on Olympic inscriptions (*I.Ol.* nos. 47, 48, 52). The dearth of athletic victor statues from this period can also be explained by financial circumstances (*I.Ol.* nos. 211–13). Economics also certainly limited the Olympic hippic events almost exclusively to the noble Eleans who were renowned for their horse-breeding in the area. Numerous inscriptions document Olympic victories in horse or chariot races during this period (*I.Ol.* nos. 191–218), and the victors are all Eleans. In fact, the last *non*-Elean hippic victor was a Trojan man, Akestorides, who won in 212 B.C., and if we exclude the victories by Roman emperors or nobility in the centuries to follow, it is not until about A.D. 193 that we meet another non-Elean among known victors in the hippic events.[10] Lack of serious competition for the Eleans in the Roman period may also be explained by the fact that the Roman circuses occupied the attention of profit-minded horse-breeders and offered a market that was absent in Hellenistic Greece or earlier.

The Romans could offer no rival, however, to the purely athletic contests of Greek festivals. If gladiatorial games were popular throughout the Roman world, they were still no substitute for the beautiful, graceful, and skilled contests of the Greeks. It is clear that the Roman people themselves admired Greek athletics from the frequent exhibits of athletes, sometimes even together with gladiatorial and musical contests, sponsored by Romans during the Republic.[11] The first appearance of Greek athletics in Rome was in 186 B.C. at games sponsored by M. Fulvius Nobilior (Livy 39.22.2). M. Aemilius Scaurus held games with athletes in Rome in 58 B.C., as did Pompey in 55 B.C., M. Curio in 53 B.C., and Julius Caesar in 46 B.C.

It is not surprising, therefore, that when an earthquake struck Olympia in about 40 B.C. and caused the roof of the Temple of Zeus to collapse, a prominent Roman, Marcus Agrippa, friend of Octavian (later the Emperor Augustus), assisted in the restoration of the sanctuary.[12] Nor is it surprising that when the Olympics were in serious financial difficulty in 12 B.C. they were subsidized by a large donation from King Herod I of Judaea, who saw the festival as "the only remnant of ancient Greece."[13]

All tables are based on Moretti (1957). In each table, a city or region is counted once for each recorded victory and not for each victor. Thus, in cases where a single victor has several victories over his career, all his victories are listed in his city's total

Table 2.1. Regions and Cities of Olympic Victories in the Late Roman Republic, 144–40 B.C. (Roman province in parentheses)

A. Asia Minor (and islands)	B. North and Central Greece	C. Peloponnese (all Achaea)	D. Egypt/N. Africa (all Aigyptos)	E. Italy/Sicily
Adramyttium, l victor (Asia)	Athens, 1	Akriai, Lakonia, 5	Alexandria, 6	Tauromenion, 1 (Sikilia)
"Asia," 1 (Asia)	Delphi, 1	Argos, 2	Cyrene, 1[c]	Thurii, 1 (Italia)
Hypaia, Lydia, 1 (Asia)	Epirus, 2	Elis, 25	total, 7 (= 9.5%)	total, 2 (= 3%)
Kos, 2 (Asia)	Kerkyra, 2	Kyparissa, Lakonia, 2		
Kyzikos, 1 (Asia)	Larissa, 1	Messenia, 2		
Magnesia, 2 (Asia)	total, 7 (= 9.5%)	Sikyon, 4		
Miletus, 2 (Asia)		Sparta, 2		
Nikaia, 2 (Bithynia)[a]		Tritea, Arkadia 1		
Philadelphia, Lydia, 1 (Asia)		total, 43 (= 58%)		
Seleukia on Tigris, 1				
(Mesopotamia)[b]				
Tralles, 1 (Asia)				
total, 15 (= 20%)				

[a]not a province until 75–74 B.C.
[b]not a province until A.D. 197–99
[c]not a province unitl 75 B.C.

as evidence of the continuing attraction of the Olympics for an individual from that region. Victors with more than two wins for their city will be noted in the narrative.

From table 2.1, we can see that in the late Republic the majority of known Olympic victories (43 = 58 percent) came from the Peloponnese, followed by those from Asia Minor (15) and the northern and central Greek mainland or islands (7). By city, Elis had by far the most known victories (25, by 23 different victors, mostly [18] in hippic events), followed by Alexandria with six victories (by three victors) and Sikyon with four victories (by as many victors). Sikyon's success is understandable since the city was relatively close to Olympia, but Alexandria's number of victories is less obviously explainable. Egyptian Alexandria had been a center of Hellenism since its founding by Alexander in the fourth century, and prior to 144 B.C. had to its credit a total of six known Olympic victors, all between 296 and 212 B.C.[14] In view of the status of Alexandria as an educational and cultural center, it is indeed surprising that it was not more successful at the Olympics during the late Republican period. It is also noteworthy that at least three victors in this period came from the far reaches of the Mediterranean world not yet incorporated as Roman provinces: one from Philadelphia (Lydia), another from Seleukia on the Tigris (Mesopotamia), and a third from Cyrene (North Africa). These areas all sooner or later become Roman provinces, but their presence on the lists in this period is a great testimony to the extent to which Greek culture has spread ahead of Roman hegemony. This period also witnesses the last victor from the province of Macedonia (Larissa); Macedonia proper had previously given at least nine victors to the Olympics between 408 and 264 B.C.[15] The series of Macedonian wars with Rome had not only reduced that province's political power but caused it to lose its place of honor at Olympia.

All of the known hippic victories in this period are the 18 by Elis, which suggests that the patron city of the games held the great advantage of not having to transport horses during this economically depressed period. It may have been a matter of Olympic pride that the Eleans decided to continue the hippic events despite the lack of serious competition from other states, lest the prestigious noble contests lapse from the program, which happened later on two separate occasions.

The Julio-Claudian Era, 36 B.C.–A.D. 67

If the last century of the Roman Republic was the nadir of the ancient Olympics, the establishment of the new political order of the Roman Empire under Augustus was the fortuitous gift of a second life that maintained the games for another four centuries. The boon of Augustus' political and cultural enlightenment to Olympia and Greek athletics in general is well known. The victory of the emperor-to-be, Octavian, over Anthony at Actium in northwestern Greece in 31 B.C. secured for him supreme power in Rome. The Actian Games were established by Augustus in

28/27 B.C. as a quadrennial celebration of his success, and the festival was included in the sacred "Circuit" (*periodos*) of traditional Greek festivals—the Olympia, Nemea, Isthmia, and Pythia. "Circuit victors" (*periodonikeis*) proudly listed the "Aktia" in their honorary inscriptions, often higher than the Isthmia or Nemea.[16] Romans even began to reckon years in "Aktiads," that is, four-year periods analogous to Olympiads and counted from 28/27 B.C.[17]

The establishment of Olympic 'spin-offs' or "isolympian games" was in itself no innovation. Such games had been popular especially in Asia Minor since Hellenistic times and they show, in their initiation, the sincerest form of flattery for the 'mother festival' at Olympia. So Augustus and later Roman emperors themselves imitated the practice with their own isolympian festivals. An "Augustalia" was held in Rome and Naples (A.D. 2) to honor Augustus.[18] The "Kaisareia" or "Emperor's Games" were eventually held in seven cities, "Aktias" in local versions were held in nine cities, and "Rhomaias" or "Roman Games" were held in 16 cities.[19] The Roman Senate in A.D. 28 added the quadrennial "Games for the Health of the Emperor" (*Ludi pro salute Caesaris*), and Nero contributed his own Neroneia in A.D. 60, with a special place on the program for musical events, the favorite contests of the ruler.

Augustus had no special love for the Greeks, the former allies of his enemy Anthony, but his admiration for 'classical' Greece and his desire to revive religiosity and cults throughout the empire were part of his larger plan to conquer by assimilation of cultures, or by what we may call 'syncretism,'[20] the attempt to combine or reconcile differing beliefs. It is usually applied to the natural amalgamation of religious or philosophical beliefs that try to accommodate one another. But the term is particularly apt for the historical process whereby the religious beliefs and cultural (including athletic) customs of Greece and Rome were accommodated to one another during the early Roman Empire. As it became less and less possible to retain one's 'pure' ethnic identity in the Mediterranean basin, and as Rome unified by a single leader assumed more and more financial and military power, both Greece and Rome took on a more international, pluralistic or 'ecumenical' character. Imperial Rome incorporated individual Greek (and other) states by granting citizenship to powerful and sympathetic civic leaders, by granting a degree of autonomy to cities that were held ultimately accountable to Rome, and by fostering the identification of Greek and Roman religions, a phenomenon particularly evident at Olympia.

The centerpiece of Graeco-Roman religious syncretism at Olympia was the "Metroön" or "Temple of the Mother Goddess," a Hellenistic structure just east of Hera's temple and just north of the Altar of Zeus in the oldest part of the sanctuary. Shortly prior to Octavian's assumption of the semi-divine title Augustus in 27 B.C., the Achaean League set up in his honor a two-and-a-half-times life-size, gold and silver alloy statue of the Roman leader in the center of the Metroön (*I.Ol.* no. 367). The statue portrayed Augustus in the image of Zeus with all of his attributes—scepter and lightning bolts in hand. The political implications of the monument are clear: the Greeks accepted the divinity of the emperor even before Octavian himself would acknowledge it, and the Greeks assumed the politico-religious leader into their pan-theon to recognize his ultimate power in the very image of a 'Zeusified' Augustus. The iconography is a marvelous gesture of the final willingness of Olympia and Greece, if not their enthusiasm, to accept the Roman overlordship that had been present for over a century. The presence of the Imperial Cult in the sanctuary is all the more remarkable when one recalls that no other 'foreign' gods, even the more popular ones like Mithra, or Isis and Osiris, were admitted there before or after this time. Statues of other emperors—Claudius, Domitian, and Titus—and their wives were later placed in the temple, and statues of still others were placed elsewhere in the Olympic Altis (Paus. 5.20.9). Above the architrave of the Temple of the Cult of the Emperor was emblazoned an inscription that advertised the role of the emperor in this new period of ecumenism: "Augustus, Son of God and Savior of Greece and the Whole Inhabited World" (*I.Ol.* no. 366).

Another sign of Olympic revival and a renewed sense of pride is the appear-ance of inscribed lists of Olympic cult officials kept in the sanctuary and dating from 36 B.C. to A.D. 265.[21] Most of the offices were indeed much older, and their names give us a fascinating glimpse of the sophisticated religious hierarchy that was honored by the monuments of the Roman Imperial period: "ministers of god" (*theokoloi*), "festival heralds" (*spondophoroi*), "seers" (*manteis*), "sacred key keep-ers" (*kleidoukhoi*), "flautist" (*aulētēs*), "guide" (*exegētēs*), "priest of daily sacrifices" (*kathēmerothutēs*), "secretary" (*grammateus*), "wine pourer" (*oinokhoös*), "libation priest" (*epispondorkhēstēs*), "wood cutter" (*xuleus*), "housemaster" (*steganomos*), and "cook" (*mageiros*). This is in fact the order in which they were recorded, with the most important first, in inscriptions from Augustus onward with some minor changes. Some of their ranks are augmented in the second century, presumably to deal with increased tourism. The "guide," for instance, would have shown visi-tors like Pausanias around the site and explained the mythical traditions, and the "seers" would have helped to interpret private sacrifices (*I.Ol.* p. 139).

Attention was also given to improving athletic facilities and to increasing im-perial visibility in the contests during the early Empire. The ceremonial entrance tunnel into the stadium from the sanctuary may have been constructed in the late Hellenistic or early Imperial times. The stadium in its "fourth" stage was renovated during Augustus' reign when the south wall was raised to provide more room for spectators and the "judges' box" area was refurbished.[22]

Augustus himself never competed in or even attended any Olympics, but mem-bers of the imperial family are recorded as victors in chariot races: Tiberius, soon to be adopted as Augustus' son and later made emperor, had won in the four-horse chariot race by 4 B.C. and Germanicus, adopted son of Tiberius, won in the same event in A.D. 17.[23] Tiberius seems to have had less interest in, or need to be inter-ested in, the Olympics during his reign (A.D. 14–37) than had Augustus. Perhaps his own previous participation and the firm establishment of the Imperial Cult under Augustus provided enough stability in Rome-Olympia relations that no intervention or improvements were needed.[24] But with Caligula (37–41), his mad, autocratic successor, there occurs another incident of the sort perpetrated by Sulla in which the Roman leader attempts to steal the Olympic 'thunder,' this time literally. Caligula ordered the colossal statue of Zeus of Phidias to be brought to Rome, where he intended to replace its head with his own. This seems to have been one of the emperor's many attempts to style himself as a Hellenistic monarch. Legend has it that the transport ship was struck by lightning on its way to Greece and that when workers attempted to dismantle the statue at Olympia the monument laughed and shook the scaffolding, which sent the workers into a panic.[25] It is more likely that such wondrous excuses were invented to dissuade the emperor from a task that the Eleans strongly opposed, one that would have incited revolt. In any case, Caligula's attempt at usurpation of Olympian tradition failed even worse than did Sulla's, and the episode illustrates the durability of the sanctuary even in the face of imperial threats.

Little of note regarding relations between Rome and Olympia happened under Claudius (A.D. 41–54), perhaps, again as with Tiberius, out of benign neglect, but relations under his successor, Nero (A.D. 54–68), were notorious. Among Nero's passions were horse racing and music, and he indulged in both of these in his tour of Greek festivals in A.D. 67. Three honorary inscriptions at Olympia (*I.Ol.* nos. 370[?], 373, 374) attest to Nero's special interest in the sanctuary, but the erasure of his name after his death on another (287) reminds us of his unpopularity among officials there at least after his visit. Nero felt drawn to Greece since his talents were not appreciated by Romans: "The Greeks alone are worthy of my genius; they really listen to music" (Suet., *Nero* 22.3). The emperor arranged for all of the Circuit Games to be held in one extraordinary year, A.D. 67, so that he might compete, win at each one, and become a *periodonikēs*. The Olympics were thus postponed from A.D. 65.[26] The Eleans hurriedly built a villa for Nero in the southeast corner of the Altis, adjoining the southwest corner of the stadium. A monumental gateway was built to enter the sanctuary near the villa. Nero entered and was of course victorious in the contests of heralds, foals, and regular four-horse chariots, all normal parts of the program. But he also ordered the inclusion of musical contests in lyre and tragedy to display his talents in those areas, as well as the exceptional ten-horse chariot. Of the latter event, Suetonius (*Nero* 24.2) reports, "[H]e lost his balance, fell from the chariot, and had to be put back in; but though he was not able to go on, and quit before running the course, he was nevertheless crowned victor." On account of this, Dio Cassius relates (63.14), he gave to the Hellanodikai, the judges, an award of 250,000 drachmas, which the Emperor Galba, Nero's successor, later ordered them to pay back.

But Nero's most hypocritical and transparent attempt to use games in the service of politics was his speech at the Panhellenic site of Isthmia on the eve of his departure back to Rome, when he presented the entire province of Achaea with its freedom (Suet., *Nero* 24.2). The gesture was an obvious imitation of Flamininus' real donation of freedom to Greece in 196 B.C., also in the stadium at Isthmia. If the Greeks cheered Nero's proclamation of freedom in A.D. 67, it was probably not because they believed it would truly come to pass, but because by their cheers they could let the emperor know that they sincerely desired their freedom. Nero is said to have returned from Greece with a total of 1,808 crowns from his victories (Dio Cassius 63.20)—and the number is credible. Likewise, the pomp and splendor of his triumphal return to Rome in which he wore both the Olympic and Pythian crowns parodied the return of an athlete and a military hero all in one (Suet., *Nero* 25.1–2). Nero's achievement was, of course, one of illusion built upon illusion which vanished quickly after his death a year later. Not only did he fail to foster the new spirit of the ecumenical games revived under Augustus, but he even brought upon himself the enmity of the Olympic officials, who declared these games invalid, an "Anolympiad." Nero had supposedly also ordered the destruction or removal of all victor statues in the Altis, but this was probably never carried out since many survived until Pausanias' time. A few statues were, however, taken from Olympia back to Rome by Nero (Paus. 5.15.8; 5.26.3).

Table 2.2 illustrates the pattern of regional origins of Olympic victors in the early Empire. The regional origins of known Olympic victors from 36 B.C.–A.D. 67, the Julio-Claudian era of the early Empire, show that the Peloponnese with 13 victors has slipped to a distant second to Asia Minor with 43 (table 2.2). North and Central Greece has also fallen to a miserable 2 native victors after having boasted 41 in the Hellenistic period, and dropped to 7 in the late Republican periods (see appendix 2.1 to this chapter). And Egypt can show only one known Olympic victor from this period. Italy has a respectable 11 victors, but 10 of these are from Rome, including the suspicious 6 victories of Nero, and 2 others by members of the imperial family. For the record, multiple victories by individual athletes do not distort the picture of geographical diversity suggested by the statistics here. There were a few victors with 2 wins, but otherwise only 2, from Antioch and Miletus, achieved 3 wins each. In sum, the only truly healthy display of Olympic talent at this time comes from Asia, and we must ask why this is so in the face of declining success from every other sector of the Graeco-Roman world.

The reasons for Asia's success and other regions' decline is to be sought in the traditional realms of economics and politics. The impoverished cities of the Greek mainland had little to offer the Roman imperial economy except the excellent ports of Patrae, refounded by Augustus, and Corinth refounded by Julius Caesar. But even these were more international centers of mercantile exchange than centers of the old Hellenic spirit. The problem for mainland Greece was not, as Gardiner argues, that the Olympics became more commercialized under the Romans, who saw the games as "the greatest market" (*maximus mercatus*, Cicero *Tusculan Disputations* 5.3), but that Greece was not commercialized enough, nor unified enough in the Classical and Hellenistic periods, to support the luxury of elaborate training schools with surplus capital.[27] In fact, Cicero's allusion to the Olympics as *maximus mercatus* is

Table 2.2. Regions and Cities of Olympic Victors in the Julio-Claudian Era, 36 B.C.–A.D. 67 (Roman province in parentheses)

A. Asia Minor	B. North and Central Greece	C. Peloponnese (all Achaea)	D. Egypt	E. Italy	F. Crete
Aigai, Kilikia, 1 (Syria) Aiolia, 1 (Asia) Alexandria, Troas, 1 (Asia) Antioch. Syria, 6 (Syria) Ephesos, 3 (Asia) Halikarnassos, 1 (Asia) Karia, 1 (Asia) Laertes, Kylikia, 1 (Syria) Laodikaia, Phrygia, 2 (Asia) Magnesia on Maiander, 4 (Asia) Miletus, 7 (Asia) Olympos, Bithynia, 1 (Bithynia) Perge, Pamphylia, 1 (Gallatia) Pergamon, 2 (Asia) Philadelphia, 4 (1 in Asia, 3 in Lydia-Pamphylia) Seleukia, Pieria, 1 (Syria) Sidon, 2 (Syria) Stratonikaia, Karia, 2 (Asia) Tiatira, Lydia, 1 (Asia) Tyana, Kappadokia[a] total, 43 (= 59%)	Antikyra, Phokis, 1 (Achaia) Nikopolis, 1 (Epiros) total, 2 (= 3%)	Aigion, 3 Argos, 1 Elis, 6 Epidauros, 1 Patrae, 1 Zakynthos, 1 total, 13 (= 19%)	Alexandria, 1 (Aegyptus) (= 2%)	Rome, 10 Thurii, 1 total, 11 (= 16%)	Kidonia, 1 (= 2%)

[a] not a province until A.D. 17

actually a quote from the sixth-century B.C. Greek philosopher and statesman Pythagoras, who compares life to "that marketplace which was considered in renown to be of the greatest pomp of the games of all Greece; for just as in that place some seek the glory and fame of the crown by exercise of their bodies, others are led by the search for eating and drinking and by profit" (*ap.* Cicero, ibid.). Similarly Livy compares Corinth as the administrative site of the contemporary Isthmian Games to a *mercatus* (Livy 33.32.3). Livy and Cicero are possibly both translating an original Greek description of and pun on the name of the "athletic festival" (*agōnes*) as "marketplace" (*agora*), and so the designation of games as *mercatus* may be a Roman translation of a Greek characterization of the games as a commercialized center at least since Archaic times.

So the decline in the athletic market in Greece and its success in Asia results from a shift of capital by Rome and others to the large, wealthy, and resource-rich cities from Byzantium to Alexandria. The single most successful city in number of Olympic victors in this period (if we discount Rome, whose numbers are padded by "imperial" victories) is Miletus with eight *Olympionikai*. Prior to Rome's annexation of Greece as a province in the second century B.C., Miletus had produced only 6 known Olympic victors in some six hundred years since the founding of the games, including 1 in the Archaic period (596 B.C.), 1 in the Classical period (472 B.C.), and 4 others with a total of 6 victories in the early Hellenistic period (388, 324, 320, 316, 308, and 296 B.C.). A century and a half elapsed before Miletus' next victory at the start of the Roman period (144 B.C.), followed by the triple victory of one Milesian in the 72 B.C. Olympiad, but it was not until the early Empire, from ca. 24 B.C. to A.D. 17, that the city gained a noteworthy seven victories.[28] This was no doubt due to the prosperity of the city under Augustus' reign, when capital became free enough to spend on gymnasia and talented youths were encouraged to represent the city in the great festivals. We know of one such boxer, Nikophon, an Olympic victor in 8 B.C.(?), who probably came from a wealthy, noble family and later became "chief priest" of the local Cult of the Emperor. Another, Demosthenes, thrice victor in the Olympic trumpeting competition, had an epigram written in his honor by Crinagoras of Mytilene, and he may have even been a lover of Augustus' daughter, Julia.[29] And regarding political patronage of the city, we know, for example, that Augustus twice assumed the titular office of Asymnetie of Miletus (17/16 and 7/6 B.C.), as did Tiberius (8/9 B.C.). The "Friends of Augustus" (*Philosebastoi*) at Miletus even built a temple to the Emperor Caligula for the province of Asia as a whole.[30] The case of this one Asian city may illustrate how others managed to maintain a successful agonistic program in the atmosphere of imperial patronage and commercial prosperity.

Less easily explained is the dearth of Olympic victors from Egypt and Alexandria during the early Empire, when the area prospered financially (table 2.2). Even in the Hellenistic period, there were relatively few victors from an area that was a booming center of Greek culture and the arts (see appendix 2.1 to this chapter). The gymnasium and ephebic education was certainly well established there by the third century B.C., but perhaps the emphasis was more on the education of select youth for magistracies and civic duties than for a professional athletic career.[31] And perhaps internal, ethnic unrest between Greeks and Jews in the early Empire required stricter regulation of gymnasium enrollments, since Roman administrators might have discouraged youth organizations of Greeks who might band together for political reasons against Jews or even Romans. The fact that the Emperor Claudius issued a special decree of Alexandrian citizenship to all who had become *ephēboi*, that is, members of the youths' athletic training schools, down to his reign suggests that at least some members of this group, for example, sons of slaves, had previously been disenfranchised and possibly discouraged from active participation in athletics.[32] Whatever the reason for the absence of Egyptian victors in the early Empire, we will see that this group makes a respectable showing in the late first to third centuries.

Two noteworthy developments in the Olympic program occur during this period concerning the "heavy" events and the hippic contests. After A.D. 37 no one was allowed to enter both boxing and pankration and thus win the title "Successor of Heracles" as others had done previously.[33] Whether this was due to violation of the old Hellenic ideal of "nothing in excess," as Gardiner suggests, or whether officials simply wished to avoid too many 'sweeps' by specialized heavy athletes in these events is uncertain. At least two contemporary athletes testify that *sōphrosunē*, the traditional ideal of "restraint" or "moderation," was still alive, namely the boxer Melanchomas (Dio Chrysostom, *Orations* 29–30) and a pankratiast, Tiberius Claudius Rufus (*I.Ol.* no. 54), but this is not to suggest that the ideal had ever died, nor that it was less frequently observed in the Roman period.

Regarding the hippic events of this period, we learn from Africanus in the entry for the 199th Olympiad (A.D. 17) that "the horse races that had been withdrawn for some time were restored and [Germanicus] son of the Emperor Tiberius won in the four-horse chariot."[34] Similarly, under the 222nd Olympiad (A.D. 109), Africanus mentions that "the hippic events were revived." The reasons for the hiatus on these two occasions can only be surmised, but financial hardship in Elis and the rising popularity of the Roman circuses may have contributed.

No substantial building or renovation was undertaken at Olympia after the reign of Augustus (ending in A.D. 14) and before that of Hadrian (beginning in A.D. 117), apart from the aforementioned Villa of Nero, and a more recently unearthed 'luxury gymnasium' faced in marble and housing a warm bath adjacent to a palaestra exercise room, in the mode of the Stabian Baths at Pompeii, and located southeast of the Altis.[35] Rather than a mark of 'degenerate' taste, the latter is better understood as an adaptation to the new standards of facilities pioneered by Italian architects.

The Middle Imperial Period, A.D. 69–177

It is clear from the example of the Julio-Claudian emperors that the prosperity or neglect of the 'ecumenical Olympics' was directly related to the degree of enthusiasm of each emperor toward the games. It seems that after Nero's farcical Olympics, the games do not again assume a significant political role until the great 'Olympic revival' under Hadrian (A.D. 117–38) and his successors. The Flavian Emperor Vespasian (A.D. 69–79) is better known for his benefaction of the Colosseum, technically the "Flavian Amphitheater," but some inscriptions at Olympia do mention him in unclear contexts (*I.Ol.* nos. 350, 376). Titus (A.D. 79–81) and Domitian (A.D. 81–96) were honored with statues in the Cult of the Emperor's Temple. In Domitian's time was undertaken a general rebuilding that included notably a guildhouse for athletes and the Leonidaion, a kind of summer palace or hostel for 'V.I.P.'s'.[36] Thus, visitors' and other facilities were also improved during the late first century A.D. Nerva's (A.D. 96–98) and Trajan's (A.D. 98–117) connections with Olympia were not particularly close, to judge from inscriptions (*I.Ol.* nos. 437, 378) and other evidence, although the revival of the hippic events in A.D. 109 in Trajan's time marks the beginning of what becomes a full scale Olympic renaissance under Hadrian.

Olympia had never lost its attraction for men of learning, but their enthusiasm for Classical Greek and Olympian culture seems to have been rekindled in the late first and through the second centuries A.D. For instance, we learn that the philosophizing mystic, Apollonius of Tyana, took refuge from Nero at Olympia, where he preached from the steps of the Temple of Zeus on wisdom, manliness, and moderation.[37] The temple and its magnificent colossal, chryselephantine cult statue of Zeus by Phidias, one of the Seven Wonders of the ancient world, became a kind of trendy forum and a focus for intellectuals of the day during this classicizing era. Quintilian, in his *Institutio Oratoria* (12.10.9), published ca. A.D. 95, mused that the "beauty [of Phidias' Zeus] added something to the received religion; to such an extent did the majesty of the work rise to the level of the god." Similarly, Dio Chrysostom's great "Olympic Speech," *Olympiakos Logos*, published in A.D. 97, praised Zeus in our almost monotheistic, Christian picture of the "peaceful and mild . . . giver of life, . . . Father of all, Protector and Savior of men. . . ." And the Stoic philosopher Epictetus (A.D. 55–135) warned his disciples that it would be "a misfortune if one dies without having seen the Zeus of Phidias." These outpourings of praise for a statue from intellectuals of various persuasions and of Greek, Roman, and Asian origin show not mere iconolatry or art appreciation, but an almost spiritual, aesthetic bond among 'idea men' of the middle Imperial period, who could find great solace in the old cult of classical Olympianism. The fact that both the religious and the athletic traditions of old Panhellenism could find new cultural life in an ecumenical world ensured the survival of the Olympics so long as the 'paganism' of Rome flourished.

The strongest imperial endorsement of this 'Olympic renaissance' came under Hadrian (A.D. 117–38), the great philhellene, and his Antonine successors. Hadrian admitted Greeks to full citizenship of Rome and propagated Greek ideals and values. He showed personal devotion to the cult of Zeus by completing the construction of the Temple of Olympian Zeus in Athens, which had been incomplete for over six hundred years. Hadrian even accepted the title "Olympian" (*Olympios*) for himself in A.D. 128; and in the East, he was worshipped as "Zeus Panhellenios."[38] Hadrian's coins carried the image of the Zeus of Phidias on them in a wonderfully effective propagandistic strategy promoting almost complete syncretism of Greek and Roman ideals of leadership.

That Hadrian's propaganda and his real benefactions to Greece were effective and were gratefully received by the Achaean League is evidenced by an inscription (*I.Ol.* no. 57, A.D. 128) that details numerous honors given to the "most divine" emperor in thanks for his manifold grants of assistance to Greek cities, temples, festivals, and games. It is a testimony to the continued political sensitivity of the Achaean League that they also set up honorific statues at Olympia to individual family members of Hadrian's successor, Antoninus Pius, namely one to his wife, Faustina (*I.Ol.* no. 613), one to his adopted son, L. Aelius Aurelius Commodus (*I.Ol.* no. 618), and one to his daughter, Faustina (*I.Ol.* no. 382), later the wife of the Emperor Marcus Aurelius (*I.Ol.* no. 614).

The most significant alteration to the athletic facilities at Olympia during Hadrian's reign was the enlargement of the stadium in phase 5, with a higher south wall and an enlarged judges' box.[39] This was the last significant stadium alteration since Augustus and indicates the revived interest in Greek athletics under Hadrian. The Prytaneion, a council house, and the Theokoleon, a priest's house, were then modernized. Following the lead of the Neronian bath *cum* luxury gymnasium, larger Roman hot baths, the Cladeus Thermae, were built west of the Altis in the early second century A.D. Hot baths were also built opposite the gymnasium and north of the sanctuary at that time.[40]

The greatest display of touristic munificence and perhaps the most controversial structure of this period was the so-called Nymphaeum of Herodes Atticus, a monumental fountain built by the Athenian millionaire, sophist, and cultural philanthrope. The fountain, which was properly called the Nymphaeum of Regilla (Herodes' wife, *I.Ol.* no. 610), was the crowning glory of a water channel built by Herodes ca. A.D. 160. There is no doubt that a good, permanent water source was needed for the great number of tourists. But more probably the appearance and location of the private citizen's monument to himself caused more scandal among the conservative Olympic officials than the fact that the amenity was even offered to alleviate the traditionally hot and dusty site. The Nymphaeum, situated in the oldest part of the sanctuary on the east side of the Temple of Hera, was a curved exedra shape on which were placed statues of the Emperors Hadrian, Antoninus

Pius, and Marcus Aurelius, as well as Attica personified and Herodes' entire family. The fact that Pausanias passes by the monument in silence despite his otherwise thorough tour of the site in A.D. 174 may indicate that the structure was controversial and the author thus avoided taking sides. There is some indication in Lucian's *On the Death of Peregrinus* 19 (late second century A.D.) that a conservative Elean element objected to the introduction of such conveniences: the Cynic Peregrinus is nearly stoned by the people when he objects to the fountain as an effeminate innovation.[41] Yet hot baths were added in less ostentatious locations in this period without any adverse comments.

It is difficult to uncover the truth behind the Nymphaeum controversy, Lucian's joke, and Pausanias' silence, however, since Herodes himself doubtless enjoyed favor with the conservative Eleans. His wife, Regilla, held the most sacred Olympic position open to a woman, that of the priestess of Demeter Chamyne. Pausanias (6.21.1–2) tells us that "Herodes Atticus has dedicated statues of Demeter and Kore in Pentelic marble in place of the ancient ones."

One of the greatest testimonia to the Olympic fascination of both tourists and men of letters in the second century is the simple fact that Pausanias devoted nearly a full two of his ten books in the *Guide to Greece* to Olympia (i.e., books 5 and 6). It is fortunate that Pausanias' visit to Olympia occurred in A.D. 174, at a period when the Hadrianic-Antonine renaissance had taken place. We are availed of a description of the site toward the end of its thousand-year history, but before its third-century decline. The amount of space devoted to Olympia may be a greater indication of the keen interest of Pausanias' wealthy Roman and Asian audience than his own personal tastes, although both are present in the *Guide*. Thus, the tourist and the man of letters is synthesized in a work epitomizing the ecumenical interests of the second-century citizen in the site.

One indication of the emperor's endorsement of athletics in the middle Imperial period is the foundation of games by or in honor of the ruling Caesar. The Capitolia was established by Domitian in A.D. 86, became one of the sacred "Circuit Games" with the Olympics, and, at least in its early years, included a footrace for girls.[42] Hadrian's tremendous popularity in Greece and Asia is attested by the proliferation of games in his honor, at least twelve in various cities: Alexandria, Ankyra, Antiochia, Anazarbos, Athens, Ephesos, Gaza, Hadrianeia, Herakleia, Cyzicus, Smyrna, and Tarsos.[43]

By this time popular tastes for athletic events were also changing in Greece and the East. The fact that musical and poetry contests are listed ahead of athletic contests by A.D. 127 on some victor lists, whereas athletic contests had come first in the Augustan period and earlier, indicates an increasing popularity in nonathletic entertainment and skills.[44] The Olympic organizers resisted the trends and never admitted musical or poetry contests, but certain singers were honored for their "Olympic hymns," which may have accompanied the opening procession, the central sacrifice to Zeus, or the prize ceremony.[45] The contests for heralds and trumpeters with which the Olympics opened were not classified as musical, since the volume and not the beauty of voices or tone counted most (Paus. 6.14.10). Such flute playing as accompaniment for events like discus- and javelin-throwing and jumping probably held a customary but purely honorary position at the Olympics.

There is also an indication that, with regard to athletic contests themselves, popular taste was shifting from the more traditionally prestigious track and field events to the more violent and showy "heavy" events in boxing, wrestling, and the all-out, karate-style pankration. In an inscription recording the prizes for the local games at Aphrodisias during Imperial times, "heavy" events receive much bigger prizes than do footraces and pentathlon, whereas a fourth century B.C. prize list from the Panathenaic games in Athens gives more money to the stade race winner than to any other athletic victor.[46]

It is not surprising that public or even imperial subsidies to successful athletes continued into late Imperial times. Subsidies in some form had been given to victors in the "Circuit" games since Archaic Greek times to encourage participation in the Olympics and other crown games without value prizes. Dio Chrysostom (*De gloria* [66].11, ca. late first, early second c. A.D.) mentions that victorious athletes were paid 5 talents in his day. The Emperor Carinus (A.D. 283–84, *Historia Augusta, Carinus* 19.2) gave gold, silver, and silken garments as gifts to athletes during his reign.

Table 2.3 charts participation by local regions during the middle Empire. The regional origins of Olympic victors in this period (table 2.3) generally maintain the trends seen in the early Empire. Asia Minor continues to boast the majority of victories (46 = 59 percent). The Peloponnese declines further from 13 victories (19 percent) in the early Empire to 8 (10 percent) in the middle period. Italy declines surprisingly further from 11 to one, indicating, perhaps, a disinclination for noble Romans to be involved in Greek athletics even though Philhellenic interest as benefactors and tourists was obviously high. But the most radical shift comes in victories from Egypt and North Africa, who tallied only one victory in the previous period but have 19 (25 percent) in the middle Empire. Of these, 17 were won by 15 Alexandrian athletes. It may be that Alexandria has finally adopted Hellenism wholeheartedly and has overcome internal problems of finance and civil strife from previous periods. The acceptance of athletics indicates the adoption of Greek culture at a popular level in Egypt, a change that had been centuries in coming but was to endure into the late Empire. With the extension of participants into Egypt, the 'ecumenical Olympics' were now more truly international than ever.

Ephesos, which previously had only 3 victors in the Classical period[47] and 3 in the early Empire, now boasted 9 Olympic victors at a time when the city prospered. Sikyon, which has no known victors in the early Empire when it ceased to sponsor the Isthmian games, is again visible with a brief streak of 6 victories within four Olympiads, the strongest showing in the Peloponnese, largely thanks to the talent

Table 2.3. Regions and Cities of Olympic Victors in the Middle Imperial Period, A.D. 69–177 (Roman provinces in parentheses)

A. Asia Minor	B. North and Central Greece (all Achaea)	C. Peloponnese (Achaea)	D. Egypt (Aegyptos)	E. Italy (Italia)
Adana, 2 (Kilikia)	Aigina, 2	Elis, 1	Alexandria, 17	Rome, 1 (= 1%)
Aigai, Aiolis, 1 (Asia)	Athens, 1	Sikyon, 6	Arisonoite, 2	
Antioch, 1 (Syria)	Elatara. Phokis, 1	Sparta, 1	total, 19 (= 25%)	
Apamea, 2 (Bithynia)	total, 4 (= 5%)	total, 8 (= 10%)		
Chios, 2 (Asia)				
Ephesos. 9 (Asia)				
Iasos. 1 (Asia)				
Kappadokia, 1 (Galatia)				
Keramos. Karia. 1 (Asia)				
Kyme, Aiolis, 1 (Asia)				
Laodikaia, Lykaonia. 1 (Galatia)				
Magnesia on Maiander, 1 (Asia)				
Magnesia at Siphylos, 2 (Asia)				
Miletus, 2 (Asia)				
Pergamon, 1 (Asia)				
Philadelphia. Lydia, 1 (Asia)				
Rhodes, 2 (Asia)				
Sardis, 3 (Asia)				
Seleukia. 1 (Syria)				
Side, 2 (Lykia-Pamphylia)				
Smyrna, 2 (Asia)				
Tarsos, 2 (Kilikia)				
Tenos, 1 (Asia)				
Tralles, 1 (Asia)				
Xanthos, 3 (Lykia-Pamphylia)				
total, 46 (= 59%)				

of one athlete, Aelius Granianus, who won 5 victories in running events and the pentathlon and was hence more an individual than a regional phenomenon.[48]

Only two hippic victories are recorded for this period, a Roman in the four-horse chariot.[49] Africanus reports that the hippic events were only revived in A.D. 109 after an indefinite moratorium at Olympia, but does not name any hippic victors in that Olympiad. The last previous known hippic victories were those of Nero in A.D. 67. This and other sources discussed earlier seem to indicate a decline in both available funding and the quality of competition at Olympia in the period between Nero and Trajan, followed by the Hadrianic 'renaissance.' The hippic events, however, even with their revival, probably still lacked a good international field of competitors that, apart from Romans, seems to have been absent throughout the Roman era. Perhaps the best stock of horses were being diverted into the more lucrative contests of the Roman circus, widely and wildly popular in this era.

The Late Imperial Period, A.D. 181–393

After the final burst of Olympic splendor under the Antonines, the games, like the Roman Empire itself, undergo a slow process of disintegration and ultimately death. The late second and third centuries show inferior architecture, no major improvements, and, to judge from coin finds, a decrease in visitors and deflated currency.[50] Africanus' list of Olympic victors ends in A.D. 217, and thereafter we find numerous Olympiads for which we know of no individual victors. Indeed, it is to some extent only an assumption that the Olympics did take place without exception every four years from A.D. 217 until their demise in the late fourth century.

We can, however, reasonably assume that the games were flourishing under imperial patronage into the first half of the third century A.D., since we find honorary inscriptions for a dedication to Julia Domna, wife of the Emperor Septimius Severus (A.D. 193–211; *I.Ol.* no. 387), and one for the Emperor Caracalla (*I.Ol.* no. 386, dated to A.D. 211–15). But no later emperors are mentioned in the monuments at the site. Certain emperors who showed an interest in Greek athletics may have supported the Olympics. Severus Alexander (A.D. 222–35) even participated in wrestling (*Historia Augusta, Severus Alexander* 27); and the Emperor Carinus (A.D. 283–84) gave gifts to athletes in the games that he sponsored (*Historia Augusta, Carinus* 19.2). Gordian III (A.D. 238–44) had games in his honor in at least two Greek cities, Athens and Aphrodisias.[51]

Olympia also continued in its tradition as a center of the arts. Aurelios Apollonios, an orator from Antioch, was honored by the Olympic Council in Olympiad 225 (= A.D. 221–24) with a statue.[52] And Sperkhios of Pisa in A.D. 233 was honored as "blameless on account of his song" written for some sacred ceremony at the games (*I.Ol.* no. 482). But the greatest testimony to the cultural syncretism of this ecumenical age is the history written by A. Asinius Quadratus, whose complete history of

Rome was entitled "The Thousand Years" (*Khilietēris*), covering the period 776 B.C.–
A.D. 223 and making the foundation of Rome coincide with that of the Olympic
games. The Eleans honored him with a statue for "honoring Olympia in word and
deed" (*I.Ol.* no. 356). Here we find that the Olympic reality is validated and acknowledged in that the site becomes a kind of twin sister to Rome. According to Quadratus at least, both great historical movements shared an antiquity, a tradition, and
a greatness that survived a millennium. The spirit of the ecumenical games is
thereby celebrated jointly with Rome's in this work written toward the end of the
period of Olympic greatness.

It is no accident that the lists of Olympic cult officials end in A.D. 265 (*I.Ol.*
nos. 138–42), since the East German Heruli invaded Greece in A.D. 267, attacking
Athens, Corinth, Argos, and Sparta. Olympian authorities built a great wall around
the Temple of Zeus and the Council House (Bouleterion) from the materials of other
buildings in the Altis. The idea was to guard the core of the sacred sanctuary and
the great statue of Zeus.[53] The invaders probably never reached Olympia, but the
siege preparation scarred the site permanently. The Herulian invasion did not de-
stroy Olympia, but it did mark the "beginning of the end." Around A.D. 300, an
earthquake damaged the Temple of Hera and the main palaestra. It may have also
damaged the roof of the Temple of Zeus, which was repaired in A.D. 303 during the
reign of Diocletian.[54] Olympia showed the will to survive despite even natural disaster and the weakening financial state of Greece during this period.

One hundred years passed before the death blow came to the festival that had
strained under but survived all previous external threats. We are told by an eleventh-
century historian, Kedrenos (*Historia comparativa* 322B and 348A), of the last Olympiad (293rd), which occurred under Theodosius I in 393 or 394 before his edict
against pagan festivals. Kedrenos reports that the Zeus of Phidias was moved to
Constantinople, where it was kept in the palace of the patrician Lausos and was
eventually lost in a fire. But the source may well be in error.[55] The Edict of Theodosius II on November 13, 426, ordered the destruction of all pagan temples. A late
source records the burning down of the Temple of Zeus at that time (Scholiast to
Lucian's *Rhetorical Precepts* 6 [22 Jacobitz]). Archaeology shows rather that another
earthquake brought down the temple, and traces of burning are absent. The cult
statue was probably dismantled by opponents of paganism. In A.D. 395, two years
after the Edict of Theodosius I, the Goths under Alaric invaded as far as the Peloponnese, although Olympia was probably passed by. Phidias' Zeus statue probably
suffered from both Christians and barbarian invaders and was not to have survived,
at the latest, the 426 edict. During the first half of the fifth century, a Christian
church was built on the site of Phidias' Olympic workshop. Thus, the Olympic religion and the ecumenical festival were literally and figuratively subsumed by new,
more dogmatic or more barbaric forces in Greece.

One fallacy regarding the late Olympics which has been perpetuated in the
handbooks is that the games in late antiquity "were rather victims, like most things

in history, of an inner decline and the external effect of force."[56] The real threats to the Olympics in the Roman era were external—adverse ideologies, natural disasters, barbarian invasions, a failing economy on the Greek mainland, and the eclipse of the stabilizing central authority of secular Rome. Even if Quadratus' chronology regarding the simultaneous founding of Rome and the Olympics is false, the roughly simultaneous falls of pagan Rome and the Olympics are not coincidental. The evidence typically mustered for internal decline of the games is slim. Philostratus' *Gymnastics* (A.D. 215–25), the last literary assessment of Greek athletics, contrasts the ideals of the old system of training in Archaic and mythical Greece with the inferior contemporary practices. But Philostratus is preoccupied with his own ideological preconceptions, which leave him in error and out of step with his times on many issues.[57] It is equally dangerous to assume decline in the quality or ideals of the Olympics because of a lack of monuments associated with them. The fact that the last recognized victor statue was erected in A.D. 261 (*I.Ol.* no. 243) and the latest cult records date to A.D. 265 (*I.Ol.* p. 138) only suggests that capital was lacking to erect such monuments. Similarly the last known horse races were in the mid-third century,[58] but the events may merely lack documentation from this period, or they too may have again suffered a moratorium for financial reasons.

The geographical distribution of victors in the late Empire is illustrated by table 2.4. A greater testimony to the continued popularity and prestige of the ecumenical games to the end is the international pool of known victors. The record of victors is very patchy after 261, with one perhaps in 277, followed by a gap of nearly a century to a few known from the late fourth century, with 2 possibly in 369, one in 381, and one in 385. The last known Olympic victor was the Athenian boy boxer, M. Aurelios Zopyros, in 385.[59] The last known hippic victors mentioned were from Rhodes and Athens. By region, Asia still held virtually the same majority of victories (54 percent) in the late Empire as it had since the early Empire (table 2.4). And Egypt still provided the second greatest number (29 percent) as it had since the middle Empire, a testimony to the continued presence of capital in Egypt and Asia in the later Empire. By city, Alexandria still had the most victors (11, by nine victors) and Ephesos still the second most (5, by five victors). Salamina in Cyprus is also credited with 5 athletic victories, though the number may be 3, and in any case they are all won by a single individual, Demetrius. One Bithynian athlete, Graus, distinguished his region with 3 victories in the long-distance race in three successive Olympiads from A.D. 213 to 221. Sinope, a city of Paphlagonia in Bithynia-Pontos on the eastern edge of the Empire, boasted 4 victories, but these all by the same Valerius Eclectus, in the four Olympiads spanning A.D. 245–61, and in the nonathletic event of herald. North and Central Greece, with 5 recorded victories, and the Peloponnese, with 4, are at their nadir, again probably for economic reasons. The total absence of recorded victories by Italians or Sicilians is puzzling but shows a lack of interest perhaps due to stronger absorption in domestic Roman festivals, games, and circuses.

Table 2.4. Regions and Cities of Olympic Victors in the Late Imperial Period, A.D. 181–385 (excluding the Olympic years 265 and 273 for which no victors are known)

A. Asia Minor	B. North and Central Greece	C. Peloponnese (Achaea)	D. Egypt/N. Africa	E. Crete
Armenia, 1 (Kappadokia)	Athens, 4 (Achaia)	Sparta, 3	Alexandria, 11 (Aegyptos)	Gortyn, 1 (Crete-Cyrene)
Bithynia, 3 (Bithynia- Pontos)	Augusta Traiana (Stara	Korinth, 1	Antinoe, 1 (Aegyptos)	(=1%)
Daldis, 1 (Asia)	Zagora), 1	total, 4 (= 7%)	"Egypt" (Aegyptos) 1	
Ephesos, 5 (Asia)	total, 5 (= 8%)		Hermopolis, 1 (Aegyptos)	
Kyzikos, 2 (Asia)			Cyrene, 1 (Cyrene)	
Magnesia on Maiander, 1 (Asia)			Naukratis, 1 (Aegyptos)	
Miletus, 1 (Asia)			Oxyrhynchos, 1 (Aegyptos)	
Nysa, Karia, 1 (Asia)			total, 17 (= 28%)	
Philadelphia, 2 (one in Asia, one in Lydia)				
Phoinikia, 2 (Syria)				
Rhodes, 1 (Asia)				
Salamina, 5 (?) (Cyprus)				
Sinope, 4 (Bithynia-Pontos)				
Smyrna, 2 (Asia)				
Tiatira, Lydia, 1 (Asia)				
Xanthos, Lykia, 1 (Asia)				
total, 33 (= 55%)				

The relations between Rome and Olympia are a particularly clear example of how Rome slowly 'fine-tuned' its responses to foreign cultures incorporated into the Empire. Alternations between abuse and neglect by the central government were finally tempered into standard policy. Augustus knew the value of adaptation and quickly established the presence of the Cult of the Emperor next to that of Zeus at Olympia. The extremes of Caligula and Nero were typical of all else in their reigns, but the more usual benign support of the Olympic cult and festival is exemplified by Hadrian and the Antonines. Rome never truly dominated Olympia but rather joined it to control political allegiance, just as Olympia welcomed Roman rulers in order to finance the games. As the graph in appendix 2.1 to this chapter shows, mainland Greece was never strictly ousted from the competition, but it simply could not compete with Asia and Egypt in wealth and leisure devoted to training. Victories by athletes from northern and central Greece and the Peloponnese consequently all but disappear in the middle and late Empire.

It has recently been argued that the diminished amount of literary and inscriptional evidence for victors after about 200 B.C. may point to a relative dimunition of interest in Olympia generally.[60] But neither the quality of athletic performance nor the standards of Olympic ideals were compromised in this Roman era, so far as our limited sources reveal. The local Elean organizers still supplied the officials and controlled the content of the festival. The later Olympics retained the fame and the conservative values of those of Classical Greece, and added to it the more international dimension of ecumenism, which is the inheritance of the modern Olympics.

Since the ancient Olympics for their entire life were of international importance in the eastern Mediterranean, their history uniquely combines a ritual core of the Olympian religion and a purely Greek program of competition with occasional acknowledgments of Roman imperial presence. To this extent, the Olympics can be distinguished from many of the festivals to be examined later. Lesser athletic festivals, like the Heraia at Olympia and the Erotidaea of Thespiae, show little or no external political or economic influence from outside mainland Greece. Though these lesser festivals were very likely influenced in part by the Olympics as a model for their program, prizes, and rituals, they also maintained their unique character and function in accordance with their own origins and cult interests. But the pervasive influence of that great Panhellenic festival requires us to consider its history first, and to keep it in mind as an important presence under which these local games flourished.

APPENDIX 2.1: Graph of Regional Origins of Olympic Victors, 776 B.C. to A.D. 277[a]

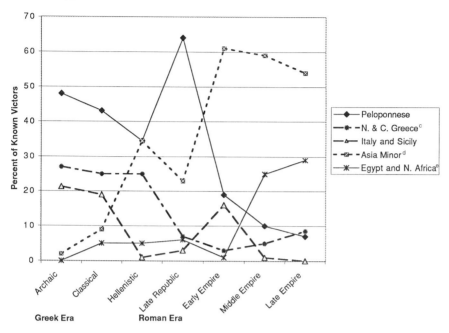

Period:[b]	Archaic	Classical	Hellenistic	Late Republic	Early Empire	Middle Empire	Late Empire
# known victors	187	236	160	74	71	78	60
				(incl. 1 from Crete)			

a. All numbers of victors, determination of regions or native cities of victors, and estimates of the dates of victories are based upon Moretti (1957 and above, note 28, 1987) and Ebert (above, note 59, 1994).

b. The following concordance of Moretti's numbers with dates has been followed in the compilation of this graph:
   Moretti (1957), nos. 1–195 = 776–484 B.C. (Archaic Greece); Moretti nos. 196–461 = 480–336 B.C. (Classical Greece); Moretti nos. 462–639 = 332–148 B.C. (Hellenistic Greece); Moretti nos. 640–718 = 144–40 B.C. (Late Republican Rome); Moretti nos. 719–795 = 36 B.C.-A.D. 67 (Early Imperial Rome); Moretti nos. 796–882 = A.D. 69–177 (Middle Imperial Rome); Moretti nos. 883–942 = A.D. 181–277 (Late Imperial Rome).

c. "North and Central Greece" includes Macedonia, Epiros, and the cities of Achaea north of Corinth, namely Antikyra, Aigina, Athens, Delphi, Elataia, and Megara.

d. "Asia Minor" includes the Roman provinces of Asia, Bithynia, Gallatia, Kappadokia, Kilikia, Cyprus, Lydia, Lykia, Mesopotamia, Pamphylia, Pontos, and Syria.

e. "Egypt and North Africa" includes Aigyptos and Cyrene. Crete, which was included in the province of Cyrene in the Roman era, has not been included in the statistics in the appendix nor in tables 2.1 to 2.4, due to the small number of its Olympic victors and the difficult of assigning it to any one of the geographical regions as defined here. We should in any case note that Crete had 2 known Olympic victors in the Archaic period (Moretti [1957], nos. 158 and 181), 5 in the Classical period (Moretti nos. 274, 296, 367b, 390, 398), one in the Julio-Claudian era (Moretti no. 752), and one in the Late Empire (Moretti no. 906). Its reputation as a haven for pirates in the Hellenistic period and after may in part account for the dearth of known victors from that time on.

3

ATHLETICS, INITIATION, AND PEDERASTY

Though it is essential to understand the character and history of the Olympics as the earliest known regular athletic festival among the Greeks, a myriad of other games testify to the use of athletics in constructing Greek society. The athletic contests of Greek myth and history were held in a variety of contexts: pure entertainment, physical education, funeral games, sacred festivals, and initiation rituals. The last of these occasions may be the least obvious, since it has not received much scholarly attention lately, but it is an essential strand in the complicated social nexus of Greek athletics. Moreover, in recent decades some scholarship has argued that Greek initiation had its origins in a prehistoric, Indo-European ritual that assigned a significant role to homosexuality, or more specifically pederasty, in Greek culture.[1] Since much of this work discusses issues of gender and sexuality in relation to Greek sports, it is crucial that these theories of an initiatory origin of pederasty be examined in relation to athletics. Though origins per se are of less interest here than later historical manifestations, most of the initiation theories claim that the initiation-pederasty nexus continued to function in various ways in the historical period. Thus the theories may shed light on historical practice. A critique of these theories is also important because, in their view, men's athletic training and gymnasium life were frequently associated with the education of a young initiate by his male lover. It is generally accepted that from the sixth century B.C. onward the gymnasium was "a hotbed of homosexuality," a topic addressed fully in chapter 8.[2] Whether or how pederasty in an athletic context may be related to a notion of 'initiation' of young men into adulthood is part of the concern of this chapter. The topic of female initiation and contests, which largely differ in character and orientation, will be treated separately in chapters 4 to 7.

We begin the study of Greek athletics and initiation with the earlier theories of Jeanmaire and Brelich, who posited initiatory origins for many athletic contests, most significantly for the Olympics.[3] In contrast to the more recent pederasty-centered theories that depended on the work of Jeanmaire and Brelich, the latter saw the public games as offshoots of primitive, local initiation ceremonies, without emphasis on the sex roles of participants. While a number of local religious rituals or festivals required of the citizen youths participation in contests of an athletic or quasi-athletic nature, it is not clear whether these gave rise to the more conventional athletic festivals such as the Olympics, or whether they are primarily rituals that incidentally took on an athletic character. In other words, can we make a generic distinction between two independent uses of the contest form in festivals—rituals with incidental contests and festivals with a full athletic program—or can we show an evolutionary relation between them?

The problem, then, is to establish the relation between athletics, initiation, and pederasty on the basis of historical evidence and with a critique of current theories. Let us begin with the definition of initiation itself. According to Mircea Eliade, "the term initiation in the most general sense denotes a body of rites and oral teachings whose purpose is to produce a decisive alteration in the religious and social status of the person to be initiated. In philosophical terms, initiation is equivalent to an ontological mutation of the existential condition. The novice emerges from his ordeal with a totally different being: he has become *another*."[4] Initiation as a universal phenomenon is generally divided into three types: (1) collective rituals whose function is to effect the transition from childhood or adolescence to adulthood, a process to which ethnologists refer as the *rite de passage* called "tribal initiation" or "puberty rites"; (2) rites for entering a secret society, like a mystery religion; and (3) initiation into a mystical vocation, like shamanism.[5] We will concern ourselves with the first type, so-called tribal initiation, which has certain general characteristics that can be grouped under three stages of the process of transition: separation from society, life in isolation, and reintegration into society.[6] There are also a number of more specific characteristics that often, but not always, belong to tribal initiation; namely, that it is compulsory, communal, sexually segregated, prenuptial, and instructive in adult activities and tribal traditions. Most significant for this study is that tribal initiations often require a test of physical strength (sometimes a contest), they impose definite restrictions on dress and diet, and their rituals occur periodically according to age groupings.[7] Since these initiations are usually the central festival of the tribe, through them takes place also the renewal of the community.[8] Only the formal aspects of life remain the same during the change of generations. The initiation ceremony, then, has the real function of introducing youths to established religious and social institutions and testing their fitness to inherit them.

Brelich has argued that initiation as a clearly identifiable and independent institution is usually absent from 'high civilizations,' since the latter depend upon an elite group of rulers and the division of duties among citizens, whereas tribal societies require of the individual direct participation in public matters and a diversity of practical skills.[9] According to these broad criteria, Greece may be called a 'high' or 'advanced' civilization, at least for the period post ca. 700 B.C. and possibly much earlier. Whereas tribal societies can impose uniform initiation rites that instruct all participants and test their worthiness, in advanced cultures, like ancient Greece, the state largely replaces the tribe as the primary unit of organization. Though tribal initiation that survived in some form in post-eighth-century Greece may have been less clearly demarcated, scholars have sought to identify it in two ways, by seeing either its function or its form reincorporated in the rituals, institutions, or myths of a state.

The prior existence of an institution of initiation in an advanced culture may be indicated by several formal characteristics mentioned above (communality, sexual segregation, special ordeal, etc.). But there should also be evidence of a primary criterion for initiation, the function of introducing the adolescent to adulthood.[10] Function of a practice cannot be defined by origin alone: according to Vidal-Naquet, "[t]he past is influential only inasmuch as it is present in the structures of thought, manners, and interpretations."[11] When, in 'high civilizations,' institutions of initiation have become weakened or changed, this function can still sometimes be detected in the myths with which they are associated. The myth itself may relate the transition to adulthood, like the myth of Theseus' return from Crete associated with the Athenian Oschophoria festival, and it may contain initiation motifs, like the transvestite dress of Theseus' comrades, also reflected in the Oschophoria, to be discussed later. Yet the use of myths in the reconstruction of historical practices like initiation rituals is notoriously fraught with speculation and guesswork.[12] Myths often better reflect the age in which the particular version was fixed than a hypothetical earlier stage. To this extent, a myth is useful as a reflection of historical practice when it is viewed as a later invention to reinvest a prehistoric ritual with meaning. But even if the reconstruction of a primitive ritual from myths and other sources is convincing, it often yields, in the case of ancient Greece, "fossilized rites which had lost their original function . . . and had acquired new functions within a complex society of the kind that eludes meaningful comparison with non-literate, primitive groups."[13] In any case, it is not of primary interest here to identify origins, but rather the workings of the ritual in later historical periods.

'Primitive' and 'Historical' Initiations

This leads us to another, in my view more profitable way of investigating initiation. Alongside the limited phenomenon of 'primitive' tribal initiation, there is the more clearly discernible historical establishment, or re-establishment, of an initiatory institution that serves the same function as, and shares the characteristics of, the primitive variety. This proposed distinction, then, between 'primitive' and 'historical' initiations is not merely an arbitrary one based on the period of institutionalization but argues, against Brelich, that initiatory rituals, whether newly created or of long survival, are of equal importance in 'high' civilizations where they serve a similar function of introducing youths to adulthood. Among the Greeks, initiation could be functionally described as the "accession to the condition of a warrior" for boys, and preparation for marriage for girls.[14] It has been pointed out that, in the course of Greek history, youth societies became prolific by the Hellenistic and Roman eras, when their gymnasium and athletic functions surpassed and supplanted what had originally been military uses.[15] In some sense, initiation is a species of the genus 'education' or 'upbringing,' Greek *paideia*, which was discussed earlier in the introduction. Initiation differs from education generally in its use of secrecy (seen in the schema of separation, life on the margin, reintegration) and of symbolism (primarily of death and rebirth). Both secrecy and symbolism are evident in initiations established in the historical period, certainly in Greece.[16] Absent any likely prehistorical connection, an initiation ritual that has probably been established in the historical period is still a rich source for understanding its contemporary context. If, on the other hand, there is strong evidence for a 'primitive' initiation that has survived with a similar function—not just a fossilized trace—into the historical period, it may indicate the longevity of the cultural phenomenon, and in some cases a long-term association between initiation and athletics, or initiation, athletics, and pederasty.   *→ father figure?*

   Sergent, Bremmer, and other scholars see pederasty as an institution that evolved from Indo-European initiation rituals in the prehistoric period, in which an older male became the lover of the initiate and his mentor in hunting, sports, and other aspects of adult life.[17] With the lapse of initiation per se in historical times, they argue, pederasty survived, and its conventions, including contest-trials, reflected its origins. Kenneth Dover has offered a convincing refutation of these theories and an alternative hypothesis as follows: Greek overt homosexuality began in the seventh century B.C. and spread rapidly among Greek states; Greek myths and initiation rituals were subsequently invested with homosexual content to validate the tastes and customs of their culture; a didactic relationship was superimposed on the pederastic one, not vice versa.[18] Dover concedes the possibility of an Indo-European initiation system that partly survived in later Greece, a possibility also admitted here, but he challenges whether pederasty was part of this phenomenon and continued after its lapse. His objections are several, both historical and philological, but most cogent are the following: these theories read initiation into many myths by a biased selection of detail; there is no literary evidence for overt homosexuality prior to the seventh century B.C. and its absence in Homer and elsewhere is unexplained by these theories.

   The reason for homosexuality's 'coming out of the closet' in the seventh century is not readily explained by Dover, beyond the general observation that

> a very slight shift in one social variable can trigger major and lasting
> changes, and, once social approval has been given to an activity which
> is physically, emotionally and aesthetically gratifying *to the adult males*
> of a society, it is not easily suppressed.[19]

One factor that may have hastened the shift is the hierarchical and competitive character of Greek homosexuality in which a subordinate youth becomes the beloved of an older male of the community. Ethologists identify the "rank-demonstrating significance" of the pederastic sex act even outside of Greek culture.[20] Public competitiveness also emerged in athletic festivals in the same period, from the seventh to sixth centuries B.C. Athletics and overt homosexuality therefore arose contemporaneously in a context of heightened social competition for status. A competitive spirit in Greek culture had of course been present since the eighth-century genesis of the Homeric texts, or likely even earlier, but the more open expression of the spirit both in sports and in sexuality was particularly characteristic of the sixth century and later.

There remains the question of what social circumstances, in addition to the 'agonistic spirit' seen in the rise of public games, may have encouraged more public demonstrations of pederasty by itself and in connection with the gymnasium and athletics, a complex problem beyond the scope of this study. I may, however, briefly suggest some of the possible causes of these related phenomena. Age-classes, which later found public expression in pederasty and in age-classes of athletic contests, may well have been part of Greek social organization before the eighth century B.C. and hence served as a foundation for the more public demonstration.[21] Age was, inter alia, a demonstration of rank and hierarchy on which Greek society was based. No doubt the emergence of the *polis* and increasing economic and military strength of the Greeks contributed to their new-found self-confidence, which allowed the public show of sexual and competitive hierarchy among male citizens. It is likely also that the popular reception of the Homeric epics was also instrumental in fostering athletic games that mimicked the heroic contests. Whatever the full nexus of historical and social reasons, it seems unlikely, given Dover's objections, that the survival of primitive initiation rituals involving pederasty per se were major factors.

The other body of theory mentioned earlier, that of Jeanmaire, Brelich, and others, argues for the prehistoric association between initiation and athletics without highlighting the role of pederasty. These studies posit the widespread existence of tribal initiation in prehistoric Greece which can be detected in many of the historical rituals and institutions, including athletic contests. While these hypotheses generally contain much that is valid and of interest, the findings with regard to a broad influence of initiation on athletic contests are open to criticisms of inadequate or unduly selective evidence. One major problem with these approaches is their detection of initiation ritual as the basis for the Olympics and other later athletic festivals solely on the evidence of characteristics that are seen to be 'initiatory,' for example, special dress, diet, celibacy, periodic occurrence, and age categories.[22] Yet in many cases these characteristics are late accretions to the athletic festival.

Brelich, for example, attempts to explain how the Olympics might have begun as a tribal initiation when two cities, Elis and Pisa, contended for patronage of the games over a long period. He posits, without evidence, an 'intertribal' initiation shared by both places in a prehistoric period.[23] It has long been recognized that the various and conflicting legends of the foundation of the Olympic festival by Eleans or Pisans are very likely a product of competitive myth-making by the two cities in later periods as they tried to claim priority in sponsorship of the games.[24] Yet there is no secure historical basis for discovering intertribal initiation in these politicizing legends. Brelich also fails to address the crucial fact that there were no age categories at the Olympics until the 37th Olympiad in 632 B.C., when the stade race and wrestling for boys were added. Prior to that, it is a safe assumption that the great majority of contestants were 17 or older.[25] Male and female contests were segregated, but there are many practical reasons for that provision. Special diets became widespread only in the fifth century B.C. and afterward; here again practical considerations rather than ritual would best explain the usage.[26] Jeanmaire reasons that the original Olympic event, the footrace, suggests that the games began as a ritual, since other later contests which were more clearly part of rituals frequently included the footrace. Moreover, theorists like Brelich and Jeanmaire fail to explain why the earliest literary representations of athletic contests, those in the *Iliad* and *Odyssey*, do not in any way reflect supposed initiatory rites. The footrace is given no special treatment or prestige in the epics; in fact the chariot race comes first and receives the lengthiest treatment of all the contests in *Iliad* 23. There are no age categories in Homeric athletics, and in fact older men are shown competing more often than younger boys. Periodic cycles are not evident, and competitions are more often at irregular occasions than in the context of recurring festivals.[27]

There are, then, serious doubts about placing athletics in contexts of 'prehistoric initiation,' as argued for either by those seeing connections with pederasty or by those detecting links with athletics in local rituals apart from pederasty. These doubts lead us to adopt the more cautious, alternative view that what some call 'prehistoric initiation' can be more reliably described as a form of social formation or *paideia* which was widespread in many cities of ancient Greece but only after the eighth century B.C. Ancient sources describe various educational systems in each *polis* as institutions whose main function was to bring youths to adulthood. Though secrecy and symbolic rituals, which are characteristic of many forms of initiation, were not always present, age categories, segregation, tests of strength, special diet, and other features were present in many such institutions. As noted previously, many of these features, such as diet and age categories, may have been established for pragmatic reasons in the historical period; they became customary, institutionalized, and at times even legislated. The adoption by athletic institutions of such formal characteristics that resemble initiatory practices brought athletics closer to initiation rituals in their common function of ushering youths to adulthood. I am making here an arbitrary, though useful, semantic distinction by calling athletic *paideia* in function an 'intiatory ritual,' and by doing so I see it as a form of ritual reflecting its context in the historical *polis*. Though athletic *paideia* may evidence traits or terminology inherited from a prehistoric period, or may conform to general anthropological patterns of initiation, its existence in the historical *polis* implies that it had contemporary significance and a social function.

Paideia with intiatory characteristics was, then, virtually omnipresent, though of varying degrees of complexity in different states. Most of these educational systems, moreover, are marked by pragmatic provisions to separate the youths from society: athletic training for youths, regular athletic contests sponsored by the state, and the formally defined spaces of gymnasia or tracks (*dromoi*) where youths underwent their training. And most athletic education was directly or indirectly associated with pederasty in the period after the sixth century, as will be discussed at greater length in chapter 8. But how can we account for the pragmatic aspect of pederasty? It is not only a demonstration of the rank of elders over youths, but it was thought to help maintain order in the state. Here we turn to an important passage from Plutarch:

> [Before the legendary pederastic passion of Laius in Thebes] the lawgivers, wishing to relax and soften at once from boyhood [the young men's] natural hot temper and vigor, strongly established the use of the flute both in all their serious and playful pursuits, giving the instrument a place of honor and prominence, and they also fostered within them an *erōs* to be conspicuous in the palaestrae, tempering the characters of the youths. Rightly so in view of this did they give a home in their city to the goddess [Harmonia] who is said to have been born of Ares and Aphrodite, so that in that place where the fighting and warlike spirit most closely associate with and unite in the one who partakes of persuasion and grace, there all are brought by Harmony to a most consonant and orderly form of civic affairs.[28]

Thus, the second century A.D. author ascribes to the legendary lawgivers of Thebes the practice of tempering youthful wildness by requiring boys to discipline and soften themselves by practicing the flute and indulging in pederasty in the wrestling schools. Plutarch had related how in the fourth century B.C. a certain Gorgidas established in the Theban army the "Sacred Battalion," composed entirely of homosexual lovers; here we see an extension of that tradition to the legendary past, at once legitimizing the later practice and rationalizing the benefits of Eros among the Theban male citizenry.[29] In short, Plutarch explains the introduction of Eros into institutionalized, athletic education not by reference to any formal initiation ceremony but to the pragmatic motivation of civic harmony.

The rise of pederasty can also be seen as a pragmatic product of the 'contest system' of Greece in the historical period as outlined in the introduction. Rather than seek the origin of socialized homoeroticism in a prehistoric or Indo-European culture, as Sergent and others have done, it is safer to posit the following: homosexuality is a universal phenomenon in human societies, and in cultures that are based on patriarchal and age-class hierarchies (including but not exclusively characteristic of Indo-European systems), male homoeroticism is more likely to take place between lovers and beloved of different age groups than among coevals. Homosexuality among peers striving in a zero-sum social contest for honor would inevitably give rise to internal civil strife. Sexual relations between an elder of pre-established honor and a youth seeking to gain honor would therefore normally promote social harmony (though exceptions certainly exist).

Robert Sallares has suggested another plausible, pragmatic explanation for the institutionalization of pederasty at Thebes and elsewhere: the practice helped to enforce a late age at which men typically married, between 25 and 37 in various Greek city-states. The diversion of sexual roles into pederasty among men who were well past sexual maturity and the biological age for procreation and marriage was a useful device to restrain population growth among the ruling élite: "[A]ge-class systems have the effect of a birth control plan."[30] It is not likely that this was a conscious social plan. There may have been several reasons why a system evolved with the de facto result of delaying marriage, for example, a less complicated inheritance situation with fewer heirs, the longer retention of male manpower in an agricultural household, enforcement of age-hierarchies in the *polis*, and stronger social bonds for young citizens. William Percy has plausibly argued that the institutionalization of pederasty began in Crete after a population increase of the eighth century B.C., and thence the practice was diffused to Sparta and elsewhere.[31] Such a time frame of seventh- to sixth-century establishment of regulated and socially useful pederasty corresponds to other evidence, notably that of Dover, which sees the seventh century as the period of pederasty's 'coming out' and being acknowledged more publicly in Greek society. It also corresponds to the rise of athletics, athletic nudity, and gymnasia over the same period, as will be discussed more fully in the conclusions. For the moment, it is important to note that the explanations of Sallares and Percy, like that of Plutarch, appeal to pragmatic grounds rather than 'primitive initiation' for the institutions of a pederasty, age-classes, and formalized *paideia*.

A passage in Plato's *Laws* (636B) gives further evidence that the functional utility of traditionally inherited *paideia* was open to question and a subject of interstate differences. In other words, traditional *paideia* was relative and changeable. Plato's work, of course, has its own philosophical aims and historical context, but I cite it here mainly to illustrate two points, namely awareness of the pragmatic effects of pederasty and gymnasia in *paideia* and a viewpoint at odds with that of Plutarch's Thebans regarding the usefulness of those social institutions. In this passage, the Athenian stranger responds to the Spartan Megillos' assertion that bravery and moderation (*andreia, sōphrosynē*) are fostered by the Spartan and Cretan customs of common meals (*syssitia*) and gymnasia:

> Gymnasia and *syssitia* on the one hand benefit states in many other
> ways, but are injurious in promoting civil strife (as shown by the cases of
> the youth of Miletus, Boeotia, and Thurii). Moreover this custom, which

is long-standing, seems to have corrupted the lifestyle and pleasures of
sex which are natural not only for humans but also animals. Someone
might make these accusations first of your states and of whatever other
states are particularly inclined to the gymnasium. . . . [I]t must be noted
that when males unite with females for procreation, the pleasure in it is
considered natural, but when males are with males and females with
females, it is contrary to nature, and the boldness of those first doing
this is due to the lack of restraint in pleasure.

The Athenian's objections, then, are based on lack of self-restraint, which can,
on the civic level, give rise to civil strife. The argument runs directly counter to
Plutarch's report of the positive effects of pederasty in the palaestra adopted by
Theban lawgivers and illustrates the diversity of views toward the practice. Plato,
like Plutarch, shows a concern for the effects of pederasty in its gymnastic and social context. Plato, however, through his Athenian speaker, criticizes the pederastic and social customs of the Spartan and Cretan interlocutors in this work.[32] This
is not to say that pederasty in the context of *paideia* was absent from Athens in Plato's
day (it certainly was not), but only that it was less formally 'institutionalized' there
than in those other states. We can at least conclude that in Plato's day, whatever
the criticism and differences of opinion among individuals within a *polis* or among
several *poleis*, pederasty was felt to provide an important form of education for a
society's youth.

Change and reform in systems of social formation were no doubt constant in
ancient Greece, and the consistent, overriding concern with the good function of
the state resulted in transformations of prehistoric customs into ones with contemporary utility. To adapt one scholar's formulation, Greek homophilia and athletic
customs were 'polycentric,' that is, subject to countless local variations emerging
in each region from its own proper prehistory and not necessarily or consistently
determined by Indo-European or other early transnational cultures.[33] We are safer
therefore in positing *paideia* as an historical form of initiation without appeal to its
prehistoric origins.

Pederasty, Initiation, and Contests in Greek Myth and History

Let us now turn to some specific manifestations of the conjunction of pederasty,
initiation, and athletic contests in Greek myth and history, examining each according to the hypotheses discussed earlier. Some of the examples surveyed are those
proposed by scholars proposing theories of an Indo-European or an otherwise prehistoric origin for athletic contests associated with initiation or pederasty, and part
of the task here is to examine the solidity of these proposals. But the main point is

to look at the evidence of texts and archeological documents for likely links between homosexuality and athletics in the context of what we have described as historical *paideia* with initiatiory characteristics serving pragmatic, contemporary functions.

Myth

It has been proposed that the myth of Pelops, one legendary founder of the Olympics, shows the characteristics of a prehistoric initiation myth.[34] The hero is "sacrificed" by Tantalus, he undergoes separation when he is abducted by a lover, Poseidon, and he emerges victorious from a contest to win Hippodameia as bride, a kind of rite of passage combining a bride-contest with succession to kingship. This story, it is maintained, parallels the general initiation triadic structure of separation–life on the margin–reintegration, and it also recapitulates the Cretan ritual of abduction (symbolic death), sojourn (education and training by an older male lover), and exit from marginal status (final victory, symbolic resurrection). The basic problem with such a characterization of the Pelops legend is a methodological one, as Dover has pointed out.[35] The use of evidence is highly selective and ignores contradictory variants. Furthermore, the evidence for Poseidon's homosexual motives in the abduction is a late variant in the tradition, first found in Pindar, *Olympian Odes* I (lines 40–45; written 476 B.C.), which is likely to be a 'homosexualization' of the myth derived from the sixth or fifth century versions that reflect a more open, contemporary glorification of homosexuality.[36]

The other famous myth connected with the 'invention' of homosexuality in a supposedly initiatory context is that of the Theban King Laius. When Laius' throne was usurped by Lycus, he served in exile as tutor to Chrysippus, son of Pelops, in the art of chariot racing, fell in love with the youth, and abducted him back to Thebes.[37] In a variant of this myth, Laius takes the boy to the Nemean Games, not to Thebes.[38] Again, the sources are late for both of these versions, and we can draw no conclusions about their prehistoric pedigree. The consistent motifs of abduction by a lover and participation of the beloved in contests may well, however, reflect later connections between athletics and social formation of a youth through pederastic liaisons.

The Spartan-based story of Hyacinthus' death from a discus thrown by Apollo is also recalled as one reflecting the themes of initiation (a youth who dies and is 'reborn' as a flower), athletics (the boy dies from a discus thrown by Apollo), and pederasty (Hyacinthus is Apollo's beloved). Yet Hesiod (fr. 171.6–8 M-W), our earliest source, says nothing of the pederastic relationship:

She then bore the blameless and brave Hyacinthus
[. . .] whom [Phoebus] himself at one time
[unwittingly killed with the pitiles]s discus.

Euripides (*Helen* 1469–73) also mentions the death of Hyacinthus, adding little to Hesiod's basic story. The Hellenistic poet Nikander (floruit ca. 130 B.C.) follows the same essential myth, that Phoebus unintentionally killed Hyacinthus "still in early youth" but hints more openly at the love between the god and the boy by adding that Apollo "lamented" the death (*Theriaka* 903–6). Apollodorus' brief allusions to the myth (*Bibliotheca* 1.3.3, 3.10.3) note that the youth was Apollo's beloved, but later authors describe the affair as a love triangle. Lucian (*Dialogus deorum* 16 [14]2), Philostratus (*Imagines* 1.24), and Libanius (*Progymnasmata narrationes* 2) all describe the revenge that the wind god, Zephyrus, exacts when the boy favors Apollo, and the discus is blown onto a fatal trajectory. Thus, the pederastic element is added to this tale first in the Roman period, and it is therefore incorrectly interpreted as evidence of prehistoric initiation involving homophilia.[39]

Generally, we may conclude with Dover regarding the use of myths as sources:

> Consequently there was never a 'canon' of Greek myths, never a period when poets were not accorded great freedom to manipulate inherited material, assimilate one myth to another, and invent. Audience-response will have been by far the most important criterion in this process, and the fundamental structure of a myth could well have been sacrificed if the poet's ambition to excite, impress and move his audience demanded the sacrifice.

In short, we are much safer in interpreting each version according to the historical date and circumstances of its composition by an author than in forcing a cluster of variants into a pattern that endorses a thesis of prehistoric origins unsupported by extrinsic evidence.

Crete

The Cretan system of social formation, with Spartan parallels to be investigated below, had institutionalized pederastic relationships in a rigid system of segregating youths into groups, each called a "herd" (*agelē*), and it had rites of passage involving initiatory segregation, life on the margin, and reincorporation into society.[40] Here too, 'primitive' initiation has often been seen as the origin of the custom, and though that may be possible, the lateness of all literary testimonia precludes us from any certainty on the question. As with Sparta, the Cretan system is likely to have gone through a 're-institutionalization,' perhaps in the seventh or sixth centuries B.C. when a militaristic motivation may have caused the changes in both cultures.[41] Cretan pederasty and age-classes undoubtedly had the same pragmatic effect as at Sparta, namely, the restriction of population growth. And as at Sparta, the Cretan system incorporated physical education into their formal upbringing, though this aspect was much less central to the Cretan system than it was to the Spartan.

The fourth-century B.C. historian Ephorus describes an institutionalized form of homosexual initiation peculiar to historical Crete in which a beloved (*erōmenos*) is abducted by a lover (*erastēs*).[42] The beloved, called *parastathentes*, "enjoy certain honors: at choral dances and at races [*dromois*] they have the most honored places." Before the boys are ritually abducted by their lovers, they are entrusted to an instructor (*paidonomos*) and later formed into *agelai* (lit., "herds"; singular, *agelē*), troops of youth; the father of the leader of the *agelē* leads the youths in hunting, "in exercising themselves and in running" (*exagein epi thēran kai dromous*).[43] Though several scholars have sought through this example to attach homosexuality to initiation ritual, Dover has pointed out that *erōs* is not presented by Ephorus as an aspect of the Cretan *agōgē*, but *erōs*' exploitation of the *agôgē* is given as a distinctive feature of Cretan *erōs*.[44] Of equal interest here is the fact that competitive running is a crucial aspect of boys' institutional *paideia*: they are taught the skills of the contest prior to becoming a "beloved," and they enjoy front-row seats at public competitions.

Other sources tell us that the Cretan *paideia* system had, along with initiatory characteristics, names for age grades which echoed athletics, in particular footraces. Until the age of adulthood (perhaps 18 or 20, the precise age not being known), the young man is called a *dromeus* or "runner," a minor is conversely called *apodromos* or "one excluded from the track."[45] Cretan nudity, special meals, and dress with special symbolism also mark the system as an initiation. Inscriptions record the fact that athletic nudity was practiced among the "herds of the undressed" at festivals to the gods. *Ekdramein*, "to run forth," but perhaps with the special meaning "to strip and enter the stadium," is used on historical Cretan inscriptions from the cities of Lato and Olous of the graduation of youths to adulthood.[46] So the 'graduates' may have disrobed to take part in the adult custom of athletic nudity. The herds separated boys by age and required them to attend communal meals (*syssitia*) with elders. It is significant that those promoted from the *agelē* were obliged to marry at the same time.[47]

Although most sources report initiation ceremonies for boys, the *Ekdysia* or "Festival of Undressing" at Phaestus required girls about to marry to shed their robes in honor of the goddess Lato Phytia and a local hero, Leucippus, who was changed from a girl to a boy. Recent archeological finds indicate that this legend may evidence initiatory homosexuality of the type described by Ephorus as early as 1000 B.C. or even into the Minoan Bronze Age, yet the isolation of this early evidence does not support the assumption of any Indo-European connection nor of any widespread adoption of similar customs until much later in Greece. As Andrew Stewart has remarked, "Though institutionalized pederasty existed in Dark-Age Crete, it was perhaps not practiced formally elsewhere until the seventh or sixth centuries, when it received a huge boost, for other reasons, of naked sports."[48] I earlier mentioned Percy's idea that the population expansion of the eighth century may have given impetus to Cretan pederasty. Whatever the antiquity of the Cretan *agelai*, it can at least be observed that in historical times their external features suggest that they were initiatory. Cretan *paideia* therefore exemplifies an initiation of a pragmatic type which may have included homosexuality earlier than elsewhere in Greece, and, in later periods, also combined athletics with its initiatory rituals.

Apart from the Cretan educational system and local rituals, general sources on Cretan athletic victors and athletic festivals can shed some light on that culture's interest (or lack of it) in public contests between city-states. A survey of known victors in the Panhellenic games suggests that Cretans were never very successful in these competitions. There are only eight known Olympic victors from Crete. Three of these, according to the standard study by Moretti, are of uncertain homeland or date, namely: a certain Titas (of Crete?), victor possibly in 504 B.C. in an uncertain event; Diognetos, a Cretan victor in boxing possibly in 488; and Ikadion, a (Cretan?) victor in the boys' stade race. Three others are victors in running events between 448 and 380 B.C., and the final two are victors in the stade race in the Roman imperial period (A.D. 25 and 209).[49] The aforementioned Titas is known only from a late-sixth-century graffito from the Athenian Agora, saying simply "Titas the Olympic victor is buggered" (*Titas Olympionikas katapugōn*).[50] If he is a Cretan, the opprobrium from an Athenian sports fan suggests not only the expected interstate rivalry, but possibly that Cretans had a reputation for pederasty connected with their formal *paideia*. There are no known Cretan victors in the Pythian or Nemean Games, and only one boxer won the crown in the Isthmian Games, probably in the fifth century B.C.[51] Nor were there any significant athletic festivals held at Cretan cities at any period.[52] The fifth and early fourth centuries B.C. were apparently the high point of Cretan achievement in the Panhellenic games, and then only at Olympia, in sparse numbers and mostly in running events, never, so far as we know, in the more elitist equestrian contests. Since Crete was not a land known for horse-breeding, that observation is perhaps not surprising. And the fact that six of the eight Cretan Olympic victors are runners is in accord with the tradition of Cretan running preserved in their nomenclature of "runner" (*dromeus*) for an age-grade of youths. If Cretan education underwent a 'reinstitutionalization' in the seventh or sixth centuries, as suggested earlier, might this event partly account for the brief success of Cretan athletes in the fifth century, after the new system had taken root? Speculation on the possible connection must remain tentative.

We cannot know for sure the reason for this lack of participation generally in contests outside of local Cretan festivals and rituals for most of the island's history. It may be due simply to the difficulties of travel from Crete to the mainland and elsewhere, either because of sheer distance or the island's infamous pirates.[53] Or the economy may not have been strong enough to support the leisure and expensive infrastructures required for athletic festivals and competitive training. Or the problem may simply have been an attitude of self-sufficiency and cultural isolationism. In any case, the lack of participation in public festivals elsewhere and the absence of festivals on Crete itself gives all the more prominence to the athletic contests which did play an apparently important role in local ritual. Contests as part of their *paideia* system, particularly running events, may have satisfied Cretan ambitions in that sphere.

Sparta

Many scholars over the last century have claimed to detect traces of 'primitive' initiation rituals in the contests and practices of the Spartan *agōgē*, the peculiar system of *paideia* that is widely understood as deriving from the same source as that of Crete, possibly but by no means certainly from a common 'Dorian' culture. Spartan age-classes were not unique, since they are used by many societies for conscription and social organization; Sparta's *agōgē* is noteworthy, however, in its greater stress on physical training and brutality and in the formalization, complexity, and prominence of its rites.[54] Paul Cartlege has made the following suggestion about the early history of this system:

> Though it is uncertain whether the predecessors of the classical Spartans, who arrived in the tenth century B.C., had an initiation-cum-education cycle of age-sets and *rites de passage*, they did establish after their arrival an *agōgē* which was essentially secular in educating and socializing with a military character and objective.[55]

How soon "after their arrival" this system was established is of course debatable. Nigel Kennell has cogently demonstrated that the *agōgē* known from our literary sources was probably first established no earlier than the sixth century B.C., the same period in which athletic festivals first flourished widely in Greece.[56] Nigel Kennell disputes Cartledge's characterization of the institution as "mainly secular" with reference to the Classical period, where Kennell believes that it had a "fundamentally religious, initiatory character" and the distinction draws "an anachronistic division between the sacred and the profane."[57] From a modern and pragmatic viewpoint, Cartledge's description is arguably very accurate for any period, when the more important social function was the effect of the institution on the political and military workings of the state. The religious dimension is for the ancients certainly inseparable from the secular, but the direct social effects of religion are less discernible. Religion, on the other hand, did provide a crucial, cultic foundation for the *agōgē*, notably in the cult of Artemis Orthia, whose popularity increased immensely in the sixth century B.C. We may conclude then, that the *agōgē* inextricably combined both religion in social context and pragmatism in its objectives. Since the antiquity of the initiatory aspects still remains in question, we can also most safely conclude that the probable foundation of the historically attested form of *agōgē* in the sixth century did not occur until initiatory and pederastic characteristics had become formally attached to upbringing.

Pederasty was certainly well established as customary within the *agōgē* by the fourth century B.C. when Xenophon first alludes to the practice, and female homoeroticism is evident in Alcman's poem *Parthenion*, dated to ca. 650–600 B.C.[58] Cartledge has reasonably argued that in Sparta after 700 B.C. "[t]he emulation generated by the 'Greek contest-system' reached a pitch of intensity rarely paralleled elsewhere," and "concepts of role-status" were one variable governing the incidence of homosexuality in societies generally.[59] Xenophon's apology for Lycurgus' endorsement of pederasty may or may not evidence the peculiar élite and Athenian views of that writer, but the apology may well contain an element of ideological truth, arguing that Spartans were concerned that the lovers show greater concern for the soul of the beloved and for true friendship with the boy than for his outward beauty. It is likely that the lover-beloved relationship was a strongly functional and tutorial one in which the adult helped usher the youth to adulthood.[60] Of the three age-groups outlined by Xenophon, namely *paides*, roughly 7–14, *paidiskoi*, roughly 14–20, and *hēbōntes*, roughly 20–30, boys generally first took on the role of "beloved" in the second group, then "lovers" in the third. The youths were first admitted to the communal dining clubs, *phitidia*, as *paidiskoi*, then became full members in the clubs as *hēbōntes*.[61] Thus the pederastic relationships were accompanied by gradual introduction to full citizen socialization and rights.

Plutarch gives us the narrative for the introduction of boys into pederastic relations in the *agōgē*:

> Lovers from among suitable [older] youths were received by boys
> already of this age [teenagers]. The elder men also kept watch over
> them, both visiting the gymnasia more frequently and being present at
> their battles and jesting with one another, not inappropriately, but in
> some way all serving as fathers, tutors, and governors for all of them.[62]

The system of oversight suggests that the boys at the status of "beloved" required the supervision of elders in certain social contexts, including notably gymnasia, presumably to maintain order and decorous behavior between pederastic couples.

Spartans realized that their rigid age-class systems and pederasty reduced the population to an undesirably low level by the fifth century B.C. and so set up other measures to increase procreation. They established sexual relations outside of marriage proper; they paraded nude or scantily clad girls who competed at public athletic contests to arouse the attraction of young men; and they offered special privileges for fathers of three sons.[63] The topic of Spartan girls' athletics will be treated in chapter 5; the phenomenon reveals a very interesting aspect of the overtly erotic Spartan "body culture," which encouraged both hetero- and homosexual attraction between audience members and participants.

We have seen that the Spartan *agōgē* was probably established in the sixth century B.C., that it included many initiatory characteristics, and that pederasty, which was likely to have been practiced openly at Sparta in the seventh century, was incorporated into the *agōgē* by the sixth century. It remains to investigate when and how athletic prominence may have figured into this *paideia*. In brief, it seems that the physical contests associated with the *agōgē* neither encouraged participation nor contributed to Spartan success in athletics outside Sparta; on the contrary, the inwardly focused system may have discouraged general enthusiasm for participation in non-Spartan games. Spartan athletes were distinguished by their success in the Olympic games for the period 720–580 B.C., for which we have thirty-six victories by Spartans in gymnic events, though none in the equestrian contests which first appeared in 680 B.C.[64] Most Olympiads in that period show at least one Spartan victory. From 576 to 372, by contrast, there are only six (or possibly seven) known Spartan victories in Olympic gymnic events, and eleven in equestrian events. The decline in gymnic victories by Spartans seems too sharp to be attributed to an accident of preservation. If the extant victories reflect a true shift in participation, this may be due to a new cultural focus after the sixth century 'revolution' in which the *agōgē* was established. Perhaps the *paideia* system placed greater emphasis on athletic training displayed only in local festivals, while the Spartan élite could enjoy greater Panhellenic visibility through equestrian victories. A hippic victory was not considered a test of manly courage, but of wealth, so defeat in that area did not entail the same quality of shame.[65] A greater focus on the military aspects of youths' training may also have contributed to this reorientation; team-sports that were atypical of the rest of Greece were established, including ball games and a team battle at Platanistas. This new, isolated orientation may be reflected in the report of Philostratus (ca. A.D. 230): "After a time, however, they abandoned boxing as well as pankration because they considered that these were contested in such a way that when a person was defeated it would be possible to slander Sparta for lacking courage."[66]

Apart from the Olympics, only three Spartan athletes are recorded in Moretti's collection of victors in local festivals between 576 and the fourth century B.C., and even these are noteworthy for competing only in contests at Sparta.[67] Aiglatas was a Spartan runner who won in two local festivals, the Athanaia and the Syrmaia in ca. 500–480 B.C. (Moretti, no. 9). An inscription dated ca. 440–431 B.C. lists a series of victories by a certain Damonon in footraces and chariot racing and by his son Enymakratidas in footraces (Moretti, no. 16). Remarkable here is the long list of festivals exclusively in the vicinity of Sparta where they competed: Gaiwochos, Athanaia, Posoidaia (one at Helos and one at Thuria), Ariontias, Eleusinia, Lithehia, Maleateia, and Parparonia.[68] Since most of these festivals are known only from this list, we cannot be certain if participation was limited to Spartans only, nor can we judge whether the festivals were short-lived or not. One would expect other references to them if non-Spartans had contended or if the games had lasted long. Also in Moretti's collection, the Spartan boy (*pais*) Arexippos won at Sparta in the first half of the fourth century in an uncertain event, possibly in one of the several contests unique to Sparta, poorly understood, and later known collectively as the "Boys'

Contests" (*paidikoi agōnes*).[69] Klee's survey of victors in gymnic contests reveals that, Olympics aside, there are no Spartans among the 670 known victors of the Panhellenic festivals, the Pythian, Isthmian, and Nemean Games, all instituted between 586 and 573 B.C., roughly the time at which we see the sharp decline in Spartan victories at Olympia.[70] Furthermore, Klee's record of the state affiliation of victors on six victor lists from local festivals shows that there were only twelve Laconian victories among the total of 340, including two at the Lykaia Games in Arcadia in the fourth century B.C., two at the Eleutheria Games at Larissa in the second to first century B.C., and eight at the Amphiaraia Games at Oropus (Boeotia) in the first century B.C.[71]

Even if we keep in mind the fragmentary nature of such records, we can venture a reasonable characterization of Spartan participation in public games. Generally, Spartans in the Classical period and later seem to be disinterested in the Panhellenic Games and, indeed, in any athletic festivals outside those of Sparta itself. If the *agōgē* was established in the sixth century, the institution may have contributed to Sparta's athletic self-centeredness in the subsequent three centuries. Perhaps the shift reflects a generalization of the attitude seen in the Philostratus quote above: the Spartans were reluctant to risk athletic defeat lest it tarnish their image of corporate, military invincibility. Diminished participation may also reflect a cultural conservatism or insularity uninterested in investing in the considerable expense needed to maintain the increasingly specialized training regimens in the fifth century and later. And the change may evidence a chauvinistic self-confidence that says, in effect, that Spartans do not need to prove their courage in contests with other Greeks. The truth may well include all of these (and doubtless other) motivations.

In any case, we may note that, like Crete, Sparta fostered its system of athletic festivals and its own athletic *paideia* in relative isolation from other Greek states. Moretti lists only nine total known Olympic victories by Spartans from 316 B.C. until the end of the Olympics in A.D. 393. From the Roman Imperial period onward, beginning with Augustus, Sparta did institute several new local festivals that included athletic programs, namely the Caesarea, the Urania, the Euryclea, and the Olympia Commodea. At these and possibly at other festivals whose names are undetermined, scholars have counted thirty-four known victors who came to Sparta from all over the Mediterranean.[72] Even though Spartans seem not to have been eager to compete elsewhere, Sparta was eager to attract competitors on the athletic circuit, in accord with the practice of other Greek cities in this period. Under the *pax Romana*, the city was induced to take advantage of the visibility and economic capital of such cultural events.

Let us now summarize our findings on the earlier question of how the Spartan education system related to their general participation in Greek athletics. The chronology of Spartan athletic victories and local festivals outlined earlier suggests that their athletic engagement outside of Sparta reached its acme before the establishment of the *agōgē* in the sixth century B.C. Indeed, a direct link between the decline in athletic victories and the formation of the *agōgē* has not, to my knowledge, been previously observed, but the connection does support the hypothetical date for the 'invention' of the *agōgē*. From the late sixth century B.C. to the fourth century A.D., Spartan athletics took on a very parochial character, which seems to underscore the greater importance attributed to unique local competitions, and to the *agōgē* system itself. The Spartan *agōgē* had seen its final revival after 146 B.C., in the Roman era, and had remained relatively unchanged thereafter. Local Spartan agonistic festivals in which non-Spartans and Spartans could both compete were also established in the Roman period, but Spartans still seem to have ventured afield rarely to compete elsewhere. The *agōgē* sufficiently occupied the interest and the competitive skills of the able youth. It was, in short, the most comprehensive system of initiatory *paideia* and one that most preoccupied youths among all such systems in Greece.

We now turn to the system itself, highlighting the 'initiatory' aspects that characterized the *agōgē*. As noted earlier, Spartan upbringing resembles the Cretan system enough to indicate either a common tribal heritage or mutual borrowing.[73] At age 7 boys entered the *agōgē* until age 30, when they became full adult members of communal meals (*phitidia*). Spartan youths spent a period in isolation, called *krypteia* or "hiding."[74] Plato, in the context of a discussion of how courage is developed (*Leg.* 633a–c), mentions the Spartan "tests of strength," namely common meals, physical exercise, the hunt, *krypteia*, whipping, and a number of other trials.

As members of the Spartan *agōgē*, boys regularly participated in certain festivals that had initiatory characteristics including physical tests of strength. Most famous and brutal was the rite of Artemis Orthia, in which youths were severely scourged at the goddess' altar and the one who could endure the most with the least sign of suffering was called *bōmonikas* or "victor at the altar."[75] This cruel custom is at least an illustration of the Spartan youths' hardiness, but probably also a part of their initiation meant to instill moral strength. The fact that there may have been age-classes in this ritual and that it concluded with a procession in special dress (of Lydian style) further indicates an initiatory character, though it appears to be a late, archaizing invention, meant to retrieve the 'Lycurgan' past.[76]

Another important Spartan festival with initiatory characteristics is the Carneia held in honor of Apollo Carneius.[77] A sacred truce (*hieromēnia*) was observed during the festival (Paus. 3.13.3). Apollo may have displaced an older ram god, Carneius, also known by the epithet *Dromaios* or "runner."[78] The Spartan *Dromos* or "track," which may have been the site of the festival, was near the sanctuary of Apollo Carneius (Paus. 3.14.6).[79] The festival was celebrated by certain unmarried men chosen by lot, perhaps from the five Spartan tribes (Hesychius, s.v. *Karneiatai*). The youths served a four-year office, suggesting a penteteric celebration on a larger scale like the Olympics. Though the Carneia itself was not strictly a part of the *agōgē*, the use of unmarried men in its ritual suggests that it had a quasi-initiatory character. The *agōnes*, which seem to have been established in the twenty-sixth Olympiad (672 B.C.), included most notably a footrace of the *Staphylodromoi* or "Runners with Grapes," again employing unmarried men and possibly connected with the *agōgē*.[80] The competitors were chosen from among the *Karneiatai* (Hesychius, s.v.). The chief source is a lexicographer (Anecd. Bekker I.305), who reports:

> *Staphylodromoi*: during the Carneia a certain youth on whom some wool bands were tied runs and prays for something beneficial for the state; youths called *staphylodromoi* pursued him. And if they should catch him, they would expect some good in the region for the state. If not, the opposite.

The name of the runners probably suggests that they carried bunches of grapes. The leading runner may have been a substitute for what was originally an animal in a staged hunt, while the pursuers may have been the hunters. Yet Demetrius (*Troicus ap.* Ath. 4.141E) calls the Carneia an "imitation of military training." Nilsson argues that the festival may have only later been associated "with Zeus as leader of the *agelē* and with his military spirit."[81] We may note that, apart from the incidental initiatory characteristics, the race of the *Staphylodromoi* mainly concerns the symbolic renewal of the state through tests of strength. If other contests of the Carneia imitated military training, then the festival as a whole may be considered a symbolic revival of Spartan military might.

A Spartan ritual called the *Platanistas* or "Contest in the Plane-tree Grove" includes a test of strength with clear military associations (Paus. 3.14.8–10).[82] After preliminary sacrifices to Achilles (Paus. 3.20.8) and the war-god Enyalios, two teams of youths (ephebes) wage an unarmed battle on an island, the object of which is to throw the opponent into the water (Lucian, *Anacharsis* 38). The no-holds-barred fight allows biting, kicking, gouging, and hand-to-hand combat. The "battle" (it is referred to by Pausanias as *machē*, not *agōn*, "contest") may have developed from a standard practice exercise for youths before a campaign, but its viciousness and military associations mark it as a purely Spartan ritual meant to strengthen young men during the initiation period.[83]

Plato (*Leg.* 633c4) includes among the Spartan tests of strength the festival of *Gymnopaedia* (naked playfulness) held in July for Apollo, Artemis, and Leto.[84] The participants were divided by age and tribe primarily for choral dance competitions in the theater; the chorus is said to have imitated the pankration and wrestling events with slow movements.[85] The Scholiast to Plato speaks of a kind of violent football contest as part of the festival in which a ball or some other object was thrown around. Though the choral performances are quasi-athletic, they are not strictly conventional contests and hence are best seen as symbolic rituals as part of the *agōgē*. The function was, like the similar festival of the Hecatombaea at Athens, to enroll a new class of young men into adulthood.[86] The highlighting of male nudity at this festival is also noteworthy. If we accept the traditional foundation date of 668/7 for the Gymnopaedia, the festival origin corresponds to the period in which pederasty began to be openly practiced not long after 700, as noted earlier. Athletic nudity is one of the factors that undoubtedly fostered and was fostered by pederasty in Greece generally. Thus, the Gymnopaedia indirectly supports the chronology for associating the two phenomena; we will see later (chapter 8) that nudity was likely to have been introduced into the Olympics by the end of the seventh century, and some sources name the Spartans as the originators of this custom.

Ball games were such an important part of the Spartan *agōgē* that Spartan youths entering manhood also have the name *sphaireis* or "ballplayers."[87] Spartan ball games became large-scale combative exercises contributing to the typically harsh moral and military training.[88] Kennell has persuasively argued that the ball games, which took place near the civic center in the theater and marked progress from ephebe to full adult, contrast neatly with the whipping test of strength for younger boys, endurance tests that were held at the city's margins at the sanctuary of Artemis Orthia.[89] In becoming "ballplayers" (*sphaireis*), boys became adults literally and symbolically admitted to the center of civic life. It is obvious that the team format of this sport, virtually unique in ancient Greece, reflects the very great importance of united enterprises among Spartan citizens.

Thera

Archaic Thera, the island in the Aegean Cyclades, was a Spartan colony archaeologically dated to a little before 750 B.C. A 'sacred precinct ' contains inscriptions to divinities dated to the eighth or seventh centuries B.C., and from the mid-sixth to fourth centuries B.C., a series of inscriptions recognized by their erotic content as 'pederastic.'[90] The pederastic inscriptions are 50–70 meters west of a sanctuary of Apollo Carneius, and some have taken this as an indication of their initiatory importance, since Apollo was frequently a god of ephebic initiation and hence athletics. The inscriptions are also the location of a later grotto to Hermes and Heracles, at the entrance to the Hellenistic gymnasium just below.[91] Many youths are named in the inscriptions with the epithets "good" (*agathos*), "honorable" (*timios*), or "a good dancer" (*orkheitai agathōs*). The latter attribute is connected by Sergent with the fact that Spartan festivals related to their *agōgē* often include dances, for example, the Gymnopaedia, Carneia, and Hyacinthia. Dances, it is argued, may have taken place outside the temple of Apollo at Thera, and the proximity of the gymnasium suggests a possible continuity in the use of this area also for training or contests of young initiates, again similar to the customs at Sparta. Finally Sergent, following Jeanmaire, interprets an enigmatic verb, *ōphein*, found on several of the inscriptions (nos. 536–38) to be a term for homosexual copulation, for example, IG XII 3.536: "Pheidipidas copulated [*ōiphe*]. Timagoras and Enpheres copulated [*egōiphomes*].

Enpylos [was] here a fornicator [*pornos*]. Enpedokles inscribed this [and] danced by Apollo." "It seems that the youths are here not only *erōmenoi* [beloved] but athletes and dancers. . . ."[92] It has been convincingly shown that *ōphein* is in fact used pejoratively and, though the precise meaning remains unclear, it may indeed be connected with a term for the male organ.[93] The pejorative sense of the verb, the fact that two of the graffiti proclaim that the act was performed "here," and the virtually universal Greek prohibition against sex in sacred places suggest that the graffiti are, in Dover's terms, "a jocular obscenity" rather than a record of initiatory achievement.[94]

There are further indications that the Theran graffiti are probably informal and that pederasty cannot, from this evidence, be seen as a formal part of Thera's initiation or *paideia*. The graffiti do, on the other hand, indicate that pederasty was practiced there in Archaic times, and the context suggests that pederasty may have been at least an informal part of an upbringing otherwise including contests among these youths. Located among the 'pederastic' inscriptions and in the same style are numerous inscriptions of some individual names, without epithet or qualification (IG XII 3.550–601). All of these inscriptions, including the pederastic, may therefore be taken simply as the normal, secular type of graffiti found in gymnasia or public areas frequented by youth, namely securing some kind of fame by proclaiming "so-and-so was here," taking pride in an individual's beauty or nobility, skill in dance, sexual prowess, and occasionally maligning an out-of-favor colleague. The closest parallel is found in the inscriptions of a later date (320–270 B.C.) on Thasos, most of which proclaim "so-and-so is beautiful" or "sweet" or "lovely," and so on (*kalos, ōraios, hēdus, eucharis, euschēmōn*).[95] We may also compare the graffito from Naxos, originally giving just the names of a boy and girl, "Karion [loves] Dorophea," to which a later jokester supplied the rude epithet for the boy "fornicator" (*oipolēs*), using the same pejorative vocabulary found on the Thera inscriptions.[96] The heterosexual and non-Dorian context of the Thasian graffito diminishes the likelihood that the Theran examples reflect an exclusively Dorian or homosexual practice. A similarly joking, here homoerotic, "metagraffito" has been found in the entrance tunnel to the (fourth century) stadium at Nemea.[97] The Hellenistic gymnasia at Priene and on Delos are also filled with graffiti from the young habitués, mostly of the "so-and-so-was-here" type.[98] We may at least conclude that the site of the Theran graffiti was frequented by local youths, and, from the above parallels and additional evidence to be supplied, it seems likely that the site was near or at an early track, dance floor, or place used for communal education.

Though it seems unlikely that the Theran inscriptions record any formal or sacred initiations involving pederasty, there are one or two indications that they may have associations with local competitions among youths. Though no inscriptions on the Thera site mention athletic prowess, that area may have been used for athletic training prior to the later formal gymnasium. The graffiti site is located at the terminus of the 'sacred way,' 50–70 meters before the temple to Apollo Carneius, and there is a flat stretch of ground long enough to have served as a stadium.[99] In the sixth and early fifth centuries, stadia and gymnasia were often no more than open ground sufficiently large for athletic activities.[100] The inscriptions therefore occupy a place that may have served as an area of public competition or training when they were written. There are, in addition, several graffiti mentioning 'dancing' skills (*IG* XII 3.536, 540, and 543), possibly in allusion to competitive dancing.

One inscription in particular is of interest (540 with *IG* XII Suppl., *ad* 537) proclaiming, "Eumelas is the best dancer. Krimion, first (*pratistos*) in the Konialos, charmed (*iane*) Simias." Certainly Eumelas' claim signals a boast of superiority, which implies a formal or informal comparison of dancers, in short, a competitive spirit. We may compare the fragmentary inscription no. 543, "Barbax dances well and he gave [. . .]," which may record the dedication of on offering to a god in thanks for his winning at a dance contest. The boast of dancing "well" may also have prompted inscription no. 540 as a rejoinder by Eumelas who either proved to be superior later or felt he was indeed the "best." In any case, in Krimion's case in no. 540, "first" (*pratistos*) seems also to be a competitive boast, here attached to a specific type of dance, the *Konialos*.[101]

Konialos was indeed the name of an obscene dance, the Attic *Konisalos*, which Hesychius (κ 3522, s.v. *konisalos*) glosses as "a leaping satyric dance of dancers inserting their genitals" or, in the plural, (κ 3521) "(dances?) to do with Aphrodite."[102] Since the graffito term *Konialos* is one of the few clues to the significance of the activities commemorated in the Theran pederastic texts, the following digression attempts to discover the possible significance and associations of the dance. Plato the fifth-fourth c. B.C. comic poet informs us that *Konisalos* is also the name of a Priapic deity from Attica, perhaps the namesake for the dance.[103] Moreover, the term may also have an athletic association, since it is the name for the residual substance scraped from athletes after exercise, in which sweat, dirt, and oil are mixed; this is otherwise known as *gloios* and is valued for its magical, pharmacological powers.[104] What, if any, connection might there be between the priapic god, perhaps the lord of a lusty dance, and the athletic residue?

The philosopher Synesius (4–5 c. A.D.) portrays Konisalos as a god in fact antithetical to athletic enterprises when he criticizes a licentious slave whom he purchased as a trainer: "[he is] not in the least suitable to the overseers of the palaestra, Hermes and Heracles. But he serves Kotus and the other Attic Konisaloi" (*Ep.* 32). Synesius, like many philosophers before him, sternly disapproves of the widespread role of Eros in the gymnasium (ch. 8). The point of Synesius' criticism is that his slave is more suited to the conventional *après*-sports activities of drinking and sex, the domains of Kotus and the Konisaloi, than to the athletics itself; a slave inclined to such indulgences would inevitably take advantage of the young athletes in his charge. Apart from the philosopher's moral stance, the censure illustrates the real social tension between the conventional deities of the palaestra and those like Konisalos, whose marginal presence may tempt trainers and athletes to nonathletic activities. *Konisalos* was also the name of a play by the fourth century B.C. comic poet, Timocles; worship of the divinity may have given rise to the Konisalos satyr dance, and hence also the topic of the play, or alternatively, the dance may have given rise to the invention of a patron deity. We can only speculate on the subject of the play, but it may be relevant that satyr plays frequently incorporated themes of athletics.[105] Perhaps Timocles' piece played on the tensions between lusty satyrs and handsome, sweaty athletes.

The word *konisalos* contains the element "dust" (*konis*) and was first used in Homer to mean simply "cloud of dust" stirred up by warriors on the march. Might the lofty epic word have been reapplied first to the athletic mixture of dust and sweat? If so, the athletic name could then have been transferred to the popular dance that mimicked the sweaty, dirty, oily, and potentially sexy grappling of the wrestlers. The athletic term *konisalos* could also have been transferred directly to the god who was invented to embody the pharmaceutical powers of the ointment. Clearly the god had taken on the identity of having phallic potency by the time fifth to fourth centuries B.C.[106] Though the actual semantic changes of the term *konisalos* cannot be traced, we know that sometime after Homer, the term for "cloud of dust" was applied to the Priapic divinity of Attica, an obscene satyr dance of Attica, and a potent ointment of the residue of athletes' scrapings. The closest semantic connection among the different meanings of the term is between the earliest, general association with dust and the athletic dust (*konis*) commonly used by wrestlers. We can otherwise only speculate how *konisalos/konialos* became attached to a god, an obscene dance, and a comic drama, but the association of athletics and Eros may furnish the link. The athletes' dirty residues contained potent and possibly even erotic properties; the dance by satyrs may mimic wrestling or sex or both; a divinity antithetical to athletic activity is given a name from the athletic substance, perhaps out of deliberate irony—the erotic domain competed with athletics for the bodies, time, and energies of the youths. We can reasonably surmise that the Theran graffito expressing a competitive boast refers to a local dance there, similar to the Attic dance, and performed as part of a formal or informal contest. The readiest parallel is the Spartan Gymnopaedia, although it lacks the obscenity of the Koni(s)alos but may have resembled it by including mimetic representations of athletic competitions such as wrestling and pankration.

Nothing is known of a formal *paideia* in Archaic or Classical Thera, but the graffiti and their context evidence that pederasty was practiced in the Doric culture there, as at Sparta and on Crete. The authors of the graffiti probably engaged in competitive dances, as at Sparta, and, we may speculate, the competition among the youths extended to athletic contests as well, perhaps practiced at or near the site of the graffiti. These practices date to the mid sixth century B.C., the very period when Spartan *paideia* seems to have been established with similar components. There is no evidence that the Theran *paideia* went much farther back into the prehistory of that island, and we may suppose that it paralleled a more general, contemporary trend found in the Doric cultures of Crete and Sparta.

Athens

The Athenian *ephēbeia* or "Youth Corps" was formally instituted in the fourth century B.C., probably in the 330s, as compulsory military training for youths aged 18–20, *ephēboi* ('ephebes' or 'mature youths').[107] But the institution is probably the evolution in Attica of the initiation process common to all Greeks.[108] What may have been an earlier, more religiously oriented *ephēbeia* became a more secular institution whose function was the military, athletic, educational, and ethical formation of maturing citizens.[109] The *ephēbeia*'s formal initiatory characteristics include separation of youths from family and introduction to the cult of the *polis*. Athletic exercises, including torch races, hoplomachy, javelin-throwing, boat-races, and numerous other contests, were an important part of an ephebe's education.[110] A two-year period of seclusion for each ephebe, according to Vidal-Naquet, has "been connected with the latency period that marks the transition from childhood to adult in a number of societies."[111] This period corresponds roughly to the Spartan period of "hiding" (*krypteia*), but youths had to undergo a two-stage formal registration into their local demes and phratries created or reorganized from Cleisthenes to Pericles in the late sixth to fifth centuries B.C.

Prior to the *ephēbeia*, Athens lacked the highly structured age-class *paideia* of Sparta and Crete; Athenian civic institutions that did involve youths grew gradually over the sixth and fifth centuries.[112] One commentator remarks:

> Schooling [at Athens] was not compulsory, nor were schools organized
> and staffed by the community though education was encouraged and
> schools were regulated by law; attendance was essentially a private
> matter between a boy's father or guardian and the teacher, an independent entrepreneur.[113]

The first informal schools were the walled gardens—the Academy is one of the earliest in Athens—and they consisted mainly of a track and palaestra for practicing the physical education that was at the core of aristocratic upbringing.[114] Solon's reforms, probably enacted in 594/3 B.C., may plausibly be seen as an attempt to bring harmony to a society that had suffered internal conflict along the lines of age-classes among the elite. What was said of Greece generally applies well to the situation at Athens: "In an age class system there is no age as one moves through life at which a *complete* set of political rights and duties is suddenly granted . . . '[power] is gradually distributed in turn through succession."[115] So it was a concern at least from Solon's day to regulate the progress of youths to adulthood through the agency of communal institutions. No single Athenian festival has a purely initiatory function, although the Arrēphoria for girls and even the Panathenaia, traditionally founded or organized in 566 B.C., are thought to have traces of initiation ritual.[116] The Athenian festival of Genesia has been seen as originally a clan festival with an athletic program reorganized by Solon into a general festival honoring Athenian ancestors, yet no traces of this festival exist in the fifth century, and the hypothesis seems untenable.[117] Of great interest in the present context is the seemingly reliable tradition of a law of Solon:[118]

> The law prohibits a slave from frequenting the gymnasium [*gumnazesthai*] and from anointing themselves in the palaestrae . . . [and it prohibits] a slave from loving or following a freeborn boy on the penalty of being given fifty lashes with a whip. (Solon fr. 74e Ruschenbusch, *ap.* Aeschines 1.138–39 [*In Tim.*])

This evidence will be reviewed in more detail later (ch. 8), but we may presently note that the purpose of these regulations was probably to guard against slaves fraternizing with freeborn youths in the palaestrae and taking such boys as lovers. A later law attributed to Solon but likely from the fifth century B.C. sets hours for the opening and closing of palaestrae to protect against pederastic liaisons taking place there after dark without proper supervision:

> The teachers of the boys shall not open the school before sunrise, and they shall close them before sunset. . . . [N]o one over the age of the boys is to enter when the boys are within. Anyone who disobeys and enters is to be punished with death. (Aeschin. 1.10 [*In Tim.*])

Such laws illustrate that by the late sixth century the palaestrae were prime locales for forming pederastic relationships and that the protocol for these relationships was an object of extremely serious civic concern.[119] The school-hours law was not meant to prohibit normal pederastic relationships but to ensure that such liaisons were formed literally and figuratively in broad daylight for communal knowledge and approval. Though there is not the formal attachment or ritual behavior found in Crete and Sparta, Athenian pederastic and athletic *paideia* were normally associated by the late sixth century. Classical and later literature and art from Athens are replete with additional examples (ch. 8).[120]

One salient artistic example of the association is pointed out by Alain Schnapp, who traces the shift from Attic black-figure vases (pre-520 B.C.) showing pederastic couples in aristocratic contexts of hunts of wild animals to red-figure Attic vase paintings (ca. 520 B.C. and later) placing homoerotic scenes in gymnasia with tamed animals in the background: "An urban eroticism, more artificial and allusive, replaces the cheerfully aggressive images of capture of the archaic period. . . . Interest is displaced from the fields to the doors of the gymnasium, from the country to the city, from the wild to the tame."[121] Sergent detects in this change of iconography a deeper allusion to an Indo-European pattern in which hunting as an ephebic activity is connected with the Cretan initiation of the youth in the wilds, which also involves training in hunting. The symbolic relation of hunter:hunted::lover:beloved is a typical erotic metaphor, and hunting as an activity "in the wilds," can hence easily be taken as characteristic of the initiate's marginal status. Vidal-Naquet describes the Attic ephebe as a light-armed, solitary creature of the margins (*eschatia*) prior to becoming a fully mature, heavy-armed, and socialized hoplite.[122] Yet there is no need to join it specifically to an Indo-European initiation pattern. Hunting is such a common prehistoric human occupation that it is perhaps inevitable if some of its practices are reflected in the sports of many world cultures.[123] More significant for our discussion is the artistic translation of hunting specifically into athletics as an erotic setting, and the fact that this was done in the very period in which gymnasia became more popular in Athens. This provides further evidence of the increasingly pederastic focus of Athenian athletic culture in that period and also simply signifies that the gymnasium was literally becoming more popular than hunting among the élite in the late sixth century.[124] Both hunting and athletic competition provide excellent stage settings for the performance of individual deeds of glory in the 'contest system.'

Alan Shapiro has pointed out that the production of homoerotic courtship scenes on Attic vases is almost exclusively a sixth-century phenomenon, which flourished especially from 550–500 B.C.[125] Thus the scenes appear to validate our inference from Solon's law, that pederasty was well established and generally accepted after 600 B.C. The sharp decline of artistic portrayals of pederastic courtship in the late sixth century is coincident with the fall of the Athenian tyrants in 511, which has led to the conclusion that there was "a popular sensibility which made depictions of this upper-class activity less acceptable in an essentially popular art form."[126] Yet, as we shall see later (ch. 8), scenes of athletes with the god Eros or in homoerotic scenes in gymnasia continue into the fourth century B.C., which may indicate that athletics was a safe context for illustrating pederasty in the popular art form. The reason undoubtedly is that athletics became ever more open to the non-élite in Athenian culture and more imbedded in the system of civic upbringing of youth. Vase-paintings do not avoid illustrating homoeroticism after 500 B.C., but only placing it in the élite contexts of courtship with hunting and gift-giving.

Another monument that is significant to this discussion is the first Athenian altar to Eros, set up by a certain Charmus, the beloved of the tyrant Peisistratus, who himself set up a statue to Eros, both installed at an entrance to the Academy prior to 527 B.C.[127] These dedications will be discussed more fully later (ch. 8), but it is sufficient to note here that the altar also served as the site at which the torch was lit at the beginning of the torch race in the Panathenaia, and that the other terminus of the race was probably the altar of Anteros (Reciprocal Love) at the base of the Acropolis. Though the torch race itself was a ritual of communal renewal of the sacred fire and not specifically an 'initiation' ritual restricted to boys, the symbolism behind the use of Eros-Anteros altars as the termini of this prestigious event illustrates some important points. It shows a strong civic commitment to Eros in association with the welfare of the state, and it underscores the strong bonds between pederasty, athletics, the gymnasium, and formal and informal political affiliations from the sixth century B.C. onward in Athens.

Though there are no rituals of an exclusively initiatory nature for Athenian males, one festival important in this connection is the Oschophoria, with a legendary foundation myth but possibly begun in the sixth century B.C.[128] The festival apparently takes its name from the *oschos* or "vine-branch" carried by two youths who led the festival procession and possibly also from vines carried by runners in the central footrace, a contest reminiscent of the Spartan *Staphylodromoi*. It has been suggested, perhaps rashly, that the name Oschophoria may be derived from *oschē* (*oschea*, *oscheos*), meaning "scrotum" and thus alluding to the function of the ritual as a dedication of young men. Although this suggestion is untenable, it does remind us that *oschos* and *oschē* are etymologically related through the idea of a "sprout"[129] and that the two words were played upon as a double entendre in Aristophanes (*Acharnians* 995, 997).[130] Thus, there may be a metaphor for assuming one's manhood inherent, consciously or unconsciously, in the activity of carrying the bunches of grapes on a vine-branch.

There are in addition a number of initiatory characteristics in the Oschophoria. In the procession that likely came before the contest, two boys in transvestite dress led the parade on the same route as the race. The transvestite youths supposedly recall two boys smuggled amid the maidens sent as tribute to King Minos on Theseus' Cretan expedition. The central contest is a footrace from a temple of Dionysus (probably the Lenaeum) in Athens to the sanctuary of Athena Sciras in Phaleron, a distance of 7 kilometers.[131] The participants of uncertain number are noble youths selected from each of the tribes of Attica. The runners are referred to either as 'ephebes' or as 'children with both parents living' (*paides amphithaleis*), and in any case representing different tribes (*phylai*). The restrictions to participants emphasize the need for communal health and broad representation in the ritual race. There was only one victor who won the right to taste of a punchlike drink called the *pentaploa*, that is, "having five ingredients," representing the chief local products: wine, honey, cheese, barley, and olive oil. There was also an element of transvestism, common in initiations, whereby two youths leading the procession after the race wore women's clothes. The festival therefore includes a test of strength, intertribal rivalry, association with the state's welfare through the special drink, and regulations regarding dress. The Oschophoria was associated with the myth of the celebration of Theseus' return from Crete. That legendary, archetypically Athenian youth had just undergone a kind of initiation in the Minoan labyrinth. The festival, which is held during the grape harvest and is associated with Dionysus, is naturally also an agricultural celebration. Though not properly an initiation festival, it has the civic function of associating youths with the legendary founder and ideal ephebe, Theseus.[132]

Another Athenian festival, the Hermaia, also combines some characteristics of a historical initiation with contests, and it has additional indications that pederasty was a concern of the organizers.[133] Aeschines in his speech *Against Timarchus* 9–12 (345 B.C.) suggests that Solon had made provisions about palaestrae in which the youths are safeguarded from the instructors and supervisors:

> [Solon] seems to have mistrusted teachers—to whom we necessarily entrust our boys, and whose livelihood depends upon self-control, the lack of which means poverty for them. . . . He also provides regulations for who the youths ought to be in order to matriculate, and at what age, and for an official who is responsible for them and for the supervision of the tutors [*paidagōgoi*], and . . . for the Hermaia in the palaestrae. . . . And the gymnasiarch [i.e., gymnasium director] shall in no way allow anyone outside the age limit to participate in the Hermaia. The gymnasiarch who allows this and does not exclude an overage person from the gymnasium is to be subject to the law about the ruination of the freeborn.

It seems unlikely that these Hermaia laws were truly established by Solon or Draco, as Aeschines asserts, because the office of gymnasiarch is not reliably attested before the fourth century.[134] And from Plato's portrayal of Socrates attending the Hermaia, it appears that the restriction against adults attending the festival was probably a fourth-century innovation (*Lysis* 206d). Nevertheless the festival is remarkable for being a 'boys-only' contest, otherwise unknown for Athenian festivals in the classical period. The Hermaia itself may have originated in the sixth century and was certainly established by the time of Socrates in the later fifth, but we have no explicit evidence about its founding date, unless we accept Aeschines' (erroneous) retrojection of festival laws to Solon or Draco as an implicit indication that fourth-century Athenians would find plausible a founding date anywhere from the late seventh to the early sixth centuries. Though one scholar has argued that all festivals of Hermes share characteristics of initiations to adulthood,[135] this goes too far with the evidence for the Athenian Hermaia. Certainly Hermes was a god of transitions in general and, with Heracles, one of the chief gods of the gymnasium. Thus, his divine roles and the restriction of this festival to youths does make this festival closer than most to a historical 'initiation' through athletic *paideia*, but there is no special requirement, strictly speaking, by which Athenian boys had to attend the Hermaia as a rite of passage.

Equally noteworthy is the apparent reputation of the Hermaia as a good festival at which Athenian men might meet boys as their potential beloved. This is made clear by the context of Plato's *Lysis*, in which Socrates accompanies another adult male, Hippothales, to meet his beloved Lysis amid the throng of boys and youths. The later law against adults attending the Hermaia was therefore probably enacted to prevent men flocking to this particular all-boys festival. Pederastic courtship was not generally discouraged, only the inappropriate use of a sacred festival as a popular 'pick-up' point. The focus on the erotic attraction of the Hermaia, both before and after the attendance law, provides a good illustration of the conjunction of pederasty and athletic *paideia* in Athenian culture.

Boys divided into two age categories, 'youths' (*ageneioi*, roughly 17–20) and 'boys' (*paides*, roughly 13–16), could and did compete alongside men (*andres*) in the numerous other athletic festivals of the Athenian calendar, including the Theseia, the Genesia, the Epitaphia, the Heracleia at Marathon, the Eleusinia, and, of course, the Greater Panathenaia.[136] All of these are properly 'civic' and not initiatory occasions, though the very participation of citizen youths was in some sense part of a common program of upbringing: even the dramatist Sophocles is said to have been an athletic (and musical) victor as a boy.[137] The fact that Athenian youths generally took part in athletic festivals held in their own city and elsewhere in Greece testifies to the vigor and success of Athens in training its young as athletic ambassadors of their *polis*. According to Kyle's catalogue of known Athenian athletes to 322 B.C., boys from Athens won three times at the Olympics, twice at the Isthmia, twice at the Panathenaia, and ten times at the Amphiaraia Festival in Oropus, Boeotia.[138] None of these occurs earlier than 468. After 322 B.C., we know of no further Olympic victories by Athenian boys, and only one nonadult victory in the other Panhellenic games, namely in youths' wrestling in the Nemean Games ca. 150 B.C.[139] Athenian athletes of all age groups were not as successful as their Spartan counterparts in victories during the first two centuries of the Olympics: Athenians had only six, compared to the thirty-six by Spartans in that period. From 576 to 322 B.C., by contrast, when there were only seven (or possibly eight) Spartan Olympic victors in gymnic events and eleven in equestrian events, there were fifteen Athenian Olympic gymnic victors and ten hippic victors. These records suggest about equal participation in hippic events but somewhat more Athenian participation, or at least success, in gymnic contests. And where records show no Spartan victors in any events or in any period of the other three Panhellenic festivals, we find a total of thirty-seven Athenian victories, nineteen of those in gymnic events (and three of those by youths).[140] The fourth century B.C. inscription recording victors at the Amphiaraia festival in Oropus, at that time part of Attica, shows, not remarkably, six Athenian victors (of the twenty-two total listed).[141] More noteworthy is the fact that none of the six are in adult events, but five are in the boys' categories and one in the youths'. If this inscription dates to 331 B.C., as Klee argues, the successes of the Athenian youths and boys may reflect the focus on the training of boys generally and on the *ephēbeia* in particular, which seems to have been formally instituted, or at least reorganized, around this time.[142] Perhaps Athens was eager to parade *la crème de la crème* of its youth corps at the games in its newly acquired territory of Oropus. The strong showing by its youth at this festival must have been a very positive reflection on Athens' athletic *paideia*.

One young athlete of interest here is Eualkes, who is said to have had the help of the Spartan King Agesilaus to gain entry into the Olympic stade race for boys in 396 or 392 B.C., though Eualkes was bigger than the other entrants. Agesilaus is said to have done this either as a favor for a guest-friend, the son of Pharnabazus, satrap of Asia, who was in love with the boy, or because Agesilaus himself was in love with him.[143] In any case, we find an Athenian boy whose athletic, and possibly his political, career is fostered by his pederastic affiliations. The boy seems to have lost the race, since his name is not among the (complete) record of stade victors in that era.

Although Athens lacked Sparta's formal institutions and more rigid rituals of initiation, Athenian *paideia* nevertheless reflects a similarly harmonious combination of separate *paideia* for youths, socially regulated pederasty, and athletic training and competition for boys. Training, pederasty, and education were more the concern of the élite at least in the sixth century, but the fifth century saw a broadening of access to gymnasia and the fourth century marked the formal union of education, athletics, and initiatory and military rigor in the *ephēbeia*. Each age of Athens of course transformed *paideia* to suit its own pragmatic ends, but Athens consistently maintained the aim of initiating youths to adulthood. Prior to the sixth century, the fundamental components of age-classes, homoeroticism, and an athletic tradition were undoubtedly present, though there is no evidence, *pace* Sergent and Bremmer, that a 'primitive' initiation existed as the basis for a later synthesis.

Thebes

Though little is known of the Theban system of *paideia*, Thebes has been an important case-study for theorists of pederasty and initiation.[144] Thebes is, as discussed earlier, the home of the legendary King Laius, who introduced homosexuality to that city, the place where the 'lawgivers' after Laius fostered Eros as part of the education in the palaestra (according to Plut., *Pelop.* 19.1–2 [287–88] quoted earlier), and the place where a "Sacred Battalion" of homosexual lovers was formed.

The city is also the locus of a sanctuary that has been cited as evidence of primitive, homosexual initiation, with links to athletics and initiation of Theban youths. The sanctuary of Iolaus is located in front of the Proitian gates and alongside the 'Iolaus' Gymnasium, a stadium, and a hippodrome.[145] Iolaus was Heracles' squire and beloved, and Pindar alludes to his tomb near the stadium in Thebes, presumably within his own sanctuary.[146] Since it was conventional to have the tomb of a local hero near athletic festival sites in conjunction with legendary funeral games in his behalf, we ought not take the historicity of this tomb too seriously. It is likely that it was a later archaization after the pattern of the Pelopion at Olympia or the Palaimonion at Isthmia—neither of which, according to archaeologists, actually contain the grave of a Bronze Age hero within the classical hero sanctuaries.[147] The more certain importance of the testimony is that Iolaus was upheld as an image of the ideal ephebe and beloved, closely associated with the agonistic sites of Thebes. Iolaus was himself the victor in the chariot race at the legendary games for Pelias.[148] And he was known above all in his cults for his embodiment of youth: Euripides has him retrieve his youth for a day.[149] Plutarch tells us in one place that "believing Iolaus to have been beloved by [Heracles], to this very day lovers worship and honor Iolaus, exchanging vows and pledges with their beloved at his tomb" and adds in another context, "Aristotle says that even down to his day the tomb of Iolaus was a place where lovers and beloved made pledges to each other."[150] The oaths of the beloved may recall the homosexual graffiti at Thera, though only to the extent that both testify to the proximity of a homoerotic meeting spot.[151] There was also a festival at Thebes called the Iolaeia (or Heracleia) in honor of Heracles and Iolaus, with competitions in both equestrian and athletic events.[152] The dual naming of the celebration seems to celebrate the legendary friendship itself. Through the cult of Iolaus, the Thebans were clearly promoting the conjunction of *erōs* and athletics among their young citizens.

The Iolaus sanctuary in Thebes incidentally recalls a similar worship of that hero in Agyrion, Sicily, where the companion of Heracles was said to be a native and there is a sanctuary for him and an annual cult festival in his honor:

> Boys who fail to perform the customary rites lose their power of speech and are like dead men. . . . [At the Heraclean gates they gather each year and] with utmost zeal they hold games which include gymnastic contests and horse races. And since the whole populace, both free men and slaves, unite in approbation of the god [Heracles], they command their servants . . . to gather in bands. . . .[153]

The Sicilian cult is a double one, like the Laconian one to Apollo and Hyacinthus, honoring both lover and beloved. Again we see the worship of Iolaus in conjunction with athletic contests and may infer that in this sanctuary, too, Iolaus was an ephebic hero whom local youths could emulate by taking part in the games and accepting the role of beloved. The tradition that threatens muteness and virtual death to boys who neglect the rites of Iolaus is a strong incentive for all youths to acknowledge and emulate the ideals that the hero represents.

Back at Thebes, we find one more example of the conjunction of pederasty, athletic *paideia*, and a hero's tomb all combined in the legend of Diocles and Philolaus, as explained by Aristotle:

> Philolaus of Corinth became a lawgiver for the Thebans. Philolaus was of the family of the Bacchidae and became the lover of Diocles, the Olympic victor [in the stade race in 728]. When Diocles, disgusted at the lust of his mother Alcyone, left Corinth, he went to Thebes, and there both of them lived out their lives. Even now people point out their

tombs, which are easily in view of one another, but one is open to view in the direction of Corinth, the other is not.[154]

We learn, moreover, from Theocritus, that Diocles' tomb was the site of a kissing competition in which boys gathered to be judged by older men. The Olympic victor and beloved is aptly remembered in an event which puts *erōs* itself into an agonistic context. Both Corinthian exiles thus take on special significance for the community.[155] Since Philolaus was an honored lawgiver and his beloved epitomizes ephebic beauty, their tombs and the kissing contest give prestige to the association of homoeroticism and the athlete-ephebe at Thebes. It is more likely to see a true historical core to this story than to take it as a myth reminiscent of prehistoric initiation, as Sergent does, since the name of Diocles is elsewhere recorded as Olympic victor.[156]

This historical legend is also significant in dating the kissing competition sometime between the late eighth century and the time of the composition of the *Politics*, ca. 340–322 B.C. Given the pattern of emergence of homosexuality elsewhere in Greece in the sixth century, we may surmise that this contest likely began no earlier than that period. Philolaus might indeed have been one of the anonymous 'lawgivers' mentioned by Plutarch as one who fostered *erōs* in the palaestra in Thebes, and thus the foundation or reform of Theban *paideia* would be roughly contemporary with the reform of the Spartan *agōgē*, with the establishment of a sanctuary to Eros in the Athenian Academy, and with the earliest Theran graffiti.

Conclusions

From this survey of the historical association of boys' athletic training and competitions, pederasty, and the establishment of rituals and institutions of *paideia* with initiatory characteristics, we can draw several conclusions. Each of the states surveyed, Crete, Sparta, Thera, Athens, and Thebes, shows significant differences in its specific practices; *paideia*, pederasty, and athletics are 'polycentric' in their historical manifestations and cannot in any meaningful way be ascribed to a common pattern derived from an Indo-European or 'prehistoric' culture. Though we can detect initiatory patterns of 'separation–life on the margin–reintegration' in certain rituals and institutions structures, the local differences are significant and suggest unique functions within the greater context of each culture. Furthermore, most or all of the customs of 'initiatory' *paideia* in conjunction with athletic and pederasty take place in the sixth century and cannot be traced to earlier sources.

In one sense, these are negative results in reference to the theories of Sergent, Bremmer, Brelich, and Jeanmaire, yet our survey has also yielded a very positive finding in the historical outline of the development of these three cultural streams in Greece from the eighth to fifth centuries B.C., which may be sketched as follows.

Most of our findings pertain to phenomena attached to historical dates of the sixth century or later, yet we must begin our sketch with some speculation about the possible evolution of culture beginning with the earliest evidence from the Homeric epics of the eighth century. Homer's texts reveal little of institutions that might be called 'initiation,' nothing of overt pederastic relationships, and indeed nothing of athletics restricted to the cultural formation of youth. Assuming that Homer's epics to some extent reflect their contemporary society or at least the ideals and values of its élite stratum, we may conclude that in the eighth century, homoerotic expression was exhibited only modestly and with euphemism, the contest was a display of heroic valor and not yet 'socialized' as a civic or Panhellenic enterprise, and the upbringing of youths was accomplished in a relatively informal manner.[157] After Homer and with the early Olympic Games in the eighth to early seventh centuries, we may posit the existence of local athletic events, particularly funeral games for local heroes and ancestors.[158] In the early- to mid-seventh century, the establishment of hoplite warfare, the growth of the *polis*, and the continued influence of Homeric poems and the Olympics all probably contributed to the slow growth in the popularity of athletic events and tracks in each city.[159] Pederasty seems to have 'come out of the closet' in the seventh century, perhaps as a measure for birth control spurred on by a population expansion in eighth-century Greece. Then comes the real 'boom' in athletics in the early sixth century. Athletic nudity, it has been cogently argued, appeared around 650–600 B.C., likely fostering and simultaneously fostered by the newly open homosexuality, though both openly displayed pederasty and formal Olympic athletics precede the custom of nudity.[160] Solon's laws relating to regulation of pederasty in the palaestra affirm that the two phenomena were associated by the beginning of the sixth century. The Pythian, Isthmian, and Nemean Games, begun within the first thirty years of the sixth century, testify to the burgeoning popularity of athletic festivals. From that point on, most *poleis* doubtless felt the pressure to provide tracks or wrestling grounds available to citizens, and male citizens were attracted to participate in athletic contests in greater numbers.

Thus far, our sketch says little of formalized *paideia*, since the evidence for this points mostly to sixth-century origins. The Spartan *agōgē* and the Cretan system of *paideia* were probably largely and formally established in the sixth century, and pederasty occupied a formal part of both, but the existence of these institutions seems not to have encouraged the youths who went through them to translate the rigors of physical tests of initiation into success in conventional, interstate athletics. Sparta's athletic acme at Olympia had ended by 520 B.C. And the initiatory rituals of Crete and Sparta seldom took on the form of conventional athletic contests. From the shadowy culture of Thera surrounding the obscene graffiti of the sixth century and later, we can observe only that pederasty and competition were connected, and athletic competitions may have played a part of their *paideia* alongside dance, but this relies on some speculation based on parallels with the better attested states. The participation of Athenian youth in interstate athletics seems also to bear little relation to its initiatory *paideia*, either in the Oschophoria festival, the Hermaia (possibly both sixth-century innovations), or the *ephēbeia* (a fourth-century institution). Theban evidence points to a possible linking of pederasty and athletics in the early seventh century in emulation of the locally honored couple, Diocles and Philolaus, also leading to the (seventh century?) endorsement by 'lawgivers' of pederastic relationships among youth in the palaestra, though we do not know whether they had a formalized initiatory *paideia* resembling those found elsewhere.

In sum, the systems of upbringing with initiatory characteristics in the several Greek states surveyed indicate that these forms of *paideia* were established generally in the sixth century, only after the liaison between pederasty and athletics had already been formed in the seventh century. Historical *paideia* naturally often adopted the characteristics found by anthropologists in the initiation rituals of 'primitive' cultures, but this does not mean that the Greek rituals and institutions were themselves 'primitive' or prehistoric in origin (though some of their terms and traits may be prehistoric). We can more reliably trace the functional integration of both athletics and pederasty as part of the 'package' of youth formation when those institutions were established, mostly in the sixth century. Since our interest has been on the early history of these phenomena, we have of course been selective in looking at those cities for which the best early, relevant documentation survives. In the Hellenistic and Roman periods, the *ephēbeia* and public or private gymnasia, all with their own local magistrates and legislation, had spread as civic and educational institutions all over the Greek Mediterranean. Chapter 8 will survey the topic of athletics and eros in later periods; a full history of athletics and education for any given city-state, as Kyle has done for classical Athens, is of course beyond the present scope. Keeping in mind that this chapter's picture of *paideia* linked to athletics and pederasty was for men only, we will next, in chapters 4 to 7, turn to the few known examples of girls' festivals and rituals that combined female social formation with athletic or quasi-athletic events. For girls, these socializing practices apparently did not, with few exceptions, foster female homoeroticism, but they did strongly validate the roles of wife and mother.

4

RACING FOR HERA—
A GIRLS' CONTEST AT OLYMPIA

Athletics in ancient Greece is normally, and correctly, considered a male domain. Yet there were exceptional instances of young women, prior to marriage, participating to different degrees and in different ways in this area of the man's world. These next three chapters examine the regional athletic rituals for girls at Olympia, Sparta, and Attica, events that were effectively the female counterpart of boys' *paideia* or initiations. Then chapter 7 looks at the mythical example of the legendary Atalanta, an exceptional, fictional female athlete proving the rule that the contests are for men. In all the regional contests, it is noteworthy that only unmarried girls could participate and the events were seen as part of their passage to adulthood. And the instances of girls' games are much rarer than those for boys or men. Married women mostly kept to the domestic sphere, while their husbands were publicly active and continued to take part in athletic activities so long as they were physically able.

The Olympian Heraia is the most clearly described ancient athletic event for women.[1] Given its visibility through associations with the Olympic festival for men, the festival was possibly also the most influential model for similar local events elsewhere in Greece. Two fundamental questions arise: when did the contests, which consisted solely of footraces for maidens, originate; and, second, why were they instituted in conjunction with a festival of Hera? Both of these are difficult to answer because we have only one literary source for their existence, namely Pausanias (5.16). Mehl saw in the festival evidence of a Bachofenian-type matriarchal culture suppressed by the later men's Olympics, and von Vacano has placed their origin in the fifth century B.C., while other scholars subscribe to a sixth-century date.[2] I wish to propose here some new insights into the origin and nature of the Heraia based upon recently revised notions of athletics, history, and cults in archaic Greece. The first part of Pausanias' account describes the festival (5.16.2–3):

> Every fourth year the women weave a *peplos* for Hera. These same
> women also hold an *agōn* called the Heraia. The *agōn* consists of a
> footrace for maidens. Indeed not all girls of the same age compete, but

the youngest run first, and after these the girls next oldest, and finally whoever are the oldest of the maidens. They run as follows: their hair is let down, and the *chitōn* reaches a little above the knee, and on the right they bare their shoulder as far as the breast. The Olympic stadium is reserved for their *agōn* also, but they shorten the course of the stadium by about one-sixth for the girls. They give to the winners both crowns of olive-leaves and a portion of the cow sacrificed to Hera. It is also possible for them to dedicate portraits of themselves which they have had inscribed. Those who administer to the Sixteen Women are, like the *agōnothetai*, married women.

The passage then relates the story of the first victory in the Heraia by Chloris, the only surviving Niobid, and to recount the alternate tradition that the Sixteen were chosen from the villages of Elis to settle the differences between Elis and Pisa after the death of the Elean tyrant Damophon in the 580s B.C. (cf. Paus. 5.16.4–6; 6.22.3–4). "Later on" (ὕστερον) the Sixteen were entrusted with holding the Heraian *agōn* and weaving the *peplos* for Hera. Pausanias then describes the other cult duties of the Sixteen, including the arrangement of the choral dances for Hippodameia and for Physcoa. The latter was a heroine from Elis Coile, where she lived in the deme Orthia and was credited with introducing the worship of Dionysus to Elis. It has even been suggested that Physcoa's cult appears to have been substituted for an earlier cult of Artemis Orthia, suggested by the name of the heroine's deme.[3] While that association is highly speculative, the unusual name Orthia may alternatively indicate some regional ties between Sparta and Elis.[4]

Several aspects of Pausanias' account are of interest in the investigation of women's athletics in ancient Greece, namely the program of the Heraia and its resemblance to other early women's festivals with footraces, the organization of the Sixteen Women, the cult associations of the festival at Olympia, and its relation to the Olympic festival for Zeus. It has been observed that the program of the Heraia resembles the earliest Olympics in its basic structure of offering, *agōn*, crowning of victors with an olive branch, and final meal.[5] Presumably the *peplos* woven every four years by the Sixteen Women for Hera was offered to the goddess as a part of her festival, although the tradition is not explicit on this.[6] The most famous analogy is the *peplos* for the cult statue of Athena Parthenos in Athens. There the weaving was begun by priestesses together with Arrēphoroi maidens and carried on by a specially selected team of aristocratic maidens, the *Ergastinai*.[7] At Athens, the weaving of the *peplos* began about nine months before the presentation at the Panathenaia. Perhaps an even better parallel is the ritual of the maidens from Locri Epizephyrii in which a *peplos* woven for Persephone was offered to the goddess as part of the maiden's prenuptial rites.[8] At Elis, the weaving took place in a special building for the Sixteen in the agora (Paus. 6.24.10), where the process possibly also began about nine months before the Heraia.[9] The

Panathenaia and presentation of the *peplos* probably existed at least since the seventh century and probably long before it, but an athletics program was attached to that festival only since 566 B.C.[10] The donation of new robes to a goddess may even go back to Minoan times.[11]

Sappho mentions that Lesbian maidens brought a *peplos* to Hera at her festival on the island.[12] At Sparta the Leucippides, or "Daughters of Leucippus," weave a tunic for Apollo at Amyclae each year; like the Sixteen, the Leucippides do this in a special weaving house called the "Tunic" (Χιτών; Paus 3. 16.2). These are the same Leucippides who, together with the Dionysiades or "Daughters of Dionysus," organize regular sacrifices to Dionysus, and who may also have helped the Dionysiades to organize the maiden's footraces for Dionysus Colonatas (Paus. 3.13.6; see ch. 5). There may also be an allusion in Alcman's *Parthenion*, lines 60–64 (Page), to Spartan maidens carrying a robe for Orthia:

ταὶ Πεληάδες γὰρ ἇμιν	60
ὀρθρίαι φάρος φεροίσαις	61
. . . μαχόνται	63

For the Peleiades
. . . fight against us
as we bear the robe for Orthria.[13]

Other parallels between Spartan and Heraian rituals associated with female cults—to be discussed later—support the interpretation of Alcman's test as a "robe for Artemis Orthia." It seems, then, that in analogy with the Panathenaic procession and with the ritual presentation of robes elsewhere, notably at Sparta, the *peplos* was presented to Hera in a procession as part of the Heraian festival.

The Heraian *agōn*, like the contests of the first thirteen Olympics (776–728), consisted solely of the stade race, although it was shortened by one-sixth for the maidens. The shorter (500 vs. 600 Olympic feet) length of the women's stade could be cited as proof both for and against their greater antiquity.[14] Late sources report that Heracles determined the length of this stade by pacing it out or by the distance one could run on one breath (Sextus Julius Africanus in Eusebius, *Chronicon* vol. 1, p. 197, Schöne; Gel. 1.1; Isidor. *Origines* 15.16.3), but the legend is scarcely decisive. The difference in the lengths of the men's and women's stade may simply reflect the fact that women's average stride is shorter.

It is clear that other women's festival contests in historical times also consisted solely of the footrace. Spartan women may have taken exercise in a variety of contests, but the footrace for Dionysus Colonatas and another cryptically called *en Drionas* (cf. Hsch., s.v., E2823 Latte) were the only known festival contests for them. Similarly, the ritual contest in the Brauronian Arkteia seems to have been a race or chase. As the first contest at Olympia and the one contest whose victor gave his name to each Olympiad, the stade race had special popularity and traditional prestige. It seems to have also gathered prestige as the contest of women's festivals.

The division of the girls into three age-groups is reminiscent of a passage in Plato's *Laws* (8.833c–834d) in which he suggests that unmarried girls up to the age of 18 or 20 compete in footraces of various lengths. He prescribes that those under 13 should compete nude while these older, who were awaiting marriage, were to wear proper attire: πρεπούσῃ δὲ στολῇ ταύτας ἐσταλμένας καταβατέον ἐπὶ τὴν ἅμιλλαν τούτων τῶν δρόμων. It has been suggested that Plato's two groups according to nudity or dress correspond to naked and clothed girl runners in the Arkteia as depicted on Attic kraters. The limits of the age divisions in the Heraia are uncertain, but we may guess that one division was under 13 and two older had an upper limit of 18 to 20. The division of the Heraian contests into three age categories also finds its closest parallel in the Spartan practice by which boys and presumably girls were divided into three age-classes of six years, each between the ages of 6 and 24, for the purposes of education and sport. We may recall that girls' races were instituted at Sparta, allegedly by Lycurgus, as a regular part of the girls' education, and this would have served as a ready model for the organizers of the Heraia (Xen., *Respublica Lacedaimoniorum* 1.4; Plut., *Lycurgus* 14.2; Philostratus, *Gymnastica* 27; Theocr. 18.21–36; Euripides, *Andromache* 595–602). In any case, it may be significant that the races are restricted to *parthenai*, as at Sparta and Brauron, and may, like those races, have some significance as an initiatory trial before marriage.[15]

The light style of dress by the Heraian runners not only afforded greater comfort but also clearly distinguished the girl athletes from women in their regular activities. Spartan girls were notorious in Classical times for being "thigh-showers" (*phainomerides*) when they wore short chitons, presumably for exercising (Ibykos, sixth c. B.C. ap. Plut., *Comparatio Lycurgi et Numae* 3.3–4, cf. also Eur., *Andr.* 597–98; Sophocles fr. 788 Nauck), and they may have inspired the organizers of the Heraia to adopt for their competition a distinctive dress that was both unconventional for women and somewhat different from the Spartan style.[16] "Mini-chitons" of a specifically Heraian style are known from two statues. The first is now in London, probably found in Albania, ancient Epirus, done in a Laconian style, and dated to ca. 560 B.C.; it may have been one of several attached to a large bronze krater.[17] The London statuette is remarkable in that it corresponds exactly to Pausanias' description of the Heraian runners: hair let down, chiton a little above the knees, and shoulder bare as far as the breast (see figure 4-1). The same is true of the second Heraian figure, a marble statue of a girl runner in the Vatican Museums, apparently a copy of a fifth-century original bronze, dated ca. 460 B.C., and almost certainly depicting a victor in the girl's race at Olympia (figure 4-2).[18] Whereas the London statuette is 11.4 cm. high (ca. 4.5 in.), the Vatican figure is 1.54 m. high (ca. 5 feet, 1/2 in.) and thus may be a copy of a life-size statue originally dedicated

Figure 4-1. London, British Museum Br.208, from Prisrend (?), Albania (ancient Epirus), ancient Greek bronze statuette, left leg restored, dated to ca. 580 B.C. Courtesy of the Trustees of the British Museum, London, U.K.

by a Heraian victor or by her family at Olympia or in her home city. The depiction of a "victor's palm-branch" on the trunk of the marble support for the figure seems to clearly indicate that the girl has won a footrace.

There are three other archaic bronze statuettes portraying girl runners, possibly all of Spartan workmanship or in Laconian style, which are not identical to but useful for comparison with the Heraian runners. One is of apparent Laconian workmanship, dated to the sixth century, now in Athens but found in ancient Epirus (Dodona), and, like the London girl, hitches up her dress with the left hand as she runs.[19] But the bodice of the Athens girl's chiton covers both breasts (see figure 4-3). Another statuette of a running girl, certainly of Spartan origin and now in the Sparta Museum, dates from 570–560 B.C.[20] A third figure of ca. 540–530 B.C., a bronze girl runner from Palermo, is also apparently of Spartan style and wearing a Spartan short *peplos*, but of Sicilian provenance (see figure 4-4). The Palermo runner may be modeled on the relief figure in a metope from the Silaris Treasury, c. 550–540

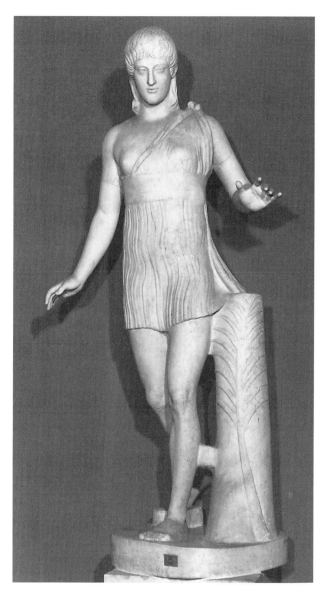

Figure 4-2. Marble statue of a girl runner in the Vatican Museum, apparently a copy of a fifth-century original bronze, dated ca. 460 B.C.; Rome, Vatican City, Vatican Museum Galleria dei Candellabri, XXXIV.36.1, inv. no. 2784. Courtesy of the Vatican Museums, Vatican City.

Figure 4-3. Athens, National Museum, Collection Carapanos no. 24, bronze statuette from Dodona (ancient Epirus), Greece, ca. 550 B.C. Courtesy of the National Archeological Museum and the Archeolgical Receipts Fund, Athens.

B.C. (?) (figure 4-5).[21] This metope scene has been interpreted as a depiction of the mythical Leucippides in flight from the Tyndaridai before their capture and marriage. The connection of the Spartan-style figure from Palermo with the Leucippides recalls the Spartan priestesses, namesakes of the Leucippides, who were affiliated with another group of Spartan women, the Dionysiades, who organized races for girls as a part of their cult duties.[22] If it is correct to identify these three figures as of Spartan style, it may well be that they represent, or at least were modeled on, the ancient Spartan girl runners rather than the Olympian Heraia participants. Unlike the Heraia costume, the ones worn by these three cover both breasts. It is, of course, also possible that any one or all three of these may represent legendary female run-

Figure 4-4. Palermo, Museo Nazionale, inv. no. 8265 (42), of unknown provenance, possibly from Tarentum or Paestum, Italian bronze statuette, ca. 540–530 B.C. Courtesy of Museo Archeologico Regionale "A. Salinas," Palermo, Italy.

ners, such as Atalanta,[23] the Amazons, or the Leucippides, but the Spartan associations by themselves make the connection with Spartan girl athletes more likely. It is much more difficult to determine the reasons for the provenience of the statuettes from Dodona[24] and Palermo, beyond speculating that they were dedications by Spartan girls, or their families, to commemorate their special education or even to honor them for specific victories in local races. In the latter event, the local races may have been either at Sparta, like that of the Dionysiades, or at sites in Epirus or South Italy.[25] In any case, the "Spartan" type statuettes are to be distinguished clearly from the Heraian figures by their dress.

The iconographic association of the Palermo statuette with mythical Lecippides in their prenuptial flight, though speculative, at least reminds us that the female race at Sparta, as at Olympia, was restricted to girls before marriage. If, as argued later, the races at Olympia and Sparta helped girls to make the transition to marriage and adulthood, figurines of girl runners might well have reflected this function by alluding, through visual clues, to other myths of prenuptial flight and pursuit. Running, in other words, celebrates the wildness of the untamed girls before

Figure 4-5. Metope from the Silaris Treasury, ca. 550–540 B.C. (?); P. Zancani Montuoro and U. Zanotti-Bianco, *Heraion alla Foce del Sele*, vol. 2 (Rome, 1964), fig. 86. Courtesy of Soprintendenza Archeologica per le Province di Salerno Avellino e Benevento.

they are "caught" or "tamed" in marriage.[26] One aspect in particular of the iconography of the statuettes may suggest a prenuptial contest, namely the gesture of hitching up the hem of the chiton while running. This is seen in the London bronze of the Heraia, and in the "Spartan" type bronzes in Athens and Palermo.[27] It is also seen on two vase paintings of Atalanta shown in the midst of her legendary flight from Melanion (Hippomenes).[28] On both vases, which date from the early and mid fifth century, the Atalanta figure lifts the hem of her chiton with her left hand, but the chitons are longer and more elaborate, clearly distinguishing them from the simple, short Spartan ones. The gesture makes more sense when used with the long, cumbersome garments in the Atalanta scenes, but much less in the figurines with hems well above the knees. The Spartan and Heraian iconography therefore prefigures the later representations of Atalanta and may share with it the visual highlighting of the "female" quality of the chiton, its typically cumbersome length even when it is not actually long. It links real races of maidens with mythical flights of those seeking escape from marriage.

Special dress for girls participating in the races also has a ritual significance. At Sparta and in Attica, girls in festival races either wore short skirts, competed in the nude, or wore only trunks.[29] The prescription for certain dress or nakedness is not only a practical consideration but may have religious significance. Dress codes or enforced nudity are often part of initiatory ritual,[30] as were segregation of the sexes and age classification. Certain dress may serve as part of the initiatory ritual and at the same time have special significance for the presiding goddess or god, for example, the saffron robes worn by girls who "played the bear" in the Brauronian Arkteia. The short chitons of the girls participating in races for Artemis' Arkteia depicted in late-sixth- to late-fifth-century Attic kraters[31] generally resemble the chitons of the Heraia as described by Pausanias. The short chitons of Spartan girls have already been mentioned. So by comparison of the Heraian dress code for girl athletes with that of Sparta and of Brauron, we may observe that the style of short chiton was common to all three and that the history of it extended eight centuries, from the first half of the sixth century B.C. (date of the London bronze statuette, Br. 208, fig. 4-1) to the second century A.D. (Pausanias' day). But the complete nakedness (or wearing of trunks only) that is associated with some female athletics in Sparta and Attica is not known for Olympia.

Nevertheless, the short chiton of the Heraian maidens at Olympia cannot be explained as a temporary trend in fashion or a garment designed purely for comfort. The style that remained unchanged for 800 years probably would have undergone further modifications for greater comfort if it had not been preserved by religious custom. It was adopted sometime before 560 B.C., when the style is first evidenced in Greek art, and maintained because it had some religious (initiatory?) significance and carried with it traditional connotations of the young, independent, and athletic woman known otherwise primarily in myth and legend among the Greeks.

Nancy Serwint's thesis may help to explain the problem of the Heraia costume.[32] To be rejected are theories that rely upon associating the Heraian costume with either the Amazons or with Artemis. The Amazonian style at Olympia cannot easily be explained. The Amazons are devotees of Artemis, if of any goddess; Callimachus (*Hymn* 3. 237–50) and Pindar (*ap.* Paus. 7.2.7.) report that the Amazons founded the Sanctuary of Artemis at Ephesus. Artemis the virgin huntress wore a short chiton that may have inspired (or been a reflection of) the costume of her followers at Brauron and elsewhere.[33] Some resemblance of the Heraian runners to the legendary Amazons might be seen in three bronze figures, originally on a tripod, from the Athenian Acropolis and one figure from Thessaly, all depicting Amazons in short chitons with hems lifted by the left hand and one with a bared right shoulder.[34] The Amazons differ, however, from the London and Vatican Heraian girls (and from the "Spartan" runner figurines) in their wearing of high-crested, "Illyrian" helmets. The "Capitoline" Amazon, dated 440–430 B.C. and one of a supposed group of monumental statues from the sanctuary of Artemis at Ephesus, has a right breast exposed in the manner of the Heraia runners. Another of the Ephesus group, the "Lansdowne" Amazon, dated to the fourth c. B.C., might ultimately be modeled on a runner resting after a race, as evidence by the unusual supporting pier that strongly resembles a turning post.[35]

Yet neither the Amazons nor Artemis have any direct connection with the Heraia. The Heraian costume, as Serwint has convincingly argued, in fact precedes the appearance of the Amazonian dress with the exposed breast, and we cannot therefore see it as a reflection of an "Amazonian" style. Chronologically, then, I suggest that the inspiration for the "Capitoline" and "Lansdowne" Amazons might have been statues of Heraian victors. It would then follow, also as a speculative suggestion, that the Amazonian "runner" style having one breast bared might generally have been modeled on the Heraian costume rather than vice versa. This suggestion relates to the present question only insofar as the "Amazonian" style may reflect an extension of the "spirit" of the costume of the Olympic girl runners.

A more productive line of inquiry is Serwint's convincing theory that the Heraian garment is probably modeled on the men's lightweight, short chiton, named the *exōmis*, or literally the "off-the-shoulder" garment. The *exōmis* is known and attested in Greek art and literature prior to the 560 B.C. date of the British Museum sculpture of the Heraia runner, and it was worn widely by men in hot weather and while performing active labor. The Heraian costume is therefore a striking example of "cross-dressing," one aspect of the symmetrical inversion of gender roles commonly attested for men, but very rarely for women, in Greek myths and rituals. Cross-dressing in ritual is one common aspect of initiation rites marking an adolescent's transition to adulthood in Greek and other cultures.[36] The logic may be explained in one of two ways, either from a psychological perspective in which, for example, the initiate adopts the state of "the other" to experience to some degree the "totality" or wholeness of social roles before embarking on one's individual role, or from a structuralist view in which the dress of the other is worn to mark the marginal status of the initiate by inverting or confounding the usual categories of gender.[37]

The dress of the Heraian girls therefore suggests that the race is part of a preparation for their status as adult females, and at the same time it suggests that the very activity of a footrace is unusual for females, more normally a male activity that calls for a special "male" costume. Why then, we might ask, do the girls not don the appropriate male costume for the footrace, namely total nudity? Or, if the ritual went back before the period when nudity was introduced, why not a simple loin-cloth?[38] Here we can only speculate. Perhaps it was worn to emphasize the essentially nonathletic aspects of the footrace which was more initiatory ritual than contest. To compete in the nude would then have looked like a simple mimicry of a men's activity. So dress was chosen which was unmistakably typical of the "everyday" activity of men, allowing freedom of movement and also socially "proper" in not being too revealing (cf. Pl., *Leg.* 833d, πρεπούση δὲ στολῇ). Yet the experts in couture often contend that a costume that reveals only some of the body is much more erotic than total nudity, so, paradoxically, the Heraian garb showing much of the legs and one breast may have pushed the limits of societal definitions of "propriety." The *exōmis* is therefore an ambiguous costume that well suits the status of the maidens, alluding to the masculine yet revealing the feminine, maintaining nominal sartorial modesty yet unveiling the body as an erotic object.

The fact that the Heraia race in Pausanias' time was held in the Olympic stadium tells us little about the antiquity of the Heraian games. The first archaeologically attested stadium (designated "I" by scholars), which extended into the Altis 80 meters farther west than the Classical stadium, dates to the mid-sixth century B.C. Although it remains uncertain where the earlier racecourse was situated, it has been suggested that the earliest track for runners ended directly at, or at least at the stadium end nearest to, the Altar of Zeus (according to Philostr., *Gymn.* 5–6).[39]

Weniger argues that it was originally located in the Altis between the Hippodameion and the Chamynaion and consequently subsumed the sanctuary of Demeter Chamyne when it was lengthened one-sixth eastward.[40] Thus, according to Weniger, Demeter's priestess was allowed the compensatory privilege of being the only married woman allowed to witness the Olympic Games (Paus. 6.20.9; 21.1).[41] This hypothesis cannot be proved, since it presumes the priority of the women's stadium and knowledge of the location of the Hippodameion—both very uncertain presumptions.

In any case, the location of the earliest stadium was closer to the sanctuary proper, and, if Philostratus' account contains any truth, the course was oriented to an altar, probably that of Zeus. Thus, not only the original Olympic footrace, but also that of the Heraia, may have literally and figuratively been oriented toward the sanctuary. Orientation of a race to an altar recalls the late sixth/early fifth century black-figure vases from Brauron and Salamis showing girls with short chitons running near an altar (of Artemis?).[42] The altar of Olympian Hera was like that of Olympian Zeus, an ash altar of the oldest type and located only a little north of Zeus' altar.[43] According to legend, it was dedicated by Clymenus of Crete, a descendant of Idaean Heracles, fifty years after the flood, ca. 1380 B.C.(?) by some ancient reckoning, untenable today. So the altar of Hera seems close enough to that of Zeus and old enough to have been in view at the finish line of the first attested stadium (ca. 550 B.C.).

Pausanias tells us that the victors in the Heraian race received a portion of the cow sacrificed to Hera, presumably on this altar at the beginning of this festival (Paus. 5.16.3). This is a more modest version of the hecatomb offered to Olympian Zeus, which presumably supplied the meal at a final banquet for victors.[44] The olive crown given to maiden victors provides another parallel to this crown given to victors in the Olympics, and the Heraian crown may have even been cut from the same sacred olive tree as the Olympic crown. This tree, whose branches were supposedly used first for victory crowns by King Iphitus of Pisa in the 6th Olympiad (756 B.C.), was later seen by Pausanias behind the temple of Zeus.[45] The sacred tree may have been associated with the "Beautifully Crowned Nymphs" (*Kallistephanoi*) whose altar was nearby (Paus. 5.15.3). In the vicinity of the olive tree was found an eighth c. B.C. bronze statuette of a group of "nymphs" dancing in a circle. Could this have been a votive offering to those divinities whose dances may have been imitated in later dances (to Physcoa and Hippodameia) staged by the organizers of the Heraia at Olympia (Paus. 5.16.6)?[46] Might some early ceremonies honoring the nymphs have been forerunners of the later cult dances? We can only speculate about the possibility. Iphitus, according to legend, adopted the olive crown in 756 B.C. due to a command of the Delphic Oracle, but it has been suggested that the tree was the remnant of a pre-Greek tree cult whose ceremony for cutting preserves an early ritual (Schol. *ad* Pind., *Ol.* 3.33; Paus. 5.15.10).[47] This early cult would have had no special association with Zeus, Hera, or Heracles (despite Pind., *Ol.* 3.14ff., a later attempt to explain the tree's importance) but more closely resembles Minoan-Mycenaean tree cults including ecstatic cult dances.[48] The adoption of the olive crown for victors in the Olympics and in the Heraia may have occurred in the eighth century to subsume earlier cults into later ones. But we cannot decide from this practice common to both athletic festivals which adopted the crown first or whether it happened simultaneously.

Pausanias mentions that the victors may also set up inscribed "likenesses" (εἰκόνας) of themselves—the term includes paintings or sculptures—in honor of Hera (5.16.3). There are in fact cuttings on many of the columns of the Heraion which probably held the paintings of victors near the well-used entrances to the temple.[49] No similar paintings for Olympic victors are known on the columns of the temples for Zeus, and no similar customs are known for other sanctuaries where women's races were held.[50] Nor have any statue bases for Heraian victors been found, but this does not preclude the possibility of the custom. Female victors in the Olympic chariot races, beginning with the Spartan Cynisca in ca. 390 B.C., could and did erect statues to commemorate the victory of chariots they sponsored.[51] The setting up of likenesses of Heraian victors generally parallels the custom of dedicating victor statues for male Olympic victors in the Altis. The first attested victory statue, made of cypress, was for Praxidamas the Aeginetan boxer in the 59th Olympiad (544 B.C.).[52] In this further parallel between the Heraia and the Olympics, it is again impossible to determine which festival began the custom.

It cannot be determined with certainty whether the participants in the Heraia were local girls from the villages of Elis or whether the festival was open to all Greeks. Pausanias relates (5.16.4) that an early victor in the Heraia was Chloris, daughter of Amphion of Thebes, but the legend need not accurately reflect historical practice. The Chloris legend is evidently connected with that of Hippodameia's institution of the original games since Pausanias mentions both together.[53] It is difficult otherwise to understand the Niobid's association with the first Heraia. It may simply be that the sole survivor of Leto's wrath sought Hera's patronage in finding a husband by competing in the wedding games. If so, Chloris was successful later in marrying Neleus and bearing him Nestor.[54] The Chloris myth may generally reinforce the nuptial character of the games. Chloris was well-known as a favorite of Leto and depicted as a young girl next to the cult statue of Leto in Argos by

Praxiteles.[55] The Chloris legend also serves as a validatory myth of early political ties between the royal families of Thebes and Pisa.[56]

The only other clue to the origins of participants in the Heraia is the London bronze statuette from ancient Epirus, dated ca. 580 B.C., and of Laconian workmanship (fig. 4-1).[57] The iconography would suggest that the piece was made for a girl who was a victor in the Heraia and that it came from Olympia. The style, however, would suggest that it was made by Spartan workmen, or in their style, possibly by artists in Sparta, but possibly elsewhere; it might also indicate that the girl honored by the statuette was Spartan. The provenience of Epirus presents other possibilities. Might this have been a decoration on a tripod honoring a Heraian victor from northwestern Greece and set up in her homeland? Or was it a dedication of a Heraian victor at Olympia which somehow found its way to northern Greece, either as a collector's piece or a souvenir? Or was it made for a girl victor in some unknown local contest in Epirus modeled on the Olympian Heraia? If these statuettes do imply that the Heraia was open to non-Eleans as early as the sixth century, the practice would be a further parallel to the Panhellenic Olympics.

If the Heraia was "Panhellenic" by archaic times, it differed in this respect from the local girls' races at Brauron and Sparta. Those latter races may have had something of an initiatory function as "tests of strength" for local maidens prior to marriage. The Heraia does resemble these local contests by including only unmarried girls as participants and by its celebration of Hippodameia's marriage in honor of Hera, patroness of all marriages. So even if this Heraia were Panhellenic in historical times, it may have developed from an original, prenuptial festival for local maidens like the Arkteia and the girls' race at Sparta.

Several aspects of the program are thus reminiscent of girls' races at Sparta and at Brauron. So far as we can tell from recent archaeological evidence, the Arkteia contest, like the Heraia, consisted of a simple running event with girls in short chitons and was held near the patron goddess' altar; contestants may have been divided into age categories. The race for Dionysus at Sparta also resembled the Heraia in its simple program of a race and in the fact that the organizers of the contest, the Leucippides, also had the duty of weaving a robe for a local cult statue.[58] The possible Spartan workmanship in the London statuette of the Heraia runner (fig. 4-1), the presence of other statuettes of Spartan-style girl runners in the same period, and the independent, athletic reputation of Spartan girls suggest possible Spartan participation in the (Panhellenic?) Heraia and the possible influence of Spartan custom on the Heraian festival.

But many aspects of the Heraia also recall the earliest men's Olympics: the basic structure of the program of offering-*agōn*-feast, the practice of crowning victors with an olive wreath, the footrace as the sole contest, use of the same stadium, the sharing of the sacrificial victim by the victor, and the dedications of images of victors to the patron divinity in the Altis. Yet in later times, the men's games changed in some of these aspects when a number of new events were added and the program became more elaborate. Some have even argued that the very stability of the Heraia program and its presumed date on the festival calendar attest to its greater antiquity in contrast to the more flexible program and date of the Olympic festivals.[59] It has since been demonstrated that the date of the Olympics was consistently at the second full moon after the summer solstice.[60] The exact calendar date of the penteteric Heraia is not known. The reasons why the Olympic program changed, albeit quite slowly, and the Heraia program did not, are unclear. It may simply be that the conservative attitude was more strictly applied to women's event not requiring the great strength of other events. Or it may be that the Heraia was more conservative for religious reasons. The general resemblance of the two festivals is so striking that one cannot help but suspect some common origin or the influence of one upon the other. The question remains whether the later changes in the Olympic program and the stability of the Heraia may indicate that the women's festival came first and the Olympics imitated it.

The origin of the Heraian games has been one of the most vexed questions of scholarship on Olympia mainly because it cannot be treated apart from the question of the origin of the Olympic festival for Zeus.[61] Although it is impossible to present conclusive proof of any theory on the Heraian origins, it seems worthwhile to offer reasonable suggestions based on comparative evidence from the other women's games observed in this study. From apparent similarities in cult practice and structure of the Heraia, the Spartan festival for Dionysus Colonatas (Paus. 3.13.7), and the Arkteia of Attica, it can be suggested that women's footraces were at least fostered in similar cult environments even if they evidence no historical connection. Before entering marriage, girls competed in "tests of strength" (usually footraces) reminiscent of or derived from initiation rituals in honor of a form of a goddess associated with fertility and nourishment of the young (Artemis Orthia at Sparta; Artemis Arkteia at Brauron; Hera and perhaps Physcoa at Olympia).

Pausanias (5.16.4–8) gives us the only direct testimony of the Heraian origin and in fact offers two seemingly contradictory, aetiological legends. He first traces it "to ancient times" (ἐς τὰ ἀρχαῖα) when Hippodameia out of gratitude to Hera for her marriage to Pelops assembled the Sixteen Women and inaugurated the Heraia. Pausanias then relates an alternate tradition of the origin of the Sixteen, according to which one of the oldest, noblest, and most highly reputed women was chosen from each of the sixteen *poleis* of Elis to form a college as part of the alliance between Elis and Pisa ca. 580 B.C. The occasion was the death of the tyrant Damophon of Pisa, which allowed the two states to resolve their differences and symbolize this occasion with the newly formed group of women. This second tradition maintains that the Sixteen were only later given the task of managing the Heraian games and weaving the *peplos*. The Sixteen also arranged two choral dances, one in honor of Physcoa, a local heroine, and one for Hippodameia to be discussed below.

The passage, like many in Pausanias, contains much of general interest on the local cults, but few clear or decisive details. The tracing of the games back to "ancient times" has been dismissed as "an invention of aetiological myths . . . a commonplace of (Pausanias') time."[62] Yet as the only definite statement we have on the Heraian origin, it cannot be ignored any more than those that associate the Olympic origin with her husband Pelops.[63] Let us then investigate the possible basis of the origin of the games from prehistoric cults at Olympia.

The tradition of the founding of the games by Hippodameia may be mythic shorthand to suggest that the Heraia was founded simultaneously with Pelops' games. Furthermore, the nature of this festival as a thanksgiving for marriage dedicated to the patroness of marriages reinforces the importance of the festival for marriage at least by Pausanias' time. Since the participants are maidens, one might well expect Artemis, a very popular goddess at Olympia,[64] to be the patroness of the festival. But it has been suggested that Hera, due to prior and predominant influence in the area, may have become patroness of adolescent prenuptial rites that were elsewhere associated with Artemis.[65]

The association of the Heraian games with Hera and Hippodameia in historical times does not preclude the early origin of the games at Olympia and an association with goddesses who were later identified with the Olympian Hera and the heroine Hippodameia. Hera's cult came to Olympia with that of Zeus, perhaps as early as the tenth or eleventh century, according to archaeological evidence.[66] Hera's worship was established at Olympia at least by the late seventh century, the probable date of the earliest Heraion.[67] It has been argued by Joan O'Brien that Hera in the *Iliad* might have been patroness of athletic contests in Elis before the eighth century. According to this thesis, Hera was known there by the epithet Hippodameia, "tamer of horses," and her functions included the "taming" of youths (male and female) in marriage.[68] Attractive and neat as the thesis may be, it remains ultimately somewhat conjectural.

If, on the other hand, Hippodameia was not a local by-form of Hera later demoted to heroine status, she may have arrived with Pelops from the Argolid as an import from the Argive-Mycenaean realm of myth.[69] Admission to an annual cult festival in Hippodameia's honor held in her sanctuary at Olympia was restricted to females (Paus. 6.20.7), as was participation in the races instituted by the heroine. So the cult of Hippodameia, like that of Hera, may have been introduced at Olympia as early as late Mycenaean times, and at least by the late seventh century with the earliest temple of Hera.[70] One can only speculate on the date of arrival of these particular cult figures, and it is also uncertain whether they supplanted similar earlier cults. Olympia was certainly a settlement as early as the Middle Bronze Age (2000–1550 B.C.) and, perhaps with interruption, into the Late Bronze (Mycenaean) Age (1550–1100 B.C.).[71] As we saw in chapter 1, evidence is unclear whether Olympia was a cult place in Mycenaean times, and there is no archeological indication that Hera was worshiped there at the time. A dearth of votive offerings before the first half of the seventh century B.C. and the problems associated with a shrine of Pelops (Pelopion) earlier than the fourth century B.C. have led many to conclude that there were no cults to Hera, Pelops, or Zeus at Olympia before about the eighth century.

There is apparently a stone circle under the later Pelopion and even under (and so earlier than) a Middle Helladic building, the so-called "House 5" built over a northeast section of the circle.[72] Did the circle enclose a sacred precinct of a god or hero? The stones certainly are not those of a dwelling of any sort but are rather reminiscent of the 2200–2000 B.C. circle of stones around a sacred area at Lerna grave or the Middle to Late Bronze Age grave circles at Mycenae and elsewhere.[73] That only about one-quarter of a circle was found and the section of the circle toward House 5 is missing could indicate that the "House" was actually an intermediate shrine or temple replacing the circle. Similar, early apsidal structures used as shrines and located approximately next to later structures are known from several Greek sanctuaries, for instance, those at Thermon and Eretria.[74] The religious and official function of the apsidal house may be reflected in the sixth-century apsidal architecture of the Bouleterion at Olympia; E. N. Gardiner conjectured that the Bouleterion may have been built in direct imitation of an earlier structure on the site which fell into disrepair.[75] The irregular hexagonal wall of the fourth-century Pelopion may have been built over the earlier circle to restore the boundaries of the original precinct, perhaps during a period in which patronage of the entire Olympic sanctuary changed hands. Thus far then, archaeological evidence at least allows for the possibility that Olympia may have been a sanctuary in the Mycenaean period. Although no objects clearly identifiable as votive or ritual have been found at the Bronze Age site, there is a variety of pottery, local in manufacture but with decoration inspired by styles from elsewhere in Greece.[76] If Olympia was a sanctuary in the Bronze Age, it would most likely have been primarily of local importance and interest, as lack of any mention of it in Homer would suggest.

If the circle was a shrine to Pelops, was Hippodameia also worshiped nearby in some early form? And were they heroes or divinities? Were there possibly other gods there in that period, perhaps, in some early forms, Cronus and Gaia, or Sosipolis and Eileithyia, gods of male and female fertility respectively, whose cults are preserved in later worship?[77]

Archaeological evidence does not support such conjecture, except for one possibly important monument. Beneath the site of the later Prytaneion and a ceremonial hearth (of Hestia?) has been found a uniquely boat-shaped construction made of large boulders. Its date is clearly prehistoric (ninth or eighth century?), and its function undetermined.[78] Pausanias relates the following about the hearth on the site: "This hearth is made of ashes and on it a fire burns all day and night. From this hearth, so they tell me, they collect the ashes and bring them to the altar of Zeus. What is brought from the hearth contributes greatly to the size of the altar" (Paus. 5.15.9). This odd ritual seems to preserve a significant symbolism of exchange of sacred material possibly from a female shrine to a male altar. If the navicular structure was itself some early form of an altar to Hestia, or to some other goddess like

Artemis, whose altar was nearby, or Gaia, whose prehistoric oracular shrine had been displaced, the ritual of carrying ashes may be a remnant of a prehistoric association between this female deity and Zeus. The shape of this prehistoric construction might just as accurately be described as vulviform, that is, embodying in its architecture the image of female fertility. The symbolism of the ritual of the ashes would then be a ritual imitation of the *hieros gamos* of the divine partners. It may be more than coincidence that the temple and sanctuary of Hera is located directly between the altar of Zeus and the vulviform structure.

While this evaluation of the Hera festival does not rely upon prehistoric origins of cults of Hera or Hippodameia, the possibly greater antiquity of these cults suggests that there may be some truth behind the myths that place the founding of the Olympics and the Heraia in the Bronze Age. It is of course uncertain what form the Heraia or its precursor would have had at that time and whether it would have included games. But we should not reject Pausanias' tracing of the games back to "ancient times," as we now proceed to investigate his account of the origin of the Sixteen Women for what it may contribute to our knowledge of the Heraia.

The mythical tradition associating the Sixteen with Hippodameia is essentially contradicted by the historical tradition that relates their institution to the treaty of Elis and Pisa after the death of the tyrant Damophon in the 580s B.C. The latter tradition maintains that only after the institution of the Sixteen ca. 580 B.C. were the women entrusted with the management of the Heraia and the weaving of the *peplos* for Hera.[79]

Political and religious circumstances make the period around 580 B.C. a most appropriate time for the reorganization of the games to Hera. The Heraion was built in its present form by ca. 600 B.C. The long rivalry between Elis and Pisa ended ca. 576 B.C. after the reign of Pyrrhos, Damophon's brother and successor, and Elis enjoyed the restoration of its power. This was also the period when Sparta, the rising power, could have exerted her strongest influence on the reorganization of the Heraia. In addition to the archaic bronze figurines from Sparta mentioned earlier, the head of the Hera cult statue in the temple of Hera is by a Spartan sculptor (Paus. 5.16.2). Pisa had been allied with Messenia in the Second Messenian War (ca. 640–610 B.C.; Strabo 8.362), while Elis had close political and military ties with Sparta in the sixth century.[80] Elis perhaps strengthened its ties to Sparta by reorganizing the games, which featured a girls' race after the Spartan model of competitions for girls. If the sixth-century organization (or reorganization) involved creating (from a local initiatory ritual?) a girls' festival open to all Greeks (i.e., "Panhellenic"), Spartan girls would have certainly had the advantage in the competition through their unique athletic training. The reorganization of other Panhellenic festivals around this period attests to a similar trend for men's public contests.[81]

The two traditions regarding the institution of the Heraia may be reconciled if the 580s founding date of the Heraia refers rather to the reorganization, under new Elean management and with Spartan aid, of a festival that had existed in a similar form since early times. Similarly in 586 B.C. the Pythian Games at Delphi were re-organized after the conclusion of the First Sacred War (595–586) between the Phocian states of Delphi and Crisa, although the festival was much older and its mythical founding is traced back to a celebration of Apollo's slaying of the Python.[82] Tradition also reports that the Olympic Games were not begun but renewed in the reign of Iphitus of Elis (Paus. 5.4.5). If the Heraia was merely reorganized and opened to girls of other states on analogy with the men's great Panhellenic festivals during the sixth century, this would also account for the sixth-century Laconian bronze statuettes (figs. 4-3 and 4-4), perhaps in commemoration of Spartan girl victors during those early contests. It was perhaps also at this time that the legend of Chloris of Thebes as first Heraian victor was initiated to justify the Panhellenic character of the contest.

The Sixteen Women may also have existed prior to the 580s B.C., in which case their membership was reorganized at the time of the treaty between Elis and Pisa to suit political circumstances, as the membership had changed again before Pausanias' day (5.16.7). If the Heraia did exist in some form prior to the 580s, it seems likely that the Sixteen or some earlier form of them organized the festival and had other sacred charges during that time. They may have resembled the *Heresides* at Argos and perhaps been under the direction of the Pisatans.[83]

According to the tradition dating the institution of the Sixteen to the 580s B.C., the woman selected from each of the sixteen cities of Elis was "whichever one was oldest, and outstanding among women in both rank and reputation" (ἥτις ἡλικίᾳ τε ἦν πρεσβυτάτη καὶ ἀξιώματι καὶ δόξῃ τῶν γυναικῶν προεῖχεν, Paus. 5.16.5). Three first century A.D. statues of Elean women honored for their virtue and modesty were found in the pronaos of the temple of Hera and may represent later members of these noble sixteen priestesses.[84] Similar distinction was bestowed upon the older Elean women chosen as priestesses of Sosipolis and of Demeter Chamyne (Paus. 6.20.2–3; 6.20.9). In the former instance, the older woman (πρεσβῦτις) may enter the temple of Sosipolis while the other women and maidens wait in the adjacent sanctuary of Eileithyia and chant hymns.[85] The priestess of Demeter Chamyne was the only married woman allowed to attend the Olympic Games, while maidens were not debarred from watching.[86] Thus the priestesses of Sosipolis and of Demeter Chamyne, like the Sixteen, enjoyed a privilege over other females attending their respective festivals. Though married women were normally more shielded from appearance in public events than unmarried women, this privilege seems to be one normally granted to Greek women in their special status as priestesses.[87]

At Sparta, the Leucippides who joined the Dionysiades in the festival to Dionysus Colonatas and set up the footraces were composed of young maidens (Paus. 3.16.1). The Dionysiades themselves who ran the actual footraces during the festival were eleven women of unspecified age, but probably also maidens (Paus. 3.13.7). The fact that the Sixteen were also responsible for the staging of dances to Hippodameia and Physcoa may provide a further clue to their origin (Paus. 5.16.6). The dance for

Hippodameia is a natural complement to the Heraian race initiated by the heroine. Probably this same group of Sixteen organized the annual sacrifice to Hippodameia for women only in the Hippodameion within the Altis at Olympia (Paus. 6.20.7). Little is known of Hippodameia aside from her establishment of the Heraian games and a legend of her exile and death at Midea in the Argolid (Paus. 6.20.7).[88] It is possible that she, like Pelops, was imported from the Argolid. Pelops, namesake of the peninsula, was patron of the monumental cult place, the stone-encircled "Mound of Pelops" that dates to the Early Helladic times (pre-2000 B.C.). The early worship of this hero or god may have included the worship of his new bride Hippodameia.[89] Whether the introduction of these cults was immediately followed by games, as the legends say, cannot be ascertained.

Though possible Bronze Age origins of the Olympic Games have been suggested by some, but more often refuted in current scholarship,[90] there has been more consensus over the existence of a centuries-long struggle by Elis and Pisa for control of the festival in historical times, and for the probable existence of some form of athletic competitions at the site prior to the eighth century.[91] The traditional date for the founding of the Olympic games in 776 B.C. may be merely the date for their change in form and revitalization under the influence of a Dorian spirit and Pisatan leadership.[92] In this case, did an eighth-century revision and revival affect only the men's Olympic games to Zeus, thereafter held on a Panhellenic scale? Were the women's games, in view of the Chloris legend, also Panhellenic from the eighth century on, or possibly only from the early sixth century on due to strong Spartan influence during a reorganization then (Paus. 5.16.5)? The integral importance of the cult and legend of Hippodameia alongside the legacy of Pelops, and the presence of other female cults and groups of priestesses at Elis suggest that at least a women's festival for Hippodameia and Hera existed in early times alongside the men's for Pelops and Zeus. It is rather more certain that a festival with footraces for girls existed at Olympia and elsewhere by the sixth century in view of the sixth-century evidence for statues of Heraian runners and in light of Pausanias' historical commentary on the festival's origins. Whether wide popularity also indicates Panhellenic status cannot be known for certain, but it seems likely that the Heraia became Panhellenic, at least by the sixth century.

The Heraia was quadrennial, Pausanias writes, and if it was Panhellenic, that is, open to girl participants from all over Greece, practical considerations suggest precisely when the games may have taken place, namely during the Olympic year, just prior to the men's games. The females who traveled from outside the immediate region of Olympia to participate probably would have most likely traveled to the sanctuary with the males in their family who went to the Olympics. And since the Greeks were well aware of the factor of dramatic sequence in public events, it makes most sense to hold the Heraia in the days just before the Olympics to avoid the anticlimactic position of following those games. The arrangement of holding the Heraia at the time of Olympics helps solve another practical problem, namely Pausanias' statements (5.6.7, 6.7.2) that adult women were excluded from attending the men's Olympics on pain of death whereas maidens could attend. The double standard of admission suggests a religious taboo against married women at Zeus' games, analogous to (but much stricter than) the prohibition of men from attending the ritual for Hippodameia in the Olympic sanctuary (Paus. 6.20.7). But it is difficult to imagine unmarried girls traveling all the way to Olympia for a Panhellenic Heraia unless it was held in conjunction with the Olympics. Thus, the joint festivals would allow entire Greek families, including girls and possibly even their mothers, to attend the Heraia, and then men, boys, and girls to attend the Olympics while the adult women stayed in an encampment apart from the sanctuary and contest locations.

The sponsorship of a cult dance to Physcoa by the Sixteen further informs us about the cult affiliations of that Elean college and possibly the affiliations of the Heraian Games (Paus 5.16.6–7). Plutarch in fact calls the Sixteen Women "the women sacred to the service of Dionysus"(αἱ περὶ τὸν Διόνυσον ἱεραὶ γυναῖκες, ἅς ‹τὰς› ἑκκαίδεκα καλοῦσιν, *Mulierum virtutes* 251e), which seems to indicate that their chief function was to organize the worship of Dionysus in Elis. Pausanias tells us that Physcoa came from the deme of Orthia in Elis Coile and that after a liaison with Dionysus she bore him a son called Narcaeus. Narcaeus became a local war hero who established a sanctuary to Athena Narcaea and, together with Physcoa, established the first worship of Dionysus in the area. Dionysus had no altar to himself at Olympia, although he had a late altar donated by private patrons, and he did share an altar with the Charites near the Mound of Pelops (Paus. 5.14.10). One tradition reports the birth of Dionysus on the banks of the Alpheus (*Hom. Hym.* 1.3 (Allen) *ap.* Diod. 366), and the grapevine was supposedly discovered in Olympia next to the Alpheus (Theopompus, *ap.* Ath. 1.34a). The name of Oenomaus, father of Hippodameia, has been taken as a reflection of this myth, since it may mean "the one who yearns for wine" or "the wine-greedy one," perhaps an epithet of the local wine god.[93] Similarly Narcaeus, meaning "the numbing one," may also be associated with a local early wine cult. In contrast to the poverty of the Dionysus cult at Olympia, the Eleans worshiped Dionysus with greatest reverence in their own city at a theater and a shrine to the god, as well as a special festival, the Thyia, held annually at a site 8 stades from the city (Paus. 6.26. 1–2).[94] Two details of the rituals are preserved, namely, the miraculous overnight filing of three empty pots in the sealed temple of Dionysus, and the summoning of the god by the Sixteen Women (Plut., *Mul.vir.* 251e), who call upon him to appear "rushing on a bull's foot" (τῷ βοέῳ ποδὶ θύων, Plut., *Quaestiones Graecae* 299a–b; *id., Isis at Osiris* 364).[95] The invocation of rushing (θύων) plays on the name of the festival (Θυία), and the Sixteen here take on a role analogous to the female college of the Thyiads at Delphi, who hold their *orgiai* on Mt. Parnassus (Paus. 10.4.3). The Elean festival is thus a milder version of the famed orgiastic rites of women maenads who roam the hills at night.

The Thyia at Elis and the dance for Physcoa seem to be related as services for god and attendant heroine in much the same way as the Heraia is related to the dance for Hippodameia. Whether the Dionysus-Physcoa cult is further related to that of Hera-Hippodameia in any way other than their sharing of a common sponsor, the Sixteen, is uncertain. It has been maintained that the independence of the two cults was preserved and that the Sixteen organized two distinct choruses, one to Hippodameia and one to Physcoa.[96] The text of Pausanias mentions two choral dances, not one with mixed participation by devotees of the two heroines, and it specifies that the Sixteen establish or institute the choruses, not that they themselves participate (χορούς δύο ἱστᾶσι, Paus. 5.16.6).

Whether or not the cults of Hera-Hippodameia and Dionysus-Physcoa were actually related in membership or ritual, they seem to have complemented each other well enough in function to be organized by the same group of Sixteen. Both cults were of primary interest to women, and the heroines of each instituted service to the god in honor of their respective marriages. There may be a trace of a closer, original association of the two cults in the name of Hippodameia's father, Oenomaus, "Wine Greedy."[97] Women are the chief officiants at both festivals, actually performing the races at the Heraia and calling upon Dionysus to come running as a bull. It has been suggested that the Elean Thyia may be a less frenzied form of the thyiadic activity of running maenads which is imitated in the dances and footraces of maidens.[98]

The evidence here is that in the Agrionia festival to Dionysus at Orchomenos, *thyiades* practice "flight and pursuit" (φυγὰ καὶ δίωξις) with a knife-wielding priest (Plut., *Qu. gr.* 299F).[99] "Flight and pursuit" are the essence of the agonistic footrace according to Plutarch (*Moralia* 640q: δρόμῳ δὲ μελετῶσι φεύγειν καὶ διώκειν), and, as will be argued later, the essence of the normal relation of beloved and lover.[100] Thyiades have also been addressed as "running hounds" (δρομάδες . . . κύνες, Eur., *Bacchae* 731) pursued by men in the *orgiai*, and at Thebes the Dionysian Agriania involved contests (ἀγῶνες, Hsch., s.v. Ἀγριάν). So the association of Elean women with both the Dionysus and Hera-Hippodameia cults suggests that some form of symbolic, prenuptial pursuit of the maidens may have been the functional notion behind the Heraian races.

The closest parallel to the Hippodameia-Physcoa cult complex at Elis is that of the Leucippides and Dionysiades at Sparta to be examined in chapter 5. At Sparta the festival in honor of Dionysus Colonatas and the nameless hero who led him to the area is celebrated by two groups of girls (Paus. 3.13.7). Both offer sacrifice to the hero and the god, and the Dionysiades, a group of eleven girls, hold a footrace (Hsch., s.v. *Dionysiades*). This cult activity differs from those organized by the Sixteen, since at Sparta there is one festival but two organizing groups. But the object of both the Physcoa dance and the festival for the Spartan hero is to honor the one who introduces worship of Dionysus to the area. The fact that the footrace at Sparta has been combined with worship of Dionysus supports our earlier suggestion that the Heraian footrace and Dionysus worship including the Thyia and the Physcoa dance may have been related in origin or at least were rites compatible in function.

The importance of the dance for Hippodameia and Physcoa and the Heraian foot-race as prenuptial initiation rites has already been suggested. The festival for Dionysus Colonatas at Sparta has been seen to serve a similar, initiatory function, since Dionysus is patron of adult women, and the Leucippides are usually repre-sented as maidens (Paus. 3.16.1; Eur., *Helen* 1466). The Leucippides, who are also worshiped as "mothers" (μητέρες) at Corinth (Paus. 2.22.5), are mythically re-nowned as the fiancées of the Dioscouroi.[101] Thus, the simple Spartan festival to Dionysus and the complex of festivals to Hera and Dionysus at Olympia and Elis can be understood as serving the same function, that of introducing the girls who are on the verge of being married, adult women into the mysteries of Dionysus. In other words, the footraces at Sparta and Olympia may both be initiatory tests that are part of the introduction of girls to adulthood.

In summary, the similar structures of the Heraian and Olympian festivals sug-gest either a common origin or the influence of one upon the other. The cults of Zeus and Hera were possibly both established at Olympia by the eighth century or even as early as the eleventh. Aside from inconclusive, legendary testimony, there is no confirmation of the priority of one festival over the other. Ultimately, on the basis of the known evidence, it must remain uncertain which festival first incorporated the program of offering-*agōn*–crown–meal into its worship of a patron god at Olym-pia. The comparative evidence of other known footraces for women in early Greece, namely, the race organized for Dionysus at Sparta and the one of the Arkteia for Artemis at Brauron, aids our understanding of the Heraia. Like those others, the footrace for Hera was performed by maidens and seems to have had the character of a prenuptial, initiatory trial.[102] The origins of the Heraia thus appear to antedate the historical institution of the Sixteen Women as festival organizers ca. 580 B.C., and the latter date may be better understood as the time when the games were re-organized for political reasons, and possibly the date when a footrace was added to Hera's festival under the influence of contemporary athletics for girls at Sparta. The Olympian Heraia appears to be no older than the Olympics, although it may be as old, and seems to preserve the traditions of archaic initiatory ritual in its struc-ture and practices.

5

"ONLY WE PRODUCE MEN"—
SPARTAN FEMALE ATHLETICS AND EUGENICS

With typically erotic overtones, Propertius sang the praise of Spartan maidens: "I marvel at the many rules of your palaestra, O Sparta, but even more at the blessings of your gymnasium for girls [*virgineum gymnasium*], since a naked girl may take part in the well-known games amidst men as they wrestle" (3.14.1–4). As with the Olympian Heraia, Spartan girls' contests offer a unique perspective from which to observe young women engaged in the rites of passage from adolescence to adulthood. Unlike men's athletics, which was an expression of heroic and martial *aretē* at Sparta and elsewhere, Spartan girls' games, like their counterparts in the Heraia and the Attica Arkteia, were ultimately an expression of prenuptial strength for the wives- and mothers-to-be of warriors. At Sparta, however, the girls' athletic regimen more closely resembled the men's in form and variety than anywhere else. As in the Heraia and the Arkteia, Spartan female contests were open only to maidens (*parthenoi*) and, in part, the contests functioned as ritual tests of strength prior to marriage.[1]

Source material for this study poses two problems: first, it is scanty, since we have only a few clear examples of women's participation. And second, it has relied upon men for transmission, which probably explains the paucity of evidence, since women's sports were both uninteresting and unimportant to them. We may infer from the few extant examples that women's athletic contests, particularly footraces in cult contexts, were probably more widespread than our sources indicate.[2]

The ritual contests for women at Olympia and in Attica, discussed in chapters 4 and 6, are in some ways analogous to the Spartan phenomenon, but at Sparta female participation was the earliest and possibly the most influential as a model for the other rituals. The important focus on this topic, which others have treated only in passing, is to examine Spartan female athletics as part of a prenuptial initiation, to review the archaeological evidence for Spartan girls' physical education, and to suggest how Sparta may have influenced practice at Olympia.

The case of Spartan women's athletics is strikingly anomalous among Greek *poleis*, since there the girls apparently took part in the famous education system, the *agōgē*, an institution allegedly founded by the shadowy figure of Spartan reform, Lycurgus.[3] The dates and the existence of this lawgiver are justly doubted, and there are further difficulties in our literary evidence for early Spartan society, namely that the authors are all late, from the fourth century B.C. to the third century A.D., and that they each write with a particular *ira et studio* that strongly defends or condemns that communal *polis*.[4] Despite varying opinions on its origins and its success, the majority of authors agree on the form and purpose of Spartan education. Modern scholars maintain that the unique structure of the *agōgē* with initiatory institutions found in other primitive cultures suggests that its roots predate the Archaic period. Male messes, age-classes, separation from society, and trials of strength are well documented for males and have analogues with initiation elsewhere. The system thus may have been first established in the sixth century, a period associated with other 'Lycurgan' measures.[5]

That Spartan girls were organized in age-groups like the boys is indicated by references in Alcman (*Parthenion* fr. 1 v. 52, second half of seventh c. B.C.), who calls a chorus of girls "cousins" (*anepsiai*), a term also used of boy colleagues, and Pindar (fr. 112, first half of fifth c. B.C.), who calls a Spartan girl chorus an *agelā* or "horse-herd," the very term used for the boys' regiments in the *agōgē*.[6] Other terms, namely *kasioi* or *kasēn*, meaning "brothers," "sisters," or "cousins," appear in numerous inscriptions, mostly from the Roman period, and these suggest educational reform whose inception is possibly even dateable to ca. 184 B.C. when Spartans revived the archaic system after a crushing defeat.[7] Callimachus (ca. 305–240 B.C.) also refers to a group of Spartan maidens as a "company" (*ila*).[8] One of the latest indications of the girls' *agōgē* is a second c. A.D. inscription (*IG* 5. 1. 170) mentioning a board of six *gunaikonomoi* or "regulators of women" corresponding to the young men's *paidonomoi*.[9] That Spartan girls are on occasion metaphorically compared to "fillies," for example, in Alcman (*Parth.* 59) and Aristophanes (*Lys.* 1308–13) is further evidence that they belonged to "horse-herds" in Archaic and Classical times.[10] An inscription mentions that the officials who administered contests for young men, namely the *biduoi*, also managed the race of the "daughters of Dionysus," suggesting that the girls were as much a part of Spartan educational system as the ephebes.[11]

Before looking at the widely attested physical education of Spartan girls, we should not overlook the fact that their education probably included "arts and letters" as well, since Plato mentions that they are well schooled in philosophy and speaking, and there are other indications of their literacy. Their glibness in fact gave rise to a series of apophthegms illustrating the free speech of Spartan women, many in the bold spirit of the exhortation to warriors to come back "with your shield or on it."[12]

Alcman's poetry, it has been observed, reveals another aspect of the girls' upbringing which parallels that of the boys, namely a homoerotic element. Fragments 1 and 3 of the choral poem *Parthenion* use erotic language to describe an amorous attraction of the Spartan chorus girls for their female chorus leader (*chorēgos*). A passage in Plutarch confirms the implication: "Though this [pederastic] love was so approved among [the Spartans] that good and noble women loved the maidens, there was no rivalry. But those men who loved the same boys rather used it as the basis for a friendship with one another, and they continued to pusue zealously and in common the aim of producing a beloved who was as noble as possible."[13] Plutarch is clear on the noble character of the women lovers, since a major function of Spartan homoeroticism was the transmission of virtue from lover to beloved; as in male pederasty, the female equivalent focused on formation of the youth to adulthood. Though the evidence is much more meager than that for Spartan male homoeroticism, it seems clear that female homoeroticism was an important aspect of their upbringing.

We should here mention the obvious cultural parallel to Alcman's female choral poem, the poetry of Sappho of Lesbos (second half of the seventh century). Interestingly, Alcaeus (fr. 130.32 Lobel-Page) alludes to beauty contests for women on Lesbos in Sappho's day, competitions that recall the later manly beauty contests of the Panathenaia: "where the Lesbian females go, with trailing dresses, having their bodily form judged, and all around resounds the wondrous noise of the sacred cry of the women each year" (trans. Dover, 1989, 181, adapted). On the internal evidence of Sappho's poems, there is little doubt that there was a homoerotic element in the circle of girls under Sappho's tutelage, though it is difficult to know how extensive or long-lived such an institution was. There is one Sapphic fragment that suggests that, among the training, was skill in the footrace: "[Sappho] instructed Hero of Gyara, that fleet-footed maiden" (Ἥρων ἐξεδίδαξε Γυάρων τάν ἀνυόδρομον).[14] Physical training would accord with the existence of beauty contests. The date of the Sapphic institutions and customs, roughly contemporaneous with the earliest female *paideia* in Sparta, suggests that female upbringing including sexual segregation, athletic training, and homoerotic relations, was dispersed and localized from at least the late seventh century. An argument from silence suggests that such female education and homoeroticism was rare outside of Lesbos and Sparta in the archaic period, though this must remain conjectural.

We cannot say with any certainty whether Spartan female pederasty was as structured or formalized as the male counterpart. It does seem likely that the female phenomenon developed simultaneously with the male in the seventh century, given the testimony by a source as early as Alcman. We have seen that the complexly developed system of Spartan *agōgē* as it was represented in later sources was probably instituted in the sixth century (ch. 3). But the coincidence of female homosexuality and athletic training from the seventh century B.C. suggests that some system of cultural upbringing existed then in Sparta, and it was at least generally of the same form for youths of both genders. The difference, to be examined in the following paragraphs, is that the goal for females upon reaching adulthood differed fundamentally from that for males, and the different goals called for different motives for pursuing similar activities like athletic contests.

Theocritus (ca. 300–260? B.C.), in his "Epithalamy of Helen" (*Idyll* 18), gives the best idealized portrait of the legendary Spartan beauty who doubtless served as a role model for younger girls. In the poem, twelve Spartan girls, former companions of the queen-to-be, praise her beauty, her skill at weaving, and her musical talent (26–37).[15] They recall their former activities: "We all as age-mates (*sunō-malikes*) who practiced the same running course and oiled ourselves down like men alongside the bathing pools of the Eurotas, we are the four-times-sixty maidens, the female corps of youth (*neolaia*)" (22–25). The poem, though not overtly homoerotic, does portray younger girls' idolization of the archetypical Spartan female heroine and alludes to the many skills prized in their upbringing.

The irony with regard to Spartan girl's physical education is that however much it resembled that of the men in form, it was essentially different in its goal of producing beautiful and fit young women who could endure childbirth and nourish their offspring until they, in turn, could enter the *agōgē*. Boys underwent the stages of initiation to become strong and virtuous warriors, girls to become wives. "Marriage is for the girl what war is for the boy," namely the fulfillment of their natures in service of the state.[16] Analogy of the types of education has led authors, especially at Rome, to attribute to the female *agōgē* the value of preparing female soldiers.[17] Plutarch (fl. 100–120 A.D.), for instance, in the context of explaining that Spartan girls exercised to produce strong offspring and contend with birth pains, adds "and moreover, if the need arise, they might be able to fight for themselves, their children, and their country" (*Moralia* 227 D. 12). The corrective for this view is found in Plato (*Leg.* 7. 805e–6a, written ca. 355–347 B.C.) who, in the words of the Athenian interlocutor, complains that the Laconian system of female education is a "half-way measure" (τὸ . . . διὰ μέσου) in which girls share in gymnastics and music, but women abstain from military service. Aristotle (384–322 B.C.), in a typical anti-Spartan tirade, gives an historical exemplum: "Even in regard to courage, which is of no use in daily life, and is needed only in war, the influence of the Lacedaimonian women has been most mischievous. The evil showed itself in the Theban invasion [370 B.C.], when unlike most women in other cities, they were utterly useless and caused more confusion than the enemy" (*Politics* 2. 6. 7, 1269B).

Our earliest explicit source on the eugenic aim of Spartan female education is Critias (*Respublica Lacedaemoniorum*, Diels-Kranz, vol. 2, 88, fr. 32, written ca. 425–403 B.C.), followed by Xenophon (*Lac.* 1. 3–4, written ca. 396–383 B.C.), naming specifically "contests of running and strength" and first giving Lycurgus credit for instituting the system. Plutarch (*Lycurgus* 14. 1–15. 1) much later (ca. 100–120 B.C.) lists the fullest program of female sports: "[Lycurgus] made the maidens exercise their bodies in running, wrestling, and the throwing of discus and javelin, so that the root of these born might better mature by taking a strong beginning in strong bodies . . ." (14. 2). By way of arguing against Aristotle's criticisms, Plutarch claims that the girls were, no less than boys, "freed from all delicacy and effeminacy" by requiring them without clothes to process, dance at certain festivals, and sing in public. The nudity in fact inspired lofty sentiment "since they partook no less than the men in bravery (*aretē*) and ambition (*philotimia*). Wherefore they were led to speak and think like Gorgo, the wife of Leonidas, is said to have done, when some-one, apparently a foreigner, said to her, "'You Spartan women alone rule over your men.' [S]he answered, 'That's because only we give birth to men'" (14.4). Philo-stratus (*Gymn.* 27, written A.D. 230) echoes Plutarch's report by explaining that Lycurgus instituted female exercise to produce more and better "warrior-athletes" (*polemikous athlētas*).[18]

The introduction of nudity to women's public events, as noted by Plutarch, may be an important clue to the ritual character and eugenic aim of their athleticism. Plutarch quotes Plato when he addresses the incentives to marriage in public nu-dity: "I refer to the processions of maidens, their undressing (*apoduseis*) and their games in the sight of young men drawn on by erotic, not geometrical, necessity!" (Plut., *Lyc.* 15. 1, cf. Plato, *Republic* 458d). Note that nudity in these contexts may mean "scantily clad," with less clothing than is customary for Greek women, that is, the short Doric *chitōn*, also called *chitōniskos*, the *monochitōn*, or *chitōn exōmis* worn without undergarment, pinned at the shoulder, open on one side exposing the thigh, and hemmed above the knees.[19] This scandalous garment won them the epithet *phaineromērides* or "thigh-flashers" from Ibycus (sixth c. B.C.)[20] and gave rise to the censorious words of Peleus in Euripides, *Andromache* (595–602, written ca. 430–424 B.C.):

> No Spartan girl could ever be restrained (*sōphrōn*) even if she wanted to be; they desert their homes to go out with young men with their thighs bared and robes ungirt and they hold races and wrestling contests with them—I would not stand for it! Is it any wonder that you do not raise chaste women?

He then compares the girls with their archetype Helen, who was also known as a home deserter, a licentious and immodest woman, as Spartan females must have appeared to most Athenians.[21] How much greater the scandal was to imag-ine those girls entirely naked in public, as they probably were, in light of Plutarch's reference (*Lyc.* 15. 1) to their "undressing" (*apoduseis*) before youths, namely their removal of their *chitōniskos*. Similarly Theocritus referred to girls "oiled down" for the footrace like men (18. 23).

Athletic nudity in the Olympics, so the legend goes, began with Orsippus of Megara in 720 B.C. or possibly Acanthus of Sparta in the same year.[22] Plutarch (*Lyc.* 14. 1–4) claims that Lycurgus introduced it at Sparta. But Plato suggests that it came to Sparta from Crete: "When first the Cretans, then the Lacedaemonians began the practice of naked exercise, the wits of the time could have ridiculed this whole cus-tom" (*Rep.* 5. 425c). As we shall see in chapter 8, the custom of athletic nudity may have been a Spartan innovation of the eighth century, but it seems not to have been adopted widely until the second half of the seventh century. Whatever the role the Spartans played in the institution of athletic nudity, they significantly claim to have used the practice to encourage male-female erotic attraction before marriage. More than a simple athletic convenience, nudity is the primitive human state in our natural innocence and passion—one is reminded of the sublime eroticism of Odysseus, brine-covered and washed up on the shores of Phaeacia, standing naked before the maiden Nausicaä.

Nudity is known to have served several religious and magic functions in ancient society, but cultic nudity among Greek girls and boys seems to have had the special significance of designating youths involved in special rituals at a stage prior to adulthood.[23] Spartan boys, for example, competed in age-groups in the Gymnopaedia, or "Festival of Naked Youths," in honor of Apollo as a test of strength in preparation for real warfare.[24] Whether the boys were entirely naked or simply unarmed, their relative "undress" points to the special role of cultic nudity in the males' festival. Similarly, at Phaestus on Crete, young boys practiced transvestism at the Ekdysia, or "Festival of Undressing," in honor of Lato Phytia; new brides at the same festival slept next to the statue of Leucippus, patron hero of the festival.[25] The name of the Cretan festival and other references to "the undressed youths" (*ekduomenoi*) suggest that cultic nudity played a role in this festival, which has the character of a prenuptial initiation for boys and girls. The vases from Brauron and Munichion in Attica showing girls, both naked and clothed in short chitons, running races for Artemis at the Arkteia Festival also suggest that cultic nudity played a role in this prenuptial ritual.[26] By analogy with customs elsewhere, we may assume that the athletic nudity of Spartan youths also served a religious and socializing function of preparing adolescents for marriage and adult life.

So when Plato recommended that youths associate in gymnastic exercise in order to be drawn to one another by an erotic necessity, he may have been following the "Lycurgan" custom reported later by Plutarch. Euripides suggests that exercise in common may have been the rule, and he is followed by the less reliable, but perhaps here accurate, restatements of the principle by Propertius (3.14), and Ovid (*Heroides* 16.149–52), the latter of whom addresses Helen: "And so Theseus rightly felt love's flame, for he was acquainted with all your charms, and you seemed fit spoil for the great hero to steal away, when, after the manner of your race, you engaged in sports of the shining palaestra, a nude maid mingled with nude men." Only Stobaeus, writing in the fifth century A.D., explicitly denies this and states that the sexes exercised separately. And his claim is further weakened by the fact that only one exercise area, the *Dromos* or "Track" is mentioned in Classical and Hellenistic times, and both boys and girls are said to frequent it.[27]

If the athletic nudity of Spartan females had deliberate erotic ends, they were certainly fostered by the legendary Spartan female beauty, perhaps comparable in our day to that of "California girls." "Sparta of the beautiful women" is first mentioned in the *Odyssey* (13.412; a *hapax* there), but the sensuous beauty of the chorus girls in Alcman's *Parthenion* of ca. 600 B.C. carries on the legend. Similarly, Aristophanes' *Lysistrata* praises the beautiful skin and firm breasts as well as the muscular virility of the Spartan woman Lampito (*Lys.* 79–83); compare the similar remarks of Athenaeus (12. 566A) and Strabo (10.13). Beauty symbolizes the possession of virtue in the girl ready to marry. Physical exercise has bestowed on her a quality that will find its culmination through the initiation process, in marriage perhaps at age 18 to 20, and then the procreation of beautiful infants. The whole educative process aims at the acquisition of beauty for real, practical aims in service of the state. Whereas boys become good soldiers, girls become mothers who produce good warriors.[28]

If beauty and the revealing Spartan costume, or lack of one, are important or indeed essential elements of the Spartan female *agōgē*, then recognition of the Spartan ideal of female beauty by Homer and Alcman suggest that Spartan society was at least predisposed to that ideal in the seventh or even late eighth century. Ibycus' complaint about Spartan "thigh-flashers," on the other hand, gives a *terminus post quem* of the 560s to 530s B.C. for the athletic costume, and hence for the social system of female initiation.

This date in the sixth century is nicely supported by the archaeological evidence of a series of sixth- and early-fifth-century bronzes, mirror handles, and votive statues, apparently from Laconia or Laconian workshops. They have been variously interpreted as dancers and acrobats, that is, secular entertainers, but in view of the literary evidence, it seems probable that they depict Spartan girls performing the dances, processions, and contests mentioned by Plutarch and others. Their existence is all the more remarkable in view of the general absence of naked females from sixth-century sculpture. I am not the first to suggest that the bronzes represent Spartan female athletes, but I am the first, as far as I know, to investigate the possibility fully and in some detail.[29]

Our discussion includes twenty-six bronzes of naked girls in the form of both mirror handles and votive statuettes, whose provenances include sites in Laconia (eight), elsewhere in the Peloponnese (two), Greece above the Peloponnese (three), Ionia (two), and Italy (two). Nine are of unknown provenance.[30] The fact that the majority of the bronzes with known provenances come from the Peloponnese, and indeed from Laconia, suggests a Laconian origin for the style. It has been argued that many of those from outside Laconia show Laconian influence. If, indeed, the naked girls are not entertainers or *hetairai* of some sort, as will be argued later, it would be difficult to explain their presence in the sixth century as anything but a reflection of the cultic and athletic nudity best known from Sparta.

Praschniker discusses thirteen mirror handles or statuettes representing naked females (appendix 5.1 to this chapter, nos. 1, 3, 4, 10, 12, 13, 14, 15, 19, 20, 22, 25, 26) which he considers to be of Spartan manufacture or under Laconian influence. Langlotz discusses five mirror handles of naked females as Laconian bronzes, although he does not identify them as representations of athletes or of entertainers (app. 5.1, nos. 3, 15, 20, 25, 26).[31] Richter discusses two of the naked figures (app. 5.1, nos. 17, and 18) and argues against Praschniker and Langlotz that this type of mirror handle need not be Spartan in style, since individual features can be found elsewhere in Greek sculpture and painting of the period.[32] Yet the Peloponnesian provenance of the majority of the statuettes along with other factors indicates Spartan influence if not Spartan workmanship. Richter observes that the girls do not answer to the description of Aristophanes' firm-breasted Lampito, but we should remember that Lampito was married and older and so more full-breasted than the Spartan maidens possibly represented by the mirror handles: "They are not muscular athletes, but dainty dancing girls, as shown by the fact that three of them hold castanets. Probably they are *hetairai*."[33] Häfner notes that the cymbals held by the girls in fact contradict the notion that they are *hetairai*, since *hetairai* only first appear with cymbals in Roman times.[34] The naturally wiry muscularity of modern female athletes, like the Romanian gymnast Nadia Comaneci or the American track star Mary Decker Slaney, corresponds closely to the images of the Greek bronzes. U. Jantzen suggests that naked male figures on Locrian mirror handles were devised in imitation of naked girl figures, of which eleven are mentioned.[35] Of the eleven, Jantzen classifies five as Spartan work, one other being from Hermione in the southeastern Peloponnese (app. 5.1, 14), one possibly a Chersonese product (app. 5.1, 8), and three of unknown provenance. He mentions one other freestanding votive statuette from Sparta (p. 67, sec. D. 5 = app. 5.1, 6). No dates are given for any of these. The five that Jantzen identifies as Spartan are listed in appendix 5.1 to this chapter, nos. 3, 9, 10, 15, and 25.

Häfner identifies only three mirror handles as certainly Spartan (app. 5.1, nos 3, 14, 21).[36] She is reluctant to ascribe all thirteen under discussion to Sparta:

> To consider the mirror handles as Laconian creations, since dances for naked girls are attested only for Laconia, is a hasty conclusion. Similar dances may have been practiced in other places, only the traditions of them have perished. Also it is questionable whether one should ascribe the creation of such costly objects to Sparta, a state little inclined to luxury.

Rather, Häfner would relate the mirror handles "to the realm of Aphrodite." Yet Spartan preoccupation with physical beauty as manifest in the mirrors is not a sign of societal luxury, but a concern with health, childbirth, and the eugenic aims of female education. Similarly, the absence of testimonia concerning female public nudity elsewhere in Greece does not argue strongly *ex silentio* against identification of the naked-girl handles with Spartan girls; the multitude of testimonia recording Spartan female nudity in public is a much stronger argument in favor of this identification. Häfner notes that, on stylistic grounds, the handles are too varied to be assigned to one common Laconian workshop, and that certain features are not otherwise common in Laconian art (pp. 13 and 36). Häfner presumes an austerity in Laconian art and postulates that certain Ionian features in the treatment of hair, eyes, dress, or body on Spartan figures are a result of Ionian influence and perhaps of Ionian origin of the mirror-handle style. Yet we may ask why Sparta, if it was so disinclined to refinements and luxury, ever bothered to produce even a few bronze female figurines. How could a sixth-century Spartan *not* identify the naked figures with the practice of female nudity in contemporary Sparta? It is easier to postulate Spartan influence on Ionian-style handles, since the actual models for such figurines were evident in Spartan daily life. Or there may have been Ionian stylistic influence on an originally Laconian subject. Herodotus (1.70; 3.39, 44ff., 55, 148) mentions Spartan relations with Samian and Ionian oligarchs in the late sixth century, including the gift of a bronze mixing bowl once sent to King Croesus of Lydia. Laconian pottery and bronzes have been found on Samos.[37]

The reason that Spartan nude female mirror-handles were exported and perhaps even copied by non-Spartan artists abroad cannot be known for certain but can plausibly be ascribed to their attraction as novelty items. It may be more than coincidence that the only other widespread representation of a female nude in the sixth century is the popular portrayal of Atalanta wrestling with or standing in the palaestra beside Peleus.[38] Most of the Atalanta wrestling vases date from 550–500 B.C., that is, exactly the same period within which most of the naked female bronzes were produced. The novelty and perhaps subtly erotic appeal of the Atalanta illustrations contributed to their popularity independent of numerous other depictions of heroic athletic contests in funeral games. So, too, the nude female bronzes, which may have originated as representations of actual or ideal Spartan athletes, were copied by non-Spartans when the subject gained trendy popularity. Therefore, despite Häfner's objections, it seems probable that the bronze representations of naked females on mirror handles and statuettes from the mid-sixth to the early fifth centuries B.C. originated as portraits of contemporary Spartan girls performing athletics or cult dances. The fact that the majority of those whose provenance is known came from Laconia and the unique and widespread renown of Spartan girls' nudity from literary sources of the sixth century and later argue in favor of identifying the bronzes as portraits of Spartan girls.[39] Regarding the bronzes, Cartledge conjectures: "They were almost certainly made by men, some of whom could have been Spartan citizens. But the mirrors at least could have been commissioned and/or dedicated by women."[40]

A few of the figures have musical accoutrements that were probably used in public dances mentioned by Plutarch.[41] There is a badly preserved girl flautist from Sparta and a mirror handle from Amyclaeon showing a girl holding cymbals and wearing a mysterious baldric or shoulder strap seen on five other statuettes.[42] The long hair that was a mark of Spartan maidens was shorn at marriage and wives wore only short hair.[43] Incidentally, the reverse is true for Spartan boys, who had to wear short hair until manhood when, as warriors, the hair was kept long. Hair length is in fact an important indicator of the status of initiates in many societies.[44] The cymbals are also in evidence in a figure from Curium (Cyprus) (fig. 5-1). Her hair has been bound up in a net or cap of the type also worn my male athletes.[45] Among these bronzes I have counted nine female figures with hair similarly bound up by a headband, net, or cap in athletic style.[46] The cymbals, besides being instruments to accompany the cult dance, were common as the toys of maidens dedicated to Artemis Limnatis at Sparta.[47] They might thus be called symbols of the transition to adulthood. This statuette is also of interest, since on the baldric can be seen a lunate crescent object that has gone unidentified but could be a strigil used by athletes for cleaning themselves after exercise, or, more likely, a sickle of the sort found on late Spartan *stelai*.[48] The sickles were dedicated to Artemis Orthia by boy victors in athletic contests, so that their presence on the naked girls may be an identification of that girl as a victor in a certain competition. The girls thus wear their prizes around their chests, an unusual custom to my knowledge, otherwise found only much later among those practicing Greek athletics in Rome.[49] We do know, however, that children sometimes wore their favorite amulettes on a shoulder strap.[50]

Another mirror handle of unknown provenance now in New York also shows the shoulder strap with the curious crescent (fig. 5-2). Note again the athletic hair net. Also of interest is the spherical object in the girl's left hand, which has been identified as some piece of fruit but is more likely an oil flask, again a common implement for athletes and found on at least three of the girl statuettes.[51] A mirror handle from Cerveteri also holds the oil flask in her left hand, but here with a blossom in her right. The blossom, commonly identified as a lotus, is found on six mirror handles and is seen on numerous other clothed figures, male and female, from bronze sculpture and vases.[52] It may be a victory prize similar to the more usually awarded palm branch, or it may be a symbol of the maidens' fertility, vitality, and virginal purity. Compare our expression "to deflower" and the Greek expression "to lose one's bloom" (*apanthein*) applied to athletes debilitated from sex. Further examples of girls holding the blossom are a votive statuette from Sparta wearing the athletic cap and a mirror handle from Hermione. One example of a peplos-clad Spartan maiden with flower is a statuette of unknown provenance but showing Ionic influence.[53]

Most of the bronze maidens, in fact seventeen altogether, are without any clothing, but six do wear the *diazōma* or trunks that are otherwise shown on fifth- to sixth-century B.C. vase paintings of the legendary Atalanta as she wrestles Peleus.[54] This is a clear indication of athletic garb, seen in the mirror handle now in New York (fig. 5-3) and also in the mirror handle now in the Trent Museum as well as the figure in the Hamburg Museum (fig. 5-4).[55] The Hamburg girl is unique and noteworthy in that she is holding up a strigil in a victorious attitude also seen in a mid fifth century statuette group from Delphi.[56] That the Delphic victor has won in the pentathlon is evident from the jumping weight he carries. The inference is that the Hamburg girl is perhaps the only certain female victor statuette.

The nudity or near nudity of these girls recalls the nudity of girls in the Brauronian rites where girls "play the bear." Separation from society and existence "in the wilds,"

Figure 5-1. Nude female bronze mirror handle from Curium, Cyprus, ca. 530 B.C., N.Y. Met. no. 74.51.5680. Note "hair net" of type also seen on male athletes, and sickle (?) on shoulder strap, a possible prize for victory in a contest. All rights reserved, The Metropolitan Museum of Art, New York.

Figure 5-2. Nude female bronze mirror handle (unknown provenance) possibly from a Spartan workshop, c. 550 B.C. N.Y. Met. no. 38.11.3. Note athletic "hair net," sickle "prize" on shoulder strap, and oil flask (?) in left hand.

literally or symbolically, is typical of initiatory rites for youths.[57] The "wild" element is represented on many of the mirror handles by lions or griffins supporting struts, but also by animals under their feet, like turtles, or the frog under a Laconian figure from Cyprus (fig. 5-1).[58] The marsh animals may allude to the fact that the girls danced and ran near the bathing pools of the Eurotas River as mentioned by Theocritus (18.22–25) and Aristophanes (*Lys.* 1308–13).

Among the contests for girls, the footrace held a special, sacred prestige like the Heraia at Olympia and the Arkteia of Attica. The *Dromos* or "Track" at Sparta also served as the gymnasium in the probable absence of any proper building before Roman Imperial times.[59] We may locate the *Dromos* on the banks of the Eurotas in the vicinity of the Sanctuary of Artemis Orthia. The Eurotas is mentioned as the place of girls' exercise by Aristophanes, Theocritus, Cicero, and Pausanias.[60]

In addition to the naked female bronzes studied here, there are five bronzes of girl runners apparently in Laconian style.[61] Besides an Amazon-style girl wearing the dress of the Olympian Heraia, now in London, there is the female runner from Dodona in a similar pose in a short chiton, one from Palermo, and two others in the Delphi and Sparta Museums.

Pausanias relates the only detail we have for the actual ritual of a race for girls at Sparta (3.13.7):[62]

Figure 5-3. Nude female bronze mirror handle (unknown provenance), ca. 540 B.C., N.Y. Met. 41.11.5. The *diazōma* or trunks are of a type worn by Atalanta depicted in wrestling scenes on Greek vases of this period. All rights reserved, The Metropolitan Museum of Art, New York.

Figure 5-4. (a, left) Nude female bronze mirror handle (unknown provenance), sixth c. B.C., Trent, Museo Provinciale d'Arte—Castello del Buonconsiglio inv. no. 3061. Figure wears athletic *diazōma*. Cp. Figure 5–3. Courtesy of Ufficio Beni Archeologici- Provincia autonoma di Trento, Italy. (b, right) Nude female bronze figurine, Hellenistic on Roman era. Hamburg, Museum für Kunst und Gewerbe inv. no. 1917.362. Figure wears athletic *diazōma* and victoriously holds up strigil. Courtesy of Museum für Kunst und Gewerbe, Hamburg.

> At Sparta next to the Temple of Dionysus Colonatas there is a precinct of the Hero, who, they say, guided Dionysus on his journey to Sparta. The Dionysiades and Leucippides sacrifice to this Hero before they do to the god. As for the second group of eleven women called 'Dionysiades,' for them they hold a footrace. The custom for them to run a race came from Delphi.

Whether the Delphic origin indicates imitation of an actual race at Delphi, or merely the institution of the custom at the behest of the Pythian oracle is unclear. More informative are the two colleges of priestesses who organize the race. The Leucippides are maidens, namesakes of the mythical brides of the Tyndaridai, Castor and Pollux, who are local Spartan heroes.[63] The duties of the two priestesses are to attend to the shrine of the mythical sisters and to weave a tunic for Apollo Amyclae each year. The Palermo runner, it has been said, was modeled on a metope of the Silaris treasury near Paestum, which may well represent the mythical Leucippides in flight from their husbands-to-be, the Tyndaridai.[64] Castor and Pollux are said to have caught the maidens and carried them away as brides. Thus, the priestesses of the Leucippides are natural overseers of the race of the maiden Dionysiades, a race with probable prenuptial significance.[65]

The identity of the Dionysiades is less clear, since they are otherwise unknown and the worship of Dionysus at Sparta outside of this temple is restricted to mountainside *orgiai*. Nilsson has suggested that their number at eleven may indicate one leader who is chased by ten runners in a rite for the salvation of the state, as in the footrace of the Spartan *Staphylodromoi* or "Grape-runners," which is held during the Carneia.[66] Calame has proposed that the presence of Dionysus, as the divinity of the adult female, indicates that the footrace of the Dionysiades is an initiatory race for maidens moving from adolescence to adulthood.[67]

We find in the Dionysiades race striking formal and structural parallels with the Heraia at Olympia which characterize both as prenuptial rites.[68] Cult affiliations of the colleges organizing both races include a hero or heroes who introduce Dionysus to the region and a young bride or brides devoted to a maternal goddess, thus tracing the progress of girls to the married state. The mythical affiliations of the Leucippides at Sparta and Hippodameia at Olympia include the winning or carrying off of a young bride. Participation in both footraces is limited to maidens. And the organizers in both cases hold special rites for Dionysus as well as for the hero or heroes who introduced him.[69] Moreover, the name "Leucippides" or "daughters of Leucippus" literally means the "white mares," whereas their spouses, the Tyndaridae, are known by the epithet *Leukopoloi* or "white colts."[70] The associations with horses recall the organizational term *agelai* or "horse-herds," used to designate companies of girls and boys in the Spartan *agōgē* and are further supported by metaphors in Alcman (*Parth.* fr. 1, v. 59) and Aristophanes (*Lys.* 1308–13), which compare the troops of dancing or racing girls to fillies. There may be a similar metaphorical association of maidens with horses in the name of Hippodameia, literally "tamer of horses," a possible allusion to her direction of young maidens with the original institution of her footrace to Hera.[71] The equine image in the realms of matrimony is not new; compare the equine image in English "bridegroom," derived by folk etymology from Middle English *bridegome*, meaning simply "bride man."

The Sparta-Olympia parallels in the cult race suggest that at least a similar cult environment fostered prenuptial trials for girls devoted to heroines, to Dionysus, and to a maternal goddess. I suggested in chapter 4 that the Heraia may have been reorganized ca. 580 B.C. under contemporary Spartan political influence in Elis. If that is so, the parallels between the Olympian Heraia and the Spartan footrace evidence the influence of Spartan female athletics over cult practices for girls elsewhere. Sparta was a natural model in the area of progressive social reform for women, as Plato amply illustrates.

So the footrace stands out in the Spartan athletic program for girls as one way to foster progress toward womanhood in a religious and athletic context. The other contests, listed in appendix 5.2, including wrestling and discus-, and javelin-throwing as well as the exercises of *bibasis* or "jumping in place" and dance, are to be distinguished as religiously less significant, but important for eugenic purposes to serve and preserve the state.[72] Sources indicate that Spartan girls' and boys' physical education waned between the fourth and second centuries B.C., when there was a renewal of the vigor of the Lycurgan system and the legend of the muscular vigor of Spartan women lived on until Philostratus in the third century A.D.[73] Despite the de facto and de iure suppression of Spartan women's rights in our own terms, the fact that we still marvel at the Spartan female in an age of progressive liberation is a testimony to their remarkably unique social achievement in Western history. To this Gorgo might have added, "Because only we give birth to men."

APPENDIX 5.1: Naked Female Bronzes

The following is a catalogue of bronze figurines representing young girls, naked or wearing only the *diazōma*, and used mostly as mirror handles or mirror supports. Those few that are statuettes not attached to mirrors are so designated. Museum, inventory number, and provenance are followed by approximate date and suggested origin according to Häfner, 1965 (= H), Praschniker, 1912 (= P), Lanzlotz, 1927 (= L), Jantzen, 1937 (= J), Richter, 1915, 1938, and 1942 (= R), Schröder, 1927 (= S), and Charbonneaux, 1958(= C); numbers indicate pages of the works cited.

1. Athens NM (no number or provenance given) (with *diazoma*). Sixth c. Spartan: P. 226–27.
2. Athens NM 6631 from the Acropolis. c. 525–500 uncertain origin: H. 12, 90–91.
3. Athens NM 7548 from Amyclaeon. c. 530–320 Spartan: H. 117–18, J. 9–10, P. 229, L. 87.
4. Athens NM 7703 from Aegina (with *diazōma*). Sixth c. Aeginetan: P. 239–40, L. 99.
5. Athens NM 13975 from Argos. c. 525–500, Magna Graecia (?): H. 90–91.
6. Athens NM 15897 from Sparta (statuette). Late sixth c. Spartan: H. 34–35 and 123, J. 67.
7. Athens NM 15900 from Sparta c. 520 Spartan: H. 123–24.
8. Berlin Charlottenberg 10820 from Anaktorion, Akarnania. sixth c. Spartan: L. 86; N.W. Greece (?): H. 132–33, Chensonese: J. 66.
9. Berlin Charlottenberg 31084 (provenance unknown). Sixth c. Northeast Peloponnese: H. 133, J. 116–17.
10. Dresden Skulpturensammlung H⁴ 44/16 from Cerveteri. c. 500, East Ionic: H. 137–38, J. 9–10, P. 227.

11. Hamburg, Museum für Kunst und Gewerbe inv. no. 1917. 362 (with *diazoma*), from Egypt (?): Roman, of Spartan type (here, fig. 5-4b). Uncertain origin. S. 196, pl. 110b.

12. Leningrad, Hermitage (no number). From Odessa. Aeginetan P. 240–42, L. 99; c. 500–475 Ionian (?). H. 144.

13. Collection Löser (unknown provenance) (statuette). C. 490–480 Spartan (?): H. 158–59, P. 236.

14. Munich, Museum antiker Kleinkunst 3482 from Hermione (Southeast Peloponnese). c. 510 Spartan: H. 147–48, J. 9–10, P. 236.

15. Met. Mus. 74.51.5680 from Curium, Cyprus. c. 530 (here, fig. 5-1) Spartan: J. 9–10, L. 87, P. 222; Ionian (?): H. 148.

16. Met. Mus. 06. 11. 04 (unknown provenance). Sixth c. Spartan: R (1915) 11–2, L. 87; South Italian/Etruscan (?): H. 149.

17. Met. Mus. 38. 11 3 (unknown provenance). C. 550 (here, fig. 5-2) Corinthian: R (1938) 344; S. Italian/Etruscan: H. 149.

18. Met. Mus. 41. 11. 5 (unknown provenance) (with *diazoma*). C. 550 (here, fig. 5-3): R (1942) 324.

19. Paris Louvre (no number) (unknown provenance ex Coll. Gréau). Early sixth c. Spartan: H. 157, C. 69, P. 240 no. 40.

20. Paris Louvre 138 from Amyclae, mid-sixth c. Spartan: H. 157, P. 251, C. 69 and 141, L. 87 and 94.

21. Sparta Mus. 27 from Sparta. Early fifth c. Spartan: H. 173.

22. Sparta Mus. 28 from Sparta. Fifth c. Spartan: H. 173, P. 238.

23. Trent, Muzeo Provinciale d'Arte inv. no. 3061 (Magna Graecia) (with *diazōma*). Sixth c. (here, fig. 5-4a): S. 196 and pl. 110a; P. 240 no. 41; J. 9 no. 1.

24. Versailles Coll. Morgenroth (with *diazōma*) (unknown provenance): c. 525–500: H. 12, 90–91; J. 66.

25. Vienna Kunsthist. Mus. VI 2925 from Nemea (?). C. 500 North Peloponnese: H. 176–77, P. 219; Spartan: J. 9–10, L. 86.

26. Vienna Kunsthist. Mus. VI 4979 from Sparta (?) statuette. C. 500 Spartan: H. 177, L. 86, P. 235.

APPENDIX 5.2: Spartan Female Physical Activities According to Sources
Chronologically Arranged

Source	Date	R	E	W	Di	J	Da	O
1. Eur., *Andr.* 595–602	430–424 B.C.	X		X				
2. Critias DK 2.88 fr. 32	425–403 B.C.	X		X				
3. Aristoph., *Lys.* 78–84, 1308–13	413 B.C.						X	X (bibasis)
4. Xen., *Const. Lac.* 1.3–4	396–383 B.C.	X	X					X (strength)
5a. Pl., *Rep.* 458D	ca. 375 B.C.		X					
5b. Pl., *Leg.* 7.805E–806A	ca. 355–347 B.C.		X					X (music)
6. Theocr. 18	300–260 B.C.	X						X (music, weaving)
7. Cic., *Tusc.* 2.15.36	45 B.C.		X					
8. Prop. 3.14	ca. 23 B.C.				X	X		X (ball, hoop, pancratium, boxing, hunting, equitation, military drills)
9. Ov., *Her.* 16.149–52	A.D. 2–18		X					
10. Schol. Juv. 4.53	A.D. 54–68			X				
11. Mart. 4.55.6–7	A.D. 88		X					
12. Plut., *Lyc.* 14.1–15.1	A.D. 100–120	X		X	X	X	X	
13. Pollux, *Onom.* 4.102, I, 231(13)	third quart second c. A.D.							X (bibasis)
14. Philostr, *Gymn.* 27	A.D. 230	X	X					

R = running; E = "exercise" (unspecified); W = wrestling; Di = discus-throwing; J = javelin-throwing; Da = dance; O = "other" (specified).

6

RACE OR CHASE OF "THE BEARS" AT BRAURON?

Our final study of girls' historical *paideia* moves to the region of Attica and a festival of Artemis Arkteia much studied in recent years. Since the 1960s, Lilly Kahil has published a series of important articles on the unique vases, mainly from Brauron, associated with the worship of Artemis in Attica.[1] These documents have stimulated a number of reinterpretations of the local festivals of Artemis, particularly the Brauronia and Munichia. There seems to be scholarly consensus that the activities of the young girls shown on the vases are some form of prenuptial initiation, and that the foundation myths of the Brauronia and Munichia support such a ritual representation by stressing the elements of tameness and wildness which would suit such ceremonies.

The chief interest of the present study of the Brauron vases is their frequent depiction of running and the problem of how running might be associated with Artemis' cults.[2] Does the running depict a chase or a race, and what is the cultic significance of this activity? No previous study has addressed this problem directly, apart from citing possible parallels with the girls' footrace of the Heraia at Olympia or that of the Dionysiades at Sparta.[3] For the latter two festival contests we have scant literary and no certain iconographic evidence.[4] For the Attic festivals of Artemis, therefore, the vases may preserve unique visual evidence of girls' races in a cultic context, if indeed the running does represent races, and if the activity can be associated with the festivals of Artemis. A review of the available iconographic evidence is followed here by an analysis of the relevant foundation myths of Artemis at Brauron and Munichion, and by a comparison with other myths of Artemis preserving similar motifs, especially in the imagery of the bear.

The Iconography

In appendix 6-1 are listed the thirty-four vases or fragments of vases which are of central interest to this discussion and that are called *kratēriskoi*. They were selected from among those published by L. Kahil and L. Palaiokrassa in view of their subject matter, which includes girls, clad in short chitons or nude, apparently running, dancing, or standing near an altar, women apparently officiating in some rituals near an altar, sometimes in the company of the girls, and other mythical individuals, presumably associated with the cult. The provenances of the vases under consideration includes Brauron (app. 6.1, nos. 1–11), the Athenian Agora (app. 6.1, nos. 12–15), Salamis (app. 6.1, no. 16), the Athenian Acropolis (App. nos. 20–23) and Munichion (app. 6.1, nos. 25–34); unfortunately the three vases of greatest importance iconographically are of uncertain provenance and in a private collection (app. 6.1, nos. 17–19; = figs. 6-5, 6-6, and 6-7), although the homogeneity of subject and style with the other pieces justifies their inclusion here.[5]

In any case the known provenances correspond to the sites of known festivals of Artemis Arkteia at Brauron, or to her sanctuaries on the Acropolis or at Salamis. Vases of a similar style and showing the palm and altar motifs typical of the twenty-three studied here were also found at Munichion, the site of Artemis' festival with close ties to the Brauronia. The Munichian vases depicting girls or other individuals have been published by L. Palaiokrassa and discussed in the work of C. Sourvinou-Inwood.[6] The vases date from ca. 510–500 (app. 6.1, nos. 20–23) to the first half of the fifth century (app. 6.1, nos. 1–11, 13, 15, and 25–34), mid-fifth century (app. 6.1, nos. 12, 14), and ca. 430–420 (app. 6.1, nos. 17, 18, and 19). The cult of Artemis Brauronia and its penteteric festival may date as far back as the sixth century.

Certain elements of iconography distinguish running from dancing or movement in a procession. Philostratus (Gymn. 32) vividly describes the movements of short- and long-distance runners:

> [The runners in the stade race] by the aid of their hands stir their legs into the quick run just as though their hands were wings. The runners in the long distance race do this near the goal but the rest of the time move almost as if they were walking, holding up their hands in front of them, wherefore they need stronger shoulders. (trans. R. S. Robinson, 1955)

The movement of sprinters, including runners in both the stade and diaulos races (about 200 and 400 meters, respectively), is, therefore, characterized by a high kicking of the legs and a high swinging of the arms with palms open and fingers sometimes splayed. Long-distance runners can be recognized by the more moderate lifting of the legs and the holding of the arms close to the side with the hands held in front often in a fist. Such positions can be seen in vase paintings of male runners, and in the practice of modern short- and long-distance runners.[7] The movements of dancers, by contrast, cannot be so easily defined, except to note that dancers are often shown with symmetrical arm and leg movements, but not ordinarily with the typical movements of runners just mentioned. Moreover, individuals in a processional or ritual attitude show more restrained, solemn, and not necessarily symmetrical movement, often in the vicinity of an altar with ritual paraphernalia.

Of the vases under study here, the following are fairly clearly representations of girls running with the movements of sprinters, based on the criteria stated above: app. 6.1, nos. 1–6, 11, 13, 16–18, and 25, among which nos. 5 and 6, figs. 6-1 and 6-2, offer clear illustrations. Of those eleven pieces, five show nudes (2, 3, 11, 18, and 25), and the rest girls in short chitons. Twelve vases may show either running or dancing (app. 6.1, nos. 7, 9, 12, 14, 27, 28, 29, 30, 31, 32, 33, and 34). Six of these twelve depict girls in chitons, and some carry either a torch (7, 14, and 29) or a corona-shaped wreath (9, 12, and 31), possible accoutrements of a ritual chorus. Only appendix 6-1, nos. 7, 28, and 32 have the legs clearly bent in a forward pace, but not a high kick. And many of these possible dancers or runners show the head turned looking backward (7, 9, 12, 14, 31 [?], and 32), an attitude that is seen in some depictions of runners, but that by its recurrence here suggests rather a dance pose. Figure 6-3 (app. no. 7) shows one such girl with a torch. Significantly, none of the girl run-

Figure 6-1. Appendix 6.1, no. 5 (Brauron Museum 568, *kratēriskos* fragment no. 6). Courtesy of the Brauron Museum, Brauron, Greece.

Figure 6-2. Appendix 6.1, no. 6 (Brauron Museum 567, *kratēriskos* fragment no. 7).
Courtesy of the Brauron Museum, Brauron, Greece.

Figure 6-3. Appendix 6.1, no. 7 (Brauron Museum 915, *kratēriskos* fragment no. 8).
Courtesy of the Brauron Museum, Brauron, Greece.

ners is in the pose of the long-distance runners known from many representations on vases, namely a low stride, arms at the side, and hands held in fists.

Three vase fragments (appendix 6-1, nos. 10, 24, and 26) fairly certainly represent girls dancing, an activity commonly associated with cults of Artemis.[8] In one (10) two girls, entirely nude, are taking short steps from left to right and swinging their arms up in an exaggerated, but asymmetrical manner reminiscent of the arm movements of sprinters. Might this dance indeed be a ritual imitation of the running seen elsewhere? On one of the other fragments (24), two girls in short chitons hold hands and dance toward the right while glancing back in the direction of a doe. The presence of a doe may indicate that the animal is imagined to be present, or that the dance is in a mythical context. The final dance vase (26) shows girls in long chitons stepping briskly forward with arms swinging in front and back in unison.

In either case this dance scene can be associated with three other fragments, all from the Acropolis (app. 6.1, nos. 20–22), which depict women playing the double flute in the presence of other women in *himatia* who appear to be dancing. A doe and a siren in the background of the flautists suggests that these scenes may also be mythical or may show these creatures imagined to be present at actual rituals. The fact that none of the young girls is evident in these latter three fragments may be an indication that some ritual dances were restricted to older women (the officiating priestesses?) and others were just for the girl initiates. Flautists and women in *himatia* are, on the other hand, notably absent from the other scenes in which the young girls appear.

There are, additionally, representations of ritual processions or activities on five or six of the vases (app. 6.1, nos. 8, 15, 17, 23, possibly 19, and 27). On one fragment (8, = fig. 6-4), three girls in short chitons similar to those of the runners approach an altar on which there is a flame. Their steps are measured and symmetrical, perhaps in a solemn procession, and their empty right hands are held forward while their left is at their sides or holding their chitons. Another fragment (15) shows a woman in a long chiton and apparently standing still while she holds up a wreath in her extended left hand. This woman may be a priestess presiding at the girls' ceremony, similar to the three women in appendix 6-1, no. 17 (= fig. 6-5) who attend girls near an altar apparently at the beginning of a running course. The important evidence of this latter, fragmentary *kratēriskos* suggests that the women are busy readying the girls for their run by arranging the *chitōniskoi*, and holding palm branches and baskets. The altar and the nearby palm tree clearly echo the ritual setting for Artemis seen in the other vases, such as fig. 6-6 (app. no. 18). Another fragment, appendix 6-1, no. 23, some ninety years older than the previous vase, also shows women at the same or a very similar altar with a flame, attending to some sacrificial task. A similar activity appears to be taking place with the dancing on a Munichian vase (no. 27). One other important piece (app. 6.1, no. 19, = fig. 6-7) has been taken by some to be a ritual scene with a priest and

Figure 6-4. Appendix 6.1, no. 8 (Brauron Museum no. 572, Brauron *kratēriskos* fragment no. 9). Courtesy of the Brauron Museum, Brauron, Greece.

priestess in the ceremonial masks of bears, but it may better be understood as a representation of the legendary metamorphosis of Callisto and Arcas.[9]

The iconography of the girl runners presents some elements rare or alien to comparable images of male runners. Many of the girls do swing their arms in the natural motion of sprinters, one high and forward, one bent back (app. 6.1, nos. 5, 6, 11, 16, 17, and 25). But several of the girls run in the awkward position of having one or both arms extended in front palms upward (app. 6.1, nos. 4 [one arm], 17, and 18 [both arms]; the latter two = figs. 6-5 and 6-6). The pose is comparable to the attitude of the girls processing to the altar with one palm forward (app. 6.1, no. 8, = fig. 6-4). But if the attitude is one of prayer, it is to my knowledge unparalleled among depictions of male runners. Furthermore, several of the girl runners hold their fingers together or cupped as they run (app. 6.1, nos. 4, 5, 6, 17, and 18; the latter four = figs. 6-1, 6-2, 6-5, and 6-6).[10] Among those having girls with cupped hands are the three vases in which the girls' arms are extended in front (4, 17 and 18; the latter two = figs. 6-5 and 6-6). The cupped-hand gesture is also present in the dancing and processional scenes mentioned above (respectively, app. 6.1, nos. 10 and 8).

The significance of this peculiar iconography is not obvious but may be associated with the role of the girls in "imitating the bear" (*arkteuein*) during the Arkteia. The gesture of cupped hands is certainly not restricted to girls holding garlands, although some are doing this in one vase showing nude runners (app. 6.1, no. 18, = fig. 6-6). Nor is this unusual position of the arms and hands specifically restricted to running, dancing, or ritual processions. It furthermore occurs in depictions of girls both nude and clad in short chitons. The simplest explanation for the ubiquity of these gestures would be that they represent girls literally adopting the characteristics of bears, whose paws are naturally closer to a closed fist than a splayed hand and who, when standing on their hind legs, ordinarily hold their front paws before them. This hypothesis also supports the further interpretation of the bear iconography that will be explored later.

The appearance of the girls both nude and dressed in short chitons (*chitōniskoi*) while running or dancing has given rise to various interpretations. The *chitōniskoi* have been erroneously identified as the saffron robes or *krokōtoi* worn by the girls during the Arkteia, and mentioned in Aristophanes' *Lysistrata* 643, where a girl boasts of her religious services in Attica:[11] "And shedding my saffron robe I was a bear at the Brauronia."

Figure 6-5. Appendix 6.1, no. 17; face A, 2 right fragments; face B, 2 left fragments (red-figure Attic krater or *kratēriskos* [I], Collection of Herbert A. Cahn, Basel, Switzerland, inv. no. HC 501). Courtesy of the Collection of Herbert A. Cahn, Basel, Switzerland.

Figure 6-6. Appendix 6.1, no. 18; face A, top 2 fragments; face B, bottom right fragments (red-figure krater or *kratēriskos* [II], Collection of Herbert A. Cahn, Basel, Switzerland, inv. no. HC 502). Courtesy of the Collection of Herbert A. Cahn, Basel, Switzerland.

Figure 6-7. Appendix 6.1, no. 19 (red-figure krater or *kratēriskos* [III], Collection of Herbert A. Cahn, Basel, Switzerland, inv. no. HC 503). Courtesy of the Collection of Herbert A. Cahn, Basel, Switzerland.

It has been suggested that the *krokōtos* may have been adopted because it resembled the tawny coat of a bear, and Brauronian inscriptions have recorded the dedication of these garments.[12] The *krokōtos* can at least be recognized as a quintessentially female garment in the classical period, a robe in which effeminate men or gods are occasionally garbed; brides wore saffron veils and the saffron plant was used as a cure for menstrual cramps.[13] Yet the *krokōtos* cannot be identified with the short chitons of the vase paintings, since it is a long *himation*, and since Brauronian inscriptions list separately the dedications of *chitōniskoi*. While the saffron robes played some role in the Arkteia ritual, they are not shown on the vases. Perhaps they were worn by the girls on the journey from Athens to Brauron, before being "shed" for the *chitōniskoi* or for total nudity at the sanctuary.[14]

The nudity of the girls which appears on five vases (app. 6.1, nos. 2, 3, 10, 11, 18, and 25) has stimulated various interpretations, all of which seem to agree that this unusual ritual practice is meant to evoke a sense of primitive wildness appropriate to devotees of Artemis, archetypically "Mistress of the Beasts." Kahil compares the Amphidromia in which mothers carrying their newly born infants run around an altar. Following C. Sourvinou-Inwood, Kahil further hypothesizes that the girls running in *chitōniskoi* in app. 6.1, no. 17 (= fig. 6-5) are at the beginning stage of their initiation, while those running nude in app. 6.1, no. 18 (= fig. 6-6) have reached puberty and perform the race one final time before leaving the "convent" of the Brauron sanctuary. Perlman disputes this proposed sequence on the grounds that it is difficult to judge ages of infants, children, and adolescents in Greek art. Adducing the parallel of Plato *Leg.* 833c–834d, Perlman has suggested that "we see on the *kratēriskoi arktoi* below the age of thirteen competing nude while those older than thirteen are 'properly dressed' in short chitons." Christiane Sourvinou-Inwood has convincingly proved through careful analyses of the iconography that the girls on the Arkteia vases are aged 5 to 10 years.[15]

While absolute ages may not be ascertained from the vases, there are younger girls in *chitōniskoi*, certainly prepubescent relative to the older girls and women priestesses in the same scene, on appendix 6-1, no. 17 (= fig. 6-5) and, conversely, there are clearly older, nude girls with well developed figures on appendix 6-1, nos. 18 and 25 (= figs. 6-6 and 6-8). It seems, then, that there were no

Figure 6-8. Appendix 6.1, no. 25 (Piraeus Museum Kk55, fragment of the lip and body of a *kratēriskos*, from Munichion). Courtesy of the Piraeus Museum, Piraeus, Greece.

fixed age limits to participation in the clothed or nude portions of the ritual. This is not to say that age per se was irrelevant in the admission of participants, and the question of age limits will be discussed further later. If, as it seems, the question of age is not linked to that of dress or nudity, and girls of all age groups do participate in the same rituals, then another rationale must be found for the dress and nudity practices.

Kahil elsewhere proposes that the nude girl *arktoi* are meant to recall their heroine Iphigeneia, who, in Aeschylus, *Agamemnon* 239, "let fall to the ground her saffron robe" before being sacrificed. The association of Iphigeneia with this ritual detail is supported not only by the existence of Iphigeneia's cult at Brauron, but also the tradition in the Scholia to Aristophanes, *Lysistrata* 645, which says that Iphigeneia was sacrificed at Brauron, not Aulis, and a bear, not a deer, was sacrificed in her stead. In view of the distinctions between the saffron robes of the texts and the short chitons of the vases, however, it is impossible to know exactly what relationship the *krokōtos* had to the activities seen on the vases. "Shedding the *krokōtos* might just as well be a prelude to wearing the *chitōniskos* as to complete nudity."[16]

Both Vidal-Naquet and Osborne have argued that the change from clothes to nudity dramatizes the passage from civilization to savagery, from the tameness of clothes to the wildness of nature. Yet neither scholar is dogmatic in stating that the order of the ritual was from clothes to nudity. Osborne notes that by their association with Iphigeneia, the *arktoi* maidens are at once returned to the nakedness of birth, a necessary precondition here for "taming" in marriage and for a strong birth. Here the parallel with the nudity of the new mothers running in the Amphidromia is striking. One can only surmise that the unusual practice of nude dances or running would be more dramatically effective as a final ritual in the ceremony, reminding those about to depart for the next stage of life of the earliest stage of infancy.[17]

Torches are found in three scenes of the running maidens, and these girls are both nude (app. 6.1, no. 3) and in short chitons (app. 6.1, nos. 7 [fig. 6-3] and 14). There is nothing to suggest that these torches are used in races, as they are in the men's *lampadēdromia* at the Panathenaia and elsewhere.[18] It may be assumed that they were carried in running ceremonies that were held at night and may have had a special significance for Artemis Phosphoros or Purphoros, epithets respectively associated with Artemis in the tholos of the Athenian Agora, and with the goddess as she ran in the Lycian mountains.[19]

Wreaths appear on several of the vases, either carried by the girls (app. 6.1, nos. 9, 12, 15, 18, and 25), or in the background of the scene, perhaps on a sanctuary wall (app. 6.1, nos. 1, 8, and 29). Furthermore, the wreaths appear in scenes with girls in the nude (app. 6.1, nos. 18 and 25 = figs. 6-6 and 6-8) and in the *chitōniskos* (app. 6.1, nos. 1, 8 [= fig. 6-4], 9, and 12; 15 has a woman in a himation; dress on 29 is uncertain). And the objects are seen both in running scenes (app. 6.1, nos. 1, 9, 18, and 25) as well as in stationary or processional rituals (app. 6.1, nos. 8 [= fig. 6-4], 15, and 27). Most of these wreaths seem too large to be crowns, and none of the girls wear crowns in the manner of athletes. Rather, the objects may be personal dedications to Artemis. In one scene (app. 6.1, no. 18 = fig. 6-6), not all girls carry wreaths while running. One indication of the nonathletic function of such crowns may be the fact that they do not appear in dedicatory inscriptions from Brauron, unlike men's victory crowns that often are listed on dedicatory inscriptions. The ubiquity of the wreaths, like the torches, suggests that they were not de rigueur as implements for a particular ceremony, but rather optional and appropriate accoutrements for the worship of Artemis.

There are two interesting parallels to the practice of runners carrying flora in the context of festival rituals, namely the Attic Oschophoria/Scira and the Spartan Staphylodromia. In the former, apparently agricultural festival, a race was held from a sanctuary of Dionysus (Lenaion?) in Athens to that of Athena Sciras in Phaleron. This involved young men representing their tribes and carrying vine branches during the race.[20] The winning tribe received a special punch called the *pentaploa* or "fivefold."[21] The ingredients of this mixture included the primary products of the region, and hence the victory took on a special communal significance. The Staphylodromia was a similarly agricultural and communal ritual in the context of the Carneia at Sparta, in which one youth wearing fillets runs and prays for something beneficial for the state, while the others, the *staphylodromoi*, pursue him.[22] If the youth was caught, they expected that some good will come to the region; if not, something bad would happen. Nilsson suggested that the pursuers carried bunches of grapes, but the one in flight may have carried the fruit. In any case, both the Attic and Spartan rituals illustrate the possible importance of the wreathes carried by the girls running in the Arkteia. The wreaths may have special local significance portending the welfare of the community, and they may symbolize the hoped-for fertility of the maidens. The wreaths, however, seem not to be essential to the Arkteia as they are to the other men's races, because they are carried neither by all participants, as in the Attic men's race, nor by a single runner leading the others, as in the Spartan ritual. Perhaps the wreaths were personal offerings from individual participants.

Altars and palm trees are found in the background of many of the scenes, but without specific restriction to the iconography of the girls (altars: app. 6.1, nos. 1, 2, 4, 8, 11, 16, and 17, cf. figs. 6-4 and 6-5; palms: nos. 1, 6, 17, and 18, cf. figs. 6-2, 6-5, and 6-6). Presumably these two objects serve to identify the setting as that of Brauron, or of another shrine of Artemis to whom the palm was, of course, particularly sacred.[23] It is noteworthy that the palm, understood broadly in Greek culture, symbolized immortality, for instance, in its association with

Heracles.[24] Here also the palm-fronds as tokens of victory for athletes may reflect this tradition.

Running near an altar recalls not only the activity of the women in the Amphidromia, but also that of the men in their own footraces at the Olympics. There, according to Philostratus (*Gymn.* 5-6), the earliest victors in the stade race were given a torch by a priest at the end of the race near the Altar of Zeus; the victor then had the honor of lighting the fire for the central sacrifice to Zeus. Philostratus also mentions that the diaulos, or two-stade race, began and ended at the Altar of Zeus.[25] So there is precedent in the men's races for orienting a race course so that the running ends at the altar of the chief god of the festival.[26] Girls, both nude and in short chitons, are shown running toward or away from altars in appendix 6-1, nos. 1, 2, 4, 16, 17, 28, and 32.

Did the altars on these vases represent either a starting or a finishing point, or both, for the runners? The altar on (app. 6.1) vase 2 is above the handles and the girls are running both away from and to it. In the fragmentary (app. 6.1) number 4, the girl appears to be running to and just behind the altar with one arm extended over it. Vase 16 (app. 6.1) from Salamis shows three girls apparently running from the altar; the hindmost runner's foot overlaps the monument in the background. But the foremost runner is arguably running around the vase back to the altar. The activities of this vase are, however, less certainly associated with the activities depicted on the other vases from Attica, and so only tentatively mentioned here as evidence for the relation of running to the altar. On vase (app. 6.1) no. 17 (fig. 6-5), the most informative ritual scene, girls appear to be beginning their run just to the left of the altar, running on behind it, and in full course to the right of it. On fragment (app. 6.1) no. 28 from Munichion, the girl seems to be at the start of a run to the right and goes away from the altar; her skirt flies back but her legs do not yet kick high. In sum, the altar occupies a central place in the running activities, and the girls seem to begin running very near it, and perhaps back to it. While analogy with the Olympic races for men would suggest that the altar served as both start and finish, the model of the women's Amphidromia suggests rather a course "around" the altar. Perhaps also at Brauron the altar served as the focal point around which the girl participants ran. The possibility that the run was not an actual race, but an initiatory task, is further suggested by the absence of any scene of the close clustering of runners, a scene familiar from depictions of men's races.[27]

Three of the vases under consideration, (app. 6-1) nos. 17, 18, and 19 (figs. 6-5, 6-6, and 6-7), require special examination since they present the fullest depiction of what may be rituals of the Arkteia. Appendix 6-1 no. 17 shows on face A (fig, 6-5) four girls in short chitons positioned alternately among three older girls or young women who appear to be officiating at the ceremony. The girls resemble those in chitons on other *krateriskoi* from Brauron or the Athenian Agora (cf. espe-

cially app. 6.1, nos. 4, 5, 6, 8, 13, 28, 30, 31, 32, 33, and 34; see figs. 6-2 and 6-4).
The girls, who are moving left to right, seem to be preparing for the beginning of
the running, also in a left to right direction, which takes place on face B (fig. 6-5,
bottom left fragment). The older females are engaged in assisting the girls in their
preparations, namely arranging one girl's *chitōniskos*, motioning with tree branches
seemingly to direct a (staggered?) start of the running, and holding baskets, possibly with offerings from or prizes for the girls.[28] The girls and the two women to the
far right of face A (fig. 6-5, top and bottom right fragments) stand behind an
altar, a position which suggests the ritual nature of the actions depicted.

Face B (app. 6.1) no. 17 (fig. 6-5, bottom left fragment) shows four girls, possibly even the same four from face A. The only visible face on B, that of the girl running second from the left, very closely resembles that of the girl engaged in preparations second from the left on face A (fig. 6-5, top right fragment). Both wear fierce,
almost scowling expressions. Furthermore, these same two girls on both faces hold
their hands extended in a gesture that may represent a bear's front paws, as was suggested above. If this hypothesis is correct, the scowling girl may be imitating the bear
which, according to the foundation myths of the Brauronia (to be examined later),
either maimed or killed a young girl. The other girls in full flight with their arms swinging may then, as a group, represent the unfortunate girl of the legend, or they may
represent her accompanied by friends. The one "caught" in this morbid version of the
game "tag" would thus have the honor of being symbolically sacrificed to Artemis.
The fact that on figure 6-5 face B one girl in flight is actually behind the supposed
pursuing "bear" is not problematic if it is seen as the artist's attempt to represent the
bear in the midst of the a group of fleeing maidens. We cannot be certain or dogmatic
regarding the details of the ritual game depicted, but the interpretation of the scene
as a chase rather than a race has the advantage of explaining the apparently staggered "start" on figure 6-5 face A. In any case the start looks nothing like the start
of any conventional Greek race for men, though it does not disallow the possibility
that this activity for girls had an agonistic element of the "bear" catching the girls,
which would have made it more dramatic and interesting for all involved. If so, the
Arkteia chase was a unique, alternative type of contest, purely for females.

Appendix 6-1 no. 18 (fig. 6-6) seems to support this interpretation since it also
depicts scenes of flight and pursuit. Face A, figure 6-6 (top two fragments), according to Kahil's very plausible reconstruction, shows five nude girls running from right
to left with a palm and a rocky hill behind on the far right. The four in the lead are
significantly larger, better developed in figure, and very probably older than the one
bringing up the rear. At least two of the older girls carry garlands in both hands extended in front. The younger one appears not to carry anything but holds both hands
cupped and extended in front in the manner of the "scowling girl" of appendix 6-1
no. 17. Face B (fig. 6-6, bottom right fragment) shows four nude girls, apparently of
the same age as the older girls on face A. They also run in full sprint, but in a left-

to-right direction and with a fragmentarily preserved bear under a palm tree behind them on the left (fig. 6-6, bottom left fragment). At least two of these girls hold a wreath in one hand while the other hand is extended straight forward.

Of greatest interest is the presence of the bear. It is not impossible that a real bear was kept in the sanctuary at Brauron in the Classical period, in which case the scene portrayed here is not part of legend, but of actual ritual practice.[29] But even if it is a scene from legend, it explains the spirit of the running scenes generally on the vases, namely the spirit of flight and pursuit. The girl in the rear on figure 6-6, face B (bottom right fragment) turns and looks at the bear with wide-eyed astonishment. All girls on both faces flee the animal at full speed. If, as has been suggested above, the extended-hands gesture of the running girls indicates that they themselves are assuming the *arktos* identity, this does not preclude their taking flight from a real bear. Perhaps they, like Callisto in Ovid's version of her transformation into a bear, retained vestiges of their human nature and took fright at the sight of real bears:

> venatrixque metu venatum territa fugit.
> saepe ferris latuit visis, oblita quid esset,
> ursaque conspectos in montibus horruit ursos. . . .
> *Met.* 2.492–94

huntress though she was, fled in fear before the hunters.
She often hid when the beasts appeared, forgetting her own nature,
and, though a bear, she shuddered when she caught sight of bears on
    the mountains. . . .

In this case the girl *arktoi* on (app. 6.1) vase no. 18 may be seen as a type of ritual half-breed, girls and not girls, bears and not bears, on the margin between savage and civilized, maidens and married women. And again as in the Callisto myth, the humans who are ordinarily the hunters become the prey of the bear in the scene on the vase.[30]

This interpretation is supported by a hunt scene with hounds chasing a fawn in the lower register of (app. 6.1) vase no. 18 (fig. 6-6, faces A and B). This scene has never before been recognized as a parallel to the one in the main register, but it has striking parallels in repetition of the motifs of savagery and civilization, or tame and wild, in the context of flight and pursuit. In the lower register are preserved, in all, four hounds (there may be a fifth, unpreserved) on both faces in pursuit of a fawn (not an older deer, to judge by its size, smaller than that of the hounds). The fawn is positioned as closely as possible beneath the bear figure in the upper register (a handle makes it impossible to put it directly beneath). The hunting scene is a mirror image of the scene above it, because the domesticated dogs are pursuing a wild animal, while the upper scene has a wild animal chase "tame" girls. Yet there is ambiguity inherent in the definitions of "tame" and "savage" in both scenes. The "tame" girls are in a natural state of undress and may even be "playing the bear" in the Arkteia ritual. The bear was considered a very anthropomorphic animal in appearance and habits, and in some versions of the foundation myth the bear kept in Artemis' sanctuary is even said to be "tame."[31]

The dogs are the agents of men in the hound hunt (*kunēgesion*) and yet follow their native instincts in chasing wild animals. The fawn is often associated with Artemis as Mistress of the Beasts, and yet the youth and helplessness of the animal evokes human pity in this scene as the victimization of the young innocent girls in the scene above it. Like a nature metaphor in Greek poetry, the hunting scene contributes to the understanding of the ritual scene. It literally underlines the ritual to emphasize the common spirit of the chase in both, and to express the irony of the symbiosis of nature in which humans can both victimize and be a victim. But in both cases the temporary and very natural exercise of the chase gives way to the final catch in which civilized humans benefit, the *arktoi* girls of the ritual are destined to be "tamed" in marriage, and the fawn to serve as food and clothing.[32]

Both scenes in (app. 6.1) vase no. 18 (fig. 6-6) are further related to one another through Artemis as patroness of the hunt and of the Arkteia.[33] In this regard, there is a noteworthy literary reference to to *hieron kunēgesion*, "the sacred (hound-) hunt" of Artemis in the Hypothesis to Demosthenes 25. Although the identification is not certain, it is likely that "the sacred hunt" is another name for the Arkteia.[34] It seems probable, then, that the scene on (app. 6.1) vase no. 18 does depict the Arkteia ritual of "the sacred hunt," and that the character of the running scenes on all the vases is not that of a race, but of a chase.

Another very important document is vase (app. 6.1) no. 19, which shows on face A (fig. 6-7, top fragment), from left to right, Leto (?) veiled, Artemis wearing a short chiton and taking aim with her bow, and Apollo, nude, holding a staff and a belt, and facing Artemis. Face B (fig. 6-7, bottom two fragments) shows, left to right, a tree, a young nude male figure with a bear's head (or mask?), an older female with a long chiton and arms raised in surprise (or prayer?), and finally a fawn or doe prancing in midair away from the woman. The importance of this piece for the present analysis is twofold. First, the scene with the gods emphasizes the centrality of Artemis in her role as huntress, a function that supports the interpretation of the running scenes on the other vases as flight and pursuit of the hunt.[35] Second, the bear-headed figures can best be understood as Callisto and Arcas, an identification that brings other bear myths of Artemis into the orbit of the Arkteia ritual. The importance of this latter association will be investigated later under a more general discussion of literary sources.[36]

Several other iconographically related vases contribute incidental information concerning the activities performed in the Arkteia rituals. Vase no. 20 (app. 6.1) shows a prancing fawn behind a woman wearing a long chiton and playing a double aulos, in front of whom is a fragmentarily preserved second woman, probably also in a long chiton, and apparently dancing. The fragmentary (app. 6.1) vase no. 22 shows the lower half of a chiton-clad dancer very similar to the dancer in vase no. 20. The fawn in vase no. 20 resembles the fawn in the mythological scene in vase no. 19, and the aulos player and dancer recall the (male) flautist with female dancers in another Brauron piece. The women dancers holding hands in the latter vase in turn very closely resemble the girls dancing in appendix 6-1, no. 24. The aulos player of vase no. 20 is also paralleled by the female double-aulos player of the fragmentary vase no. 21, with the difference that a siren appears instead of a fawn in the background field of the latter piece. The fawn and the siren in the context of flute-playing and dancing seem to be emblems of the Brauronian ritual, iconographic indications of the association of the pieces with the Brauron sanctuary.[37] The fragment of (app. 6.1) vase no. 23 shows an altar with volutes and burning firewood on top very similar in appearance to the altars in the other scenes of running or ritual activity reviewed here. At the altar in vase no. 23 are two women, one in a himation pouring a libation, the other in a chiton (identical to those in vases no. 20, 21, and 22). A basket (*kanoun*) sitting on the ground near the altar is also reminiscent of one held by the woman officiating at the altar in the running ritual of appendix 6-1, no. 17. Women of indeterminate age stand around or dance toward an altar in appendix 6-1, no. 27.

Taken together, appendix 6-1, nos. 20 to 24 indicate that older women, possibly the same as the officiating women in appendix 6-1, nos. 15 and 17, provide music for and possibly supervise dances as a part of the Arkteia. It is, of course, not surprising that dances are a part of the rites of Artemis, one of whose realms is dance.

The Foundation Myths

W. Burkert has reminded us that myth and ritual can overlap but are distinct.[38] Both function similarly, to communicate and to promote understanding and solidarity in a community. Yet ritual is a form of action, often of primitive or even animal origins, which is redirected to serve as communication, whereas myths are traditional tales structured after some typical human pattern of action that can often be reduced to a simple imperative notion such as "Get!" or "Find!" or "Go!" The ritual action of the vases analyzed above is, however, unclear in communicating any message beyond the vague notions of tameness and wildness somehow related to chase and flight among adolescent girls in a sanctuary of Artemis.

These rituals are greatly informed by the foundation myths of the Attic festival of Artemis, the Brauronia and Munichia.[39] The fullest sources for the Brauronia are the Scholia to Aristophanes *Lysistrata* 645 (Ravenna and Leyden) and the Suda, s.v. *arktos ē Brauroniois*. They present a tale that may be outlined as follows:

1. A bear is donated to (or wanders into) a sanctuary and is tamed.
2. A girl plays with the bear, which acts wild and blinds her.
3. The girl's brother(s) slay(s) the bear.
4. Artemis orders (or a plague causes the Athenians to consult an oracle that requires) all girls of Attica to "serve as bears" (*arkteuesthai*) before marriage and to wear a saffron himation.

The Leyden version supplies the additional variant that Agamemnon slew Iphigeneia at Brauron, not at Aulis, and that a bear, not a deer, was substituted for her in the final sacrifice. This gave rise to the *mystērion* of the Arkteia. This variant, which is certainly a significant allomorph for mythological studies, will not be considered here since it appears to be a true foundation myth for Brauron, but a later one either devised to rival the more broadly accepted Aulis myth, or arising from association with the prominent Brauronian tradition of Iphigeneia's death at that sanctuary. The Leyden version also contributes the information that the girls were aged 5 to 10; the Suda gives the age limits as 5 to 9. The question of age will be discussed later.

Tameness and wildness are salient motifs in the Brauronia myth, as has been mentioned earlier.[40] Osborne (1985) 163 has noted that the bear in the Brauron myth is tame: *arktos tis . . . hēmerōthē* in the scholiasts, and *hēmerōtheisan autēn* in the Suda, whereas the one in the Munichian version is not. Tameness of the ordinarily wild animal thus becomes an explicit issue. The scholia proceed: "Then at some time a certain maiden played with it (*epaixe pros autēn*) and her eyes were scratched out by the bear." The Suda gives a slightly fuller version: "They tamed it to be familiar with humans, but a certain maiden played with it (*prospaizein*), and when the girl mistreated it (*aselgainousēs tēs paidiskēs*), the bear was aroused (*paroxuthenai*) and tore up the maiden." There are erotic overtones, as Montepaone (1979) 348–49 and Osborne (1985) 165–66 have noted, in the vocabulary of the passage: (*pros*)*paizō* can also designate erotic play, *aselgainō* can also mean to "behave outrageously or lewdly," *paidiskē* can also mean a "prostitute," and *paroxunesthai* can mean to "excite" or "arouse" erotically. So the *parthenos/paidiskē*, yet unyoked in marriage, literally plays with the supposedly tamed bear, and in so doing she arouses his wildness. Just as the untamed human behaves outrageously in an unusual act of wildness, the supposedly tamed bear reverts to his usual wild instincts. Both interact in the domain of the wild. After the bear is slain, it seems only a fitting ritual resolution for other girls also to interact with the wild in a final acknowledgment of that aspect of their nature—their 'Artemisian nature,' we may term it—before proceeding to their Aphrodisian or Heraian roles as mature, married women. A somewhat similar dynamic occurs in Euripides' *Hippolytus* 1425–27, in which Artemis establishes the cult ritual of maidens cutting their hair before marriage to commemorate Hippolytus and his terrible fate.

Most scholars agree that, as a prenuptial requirement for the girls of Attica, the Arkteia is a form of initiation ritual, a rite of passage to mark transition from girlhood to maturity and to prepare girls for marriage and childbirth.[41] Some have added that the Arkteia is also an expiatory ritual derived from the practice of primitive hunting culture in which the death of an animal calls for the compensatory 'sacrifice' of a human victim. Henrichs has noted that the context of a female, prepuberty ritual in this hunting practice is especially appropriate for Artemis as patroness of both "the natural supply of young life and the dangers which threaten its survival."[42]

Beyond these general interpretations, few have ventured to reconstruct the ritual itself by a careful comparison of the iconographic evidence with the literary sources. Since nudity and the wearing of special *chitōniskoi* are the most prominent emblems, respectively, of savagery and civilization on the vases, we might ask whether literary sources offer any clues as to the progress from one state to the other during the ritual. And if the *chitōniskoi* are not to be identified with the *krokōtoi* garments mentioned in Aristophanes, *Lysistrata* 645, how do the *krokōtoi* fit into the ritual? Osborne's comments suggest that some (unspecified) garment was worn by the girls as they "played the bear" and that the shedding of this is the symbolic abandonment of their prepubescent "wildness." This scholar also notes that the evidence does not allow us to reconstruct "a day in the life of the Brauron sanctuary," although an interpretation may be offered for the symbolic activity of the ritual.[43] Yet more can be made of the evidence with regard to details and structure of the ritual, as has been demonstrated in the examination of the iconographic evidence above.

Montepaone presses the evidence farther for the following explanation of the Arkteia:

> Consider, in fact, that for the very reason that the myth was a dramatization of the passage from savagery to civilization, the order [of ritual action] ought to be this: mimesis / (*himation krokōton* [*sic*])—nudity/ dressing in civilized clothes. This ought to have been the significant moment of the ritual.[44]

Others see the ritual process as the reverse, namely the wearing of the *krokōtos*, then the shedding of it to assume the state of nudity seen in the vases.[45] Support for this interpretation comes from the readings of Aristophanes, *Lysistrata* 645, which mean "shedding the *krokōtos* I played the bear at the Brauronia."[46] Sourvinou-Inwood's very careful analysis of the modalities of dress on the Arkteia vases has arrived at the following hypothesis: first the short chiton of the child was worn, symbolizing the childhood to be abandoned, then the *krokōtos* for the segregation period, followed by shedding of this garment and adoption of nudity, and finally the long chiton and himation for the marriageable *parthenos*.[47] As was discussed above, no one has yet ascertained the role of the *chitōniskoi* in the ritual, and, failing new literary evidence, there can ultimately be no certainty as to the order of activities or states of dress. Yet we may surmise that the *krokōtoi* with which Aristophanes' audience was familiar were worn in the long, public processions to Brauron, and the *chitōniskoi* were generally worn by the younger and newer initiates, while nudity was reserved for those about to quit their service, that is, those generally, but not exclusively, older.[48]

The literary tradition for the foundation myth of the Munichia has a somewhat similar structure to that of the Brauronia, but with significantly different details:[49]

1. A certain Athenian, Embaros, founds a sanctuary to Artemis at Munichion.
2. A bear "appears" in the sanctuary, harms many people, and is killed by Athenians.
3. A plague/famine ensues.
4. "The god" [Apollo] promises relief if a daughter/girl is sacrificed to Artemis.
5. Embaros/Baros promises his daughter in return for priesthood of the cult for his *genos* in perpetuity.
6. He hides his daughter (in an *adyton*) and sacrifices in her place a goat named after his daughter/dressed in human clothes.
7. Athenians distrust the man and ask Apollo, who confirms the man as perpetual priest; the man confesses to his deception.
8. Girls thereafter "play the bear" before marriage "to purify the events concerning the wild beast."

Of the three sources of this myth, only the *Lexeon Chresimon*, s.v. *arkteusai* (Bekker, *Anec. Graec.* 1.144f.) gives the information in sections 7 and 8, notably including the requirement of "playing the bear."[50] Given the absence of girls on the vases found in the Piraeus sanctuary, it may be that these last two sections were not original, but a contamination from the Brauron tale.[51] In any case the association of humans with bears is not a central motif here as it is in the Brauron myth.[52] Certainly this, like the Brauron myth, presents an *aition* for the sacrifice and the expiatory ritual to Artemis for the killing of a bear. The focus here, however, seems to be on the unreliability of appearances and on deception practiced by both humans and gods. The bear is not recognized as an animal particularly sacred to Artemis and is nevertheless slain (that is, men act blindly against a quasi-divine animal and offend a divinity). Embaros/Baros cleverly attempts to deceive both the Athenians and Artemis. He agrees to offer up his daughter to the goddess in return for the office of the priesthood, yet he substitutes for his daughter a goat dressed as a girl (that is, a man offers a quasi-human animal to appease the divinity).[53] And (if this section is accepted as an original part of the myth) thereafter the girls of Attica "play the bear" (*arkteuein*) before marriage, so that they might purify the events concerning the beast (i.e. quasi-animal humans perform a ritual to atone for both the slaying of the quasi-divine animal and the consequent deceptive sacrifice of the quasi-human animal). Even the folk saying attached to the myth by Eustathius and the Suda, "I am/you are an Embaros, sensible, intelligent," conveys the theme of clever deception.

The Embaros legend of Munichion is clearly an aetiological tale of the traditional priesthood of the sanctuary, and as such it is more concerned with the clever character of the founding priest than with the ritual significance of the "playing of the bear" by the girls. The difference of focus between the foundation myths of Munichion and Brauron therefore corresponds to the difference in iconographic evidence, where depictions of girls running or performing ritual actions are later and rarer in the Munichion vases.[54] These discrepancies suggest that the Arkteia rituals for girls may have been performed first at Brauron and were adopted only later at Munichion due to the popularity of the ritual.

Scholarly opinion is divided with regard to exactly which girls participated in the Arkteia. Some take the ambiguity of the sources to indicate that all girls in Attica of the requisite age took part.[55] Most, however, argue that on practical grounds only a representative few took part.[56] The age-limits of participants seems to be from 5 to 10 years old in view of literary and archaeological evidence.[57] These ages seem to some to be oddly young for a prenuptial ritual, but the important point is that the age-grouping is very safely before menarche. Perhaps the ancients took such limits less rigidly than we do with our more precise documentation. A parallel may be adduced from the age categories for men's athletic competitions, where participants' status as boys, youths, or men was adjudicated on an ad hoc basis by local judges of the contest, sometimes with disputes over the decisions.[58] It may also be that the 5-to-10 limits defined the years within which a girl might be inducted into the cult as an *arktos*, not the age at which she left the service of the goddess.

There is one cryptic literary tradition in Aristophanes, *Peace* 873–76, its scholia, and Suda, s.v. "Brauron," which some have seen as a link between the Brauronia to Artemis and a Dionysian Theoria at that site.[59] The association is made since Brauron is mentioned and the Theoria, like the Brauronia, is a penteteric festival. During the Theoria men got drunk and seized the many prostitutes who were found at Brauron. The Scholiast's report sounds to some like "a feeble attempt to explain the text."[60] But certain information in the report offers details that cannot be extrapolated from Aristophanes: such Theoriai were held "in each deme" of Attica, and there were specifically "many" prostitutes at Brauron. Some plates from Brauron also show maenads and hetairai.[61]

Brelich accepts the Theoria as historical, and in view of reports of similar abductions, he sees the Brauronian Theoria as a men's Dionysian ritual held in close
association with, perhaps as a conclusion to, the women's Brauronian Arkteia.[62]
Deubner takes the Theoria as a reference to the male legation that accompanied the
women from Athens to Brauron. Arrigoni draws a parallel between the worship
of Artemis and Dionysus at Brauron to their coexistence at Sparta, where maidens, named Dionysiades or "the Daughters of Dionysus," held a race in honor of
Dionysus, and the boys participated in rituals for Artemis.[63]

In a similar cultic context, the Heraia at Olympia involved a footrace for girls,
was a premarital ritual, and was complemented by rites to Dionysus held by the
same organizers. According to legend, as discussed in chapter 4, the Heraia
was instituted by Hippodameia in thanksgiving to Hera for her marriage to Pelops
(Paus. 6.16.4). Participation in the festival footraces was restricted to maidens.
The girls are not necessarily local natives, although the festival may have begun
like the Brauronia as a local celebration and may have then later been opened
up to girls from all over Greece who accompanied their parents to the men's Olympics. The priestesses who presided over this festival, the Sixteen (Elean) Women,
also established two choral dances in honor of Hippodameia, and another local
heroine, Physcoa, who mated with Dionysus, bore him a son, and introduced
his worship to the region (Paus. 6.16.6). Pausanias also notes that Dionysus
was particularly reverenced by the Eleans, who held a special wine-festival to him,
the Thyia (6.26.1). The Thyia is named after the fact that the organizers of this
festival, again the Sixteen Women, invoke the god to be present "rushing with
rage on his bull's feet" (*tōi boeōi podi thuōn*, Plutarch, *Quaestiones Graecae* 299a).[64]

Dionysus, who is ordinarily at odds with his stepmother Hera, is here linked to
the goddess through the choruses set up by the Sixteen Eleans. Dionysus is, like Hera,
associated with adult females, although his rituals promote temporary *ekstasis* or
liberation from matronal roles, while Hera's reinforce the status of wife.[65] On the
other hand, Hera's functions at Olympia correspond to those of Artemis at Brauron
insofar as both can oversee the stage of transition from maiden to married woman,
a status generally encompassed in the term *parthenos*. Hera's patronage of Hippodameia's marriage and of the Heraia ritual therefore closely resembles Artemis'
function in the Attic Brauronia.

The presence of Dionysus at Sparta, Elis, and Brauron in association with the
ritual running of maidens need not suggest a common origin or some mutual influence. There is in all three at least a similar complementarity of cults and ritual
motivation whereby the community provides for its maidens an experience of solidarity in the celebration of their untamed state before it is sacrificed in marriage.
Dionysus, Hera, and Artemis are appropriate as the respective patrons of adult,
newly wed, and premarital females. Complex local traditions have dictated the
choice of one over another in the three festivals, but all are linked by the presence
of Dionysus, the "female Zeus."

Artemis and Other Bear Myths

There remains for our investigation one central feature of the Brauronian Arkteia in literary sources, namely the figure of the bear itself. Artemis' very name may well be derived from the same root as arktos, and the goddess would then naturally have close ties to that animal, even if it cannot be known whether the bear was originally a theriomorphic aspect of the goddess.[66] As mentioned earlier, the bear was considered very human in appearance and characteristics, and the beast therefore bridges the gap between the savage and the tame. Artemis' association with bears in several of her myths, namely Atalanta, Callisto, and Polyphonte, can help us to define more generally the significance of bears in those tales, and to understand better the bear's function in the myth and ritual of the Arkteia.

The Atalanta, Callisto, and Polyphonte myths also define Artemis' relation to her young female followers on the border between *parthenos* and *gunē*, savage and tame, human and divine. Artemis has been called a *Herrin der Draussen*, a border goddess whose domain was chiefly the frontier outside of the city, a spatial designation that corresponds to her social role as one who ushers *nymphai* or *parthenoi* into marriage. Artemis was also naturally averse to marriage or sexual contact generally for her devotees in myth. The first sex act is rejected as an act of violence and brutality, "the common terror of virgins" (*Palatine Anthology* 9.245), and "a struggle which resembles the hunt and warfare, a wounding which makes blood flow."[67] In the myths of Artemis, the bear can either reinforce a maiden's devotion, as in the case of Atalanta, or widen the gulf between the sexually indulgent maiden and the goddess, as in the cases of Callisto and Polyphonte.

As an infant, Atalanta is nourished by a bear before she pursues a career as huntress under Artemis' patronage. Later she breaks with the goddess when Melanion/Hippomenes, aided by Aphrodite, wins her in marriage as a prize for defeating her in a footrace. In Propertius' words,

> Milanion . . . saevitiam durae contudit Iasidos.
> . . . ergo velocem potuit domuisse puellam.
>
> (I.1.9–10, 15)

> Milanion . . . broke the savageness of the tough daughter
> of Iasus. . . . Therefore he was able to tame the swift girl.

As will be discussed at greater length in chapter 7, the extent of Atalanta's prenuptial *saevitia* is made clear from her myths, which include the killing of centaurs who try to rape her, and the execution of all the suitors prior to Melanion who fail to overtake her in the footrace:

Praemia veloci coniunx thalamique dabuntur,
mors pretium tardis. ea lex certaminis esto!
Illa quidem inmitis. . . .

$$\text{(Ovid, } Met. \text{ 10.571–73)}$$

[She proclaimed] "The prizes for the swift will be a wife and the
bed-chamber. For the slow the reward is death. Let this be the rule
of the contest!" Indeed she was pitiless. . . .

Once, while on a hunting expedition, the couple made love in a precinct of Zeus
and were changed into lions (presumably by Zeus).[68] Like the Arkteia girls, Atalanta
maintains her virginity zealously in devotion to Artemis. Her singular accomplishments, epitomized by her being first to wound the Calydonian boar, distinguish her
as a hunter, again like the girl *arktoi* who participate in a sacred hound hunt as part
of the Arkteia. The Atalanta myth in its various versions communicates literally
what the Arkteia does ritually, namely the progression of young girls from *parthenos*
to *gunē*, from savage to tame, from status as huntress to that of prey.

Atalanta's being reared by a bear and her unnatural strength during her maidenhood mark the girl as a quasi-bear, an *arktos* in the manner of the Brauronian
girls. After marrying, she and her spouse are transformed into lions, beasts prover-
bially forbidden to copulate.[69] Atalanta's associations with a she-bear more closely
unite her to the domain of Artemis. The union is severed by Melanion/Hippomenes
with the aid of apples from Aphrodite's sacred grove on Cyprus.[70] And the balance
is ultimately redressed by metamorphosis of the female into a wild animal, here with
the added irony that the transforming agent of *erōs* is denied to the female in her
final wild form. The pattern is clear from the other myths. The introduction of *erōs*
into the life of the devotee of Artemis is the catalyst for her transition to adulthood.
But with Atalanta the bear is the agent to usher her into the world of Artemis, not
the one to lead her astray from it. Yet the bear still serves as Artemis' agent of transformation between the savage and the civilized. And the female's teleology, both
in the myths under examination and in the Brauronian ritual, is to be fixed as an
image of a savage animal that has passed beyond its taming and back into an eternal status of the untamed.

Artemis' follower Callisto is transformed into a bear by Artemis after she is raped
by a disguised Zeus and Artemis discovers her pregnancy.[71] Or Callisto is shot by
Artemis since she did not protect her virginity.[72] Or Callisto is changed into a bear
by a jealous Hera when she learns of Zeus' affair.[73] Whoever the agent, the transformation into a bear follows Callisto's loss of virgin status and is thus a just punishment not so much because the bear is a symbol of complete separation with the
savage state, as the beast is a marginal creature representing in one form the attributes of both the savage and the human.

Polyphonte, also a devotee of Artemis, rejects Aphrodite, who drives her mad with passion for a bear.[74] The resulting children, Agrios and Oreios, are the epitome of savagery since they savagely kill any guests coming to the house. Polyphonte and her sons are eventually changed into birds of ill omen by Zeus. Polyphonte's association with a bear, like that of Callisto and the girl of the Brauron legend, results in a rupture with the domain of Artemis. Polyphonte's break is even more abrupt, since she literally flees the wilds for the safety of her domestic setting. Her unholy commingling with a bear marks the confusion of tame and wild elements: she, a human devoted to the wilds, rejects the all-taming Aphrodite, who causes her to be 'tamed' by the eros for a bear, a wild animal who transgresses the human sphere. And again, like Callisto and the Brauron girl, Polyphonte's legend results in the transformation of humans, in myth or ritual, into animals. The common thread is the account of a girl's transformation from the status of an untamed youth to that of a tamed woman marked by an encounter with the human-like bear, a transformation later redressed by the further transformation of the offending females into animals.

Running is a salient feature of the myths and cults of Artemis, wherein her followers race through the mountains and chase animals in the hunt. Arrigoni suggests that "[i]f therefore the Arkteia is regarded basically as a sort of domestication of a force uncontrolled and intensified by the Attic girl, the function of the ritual race was perhaps that of representing in the expressive freedom of action, of costume (and especially of nudity), and of the agonistic tension the moment of breaking loose and of the liberation of such a youthful force in view of the certainly more conforming and sedate status of adult women."[75] Running can stir devotees to a frenzy, or it may be the result of a madness sent by the gods.

Atalanta, whose epithet is "swift-footed" (*podorrōren*, Callimachus, *Hymn to Artemis* 215), races with Melanion/Hippomenes when she is made mad with love for the youth (ἐμάνη . . . ἐς βαθὺν ἅλατ' ἔρωτα, Theocr. 3.42.) Atalanta's running is, however, not the chase of the hunter, but the flight of the hunted. She is the maiden seeking perennial virginity like that of Artemis, (Cal., *H.Art.* 6) and avoiding the natural fate of being "tamed" as spouse. Polyphonte, though formerly a huntress, is chased by animals, is afraid, flees (δείσασα . . . φεύγουσα, Antoninus Liberalis 21.3), and takes refuge in her father's house. As noted earlier, Callisto, "huntress though she was, fled in fear before the hunters. She often hid when the beasts appeared, forgetting her own nature, and though a bear she shuddered when she caught sight of bears on the mountains" (Ov., *Met.* 2.492–94). Callisto, like Polyphonte, is chased by Artemis' wild beasts in Ovid's version.[76] Fleeing is also a motif in the Artemisian myth of Proetus, the king of Argos, and his three daughters, the Proetids. These maidens either showed disrespect for a xoanon of Hera or refused the mysteries of Dionysus, that is, in either case they insulted deities associated with adult females (Bacchylides, *Epinician* 11

[Maehler]; Hesiod and Acususilaus *ap*. Apollodorus 2.26–29; Paus. 2.18.4, 5.5.10, 8.18.8.). The Proetids were then driven mad and fled off wildly (lit., "untamed") through the mountains.[77] The girls therefore enter the realm of Artemis in the Arcadian mountains. Proetus achieved their return either (in Bacchylides) by the intervention of Artemis, or (in Apollodorus) by a contract with the soothsayer Melampus, who, with his brother, obtained two of the daughters in marriage along with two-thirds of Proetus' kingdom in the bargain. Again the ties with Artemis are severed by marriage. But the significant contribution of this "taming" myth of Artemis is that the girls are released from their madness at a shrine of Artemis *Hēmerē* or *Hēmerasia*, "the Tamer" at the stream Lysos, the "Releaser" (Cal., *H.Art*. 233–36; Paus. 8.18.8, cf. 2.18.4, 5.5.10; Polybius 4.18.9–10; Vitruvius 8.3.21).

The taming of the Proetids, and the consequent institutionalization of Artemis as "the Tamer," support our analysis of the Brauron myths in which "taming" is an important function of Artemis. This is especially echoed in the description of the bear in the sanctuary at Brauron as "tame" (ἄρκτος . . . ἡμερώθη, Schol. Aristoph., Lys. 645; ἡμερωθεῖσαν αὐτήν [sc., ἄρκτον], Suda, s.v. ἄρκτος).

Conclusions

The pattern in the myths of Artemis therefore describes the abandonment of the civilized, flight to the domain of the wild, followed by eventual taming, and, in some cases, reversion to or retention of the wild aspect even after the taming has been accomplished. The semihuman aspects of the bear make it an ideal symbol of Artemis' function in the rituals of Attica, namely as a figure on the margin between wildness/virginity and tameness/wifehood. The all-out sprinting depicted on the vases reinforces with a ritual the transitional aspect of the girls' initiation to womanhood. Specifically, it is the running of a chase and not a race. The analogy is to the hunt, not to the agonistic battle that is more suited to the imagery of male competition. The chase re-enacts the foundation myths of Brauron and Munichion. It combines the tension of quasi-sexual play with a dangerously half-tamed bear, a desperate flight from the very same beast in his half-wild aspect sympathetic to Artemis, and sacrificial commemoration of both aspects embodied in the individual girls who assume the identity of the bear.

Though the chase is not the basis for any conventional Greek athletic competition for men, as it is, for instance, in American football, I deliberately include the Arkteia ritual in the present discussion for several reasons. The chase of the Arkteia may possibly have been a contest in which the 'winner' is the girl playing a bear who is able to tag another girl (playing the 'girl' of the foundation myth). In this hypothetical game structure, the 'bear-girl,' if successful, would overcome the 'girl-girl' and thus win the contest for the patron Artemis; and perhaps if the 'bear-girl' cannot catch her 'prey,' another girl may take her place as 'bear.' Thus, each in turn takes on the identity of Artemis' sacred animal. Even if the chase was not strictly a competition based on a tag-game, but was a running ritual, it assumed the form of a 'pseudo-hunt,' an informal leisure activity for ancients and not strictly an athletic event, and it did have several elements in common with the Heraia in particular (age categories, running for a goal, prenuptial significance), all of which make it an important alternative female ritual held in lieu of the more conventional male competitions. Whether it was a competition or a ritual, it is clearly a rite of passage requiring a test of strength that helped inform female gender identity in ancient Attica.

Postscript

The article of Richard Hamilton, "Alcman and the Athenian Arkteia," *Hesperia* 58.4 (1989) 449–72 and plates 83–86, deserves some special comment, since it presents an unusual hypothesis that is at odds with this thesis, and with much previous scholarship, on the interpretation of the Brauron vase scenes. Hamilton catalogues most of the same "Arkteia" vases from Brauron, Munichion, the Athenian Agora, and the Herbert A. Cahn collection as I have catalogued in Appendix 6-1, with the following exceptions: his no. 1 is that same as his no. 7 more fully restored (= App.6-1, no. 6 here); I have not catalogued certain fragments that Hamilton has, since they seemed too fragmentary to be informative (his nos. 15, 20, 24, and 25); he omits my Appendix 6-1, nos. 11, 16 and 20 to 23 for reasons not clear, and he excludes my Appendix 6-1, no. 19 since it probably portrays a mythological scene (included here for its iconographic relevance). Hamilton's catalogue contains certain errors of detail, noted in my appendix 6-1, which would indicate that he did not have the opportunity to study the fragments firsthand but was relying on published photographs. Even so, Hamilton's three tables demonstrating the lack of consistent iconography of dress, hair styles, and activities of the girls on the *kratēriskoi* fragments remain generally valid. Hamilton argues (459–63) that the lack of consistent detail on the vases, and the difficulties in reconciling the testimonia and the vases suggest that the vases do not portray the rituals of the Arkteia, at least not its mystery rites proper. Hamilton concludes, after a comparison of the vases with the activities apparently described in Alcman's *Parthenia* poems, that the *kratēriskoi* reflect the typical private rituals of *parthenioi* more than they do the public penteteric festival of the Arkteia and its *mystērion* mentioned in the sources (471). But Hamilton does not offer any specific alternative female rituals with which we might identify these activities, nor does he choose to emphasize the striking generic similarities in the very categories of procession, sacrifice, contest (chase?), and chorus that may surround the mystery as part of the festival. Even if the *kratēriskoi* scenes do not present strictly regimented appearance in the participants, there is no reason to assume that ancient ritual demanded it in the way, for example, the Catholic Church does of its altar boys. This study shows how the testimonia, in particular those on the foundation myths of both Brauron and Munichion, may be reconciled with the activities of running on the vases in representing in ritual the initiation of girls to adulthood (against which, Hamilton, [1989] 459 and note 22). Hamilton objects to interpreting a rite of passage as a form of initiation (ibid. 459, note 20), but see M. Eliade, *Rites and Symbols of Initiation: The Mysteries of Birth and Rebirth* (New York: Harper, 1958, repr. 1965) 2, where initiation that effects transition from adolescence to adulthood is distinguished from rites for entering a secret society (including religious cults). Although the Arkteia ritual is a *mystērion*, it does not in itself constitute a "mystery religion," and there is not necessarily a stringent prohibition against showing some of the activities. It cannot be known whether the activities shown on the *kratēriskoi* are part of a "cannon" or core of the mystery in which the *krokōtos* was worn. In fact, the absence on the published vases of any robe that might be called a *krokōtos* suggests that this unique part of the ritual was kept secret. But the absence of the *krokōtos* itself does not mean that the other activities shown were not associated, even very integrally, with the rites of the Arkteia. Indeed, the similarity of the vases at diverse sites and their provenances from Brauron, Munichion, and the vicinity of Artemis' shrines in the Agora and on the Acropolis argue that they all were associated with an Arkteia prescribing similar if not identical rituals. To posit some unknown private rites instead, as Hamilton does, is to strain credulity. For a more detailed critique of Hamilton, see C. Sourvinou-Inwood, "Ancient Rites and Modern Constructs: On the Brauronian Bears Again," *BICS* 37 (1990) 1–14.

APPENDIX 6.1: The Evidence of the Vases

The following list is an inventory and brief description of thirty-four *kratēriskoi* or fragments thereof, all those that, so far as I am aware, comprise the presently published corpus of vases or fragments representing girls running or performing other apparently ritual acts. The inventory serves as the basis for the discussion at the beginning of chapter 6. A complete publication of the Brauron pottery is highly desirable. I have studied in their museum cases in the Brauron Museum numbers 1, 2, 3, 5, 6, 8, 10, and 11; in the Piraeus Museum *apothēkē*, I closely examined numbers 25, 26, 28, 30, 31, 32, 33, and 34.

1. Brauron Museum 542, *kratēriskos* no. 4, from Brauron. First half of the fifth century (= Kahil [1965] pl. 7.2, 4, 6; Hamilton [1989 1] no. 4). A girl in a short chiton holding a wreath in front on one side runs to the right toward a palm tree; on the other side a similarly clad girl runs toward an altar on which a flame burns; in the field behind are two wreaths, one on each side of each runner. Both girls hold their arms extended in front of themselves and are looking forward. For other scenes

of running in the vicinity of an altar, see app. 6.1, nos. 4, 6, 16, 17, and 28 (cf. figs. 6-2 and 6-5). Hamilton incorrectly says that both girls "stand," and that a garland "hangs" in the background.

2. Brauron Museum 548, *kratēriskos* no. 2, from Brauron, vicinity of the classical house (= Kahil [1965] pl. 7.3; Hamilton [1989] no. 9). First half of the Fifth century. Three nude girls on each side (six total on the vase; Hamilton notes only three) run toward the right; nothing is in their hands. An altar with flames sits over one handle so that three girls run toward it, three away from it. The heads of the four girls which are preserved face forward.

3. Brauron Museum no. 546, Brauron *kratēriskos* no. 3 (A26), from Brauron, vicinity of the classical house (= Kahil [1965] pl. 7.5; *id.* [1983] fig. 15.7; Hamilton [1989] no. 3). First half of the fifth century. One nude girl on each side (two total on vase; Hamilton notes only one) runs to the right holding a burning torch. For runners with torches, see app. 6.1, nos. 7, 14, and 29 and figure 6-3. A fillet hangs in the background near each girl.

4. Brauron Museum *kratēriskos* fragment no. 5, from Brauron, near the small "Heroön of Iphigeneia" (= Kahil [1965] pl. 8.1; Hamilton [1989] no. 5). First half of the fifth century. A girl in a short chiton runs to the right at full-speed toward an altar with a flame on it. Her hand is extended before her. For other scenes of running in the vicinity of an altar, see app. 6.1, nos. 1, 16, 17, and 28 (cf. fig. 6-5).

5. [fig. 6-1] Brauron Museum 568, *kratēriskos* fragment no. 6, from Brauron, near the small "Heroön of Iphigeneia" (= Kahil [1965] pl. 8.2; Hamilton [1989] no. 6). First half of the fifth century. A very young girl in a short chiton (*exōmis*) and wearing a red fillet in her hair runs to the right at full speed. The *exōmis* is painted in very light, vertical black lines over the white body whose outline is visible underneath (no "white zigzag decoration" on her dress, as per Hamilton).

6. [fig. 6-2] Brauron Museum 567, *kratēriskos* fragment no. 7, from Brauron, near the small "Heroön of Iphigeneia" (= Kahil [1965] pl. 8.3; *id.* [1983] pl. 15.10 (with additional fragments restored); Hamilton [1989] no. 1 and 7 (!), incorrectly taken as two different fragments). First half of the fifth century. A girl in a short chiton runs to the right toward a palm tree; to her left is an altar with a palm tree; to the left of the altar is a second girl in similar, sprinting stride, looking behind her.

7. [fig. 6-3] Brauron Museum 915, *kratēriskos* fragment no. 8, from Brauron, near the small "Heroön of Iphigeneia" (= Kahil [1965] pl. 8.4; Hamilton [1989] no. 8). First half of the fifth century. A girl in a short chiton with striations runs (or dances) toward the right holding a lighted torch in her left hand and looking back behind her. The very low position of the leg in front suggests the slower motion of a dance, but a race is also possible. The style of this piece is very hurried and sketchy in comparison with other figures on *kratēriskoi*. Cf. a similar style at app. 6.1, nos. 9, 12, 14, 30, 31, and 33. For runners with torches, see app. 6.1, nos. 3, 14, and 29.

8. [fig. 6-4] Brauron Museum no. 572, Brauron *kratēriskos* fragment no. 9, from Brauron (= Kahil [1965] pl. 8.5; Hamilton [1989] no. 2). First half of the fifth century. Three girls in short chitons and wearing mid-length hair advance leftward toward an altar with a flame on top and, to the left of it, a figure (priestess?) in a long chiton. The girls seem to be walking or dancing in step with one another and holding their right palms extended, their left hands at their sides. They may be holding fillets, of which there seem to be faint traces. Cf. app. 6.1, no. 16 on face A for a similar scene of girls in short chitons before an altar.

9. Brauron Museum *kratēriskos* fragment no. 10, from Brauron (= Kahil [1965] pl. 8.6; Hamilton [1989] no. 10). First half of the fifth century. Two partially preserved girls in sleeveless chitons (not naked, as per Hamilton). One holds a wreath in her outstretched left hand; the other looks back at the first and holds her right arm bent (with her hand on her hip or with her arm simply bent at her side). Both girls are probably running in poses similar to those of app. 6.1, nos. 1, 7, 11, or 25 (also with wreaths). For other girls holding wreaths in this position, see app. 6.1, nos. 1, 12, 15, 18 (nude), 25 (nude), and 31, and figs. 6-6 and 6-8. For girls in similar, sleeveless chitons, see app. 6.1, nos. 1, 5, 6, 7, and 17.

10. Brauron Museum 570, *kratēriskos* fragment no. 11, from Brauron (= Kahil [1965] pl. 8.7; Hamilton [1989] no. 11). First half of the fifth century. Partially preserved figures of two women or girls, completely nude, dancing in matching steps toward the right, the left figure holds her left arm raised in front and her right arm dropped behind her, and the right figure has her right arm cocked at her side. Both seem to imitate running or slow jogging by the position of their arms, but, by their short strides, are certainly not running fast. They may be performing a simple dance, perhaps in imitation of the running maidens seen on other pieces. A fragment of the hand of a third girl may be seen just above the buttock of the left figure. If a dance is portrayed, the arm movements are not symmetrical.

11. Brauron Museum krater fragment no. A 56, from Brauron (= Kahil [1965] pl. 8.8; Kahil [1963] 25–26 and pl. 14.3). First half of the fifth century. An altar with a partially visible seated figure to the left (a man?), a garment visible behind the altar on the right (a suppliant or priestess?), a *kratēriskos* lying on its side, and a sprig of ivy or olive branch in front of the altar. On the *kratēriskos* image are depicted three figures in silhouette: the one on the conical stem appears to be a nude female running to the right, and, on the side of the vase, two nude female figures run or dance to the left. The left figure seems to look back and run from an altar, the right one looks forward and runs to the altar. Kahil (1965) 24 plausibly concludes from the scene that the *kratēriskoi* were ritual vases. Simon (1983) 83 suggests that the twig was used to sprinkle water from the vase; Kahil (1979) 80 also sees the branches as being used for aspersions.

12. Athens, Agora, *kratēriskos* fragment inv. no. 933, from the sanctuary of Artemis Aristoboule, near the Agora. Mid fifth century (= Kahil [1965] pl. 9.6;

Hamilton [1989] no. 26). Two women or girls in long chitons (hastily drawn for shorter ones?) run or dance to the right holding wreaths in front of their left hands. For other girls holding wreaths in this position, see app. 6.1, nos. 1, 9, 15, 18 (nude), 25 (nude), and 31, and figs. 6-6 and 6-8.

13. Athens, Agora P 128, *kratēriskos* fragment, from the vicinity of the Stoa of Zeus. First half of the fifth century (= Kahil [1965] pl. 9.7; *id.* [1981] pl. 62.7 [mislabeled P 14550]; Hamilton [1989] no. 29 [also mislabeled P14550]). Partial figure of a girl in a short chiton running to the right. Her arms are not preserved.

14. Athens, Agora, *kratēriskos* fragment inv. no. 934, from the sanctuary of Artemis Aristoboule, near the Agora. Mid fifth century (= Kahil [1965] pl. 9.10; *id.* [1981] pl. 62.8; Hamilton [1989] no. 27). Partially preserved figure of a chiton-clad girl, running (?) to the right with head turned back and left arm extended, holding a burning torch. For runners with torches, see app. 6.1, nos. 3, 7, and 29 and figure 6-3.

15. Athens, Agora P 14550, *kratēriskos* fragment, from the vicinity of the Stoa of Zeus. First half of the fifth century (= Kahil [1965] pl. 9.11; *id.* [1981] pl. 62.8 [mislabeled P 128]; Hamilton [1989] no. 28 [also mislabeled P 128]). Partial figure of a woman or girl in a long chiton stepping (in a dance?) to the right with her left hand extended back and holding a wreath. Cf. app. 6.1, no. 12, also in a chiton and holding a wreath. For other girls holding wreaths in this position, see app. 6.1, nos. 9, 12, 18 (nude), 25 (nude), and 31, and figs. 6-6 and 6-8.

16. Athens, National Museum 548 (C884) = J. Beazley, *Paralipomena*, 2nd ed. (Oxford: Clarendon, 1971) 292; black-figure Attic lekythos, attributed to the Bedlam Painter of Athens, but from Salamis (= Kahil [1965] pl. 10.6–7). Three girls in short chitons run to the right, away from an altar. Implausibly associated with the Olympian Heraia race by J. W. Kyle, "The Maiden's Race on an Attic Vase," *American Journal of Archaeology* 6 (1902) 53. For other scenes of running in the vicinity of an altar, see app. 6.1, nos. 1, 4, 17, and 28 (cf. fig. 6-5). The sleeves of these short chitons are very similar to those on the long chitons of app. 6.1, no. 26.

17. [fig. 6-5] A partially preserved, red-figure Attic krater or *kratēriskos* (I), Basel, Collection of Herbert A. Cahn, inv. no. HC 501, provenance unknown, from an Athenian workshop and of the Brauronian type, dated ca. 430–420 B.C. (= Kahil [1977] pl. 18; Hamilton [1989] no. 31; Reeder [1995] 322–25, cat. no. 98). Face A [fig. 6-5, fragments on upper and lower right] shows four young girls in short chitons positioned alternately between three older girls or young women in chitons and himatia. The young girls resemble those shown running on the Brauronian vases, but here the one on the far left seems to be preparing to run, and the other three actually beginning to run a course. The older females seem to be aiding in the preparations, (from left to right) one arranging a girl's chiton, or otherwise officiating, one holding (laurel?) tree branches, and one holding baskets, evidently as part of a ritual. The girls and two women to the far right stand

behind an altar, which also suggests a ritual context. Face B (fig. 6-5, fragment on lower left) shows four girls, possibly the same four as on face A and so in a narrative sequence, also in short chitons, in full stride running to the right. To their left is a palm tree. The girl on the farthest right is only partially preserved; the other three have one or both hands extended in front. Certain details argue that the two faces show two phases in narrative sequence: on each face the second girl from the left runs with both arms extended and with a fierce, scowling expression. The backward glance of the third girl from the left on face A suggests that she is fleeing from the fierce-looking one immediately behind her. The fierce girl, I would suggest, "plays the bear" in pursuit, while the others assume the ritual role of the mythical girl who fled the wild animal. Kahil (1979) 80–81 sees faces A and B as representing, respectively, "les preparatifs de la course sacrée des petits filles" and "la course elle-même" but does not comment on the possible bear imagery of the scenes. For other scenes of running in the vicinity of an altar, see app. (6-1) nos. 1, 4, 16, and 28.

18. [fig. 6-6] A partially preserved, red-figure krater or *kratēriskos* (II), Basel, Collection of Herbert A. Cahn, inv. no. HC 502, provenance unknown, from an Athenian workshop and of the Brauronian type, ca. 430–420 B.C. (= Kahil [1977] pl. 19; Hamilton [1989] no. 32; Reeder [1995] 324–29, cat. no. 99). Face A [fig. 6-6, fragments joined on upper left] shows five girls, all nude, running to the left with a palm tree on a rocky hill to the far right. The four girls in the lead appear to be larger and older than the one following behind them; two girls carry wreaths (as may the other three whose hands are not preserved). Face B [fig. 6-6, fragments joined on lower right] shows four girls, also all nude, and also all in full stride, but here running to the right. On the far left, as Kahil has plausibly reconstructed the fragments, is a palm tree [fig. 6-6, fragment on lower left] under which is a partially preserved animal, a bear to judge from its shape and ears. As on face A, the girls' hands are extended, and at least two hold wreaths. For other girls holding wreaths in this position, see app. 6.1, nos. 9, 12, 15, 25 (nude), and 31, and fig. 6-8. In the lower register of both faces A and B is a hunting scene with fours dogs chasing a fawn, suggesting the theme of flight and pursuit. The hunt is a mirror image of the scene on the body of the vase: "tame" hounds pursue a "wild" animal in the same manner in which a "wild" bear pursues the "tame" girls. Yet there is an inherent ambiguity in the motif of tameness and savagery of both scenes. The "tame" girls are in the natural state of nudity, as the bear of the Brauron myth is "tamed," and as bears generally have some human characteristics. The "tame" dogs follow their nature in attacking the fawn, which, though wild, evokes human sympathy for its fate. The Arkteia is called to *hieron kunēgesion*, "the holy hound-hunt," in the Hypothesis to Demosthenes 25. The iconography, *tout ensemble*, represents in scenes from the ritualized myth of the Arkteia and from daily life the natural state of balance between nature and the human world.

19. [fig. 6-7] A partially preserved, red-figure krater or *kratēriskos* (III), Basel, Collection of Herbert A. Cahn, inv. no. HC 503, provenance unknown, from an Athenian workshop and of the Brauronian type, ca. 420 B.C. (= Kahil [1977] pl. 20; Reeder [1995] 325–28, cat. no. 100). Face A [fig. 6-7, upper fragment] shows, left to right, Leto (?) veiled, Artemis with her bow stretched in front and wearing a short chiton, and Apollo, nude, holding a staff and a belt, and facing left back toward Artemis. Face B [fig. 6-7, lower two joined fragments] shows, left to right, a tree (curiously, *not* a palm), then a nude male figure with a bear's head or mask, next a female with half-raised arms and fingers spread apart, wearing a chiton and again having a bear's head or mask, and finally a doe or fawn prancing away to the right. The mythical scene on face A may be an analog to the scene with the bear-headed figures on face B, or the two may be linked in narrative. As analogs, the two may show a divine and a human form (with ritual officiants in bear masks) of the "sacred hunt" of Artemis. The hunting iconography would then complement the images on app. 6.1, no. 18 (fig. 6-6). Cole (1984) 241, Arrigoni (1985) 103 and Kahil (1977) 93 all construe the bear faces as masks on the priest and priestess of Artemis. Alternatively, Simon (1983) 87–88, followed by Hamilton (1989) 462–63, and by Reeder (1995) 328 has very convincingly argued that the bear-headed figures represent Callisto and her son Arcas, and that Artemis on face A is shooting not at the prancing animal on face B, but at Callisto in a state of metamorphosis. Furthermore, Ovid's version of the myth, which attributes the metamorphosis to Hera out of jealousy for Zeus' affair, would suggest that the veiled figure behind Artemis is Hera and not Leto, as Simon and other scholars have assumed; the bridal veil is a common attribute of Hera (cf. Simon [1983] 54 and figs. 43, 44, and 45). This interpretation of the scene as the slaying of Callisto is compelling in view of the smaller and younger body on the male figure, and in view of the look of consternation on the face of Callisto. The Callisto scene complements the Arkteia ritual, since in both the ursine image is associated with the transition from maidenhood to adult female. For Artemis with a quiver on another fragmentary vase from Brauron, see Lily G.-Kahil, "Quelques vases du sanctuaire d'Artemis à Brauron," *Antike Kunst*, suppl. 1 (1963) fig. 10.3 (= interior of a white ground kylix, Brauron A38, ca. 460–450 B.C.) and p. 9.

20. Athens, Acropolis 621 a, fragment of the upper part of a *kratēriskos* from the Acropolis. Ca. 510–500 B.C. (= Kahil [1981] pl. 62.1). A fawn bounds to the right (cf. face B of app. 6.1, no. 19) behind a female facing right and playing a double aulos (flute), and in front of her is another woman, of which only part of the chiton and right hand remain. The latter woman's pose suggests that she is dancing (cf. the similar position of the hand of the dancers at app. 6.1, no. 26).

21. Athens, Acropolis 621 c (face B of Acr. 621 a?), fragment of the upper part of a *kratēriskos* from the Acropolis. Ca. 510–500 B.C. (= Kahil [1981] pl. 62.2). On the left a siren with wings spread, preceded by a woman on the right playing a double aulos; traces of a seated woman (dancing or running) before the aulos player. The

siren, like the fawn of Acropolis 621 a, was probably above the double handle according to Kahil—showing parallels of composition in the two fragments.

22. Athens, Acropolis 621 d, fragment of the lower part of a *kratēriskos* from the Acropolis. Ca. 510–500 B.C. (= Kahil [1981] pl. 62.3). Lower part of a female figure in a himation, dancing or walking to the right, followed on the left by a second figure.

23. Athens, Acropolis 621 b, fragment of a *kratēriskos* from the Acropolis. Ca. 510–500 B.C. (= Kahil [1981] pl. 62.4). Altar with volutes and with burning firewood on top; a woman on the left pouring from an oinochoe wears a himation, and woman symmetrically opposite on the right wears a chiton. A *kanoun* or offering basket sitting on the ground is partly visible.

24. Athens, Agora P.27342, fragment of a *kratēriskos* from the area of the southeast Stoa. Ca. end of the fifth century (= Kahil [1981] pl. 62.9; R. R. Holloway, "Explorations of the Southeast Stoa in the Athenian Agora," *Hesperia* 35 (1966) pl. 27; Hamilton [1989] no. 30). Left to right, the fragment depicts the front legs of a doe, then two dancing girls wearing knee-length, sleeveless chitons, holding hands, with heads turned back to the left as they dance to the right.

25. [fig. 6-8] Piraeus Museum Kk55, fragment of the lip and body of a *kratēriskos*, from Munichion. First half of the fifth century (= Palaiokrassa [1983] 207–8 and pl. 52 a; = Sourvinou-Inwood [1988] pl. 5; Hamilton [1989] no. 23). One girl fully preserved in the center of the fragment and another to the right with only an arm and leg partially preserved run in full stride to the right. Each figures carries a wreath, the wholly preserved girl with it held in front with her left hand, the fragmentary figure holding it behind her. The central girl shows a breast in profile and her hair is tied back in a bun (cf. app. 6.1, nos. 4, 17, and 18 [the latter two = figs. 6-5 and 6-6] for other examples of the hair style in the Brauron vases). For other girls holding wreaths in this position, see app. nos. 9, 12, 15, 18 (nude), and 31, and fig. 6-6.

26. Piraeus Museum Kk3, fragment of the lip and body of a *kratēriskos*, from Munichion. First half of the fifth century (= Palaiokrassa [1983] 187–88 and pl. 44 g; Hamilton [1989] no. 12). A woman wearing a long chiton dances to the right as she looks back at another woman behind her of whom only the outstretched left arm is preserved. The hand of a third woman in front of the central dancer is also preserved. Compare app. 6.1, no. 16 for similar sleeves on shorter chitons.

27. Piraeus Museum Kk8, fragment of the body of a *kratēriskos*, from Munichion. First half of the fifth century (= Palaiokrassa [1983] 189 and pl. 45 b; Hamilton [1989] no. 13). Partially preserved altar with a woman standing to the right facing it (feet and bottom half of her long chiton preserved). Farther on the right, a woman (almost fully preserved) in a long chiton approaches the altar in what appears to be a dance step with arms in a position similar to the figures in app. 6.1, nos. 10 and 26. The feet of two other dancers are partly preserved on the left and right edges of the fragment. It appears, therefore, that the dancers approach

the altar from both sides while a stationary priestess at the altar officiates at a sacrifice, similar to the scene in app. 6.1, no. 23.

28. Piraeus Museum Kk9, fragment of the body of a *kratēriskos*, from Munichion. First half of the fifth century (= Palaiokrassa [1983] 189–90 and pl. 46 a; Hamilton [1989] no. 14). A girl in a short chiton with hem well above the knees (cf. app. 6.1, nos. 4, 5, and 6 [= figs. 6-1 and 6-2]) runs or dances to the right away from an altar and a palm tree (or a post?). The scene of running in the vicinity of an altar recalls app. 6.1, nos. 1, 4, 16, and 17 (cf. fig. 6-5).

29. Piraeus Museum Kk21, fragment of the lip and body of a *kratēriskos*, from Munichion. First half of the fifth century (= Palaiokrassa [1983] 195 and pl. 46 b [mislabeled 46 g]; Hamilton [1989] no. 18). Partially preserved figure of a girl's head and arm holding possibly a torch or castanets (*krotala*), running to the right. A wreath hangs in the background. For runners with torches, see app. 6.1, nos. 3, 7, and 14 and figure 6-3.

30. Piraeus Museum Kk18, fragment of the lip and body of a *kratēriskos*, from Munichion. First half of the fifth century (= Palaiokrassa [1983] 193–94 and pl. 46 d; Hamilton [1989] no. 17). Partially preserved figure of a girl's head and shoulders, shown frontally, wearing a chiton and fillets in her hair, which has two topknots or "buns" (possibly to resemble the bear's ears?). Cf. app. 6.1, no. 32 for a similar hair style.

31. Piraeus Museum Kk24, fragment of the lip and body of a *kratēriskos*, from Munichion. First half of the fifth century (= Palaiokrassa [1983] 196 and pl. 47 a; Hamilton [1989] no. 19). Torso, head, and right arm of a girl shown frontally, wearing a chiton with cross-hatched lines, and holding a wreath in her extended arm. For other girls holding wreaths in this position see app. 6.1, nos. 1, 9, 12, 15, 18 (nude), and 25 (nude), and figs. 6-6 and 6-8.

32. Piraeus Museum Kk17, four fragments of the lip and body of a *kratēriskos*, from Munichion. First half of the fifth century (= Palaiokrassa [1983] 193 and pl. 47 g; Hamilton [1989] no. 16). Part of an altar (on the left) and woman in a long chiton (on the right) running (or perhaps dancing) in full stride to the right as she looks back at the altar. The long chiton, absent in any other running scenes but seen in the dances on app. 6.1, nos. 20, 22 and 26 (a Munichian vase), suggests that the activity represented here is probably a dance. For comparison, see the scenes of running in the vicinity of an altar on app. 6.1, nos. 1, 4, 16, 17, and 28 (cf. fig. 6-5). Hamilton (1989) 454 argues that this is dancing, but the high kick and the backward glance also occur with running figures (kick: app. 6.1, no. 18; backward glance: app. 6.1, nos. 6 and 18).

33. Piraeus Museum Kk53, fragment of the body of a *kratēriskos*, from Munichion. First half of the fifth century (= Palaiokrassa [1983] pp. 206–7 and pl. 51 b; Hamilton [1989] no. 2). Torso arms and head of a girl in a chiton, shown frontally with arms stretched out left and right. Since the hands and legs are not preserved, it cannot be determined whether she is running, dancing, or stationary,

nor whether she holds anything in her hands. But in comparison with similar figures in stance and sketchy style, she may be running and may be holding a torch
or a wreath: cf. app. 6.1, nos. 7, 9, 12, and 16 (cf. fig. 6-2). Alternatively, she may
be dancing and holding hands with other girls, as in app. 6.1, no. 24.

34. Piraeus Museum Kk54, fragment of the body of a *kratēriskos*, from
Munichion. First half of the fifth century (= Palaiokrassa [1983] 207 and pl. 51 g;
Hamilton [1989] no. 22). Part of a long chiton and foot of a woman dancing (?):
cf. app. 6.1, nos. 22 and 26 for women dancing in long chitons with legs in a very
similar position.

7

ATALANTA AND ATHLETIC MYTHS OF GENDER

In view of the general exclusion of women as competitors, the legend of "swift-footed, noble Atalanta" as an indomitable athlete stands out as an exceptionally problematic narrative appearing early and often in Greek literature and art.[1] She was, in the Boeotian or central Greek version of the myth, daughter of a certain Schoeneus, who lived as a virgin huntress, despising sex but agreed to marry the suitor who defeated her in a footrace. Hippomenes (also called Meilanion) won her by the stratagem of throwing golden apples, supplied by Aphrodite, in her path to delay her as she stopped to collect them. The newlyweds make love in a sanctuary and are metamorphosed into lions by some divinity—Zeus, Cybele, or Artemis. In the Arcadian, or southern Greek version of the story, Atalanta is exposed as an infant, is suckled by a bear, becomes a man-hating huntress, and is ultimately won by Meilanion in a footrace.[2]

To these essential legends of the origin and end of Atalanta's life are attached several episodes in various versions. As a maiden living in the wilds, she encountered and killed two centaurs who tried to rape her. She takes part in the Calydonian boar hunt, where she represents her self well among an assemblage of the greatest heroes of the era. She joins another famous group adventure, the voyage of the Argonauts, and participates in the Funeral Games for Pelias, where she wrestles and defeats Peleus.

The ancient sources for these legends indicate that the stories were formed early in the literary tradition, and that they were very popular. Atalanta is mentioned by Hesiod writing about 700 B.C., and the three great fifth-century dramatists, Aeschylus, Sophocles, and Euripides, each wrote a play about some aspect of her story; unfortunately all of the above are preserved only in fragmentary lines. The fullest versions of her narrative are preserved only in the first- to second-century A.D. anthologists of Greek myth, Ovid, Hyginus, and Apollodorus, whose synthetic accounts must be read with caution for evidence of earlier Greek attitudes.

In Greek art, Atalanta's various episodes are related on vases dating from the early sixth century B.C. to the fourth century B.C., with some later representations by Roman artists. Clearly the Atalanta theme was of wide appeal to both literary and visual artists and to their public. But why would the legend of so exceptional a female who violated all norms of female behavior and all expectations of natural ability have been so popular? Was such a woman seen in any way as a role model? Was she seen as a threat to the status quo? And, most important for the present study, what does her legend tell us about the Greek view of women as athletes? To answer these questions, we must reconstruct Atalanta's legend in the context of its particular literary and artistic versions.

Atalanta in Literature

Hesiod, our earliest source, referred to the maiden's original aversion to men as follows:

> ... ποδώκης δῖ' Ἀταλάν[τη
> [Χαρί]των ἀμαρύγματ' ἔχο[υσα
> [πρὸς ἀνθρώπων ἀ]παναίνετο φῦλον ὁμιλ[εῖν
> ἀνδρῶν ἐλπομένη φεύγ]ειν γάμον ἀλφηστάων[
>   (fr. 73.2–5 Milne)

> ... swift-footed, noble Atalanta
> having the flashing steps of the Graces
> refused to associate with the tribe of humans
> expecting to flee a marriage with enterprising men.

And a poem ascribed to Theognis (sixth century?) adds:[3]

> ὡραίην περ ἐοῦσαν ἀναινομένην γάμον ἀνδρῶν
> φεύγειν ζωσαμένην. ἔργ' ἀτέλεστα τέλει
> ... φεύγουσ' ἱμερόεντα γάμον, χρυσῆς Ἀφροδίτης
> δῶρα· τέλος δ' ἔγνω καὶ μάλ' ἀναινομένη.
>   (12.2.1289–90, 93–94)

> ... beautiful though she was, she rejected the marriage of men
> and lived in flight from it. She accomplished deeds which went
>   unfulfilled
> ... in flight from a marriage which excites longing, golden Aphrodite's
> gift; but she knew the goal though she strongly rejected it.

These earliest sketches therefore emphasize her beauty, her charm that would cause men to feel desire for her, and her strong aversion to a marriage that in turn might arouse her own desire. The description of the men whom she fled as "enterprising" or "industrious" emphasizes her own distance from the normal civilizing activity of the polity and places her in the domain of nature and the wilds. Her self-inflicted isolation is at once an aversion to civilization and to all intercourse, literal or figurative, with males who are engaged in the daily commerce of civilized life. The point is made more bluntly in the later version of the mythographer Hyginus:

> Schoeneus Atalanta filiam uirginem formosissimam dicitur habuisse, quae uirtute sua cursu uiros superabat. ea petiit a patre ut se uirginem seruaret. (Hyg., *Fabula* 185)

> Schoeneus is said to have had a very beautiful daughter, the maiden Atalanta, who used to defeat men in the footrace because of her innate excellence. She asked of her father that she might remain unmarried.

She is therefore in the sphere of Artemis, goddess of the wilds, hunting, and the outdoors, and to some extent associated with the Amazons who are also renowned as hunters and as women who shun the company of men. Atalanta is therefore consistently portrayed in sixth- and fifth-century B.C. vase paintings as an Amazon figure in dress and with the characteristic bow; to a Greek eye, she is a 'foreigner,' the 'other.'[4] According to one legend illustrating her magical power over nature, she even produced water from a stone in the wilds of Arcadia by striking the rock with her javelin (Paus. 3.24.2). She can compete well in 'manly' activities, yet she is neither a man, nor in any sense a typical Greek female.

Atalanta's deeds, her adventures and accomplishments, were 'unfulfilled' in some sense. Although she knew the normal goal of female maturation in sex, "the gifts of Aphrodite," she nevertheless avoided it. By avoiding the goal, Greek *telos* that can mean "endpoint" of a race or "complete fulfillment," Atalanta assumes a position of ambiguous gender, avoiding normal female nature and adopting male behavior. She is described by the fifth c. A.D. author, Nonnus (*Dionysiaca* 35.82), as ἀντιάνειραν, which can either mean "a match for men" or "antimale"; the term is otherwise used exclusively of Amazons in Greek literature. Eustathius (*ad Iladem* vol. 2 p. 88, and vol. 4 p. 93, line 12) calls Atalanta "manly" (ἀνδρικὴν, ἀνδρεία). She is beyond normative gender categories until she is captured by Aphrodite.

Atalanta's position is very analogous to that of legendary Hippolytus and of Meilanion himself, with, of course, genders reversed, in her shunning the company of the opposite sex, complete aversion to marriage, and devotion to Artemis and hunting.[5] Xenophon's final words of his treatise *On Hunting with Hounds* (*Cynēgetica* 13.18) recalls Atalanta's special gifts from Artemis:

> For not only the men who have loved hunting have been good, but also
> the women to whom the goddess [Artemis] have given the skill,
> Atalanta . . . and others like her.

And earlier in that treatise, Xenophon presents an alternate version of the myth in which Meilanion wins Atalanta by his hunting skills:

> Meilanion was superior in his industry [in hunting] to such a degree
> that he alone of all those who were his rivals, the best men from among
> the greatest of that time, succeeded in wedding Atalanta. (*Cyn.* 1.7)

"Industry" (Latin *industria* = Greek *philoponia*) is also attributed to Meilanion by Atalanta's father, Schoeneus, as he willingly gives his daughter after the footrace in Hyginus' version of the tale. With a show of cleverness characteristic of the Greek male ephebe, the male's industry consists more of cleverness and contrasts with the superior physical strength of the female in this contest: his mental astuteness conquers her might.[6] But ephebes are not usually matched against females, and the youth's ruse and the girl's response simultaneously point up a reversal of the normal gender roles. Atalanta as a hunter demonstrates a complementary, broader quality of *aretē* (= Latin *virtus*), "excellence," generally prized in hunting, athletics, and warfare. Here the "excellence" by context must be taken to mean superior physical prowess. So Hyginus notes that the heroine was given the hide of the boar by Meleager "in view of her excellence" (*ob virtutem*) and overcame men in the footrace by her "excellence" (*virtute*). The male and female gender reversals have been observed in the historical contests and rituals studied in previous chapters; here they are underlined in legend.

The terms of the footrace for the bride also portray Atalanta as an avid hunter and a match for men in view of her physical strength. Unlike the scenario of most bride-contests, the bride herself is here the competitor. Still more striking is the penalty for the unsuccessful suitors who, in all accounts, are put to death. In Ovid's words, noted in chapter six,

> To the swift will be given the prizes of a wife and the bedchamber;
> death is the price for the slow. Let this be the rule of the contest.
>
> (*Metamorphoses* 10 571–72)

In Hyginus' account (*Fab.* 185) comes the gruesome detail that Atalanta followed her suitors with a spear with which she killed the many losers and put their heads on posts in the stadium! The footrace takes on the character of the hunt, in which Atalanta's skills were also supreme. Her athletic prowess literally enforces her celibacy by the murder of all who would subordinate her. Their desire is turned to death. By violently spearing her suitors, she avoids being penetrated by them sexually. In the end, only male trickery can overcome female strength, a complete reversal of the Greek norm.

Atalanta has, in the symbolic language of myth, received the gifts of Artemis but refused those of Aphrodite. The ancient Greek word for "sex" is *Aphrodisia*, literally "the things of Aphrodite." Like Hippolytus, Atalanta is "hated by Aphrodite," as Euripides' play *Atalanta* puts it (Κύπριδος δὲ μίσημ', *TGF* fr. 563 Nauck²). The lack of balance in both characters is put right when they are punished by the tricks of the offended goddess. In Atalanta's case, rejection of Aphrodite's gift of sex is followed by acceptance of her literal gifts, the golden apples used by Hippomenes to delay her in the footrace/marriage-contest. This is an essential element in Hesiod's original version:

> For the contest was not equal for both
> Swift-footed, brilliant Atalanta
> entered refusing the gifts [of Aphrodite],
> but for him the race was for life itself, either for her to be captured
> or to escape. Then he spoke to her devising treachery:
> "O daughter of Schoeneus, you with a relentless heart
> receive the splendid gifts of the goddess [golden Aphrodite]. . . ."
> Immediately like a Harpy she snatched [the apple] with delay to her feet
> and he let fall from his and to earth a second apple. . . .
> Then swift-footed, brilliant Atalanta held two apples.
> She was near the finish [*telos*]; he sent down a third to the ground.
> With it he escaped death and a dark fate.
> He stopped and caught his breath.
>
> (fr. 76.4–10, 17–19, 20–23 Milne)

Hesiod's narrative obviously echoes in part the famous Homeric scene of Achilles' chasing of Hector and thus implicitly compares the heroine with the greatest Achaean hero: "the two strove not for a sacrificial beast nor an ox-hide, which are the prizes for men in a footrace, but they ran for the life of horse-taming Hector" (*Il.* 22.158–60). The Achilles-Atalanta comparison is also implied in the epithets "swift-footed, brilliant" applied to the former by Homer and by Hesiod to the latter (ποδώκης δῖ' Ἀταλάντη). This implicit characterization contrasts the Achillean Atalanta all the more with the Paris-like Hippomenes.

The male opponent here employs deceit, more normally a female stratagem in Greek myth, to lure the female to the "gifts of Aphrodite." Apples, like fruit generally, are symbols of love, immortality, and victory in the language of myth; their goldenness only enhances their sensual appeal and their power to deceive.[7] Nonnus echoes Hesiod's account:

> It was such a contest for equals, as when Hippomenes
> rolling golden wedding gifts before the maiden,
> conquered Atalanta whom he pursued.
>
> (48.180–82)

The deception is perpetrated by Aphrodite not only on Atalanta, the beloved, but also on the lover, Hippomenes. So Theocritus (*Idyll* 3.40–42) notes:

> When Hippomenes wished to marry the maiden,
> How he knew, how he went mad, how he was taken to the depths of Eros!

Aphrodite controls the dynamics of the myth for the lover and beloved until her vengeance has been taken and the balance has been set right. The lovers, driven mad, then proceed to violate another taboo and have sex in a sanctuary. The divine patron of the sanctuary and the god who punishes the taboo vary in the tradition, but Nonnus names Artemis as the offended deity and the punisher:

> . . . καὶ γαμίην μετὰ νύσσαν ἀελλοπόδων Ὑμεναίων
> καὶ Παφίης μετὰ μῆλα λεοντείην ἔτι μορφὴν
> Ἄρτεμις οἰστρήσειεν ἀμειβομένην Ἀταλάντην.
> $$(12.87\text{–}89)$$

> . . . and beyond the finishing post of the Hymnaeal wedding gods driven
>   by the wind,
> after the apples of Paphian Aphrodite, into a leontine shape
> will Artemis transform Atalanta, goading her on.

"Goad" here is the Greek verb, *oistraō*, which is associated with female passion in particular (hence giving us the modern term "estrogen"). There is a poetic justice to this conclusion in which the tale comes full circle, with Artemis in turn offended by Atalanta's excess in the other direction, violating the domain of sexual purity.

Apollodorus and Hyginus, second century A.D. authors, assign the sanctuary and the punishment to Zeus, and Hyginus adds that they were changed into lions, "to which the gods deny the sexual act of Venus" (*quibus di concubitum Veneris denegant, Fab.* 185). Whichever deity punishes the couple in the end, the moral is clear. Balance and moderation (*sōphrosynē*) are needed in following the dictates of one's natural gender, and this rule holds true for both genders. Transgression in either direction results in the total denial of natural sexuality to the offenders.

The vacillation of Atalanta between the poles of Artemis and Aphrodite in earlier Greek sources undergoes an interesting transformation in Ovid's *Metamorphoses* (10.560–680). First Hippomenes is inflamed with desire (*concipit ignes*, 582) and is willing to face death even before he gets the help of Venus/Aphrodite (640–51). Atalanta then "wonders whether she prefers to conquer or be conquered" (*dubitat, superari an vincere malit*, 610). In love with the beautiful young Hippomenes even before the ruse of the apples, she hesitates to condemn him to death for daring to challenge her in a contest. Recognizing the dilemma of her position, she complains, *non culpa mea est* (629). "The universal dilemma of the woman (or man) in love: she must 'die' as an independent *puella* in order to become a wife."[8] The romanticizing Ovid projects into Atalanta's psyche the tension that had earlier been described as the external tension of two divinities, Aphrodite and Artemis, respectively representing the subordinated and the untamed aspects of womanhood.

Plato adds an interesting postscript to the Atalanta story. In his description of the afterlife and transmigration of various souls in his myth of Er at the end of the *Republic* (10.620b) occurs the following:

ἐν μέσοις δὲ λαχοῦσαν τὴν 'Αταλάντης ψυχήν, κατιδοῦσαν μεγάλας τιμὰς ἀθλητοῦ ἀνδρός, οὐ δύνασθαι παρελθεῖν, ἀλλὰ λαβεῖν.

In their midst is Atalanta's soul drawing its lot; it beholds the great honors of the male athlete, is not able to resist them, but accepts the lot.

She was, then, reborn as a male athlete in her next life. Plato's fictional reassignment has a double point. The philosopher had proposed that women receive the same athletic training as men in his ideal state, and so he would have little hesitation in the appropriateness of making a woman into an athlete.[9] But even more interesting for our present purpose is Plato's characterization of Atalanta as essentially an athlete in her soul; justice dictates that she should receive in her next life the "great honors of a male athlete" that were denied to her in her previous life. To Plato at least, Atalanta was, above and beyond all else, the quintessential athlete apart from consideration of her gender.

Atalanta's other exploits also reveal a tension between the heroine as powerful maiden and as object of erotic attraction; yet in none of these did she actually yield to her would-be lovers. The killing of the two centaurs who attempted to rape her shows her determination to resist the most forceful advances (Apollod; *Bib.* 3.106; Aelian, *Varia Historia* 13.1). In the Calydonian Boar Hunt, the maiden has proved her prowess by being first to wound the monstrous animal, and so:

. . . φασι τὸν Μελέαγρον περιγενόμενον τοῦ Οἰταίου συὸς τούτου καὶ ἀποδείραντα δοῦναι τὴν αὐτοῦ κεφαλὴν καὶ τὸ δέρμα τῇ ἐρωμένῃ 'Αταλάντῃ. (Eustath. *ad Il.* 2.802.4)[10]

. . . they say that Meleager, prevailing over this Oetaean boar and flaying it, gave its head and hide to his beloved, Atalanta.

The virtue of *aretē*, "excellence," displayed in hunting prowess is the same valiant warrior ideal as that prized in her later, more strictly "athletic" exploits. And like Hippomenes (Meilanion), Meleager falls in love with the maiden out of admiration for her beauty and her physical skill. The love interest, like that of Hippomenes, may be one-sided on Meleager's part. Intimations of love interest are depicted on several vase scenes, possibly influenced by her characterization in Euripides' *Meleager*.[11]

The heroine's wrestling match with Peleus, the episode closest to the setting of an actual ancient contest, is preserved in literary sources only with brief mentions in Apollodorus, Hyginus, Tzetzes, and Ibycus.[12] Yet the short shrift on this famous wrestling match is not evidence of the tale's late invention or earlier unpopularity. The early-sixth-century B.C. poet Stesichorus had an account, now lost, of *The Games for Pelias* in which the match would have figured, and the sixth-century Ibycus may also have mentioned the event.[13] And of even greater interest is the evidence of vase paintings.

Atalanta in Art: The Footrace

Atalanta is depicted as a wrestler on at least fourteen vases, mostly from the mid- to late-sixth century B.C.[14] Compare this with the paucity of Greek paintings, only three, portraying the famous footrace.[15] Why this discrepancy of visual and literary interest? The literary narrative of the race, as we have seen, can allow the legend to develop details of the tension between the realms of Artemis and Aphrodite, between wildness and civilization, between girlhood and maturity, between a free maiden and a subordinate woman. This is difficult to achieve in the synoptic vision of the vases, and somewhat awkward in two of the paintings that portray the race proper. One is much more effective in showing a gymnasium scene before the race.

A wedding vase from about 500 B.C. shows Atalanta running in an elaborate female costume and surrounded by three Erotes, with one behind her holding a victor's crown in one hand and a whip in the other to goad on the unwilling maiden (fig 7-1).[16] The artist has ignored the Amazonian iconography of previous hunting scenes and focused here not on the girl's athletics skill, but on her natural reluctance to marry. This is presumably to serve as an allegory for contemporary brides, apropos of the type of vase. The famously strong and skilled heroine has been made more acceptably feminine, in art as in myth, and even she eventually yielded to Eros. Another vase from 450 B.C. shows, from left to right, a female figure, perhaps Aphrodite, Victory, or "Palaestra" (Goddess of the Contest), with a ribbon to tie on the victor, a man with a hat and cape, Hippomenes, running right toward Atalanta, and to her right a bearded man, probably Atalanta's father, acting as judge (fig. 7-2).[17] Between the woman on the left and the running man are apples. Like the previous vase, Atalanta is in distinctively female dress, but here the Erotes are gone, and instead her father and a goddess remind the viewer of the result in which the girl will be make the transition from being a possession of her father to that of a husband, a process sanctioned by divine oversight. The focus has shifted from her erotic attractiveness during the race to her changed status afterwards.

The third and most effective depiction of the footrace motif, a calyx-krater from about 420 B.C., puts Atalanta in a stadium scene with Hippomenes and six other figures before the contest (fig. 7-3).[18] Trees and other vegetation make it clear that

Figure 7-1. Attributed to Douris, Athenian, 1st half 5th century B.C. *Atalanta Lekythos*. Painted white-ground terracotta, 500–490 B.C., H. 31.8 cm. © The Cleveland Museum of Art, 1999, Leonard C. Hanna, Jr., Fund, 1966.114; *CVA* Cleveland (1) Pl. 32–35. Courtesy of the Cleveland Museum of Art.

Figure 7-2. Attic red-figure hydria, ca. 450 B.C., Madrid, Mus. Arqueólogico Nac. 11130, from Cyreanaika; *CVA* Madrid (2) III ID Pl. 6.E. Courtesy of the Archivo Fotográfico, Museo Arqueológico Nacional, Madrid, Spain.

the scene is outdoors, and the start- and finishing-post (*terma*) indicates a race-course (*dromos*). On the left, Atalanta and an older man with an umpire's stick, presumably her father Schoeneus, stand near a washbasin (*loutērion*); on the right, Aphrodite near the *terma* hands an apple (?) to Eros (or accepts it from him), who holds two others, and faces a youth, Hippomenes, with a strigil. Three young men sitting in the background may represent other competitors, that is, suitors, or perhaps spectators. This rich scene encompasses many of the motifs associated with Atalanta. She is literally between her father at the basin and her future husband at the *terma*, the two male forces in the lives of Greek women, and her transition from one to the other, contrary to her will, is ensured by the divine powers of Eros and Aphrodite which conspire against her in the race. Unlike the other footrace depictions, Atalanta is here naked, except for sandals and an athletic cap, neither of which is normal apparel for a runner. The cap, more usual in combat sports and included in several of the Atalanta-Peleus scenes, seems to allude to her wrestling achievement.[19] Her athletic nudity is probably in imitation of male practice, as opposed to the short chitons of the Heraia and Spartan runners; it is less likely borrowed from the iconography of the naked girl runners at Brauron, all of whom are much younger. The graceful, contraposto stance with hands up to adjust the cap recall her pose in a wrestling scene of earlier date which will be discussed later (fig. 7-7).[20] The contrast of female grace and beauty with allusion to her wrestling prowess incorporates the contradictions inherent in the heroine.

Atalanta in Art: Wrestling

The more numerous vases with wrestling scenes, some fourteen from the sixth to fourth centuries, mostly do not reflect erotic overtones but are comparable to the early hunting vases with their concern for the 'foreign-ness' of a female participant in male activity.[21] The wrestling scenes also focus on the material prizes for the victor and the realistically 'athletic' aspects of the contest, as the footrace scenes do not. These vases uniformly depict Atalanta as more muscular than her male opponent, almost to the point of caricature.[22] In some scenes she has a short chiton skirt

Figure 7-3. Attic red-figure calyx-krater, Dinos Painter, ca. 420 B.C., Bologna, Museo Civico Archeologico 300; *CVA* Bologna (4) III I Pl. 86–87; Beazley, *ARV²* 1152.7. Courtesy of the Museo Civico Archeologico, Commune di Bologna.

Figure 7-4. Black-figure hydria, ca. 550 B.C., Adolfseck, Schloss Fasanerie 6; *CVA* Adolfseck, Schloss Fasanerie (1) 11 Pl. 10. Courtesy of Hessische Hausstiftung, Verwaltung Schloss Fasanerie, Eichenzell, Germany.

and top, as in this sixth-century vase showing a prize pot in the center (fig. 7-4).[23] But in many she wears only *perizōma* trunks allowing the artist to display her strong torso to full effect, as in this amphora from ca. 500 B.C. (fig. 7-5).[24] The *perizōma* also suggests the strangeness of Atalanta, since it is the garb typical of barbarians and long out of date, hence emphasizing her 'non-Greekness' and her antiquarian style. She is also quite muscular in this clay relief from about 460 B.C. of a presumably parodic scene in which Atalanta directly thrusts her knee into Peleus' groin (fig. 7-6).[25] In this unique variation on the motif, the viewer is, as in the footrace and hunt, again made aware of the gender differences, but the artist has comically given Atalanta a different kind of natural advantage over her male opponent.

Many of the wrestling scenes display the valuable prizes set between the two opponents locked in competition, and thus introduce as a focal point the realia of both legendary and contemporary athletic competition. True athletic contests were played for material rewards, which of course served as public monuments to the honor of the victor, the family, and the state.[26] Two shows tripods, reminiscent of Homeric contests and of the dedications found at Olympia.[27] In one wrestling scene on a 540 B.C. hydria, the hunt is even alluded to by the presence of the boar's head and hide as prizes between the two opponents.[28] The motif is echoed on an early-fifth-century scarab relief, again with the boar's head at the opponents' feet.[29] Do these scenes suggest that Atalanta has staked the chief emblems of her heroic honor as prizes to the man who can defeat her? Was there a variation on the tale in which

Figure 7-5. Black-figure neck amphora, ca. 500 B.C., Munich, Staatl. Antikensamml. VAS 1541; *CVA* Munich (9) 36 Pl. 28. Courtesy of the Staatliche Antikensammlungen und Glyptothek, Munich, Germany.

the prizes of the hunt were awarded (by Meleager?) during the later Games of Pelias? Or are the boar's head and hide meant to remind the viewers of her hunting prowess by a conflation of the two stories? The first two possibilities do not find any support in other extant evidence, literary or artistic. Most probably the hunting prize simply alludes to her other great success in the realms of male achievement.

Further athletic realism is achieved by showing umpires and spectators in a number of the wrestling scenes. Most noteworthy is a red-figure hydria of Psyax of 520–510 B.C. in which the umpire holding a stick and a club has been identified as Heracles.[30] This corresponds to Pausanias' account of the Games of Pelias on the Chest of Cypselus (5.17.9), in which Heracles is said to be sitting on a throne and presiding over the contests. Heracles was, of course, not only a famous patron of the gymnasium, but an accomplished wrestler in many of his major and minor labors.[31] His presence here as the supreme figure presiding over heroic male athletes reinforces the image that the heroine is competing in a normally male domain.

The results of the contest also have implications for our evaluation of Atalanta's role as a wrestler. Close analysis of the vase-painting scenes indicates that Atalanta is probably winning in some six depictions, Peleus possibly in four, and there is an apparently even match in four others.[32] This ambivalence over the outcome is also reflected in the literary sources for the contest: in Apollodorus Atalanta is the victor; in Hyginus, Peleus.[33] Who wins seems therefore to be less significant than the notion that such a match would ever take place. I can suggest two reasons for the

Figure 7-6. Clay relief, "Melian," fr. Attica, ca. 460–450 B.C., Berlin, Staatliche
Museen TC 8308. Courtesy of Antikensammlung, Staatliche Museen zu Berlin,
Preussischer Kulturbesitz, Berlin, Germany.

intense and wide popularity of the myth. First, it is for contemporaries an improbable scene, challenging all norms of female behavior and therefore arousing curiosity and controversy. Second, I would argue that a male-female match has more than a little prurient interest. "Imagine yourself in his or her position," it says to the viewer.

Even the costuming supports these two lines of interpretation by making the heroine appear either strange or seductive, or both. The short chiton was known from representations of Artemis, Amazons, and the exceptionally 'liberated' Spartan girls. All of these designate a status aberrant from normal Greek female behavior. One Roman statuette, which has been variously interpreted as either Atalanta or Artemis in her hunting garb, supports ancient and modern confusion of the two characters, and other representations in Amazonian dress reinforce that aspect of her identity.[34] With regard to her erotic iconography, Atalanta's revealing *perizōma* (loincloth) has been borrowed from the realm of the acrobatic girls who performed as entertainment at men's drinking parties, the sometimes bawdy symposia.[35] Or the loincloth may be seen on some sixth-century mirror handles from Sparta which allude to the scandalously scanty dress of the Spartan maidens, as discussed in chapter 5.

The most clearly erotic depiction of Atalanta is this fragmentary 440 B.C. vase showing a bearded spectator, labeled "Kleomolpos," watching Atalanta wearing athletic headgear, a *perizōma*, and a flaunty "breast-band" (*strophion*) with both breasts exposed, while a wrestler, misnamed as "Hippomenes," puts a hold on her; to the right a boxer, misnamed "Amycus," adjusts his gloves to the right; and on the far right a hand holds a hoplite helmet over a turning post (fig. 7-7).[36] There are obvious problems in the scene, which seems to be either an attempt to conflate various adventures of Atalanta or a genuine mix-up by the artist. Peleus is misnamed Hippomenes, the games of Pelias are confused with the Polydeuces-and-Amycus boxing match held by the Argonauts, and a hoplite race seems to be introduced into the bargain.[37] Amid this confusion of identities, however, the focus of the piece is on Atalanta, whose name alone among the preserved figures, unmistakable to artist and audience, is not inscribed. Her pose is that of a comely dancer in exotic costume with arms gracefully overhead, not the image of a competitive athlete. She looks serenely down at her opponent, who himself looks bemused rather than intense, his head almost buried in her bosom. The two flanking onlookers seem to grin as they watch him. The artist's error in labeling the wrestler "Hippomenes" is understandable since, in all known versions of the story, it is he and not Peleus with whom she becomes erotically involved. The transference of the love affair from the footrace to the wrestling match suggests that the chief interest of the (male) producers and consumers of these artifacts is in the parallel between erotic and athletic conquest in a mixed contest. A similar strain of interest is evident in the boar hunt, where her erotic involvement with Meleager is highlighted in both art and literature, at least after Euripides' treatment. In the Ferrara fragment, the muscular female of other wrestling scenes has become an alluring object of male desire.

Figure 7-7. Fragment of an Attic red-figure volute-krater, fr. Spina, ca. 440 B.C., Peleus Painter, Ferrara, Museo Archeologico Nazionale di Spina T.404; Beazley, *ARV²* 1039.9. Courtesy of the Ministerio per i Beni e le Attività Culturali, Sopraintendenza archeologica dell' Emilia Romagna, Italy.

The wrestling iconography of Atalanta, then, alludes at times to her hunting prowess, at times to an "otherness" strange to the male contests, and at times to her erotic attraction. All of these peculiar aspects are, however, firmly anchored in contexts that echo the realities of athletic competition in everyday Greek life—grappling before audience and umpire over valuable prizes. So the real is combined with the mythical, and in the mythical we find strong symbolism of the unresolved tensions at the heart of her myth—male strength in female beauty, strangeness and wildness in a participant in the civilized custom of athletic competition, and the erotic played against the athletic conquest. The ironies and oxymorons of the myth are what made the wrestling scenes so attractive a motif, and these same themes are also echoed in one final aspect of her visual record, the gymnasium scenes.

Atalanta in Art: The Gymnasium

The visual evidence of ten vases supplements the Atalanta myth with depictions of her in a gymnasium, all but one with a young male, Peleus or Hippomenes.[38] These scenes not found in any extant literary treatments of the myth, and may represent original attempts of the visual artists to conflate the Atalanta-as-athlete motif with popular but more mundane depictions of palaestra (or gymnasium) life.[39] The importance of the gymnasium rather than the public stadium is that it represented a more private space in which athletes, coaches, and older men lovers of athletes interacted freely.[40]

To understand the context of these Atalanta scenes, it is necessary to consider briefly an unusual group of four, fifth-century Attic vases on which several women are depicted bathing, apparently in gymnasia (fig. 7-8).[41] In all four scenes, several naked girls, apparently aged in their late teens, gather around a *loutērion* (wash basin); the presence of columns in three scenes suggests an indoor setting. Strigils and oil flasks in two of the scenes, and the Atalanta-type breast-band on one have been taken to indicate that the girls are bathing after some athletic exercise, scraping off the oil, sweat, and dust. One vase shows a variation on the all-female scenes: a young man has entered the scene and feels the breast of one girl bather who gestures resistance with one hand as another girl strides away (fig. 7-9).[42] This scene strongly suggests that the setting is not private, but public, where a male intruder would turn what is normally a serene portrait into a comic or surprising event.

These four scenes have been interpreted by Arrigoni as an Athenian depiction of Spartan girls. Bérard, on the other hand, sees them not as portraits of specific historical or mythic events, but illustrations of the ideal of female health and beauty in opposition to the male spirit of competition and rivalry. Thus, he argues, women are never shown in active competition, but only at the bath. We might add to the latter argument that, aside from the strigils, which are typically the cleaning instruments of male athletes, there are no javelins, discus-bags, picks, nor other accouterments that occur usually in the background of men's gymnasium scenes. Nor is the breast-band known from any portraits or descriptions of Spartan athletes.

There is, however, at least one other explanation for the scenes: they show the actual contemporary custom of females bathing, but we need make no assumption of 'athletic' exercise or competition that proceeded. First, the breast-band was primarily a common female undergarment without athletic use, and it

Figure 7-8. Red-figure column-krater, Painter of Tarquinia 707, ca. 450 B.C., from Cortona (formerly Raccolta Obizzi), Vienna, Kunsthistorisches Museum AS IV 2166. Courtesy of the Kunsthistorisches Museum, Vienna, Austria.

Figure 7-9. Red-figure stamnos, ca. 480 B.C., Siren Painter; private collection; formerly in the Nelson Bunker Hunt Collection. Photo courtesy of Sotheby's, New York.

may merely indicate a stage of dressing or undressing. Second, numerous strigils have been found in fourth- and third-century B.C. graves of females who were apparently *not* athletes, but who prized the implements as personal possessions.[43] The strigils come from many parts of the Greek and Greek-influenced Italian regions: mainland Greece, South Italy, Campania, Praeneste, Palestrina, and Etruria. The objects carried with them many positive connotations of status, but they seem also to be costly but useful tools for bathing even for nonathletes. If nonathletic females took up the use of strigils by the Hellenistic period, it seems probable that the custom began, perhaps in a limited way, in the Classical period. Since, on one vase, two girls wear earrings and one a necklace, we may surmise that these are daughters of the wealthy who used public baths and strigils either after some moderate exercise such as swimming, or simply as a regular means of bathing.[44] In Hellenistic times, fixed days were reserved at some gymnasia for women's use, not necessarily for athletic exercise but just for bathing.[45] Again, a Classical precedent might be expected. There are early fifth-century vases, similar to the four discussed here, showing women bathing at public basins or fountains, without strigils and without any athletic implements in sight.[46]

To these four vases, we can add three other pieces, relevant to the present context but unnoticed by commentators. A vase in the Louvre also makes explicit the erotic aspect of such scenes by depicting a naked woman washing at a basin and confronted by an Eros hovering opposite her.[47] A fifth-century oinochoe vase from Ferrara by the Brown-Egg Painter shows Eros approaching some women, one of whom holds a strigil.[48] This painter also has painted many scenes of athletes and youths, and again of Eros with youths or women; the present scene may combine both the athletic and Eros motifs. And a fourth-century Faliscan stamnos suggests that by that period the "woman-and-athlete" scene may have become generic, combining elements of the gymnasium basin scenes with those showing Atalanta and Peleus: a naked athlete holding up a strigil faces, over a basin, a woman in a peplos with one hand arranging her hair.[49]

Whatever the inspiration for these gymnasium scenes—Spartan girls' athletics, simple bathing without the presumption of exercise, or artistic licence to make a point—one point of Bérard remains true and significant: the depictions would have naturally evoked comparison with similar scenes of males bathing in the gymnasium. The comparison would not only heighten the awareness of the general absence of girls' athletics outside of Sparta, and the differences between male and female institutions for maturation in most Greek polities, but it would also arouse a kind of voyeuristic curiosity, an erotic desire, like that of the youth on the Siren Painter stamnos (fig. 7-9), to invade the female space.

The motifs of eroticism and 'otherness' of girls in a gymnasium or gymnasium-like setting thus return us to the consideration of the nine vases showing Atalanta and Peleus in the gymnasium. On strictly chronological grounds, it is possible that the bathing girl scenes inspired the Atalanta scenes; two of the bather vases, a column krater by the Göttingen Painter and a stamnos by the Siren Painter (fig. 7-9), respectively dated 500–490 and 480 B.C., are earlier than the earliest vases, from 475 to 450 B.C., showing Atalanta in a gymnasium setting.[50] Thus, the latter may have been an artistic attempt to combine two earlier themes of vase painting, Atalanta as an athlete and (actual?) girls bathing. Whatever the source of the scenes, the depiction of Atalanta in the gymnasium evokes the same motifs found in the two earlier themes.

One of the gymnasium scenes, a calyx-krater from Bologna depicting Atalanta before the race with Hippomenes, has already been discussed (fig. 7-3). It was observed in that context that the presence of the girl's father as well as Eros and Aphrodite made explicit the focus on her transition from daughter to wife. All of the other scenes of Atalanta in the gymnasium seem to represent her either before or after her wrestling match with Peleus at the funeral games for Pelias. On one, Atalanta (name inscribed), standing alone next to a *terma*, wears a loincloth, breast-band, and wrestler's cap and holds a pick to soften the wrestling floor; a strigil, sponge, and oil-flask hang on the wall (fig. 7-10).[51] The independent figure displays all the trappings of the male athlete, yet oddly wearing the feminine, deco-

Figure 7-10. Tondeau of a red-figure kylix, fr. Kerch, 475–450 B.C., The Euaion
Painter, Paris, Louvre CA 2259. © Musée du Louvre, Paris; permission and photo
courtesy of Musée du Louvre, Paris, France.

rated breast-band and trunks. The oxymoron of feminine and masculine elements,
evoking the unusual and the erotic, probably made the piece interesting to the
ancient audience. The juxtaposition of the heroine with the *terma*, an element of
the footrace but not important in wrestling, may allude to her ultimate defeat by
Hippomenes.

On all the another gymnasium scenes, she stands in the presence of her opponent, Peleus (or, on one, Hippomenes), often with a basin nearby, and with one of
the two antagonists standing, the other seated.[52] The inclusion of strigils, held by
Peleus, in some scenes where there are also basins suggests that the encounter occurs after the famous wrestling match. Yet the time of the meeting, before or after
the match, is left ambiguous in two other vases without basins, in which one of the
pair has a strigil, while the other holds a pick used to prepare the area for the contest (fig. 7-11).[53] The relation of the gymnasium scene to the actual competition
seems to be unimportant, since the focus is not on the antagonism, but on the apparently mutual attraction of the pair. Extant sources, all from the Roman period,
are silent on the topic of a love affair between Peleus and Atalanta, yet the vases

clearly suggest such a liaison. At least five and possibly six of the vases show the pair directly gazing at one another.[54] The fact that they are not touching suggests that the erotic attraction arose directly from the athletic one. We see the gaze of the moment at which Eros invades both.

On the only two gymnasium scenes on which Atalanta is clearly naked, Hippomenes or Peleus has his eyes fixed on her, but she looks away, seemingly self-absorbed (fig. 7-3).[55] Here he is the one stricken by Eros, most clearly in the Hippomenes scene on this krater where Eros and Aphrodite are present. There is one curious depiction of the scene on a bell-krater from Al Mina, unfortunately fragmentarily preserved, in which Eros again directly appears before Atalanta (fig. 7-12).[56] Only her head is preserved, and so she may be naked or dressed in female athletic garb. She is seated facing to the right and above, where Eros holds a mirror for her; to her left a naked young athlete (presumably Peleus) sits on the edge

Figure 7-11. Attic red-figure kylix, fr. Spina, ca. 475–450 B.C., Aberdeen Painter (tondeau with Peleus and Thetis), Ferrara, Museo Archeologico Nazionale T.991 inv. 1340 di Valle Trebba. Courtesy of the Ministerio per i Beni e le Attività Culturali, Sopraintendenza archeologica dell' Emilia Romagna, Italy.

of a basin with his body facing in her direction but his head turned back to the left, where a fellow young athlete holds a strigil and puts a hand on his shoulder. The scene appears to depict the tension in Peleus between his athletic and erotic desires, between the agonistic world of male competition and the amorous company of a female. The attraction of Atalanta may be increased because she embodies some elements of both the agonistic and the erotic worlds. She is in some senses an androgynous figure, with renowned female beauty and the proved physical prowess of a male.

The other scenes on the gymnasium vases also support the interpretation that the concern here is the combination of erotic with athletic themes. Exclusively male athletic scenes from everyday life are depicted on five or six of the vases.[57] An Eros scene on the other side of a calyx-krater from Locri Epizephyrii (note 53) suggests that the scene also has erotic overtones.[58] It does not matter so much whether Eros affects one or both of the opponents, nor whether the moment of desire comes before or after the competition. The main concern of the gymnasium scenes is to show that Eros is a strong presence in the peaceful setting in which the beauty of the athletes is displayed; the competitive fervor has been put aside in favor of the erotic; the external physical struggle is replaced by an inner turmoil. That in itself is not a unique aspect of gymnasium scenes generally in Greek art, as will be discussed in chapter 8. The wrestling specifically in which the pair will take part or have taken part is frequently used as a metaphor for erotic activity, as will also be discussed later. The scenes with Atalanta in a gymnasium are presumably of particular interest to the audience, since they differ from the ordinary depictions of male-male amorous interactions in the gymnasium.

Figure 7-12. Fragment of Attic red-figure bell-krater, ca. 400–390 B.C., fr. Al Mina, Oxford, Ashmolean Museum 1954.270. Courtesy of Ashmolean Museum, Oxford, U.K.

The visual versions of Atalanta's match with Peleus therefore differ markedly from those of the literary narrative. It may be that the gymnasium scenes in particular, which are generally later than the wrestling scenes and the footrace scenes proper and emphasize the amorous relation between Peleus and Atalanta, reflect a contamination or a confusion of the wrestling myth with the footrace story. There are no (extant) attempts to reconcile the relative chronology of the wrestling match with the footrace. The tradition of Hesiod, Theognis, and other authors, which characterizes Atalanta as one who flees unions with men until Hippomenes/ Meilanion catches her, seems to be at odds with these later scenes of desire between Peleus and Atalanta. Obviously, the marriage of Hippomenes with Atalanta and its unfortunate consequences form the oldest and most widespread version of her myth. Yet the wrestling-match liaison myth arises alongside it and survives despite any logical contradictions, as often is the case with Greek myths.[59] Both athletic-amorous encounters complement one another in showing that Atalanta was an anomaly, not strictly a role-model but one who proves that even the most male-like of females must ultimately be dominated by the male in the social order of marriage. The images were doubtlessly seen by male viewers as a validation of their natural dominance in the athletic domain and by females as a warning against challenging men or against rejecting their normal destiny in marriage.

About the reasons for chronology of the popularity of the Atalanta as athlete in literature and art, we can only speculate. We have seen in chapters 3 and 5 that the Spartan maidens had homoerotic relationships in the seventh century (cf. Alcman), but that the formal institution of the Spartan male, and likely female, *agōgē*, complete with athletic training, took place in the sixth century, the date of many of the bronze naked female athlete statuettes. Likewise in chapter 4 we saw that the girls' Heraia footrace at Olympia was probably instituted by the time of the sixth century, possibly inspired by the Spartan girls' activities. Hesiod ca. 700 B.C. and the sixth-century authors Stesichorus and possibly Ibycus and Theognis relate the legend of Atalanta as athlete. Vase paintings mainly from the mid-sixth century to the fifth century show a continuing fascination with the Atalanta story. Thus, we may posit one motivation behind the story's popularity, namely the opportunity for non-Spartan cities to show how Sparta's female-friendly training in athletics goes contrary to the normal gender ethos. Certainly the legend developed prior to the highpoint of the Spartan institutions, but the negative connotations subsequently attached to the Atalanta myth may have originated in the concern that such practices might catch on outside Sparta. The Heraia race itself may not have been a 'target' of this publicity against female athelticism, since that phenomenon did not infringe on the other more obviously male athletic events like wrestling, though its establishment may have aroused concern over creeping Spartanism. And in the end we can only hypothesize about the relationship of these contemporary cultural developments, absent any direct ancient commentary.

A major motif in all versions of Atalanta's athletic tales in both literature and art is the ambivalence or tension inherent in the very notion of a woman who combined the epitomes of female beauty with male strength and valor. Her tragic flaw, according to the narratives, was to resist her normative gender role and the expected natural yielding to "the gifts of Aphrodite"; her natural *telos* was in conflict with her will to adopt conventional male pursuits. It is only Plato, in his myth that allows her soul to be reborn in a male athlete, who can finally reconcile the two goals. Plato aside, and with the other exceptions noted in previous chapters, Greek athletics was normally restricted to the male domain, and in the one myth in which a mortal female intervenes in that sphere, the legend is shaped so that the heroine not only loses the contest in the end; she is even punished with loss of her humanity by transformation into a very unsexy beast.

8

EROS AND GREEK ATHLETICS

Cicero said that Greece had undertaken a great and bold plan, namely to have set up statues of Cupid and of deities of Love in the gymnasia.

Lactantius, *Divinae institutiones* 1.20

In Ionia and many other places where people live under the rule of the barbarians [pederasty] is considered base. This is shameful to the barbarians because of their tyrannical governments, as are also philosophy and the passion for athletics (philogymnasia). For, I suppose, it is not in the interests of the rulers that the subjects have high thoughts, nor strong bonds of friendship or society, which eros most especially above all these other practices is accustomed to create.

Plato, *Symposium* 182b–c

Until recently, conventional wisdom told us that sports and sex were disassociated, if not antithetical activities; but cultural experience says otherwise. Once I saw Mariel Hemingway in the men's locker room of the gymnasium at UCLA and was reminded of the Greek vase painting of Peleus gazing at Atalanta in a gymnasium. But our modern athletic heroine was surrounded by a movie crew as, some years ago, they were filming *Personal Best* (1982). A high point of the film was a passionate, lesbian love scene between Hemingway and another athlete after a bout of arm wrestling. About the same time, *North Dallas Forty* exposed, among other things, the sexual appetite of football players. The contemporary association of sports and sex is also reflected in the multi-million dollar endorsement contracts by attractive sports idols such as Dennis Rodman, Michael Jordan, Mia Hamm, and Picabo Street.

The erotic element of sports seems to have re-emerged during the last quarter century, not merely as a theme exploited by Hollywood and Madison Avenue, but as a social by-product of the more liberal sexual mores of the nineteen sixties and the narcissistic, mirror-gazing, aerobic body culture of more recent decades. Perhaps the realignment of traditional moral structures has encouraged the recognition of some primal association of sporting play with, on the one hand, private foreplay and, on the other, with an exhibitionistic display of the body in public. Exercise is associated with the newly coined "sexercise," or, according to the German pun, *Liebesübungen* (love-exercises) with *Leibesübungen* (physical exercises). Some medical studies have recently argued that the hostility in sports to the sexual activity of athletes is without clinical evidence, and social scientists have criticized the taboo as a product of capitalist repression.[1] In 1987 a survey of 999 top German athletes showed the overwhelming view that the no-sex rule was irrelevant or senseless, and that about 80 percent of them did not practice abstinence before competition. More recently, during the 2000 Olympic games in Sydney, newspapers reported that Ansell International, the official supplier of condoms for the games, announced a restocking of its product when the 50,000 items originally sent to the Olympic village had been seriously depleted to 20,000 only halfway through the events: "Ansell is mindful that demand for condoms goes up dramatically in the last few days as more and more athletes complete their events and pursue their athleticism off the field."[2]

Sexual mores are in the process of radical change in light of the spread of the HIV virus. Individuals exercise much greater caution and even abstinence in sexual relations. The announcement of the American basketball superstar, Magic Johnson, that he has tested HIV-positive after years of liberal sexual activity has had a profound effect on the American public's awareness of the high risk of all sexual activity, both homo- and heterosexual. It is not coincidental that it took a public announcement by a very popular athlete to convey this message. The general populace, particularly the young, identify with and respect sports heroes above other famous public figures like film stars and politicians. Hence, sports personalities who epitomize at least a physical ideal of excellence wield a great deal of informal power over public taste in behavior and appearance generally, including sexual attitudes in particular.[3]

Modern sporting events can arouse a variety of complex erotic responses in athletes and spectators. This is clearly part of the reason for the popularity of women's gymnastics and the late Florence (Flo-Jo) Griffith-Joyner's flashy uniforms during the Olympics, and for the tight style of pants on football and baseball players. Spectator responses may range from an animal aggressiveness to a subliminal tingle. For athletes themselves, some experts like Freud have considered sports to be a substitution for sex, while others see it as a positive stimulus to the sexual appetite. Freud theorized that sports are not so much a distraction of youth from sexual activity as they are a replacement for sexual pleasure; sports "push sexual activity back upon its autoerotic components."[4]

Baron Pierre Coubertin, the founder of the modern Olympics, wrote in a 1913 essay, "De la volupté sportive":

Yes, sport produces voluptuous sensation, that is to say, intense
physical pleasure. The man called upon to choose between the keen

pleasure which demeans him and the pleasure that exalts may well choose the second over the first. . . . Many sportsmen will swear that this pleasure reaches in certain circumstances the characteristics at once imperious and stirring of sexual passion. That these feelings are sensual is, in general, undeniable. It is infinitely probable that the animosity the Early Christians unleashed against athleticism was due precisely to the fleshy satisfaction which sport represented as well as that 'pride in life' pursued by sportsmen and denounced by the Holy Writ.[5]

We are not, however, in the throes of a renaissance of the classical Greek celebration of the athletic body. The modern European and American sporting phenomena alluded to here are complicated, to be sure, but they are at least partly tied to the revision of social strictures that are at least a century old; the ancient phenomenon, also complex, emerged from what I would argue was a more positive cultural milieu. Heroic excellence, or *aretē*, in Homer and other early authors may be defined as a primarily competitive, hierarchical, and selfish ethos.[6] Competition between cites in warfare and between citizens in the political arena was pursued to maintain the safety and increase the prosperity of the social unit. Physical beauty was considered an external manifestation of noble excellence. This sense of *aretē* was transmitted from the battlefield to the stadium and the gymnasium in classical Greece.[7] Ancient athletics, as it will be treated here, primarily concerns the "gymnic events," *ta gumnastika* in Greek, highly serious and sometimes violent events, mostly for individuals and not teams, in which winning for the sake of individual honor was the supreme goal—one even worth dying for.[8] Among other events were wrestling, boxing, the all-in pankration that combined boxing and wrestling, footraces, and the pentathlon (including the latter two events plus the long jump, and discus- and javelin-throwing). We will also be secondarily concerned with the other major aspect of Greek athletics, the "hippic events" (*ta hippika*), which are less ordinarily associated with Eros, presumably since those contests are not as expressive of an erotic spirit: drivers and riders are clothed and their physical beauty is rarely praised; owners are the victors; and the presence of horses and vehicles mitigates the spirit of a "man-to-man" struggle of gymnic events.

Eros and athletics comprised as vast and complex a set of topics in the ancient world as they do today, and my hope here is merely to suggest possible lines of intersection in ancient Greece.[9] Athletes become lovers; spectators are erotically attracted to athletes; and on the mythical and religious level, Eros the divinity is himself a habitué of the gymnasium. After some defining of terms,[10] the procedure here will be first to examine two fundamental aspects of the topic, namely athletic beauty (including nudity) and Eros the divinity with his athletic cults and festivals. A culture's standards of "beauty" are often linked to the objects of sexual desire sanctioned and encouraged in the popular view. In ancient Greece, athletics played a major role in establishing and transmitting these standards. Thus, the cults and festivals of Eros are historical manifestations of the association of desire with athletics. Along with these general cultural trends, some specific, related questions will be investigated, namely "infibulation" and self-control, and the erotic metaphor in myth, literature, and art. With regard to evidence used here to reconstruct ancient views of eros in the gymnasium, vase paintings and popular poetry, particularly certain lyric and dramatic poetry which we shall examine below, are possibly even better indicators of the popular ethos of ancient eros than are the pronouncements of the philosophers.[11] Paintings and poems were generally produced for the citizen male élite, but we can, with caution, correlate or cross-check a theme to establish its historical verisimilitude with some probability.

The following survey is approached topically rather than chronologically, though the conclusions suggest a chronological sketch of the relation of athletics to the erotic. The literary evidence for the topics includes sources mostly from the 500s B.C. to ca. A.D. 200, with a focus on events in the first three centuries of the tradition when the terms of the erotic element in athletics were established. The evidence of vase paintings and sculpture is also largely from the sixth to fourth centuries B.C., when the iconographic imagery of Greek athletics was most prolific. Certainly, within the centuries covered here and in different city-states, there were differences in athletic practices and in sexual mores which could have been highlighted in a strictly chronological study. This was done from one perspective, that of athletic *paideia* and pederasty, in chapter 3. But the purpose of this chapter is to point out several major interrelated topics that arise early in the erotic-athletic tradition and persist in more or less the same form throughout the history of ancient Greek culture. The weighting of this treatment to the three earliest centuries of the literary and visual sources is partly due to the richness of the source material itself in those periods, but, even more important, it locates the major features in the formation of attitudes and conventions that persisted over later centuries.

Defining Eros

First, some terminological considerations need to be addressed. I will in the ensuing discussion make reference to "homosexual" and "heterosexual" manifestations of *erōs*. Though these terms may be understood according to modern constructions of sexual orientation, there is a danger in their use since both are relatively modern designations and both carry with them a host of connotations not applicable to ancient sexual realities.[12] A full exposition of the various constructions of sexual orientation in antiquity is neither possible nor necessary at this point; many recent studies have illuminated various aspects of this topic. It may, however, be observed by way of brief preface that, in the sixth to mid fourth centuries in Athens and many other parts of Greece, many adult males pursued sexual relations both with women (including their wives and prostitutes) and with other males (including citizen boys and mostly noncitizen prostitutes).[13] Yet within this phenomenon of "bisexuality" (to risk using yet another anachronistic term), the relation of a lover to his beloved was constructed with different social norms and expectations according to the gender of the beloved. Thus, my distinction between hetero- and homosexual orientation is used in the present context in reference to corresponding ancient distinctions, and the reader is urged to abandon any presumptions attached to this terminology by modern conventions.[14] The investigation will, of course, not be limited to literary or artistic evidence, in which the name or image of "Eros," the god, appears in an athletic context, although these will certainly be a part of it. Rather, I have gathered any examples that came to my attention of "eros" in the sense of "desire," mostly obviously but not exclusively physical, in relation to Greek athletes and athletics. A broader discussion of the topic of "Desire in Greek Athletics," in chapter 9, explores some wider senses of "desire" in this context.

Eros itself, or himself, can be defined here with respect to three aspects of particular significance for the ancient athletic world, though admittedly the three overlap and a strictly philological distinction is at times unclear. First, Eros ("Ερως) was a divinity who, along with Hermes and Heracles, was among the most popular gods worshiped in the gymnasium.[15] A vase of about 420 B.C. from the Getty Museum shows on one side Eros offering a strigil to an athlete, that is, a suggestion to clean up and to reveal the healthy bloom of one's skin after exercising and before indulging in eros; on the other side, one athlete with a strigil seems to give advice to another who practices with the javelin, a sign of friendship that is associated with male eros (figs. 8-1a and 1b).[16] More on Eros the god later.

Second, eros, the concept of emotion designated by the lowercase Greek word (ἔρως), included hetero- and homosexual desire, which, in general Greek terminology, included both *pothos*, a longing for the absent, and *himeros*, an attraction to what is before one's eyes.[17] Conventionally among the Greeks, the "lover," *erastēs*, pursues the fleeing "beloved," *erōmenos*. Eros is therefore often a process of flight and pursuit, real or metaphorical, which is either satisfied by capture or frustrated by rejection or loss.[18] At times there was also competition among lovers for the affection of the beloved (e.g., Plato, *Charmides* 153d–154d). Eros is thus in accord with the ethos of *aretē* seen in terms of a conquest or display that often establishes a hierarchy in the relationship of individuals, rival suitors with one another or the successful lover with his beloved, each of whom seeks his own selfish aims. Friendship may or may not accompany eros, but the two lovers are not ordinarily of equal status, nor do they have equal claims upon one another, as in the modern ideal of love shared between couples.[19] Ancient Greek eros was hierarchical with the lover occupying a socially higher position than the beloved, and thus the phenomenon had an inherently agonistic aspect to it.[20]

Figure 8-1a and 1b. Attic red-figure kantharoid skyphos (handles in the form of
Heracles' knots), ca. 420 B.C., Aison (painter), The J. Paul Getty Museum, Los
Angeles 86.AE.269. Courtesy of The J. Paul Getty Museum, Los Angeles, California.

Third, there is a philosophical and abstract Eros that prescribes or defines proper
sexual or athletic activity according to a broader philosophical system. For example,
the Platonic image of eros, presented in the *Symposium*, the *Phaedrus*, the *Lysis*, and
elsewhere, is an abstract notion secondarily derived from a tradition that goes back
to Hesiod, whose divinity Eros is at once an abstraction and a real physical force of
attraction. This philosophical Eros may represent ideals that only indirectly reflect
contemporary, nonphilosophic conventions of erotic expression and of athletic practices. Here, too, caution must be exercised. It is, of course, a matter of great significance that the major philosophic schools of Plato, Aristotle, and the Cynics were located at gymnasia, the Academy, the Lyceum, and the Cynosarges, and the relation
of philosophy to athletics merits a separate study.[21] That a number of Plato's dialogues
took place in gymnasia is a natural reflection of this social context in which the ideal
of *mens sana in corpore sano*, or more accurately, "a beautiful mind in a beautiful body,"
was promulgated (e.g., Pl., *Char*. 1154d). There is a seemingly reliable tradition that

Plato himself had a career as a wrestler,[22] and so his dialogues yield many insights into the contemporary gymnasium and its social dynamic in particular.

Athletic Beauty, Athletic Nudity

One a priori association of athletics with Eros is the ideal of athletic beauty to which the Greeks adhered. From Homer on, the ancient Greek had a supreme appreciation for physical beauty combined with moral excellence, epitomized in the ideal of *kalokagathia*; thus the lowly Thersites in the *Iliad* is both ugly and morally repulsive (*Il.* 2.212–19).[23] The most fundamental Greek adjective for "beautiful," *kalos*, was used to designate anything that was socially sanctioned as excellent in form, substance, or spirit. There were, in fact, contests for beauty of the physical form per se, as well as contests of "manly beauty," *agōnes euandrias*, or "deportment," *euexia*, at several Greek festivals, notably at the Panathenaia and Theseia festivals in Athens, in which apparently not only bodily size and strength, but also mental and moral qualities and some demonstration of physical prowess were taken into account.[24] By considering outward appearance as well as performative competence, these contests thus extended the idea of contest to the contestant's cumulative inner and outer attributes.

One early text directly associating physical beauty with athletic prowess is an epigram (*Anthologia Graeca* 16.2) attributed to Simonides (b. ca. 556):

> When looking at Theognetus, the Olympic victor, know
> that as a boy he was the skilled 'chariot driver' of wrestling,
> most handsome to see, and no less impressive in the form of his athletic skill,
> (κάλλιστον μὲν ἰδεῖν, ἀθλεῖν δ' οὐ χείρονα μορφῆς)
> the one who crowned the city of his noble ancestors.

The victory by Theognetus of Aegina occurred in the 476 B.C. Olympics, and the above epigram was doubtless written for the inscription on the base of his victory statue. A statue of this victor was set up at Olympia (Paus. 6.9.1). It is noteworthy that the epigram praises the physique of the boy at the age of the beloved in a pederastic relationship, and that the physical beauty is directly matched by his 'form' in competition.

A gymnasium scene from about 510–500 B.C. reminds us of the prominence of gymnasia and supervised training from the sixth century onward; the inscription in the center, *Leagros kalos* (Leagros is good-looking), witnesses the appreciation of or attraction to physical beauty in the gymnasium context (fig. 8-2).[25] A poem of the *Greek Anthology* testifies to the erotic nature of *kalos* inscriptions commonly written on baths and city walls as a testimony to the attractiveness of the one whose name is inscribed:

Figure 8-2.   Red-figure calyx-krater, from Capua, ca. 510–500 B.C., Berlin, Staatliche Museen F 2180. Courtesy of Antikensammlung, Staatliche Museen zu Berlin, Preussischer Kulturbesitz, Berlin, Germany.

Philocles from Argos is beautiful in Argos, and Corinth's
inscribed pillars and the tombstones of Megara shout this fact.
How beautiful he is has been written even on the baths
at Amphiaraus. Just for a short time; we are missing the scratching.
For the stones are not witness to this, but Rhienos
who saw it himself, and he is better than the other sources. (Aratus,
  Greek Anth. 12.129)

The widespread use of *kalos* inscriptions on athletic vases is now supplemented by the recent and dramatic discovery of numerous graffiti, apparently by the athletes themselves, on the interior surface of the entrance tunnel of the fourth-century stadium at Nemea. The inscribed personal names are followed by the adjective "beautiful" or "handsome" (*kalos*), and we can only speculate whether they were exercises in self-praise, or expressions of admiration for fellow athletes. The latter view may be supported by a much-studied and humorous "metagraffito," where appended to the original "Akrotatos is handsome" follows the comment, "to the one who wrote this."[26] The graffiti of the Nemean entrance tunnel at least indicates a self-conscious awareness of athletic beauty, and it may even testify to a homoerotic attraction of athletes to one another literally at the competition site.

The *kalos*-graffiti is just one manifestation of the association of athletic nudity with beauty, and leads us to a broader consideration of the connection. The custom of athletic nudity, a unique feature of Greek culture, was an inherent part of the social nexus that fostered the association of athletics, male beauty, and sexuality.[27] One recent, intriguing suggestion for the significance of athletic nudity is that what began as a quasi-religious "habit" or ritual practice in imitation of Apollo-like *kouroi*, later took on civic meaning—

> the readiness to stand up and fight even though one knew one was vulnerable. It had to do with military valor which requires risking one's life, being fully exposed. . . . The relation of this manly nudity to the nudity of the gods is crucial: the gods could be nude because they relied on themselves.[28]

This notion, though it cannot be definitively proven, seems attractive and plausible at least as a partial explanation of the phenomenon. Whatever the validity of this view, nudity was an integral part of the athletic scene, and, whatever its origins, contributed to other facets of society like aesthetics and sexuality. As another scholar has remarked,

> The cult of nakedness and athletic prowess in the *gymnasion* and *palaistra*, the sexual exclusiveness of the *symposion*, and the emphasis on male courage in a society still largely organized for war must surely be connected with the rise of homosexual love among an aristocracy who invented a new compound to describe themselves, 'The beautiful and the good', (*kaloikagathoi*—'good' of course in the sense of well-born).[29]

The association of nudity with male valor in particular is illustrated by a passage in Plato's *Republic* (452a–457b), where the custom is logically extended to women who are to undergo gymnastic education similar to that of men.[30] Plato goes to some length to explain to his audience that although this proposal, and most especially the sight of women exercising in the nude alongside men in the gymnasium, may seem ridiculous, it is analogous to the adoption of male nudity:

> Not long ago, we shall remind them, the Hellenes were of the opinion, which is still generally received among the barbarians, that it was shameful and ridiculous [*aischra . . . kai geloia*] for men to be seen naked, and when the Cretans and then the Spartans began the custom of stripping for exercise, the wits of that day might equally have ridiculed that innovation: But no doubt when experience showed that to let all things be uncovered was far better than to cover them up, the ludicrous effect to the outward eye vanished before what reason had proved to be best, and the man was perceived to be a fool who directs the shafts of his ridicule at any other sight than that of folly and vice, or seriously inclines to weigh the beautiful by any other standard than that of the good. (452c–e, trans. Jowett, adapted)

Women, Plato goes on to argue, are in no way inferior to men in that aspect of their nature pertaining to administration of the state and so should enjoy the same gymnastic education. He then concludes with the exhortation:

> Then let the guardian women undress, for their virtue will be their robe,
> and let them share in the toils of war and the defense of their country,
> and let them not do other things; And as for the man who laughs at
> naked women, exercising their bodies for the best of motives in his
> laughter he is "plucking the fruit of unripe wisdom," and he himself is
> ignorant of what he is laughing at, or what he is about;—for that is,
> and ever will be, the best of sayings, "The useful is noble, and the
> hurtful is shameful." (*Rep.* 457a–b, trans. Jowett adapted)

The terms used to describe the Greek reaction to nudity before it became customary are "shameful and ridiculous" (*aischra . . . kai geloia*). And again in the final remarks, Plato expects that his suggestion of female athletics will be met with men's ridicule (*gelōn*). Laughter for the Greeks was primarily not friendly jesting, but a gesture of derision of a subordinate or hostile element of society.[31] Plato therefore attempts to defend his proposed social revision, and mostly the aspect of female nudity, by explaining the rationale behind women's gymnastics. Most important for us, however, nudity is seen as something that, when not sanctioned by established social custom, is subject to derisory scorn. This form of mocking ridicule is probably only just short of serious anger because the one laughing feels securely superior to the object of derision. As there was derision for men when nudity was first introduced, so there would be for women if the new scheme had ever been adopted (as it was not). According to Plato, then, there ought not to have been any distinction between the nudity of male or female athletes in Greek thought, *if* Greek society could have been convinced that females were, by nature, as worthy of gymnastic education as were males.

The Greeks were acutely aware that the custom of athletic nudity was unique to their culture and that it distinguished them from other Mediterranean peoples, at times to the extent that other nations ridiculed them.[32] Lucian, for example, puts in the mouth of the sixth-century Athenian statesman Solon a defense of athletic nudity against the criticisms of the Scythian Anacharsis:

> [E]xpecting to appear unclothed before so many people, [Greek athletes]
> try to attain good physical condition so that they may not be ashamed
> of themselves when they are stripped, and each makes himself as fit to
> win as he can. . . . But as things are, even from these contests they give
> you an opportunity to infer what they would be in war, defending
> countrymen, children, wives, and fanes with weapons and armor, when
> contending naked for parsley and apples they bring into it so much zeal

for victory. What would your feelings be if you should see quail-fights and cock-fights here among us, and no little interest taken in them? You would laugh, of course. . . . Yet this is not laughable, either; their souls are gradually penetrated by an appetite for dangers. . . . (Lucian *Anacharsis* 36–37, trans. R. S. Robinson [1979])

Other "barbarian" cultures that came into contact with the Greek, like Etruscans and Romans, had similar aversions to total nudity even in athletic contests copied from Greece.[33] This is most obviously illustrated in the "Perizoma Group" of stamnoi pots from the late sixth century B.C., which show athletes naked except for their *perizōmata*, "loincloths."[34] Long understood as depictions of Greek athletes who had not yet adopted the custom of nudity, these vase illustrations have now been convincingly interpreted as Greek pots produced for the Etruscan market, where there are other examples of athletes with belts or loincloths.[35] In short, the Greek custom of nudity was one to which specific values were attached, and it was not readily adopted in cultures that had otherwise imported and endorsed Greek athletic contests themselves.

One cannot posit a simple causal chain for complex phenomena in Greek society such as the association of athletic nudity with the ethos of the warrior-hero and with the conventional standard of beauty, but, at least for Athens after the sixth century B.C., the gymnasium and athletics were natural by-products of an élite class of warrior-nobles whose values and ideology, including sexual-orientation and ideals of beauty, were preserved and transmitted by those institutions.[36] This identification of the body with the individual citizen was so complete that the Greek word for "person" was also the word for "body," and hence Thucydides has Pericles in his Funeral Oration praise "the self-sufficient body/individual" maintained by the Athenian citizen for the sake of the state (2.41.1).[37] The political association gives an important insight to the Greek (or at least Athenian) connection of athletics, the body, and desire. In the same oration, Thucydides' Pericles speaks of the final "crown" and "prize" of the lives of the fallen warriors in terms of athletic metaphor, further supporting the image of citizen-as-athlete (2.46.1). And Pericles also exhorts his citizens to be "lovers" (ἐραστας) of the power of the city, again a figurative play on the literal role of the older male to his younger "beloved" frequently in gymnasium contexts.[38] The combination of these tropes in a speech idealizing the role of the Athenian male citizen illustrates a natural Greek train of thought, connecting athletic images with valor, the beauty of the physical body with that of the more abstract body politic. It is perhaps not accidental that Thucydides gives us the earliest testimonium on the origins of the practice of nudity in Greek athletics "shortly before his time" to illustrate how the Greeks progressed beyond and abandoned old customs still maintained by barbarians (1.6).[39] The omnipresence of athletic nudity served as a hallmark of Greek culture, and a symbolic display of civic self-sufficiency.[40]

For any society, ancient or modern, it is difficult to assess whether, how, and to what extent public appreciation of bodily form in contests was associated with erotic attraction. There are the noteworthy testimonia of ancient authors like Plutarch and Athenaeus, who mention boys' "erotic compulsion" (ἐρωτικαῖς ἀνάγκαις) to watch girls competing in athletic contests (Plut., *Lyc.* 15.1; Ath. 13.566e). Perhaps such notices arise out of attention to the prurient and exotic— the rare, public exhibition of girl athletes—and hence cannot be seen as typical. But these examples do testify to the at least potentially erotic nature of performances by young athletes. Further examples of eroticism in athletic contexts will confirm this impression in the discussion that follows.

One general question before us is whether widespread public approval of an ideal physical type—in Greece, notably the type of the young athlete—implies sexual desire for that type. A society's standards of beauty do imply a generally positive response to a physical form, but on a personal level the expression of the response may range from the intellectual admiration of proportion, musculature, and so on, to passionate sexual desire. The individual response to viewing a representation of the body beautiful may include a whole range of reactions, from seeing the one depicted as beloved, or as a lover, to imagining one's ideal self in the image. As one modern commentator has cautioned: "We tend to think of [the naked figure in art] as mostly erotic. Eros surely moves behind the sight of the naked human body, but its erotic significance is not the only one in art."[41]

Standards of beauty are, of course, fluid and subjective and may be manifest in numerous ways, from works of art and literary descriptions, to achetypical images alive in the popular imagination. Images can be evoked by the mere names of pulchritudinous heroes, heroines, and deities among the ancients: Heracles, Atlas, Adonis, Helen, Aphrodite. So also in contemporary ideals one thinks of the popular "stars": Schwarzenegger, Stallone, Monroe, and Madonna. And an entire class of those whose beauty is admired, all of the above included, are also conceived of as 'sex symbols.' Aesthetic admiration and sexual attraction cannot easily be separated, but the existence of certain widespread aesthetic ideals can indicate a culture's common approval of and attraction to bodily types.

The athletes of ancient Greece seem also to have conformed to physical types, which would imply aesthetic standards in operation for society generally. Philostratus described some of the types in his treatise *On Gymnastics* (31–40), and a recent study has shown that athletic sculpture of the Classical period conforms to these types in an almost mechanical way.[42] In general, however, it seems that the aesthetic admiration for the passive beauty of the beloved was less keen than the admiration for the beautiful body which was at the same time successful in competitive action. Thus the competitions that took into account the beauty of the competitors, the *euandria* and the like, were rare. Beauty was a highly desired and admired by-product of athletic pursuits, not an end in itself.

Eros in the Gymnasium: Laws and Liaisons

The quotation from Lactantius with which this chapter began (*Inst.* 120) indicates that the presence of Eros in the gymnasium, in spirit and in the material form of a statue, was a "great and bold plan" (*magnum . . . audaxque concilium*) of the Greeks which other peoples like the Romans viewed with a mixture of wonder and perplexity. "To me at any rate this custom [of pederasty] seems to have been born in the gymnasia of the Greeks," says Cicero himself, "where those loves are unrestricted and permitted (*isti liberi et concessi sunt amores*). Thus Ennius well commented 'It is the beginning of disgrace to bare bodies among citizens'" (*Tusculan Disputations* 4.70). The introductory quotation from Plato (*Symp.* 182b–c) suggests again that the devotion to eros, to the gymnasium, and to philosophy—not necessarily all together, though they could be found together—was considered unique to the Greeks, inspiring them to think "high thoughts" (*megala phronēmata*) inimical to the aims of tyranny. The ways in which the Greek plan was "bold" and its salutary effects upon the culture will be explored in this section.

A poem by Theognis of Megara, possibly from the early to mid-sixth century B.C., may provide the earliest explicit literary evidence associating eros with athletics:[43]

Ὄλβιος ὅστις ἐρῶν γυμνάζεται οἴκαδε ἐλθών
εὕδειν σὺν καλῶι παιδὶ πανημέριος.
(Theog., *Elegiae* 2.1335–36)

Happy is the lover who after spending time in the gymnasium goes home to sleep all day long with a beautiful young man.

The verb *gumnazetai*, meaning "spend time in the gymnasium" or possibly "practice gymnic competition," appears first here if a sixth-century date is correct.[44] This passage may also give the earliest clear indication that a special place in the community was established for athletic activity and that those athletes frequenting it were "naked" (*gumnos*). But even with the necessary doubt concerning the date of the above lines, we have much other circumstantial evidence suggesting a sixth-century date for the spread of nudity and pederasty in Greece. McDonnell's convincing recent argument for a date of about 650–600 B.C. for the gradual adoption of the custom of athletic nudity and other evidence for seventh- to sixth-century athletic pederasty (reviewed in ch. 3) suggest that both had become normative customs in Greek *poleis* by the mid sixth century.[45] Two generally accepted historical observations put this in the wider context of contemporary trends: the "social acceptance and artistic exploitation [of homosexual eros] had become widespread by the end of the seventh century B.C.," and the earliest gymnasia, consisting of simply delimited, open fields, became common in Greek cities during the sixth century.[46] When we add to these points the recognition that athletic nudity was becoming the norm at about the same time, we see a likely cooperative evolution between the gymnasium and the popular acceptance of pederasty. Gradually over time, the two institutions fostered the acceptance of one another, as a wealth of evidence attests.[47] The high value placed on an athletic type of physical beauty and nudity contributed to the establishment of gymnnasia and the sanctioning of homosexuality among athletes, at least from the sixth century onward.

Some ancient sources gives a clear and plausible (if not provable) response to the chicken-or-egg conundrum: pederasty took root as a consequence of the institution of gymnasia, explains a character in Plutarch's *Amatorius* in a mythological allegory:

> Like a late-born son, a bastard of some old man, and a child of the shadows, he [sc., Eros *paidikos*, "of boys"] tries to drive out his legitimate older brother, Eros. For it was only yesterday or the day before, after the undressing and stripping naked of the youths, that he entered the gymnasia, rubbing up against and putting his arm around others calmly during exercise. Then little by little he grew wings in the palaestrae and would no longer sit still, but he hurls abuse and throws mud at that brother, conjugal Eros. . . . (Plut., *Amat.* 751f–752a)

The character here does not fairly represent either early or general attitudes toward pederasty, but he does echo the view that common acceptance of the practice was an innovation that arose from the institution of gymnasia. He also reflects the notion, discussed earlier, that the practice of nudity was the most significant incentive for eros to be pursued in athletic contexts. "Rubbing up against" (*prosanatribomenos*) young men or "putting an arm around" (*prosagkalizomenos*) them are both double entendres playing on technical athletic terms and occur in both erotic and athletic contexts in artistic and literary depictions of the gymnasium (fig. 8-7).[48] The fact that one of the common titles for a trainer was *paidotribēs*, that is, "the one who rubs the boys" [with oil in preparation for exercise], suggests that gymnasium officials sought to keep the important practice of anointing literally in the hands of responsible professionals. Plutarch's allegory is of course not social history, but it does at least support the intuitive notion that athletic nudity and same-sex proximity will foster homosexuality. Another source also supports this view.

Solon, the famous lawgiver and chief archon at Athens in 594/3 B.C., is alleged to have instituted two pieces of moral legislation in Athens pertaining to homosexuality in the gymnasium.[49] The first prohibits slaves from activities of the gymnasium and from having freeborn boys as lovers:

> The law prohibits a slave from frequenting the gymnasium [*gumnazesthai*] and from anointing himself in the palaestrae . . . [and it prohibits] a slave from loving or following a freeborn boy on the penalty

of being given fifty lashes with a whip. (Solon, fr. 74e Ruschenbusch, *ap.* Aeschin. 1.138–39 [*In Tim.*])[50]

Slaves were thus forbidden from doing what normal free citizens were encouraged to do. The concurrence of sources, all fourth century b.c. or later, can be taken as an indication that some regulation of this sort was proposed and instituted by Solon ca. 580 b.c., and that homosexual eros in gymnasia was a reality in early-sixth-century Athens. Plutarch comments on Solon's alleged love affair with the young Peisistratus and the law against slaves in gymnasia as examples of the importance of pederasty in the legislator's social program:

> That Solon was not proof against beauty in a youth . . . may be inferred
> from his poems. He also wrote a law forbidding a slave to practice
> gymnastics or to have a boy lover, thus putting it in the category of
> honorable and dignified practices, and in a way inciting the worthy to
> that which he forbade to the unworthy. (Plut., *Sol.* 1.4)

So it is clear that Solon was responsible for institutionalizing pederasty to some extent at Athens in the early sixth century. He notably did not attempt to set up obligatory pederasty or kidnapping of boys by lovers, as may have been the case at some places in early Crete; nor did he adopt the 'herds' of boys as in Crete and Sparta of his day. Pederasty no doubt existed at Athens in less formalized contexts, and he maintained it as a freer practice associated, inter alia, with gymnasia and symposia. We cannot say for certain whether Solon himself or some aristocratic group of his day first introduced public or private gymnasia with nude athletic training to Athens.[51] In any case, the date of Solon's pederastic regulations corresponds neatly to our earlier hypothesis that athletic nudity and pederasty began to see more widespread acceptance by about 600 b.c.

A second "Solonian" law, this probably dating to the late fifth century, prescribes hours for opening and closing schools and palaestrae to discourage homosexual liaisons from taking place there in the dark or without the presence of the proper supervisors:

> . . . [Solon] forbade teachers from opening schools and *paidotribai* [pl. of
> *paidotribēs*] from opening the palaestrae before sunrise, and he ordered
> that they shut them before sunset, holding the deserted and dark places
> in very great suspicion. (Aeschin. 1.10 [*In Tim.*])

The law then states ages and qualifications for *neaniskoi*, bridging the categories of the older young men (*paides*) or younger adults (*neoi*), possibly anywhere between 18 and 30 years of age, according to various sources.[52] It later calls for the exclusion of males from the Hermaia (Contests of Hermes), or else the head of the gymnasium would be subject to the law concerning corruption of youth; anyone older than the boys, other than relatives of the teacher, caught entering the palaestra will be punished with death (Aeschin. 1.12 [*In Tim.*]). The restrictions on attendance at the Hermaia are enlightening, since they imply that the games themselves, and not just the gymnasia, furnished real opportunities for men to "pick up" a young beloved. Though these last aspects of the law (and chapter 12 of the speech generally) have rightly been judged as unauthentic in view of anachronisms and errors,[53] the earlier parts concerning opening and closing times and age regulations appear to be authentically Solonian. Solon's laws thus seem to reflect an early concern about the gymnasia becoming the site of illicit trysts, for example, between slaves and freeborn youths, which could not be openly observed by supervisors.

A similar law from the mid-second century B.C. was found inscribed on a stele in Beroea, Macedonia, listing those prohibited from entering the gymnasium, including slaves, freedmen, the infirm (?; *apalaistroi*, a word otherwise unknown), male prostitutes (*hetaireukotes*), peddlers, drunkards, and lunatics.[54] As in Solon's gymnasium laws, only the undesirables who might exercise a bad influence on the citizen youth are excluded, and there is even a similar clause wherein the *neaniskoi* were forbidden to speak with the junior youths, the *paides*.[55] The fundamental distinction in Greek homosexual orientation was one of active versus passive partner, and the active were customarily the adults (*neoi* or older), the passive the *paides*. One recent commentator observes:

> Consequently the Greeks considered that young men in this period of their lives (the *neaniskoi*) were people in an uncertain and ambivalent state, at the same time *paides* and *neoi*, and thus simultaneously irresponsible and reasonable, and in the sexual field simultaneously passive and active. All this meant, obviously, that they could not make good lovers. The law recognized and, so to speak, codified their status, taking care to prevent them seducing their younger companions.[56]

The Solonian regulation of opening and closing hours for the gymnasium or palaestra may also show concern over the possibility of the trainer's sexual harassment of his young charges. A Hellenistic epigram tells the following joke on the same theme:

> I dined yesterday with the boys' trainer, Demetrius,
> the luckiest of all men by far.
> One boy was in his lap, one over his shoulder,
> one brought his food, another gave him to drink.
> A notable quartet. I joked with him saying:
> "My dearest friend, even at night you act like the boys' trainer."
> (*Greek Anth.* 12.34 [Automedon])

This witticism is admittedly late, from the first century A.D., but it indicates a danger of unprofessional behavior, which had been and continued to be a concern in gymnasia for centuries. So the character of "Right Argument" in Aristophanes' *Clouds* recalls the proper behavior of boys in former times in the gymnasium:

> When sitting before the trainer, the boys had to keep their legs
> together in front so as not to display anything cruelly to those outside.
> Then when the boy stood up, he had to smooth the sand over and
>   remember
> not to leave an impression of his youth for would-be lovers.
>
> (Aristroph., *Cl.* 973–76)

The trainer is not specifically named as an admirer here, but the mention of him in this context suggests that he of all was in the best position to be aroused by the attributes of the boys. Two other epigrams by Strato of the second century A.D. also illustrate the theme. In one the trainer, apparently a type of voyeur, tells one boy how to take on the active role of a lover and thinly veils his advice as wrestling instructions:

> [DIOPHANTES, THE INSTRUCTOR]: If you go at this boy, grab his waist and bend him over. Get it on and fall on him, pushing forwards and hold him tight.
>
> [BOY AS ACTIVE PARTNER]: You've lost your sense, Diophantes. I can hardly execute these tactics. Boys' wrestling is something different.
>
> [DIOPHANTES TO CYRIS, THE PASSIVE BOY]: Let yourself be troubled and stay still, Kyris, and allow his attack. First let him learn to do it with cooperation before he does his own workouts. (*Greek Anth.* 12. 206 [Strato], trans. M. Poliakoff [1982]128)[57]

Whether this is real evidence for a trainer abusing his authority or simply a parody combining stock athletic exercises with sex education is uncertain. The erotic premise according to which the trainer acts, and the notion of "initiation" of two boys into the world of active and passive sexual roles is of interest, even if it is an artistic fiction. It suggests that these notions of the erotic trainer and the athletic-erotic initiation were near enough to reality to constitute an effectively comic situation. In another epigram, Strato tells of a trainer who himself pins the boy in an amorous wrestling grip:

> A trainer once, while giving a smooth-skinned boy preliminary lessons, opportunely bent him to the knees and gave the boy's middle a workout, caressing his nuts with his hand. But by chance the head of the

household came in, in need of the boy. The trainer quickly tied his legs
around the boy and leaned him backwards, clamping his throat with
his arm. But the master of the house was not unacquainted with
wrestling and cried out: "Stop," he said, "you're snagging the boy."
(*Greek Anth.* 12.222 [Strato], trans. Poliakoff [1982] 129)[58]

The setting here seems to be not a palaestra but a private house, and the instructor
is thus privately hired by the "master of the house" (*desposunos*) to instruct a youth
who has athletic potential. The boy may be the master's own son, a talented free-
born or even a slave—the vocabulary here is ambiguous. In any case the joke turns
on the illicit advances of the instructor, all the more risky in the house of the serious patron. The implication is that such assaults could and did occur from time to
time, violating a professional ethic of the *paidotribēs*.

The notion of a sexually aggressive trainer was later taken to the limits of heterosexual fantasy in Pseudo-Lucian's *The Ass*, where the maidservant, Palaestra,
"Wrestling School," acts as trainer to the main character, Lucius:

"You must put on an exhibition," she said, "the way I want it. I will
follow the rules of trainer and manager, and I'll call out the names of the
hold I want as I think of them. . . . " She stripped off her clothes and,
standing up stark naked, started her orders then and there. "Off with
them, my lad and rub on some of the scented oil from over there, then get
a grip on your opponent. With a snatch hold on my two thighs, drop me
on my back, then, from the on-top position, slip though my thighs. . . . "
([Lucian], *The Ass* 8–9)[59]

Wrestling is, for obvious physiological reasons, the favored metaphor for making
love in the literary sources, and the practice of this contest in the privacy of a special tutor makes it a natural topic for fiction with erotic themes. Nor was the metaphor absent from historical narrative, where we learn from Suetonius that the
emperor Domitian "possessed excessive lust and called his constant practice of sex
as a type of exercise, 'bed-wrestling' [*clinopalēn*]" (Suetonius, *Domitian* 22).

More often the public gymnasium was the setting for legitimate liaisons between those practicing athletics in the gymnasium, normally with the older man
of the pair seducing the younger. At times, the younger man may tease the older to
start a relationship, as in perhaps one of the most famous seductions related in
Plato's *Symposium*, where Alcibiades relates his attempt to seduce Socrates:

μετὰ ταῦτα συγγυμνάζεσθαι προυκαλούμην αὐτὸν καὶ
συνεγυμναζόμην, ὡς τι ἐνταῦθα περανῶν. συνεγυμνάζετο οὖν μοι
καὶ προσεπάλαιεν πολλάκις οὐδενὸς παρόντος· καὶ τί δεῖ λέγειν;
οὐδὲν γάρ μοι πλέον ἦν.

Afterward I challenged him to exercise with me in the gymnasium and I
exercised to accomplish something there. He therefore joined in with me
and wrestled often when there was no one present. What more can I
say? For I got nowhere farther with him. (Pl., *Symp.* 217.b–c)

Naked contact between a lover with his beloved under the excuse of wrestling is
obviously an opportunity for a suggestive advance, and he could claim that it was
accidental if it aroused resentment.[60] But Alcibiades, despite all his attempts at seduction, at times acting "for all the world as if I were a lover with designs on a boy"
(217 c), remained in the role of the passive, if unrequited, younger partner. There
is also here an aspect of education, or assistance to self-betterment, a kind of "initiation," which Alcibiades feels he could gain from having Socrates as his lover:
"Nothing is more important to me than to become the best man I can, and I don't
think anyone can assist me more in that than you" (218d). The athletic relationship between older and younger men, whether in competition or in simple conversation in the context of a gymnasium, normally had this aspect of instruction in
the ways of one's "elders and betters," and this, as I shall discuss further, is perhaps
the most important social function of eros in Greek athletics.

Plato's Socratic dialogues present several other examples of the gymnasium as
a place where erotic relations are commonly fostered. The *Lysis*, whose dramatic
setting in a newly erected, private palaestra in Athens, begins with Socrates asking
Hippothales about the people he will meet there:

—"First I should like to know what is expected of me and who is the
favorite beauty [*kalos*]."

—"Some of us seem to go for one," he said, "others for another,
Socrates."

—"Who is yours, Hippothales? Tell me this."

At this question he blushed, and I said: "Hippothales, son of
Hieronymus, you need not tell whether or not you are in love with
someone. For I know not only that you are in love, but even that you
are already smitten by eros.

. . . Upon entering, we found that the boys had just been sacrificing
and were already finished. . . . There were a circle of onlookers [at a dice
game]; among them was Lysis. He was standing with the other boys and
youths [*paisi te kai neaniskois*] crowned and outstanding in appearance,
not only worthy of praise for being beautiful [*kalos*] but because he was
both beautiful and noble [*kalos te k'agathos*]. (Pl., *Lysis* 204b, 206e–207a)

The casual atmosphere of the small, private palaestra is captured in this scene, as
is the erotic ambiance felt by all there, youths with a more formal program of reli-

gious and athletic activities, and the older males socializing at leisure. We might also note that the *paides* and *neaniskoi* are not rigorously separated here, perhaps because the facility is a private one and not subject to regulations like those of Solon. The scene is very similar to that in the dialogue *Charmides*, where Socrates, after a prolonged absence from the city, visits the palaestra of Taureas in Athens and asks about events there:

> . . . I, in turn, asked them about the current state of philosophy and
> about the young men [*neōn*], if any of them happened to be distin-
> guished in wisdom or in beauty or both. And when Critias looked at the
> door and saw some of the youths [*neaniskous*] entering and quarreling
> with one another and another crowd following behind, he said,
> "Concerning the beautiful ones [*kalōn*], you seem to me to see them
> entering. For those who are just entering are the precursors and the
> lovers of the one who is judged most beautiful in the present opinion,
> and he appears to me now to be not far off. (Pl., *Char.* 153d–154a)

Not only is the topic of the beauty of the boys apparently standard in gymnasia; there seems to be almost a local consensus about the most desirable beloved among them. The bitter argument of the youths as they enter is presumably over who is to be the lover of the most beautiful boy.[61] It is again noteworthy that in this palaestra there seems to be no rigid separation of *neaniskoi* from *paides*, perhaps again because it is not a "major" gymnasium under state supervision, like the Academy or Lyceum. Or it may be that Solon's law was only selectively enforced at certain places or times when an individual acted outside of what was deemed "proper."

Aristophanes, if we can read his view in a chorus, opines that his status as a poet does not require him to seek sexual favors in the gymnasium as a reward for his public success: "Formerly when I was doing well as I would have wished [sc., winning victories in the theater], not hanging around the palaestrae to try to pick up boys . . . " (Aristoph., *Peace* 762–63).[62] Aeschines (1.135 [*In Tim.*]), as one who did indulge in such activities, admitted an allegation that he made himself "a nui-sance in the gymnasia" and says "I have been erotically inclined [*erōtikos*] and re-main so."[63]

A number of erotic epigrams extol the seductive powers of athletics and the gymnasium, including an anonymous poem alluding to the custom of the victor's friend crowning him and adorning him with fillets[64]:

> When Menecharmus, Anticles' son, won the boxing match
> I crowned him with ten soft fillets,
> And thrice I kissed him all red with much blood,
> But the blood was sweeter to me than myrrh.
>
> (Greek Anth. 12.123 [Anonymous])

The tender sentiment conveys the bittersweet quality of much of Greek eros, the pain of the contest, and the passionate attraction of that very suffering to one spectator. A poem by Strato similarly extols the erotic powers of athletic sweat:

> I don't like excessive hair and ringlets,
> which are trained in the deeds of artifice, not nature.
> But I do take delight in the dusty filth of a boy in the palaestra,
> and the anointed skin of the flesh of his limbs.
> Pleasurable to me is an unadorned passion. The bewitching
> shape of a female is the work of Aphrodite.
> (Greek Anth. 12. 192 [Strato])

The opposition between artificial skill (*technē*) and nature (*physis*) is the point of this ode to athletic beauty. It seems that not just the product of a healthy body, but the process of toil itself became a source of pleasure for admirers of athletes.

Thus, the erotic attractions of the gymnasia are topical from the sixth century to the period of the Roman Empire, and local regulations, such as those of Athens and Beroea, hint at ongoing public interest in restricting various influences deemed as improper, though they in no way discourage sanctioned pederastic relations between citizen youths and adults. In short, both serious and comic literature testify to an at least 800-year-old tradition linking pederastic eros and the gymnasium from about 600 B.C. onward.

The Maiden at the Goal

While most of the above instances suggest that the gymnasium was the locus of athletic homoeroticism, other poems and anecdotes allude to the erotic attraction of athletes to women (or vice versa), a phenomenon that must have occurred ordinarily outside the precincts of gymnasia. Athenaeus' reference to boys wrestling girls in the palaestra on Chios may or may not have a basis in fact (13.566e):

> The Spartan custom, also, of stripping before strangers is highly praised.
> And on the island of Chios it is very pleasant to walk to the gymnasia
> and running tracks and watch the young men wrestle with the girls.
> (Ath. 13.566e)

We learn little of the purpose of the Chian practice from the symposiastic chatter of Athenaeus. Did it also serve as the standard training for local girls before marriage, as at Sparta? Or is it merely lascivious gossip about the notorious *vita Chiana*? If it did occur, it was an exception to the rule. Whatever the historicity or function of these contests, the mere report of them aroused heterosexual eros in men.

The other famous exception was the case of Sparta, discussed more fully in chapter 5, where, according to Plutarch, the famous Spartan lawgiver Lycurgus instituted public games with both girls and boys present for the expressed purposed of encouraging eroticism and marriage. The passage is nowhere better illustrated than by Degas's wonderful painting, "Young Spartans Exercising" (fig. 8-3):[65]

[Lycurgus] freed [the girls] from softness and delicacy and all effeminacy by accustoming the maidens no less than the young men to go naked in processions, and at certain festivals to dance and sing when young men were present as spectators. There [the girls] sometimes even made jokes and chided good-naturedly any youth who misbehaved himself; and again they sang the praises of those who had shown themselves worthy, and so inspire the young men with great ambition and ardor. For he who was thus extolled for his valor and held in honor among the maidens, went away exalted by their praises; while the bite of their playful chiding was no less sharp than that of serious admonitions, especially since the kings and elders, together with the rest of the citizens, were all present at the spectacle. Nor was the nudity of the maidens a shameful matter, for modesty was maintained, and bawdiness was absent. But rather it produced in them the habit of simplicity and an eagerness for a healthy and beautiful condition. It also gave to womankind a taste of noble sentiment, for there was for them no less of a share in both excellence and ambition. . . . Moreover, there were incentives to marriage—I mean such things as the processions of the maidens, their going without clothes, and athletic contests in sight of the young men, who were drawn on by feelings of constraint "not geometrical, but erotic," as Plato says. (Plut., *Lyc.* 14.2–15.1)

As is apparent from the adult Spartans with infants in the background of Degas' work, the object of the Spartan practice was to encourage by praise or blame eugenic procreation among the fit youth of the city. But the basic principle was that *anagkē*, the "necessity" or "compulsion" of the sex drive or "the constraints of desire," as Jack Winkler named it,[66] arose merely from watching the girls in processions and competitions. Plutarch's Lycurgus thus instituted the custom of public nudity and athletic contests for girls on special occasions. The same "constraints of desire" would presumably also result in the more normal situations of Greek athletic festivals in which nude male athletes performed in front of young females, to be discussed shortly.

Plato's proposal for coeducation in the *Republic* also includes physical education aimed at encouraging heterosexual relations:

As [male and female guardians] are mixed together both in athletic training and in the rest of their upbringing, they will be drawn by a

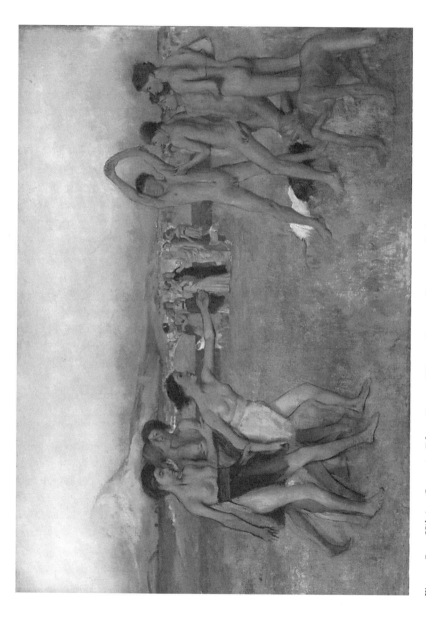

Figure 8-3. Hilaire-Germain-Edgar Degas. "*Young Spartans Exercising*," about 1860; oil on canvas. London. National Gallery. Degas NG3860. © National Gallery, London, U.K.

necessity of their nature to have intercourse with one another. Don't
you think I refer to something "necessary"?

A necessity, he said, not geometrical, but erotic that is very likely to
be keener in persuading and drawing on the majority of people. (Pl.,
Rep. 458d)

Plato's suggestion for physical education in common may be based upon the actual practice at Sparta, as Plutarch implies by alluding to this passage. Both speak
of the "sharpness" of the compulsion in the presence of the other sexes (Plut., *Lyc.*
14.3; , Pl., *Rep.* 458d6), a quality commonly associated with erotic passion.[67] Thus,
in Spartan practice and in Platonic theory, heterosexual attraction is viewed as
positive, a phenomenon to be encouraged, as homosexual relations were already
widely accepted as part of athletics and the gymnasium in the Greek world. Plato
says nothing to imply that female desire would be any weaker than male, unlike
Plutarch, who specifies that the male youths are the ones "drawn on by erotic necessity." Plato's view of mutual eros is thus more in accord with the general terminology of heterosexual relations in which male eros is answered by female *anterōs*,
"counter-love," a term more fully discussed later.

Apart from these exceptional cases in Sparta, Plato's ideal state, and possibly
Chios, a number of less formalized opportunities existed for male athletes to become
the objects of female desire, and for them to seek a female beloved, either at the public
games where citizen women were in attendance, or by means of normal liaisons
with female prostitutes or courtesans. There is much uncertainty about whether
both men and women attended any particular men's athletic festivals. It was a
strongly enforced custom of the men's Olympics that married women not attend
the festival; that is, they were not allowed into the sanctuary or stadium on actual
festival days (Paus. 5.6.7; Aelian, *De natura animalium* 5.17). And the footrace
founded by the legendary Amphissos in honor of his mother Dryope prohibited any
woman (*gunaiki*, referring to "married" women only?) from attending even in historical times (Antoninus Liberalis, *Metamorphōseōn sunagōgē* 32.5).

An ode of Pindar notes that both women and maidens were present as spectators at certain games:

As you won often in the seasonable
Games of Pallas in silence, you were watched
by the maidens and older women, who
prayed that you, Telesicrates,
might be their dearest husband or son,
and also at the Olympic Games and
at those of the deep-bosomed goddess, Earth,
and at all local games.

(Pind., *P.* 9.97–100)[68]

Telesicrates of Cyrene is honored in this poem as the Pythian victor in the hoplite race in 478 B.C.; he was also a victor in the Pythian stade race at a later date, perhaps 474 or 470.[69] He never won at Olympia, since the names of the winners of the hoplite and other footraces for this period (484–468) are known. Nor was he a victor at any other Panhellenic festival, to judge by the silence of the Scholia on Pindar and other sources. He was apparently a victor at the "Games for Pallas [Athena]," but it is uncertain whether this refers to the Panathenaia at Athens or some other games held at Cyrene. The wide popularity of this athlete suggests that he won at the Panathenaia, perhaps in 482 B.C., a festival of greater importance than one in Cyrene, and known from an early period as "the festival for Pallas at Athens."[70] The subordinated reference to Telesicrates' popularity at Olympia may indicate that he competed there in 480 B.C., unfortunately against the "super-star" athlete Astylos, who swept three running events, the stade, diaulos, and hoplite races. If the prohibitions against married women at the Olympic Games were in effect in Pindar's day, then this passage must refer only to the maidens present there, and to maidens or married women at the other festivals. Apart from a festival of Ge Chthonia at Mykonos, festivals of "broad-bosomed Ge," the earth goddess, are unknown.[71] Wherever these games took place, they are grouped with the Olympics, and hence it seems unlikely that Telesicrates was also a victor there. Perhaps these games were of special personal importance to this athlete, or perhaps the spectators held him in special honor. The mention of "all the local (games)" (*pasi epichōriois* [*aethlois*]) may refer to all those less conspicuous festivals in which the athlete has participated, regardless of his success in them.

The point, for Pindar in any case, is to show that "Telesicrates . . . has frequently been victorious and can expect to receive a fine wife."[72] The prominence of the theme of marriage in this poem has been noted, with the explanation that Telesicrates is soon to be married, or of an age to marry. This is clearly echoed in an allusion to the myth of Cyrene, namesake of the victor's fatherland, in which a footrace of suitors was staged by Cyrene's father to choose a suitable groom:

[Cyrene's] father seeking to arrange for his daughter
a more distinguished marriage, heard how once in Argos Danaus
devised that for his forty-eight maiden girls
before midday should take place
a very swift marriage. He made the whole chorus of suitors stand
then at the boundaries of the contest place.
He ordained that they decide with the contest of a footrace
whichever of the girls each hero might have, and which sons-in-law
    might come to them.
Thus Libys betrothed and gave to his daughter
a marriageable man. He made her stand at the finish-line,
to be the ultimate goal [*telos*] with her finery,

and he spoke in their midst that he would lead her away whoever
would be the first to rush forth and touch her garment.

> (Pind., *P.* 9. 111–20)

Thus, the mythical situations of the Danaids and Cyrene seem to parallel the historical one of Telesicrates' pre-eminent eligibility as a husband, and a bride as his *telos*, literally and figuratively the "goal" of his victory. The literary theme of the bride or the beloved at the *telos* may, incidentally, have its counterpart in the visual arts in a fifth-century B.C. vase-painting that shows Eros standing at the starting line of a footrace.[73] Competition in the hoplite race at the Pythia, as at most festivals, was for adult males only, that is, generally males 18 years of age or older.[74] Since males generally married at about 30 years of age, and since Telesicrates accomplished a stade victory still in his athletic prime in 474 or 470, perhaps in his mid to late twenties, we can infer that the victor described by Pindar *Pythian* 9 is a young man between 18 and 26 years old.

It has been reasonably suggested that the major games would have provided excellent opportunities for marriages to be arranged by fathers and that "fathers with eligible daughters would have attended the athletic festivals in the hopes of arranging a marriage with a young man of good background and outstanding physical ability."[75] Maidens were apparently permitted to attend the Olympics, as Pausanias reports (5.6.7, 5.13.10; 6.20.9), while married women were generally excluded. "When the Olympics are in progress," Achilles Tatius (1.18) informs us in discussing the myth of Arethusa, "it is the custom of many of those present at the festival to throw various objects into the waters of the river, and these are borne directly to the beloved girl, and are the wedding presents of the river." Thoughts of love and marriage seem to have occupied the minds of those at Olympia participating in this ritual, analogous to the modern custom of tossing a coin into a fountain or "wishing well." To the extent that athletics furnished a forum for "matchmaking," the special acceptance of eligible maidens at the Olympic festival makes sense.

Pindar's reputation for being, in Athenaeus' words, "immoderately erotic" (οὐ μετρίως ὢν ἐρωτικος, 13.601c), and for praising thematically an athlete's beauty and his talent inherited over generations is also consistent with the important erotic function of athletics. The erotic appeal of the athletic victor, Hippocleas of Thessaly, was further acknowledged in an ode honoring a victor in the boys' 400-meter diaulos race at the Pythian Games of 498 B.C.:

> . . . with my songs written for the sake of his crown [I hope] ever more
>   to make
> Hippocleas admired among his fellow youths and his elders
> and to young maidens a beloved object of care, for, as
> some loves tease some hearts, others others.

> (Pind., *P.* 10.54–60)

Like Telesicrates, Hippocleas evokes different feelings among the spectators and among those who hear Pindar's song. The victor is seen as a "beloved object of care" (*melēma*) only for the maidens, and the reference to varying responses of "loves" (*erōtes*) probably also refers only to the girls who desire him as a husband. Again, Pindar focuses on the heterosexual attraction of the athlete, and the related function of the games as an inducement for marriage. Pindar also addresses the homoerotic attraction of the athlete, as in his allusions to the mythical abductions of Ganymede by Zeus and Pelops by Poseidon in *Olympian Ode* 1 to Hiero.[76] Hence the poet treats both of the accepted forms of eros that were seen, in different ways, as socially beneficial.

The erotically charged atmosphere at major festivals is vividly described in the Greek novel of the Roman Imperial period, *An Ephesian Tale* by Xenophon of Ephesus. As the work opens, Eros plays matchmaker between a young man, Habrocomes, and a girl, Anthia, at the Festival of Artemis at Ephesus:

> The local festival of Artemis was in progress, with its procession from the city to the temple nearly a mile away. All the local girls had to march in procession, richly dressed, as well as all the young men of Habrocomes' age—he was already sixteen and a member of the Ephebes, and took first place in the procession. There was a great crowd of Epheseians and visitors alike to see the festival, for it was the custom at this festival to find husbands for the girls and wives for the young men. So the procession filed past—first the sacred objects, the torches, the baskets and the incense; then horses, dogs, hunting equipment . . . some for war, most for peace. And each of the girls was dressed as if to receive a lover. Anthia led the line of girls. . . .[77]

Scholars have rightly given serious historical credence to this literary report of marriages attached to the Festival of Artemis.[78] The festival program included musical and gymnic competition and was compared by Thucydides (3.104) to the Delian Games on Delos, particularly in that those attending brought along wives and children.[79] A (nameless) pentathlete, because of his outstanding athletic success, held the special honor of being at the head of the procession (*proagōn*) at an Artemis festival, just as the character Anthia does in Xenophon's novel. Doubtless the holders of such honors were considered to be supremely suitable husbands.

Legends also reflect the cultural ideal of the victor taking the bride. Of course, contests for the bride, German *Brautagonen*, are common in the folktales of many cultures. In Greek culture, athletic tests of strength and prowess are demanded most notably of Odysseus, Pelops, and Heracles to win their brides. The most popular legendary male-female contest among vase painters is the wrestling match between Peleus and Atalanta at the Funeral Games for Pelias, discussed in chapter 7. Greek myths and folktales generally reinforce the agonistic ideal of man-winning-woman-through-contest. Pausanias (6.6.7–11) tells one unusual variation on the story in which an Olympic victor in boxing, Euthymus, fell in love with a maiden in Temessa, Italy, but to win her he first had to fight the local ghost, a former companion of Odysseus who haunted the locals and demanded each year a local virgin as his wife. Euthymus got the girl when the ghost fled, daunted by the sight of the athlete.[80] Such folktales and myths reinforce the reality described by Pindar. The hero or athlete who has successfully demonstrated his excellence is a most suitable candidate for husband.

Athletes and Prostitutes

A much less praised form of eros, that between athletes and female or male prostitutes, is not surprisingly absent from Pindar's odes. Anecdotes and epigrams attest to the prevalence of such affairs in which athletes must have sought to earn erotic capital through their beauty and popularity. Perhaps the most notorious example is Cleomachus of Magnesia, an Olympic victor in boxing in 424 B.C. and the target of lampoons by his contemporaries Aristophanes and Cratinus.[81] Of Cleomachus, Strabo notes, "Cleomachus the boxer, who fell in love with a certain *cinaedus* and with the girl prostitute raised by the *cinaedus*, tried to imitate the manner of speech and characteristics of those among the *cinaedi*" (Strabo 14.1.41 = C 648). The *cinaedus* was an effeminate type of homosexual, thoroughly dishonored in Greek society and as such to be distinguished from other pederastic partners.[82] Another famous athlete, Dioxippus of Athens, a pankration victor at the Olympics (in 336?), was chided by Diogenes the Cynic philosopher for his sexual weakness:[83]

> For when Diogenes saw that the Olympic victor, Dioxippus, riding in his
> victory procession, was not able to take his eyes off a shapely woman who
> was watching the parade, but kept glancing at her and turning around,
> he said "Do you see the athlete who has been taken in a neck-hold by the
> little girl?" (Plut., *De curio.* 521B)

Diogenes Laertius repeats the story about the Cynic, but without naming the athlete and referring to the girl as a *hetaira* (6.61). Both Dioxippus and Cleomachus are the object of derision because they are dominated by eros despite their obvious physical excellence. The irony makes the contrasts especially poignant. Censure of these less respectable expressions of eros by athletes receives less attention than the more legitimate and productive pederastic liaisons or the intrinsic attraction of girls to athletes at a marriageable age. One cannot, however, conclude that athletes indulged in 'illicit' affairs with prostitutes, male or female, any more or less than did other Greeks, only that, when they did, their weakness was all the more scorned.

It is likely that prostitutes (*pornai*) and hired female courtesans (*hetairai*), were in attendance at many athletic festivals, though probably amid the 'fringe' events and not those held in the stadium or sanctuary. The comic poet Machon (third c. B.C.) tells the anecdote about the hetaira Mania who lives like a wife with the famous Olympic pankratiast Leontiscus and is seduced into an 'adulterous' affair by the equally famous Olympic pancratiast Antenor. When Leontiscus discovers the affair, Mania wittily replies, "Let that bother you not at all, sweetheart: I only wanted to learn what it feels like when two Olympic athletes go at it stroke for stroke in a single night."[84] Herodas' *Mime* I (third c. B.C.) portrays an older woman encouraging the younger *hetaira* to take as a new lover the (fictitious) boxer Gryllus, victor at the Pythian, Isthmian, and Olympic Games; the athlete saw the girl at a Festival of the Descent of Misē (a chthonic Asianic goddess), and "his passions swelled up when he was stung in the heart with eros, and, my child, he would not leave my house by night or by day, but he weeps over me, wheedles me, and is dying of passion." Prostitutes and courtesans likely sought the favors of young men not only at festivals, but also local gymnasia. Theocritus' *Idyll* 2 (third c. B.C.) represents a *hetaira* trying to win back with a love spell her lover, a young athlete named Delphis who is portrayed chiefly as the handsome habitué of a local palaestra. *Hetairai* may have found young athletes especially desirable since many such youths were wealthier and more handsome, or at least healthier, than other potential companions.

An interesting visual parallel to the above stories is a column-krater of about 500–490 B.C. in the Getty Museum, on which the near-identical poses of the figures wittily makes a visual pun comparing the discobolus on one side with the *krotalos*- (or castanet-) playing *hetaira* on the other (fig. 8-4).[85] The pun may be interpreted on several levels: she is 'athletic'; he is a 'courtesan' whose prizes are his payment; both place a premium on the beauty of the body; both possess erotic attraction. Was she to be the entertainment at the victory party to follow?[86] Might he, like Cleomachus, have indulged in her favors? Are the two sides merely a play on the nude form, or do they relate to one another? In any case, both sides celebrate the hedonistic pleasure of leisure activities.

Abstinence, Lead on the Loins, and the Dog's Leash

Another explicit association between Eros and athletics, the ancient view that sexual intercourse was thought to impede competitive performance, may seem at first to contradict the picture of athletic eroticism described thus far. So far as we can tell, there was no universally accepted custom of abstinence for athletes, as there seems to be today in the (apparently unfounded) popular wisdom of coaches who impose curfews and discourage sex especially on nights before competition.[87] Philostratus supplies the sole testimonium on this:

> It is better for athletes who have just had intercourse not to take a
> workout. For how can they be men if they have exchanged crowns of

Figure 8-4. *Hetaira* playing castanets, left; discus thrower, right. Attic red-figure column-krater, ca. 500–490 B.C., Myson (painter), The J. Paul Getty Museum, Los Angeles 73.AE.135. Courtesy of The J. Paul Getty Museum, Los Angeles, California.

victory and the herald's announcements for a shameful pleasure [αἰσχρὰν ἡδονὴν]? If they do work out, they should exercise openly after being warned to watch out for their endurance and breath [ἰσχὺν ... πνεῦμα], because sexual pleasures cause the most harm in these areas. A nocturnal emission is one and the same as sexual intercourse, but as we have said [ch.49], it is involuntary. Those who have had nocturnal emissions should take exercise carefully and should build up their strength more than usual, since they now have a deficit in their system, and they must get rid of the excess perspiration which they have. Their workouts should be easy to do but spread over a longer period of time than usual, so that their lungs may be exercised. They need a normal amount of oil thickened with dust. For this medicine preserves and refreshes. (Philostr., *Gymn.* 52)

It is unclear whether the recommendation is to be followed for all training periods, or only just before competition, but his remarks about the harmful effects of intercourse imply that abstinence should be maintained for all periods of training. The prohibition never addresses the matter of sex *after* exercise, or outside of the training period proper. In fact, one ancient medical author, Oribasius, perhaps reflecting the views of Galen, endorses the practice of some exercise such as a footrace or horse riding before sexual intercourse.[88] It would seem, then, that moderate fitness and moderate sexual activity were in keeping with the life of the healthy Greek, and that athletics is part of a recommended regimen for those concerned with counteracting the potentially debilitating effects of intercourse.

Philostratus' advice, it has been noted, accords with contemporary medical theories of bodily humors whereby semen was an important contributor to manly strength, despite differing views on the physiological sources of semen.[89] Aretaius, a first-century A.D. physician, discusses the power of semen, specifically as exemplified in abstinent athletes:

ἢν δέ τις ἀνὴρ καὶ ἐγκρατὴς ἔῃ τῆς θορῆς, κραταιος, εὔτολμος, ἀλκήεις μέσφι θηρίων· τέκμαρ δὲ ἀθλητῶν οἱ σαόφρονες. (Aretaeus, *De causis et signis acutorum morborum* 2.5.4)

If any man is in possession of semen, he is fierce, courageous, and physically mighty like beasts. Evidence of this is those athletes who are abstinent.

Galen, writing in the second century A.D., observed some unfortunate cosmetic side effects of those athletes who rigorously practice abstinence[90]:

Those athletes or singers whosoever from the start [of their competitive careers] lead lives chaste of all sexual relations and in all ways curb themselves from any such thought or daydream, have genitals which become thin and wrinkled like those of old men. For in the case of others who indulge in sexual relations over a long time from youth onwards, their vessels swell up in those areas, and they become enlarged both in their blood flow and in their appetitive power for sexual relations, according to the common explanation of all powers, which Plato has written, saying that lack of personal activity weakens and pursuit of it increases strength. (Galen, *De locis affectis libri vi*, vol. 8.451–52 [Kuhn])

"Strength" in this context seems to refer to the physical growth of the genitals, and not the absolute physical development of the athlete. The passage is thus evidence only for the fact that, even in Galen's day, chastity was practiced in an orthodox manner by some athletes. There seems to have been a type of athlete, then, who was known to practice sexual restraint.[91] While the abstinence upholds certain medical or philosophical notions of the virtue of restraint, it does not necessarily imply that the custom derived from theoretical biases. Rather, the historical examples of athletic abstinence show that the practice was widespread as early as the fifth century B.C. and inspired philosophers and others to cite such athletes as models of self-control.

In the *Laws*, Plato's Athenian speaker extends to the Cretan Clinias the radical proposal that men should sleep only with women by whom they wish to have children and should otherwise refrain "from sexual rage and frenzy and all sorts of fornication"; the self-imposed chastity of some athletes is exemplary:

ATHENIAN: Do we not know by report about Iccus of Tarentum, because of his contests at Olympia and elsewhere—how spurred on by his desire for victory, obtaining both skill and a courage combined with self-control in his soul, during all the period of his training (as the story goes) he never touched a woman nor a boy. And the same story is told about Chrison and Astylos and Diapompus and very many others [ἄλλους παμπόλλους]. And yet, Clinias, these men were not only much worse educated in their souls than your citizens and mine, but they also possessed much more sexual vigor of body.

CLINIAS: You report these things accurately, since the ancients affirm that these practices were truly undertaken by those athletes.

ATHENIAN: Well then, if those men had the courage to abstain from an action which most men call fortunate for the sake of victory in wrestling, footraces, and other such contests, shall our boys be unable to endure for the sake of a much finer victory. . . .

CLINIAS: Which victory?

ATHENIAN: A victory over pleasures, which will be fortunate if they endure, but the very opposite if they lose. (Pl., *Laws* 839e–840c)

Plato's allusion to anecdotal reports about individual athletes who practiced sexual abstinence, some famous as well as "very many others," implies that such restraint characterized a significant number of known competitors but was not universal. The passage also suggests that, by reputation, athletes were presumed to possess "much more sexual vigor of body" than did average individuals. And that vigor was directed, when the praiseworthy restraint was absent, toward boys or women. Caution must be exercised in using a philosophical perspective as evidence for popular views, but Plato's passage illustrates that "bravery with self-control" (τὸ μετὰ τοῦ σωφρονεῖν ἀνδρεῖον) added to a special skill (τέχνην) was one prescription for athletic success. "Self-control," which we had noted earlier was one common athletic virtue,[92] refers here to one specific type of restraint, that of sexual desire.

Aelian, writing in the latter half of the second century A.D., elaborates on the story of Iccus, an Olympic victor in pentathlon in 444 B.C. and also mentions the example of Cleitomachus of Thebes, an Olympic pankration victor of 216 B.C., in a context in which sexual abstinence is praised as a part of self-imposed training:

> Therefore Plato, son of Ariston, praises [Iccus] for remaining entirely inexperienced in sexual intercourse and unacquainted with any female for the whole period of his training. And for Iccus, who was a human being, was in love with [ἐρῶντι] the Olympic and Pythian Games, was aware of fame, and longed for good repute, it was no great achievement to sleep modestly and chastely. For the prizes of the contest both seemed to him and were for him a source of fame, the Olympic olive crown, the Isthmian pine crown, the Pythian laurel crown, so that he was respected in life and spoken well of after his death. . . . The pankratiast Cleitomachus once turned away when he saw dogs in the act of mating and got up and left a symposium if he heard licentious or lewd conversation. (Aelian, *De nat. an.* 6.1)

Aelian thus implies that Iccus' eros for athletic competition and the fame (*kleos*) and reputation (*doxē*) that these afforded were compensations or noble substitutes for indulgence in sexual relations. The fact that Iccus "remained inexperienced" in sexual matters implies that as a young man training for competition he was a celibate virgin, but that he probably lifted his self-prohibition after his athletic career ended. His restraint was apparently self-imposed, and not part of a standard training regimen to which an athlete might have subscribed.

Cleitomachus, somewhat a different case, seems to be obsessively averse to even the idea of sexual activity, whether in conversation or in observing animals in the act.[93] His reputation is also noted in Plutarch (*Quaest. conv.* 710D), who echoes the story about his leaving symposia, and in an *Appendix to the List of Victors* that relates the following:

> Cleitomachus the Theban is noteworthy as a boxer and as being
> unsurpassed in strength, as well as for his practice of self-restraint
> [σωφροσύνη]. For he did not even tolerate the mere mention of sex.
> When discussions of eros arose in symposia or elsewhere, he immedi-
> ately stood up and left. He did this so that the bloom of his strength no
> be weakened if he ever yielded to sexual pursuits. (*Anecdota Graeca
> Bibliothecae Regiae Paresiensis* II.154, lines 20–25 [Cramer])

Thus Cleitomachus' motive of preserving "the bloom of his strength" (ἡ τῆς ῥώμης ἀκμή) is spelled out more literally than in other cases, and the exceptional nature of his restraint is implied by the remarks of the commentator.

Dio Chrysostom (ca. A.D. 40/50–post 110) describes the boxer Melancomas of Caria, possibly an Olympic victor in A.D. 49, as another exemplar of self-imposed restraint.[94] "So that he not be defeated by his opponents, he did not allow himself to be overcome by exertion, heat, desire for food and drink, and sexual desire [ἀφροδισίων]", notes Dio (*Or.* 28.12). He also mentions that Melancomas died as a youth, that is, at 18 to 20 years of age, and remarks that "he enjoyed none of the delights of life" (*Or.* 28.9, 10, 13). This comment reminds us that it was considered unusual for such a youth not to have had sexual experiences, and that celibacy was still an active choice for some athletes in the Roman era.

Clement of Alexandria (ca. A.D. 50–ca. 215) reflects Plato's doctrine of self-control but argues for such exceptional restraint in the service of God:[95]

> They say that not a few athletes abstained from sexual relations while
> they were maintaining a program of physical training, such as Astylos
> of Croton and Crison of Himera. . . . Aristotle of Cyrene is the only one
> who was able to disdain Laïs when she was in love with him. He swore
> to the hetaira that he would take her back with him to his fatherland if
> he had some luck against his athletic opponents. When that happened,
> he cleverly fulfilled his oath by having as realistic as possible a statue
> made of her and sent it back to Cyrene, as the historian, Istros [writing
> in the third century B.C.] narrates in his work, *On the Character of
> Athletics*. (Clement of Alexandria, *Stromata* 3.6.50, 4–51.1)

Aristotle of Cyrene is otherwise unknown, and his vow to marry if he wins seems to reflect the mythical pattern of the hero who uses a would-be beloved only to abandon her later, for example, Theseus and Ariadne or Jason and Medea. It is here unclear why the athlete would feel compelled to make such a promise unless the hetaira was thought to have some beneficial power or some malevolent threat. Did Laïs possess magical powers, special divine favor, or simply the threat of shaming Aristotle publicly?

Aelian tells the same story of a different Cyrenean athlete, Eubatas, winner of the Olympic stade race in 408 B.C., with some informative additions or changes:[96]

> Upon seeing Eubatas the Cyrenean, Laïs fell very passionately in love with him and suggested a proposal of marriage. Since he feared treachery from her, he promised to do it. Indeed he did not have relations with her but lived his life modestly. His promise was to be fulfilled after the contest. Therefore when he won, he did not want to appear to have broken his promise to the woman and so he had a sculpture of Laïs made and sent it back to Cyrene, declaring that he was sending Laïs back to Cyrene. Wherefore the woman who was lawfully married to him had a very large statue set up to him in Cyrene, repaying him for his modesty. (Aelian, *Varia historia* 10.2)

Clearly the story had come into the realm of Cyrenean folktale, probably associated with or even inspired by particular statues in that city. In both tales, the hetaira is portrayed unsympathetically and the athlete goes to great lengths to flee her sexual advances. In the version of Clement and Istros, the athlete "disdains" (ὑπερεῶρα, lit., "looks down on") the famous courtesan by refusing to take her back with him. Clement's athlete "cleverly" (χαριέντως) avoids fulfilling his promise: the adverb suggests that he fears being labeled a breaker of promises. In Aelian's tale, the initial motive is not that he feared perjury, but that he "feared treachery from her" (φοβηθεὶς τὴν ἐξ αὐτῆς ἐπιβουλήν) if he were to reject her by not promising marriage. Only after that does he swear to marry her and then cleverly get around the promise. The final gesture of Eubatas' wife, "repaying him for his modesty" (ἀμοιβομένη τῆς σωφροσύνης), heroizes him for his self-restraint and cleverness against a woman notorious for her passion; the wife's giant statue of him balances his of Laïs as a monument to their stable relationship. Both versions relate how an athletic victor, at least in one case an Olympic victor, resists the most famous of hetairai. The preservation of his characteristic modesty or restraint is the point, explicitly in Aelian's version, implicitly in Clement's. The inclination to chastity may be a particular local custom of Cyrene, where an unusually strong law existed regulating cleanliness after "pollution" from sexual relations.[97] In any case, the stories of both athletes portray an ideal practiced by a few, the exception to the normal behavior of athletes. Ancient sources probably preserved the story because it was so unusual, philosophers and Christian authors because it served their purposes.

There seems to have been no rule about the advisability of abstinence as preparation for any specific forms of competition. Though the majority were stade runners (Astylos, Chrison, Diopompus, Eubatas, Aristotle [?]), Iccus was a pentathlete,

Melancomas a boxer, and Cleitomachus a pankratiast. It is also difficult to see any pattern in the chronology or geographical origins of these athletes. Later authors mostly cite the fifth-century B.C. examples, and only two are mentioned from later periods, perhaps for their extreme application of the practice (Cleitomachus of the third century B.C. and Melancomas of the first century B.C.). There is a solitary reference in the twelfth-century A.D. author Eustathius (*Com. ad Hom. Il.* 24.130 = vol. 4, 341.2–3), stating that at Olympia "athletes are not allowed to associate with women during the whole period of their competing in the games" (διὸ καὶ οἱ ἀθληταὶ τὸν τοῦ ἀθλεῖν πάντα καιρὸν οὐκ ἀφίεντο πλησιάζειν γυναιξὶν). But this unique mention of the custom suggests that it may be an error, confusing the prohibition against adult women attending the games with training regulations.[98] A case has been made that a Pythagorean school of training, begun in late sixth century B.C. Croton, may have influenced some of these athletes, three of whom come from the Greek colonies of South Italy and Sicily, namely Astylos of Croton, Chrison of Himera, and Iccus of Tarentum.[99] The best evidence is Iccus himself, known to be a Pythagorean. Though there may be some basis to this observation, no explicit source connects the Pythagoreans with athletic chastity, and ultimately we must leave open the question of the origins of the custom. It is clear that the practice was not restricted to Pythagoreans, and it seems just as likely to have begun as a folk custom, based on the physiological experience of weakness or the diminished aggressiveness felt after intercourse, and was later adopted by individual athletes or canonized in the training regimens of certain trainers.

There is reference in Galen to an extraordinary regimen that seems to have been adopted by some athletes for maintaining their chastity against nocturnal emission by covering the loins with leaden plates during sleep[100]:

> But a flattened leaden plate, in and of itself and without any of the other [pharmaceutical applications], is an object to be placed under the muscles of the loins of athletes in training, clearly chilling them, whenever they might have nocturnal emissions of semen. (Galen, *De simplicium medicamentorum temperamentis ac facultatibus libri vi* 12.232)

It is unclear whether the effective part of this remedy was meant to be the mineral properties, the weight, or simply, as Galen says, the chill of the lead. It is furthermore unclear whether it was meant to lessen emissions, to eliminate them, or to reverse their deleterious effects. In any case, the practice addresses the same problem noted by Philostratus and attests to the great lengths to which some athletes would go to preserve an obsessively chaste lifestyle.

Also cited as evidence of the chastity of ancient athletes is the so-called "infibulation" or *kunodesmē* (literally "dog's leash," Greek *kuōn*, "hound," being slang for the penis),[101] a practice among the Greeks whereby the foreskin of the penis is drawn up and tied back upon itself with some sort of cord. This practice is mostly known from vase paintings, where it is seen on athletes, revellers, and satyrs and only briefly mentioned in a few late ancient authors. An Etruscan painting of the early fifth century B.C. shows that the practice was widespread and subject to certain variations of style, such as being tied to a cord on the waist instead of the more usual binding of the penis bent back onto itself (fig. 8-5). Most modern commentators take the practice to be "a conspicuous symbol of an individual's commitment to chastity"[102] or, presumably in the case of satyrs, as a comic proclamation of the desire for abstinence.[103] It seems preferable to understand it as a simple practical measure taken for the sake of decorum to prevent the embarrassment of an erection in a public context, something for which satyrs were notorious.[104] Modesty does not necessarily presume chastity. This interpretation is supported by one of the few literary references to the practice:

κυνοδέσμη· δερμάτιον ᾧ τὰς ἀκροποσθίας ἀποδοῦσιν οἱ περὶ τας ἀποδύσεις ἀσχημονοῦντες

"*kunodesmē*: a small piece of skin with which those who are ashamed in stripping bind the end of the prepuce." (Photius, *Lexikon*)

Figure 8-5. Athletes wearing the "dog's leash." Etruscan painting, early fifth century B.C., Tomb of the Monkey, Museo di Chiusi. Published with permission of the Ministerio per i Beni e le Attività Culturali, Sopraintendenza archeologica di Firenze, Florence, Italy.

It has also been argued that the very practice of athletic nudity was adopted by the Greeks to show that they were superior in their exertion of self-control.[105] While this argument for the origin of the custom is less convincing than others examined so far, it does remind us of the importance of self-control. Compare Augustine's reminder of the even more modest Christian view: "But the genital organs have become, as it were, the private property of lust. . . . It is this that arouses shame; it is this that makes us shun the eyes of the beholders in embarrassment" (*City of God* 14.19). Greek culture was of course completely different in its construction of "shame" but did share with Augustine the notion that the male genitalia had, so to speak, a mind of its own which required great self-control to keep it reined in. Would it not then have been an even greater demonstration of self-control to exercise in public without the artificial constraints of infibulation? And might not wearing of the infibulation binding be taken as a sign that one did not have a sufficiently strong will to overcome the powers of physical arousal? Again Photius gives our most explicit clue to the rationale for undergoing infibulation, and that points to the fact that those who did it were ashamed of suffering an erection in public. There is no mention of advertising one's lack of self-control. Perhaps some wished to advertise their zealousness in modesty, perhaps some were easily aroused, perhaps they did not have sufficient self-control, or perhaps a few required the assistance of the device and other adopted it as a kind of ornamental fashion. It is, in any case, a measure for inhibiting overt displays of sexual arousal.

Images of Eros and Athletes

The evidence of the vases also contributes much to the theme of athletic eroticism. A number of the homosexual vase paintings catalogued by K. J. Dover relate the homoerotic to athletics.[106] One sixth-century, black-figure vase juxtaposes a courtship scene with a wrestling scene just above it (Munich 1468; Dover no. B 271). A red-figure vase shows pairs of courting couples probably in a gymnasium, youths with boys, one of the latter holding a discus (Paris G 45; Dover no. R59). The interior tondeau of a red-figure kylix shows an older man fondling the genitals of a receptive boy; a strigil, oil-flask, and sponge hanging in the background suggest that the setting is a gymnasium (Oxford 1967.304; Dover no. R 520). To Dover's vases we can add the following on similar themes. A vase in the Getty Museum dated to about 510 B.C. shows some men cleaning up after exercise, while others consort with boys in the gymnasium (fig. 8-6).[107] A late-sixth-century kylix in Berlin shows young men with boys in the gymnasium, identified by strigils and sponges on the wall, and, on the other side, men with young women, presumably hetairai or prostitutes, and apparently not in the palaestra (fig. 8-7).[108] To the central homosexual couple in a kind of wrestling embrace, we may compare the wrestling hold of Peleus and Atalanta on a vase of the same period (fig. 7-5). The Berlin kylix shows that

Figure 8-6. Attic red-figure psykter, ca. 510 B.C., attributed to Smikros (painter), The J. Paul Getty Museum, Los Angeles 82.AE.53. Courtesy of The J. Paul Getty Museum, Los Angeles, California.

the ethos among Athenian youths was one of bisexuality, while homosexual activities were most natural to the gymnasium.

Yet, as was discussed above in chapter 7 regarding scenes of women in the gymnasia, there was interest among artists, and presumably their patrons, in depicting heterosexual scenes with athletic contexts. There are some important differences in iconography between the scenes discussed earlier showing girls by themselves, bathing with strigils, and the present scenes of men with girls in the gymnasium. The former scenes are of interest since they portray the exotic, if not impossible, and hence the erotic sight of girls alone in what is ordinarily a male domain. The latter scenes of girls with men puts the girls in the place of the boy beloved and hence suggests that the girls are not quasi-athletes, but objects of love in the erotic setting of the gymnasium. A vase by the Amasis Painter, for instance, shows six pairs of amorous encounters, three on each side, two of older bearded male with younger male and one bearded male with a young female (fig. 8-8).[109] The girls, holding blossoms and circular fillets or necklaces, occupy the center of each side to

Figure 8-7. Attic red-figure kylix, Peithinos Painter, Berlin, Staatliche Museen F 2279. Courtesy of Antikensammlung, Staatliche Museen zu Berlin, Preussischer Kulturbesitz, Berlin, Germany.

emphasize their presence amid the males. An oil-flask and fillets hang on the walls, and two young men have oil-flasks, four hold spears, indications of a setting probably in the gymnasium. The older men each offer conventional lover's gifts, mostly small animals,[110] to their beloved boy or girl; two additional older men holding gifts fill in the space under the handles. There are numerous other courting scenes in gymnasia, some with males and (ordinarily clothed) females.[111]

One unusual vase, a kylix dated to about 510–500 B.C. in the Getty Museum, gives a narrative of athletic eros reminiscent of the epigrams praising the beauty of the sweaty or bloody victor (fig. 8-9a,b,c).[112] Here the exterior shows a narrative sequence of the three events unique to the pentathlon, namely discus-throwing, javelin-throwing, and jumping; the 100-meter stadion race and wrestling of the pentathlon also existed as independent events. Side A has two contestants performing in the discus-throw and long jump, while side B has one individual, apparently older contestant throwing the javelin, and, finally, dedicating his discus on the altar of a patron god in thanks for his victory (fig. 8–9a,b). Most interesting, however, is the interior tondeau that shows the clearly older victor perhaps somewhat reluctantly receiving a congratulatory kiss from a boy (fig. 8–9c). To this we can compare a gymnasium tondeau scene in which a bearded man fondles the genitals of a boy responding positively; a strigil and sponge hanging on the wall behind them indicates the athletic location.[113] Is the Getty victor simply being modest in his moment of glory? Like Alcibiades making advances to Socrates, the youth is bold in trying

Figure 8-8. Black-figure skyphos cup, Paris, Louvre A479 (MNB 1746), Amasis Painter, third quarter of the sixth century B.C., from Camiros, Rhodes. © Musée du Louvre, Paris; permission and photo courtesy of Musée du Louvre, Paris, France.

to seduce the victor. Also like Alcibiades, the boy appears to be rejected as the athlete upholds proper decorum of the homoerotic relation in which the older man should be the active party. The boy is also like the admirers in the epigrams, enamored of the athlete for his display of natural prowess. The pentathlete was, by reputation, the best all-around athlete, even if the contest did not enjoy the greatest popular favor. Incidentally, the enlarged breasts of the boy give him an almost hermaphroditic quality, reminding us again of the bisexual orientation of some Greek athletes. Presumably the arrangement of scenes on the cup was meant to allow the victor who owned the cup to enjoy the interior scene as he drank, while others in his presence could marvel at his athletic *aretē* on the exterior.

The above vases all show literal scenes of erotic relations in an athletic context. Another frequent motif adopts a more metaphoric approach, with the god Eros in a gymnasium scene, attempting to induce a youth or boy to enter into his power. A kylix cup from the early fifth century B.C. shows Eros literally invading the gymnasium and wielding what may be a sandal or a knife, sending two clothed youths to flight and perhaps on to love.[114] On the other side, one youth drops his strigil in amazement, presumably witnessing the chaotic invasion of the deity, while a colleague holds on to him to steady him; a third youth to the left continues to dress (or undress) unaware of the disturbance (fig. 8-10). A fifth-century bell-krater from Italy in the British Museum also shows an Eros approaching a startled youth who turns to run as he gestures in surprise (fig. 8-11).[115] Another fifth-century vase shows two Erotes, Eros and Anteros, in pursuit of a startled youth, possibly an athlete or symposiast, half-draped and wearing a crown.[116] This scene is unusual in depict-

Figures 8-9a (top, side A), b (middle, side B), c (bottom, interior). Attic red-figure kylix, The J. Paul Getty Museum, Los Angeles 85.AE.25; Athens 510–500 B.C., attributed to the Carpenter Painter. Courtesy of The J. Paul Getty Museum, Los Angeles, California.

Figure 8-10. Eros invades the gymnasium, top; surprised youths, bottom. Attic red-figure kylix, first third of the fifth century, attributed to Douris, Berlin, Pergamon Mus., V.I. 3168; Beazley, *ARV²* 428.13; Beazley, *Paralipomena* 374. Courtesy of Antikensammlung, Staatliche Museen zu Berlin, Preussischer Kulturbesitz, Berlin, Germany.

ing two Harpy-like Erotes, the significance of which will be discussed later. The theme of Eros-pursuing-athletes occurs on several other vases. We may include under this theme the Getty Museum skyphos depicting Eros offering a strigil to a boy (figs. 8-1a and 8-1b and note 16). Though Eros is not literally rushing after the youth, the god's power seems apparent to the boy, who modestly averts his gaze. Two vases by the Veii Painter, ca. 475–450 B.C., show, in the interior, an athlete tying up his penis with the "dog's leash," while both exterior scenes show Eros pursuing a youth.[117] A vase of the same period from Orvieto shows, in the interior, an athletic victor, and, in the exterior, Eros pursuing a boy.[118] Another of this period, possibly also from Orvieto, also depicts athletes in the interior and Erotes flying to a seated youth on the exterior.[119] A kylix, also ca. 475–450 B.C., from Heidelberg

Figure 8-11. Lucanian red-figure bell-krater, ca. 440–430 B.C., Pisticii Painter, London, British Mus. F.39 (GR 1824.5–1.38). Courtesy of the Trustees of the British Museum, London, U.K.

shows three athletes on one side and Eros pursuing a youth on the other.[120] The Washing Painter, working in the period 450–420 B.C., has two vases on this theme: a pelike vase in Brussels depicts Eros approaching a lone athlete[121]; a kylix in Brussels shows on both exterior sides a jumper pursued by two Erotes.[122] Several bell-krater vases by the Meleager Painter from the first third of the fourth century B.C. show Eros with two athletes.[123] This painter's depiction of Eros with athletes and women in the same scene suggests an interest in the heterosexual aspect of athletic attraction, as will be discussed later. Two early-fourth-century vases from Spina, Italy, attributed to the "Fat Boy Group" (so named for the frequent portrayal of fat athletes), depict Eros between two athletes.[124] By this time, even those athletes who do not conform to the canonical proportions of beauty are portrayed as under the influence of Eros. The main point of these scenes seems to be that Eros can send the gymnasium into turmoil as he works his erotic power upon the youths. They, as the beloved, the objects of desire, respond with fright and amazement. No lover is depicted, which is typical of vases with this motif. We can only assume that the viewer himself is meant to take the position of the lover, vicariously projecting himself into the gymnasium scene, wishing to pursue youths of such beauty.

Other vases with Eros and athletes convey a second prominent theme, that of Eros offering a victor's fillet, crown, or other object as a prize to a young athlete. Here the motif may be secondarily derived from the frequent depiction of a Nike offering a fillet to either a victorious athlete or lyre-player.[125] The transference would be natural, from one winged deity to another, but the change significantly also implies that the boy has acquired not just success in competition, but the attractive qualities of a beloved. A vase in the Fitzwilliam Museum, Cambridge, dated to the second quarter of the fifth century, shows a winged Eros on one side carrying a fillet, apparently to place on a victorious youth on the other side, who stands with hand outstretched to receive his token of success, a finishing post displayed prominently in the background (fig. 8-12).[126] Here we are out of the gymnasium and on the stadium floor. The significance seems to be that with victory comes enhanced beauty; the god's symbolic fillet indicates that the boy himself will become an object of the lover's conquest. A fifth-century pelike from Brussels is comparable in theme to the Getty skyphos (figs. 8-1a and 1b) in depicting Eros standing before an athlete, yet here the strigil is held by the athlete while Eros offers him a fillet, and here the athlete does not avert his gaze, but looks confidently at the deity.[127] So too a fourth-century kylix in Frankfurt shows Eros in the tondeau carrying a fillet while, on each side of the exterior, a naked athlete holding up a strigil faces a robed man who gestures to him, perhaps offering a crown or fillet (fig. 8-13).[128] The mythical Eros repeats the honoring of the athlete on the exterior and extends the significance of the victory ceremony to imply that erotic attraction is also part of his success. Two fifth-century vases in the "Manner of the Washing Painter" also embrace the

Figure 8-12. Attic red-figure skyphos, Zephyros Painter, Cambridge, Fitzwilliam Mus. GR 13.1955. Reproduction by permission of the Syndics of the Fitzwilliam Museum, Cambridge.

Figure 8-13. Eros, top; trainer (?) and athlete, bottom. Attic red-figure kylix, Frankfurt, Museum für Vor- und Frühgeschichte, Archäologisches Museum, WM 06; *CV*. pl. 68, 3–6; Beazley, *Paralipomena* 501, 12 *bis*. Courtesy of the Museum für Vor- und Frühgeschichte, Archäologisches Museum, Frankfurt, Germany.

victor theme by showing Eros with a box, perhaps a prize, approaching a naked athlete.[129] Two others of the same period by the Painter of London E 395 show Eros before a victorious athlete.[130] A fifth-century kylix shows Eros on each side with two youths, presumably a victor and a colleague. On side A, Eros offers a crown (?) to the victor, and the second youth offers the victor what may be a prize money purse; on side B, Eros offers an object, perhaps fruit or a flower, to the victor while the companion gestures recognition to his victorious colleague (fig. 8-14).[131] A fourth-century bell-krater in Athens echoes the theme, showing a winged Eros

Figure 8-14 a (top, side A) and b (bottom, side B). Red-figure kylix, 460–450 B.C., Würzburg, Wagner Mus. L 487. Courtesy of the Martin von Wagner Museum, Universität Würzburg, Würzburg, Germany. Photo: K. Oehrlein.

crouched at the feet of a youth who holds up his strigil as an apparent sign of vic-tory, while to the right another youth gestures recognition to the victor.[132] Another bell-krater in Athens shows a similar theme, with a standing, winged Eros about to place a fillet on a crowned, seated victor; a second youth to the left watches his friend receive the honor.[133] To these scenes compare the real-life image of a bearded older man, probably a trainer (note the trainer's stick), but perhaps also a lover, stand-ing before and gazing admiringly at a naked boy victor on a victory pedestal, wear-ing a crown and holding a javelin, strigil, oil-flask, and sponge.[134]

The erotic-athletic theme seems to be elaborated upon in vases of the mid to late fourth century, with the addition, in each case, of a clothed female positioned opposite the naked victor who is being given a crown or a fillet by Eros.[135] On one of these scenes, for example, Eros flies above the youth with a fillet while the female opposite him gazes over the basin between them and offers him a present of a box, perhaps as a prize for his victory (fig. 8-15).[136] Several other vases of the same period show Eros flying with a crown over the head of a clothed female in the presence of a naked young male, who appears to be a victorious athlete, wearing a fillet or crown.[137] Heterosexual attraction aroused by athletic beauty seems to be the interest in these scenes, which are all Apulian and done in the period in which the popularity of homosexuality as an artistic subject (though not as a social reality) was apparently on the wane in the Greek world.[138]

This heterosexual interest may have been present in earlier vase-painting scenes from mainland Greece dating from the late fifth or early fourth century, as in a motif on two vases on which a naked youth or youths, crowned, are shown in the presence of a clothed female.[139] The motif here is to be distinguished from that of hetairai or prostitutes with men in gymnasium scenes (fig. 8-7). The young women here do not actively consort with the athletes but gaze at them with interest, admiration, and, presumably, some erotic desire. On both vases, the clothed female leans on a *terma*; the youth on the right appears to be the victor while the one on the left offers him a fillet, a scene repeated on both sides of the vase Athens N.M. 1408, but only on one side of Athens N.M. 13908. Another vase with female and athlete, a krater in Thessaloniki, shows an athlete practicing the long-jump before a *terma* post, upon which the female leans as she watches him (fig. 8-16).[140] Three Italian bell-kraters from the second half of the fifth century show Eros with a woman and an athlete on one side; on a fourth bell-krater (Naples 82898) the woman is beside a *terma* on one side and two draped youths stand beside the other post marked *termōn*.[141] On this latter piece, the youths and the woman are perhaps depicted at opposite ends of the stadium, and she is symbolically positioned with Eros as the "prize" of their desire, as in the myth of Cyrene discussed earlier. Nine kylikes by "the Q Painter" dated to the first third of the fourth century represent an athlete and a woman together; on two kylikes he shows Eros with a youth or woman on one side, and an athlete with a youth or woman on the other.[142] Clearly this artist specialized in such scenes, presumably serving a (faddish?) demand of the fourth-century market. A kylix by the Group YZ (iii) and also from the early fourth century has an athlete with a youth and a woman together, possibly illustrating the theme of bisexual eroticism for the athlete.[143] Six fragments of vases from this same period and attributed to the Mithridates Painter show a woman with an athlete or athletes.[144] On a series of twenty-two kylikes by the Meleager Painter, whose work also dates to the first third of the fourth century B.C., a woman is depicted in the company of an athlete or athletes, and sometimes with Eros present either in the same scene or elsewhere on the same vase.[145]

Though heterosexual erotic scenes with athletes had appeared earlier, the Meleager Painter, together with the Q Painter and the Mithridates Painter, seem to have popularized the heterosexual aspect of the theme of eros and athletics in vase

Figure 8-15. Apulian red-figure pelike, ca. 310–290 B.C., Paris, Louvre K 96.
© Musée du Louvre, Paris; permission and photo courtesy of Musée du Louvre,
Paris, France.

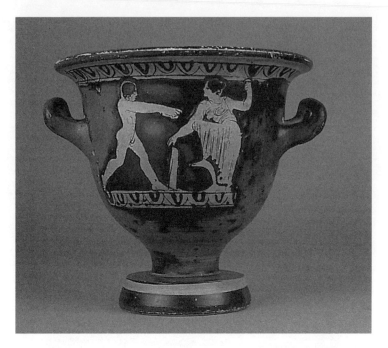

Figure 8-16. Attic red-figure krater, Archeological Museum of Thesalloniki 5206. Courtesy of the Archeological Museum, Thesalloniki, Greece.

painting. The Meleager Painter's interest in the theme of course complements his interest in the Meleager-and-Atalanta theme.[146] In both we find a woman in what is normally an all-male context, athletic activity or hunting. Her presence does not disturb the men but rather suggests the erotic possibilities. Might the woman with the athlete even be the legendary Atalanta and the athlete, Peleus? Though the painter may have been inspired by that mythical male-female wrestling bout, the fact that the female is always fully clothed and entirely without athletic accoutrements, such as a strigil, makes it unlikely that Atalanta is intended by the figure. The Meleager Painter's female-with-athlete motif, nonetheless, recalls Atalanta's famous liaisons by merely putting a lone female in the gymnasium.

The women's lack of direct interaction with the athletes, and their decorous dress, suggest that the scenes of woman-with-athlete depict a form of attraction and desire between two citizens which will lead to marriage. The "constraints of desire," which Plutarch and Plato observed arose between Spartan boys and girls during athletic displays, and which Pindar imputed to girls watching a successful athlete, may have been considered a common result of girls watching male athletes. This phenomenon is, mutatis mutandis, a part of the mythos of athletes in modern societies, and in ancient Rome where graffito proclaimed a gladiator to be "the girls' heart-throb" (*suspirium puellarum*). These vase scenes may thus document an aspect of athletic eros quite different in function from the homosexual or prostitute scenes. Athletics for youths could in part serve as a prenuptial stage in which boys saw and were seen by potential wives. Presuming that females could and did attend athletic games, as was argued earlier, the contest itself was a performance of male valor which helped both sexes make the transition to marriage or led directly to arranged marriages.

Vase paintings are not of course reliably photographic representations of societal trends. But taken together with the literary evidence examined in this chapter, the visual images seem to support the following general observations. From the survey of athletic eroticism on vases, we find, in historical perspective, that scenes of an erotic encounter between males and sometimes between males and *hetairai* in a gymnasium seem to appear earliest, from the sixth to mid-fifth centuries B.C. In the fourth century, there arises the popular depiction of the athlete with a young woman, a possible allusion to the waning phenomenon of widespread homosexuality and the recognition of the importance of athletics as a stage of socialization before marriage. Whether this is related to the institutionalization of the organized youth groups of *ephebes* in fourth-century Athens and the formation of other athletic unions elsewhere cannot be known, but one may suspect that these phenomena are at least complementary.[147] Though it is beyond the limits of this study, it should be noted that there are numerous Roman images of Eros (Amor, Cupido) as a victor, either with a crown, a palm, or the victory purse, or crowning himself.[148] These take on a life and meaning of their own for Roman culture but are undoubtedly inspired by the Greek images of Eros as victor discussed earlier.

The depiction of Eros the deity with athletes seems to consistently show the god with a younger man, that is, the beloved, and never with older bearded athletes. Thus it would seem that Eros is bestowing upon the youth a favor (*charis*) of beauty which will arouse desire in his lover. The young male beloved's proper response to his older lover is not normally "eros," but a more passive *philia*, "friendship."[149] But a female can, in the normal Greek terminology of relationships, respond to eros with the reciprocal eros called *anterōs*. These dynamics will be discussed further, but the important point here is to note that the divinity Eros may symbolize different phenomena in athletic scenes with young boys than in those with an athlete and a woman. One type of scene with young athletes by themselves portrays narratives of the god's "invasion" of the athletic realm, as if to initiate the boys into the ways of eros, just as the comic poem of Strato put the trainer into the role of teaching two young wrestlers how to act as lovers. The boys appropriately try to flee, or are in awe, or act modestly. Another type of scene shows the boys being crowned, given the victor's fillet, or given some present by the god; this acknowledges the youth's *aretē*, his internal and external beauty demonstrated by his public success.

Eros, Hermes, and Heracles

Thus far, we have discussed literary and artistic evidence documenting the association of eroticism of various sorts with athletics in Greek society. Eros the god has appeared more or less as the symbol of actual human relations. Now we turn to several striking instances in which Eros has been literally enshrined in cults in the gymnasium and worshiped in festivals that include athletic contests. Our interest is in describing the character of these cults and festivals and discussing their possible significance in the history of athletic eroticism in Greece.

From at least the Classical period onward, Eros seems to have shared pride of place in athletic cults with Hermes and Heracles. Athenaeus attempts to explain the significance:

> ὅτι δὲ καὶ οἱ τούτου πρεσβύτεροι κατὰ φιλοσοφίαν σεμνόν τινα τὸν
> Ἔρωτα καὶ παντὸς αἰσχροῦ κεχωρισμένον ᾔδεσαν δῆλον ἐκ τοῦ
> κατὰ τὰ γυμνάσια αὐτὸν συνιδρῦσθαι Ἑρμῇ καὶ Ἡρακλεῖ, τῷ μὲν
> λόγου, τῷ δ᾽ ἀλκῆς προεστῶτι· ὧν ἑνωθέντων φιλία τε καὶ ὁμόνοια
> γεννᾶται, δι᾽ ὧν ἡ καλλίστη ἐλευθερία τοῖς ταῦτα μετιοῦσιν
> συναύξεται. (Ath. 13.561d)

> But that others, also, who preceded [Zeno] in philosophic speculation,
> knew Eros as a holy being far removed from anything ignoble is clear
> from this, that he is enshrined in the public gymnasia along with
> Hermes and Heracles, the first presiding over eloquence, the second over
> physical strength; when these are united, friendship and concord are
> born, which in turn join in increasing the fairest liberty for those who
> pursue them.

Athenaeus implies that, from at least the fifth century B.C., Eros represents the friendship (*philia*) and concord that unite eloquence and strength among the habitués of the gymnasium. He significantly mentions "freedom" as a benefit of this union. Eros, as the author sees it, clearly plays a crucial role in communicating noble values to society, and athletic eros is, above all, a socially beneficial force. This is clearly an ethereal, almost Platonic notion of Eros that, although valid for the philosophical exegetes, seems unrealistically to portray a kind of Eros "far removed from anything ignoble." "Ignoble" (*aischrou*) here connotes not only spiritual baseness, but also physical ugliness. The claim is reminiscent of the quotation from Plato (*Symp.* 182b–c) with which this chapter began, paraphrased here: the barbarians consider pederasty, along with philosophy and love of athletics, to be ignoble (*aischron*), because these customs, and eros especially, promote lofty thoughts and strong bonds of friendship (*philia*) and society, characteristics of freer civilizations that tyranny denies to its subjects. Whether or not Plato himself subscribed to this line of argument put into the mouth of the character Pausanias, we can presume that it was a reasonable one for an Athenian at the time of the dramatic date of the dialogue (416 B.C.).

In Plato's last work, *Laws* (unfinished in 348; cf. *Symposium* ca. 384–79), where the elder Plato is perhaps being more cautious on the threat of carnal desires, the Athenian speaker seems to contradict the views of the earlier dialogue by arguing to the Spartan and Cretan speakers:

> While these gymnasia and common meals presently benefit polities in
> many other respects, yet they are problematic in contexts of civil strife;
> the case of the youths of Miletus, Boeotia, and Thurii illustrate this
> point. And though this custom [of pederasty] has existed for a long time,
> it also seems to have corrupted contrary to nature the pleasures of sex
> not only of humans but also of animals. And someone might hold
> responsible your states first and whichever of the others are especially
> devoted to gymnasia. (*Leg.* 1.636B)

For Plato's Pausanias and Athenaeus, then, homoerotic liaisons of the gymnasia were not per se base or ignoble, but for Plato's Athenian of the *Laws*, they can become so in certain contexts, namely civil strife, when amorous liaisons can become dangerous political alliances. Athenaeus does not distance Eros from the physical aspects of love but suggests that both physical and spiritual forms of beauty are essential to athletic eros. Athenaeus, like 'Pausanias,' believes that eros, athletics, and education in rhetoric or philosophy increase freedom by promoting free and independent interchange among citizens. Even in the *Laws* passage, we find the Athenian not wholly censorious, but only cautioning that athletics-inspired pederasty can be either beneficial or injurious depending on context (636a).

The close relation of Hermes to Eros in the gymnasium is graphically portrayed by a second century B.C. bronze statue of Eros, now in Tunis, holding a victory palm in his left hand, wearing a crown, and leaning with his right arm on a pillar of Hermes, or "herm" (now missing). A life-sized bronze sculpture of a herm, on which an Eros (now missing) once leaned, now in the Getty Museum, may in fact be the very herm of the Tunis Eros.[150] Hermes is thus a literal and figurative support for the victorious figure of Eros, and the scene reflects the vase paintings in which Eros crowns a human victor, or in which an athlete leans on a *terma* or herm.[151] Two calyx-krateres in Athens, National Museum, one (inv. no. 1669) showing Eros offering some object to two herms, a male and a female; the other (inv. no. 1460) showing Eros crowning a satyr who has one hand raised in a gesture of victory and one foot resting on a raised "victors' pedestal."[152] The herms need not be in a gymnasium but are likely to be, given the other associations cited here, and given the occurrence of the theme in at least five paintings or gems from the Roman era.[153] Satyrs are known to have portrayed athletes commonly in satyr plays, and krater

1460 may reflect a comic version of the more common scenes of Eros crowning human athletes.[154] Hermes' familiar presence in the gymnasium in his embodiment as a herm and his close association with erotic liaisons there are attested by an epigram in the Greek Anthology in which a love-stricken athlete commiserates with the herm in the gymnasium:

> —Hermes, having been shot by a young man [*ephebe*], I draw out the
>   bitter arrow.
> —Stranger, I also have suffered the same fate!
> —But a longing for Apollophanes wears me down.
> —O you lover of athletics [φιλάεθλε], you've outdone me. We two have
>   been thrown into the same fire! (*Greek Anth.* 12.143 [Anonymous])

A poem of the third century B.C. also attests to Hermes' statue as a locus of homoerotic beauty:

> I, Hermes, having departed from the steep peaks of Cyllene
> with its quivering foliage stand here guarding over the lovely gymnasium
>   ['ερατοῦ γυμνασίου].
> On me boys have often placed marjoram and hyacinth,
> and fresh crowns of violets.
>
> (*Greek Anth.* 16.188 [Nikias])

The herm here alludes to the offerings placed on it in the gymnasium, typically wreaths on its two post-like "arms." The erotic beauty of the setting is noted in the description of the gymnasium as *eratou*, "lovely," connoting the aesthetic appeal or the eros the reader might feel for the flowers or the boys themselves. Hermes is strongly identified with the gymnasium, both as guardian and as an embodiment, in part, of the spirit of the place. He was from the early Classical period onward known as a "god of the contest" (*enagōnios*) or "of the palaestra" (*palaistritēs*) and associated with the agon in myth,[155] yet he himself did not embody the ideal of strength. Thus, a poem by Xenocrates, dated sometime prior to the first century B.C., comically describes how the block-shaped pillar of Hermes is paradoxically unsuited to the palaestra (*Greek Anth.* 16.186). The herm lacks arms and feet and cannot therefore run or shadow-box. The importance of the herm thus seems to be more as a guardian figure, in general a god who watches over and assists in transitions, here perhaps related to the education of the youths to adulthood in the most general sense.[156]

Hermes is rather a god of theft and cleverness, not of strength, and if he contributes anything to the spirit of the athletic contest, his clever tactics may be the most important in wrestling. He is said to have been the first to teach wrestling to mortals, and his daughter was called "Palaestra," according to Philostratus.[157] It is therefore noteworthy that in the one myth in which he directly participates in athletic competition, it is a wrestling match against Eros in which the infant Hermes is said to have somehow cleverly "stolen away the feet" from under the young Eros:[158]

χθὲς δὲ προκαλεσάμενος τὸν Ἔρωτα κατεπάλαισεν εὐθὺς οὐκ οἶδ᾽ ὅπως ὑφελὼν τὼ πόδε· εἶτα μεταξὺ ἐπαινούμενος τῆς Ἀφροδίτης μὲν τὸν κεστὸν ἔκλεψε προσπτυξαμένης αὐτὸν ἐπὶ τῇ νίκῃ, τοῦ Διὸς δὲ γελῶντος ἔτι τὸ σκῆπτρον· εἰ δὲ μὴ βαρύτερος ὁ κεραυνὸς ἦν καὶ πολὺ τὸ πῦρ εἶχε, κἀκεῖνον ἂν ὑφείλετο. (Lucian, *Dial. Deor.* 7.3 [221])

(Apollo to Hephaestus): Yesterday [Hermes] challenged Eros to wrestle and at once somehow stole both feet out from under him. Then while he was being congratulated by Aphrodite and she hugged him for his victory he stole her girdle, and as Zeus was still laughing he took his sceptre. And if his thunderbolt had not been rather heavy and blazingly hot, he would have stolen that too.

While this tale of the infant kleptomaniac is late (second c. A.D.) and possibly a comic embellishment of similar, earlier stories, its combination of Hermes' traditional wrestling and thieving skills with the legendary wrestling prowess of Eros, to be discussed later, suggests that it may have an older origin.[159] Perhaps in earlier versions, Eros even bettered Hermes by carrying off his caduceus, as is shown on a vase from 460–450 B.C., and bettered Zeus (and the Hermes of the later version) by wielding his thunderbolts, as attested by the image on Alcibiades' shield.[160] In any case, Hermes is renowned as a teacher, an overseer, a supervisor of the skillful and sometimes clever activities of the gymnasium. His function is complementary to that of Eros, who oversees relations both friendly and erotic within the same sphere. Neither is touted for his physical strength, but this deficiency compensated for by other attributes essential to athletics and to everyday life.

Hermes and Eros both therefore complement Heracles, who in Athenaeus' words, embodies physical strength (*alkē*) in the domain of the gymnasium. First, some explanation of the relation of Heracles to athletics is necessary before we look at his relation to Eros. Heracles is, according to various sources, a founder of the Olympic games, the one to institute the olive crown, and an Olympic competitor, primarily in wrestling and pankration.[161] Some late sources also attach to Heracles the founding of the Nemean Games after he killed the lion.[162] Pindar, the earliest source to associate Heracles with the Olympics, says nothing of Heracles as a competitor, and no sixth- or fifth-century vases depict the hero clearly as an athlete, though a few show him with a tripod.[163] The images of Heracles performing his labors on the metope reliefs of the Temple of Zeus at Olympia, dated to the mid-fifth century B.C., seem to evoke athletic poses, but again the association is indirect and he is an icon for the *aretē* achieved by *athloi*, whose meaning embraces both "labors" and "contests."[164] The portrayal of Heracles as an athletic competitor thus seems to be a secondary and late attribute of the hero, most likely derived from his legendary displays of physical strength in his labors. The labors that took the form of wrestling or pankration matches, such as the struggles with serpents at his crib, the Nemean lion, Acheloüs, Eryx, and Antaeus, were not, however, set athletic contests as such, but encounters with beasts or heroes who habitually acted violently toward humans. Thus the labors that superficially resemble athletic events in the earlier Heraclean literary tradition are neither athletic contests proper, like the Olympics, nor even ad hoc contests mutually agreed upon for a special prize, like Atalanta's footrace or Penelope's contest of the axes. So too in the artistic tradition, a recent study concludes that "H[eracles]'s role in gymnasia and palaestrae is demonstrated by many monuments rather than by scenes of H[eracles] involved in athletic contests."[165] In addition to Athenaeus' mention of monuments of Heracles in the gymnasium, Pindar and Cicero mention the fact, and we find his gymnasium cult and athletic festivals in his honor attested in many other sources.[166] Heracles is then widely associated with athletics, but his presence in athletic settings seems to be an honorary one demanded by the preeminence of his legendary feats rather than his reputation as a direct participant.

Eros is most directly associated with Heracles in his acquisition of that hero's attributes, the club and lionskin.[167] Two poems in the *Greek Anthology* describe the theft, and it was portrayed at least in a fourth century B.C. painting by Aetion.[168] A second century B.C. inscriptional inventory from the gymnasium at Delos records the dedication of a statue of Eros with the attributes of Heracles: "Eros on a column, two-footed, with a lionskin and club, a dedication of Tlepolemus and Hegeus" (*Inscriptions de Délos* 1417 face A, 119–20).[169] Other representations of Eros with Heracles from the fourth century onward suggest an erotic context for various of the hero's undertakings, or simply an erotic or playful aspect of the hero's character.[170] In any case, these direct associations were successful because they were based on an interesting contrast between the brute, physical power of the massive Heracles and the tender charm of the young Eros. Eros' theft of Heracles' attributes underlines an old theme, here freshly expressed, of love conquering all. In other words, it illustrates the tension between physical and emotional powers, or the paradox of a figure of violent strife who is dominated and one of peaceful union who dominates. A similar contrast is inherent in the depictions of Eros wrestling Pan, which appear as early as the fourth century B.C. but become popular in the Roman period. But with Pan the precise contrast is somewhat different, between a divinity of wild nature and one of emotion associated primarily with humans.[171]

I have discussed some of the direct associations between the three primary cult figures of the gymnasium, yet these cults most likely became attached to athletics and the gymnasium setting for different reasons and over a period of time in the early development of organized athletics during the sixth and fifth centuries B.C. The more direct associations in myth and art probably arose in part to explain the juxtaposition of these deities in the gymnasium. Yet even such derivative and artificial associations aid in our understanding of the dynamics of athletic cults. A careful chronology of the early associations of the three main gods of the gymnasium cannot be undertaken here, and it is likely that such a chronology would be provisional, given the fragmentary evidence for athletic cults in these periods. Yet more can be said of the early cults of Eros in relation to the athletic tradition.

Eros and Anteros

Pausanias describes as follows a shrine to Eros at the Academy in Athens, mentioned briefly in chapter 3:

> In front of the entrance to the Academy is an altar of Eros that has an inscription saying that Charmus was the first to dedicate [an altar] to Eros. . . . In the Academy is also an altar of Prometheus, and they run from this to the city holding lit torches. The object of the contest is to keep the torch liighted, and if the first man's torch is out, he has no share in the victory, and it goes to the second-place finisher. If this one is also not burning, the third one wins. If all are out, no victory goes to anyone. There is also an altar of the Muses, another of Hermes, and, inside [the Academy] of Athena and Heracles. (Paus. 1.30.1, 2)

Since the altar of Prometheus, the original bringer of fire to men, is named here as the starting point of the torch race, it has been argued that the race in question here is part of the Prometheia, organized as an annual competition among the tribes of Attica.[172] In addition to the Prometheia, there was also a torch race at the Panathenaia, probably modeled after the contest for Prometheus.[173] The unique concern in the rules of these contests, and in other torch-race contests in Athens and elsewhere, was keeping the torch lighted, a symbolic display of one individual, who is distinguished in his victory by a combination of speed and careful restraint, and who, by his victory, preserves the civilizing element for the entire community. According to a fourth-century list of prizes of the Panathenaia (*IG* II² 2311, lines 76–77), the torch race is listed as a tribal event, indicating that each runner represented a segment of the Athenian people and thus assumed a greater collective responsibility than he would have in most other events. The race is also distinguished in not offering the conventional prize of special amphorae filled with olive oil, but rather "a bull and one hundred drachmas" to the winning tribe and "a water jar and 30 drachmas" for the individual victor. This distinction in prizes, and the grouping of the event among other special tribal contests, suggest that the ritual aspect of the torch race is at least as important as the athletic.[174] That training and fitness were crucial to this event, as to the *euandria* on the same program, is indicated by Aristophanes' satire of contemporary runners who cannot carry the torch or keep it lighted due to "lack of training" (*agumnasia, fr.* 1088).[175] Healthy appearance, that is, "beauty" and performance were therefore of great importance in an event in which civic prosperity was mirrored in the success of the athlete. Perhaps these calisthenic associations led to a natural association of the torch race also with Eros in the Academy.

The altar of Prometheus may have been part of a large sanctuary area at the entrance to the Academy also occupied by the altars of Eros and the other gods mentioned by Pausanias in this passage.[176] The torch race for the Panathenaia apparently began at the altar of Eros: "The long race in the Panathenaia began from the altar of Eros. The ephebes lighting their torches there ran the race and the fire for the sacrificial offering to Athena was lighted from the torch of the victor" (*Schol.* [Hermias] Pl., *Phaedr.* 231e). Athenaeus agrees with Pausanias that the altar was set up by a certain Charmus, a general, the supposed lover of the young Hippias and later his father-in-law when Hippias became tyrant (Ath. 13.609d).[177] An inscription on the altar was as follows:

ποικιλομήχαν᾽ Ἔρως, σοὶ τόνδ᾽ ἱδρύσατο βωμὸν
Χάρμος ἐπὶ σκιεροῖς τέρμασι γυμνασίου.

Eros with your many devices, Charmus built you this altar
Near the shadowy turning posts of the gymnasium. (Ath. 13.609d)[178]

The inscription suggests that the gymnasium existed by 527 B.C., and our earlier discussion of the laws of Solon suggests that the Academy may have existed by the beginning of the sixth century. I translate *termasi* of the poem as "turning posts" rather than the "limits" or "boundaries" that others read here, since *terma* is more frequently used of athletic goals or turning posts in races than of the boundaries of a plot of land.[179] Plutarch elaborates upon the erotic relations, informing us that there was also a statue of Eros, presumably at or near the altar, from which the torch races began: "It is said that Peisistratus was the lover of Charmus, and that he set up a statue [*agalma*] of Eros in the Academy, from which place the runners in the sacred torch race lit their flames (Plut., *Sol.* 1.7). The Eros statue was therefore set up before 527 B.C., the end of Peisistratus' reign, and it probably preceded the altar built by the tyrant's (presumably younger) beloved, Charmus. It has been speculated that the torch race of the Panathenaia originally (in a reorganization of 566 B.C.?) began at the altar of Prometheus and was later (in the 530s or 520s?) transferred to the altar of Eros, perhaps with Charmus' foundation of the altar during the tyranny of the Peisistratids.[180]

Between his descriptions of the altars of Eros and Prometheus with its torch race, Pausanias narrates the origin of another Athenian altar associated with Eros:

They say that the altar of the so-called "Anteros" ["Counter-Love" or "Love Returned"] in the city was set up by foreign residents when an

Athenian called Meles spurned an alien man in love with him,
Timagoras, and told him to climb up to the highest point of a rock and
jump. Thereupon Timagoras cared nothing for his life and wanted to
give the youth everything just as he asked and so went there and threw
himself off. When Meles saw that Timagoras had died, in a change of
spirit resolved to throw himself off this same rock, and so doing he died.
From then on, the foreign residents resolved to honor this spirit of
vengeance, Anteros. (Paus. 1.30.1)

Why does this apparent digression on the cult of Anteros in the city interrupt the
discussion of altars in the Academy? Is it merely to mention the only other prominent shrine to Eros in Athens, and therein to include the dramatic tale of its founding? Was there a connection between the cults of Eros in the Academy and Anteros
in the city? The dearth of cults of Eros in Athens was noted by Euripides and Plato,
and we may surmise that the ones named in this passage were the only ones known
to Pausanias.[181] It is odd that he is apparently silent about the classical shrine of
long standing to Eros in conjunction with Aphrodite on the north slope of the
Acropolis discovered by archaeologists.[182] Might the Acropolis shrine be identified
with the shrine of Anteros? The cliff looming above it would have made it a suitable "lover's leap." One study suggests that the Acropolis shrine was then also the
terminus of the race "in the city," thus making it a race from the vicinity of a shrine
to Eros to the vicinity of one to Anteros.[183] Pausanias says only that the torch race
of the Prometheia is run "to the city," without specifying the finish, possibly at the
altar of Athena on the Acropolis where the victor's flame served as an auspicious
source for the sacrificial fire at the Panathenaia. The torch race of the Panathenaia,
in this case, would have ended at the altar of Athena on the Acropolis, located directly above the sanctuary of Eros and Aphrodite (and of Anteros?).[184]

At the very least, Pausanias' juxtaposition of the altar of Eros in the Academy,
the shrine of Anteros in the city, and the altar and race of Prometheus in the Academy shows that the first two were associated as two of the few cult sites of Eros
in Athens and that the altars of Eros and Prometheus were in close proximity.
Peisistratus or Hippias may have been the one to add a torch race and to have it
begin at the Altar of Eros, modeling it on that of the Prometheia.[185] The attention
to the shrine of Eros in the Peisistratid period is evidence that this institutionalized
association of Eros with athletics began in the 530s or 520s B.C. and thus, like Solon's
earlier law on eros in the gymnasium, marks an important stage in the civic incorporation of the two customs. The fact that the race was a tribal event and that it
was run from the altar of Eros to the most prominent altar of Athena further evidences the great civic importance of this event. The choice to have the fire taken
from the altar of Eros rather than that of Prometheus suggests that, in effect, Eros
was given prominence over the original fire-bringer. Eros, not Prometheus, better
symbolized the spirit of what Athenians saw as the source of civic prosperity, the

greatest source of strength in the gymnasium. In the later words of Plato, eros is what most contributes to the bonds of friendship and society (Pl., *Symp.* 182c); in the words of Athenaeus, eros increases the friendship, the concord, and ultimately the freedom of the state (Ath. 13.561d). Keeping to the philosophical tone of his dialogue, however, Athenaeus seeks to bowdlerize the physical aspects of eros which were intrinsic to the cult from its origins: "The Athenians were so far from considering Eros as being in charge of any form of sexual intercourse that right there in the Academy, a place clearly consecrated to Athena, they set up his shrine and worshiped him in conjunction with her" (13.561e). In view of the widespread, legitimate associations of the physical side of eros with the gymnasium, Athenaeus here overstates the religious and spiritual aspects of Eros at the expense of his more worldly side. By incorporating his worship into the torch race of the Panathenaia, the Athenians were paying homage to both aspects of love.

The union of symbolism of Eros and the torch race first appears with some frequency in Hellenistic and later art, perhaps influenced by the Athenian custom and the popularity of torch races elsewhere as a tribal event for young athletes.[186] An Attic red-figure amphora, ca. 460–450 B.C., shows on one side Eros in flight with two torches, on the other a young man in flight.[187] Here are combined the motifs of Eros as patron of the torch race and of Eros invading the gymnasium in pursuit of the young athlete. This scene is, to my knowledge, the earliest depiction of Eros with a torch and may represent symbolically the erotic aspect of the Panathenaic torch race. An Apulian plate from the fourth century B.C. depicts on the exterior one Eros running with a torch and bedecked with victory fillets before an altar, while a second Eros sits holding a wreath.[188] Though from an Italian provenience, the scene reflects the torch race from or to an altar, perhaps of Eros, with the altar flame represented by a stylized ivy leaf. Another Apulian vase, a bell-krater of the same period as the plate, also shows Eros running with a torch clearly of the type used by torch racers.[189] Eros is depicted holding a torch on a second-century B.C. bronze statuette from Tunis, and on a late fourth-century B.C. terracotta from Tarentum.[190] There is an Eros *Lampadēphoros*, "Runner in the Torch Race", (literally "Torch Bearer" [in a race]), holding the torch in his raised right hand, as depicted on a relief sculpture dated to the late second to early first century B.C. and found on Delos in the Maison de Fourni.[191] There are three graffiti sketches of Eros on a stele from the Granite Palaestra on Delos and dated to the second to early first century B.C. which, in light of corresponding descriptions on a gymnasium inventory, are believed to depict statues of Eros dedicated in the palaestra.[192] Among these Delian graffiti images of Eros, there appears an infant Eros carrying a torch in both hands and running to the right. Since the graffito image corresponds to the Maison de Fourni relief and to a type of torch inscribed on the seats of the gymnasium at Delos, the Eros appears to be another "Runner in the Torch Race."[193] Next to him is a grafitto of Eros with a bow and a dedication underneath, "Boleas [dedicated this] to

Hermes" (ΒΩΛΕΑΣ ΕΡΜΕΙ). Hermes, when evoked alone in the Delian victory inscriptions, was the patron of torch racers.[194] According to one recent commentator, "Eros, though made an object of private dedications, as numerous graffiti attest, was never explicitly honored in the gymnasium at Delos, where he appears more as a guardian of the *philia* of ephebes than as an agonistic divinity."[195] This view of Eros as a "guardian of the *philia* of the ephebes" seems to rely on a literal reading of the Athenaeus passage discussed earlier, and yet, as we have seen, the agonistic Eros is not clearly separable from the god as advocate of ephebic friendship. The fact that Eros is on second century b.c. Delos, acknowledged widely in private dedications but not in public ones, seems to reflect the private nature of erotic relations in connection with the gymnasium; it does not, however, exclude the god as an important figure in the agonistic realm.

The original association between Eros and the torch race, then, seems to have arisen from the Panathenaic race from the shrine in the Academy and apparently began in the late sixth century b.c. There, too, the Peisistratid shrine was a private one, but with an important civic function. Delos and other gymnasia probably adopted the association on analogy with the Panathenaia. Eros as Runner in the Torch Race epitomizes the connections of that event with the encouragement of young men to join in the tribal contests of the ephebes. The great proliferation of images of Eros (Amor, Cupido) with a torch later in Roman art may in part be derived from this Greek tradition, though its adoption of a wholly different iconography of its own undoubtedly reflects a peculiar Roman symbolism that is to be distinguished from the Torch Runner Eros of the Greek gymnasium and is beyond the purview of this study.[196]

In addition to the Eros in the Athenian Academy, Pausanias tells us that at Elis "in one of the palaestrae is a relief sculpture with Eros and the so-called Anteros. Eros has a palm branch, and Anteros tries to take the palm from him" (6.23.5).[197] This palaestra may be part of the gymnasium called "Maltho," "the Soft Place," after its floor softened for wrestling practice, reserved for ephebes for the whole time of training before the Olympic festival under Elean supervision. Here, as in Athens, Eros occupies a place of honor in the gymnasium, and, as in Athens, he stands as an important agonistic presence expressed in an artistic medium. At Elis, Eros is not just a guardian of friendship and a reminder of the important benefits of beauty and erotic relations that result from athletic participation; he is also an active participant in the contest. He is a wrestler. As such, the god is a model for Olympic athletes, as he is for those in the Panathenaia. Though the Elean gymnasium is not in Olympia, it is the requisite training area for all Olympic athletes. Since Olympic wrestlers and perhaps pankratiasts are directly confronted with the image of Eros, the god is publicly, if somewhat indirectly, acknowledged as an important force behind the Olympic Games. The date of this relief is uncertain, but the existence of other fifth century b.c. depictions of Eros wrestling Anteros, notably including a mid fifth century relief on a terracotta altar from Sicily,[198] at least allows for the possibility that the Elean scene dates from that period. It may be that the Elean gymnasium was following a tradition of images of Eros in the gymnasium begun at the Academy.

Incidentally on the topic of images of Eros associated with Elis and Olympia, Pausanias (5.11.3) reports that on Phidias' famous cult statue of Zeus at Olympia there was placed between the feet of the statue a relief sculpture of a certain athlete binding his own head with a victor's ribbon. The figure is said (*legousi*) to resemble Pantarkes of Elis, victor in boys wrestling at the eighty-sixth Olympics (436 B.C.), who was said also to be the beloved of the artist himself. The story is plausible, since the date of Pantarkes' victory accords with the period when Phidias was working on the cult statue in the years after 438. Elis was, moreover, famous for its beautiful boys.[199] But even if Pausanias' cautious hearsay report suggests a tour-guide fiction, the story itself reinforces our thematic point that victorious Olympic athletes often became sex objects, validated here by the alleged example of the famous artist. Though Eros himself is absent from the Olympic image, his presence is conveyed by the legend.

The Eros-Anteros image was also extended for metaphorical use outside of athletics, namely to express the contest spirit in sexual relationships. An Attic pyxis vase of about 430 B.C. shows on one side a woman on a bridal couch attended by Eros, and on the other a wrestling contest between Eros and Anteros (fig. 8-17).[200] To the right of the contestants sits Aphrodite with her scepter, an attendant, and a harpist, probably Harmonia; to the left stands a goddess, perhaps Peitho in the role of umpire.[201] A fragment of a nuptial lebes shows a similar scene, Eros wrestling Anteros, with two (olive?) crowns in the background and in the presence of goddesses (fig. 8-18).[202] The juxtaposition of a marriage scene with the wrestling Erotes suggests that the agon generally and wrestling specifically were metaphors for the wedding and heterosexual eroticism. Peitho acting as umpire attests to that divinity's role in the marriage ritual, as does the attendance of Aphrodite and Harmonia, gods typically more associated with a wedding than a wrestling match.[203] A fourth century B.C. Apulian vase shows two Erotes wrestling before a woman (the 'prize'?; or a goddess?) while a third Eros flies above holding a crown.[204] The scene becomes very popular in Roman art but is transferred to sarcophagi and gems with other iconographic significance, with multiple Erotes/Amores appearing in one scene of athletic contests.[205] If the wrestling Erotes are for the Greeks a metaphor for the phenomenon of eros itself, they may have seemed more apt than other images in view of the pre-established associations of Eros with homoerotic relations in the gymnasium. Yet the precise agonic activity of the metaphor, wrestling, requires further explication.

Erotic love has often found expression as agonistic activity in Greek literature. Eros has occasionally been made into a metaphorical boxer in Greek literature. So a poem of Anacreon (ca. 570–ca. 485 B.C.) exhorts:

φέρ' ὕδωρ, φέρ' οἶνον, ὦ παῖ, φέρε <δ'> ἀνθεμόεντας ἡμὶν
στεφάνους ἔνεικον, ὡς δὴ πρὸς Ἔρωτα πυκταλίζω.

Figure 8-17. Two Erotes wrestling in the presence of goddesses. Attic red-figure pyxis, ca. 430 B.C., Washing Painter, Würzburg, Wagner Mus. L 541 (H4455). Courtesy of the Martin von Wagner Museum, Universität Würzburg, Germany. Photo: K. Oehrlein.

> Bring water, bring wine, o boy, and bring me the flowery
> Crowns. Bring them, since I am indeed boxing against Eros!
>
> (Anacr. fr. 369 Diehl)

The struggle with love is presumably set in a symposium, at which the speaker wishes to break the resistance of a beloved boy. He therefore needs the "weapons" by which to persuade the fellow symposiast: wine, water, and gifts of garlands. But why is the speaker "boxing against Eros" and not with Eros on his side? The same metaphor is used by Sophocles:

> Ἔρωτι μὲν γοῦν ὅστις ἀντανίσταται
> πύκτης ὅπως ἐς χεῖρας οὐ καλῶς φρονεῖ.
>
> Whoever challenges Eros to a match
> Like a boxer fist-to-fist, he is out of his wits.
>
> (Soph., Trachiniae 441)

Figure 8-18. Two Erotes wrestling with two crowns in the background. Attic red-figure lebes gamikos fragments, ca. 430 B.C., Washing Painter, Munich, Staatl. Antikensamml. VAS 8926. Courtesy of the Staatliche Antikensammlungen und Glyptothek, Munich, Germany.

There is a deliberate ambiguity here, I believe, since the speaker is inflicted with eros and tries to fight the passion like a disease, that is, he struggles internally with eros, and at the same time he yields to the ineluctable power and struggles with his beloved to respond to it. The response of a junior partner in a Greek pederastic relationship is not normally termed *erōs* or *anterōs* (counter-love), but rather *philia*, "friendship," "affection," or "fondness."[206] The response of a female beloved to a male lover is, however, conventionally termed *anterōs*. The difference is at least in part due to the convention that a boy beloved yields due to a self-sacrificing *philia*, while women, who are, in the Greek view, more emotionally inclined, are more likely to feel an *erōs* in response to their male lover. Whatever the terms used, the beloved conventionally resists, and a "struggle" to resist or flee the lover ensues. Eros the god both "infects" those who feel the emotion *erōs* and acts as the supervisory divinity who brings relationships to fruition. So in Aristophanes' *Acharnians* (991–94), a chorus member hopes for Eros to unite him with the female "Reconciliation" (*Diallagē*), before he resorts to a threat of force, using wrestling metaphors: "Would that somehow an Eros seize and unite you and me, just like one painted wearing a crown of flowers. Perhaps you think I'm a bit too old for that? Yet I still think I could put a hold on you and throw you for a fall."[207]

Eros then fights against himself or "wrestles" with himself in the person of the two individuals in either a homo- or heteroerotic relationship. Thus the metaphor of a wrestling Eros probably portrays the internalized eros of the lover, and his agonistic attempt to realize it with his beloved. There is, on the one hand, an internal struggle to control or channel or find satisfaction of the desire, and, on the other, a struggle between self and other, lover and beloved, to determine through passion or reason the terms of their relationship. The self-other relation between lover and beloved is, as noted earlier, usually one between partners of unequal status, and thus the heroic ethos of victory in the *agōn* becomes the most natural one underlying the erotic conquest as well. The courtship between Greek men and boys, or between men and women, was normally characterized by the resistance of the beloved to the lover's advances, though the resistance may well have been more a performance than a reality.[208] In any case, the "flight and pursuit" motif of erotic relations evidences a conventional tension that apparently found metaphorical expression in the wrestling match of Eros paired against himself.

There may also be implied the external struggle of two or more rivals, the Greek term for which is *anterastēs*, who vie for the affection of a beloved. In this case, the "wrestling match" would also be for the "prize" of a beloved's affection, and the metaphor would also describe an external struggle of self versus other for a common goal. Such a struggle also fits the athletic image well, and it may be that the wrestling iconography at once allows for all three levels of meaning: internal struggle, lover struggling with beloved, and rival lovers contesting for a beloved.

The indeterminacy of the struggle, the tension inherent in it, and the notion of a victory for the successful lover are what characterize the agonistic aspect of Eros. Plato played on this association in the *Phaedrus* with particular reference to the internalized desire of the lover:

ὅταν δὲ χρονίζῃ τοῦτο δρῶν καὶ πλησιάζῃ μετὰ
τοῦ ἅπτεσθαι ἔν τε γυμνασίοις καὶ ἐν ταῖς ἄλλαις ὁμιλίαις,
. . . καὶ ὅταν μὲν ἐκεῖνος παρῇ, λήγει κατὰ ταὐτὰ ἐκείνῳ τῆς ὀδύνης,
ὅταν δὲ ἀπῇ, κατὰ ταὐτὰ αὖ ποθεῖ καὶ ποθεῖται, εἴδωλον
ἔρωτος ἀντέρωτα ἔχων· καλεῖ δὲ αὐτὸν καὶ οἴεται οὐκ ἔρωτα
ἀλλὰ φιλίαν εἶναι. ἐπιθυμεῖ δὲ ἐκείνῳ παραπλησίως μέν,
ἀσθενεστέρως δέ . . . (Pl., *Phaedr.* 255b–e)

And when this feeling [of close friendship] continues [between lover and beloved], he is nearer to him by embracing him both in gymnastic exercises and at other times of meeting. . . . When he is with the lover, both cease in their pain, but when he is away, then he longs as he is longed for and has as love's image, Anteros, which he calls and believes

to be not love only, but friendship, and his desire is as the desire of the
other, but weaker. . . .

Plato is first to attribute Anteros to the partners in the pederastic relationship, and
he does this to further his view of the idealized form of the phenomenon. But his
description serves as a general one for both homo- and heterosexual relations. It
also describes the reciprocity of action and the internal struggle that are common
to any reading of the metaphor of Eros wrestling Anteros.

Athletic Festivals of Eros

Thus far, we have seen the cult of Eros associated with athletics primarily through
altars or artistic representations in gymnasia, the relief of Eros wrestling Anteros
at Elis, and statues or altars of the god in Athens and Delos. In at least two other
instances, however, at Thespiae in Boeotia, and on the island of Samos, fully fledged
athletic festivals were held in honor of Eros, and the character of these games will
contribute to our understanding of the social role of this god in athletic contexts.
One of the most famous cults of Eros in antiquity was at Thespiae in Boeotia where
an athletic festival, the Erotidaea, was held every four years like the Olympics and
the Panathenaia in honor of the god.[209] "The people of Thespiae celebrate the
Erotidaea just as the Athenians do the Athenaia [= Panathenaia], the Eleans the
Olympics, and the Rhodians the Halieia," reports Athenaeus (13.561e); another
source says that "various games [agōnes] are held in Boeotia: in Thespiae the
Erotidaea" (Schol. ad Pind., Ol. 7.154c). Thus, the Erotidaea seems to follow the
pattern of the major athletic festivals, and a series of inscriptions from Thespiae
record the victors at contests that included most of the conventional athletic events
found at Olympia and other major festivals.[210] Among the contests recorded are five
types of footrace (dolichos ["long-distance"], stade ["one-length"], diaulos ["two-
length"], the torch race, and the hoplite race in armor), the pentathlon, wrestling,
boxing, and pankration, all of these held for men and as many as three other age-
divisions for boys (younger boys ["Pythic" boys], older boys ["Isthmic" boys], and
youths [ageneioi]). There was also a full range of chariot races (two- and four-horse,
for both foals and full-grown horses) and horse races (for both foals and full-grown
horses). Generally, the standard "gymnic" (nonhippic athletic contests) events are
followed by the hippic events, which we may assume reflects the order of competition in the festival. In one case (IG 7.1772, lines 9–10) a poiētēs chorōn (arranger of
choral dances?) is oddly listed in a smaller script between the gymnic and hippic
events. This may be a half-time show, or it may be a scribal error to compensate for
an omission earlier in the "music" category of another festival held at the same time,
as will be discussed shortly.[211] Not all events are listed on all preserved lists, and,

even in view of the fragmentary state of most of the lists, it seems likely that the program varied slightly from festival to festival over the years, perhaps due to an occasional lack of sufficient entrants.

It is uncertain when the cult of Eros at Thespiae was established, though Pausanias considers the rough-stone cult image at Thespiae to be "very old" (Paus. 9.27.1). The cult became famous all over Greece when a statue of Eros by Praxiteles was set up there in the fourth century B.C., supposedly the result of a gift by the sculptor to the famously beautiful hetaira, Phryne, who had the statue installed in Thespiae, her birthplace.[212] Thereafter the touristic traffic probably increased as pilgrims came to see the famous masterpiece. At some point thereafter, the citizens of Thespiae decided to capitalize upon their cultic importance by instituting joint festivals of the Erotidaea and the Musaea, the latter consisting of musical contests in honor of the Muses, whose mythical home was the nearby Mount Helicon.[213] Both festivals probably took place in the city of Thespiae, where a theater has been found, though Pausanias seems to indicate that Helicon was the venue.[214] The earliest inscriptions for the festivals date to the second century B.C., and we may assume that they were instituted in that period. Both were, according to Plutarch, produced "very lavishly and splendidly"(φιλοτίμως πάνυ καὶ λαμπρῶς, *Amat.* 748f), and, as the homelands of the victors attest, they attracted an audience and competitors from all over Greece and the Eastern Mediterranean. Later, the epithets *Romaia* and *Kaisareia* (Roman; Imperial) were added to the Erotidaea, and *Sebasteia* (August) to the Musaea; presumably Rome, the emperor, and his divinity were accordingly honored in the ceremonies and rituals. The Erotidaea seems to have been held simultaneously with a festival for the Muses, the Musaea, at which the program consisted of musical contests, at times even sharing the same agonothete, the local citizen who organized and financed the undertaking.[215]

Though athletic and music contests took place together at many festivals, and some festivals were held jointly, the combination of the Erotidaea and Musaea shows a natural complementarity that organizers exploited by sharing the two sorts of contests over the two established local cults. The association of the Muses with musical contests is obvious, but the organizers, by attaching Eros to athletic contests, show a conscious association of that deity with athletics. The Eros-athletics connection had obviously grown through various paths traced earlier in this chapter, but was now overt enough to become institutionalized in a major festival.

There are few clues as to the special character of the actual events of the Erotidaea which would mark it as a festival for Eros and not just an athletic festival like many others, grafted onto a local cult. We know nothing of the public sacrifices at the Erotidaea, but we can glean from Plutarch that offerings were made by pilgrims attending privately to seek from the god some assistance in their love lives, either just after a marriage, while wooing a special woman, or seeking to settle a dispute among the in-laws.[216] Love and romance seem to have been 'in the air' during the celebrations. In the dramatic setting of Plutarch's dialogue, purporting to be based on an actual event, a boy who is the controversial fiancé of an older woman is abducted by the woman just as he emerges from a palaestra in Thespiae during the festival; the spectators thereupon lose interest in the contests (754e–755a). One citizen comments: "Let's hand over the gymnasium and the council house to the women, since the city has been completely emasculated." In a real-life scene that is reminiscent of Greek Old or New Comedy, the actual workings of Eros have thrown the formal festivities of the deity into chaos. The fact that the finest artistic attraction of Thespiae's festival was Praxiteles' Eros, dedicated by the most famous daughter, the hetaira Phyrne, can be taken as an indication that extramarital eros was also an acknowledged dimension of the cult. Though there is no explicit mention of offerings for homoerotic aims, Plutarch's *Amatorius* recounts a discussion at the Erotidaea regarding the merits of homo- and heterosexual love, and it is likely that this, the best known festival of Eros, comprehended the god in all his spheres of influence. In the context of the cult at Thespiae, Pausanias in fact recounts the multifarious aspects of Eros, including his role in cosmic creation and his prominence in the hymns of Sappho (Paus. 9.27.1–2). While public sacrifices and prayers probably addressed Eros in all his aspects, private petitioners from all over Greece likely sought divine favor for their particular *affaires de coeur*, whatever the sexual or spiritual orientation.

Eros' character may have also affected the structure of the athletic events in subtle ways, though this matter is not addressed in any literary sources. One inscription, the earliest athletic one from Thespiae, lists a torch race as the first gymnic event on the program.[217] This is the event most closely identified with Eros, as our earlier discussion has indicated. It may also be significant that the age categories for boys are given the fullest possible distribution into three groups, covering roughly ages 12–14, 14–17, and 17–20.[218] These divisions correspond to the age categories of boys available for pederastic relationships and marked in Greek terminology, younger and older *paides* (boys), and *ageneioi* (lit., "beardless," i.e., those just beginning to grow a beard = *ephêboi* = *neaniskoi*).[219] None of the Panhellenic festivals and only a few other local festivals have such a variety of categories.[220] Part of the rationale may have been to offer contestants more opportunities to win among their coevals and thus enhance the attraction to enter. But the effect, incidental if not intentional, was to display the beauty, strength, and skill of youths and boys at various stages in their progress toward adulthood. It was, of course, an implicit result of age categories at all festivals to display the beauty of the male body, but this aspect may have been more pronounced at a festival whose focus was Eros. Youths and boys may have been seen here more than elsewhere as objects of desire, as beloved of an older male, or as a potential husband.

Athenaeus is the sole source for the Eleutheria, the festival of Eros on Samos which had athletic associations and a civic function complementary to the cults at Athens and Thespiae:[221] "As Erxias says in his *History of Colophon*, the people of Samos dedicated a gymnasium to Eros and called the festival that was estab-

lished on this occasion the Eleutheria" (Ath. 13.562a). Though we know nothing more about the content of this "Freedom Festival," it has been suggested that
there were, as at the Erotidaea, athletic contests.[222] The association of the cult
with a gymnasium and the traditions of similar games make this likely. A well-
known athletic festival called the Eleutheria in honor of Zeus *Eleutherios* was established in 196 B.C. at Larisa, Thessaly, to celebrate the liberation of Macedonia
from Philip V by the Romans.[223] The most famous Eleutheria festival, also with
an athletic program and also dedicated to Zeus *Eleutherios*, was that established
at Plataea in thanks for the Greek victory over the Persians at that city in 479
B.C.[224] The occasion for the founding of the gymnasium and the games has been
associated with the fall of the tyrant Polycrates in 522 B.C., at which time a cult
of Zeus *Eleutherios* (God of Freedom) was also established, though Samos' Athenian alliances either in the later fifth century or during the fourth century B.C.
might also have prompted the custom as a political gesture.[225] In any case, the
fact that our source, Erxias, probably wrote in the second century B.C., suggests
that the festival was older than the Erotidaea.

The connection of a "Festival of Freedom" with Eros rather than Zeus requires
explanation. We may recall Athenaeus' comments, discussed earlier, about the
complementary function of the cults of Eros, Hermes, and Heracles: "when these
are united, friendship and concord come about, out of which the fairest freedom
(*eleutheria*) is enhanced for those who pursue them" (Ath. 16.561d). *Eleutheria*, "freedom," is of course a very broad and complex concept in Greek culture, comprehend-
ing both civic and private liberties, as well as the freedom of one state from undue
repression by another. It included not only the negative concept of freedom from
domination by others, but a freedom that mainly encompassed political status and
political opportunities for all male citizens.[226] For Athenaeus, the freedom arising
from the combined worship of three athletic deities is a product of "friendship and
concord" (φιλία τε καὶ ὁμόνοια), primary civic values that are practiced in the gymnasium. For Plato, eros is what most contributes to the bonds of friendship and society; it separates the civilized Greeks from the barbarians (Pl., *Symp.* 182c, quoted
in the opening of this chapter). "In the thought of this period," writes one commentator on fifth century B.C. ideals,

> the notions of justice, concord, friendship, and equality were seen as
> interdependent if not identical, and essential to the preservation of the
> political order. . . . [C]oncord is a word applied to cities when the
> citizens agree about their common interests make the same practical
> choices, and carry them out.[227]

The qualities opposite to those prescribed by Athenaeus, namely civil strife (*stasis*)
and hostility (*echthra*), would conversely result in political discord and possibly the
domination of one group by another.

In general terms, then, political order and freedom issue directly from a spirit of eros, taken in the widest sense, which is fostered in the gymnasium. Athenaeus in the passage just mentioned furnishes additional examples of how Eros is directly linked in various Greek cities to the civic well being (13.561e–f). Besides the cult in the Athenian Academy and the festivals of Thespiae and Samos, he mentions the Spartan custom of offering preliminary sacrifices to Eros before the troops are drawn up in battle line, "since salvation and victory rest in the friendship of those drawn up"; the Cretans post their handsomest citizens in the battle-lines and through them offer sacrifices to Eros; the so-called "Sacred Company" of the Thebans is composed of lovers and their male beloved [i.e. homosexual couples], indicating the solemnity of the god Eros, "since they welcome a glorious death instead of a shameful and reprehensible death"; and the Peisistratids were the first to begin defaming the actions caused by Eros, since their downfall was partly occasioned by the male lovers Harmodius and Aristogeiton (13.561e–562a). The latter incident seems to contradict the story quoted earlier of Peisistratus establishing the Eros cult in the Academy, but it can also be taken to show how Eros and his cult were flexible and vital political realities in Athens, able to be invoked by either side in political strife as suited the circumstances.[228]

Athenaeus further notes that wrestling schools and gymnasia themselves were seen as threatening to tyrants since those institutions were hotbeds of pederastic bonding that could give rise to coup attempts:

> Because of such love-relationships, then, the tyrants, to whom these friendships are inimical, used to forbid pederastic relations entirely, extirpating them everywhere. Some even set fire to and demolished palaestras, regarding them as counter-fortifications against their own citadels. Polycrates of Samos did this. (13.602d)

Perhaps the Samian Eleutheria in honor of Eros mentioned above was the peoples' reaction to Polycrates' stern measures. Another famous example of tyrannical repression of gymnasia is that of Aristodemus of Cymae (died 524) who, seeking to discourage a "noble and manly spirit," closed all gymnasia and forced all youths reared in the city to dress and wear long hair in the fashion of girls.[229]

In yet another way a century later, Eros was still invested with political imagery during the Peloponnesian War. The quasi-tyrannical Alcibiades' golden shield was emblazoned with an image of the god holding a thunderbolt (Plut., *Alc.* 16, cf. 17.2); Eros thus assumes the aggressive, martial role usually reserved for Zeus. Thucydides (6.24.3–4) says of the Sicilian Expedition at its outset, "There was an eros for the enterprise which affected everyone alike." And the general enterprising spirit of the Athenians in the fifth century has been described as a manifestation of eros, reflected at times in the drama of the period.[230] Eros could thus be invoked as a spirit seeking to preserve freedom in the state by promoting friendship and concord among citizens and a passionate unity against a common foe of the polis, whether the enemy be another state or a tyrant. It is in this sense that the god can be understood as the patron deity of the Eleutheria at Samos.

Agonistic Desire and Aesthetic Metaphor

The assimilation of Eros to athletics and to athletic festivals was so complete that the "agonistics" of desire, the similarities between the struggles of the contests and those of sexual relations, served as the basis for a number of artistic metaphors. We have already examined many scenes in which Eros is portrayed in the performance of athletic events, notably wrestling Anteros, in the visual arts. The same can be found in literature, ordinarily in comic or bawdy contexts. Aristophanes' *Peace* (894–905) fantasizes about a character's encounter with Lady Festival, *Theōria*. First love-wrestling and pankration are described, then a horse-race:

> Then you will at once be able to hold an athletic festival,
> a very fine one, tomorrow when you have this lady.
> It will have ground-wrestling, getting down on all fours,
> oiled up in the manner of a young athlete for pankration
> to hit and to gouge, all at once with the punch and the prick.
> On the third day after these events, you will go in for horse-racing,
> one jockey out-jockeying another,
> chariots piled one on another
> blowing and panting as the teams come to the finish.
> Some will lie by the side, stiff and still,
> drivers having fallen around the bends.
>
> (Aristoph., *Peace* 894–905)

There is a certain wittily feigned modesty in Aristophanes' clothing of an orgy in the double-entendre of a sports festival at which the central attraction is "Lady Festival" (*Theōria*) herself.[231] The aggressive aspects of erotic encounters are conveyed pointedly, for example, with play on the terminology of "the punch and the prick" (πὺξ ... καὶ τῷ πέει) in the pankration. This passage was a forerunner of the later love-wrestling scenes in Nonnus' *Dionysiaca*.[232]

An epigram of Lucillius, written in the Neronian period (A.D. 54–68), also plays on the aggressiveness of desire as a force stronger than athletic strife:

> Cleombrotos retired as a boxer. Then afterward married,
> And endures at home the blows of the Isthmian and Nemean Games,
> A pugnacious old woman, whose punches are worthy of the Olympics,
> And he dreads his own house more than he ever dreaded the stadium,

Whenever he gets his wind, he is pummeled with the blows of an entire match
to make him yield to her; and if he gives in, he is beaten again.

(Lucill., *Greek Anth.* 11.79)

The boxer's yielding (ἀποδῷ) here is a double entendre, using the technical term
for admitting defeat in a contest, and the term for yielding to his 'marital devoir.'
The joke of course takes point from the ironic role-reversal of the normal order, not
only in the disgrace of the victor being beaten, but also the fact that it is a woman
who beats him, apparently to spur on his sexual favors. To this compare the love
poem of Ibycus:

Eros again glances at me
from beneath his dark eyelashes with languishing eyes
and with his manifold charms
hurls me into the boundless nets of Aphrodite.
How I shudder when he attacks,
the way that a yoked, prize-winning horse close to old age,
unwillingly pulling the swift chariot goes to the contest.

(Ibyc., fr. 6 [Page])

The constraints of Eros again portray the subject as one drawn into the tension of
the contest.

A Hellenistic epigram also takes up the theme of constraints of desire, describing in athletic terms a lover, possibly himself an athlete, who is rejected by a hetaira,
a virgin, and a boy:

No longer do I love. I have wrestled [πεπάλαικα] with three yearnings;
    one sets me on fire for a hetaira,
One for a virgin, and one for a boy.
And in every way I suffer pain. For I have been worn out with exercise
    [γεγύμνασμαι],
Seeking to persuade the prostitute's door to open, the foes of him who
    cannot pay.
Continually sleepless I stretch out on the girl's couch,
Giving the child one thing and that most desirable, a kiss.
Alas, how shall I tell of the third flame? For from that [boy]
I have gained nothing but glances and empty hopes.

(*Greek Anth.* 12.90, Anonymous)

As in the other literary expressions, this poem shows that the agonistic struggle was
one basis for a concept of desire. By Hellenistic times, the metaphor has become a
common expression, almost the leading idiom, for the experience of erotic passion.

Chronology and Overview

The use of athletics as a metaphor for erotic passion signals an evolution from an earlier stage at which naked athletes in the gymnasium or at games actually inspired eros in viewers. That visual stimulus remained in later periods, but the theme of agonistic desire was reinterpreted and embellished later in visual art and literature. This evolution resulted from a complex series of events. Our survey has shown that Eros has come far from Hesiod's cosmogonic portrait of the force that unites the complementary powers of creation. From that primal aspect have evolved many others, social, philosophical, and political. At the same time, athletics evolved in Greek society and played a crucial role in the cultural customs and concepts of eros. Chronologically, the fusion and evolution of eros and athletics can be traced in brief as follows, based on the discussions in this chapter.

By the eighth and seventh centuries B.C., Olympia had become a leading political and religious center for all Greeks. The incorporation of an athletic festival and the participation of contestants from ever more distant reaches of the Greek world led, by the sixth century B.C., to an 'athletic revolution' characterized by three significant events. First, some regions established their own Olympic-style Panhellenic games at the prominent sanctuaries of Delphi (from 582 B.C.), Isthmia (from 581 B.C.), and Nemea (from 573 B.C.). This happened alongside the widespread establishment of regularly held local athletic festivals, most prominent among which was the quadrennial Great Panathenaia of Athens, organized in 566 B.C. Second, cities generally fostered participation in athletic contests by establishing local training centers, gymnasia, wrestling schools, or specially designated "tracks" (*dromoi*). With these came special trainers or coaches and training programs, the earliest of which may have been that of the philosopher Pythagoras in Croton in the last third of the sixth century. Moreover, the custom of total nudity seems to have been widely adopted in this period, as the testimony of Theognis and other evidence seem to indicate: "Happy the lover who spends time in the gymnasium" (or "practices the gymnic events" = *gumnazetai*; Theog., *Eleg.* 2.1335). While the term *gumnos* may at times mean "lightly clad," its first appearance in the sixth and fifth centuries in athletic vocabulary suggests that a new terminology has been coined to describe the phenomenon of practicing athletics in the nude.

The possibly earliest use of such terminology, in the *Theognidea*, is also tied to a lover who "returning home, enjoys the whole day with a handsome youth." In the words of Plutarch cited earlier, pederastic eros came later than heterosexual eros, entered the gymnasium, slowly "grew wings," and grew bolder as a presence there (Plut., *Amat.* 751f–752a). Lactantius saw the fusion of Eros with the gymnasium as a "bold plan." More probably, it was the natural and inexorable movement of complementary, sixth-century practices. The 'athletic revolution,' whereby once disparate Greek cities felt a new unity with one another in their sharing of festivals and training practices, called for a new and visible expression of the spirit. Nudity may have been adopted as a free expression of Greek national confidence and aesthetic inclination. Since the Bronze Age, the athletes of Greece and of various Mediterranean cultures (Minoans, Mesopotamians, Egyptians, et al.) had worn little[233]; by abandoning all vestiges of clothing, the "costume" of nudity now made Greek athletes resemble their statues of the gods. Athletic nudity attested at once to the self-sufficiency of individuals and the freedom of a civilization easily distinguished from "the barbarians."

The growth of pederasty in this context was probably fundamentally fostered by erotic desire from the visual and tactile stimuli of the gymnasia and simultaneously shaped by cultural and political agendas of the day. I will not speculate on the currently debated topic of whether "desire" itself is "natural" or "culturally constructed," partly because it is beyond the purview of this study, and partly because it is a perennially unresolvable topic. I will only state that, in my view, "erotic desire" is a complex product of individual physiological and cultural factors. And since human physiology is presumably constant across cultures, what is of interest here is the way that the cultural construction of sexual desire in athletic contexts was uniquely formed by the Greeks. For the Greeks, of course, *erōs* was popularly considered to be a "natural" force, perhaps sent by divine powers. I therefore argue (and I think most Greeks would have agreed) that pederastic *erōs* was not literally "invented" in the gymnasium, but it was to some extent given a focus there and, under the restrictions of various formal and informal conventions, allowed to flourish there. The gymnasium became a locus of erotic affiliation, and of social and political ties that resulted from legitimate relationships formed therein. We cannot, unfortunately, obtain a precise historical picture of the evolution of pederasty within the gymnasium to judge whether it was tolerated or encouraged in the early development of the gymnasium, since the literary and visual evidence is sketchy. One can reasonably conclude from the evidence at hand that attitudes differed from city to city, generation to generation, and perhaps among different classes, but generally pederasty in the gymnasium was seen as a positive phenomenon. It also seems likely that desire itself, the "all-conquering," took on a life of its own and invaded the gymnasium through the emotions of the habitués of the gymnasium apart from the moral or political attitudes of any citizens. Solon, for one, seems to have implicitly endorsed pederasty in the gymnasium and even seen it as a phenomenon properly restricted to free-born citizens. As often, it may well have been a case of policy being written to sanction the prevailing norm.

Pindar is the most noteworthy early informant on the complementary phenomenon of heterosexual eros associated with athletics. In this case, liaisons with prostitutes aside, the *telos* of eros was marriage. This eros was expressed primarily outside the gymnasium and in the stadium. There maidens first witnessed the beauty of the nude male youth, and their fathers, with or without daughters present, may have sought to establish marriage ties with a successful youth and his family. Not only could the physical suitability of the athlete be assessed, but his fame as a victor would undoubtedly enhance his marriageability. Marriage arrangements could also result from pederastic relations formed in the gymnasium, as may have happened in the case of the Athenian Charmus, who was the beloved of Peisistratus, and whose daughter was married to his own beloved, Hippias.[234]

The associations of Eros with athletics arrived at their logical full extent with the institutionalization of cults of Eros in the gymnasium, probably beginning, in Athens at least, with Charmus' altar to the god in the Academy, and most clearly expressed in the athletic festivals to Eros at Thespiae and on Samos. Altars or statues to Eros were commonly found alongside the complementary deities of Hermes, the supervisor of skilled activities, and Heracles, the embodiment of superhuman strength. To these two gods Eros contributed the spirit of passionate longing, for victory, for beauty, for fame, and for friendship with fellow athletes and citizens. Some athletes may have restricted themselves from the sexual expression of eros while training, but it was only a Cleitomachus who indulged his eros for athletics in an obsessive aversion to any hint of sexual expression. Most athletes, we may assume, took a more balanced view, worshiping and following Eros in all his manifestations, physical, spiritual, and civic. At Thespiae it was evident that Eros was to be identified with contests of the body, while the Muses were honored with musical competition. But the Festival of Eleutheria, "Freedom," on Samos is the logical and ultimate extension of athletic eroticism. Desire freely expressed, manifest in nudity freely displayed and contests freely entered, could be an emblem of Greek civilization. By a certain paradox, Eros himself could exert a natural constraint on the individual, and individuals could exercise restraint in their capitulation to him, but ultimately athletics was a free expression, outside the duties and obligations of nature and the state, where the athlete could choose to display his body, to hone his natural skills, and to test his performance publicly to honor Eros. There was always the freely assumed risk of defeat and ignominy, but this was outweighed by the freely sought fame for self, for family, and for the city.

The athletic tradition of Eros may be best symbolized in the image of the Athenian torch-runner, carrying from the altar of that deity in the Academy a flame that stood for the civilizing element given to humans by Prometheus. The victorious runner ended his race at the civic and religious soul of Athens, the Acropolis, and his flame was probably used to kindle the sacrifices to Athena, patroness of the city. In short, the athletic Eros of the Panathenaic torch race linked the gymnasium, where boys were trained in the ways of men, with the shrines and public areas where the active life of adults took place. This tradition, so prominent in Athenian ritual, was played out for similar reasons, but with different rituals and contests, in other cities. A parallel tradition of a philosophical and abstract Eros sometimes tried to rationalize, control, or regulate the erotic aspects of athletics but never denied the power of the god. Only with Christianity was the heroic exultation of the body redirected and transformed. The body culture of today, while not a direct heir to the classical past, has resurrected a spirit of vigorous competition with a somewhat less overt and differently motivated devotion to the erotic.

9

DRAMA, DESIRE, AND DEATH IN
ATHLETIC PERFORMANCE

Philostratus recounts the following myth of origin for the ancient Olympic "stade" or single-length footrace:

> The stade race was founded in the following way. When the Eleans were offering sacrifice as is required, the offerings were laid on the altar, but fire was not yet applied to it. The runners went one-stadium length from the altar, in front of which a priest stood with a torch, acting as umpire. The winner then lit the sacrifice, and departed from there as Olympic victor. (*Gymn.* 5)

However historically suspect Philostratus' information may be, as we noted in chapter 1, it is not likely that the aetiological tale is a total fabrication. Some, perhaps most, ancient Greeks believed that this was the origin of the simplest footrace at Olympia—it is the only such explanation that has survived. The story has importance, then, at least as evidence of folk beliefs about the footrace, and it implies direct associations between athletic success and ritual actions.

In his brilliant analysis of cultic symbolism at the ancient Olympic festival, Walter Burkert quotes Pausanias' description of the sacrifice of bulls on Zeus' altar (5.13.9–10) and then offers the following interpretation of the Olympic footraces:

> Thus, the foot-race presupposes the bloody act of killing; likewise Pelops was "drenched with blood" in the preliminary sacrifice. The end of the race, its goal, is the top of the ancient heap of ash, the place where the fire must blaze and burn up the thigh-bones [of the bulls]. The race marks the transition from blood to purifying fire, from encountering death to joyful satisfaction of surviving as manifested in the strength of the victor. Thus, the most important agon at Olympia is part of the sacrificial act moving between the Pelopion and the altar of Zeus.[1]

So Burkert sets up a polarity between the funeral sacrifice to Pelops and the bright fire for Zeus, discussed in chapter 1 as a cultic phenomenon. Yet the contrast goes beyond one of encounter with death and surviving it. It is a contrast between the ignominy of being conquered and the fame of conquering. The footrace can be understood symbolically as the progress from death, anonymity, and disorder to life, glory, order, and the supremacy of Zeus. This life-and-death allegorical quality of athletic activity is not, however, limited to the events at Olympia but can be extended to most, if not all, Greek athletic contests. In a sense it is the controlling metaphor of the athletic performance and its associated cult myths and rituals. The athletic *agōn* is, as we have seen earlier, a contest characterized by an all-out desire to win, the extreme effort to do so, high esteem for success, fame for the victor, and the recognition of the mortal and physical limitations of the defeated. Both the male and female Greek athletic phenomena described in the preceding chapters can be described as agonistic performances played out between the valences of life-affirming desire and death-evoking fear.[2]

In this chapter I explore several aspects of this tension inherent in Greek athletic performances: the fundamental notions of the "performative" or "dramatic" qualities applied to athletics, the "teleology" or goals ascribed to both men's and women's competition, the foundation myths and cult associations of the athletic festivals of both sexes, the broader notion of "Eros" as desire in athletic performance, and the element of death or risk associated with many contests.

Greek athletic contests, as we have seen, were closely associated with the gods, local or Olympian, and to the cultic context in which the contests are held. The three most common gods of the gymnasium, Hermes, Heracles, and Eros (Athenaeus 13.651d) illustrate certain universally complementary ideals of those cults with respect to athletics. At the gymnasium in Elis where the judges assess the Olympic contestants before the Olympic festival, is found a similar, complementary combination of cults (Paus. 6.23.3). There is an altar for Idaean Heracles, "the Supporter," in some versions the founder of the Olympics, donator of the divine olive tree to Olympia, and protector of the child Zeus. This Heracles, like his namesake, the son of Alcmene, therefore represented protection and support of the patron deity and of athletes competing in his name. There was, incidentally, a bust of Alcmene's Heracles in the wrestling pit near the Elean gymnasium (Paus. 6.23.5). There was also an altar for Eros and for Anteros, Love and Love-returned, who stand for desire, its struggle, and its fulfillment. And there was an altar for Demeter and her daughter, who together represent the principles of fertility, death, and rebirth in the cycles of nature. This last cult thus reminds those in the gymnasium of the life-and-death struggles in nature parallel to those in athletics and society generally.

The athletic aspects of rituals of initiation of youths into adulthood, a theme taken up by four of the chapters above (3–6), contribute to the overall goal of *paideia* or social formation, and the athletic events constitute what we may call a kind of "performance" reflecting and contributing to the formation of established gender roles. It is arguably less important in such initiatory trials for a given individual to emerge as victor than it is for the victor to represent the well-being of a group, often the group of youth on the verge of adulthood, sometimes also the group of citizens who see the youth as symbolic of the future prosperity of the community. Victory could be read as a portent of divine favor. While such trials can, at times, involve risk of bodily harm, most notoriously the contest of enduring flagellation in Sparta, for the most part they consist of relatively harmless footraces in which the course can symbolize the essential movement of the youth from one status to the next. The initiatory contests of girls, though formally analogous to those for boys, convey in their performances a different set of communal values that are laden with the symbolism of the roles they will adopt as women, particularly bodily and spiritual strength for marriage and motherhood.

"Desire" is present in several ways in the context of initiation contests. As at Sparta, the presence of young men and women exercising or competing nude before one another can arouse a natural *erōs* that seeks fulfillment in marriage or some other erotic relationship. But the youth in all of these contests are subject to another *erōs*, the desire to reach the status of adulthood and to absorb the attendant lessons of their gender roles. This latter form of social *erōs* is not led on by nature, but placed onto them by adults. Like the "desire for death" that the coach of the dying pankratiast Arrhichion instilled in him during his match, the "desire for adult status" is communicated to the youths by, in some cases, requiring all in the community to undergo this ritual activity, and, in all cases, by informing the contest with the symbolism and meaning of cults and myths.

"Death" and the attendant fear of the obliteration of personal identity in death may also be present in symbolic form in initiatory athletics. Since the genuine physical risks are low, the true fear in the youth is one of changing, losing the physical and social qualities that define him or her as a child or adolescent, and taking on new and strange roles. So "death" in these contests is loss of one's 'wild' status and assumption of a new 'tamed,' civilized one that the participant is taught to desire. For girls, the symbolic 'death' or transformation takes place when the girl marries, after which she pursues the female ideals of *sōphrosynē* (self-control) and silence in accordance with her new social status. For the female, public athletic, contests of any sort end with marriage. For men, athletic competitions of the initiatory sort also end with adulthood. Athletic contests of the normal festival type are, of course, open to participation by males of all ages, yet the universal use of age-divisions in men's athletics may reflect an initiatory aspect of those contests, an emphasis on the progress from boy to man. Men's athletics are a performance and a reinforcement of male virtues and qualities, most noticeably the character of the hero and the warrior.

The individual response to death, like the attitude to the transition to adulthood, was for the Greeks a crucial indication of personal excellence. "A man who achieves the things desired forgets Hades," Pindar remarks about the effect of a boy's wrestling victory on his old father (*Ol.* 8.72–73). And the poet summons Echo to go to visit an athlete's father in Hades with report of his son's victory: "in the glorious vales of Pisa, his son has crowned his young hair with the wings of the glorious games" (*Ol.* 14.22–24). The youth succeeds in proving his adult excellence, which in turn gives him death-conquering fame and also ennobles his father and ancestors in their life and even after their death.

The "performative" qualities of death and desire in Greek athletics have the qualities of being once removed from "reality" and hence can be mimetic of some aspects of daily life, particularly those like martial strife and the struggle of lovers internally and with one another. That mimetic distance makes the athletic experience valuable as a kind of *paideia*, a didactic process that facilitates both participants and spectators in transferring the lessons of the contest to the practical activities of daily life. The "rupture" of the illusion of athletic performance, or perhaps more accurately its translation into civic action, constitutes a fundamental benefit of athletic pursuits among the Greeks, and, mutatis mutandis, among ourselves.

Performance and "the Dramatic" in Greek Athletics

First let us look more closely at how athletics might be described as a "performance" analogous to drama. Since the question involves the formal aspects of competition, especially public competition, our discussion is here at least relevant to both modern "sports" as we understand it, and the "athletics" of ancient Greece. Some recent critics have dismissed the notion that sport is a form of art since art, it is argued, is a form of communication of the artist with the audience, whereas sports, and play generally, need no audience.[3] While sport and art, particularly the dramatic arts, are of course distinguishable phenomena, their analogous traits will help us to understand the social function of ancient (and modern) athletic competitions. The very structure of the contest implies an almost dramatic form, which, even without a narrative structured by an author, possesses an inherent unity of action.[4] There are, of course, a host of formal and substantive differences. With regard to the media of expression, athletic contests rely almost entirely upon bodily actions with little or no verbal embellishment, whereas drama ordinarily relies on a balance of words and actions to communicate its effect. Perhaps mindful of the coordination and physical control afforded by athletics, Cicero believed that orators' skill in gestures benefited from the physical training of athletes (Cic., *De Oratore* 3, 59.220; cf. Quintilian, *Institutionis Oratoriae* 1.11.18). In athletics, the competitors "perform" in the events themselves, while dramatic poets used actors. Yet in early Greek drama, the playwrights are known to have acted in their own productions.[5] Unlike most performing arts, athletic contests are unscripted and unrehearsed in the conventional sense; unlike drama as Aristotle defined it, athletics is not an imitation of some other type of ordinary action. The numerous rules for a contest do, however, constitute a kind of "script" within whose constraint the actors are bound, the very long and arduous training period is a de facto "rehearsal," and the contest itself is an imitation of many types of struggles that were an intrinsic part of Greek culture.[6]

Athletic competitions could be and were understood on a metaphorical level. As Lucian attests,[7] the spectators at a Greek sporting event were aroused to seek "human happiness" through excellence and hard work by watching the athletes compete. That is, the audience was aware of a symbolic level at which the games are played out as displays of excellent achievement of a sort required in daily life. The precise substance of this symbolic message of course varies with each contest and each spectator.

Let us now turn to five areas in which there are some natural and essential parallels in the two realms of performance. The following do not pretend to be a complete list of analogous aspects, but merely an overview of some of the ways in which athletic performances overlap with drama as forms of symbolic communication: 1) festival context; 2) the mimesis of heroic actions; 3) the agonal spirit; 4) stadium and stage; 5) forms of action and audience response. This is not to claim that athletics was a prototype of drama so much as an analogous form of symbolic communication in which the culture participated. The similarity in forms of participation indicates the Greeks' consistent interest in public expressions of certain shared verities. The fact that the first dramatic performances of Thespis followed the institution of the Olympic Games by more than two centuries does not make the comparison preposterous.[8] Indeed, athletic phenomena may, in some ways, have prepared the way for drama.

Festival Context

Whatever the actual origins of ancient drama, we can see in the earliest public athletic festivals a kind of precursor for dramatic festivals, and perhaps even an indirect, contributory incentive for the rise of drama.[9] Athletic festivals very probably aroused and promoted intense interest in live performances held regularly in conjunction with religious festivals, and frequently in conjunction with musical or choral contests since at least the eighth century B.C. Recently it has been claimed that drama was not a radical innovation, but the result of centuries of prior traditions of musical contests, some held in conjunction with athletic festivals.[10] Citizens gathered to see and hear the sights of the *agōn*, to witness the spectacle of the processions and oaths preceding the contest, and to feel the full range of emotions: wonder and delight at excellence in victory, fear and pity in sympathy with valiant but unsuccessful challengers. The audience was involved in scenes of heroic success and shameful defeat.[11]

The Mimesis of Heroic Actions

Some of the most successful early athletes even enjoyed the status of heroes, complete with cult shrines; to this extent they were comparable to the mythic characters of tragedy.[12] Theogenes of Thasos, to cite the most famous example, was even considered to be the son of the divine Heracles.[13] The athletic contests had other heroic associations, myths that sought the aetiology of each event in the deed of famous heroes. The chariot race at Olympia in a sense repeated the original race between Pelops and Oenomaus, Theseus (or Heracles) invented the pankration contest, the first pentathlon was held by Jason and his Argonauts, Theseus wrote the rules of wrestling, and so on.[14] Such associations ennobled and enhanced the prestige of the competitions for both athletes and audience. Dramatists, on the other hand, played upon the athlete analogy in their descriptions of characters.[15] The athletic event became, in a sense, a mimesis of the actions of the mythical founders, and in this sense it was performed in the spirit of ancient drama.

The Agonal Spirit

Not only did Greek dramas share with athletics the tension of a contest within the unraveling of the action, they were also, of course, performed as part of an artistic contest, an *agōn*, or, perhaps more accurately, a 'meta-*agōn*' in which the drama entered in the competition itself describes struggles or *agōnes* in its plot.[16] And there were, according to a recent study, as many as sixteen festivals at which *agōnes* in both athletics and dramatic performances took place.[17] So the spirit and suspense of the artistic competition only heightened the natural interest in the dramatic performances themselves. Both dramatic and athletic contests are performed in public spaces specially set aside for performance at the time of festivals. The term *agōn* probably originally signified "an assembly gathered for a contest" and is therefore etymologically a place term that complements *aethlos*, a word connoting the "strenuous labor" of the contest.[18] In short, the most common Greek terms for competition suggest by their original meanings that "place" and "action," "performance" and "setting" were the two essential components of athletic phenomena.

It has also been suggested recently that three types of *agōn* or "conflict" represented in drama can be categorized in a fashion analogous to that of athletics: competition directly between two individuals (as in wrestling), competition of one individual with "the others" in the field (as in footraces), and competition between two (or more) groups (as in torch races).[19] Without entering into the vexed question of what precisely constitutes a dramatic *agōn*, one can easily see the analogies in the first two types of contest, but less so the third, since "team" competitions were exceptional in athletics. The general analogy still holds between dramatic and athletic conflicts of characters/participants. Whereas the characters of drama represent certain human ideals that come into conflict and are ascribed by the playwright, athletes usually "represent" some of the standard and more fixed athletic virtues as well as some specific attributes of their city, their family, and their own personal reputation. There are, of course, obvious differences. One athlete emerges as "victor" from the contest, and the "character" of the opposition is normally of little interest; dramatic characters, particularly tragic ones, are less easily labeled as "victors" at the end of the action, and the character of both protagonist and antagonist is of crucial importance to the understanding of the drama. Yet the action of the conflict itself rather than the characters of the participants constitutes the drama (Aristotle, *Poetics* 1450a). In athletics as in tragedy, it is the hero's or heroine's error, his or her slip, not moral turpitude, which results in failure.[20]

Stadium and Stage

Stadia are functionally analogous to early theaters, as the use of the word *theatron*, "viewing place," for both suggests.[21] They also served similar civic purposes as outdoor assembly places where spectators could celebrate a festival and become communally involved in a spectacle. Chronologically, of course, stadia antedate theaters by almost two centuries. The first "stadium" at Olympia, probably resembling more a wide track along a hillside than an artificial construction, is presumed to exist from at least 700 B.C.,[22] and possibly even earlier, if one accepts the traditional date of 776 B.C. for the founding of the games. More formally constructed versions of this stadium were built between ca. 450 and 340 B.C., with increasingly more room for spectators. In the Hellenistic and Roman eras, the facility is estimated to have held as many as 40,000 people.[23] The earliest facilities for viewing drama in the late sixth century B.C. were temporary wooden stands set up in the Agora in Athens, followed in the fifth to late fourth centuries by increasingly more sophisticated constructions for spectators at the Theater of Dionysus site on the south slope of the Acropolis.[24] There was a surge of construction, perhaps coincidental, of athletic and dramatic facilities in the fourth century. Major building or rebuilding of stadia took place at many major athletic sites, including Olympia, Nemea, Isthmia, Athens, and Epidauros.[25] Among the many construction or improvements of theaters in this period, those at Isthmia, Athens, and Epidauros are perhaps most noteworthy since they occur roughly contemporaneously with athletic construction.[26] The great expense afforded to these building programs certainly shows political savvy on the part of the officials who contributed the funding, but it also shows the intense public fervor for spectacles at festivals in the fourth century. The great interest had no doubt been there in the fifth century as well, but political and economic opportunism combined now with widespread desire to improve facilities. What had been simple structures erected for the occasion had evolved into permanent, monumental architecture signifying that drama and athletics were permanent civic institutions of the Greeks. So theaters

and stadia naturally became a part of the building programs of great civic benefactors like Lycurgus, who greatly improved both the theater of Dionysus and the
Panathenaic stadium in Athens ca. 338–326 B.C.[27]

Forms of Action and Audience Response

What has been said about the shared sense of community at a tragic performance
in classical Greece is equally true of the feeling of attending an athletic festival:

> The sense of the group, of community, was moreover enhanced by the
> fact that the community sat together on stone benches without seat
> divisions so that arms, legs and haunches could touch, and emotions
> could race through the audience, physically making them over into one
> common response. . . . Performances were out of doors, in daylight,
> continuously, starting at dawn in a large arena, where there must have
> been constant movement. . . . A large crowd is characteristically
> animal; the atmosphere is charged with passion and a tension that
> betrays the crowd's volatile nature. Large crowds are not at all prima-
> rily rational and theater was in any case an emotional experience. The
> focus of the audience was directed to the flat area before the benches
> known as the "dancing place." . . . Finally there is a common feature to
> ancient theater architecture that needs comment. That is the generally
> splendid and compelling view that lay beyond the *skēnē*. Concentration
> must have always been a problem and yet the spectator seats look out to
> hypnotic vistas, at Delphi a marvellous valley, at Pergamon a breath-
> taking and vertiginous drop to a far off valley. . . . Tragedy was part of
> the ancient public domain.[28]

Athletic sites, too, possessed the sensual and communal energy of a crowd touching, talking, eating, and drinking, cheering, viewing the central playing area, and
admiring the sights beyond the stadium or hippodrome. Like the theater, the stadium encouraged the feeling that the individual was part of a community consisting of both people and place.

The action of the athletic contest, conveyed by the word *aethlos*, "toil of the
contest," also has certain general similarities to dramatic action. In very general
terms, the athletic contest or dramatic action is resolved in victory or defeat for each
antagonist, antagonists struggle each for his or her own goal, and there are types
of rising action, turning-point of a crisis, and resolution. The emotional reactions
of participants and audience are often a mixture of delight and sadness, hope, pity,
and fear.

At the level of dramatic competition at a festival, the dramatic poet "contends"
with other poets, and the uncertain outcome may engage the audience's interest

at that level. On the deeper level, the poet is not only a competitor, but also an exhibitor of conflicts and contests among (usually) fictional characters.[29] Certainly, the course of the action in athletics is arbitrary and often beyond the control of the antagonists themselves; to this extent athletic action does not possess the artistic unity of dramatic action artificially constructed. Yet the apparent randomness or lack of tight economy in athletic performance is closely controlled by the rules and conventional tactics of competition.[30] And for an audience watching either kind of spectacle, attention is held by the desire to witness the unraveling of mysterious events against a backdrop of familiar conventions. Where a poet prescribes the words, action, and scenery of a drama, the athlete's physical ability and shrewdness of mind determine the course of the struggle during the contest. Special roles are, in a sense, adopted when the athlete stands up in public to represent his polis and family and to follow the rules and customs in a particular event at a particular festival. Costumes are assumed to signal the change from one's everyday roles, since even nudity, infibulation, anointment with oil, and application of powdery dust are costumes of a sort.[31] And even the gods' presence can be felt influencing the course of events, as they are seen to do in drama, in that athletic events occur at religious festivals and athletes swore oaths, made prayers, gave thanks, or paid penalties to divinities before and after their competition.[32] So Hesiod recommends that athletes show devotion to the powerful goddess Hecate (*Theogony* 435–38).[33] And a recent study has collected numerous examples of "curse tablets" (Greek κατάδεσμοι; Latin *defixiones*) on which are written prayers of competitors in athletic contests seeking the help of the gods.[34]

Athletic Teleology

The analogies between drama and athletics drawn thus far involve largely formal similarities: both are performances that communicate more general symbolic truths, and public events whose setting, action, and performers function in similar ways. Within Greek society, both types of public displays delighted the audience and improved them by inspiring positive behavior. Let us now turn from the dramatic aspects of athletics to the message that it in fact communicates through these media. We have observed in the previous chapters some of the primary values imparted to spectators at the games. According to Lucian, the audience was led to "immoderate desire for excellence and hard work" (*Anacharsis* 36); the prize for citizens watching the contest was potentially one of happiness or well being, if they were inspired to follow the example of the athletes. So much holds true for those watching (and even participating in) contests for either men or women, although Lucian does not mention the latter explicitly. For both genders, there are socially desirable objects or goals sought in athletic displays. Athletics is therefore teleological, both in the literal sense that each contest has a 'goal' or 'prize' (both athletic uses of Greek *telos*),

and metaphorically in that audience and athletes both seek to attain the realization of a prescribed 'purpose' (also a sense of *telos*) in the social process.[35] So Plato
draws the analogy:

> True runners who come to the *telos* receive the prize and are crowned. Is
> it not generally also this way with just men? They maintain a good
> reputation to the *telos* of every deed, every association, and life itself.
> They carry off the prizes from their fellow human beings. (*Republic* 613c)

And in the *Cleitophon* Plato speaks of the man who becomes happy in his progress
toward the *telos* of excellence (*aretē*, 410e). Pindar, as we saw earlier, elaborates
upon the image of the virtuous athlete: in the games for men fame was the object
won by hard work and expense, by facing great risks, by avoiding *hybris*, "excessive violence," and by the demonstration of *aretē*, "excellent achievement." The
precise values conveyed in the terms "excellence" and "happiness" of course differ
widely according to their contexts in philosophy or literature, and this is not our
central concern here. Yet certain generalizations can be made about the desired
"goals" of excellence communicated to men and women in athletic phenomena.
Many of these have been discussed *passim* in the previous chapters, and they are
summarized here for a comprehensive overview of the function of athletics in
Greek society.

On a personal level, male athletes followed the models of heroic warriors in
seeking to display *aretē* by which they might win fame. On a social level, the primary functions of male athletic valor were to reinforce the traditional order of the
polis and to enhance the reputation of the community. The honor and fame obtained
from athletic victories redounded to the credit of the individual, his family, and his
polis during his life and often for years thereafter.[36] The establishment of enhanced
social status, a kind of "hierarchy" among victors, thus reflected generally the hierarchy of the empowered males in Greek society. Although athletes could indirectly
influence a city's reputation by their display of prowess in a Panhellenic contest,
they rarely obtained direct political power in a city.[37] In short, athletic values and
performance reflected those aspects of the "real world" outside the stadium and most
usually affected matters nonathletic by transmitting and validating heroic-type
ideology and behavior.[38]

In general, the social function of athletics for females was to reinforce the traditional roles of women as wives and mothers, to acknowledge and strengthen the
order of the Greek private domain, the *oikos* or "household." Female competitors
did not enjoy widespread public fame but underwent certain prenuptial, ritual contests to demonstrate publicly their transition from their roles as "wild" maidens to
those of "tamed" wives and mothers. The athletic contests in which girls participated publicly were almost universally restricted to footraces, that is, "light" forms
of competition presumably better suited to females than the more violent "heavy"

combat sports of men. In the exceptional case of Spartan maidens, athletic exercise, legendarily including wrestling, also prepared their bodies literally as well as ritually for the rigors of childbirth.[39]

Gods, Heroes, and Foundation Myths

The respective "goals" of men and women and the social functions of their athletics are reflected in the cults and foundation myths of the athletic festivals. We have seen in the previous chapters that the cult of the patron god in many ways characterizes the spirit of the contest. The foundation myths for the greatest Panhellenic athletic festivals for men at Olympia, Delphi, Isthmia, and Nemea incorporate certain "male" athletic values mentioned earlier. In Pindar's version of the founding of the Olympics, the earliest extant, Heracles' labors are characterized as "toils" (πόνων, Ol. 10.25), yet he exceeds the limits of the athletic hero by slaying several of his opponents (Ol. 10.26–42). And the very metope sculpture of the Temple of Zeus at Olympia portrays Heracles performing his labors in various poses evocative of those portrayed on athletic victory statues or on vase paintings of athletes in the course of competition.[40] Diodorus Siculus describes Heracles' labors as "contests for the prize of immortality" and consistently uses the word "contest" (athlos) for his labors.[41] Immortality is the ultimate prize of which most men share only a part in the acquisition of fame.

Another foundation myth, evidently composed later than the Heracles story, also illustrates the function of male athletic values in the Olympics:

> With regard to the Olympic Games, the Elean historians of the most ancient period say that Cronus held the first kingship in heaven and a temple was placed in Olympia by contemporary men who were called the "Golden Race." When Zeus was born . . . [his guardians, the Curetes,] came from Cretan Ida—Heracles, Paionaios, Epimedes, Iasios, and Idas. Heracles, being the eldest, organized a contest in running for his brothers and crowned the winner among these with a crown made of an olive branch. . . . Some say that Zeus wrestled Cronus himself here [at Olympia] for rule [in heaven], others that he held games for Cronus after he had been overcome . These also say that Apollo outran his challenger Hermes and beat Ares in boxing. (Paus. 5.7.6, 7, 10)

In this late attempt to rationalize the associations of heroes and gods with the Olympic games, the gods and the heroic figures of legends are not merely patrons of the festival, they become competitors in the contests.[42] The games are tied by association with the Curetes to the myth of the birth and childhood of Zeus. One of these Cretan Curetes, named "Heracles," in a spirit of play (Ἡρακλέα παίζοντα) gathers his brothers, the guardians of the newborn god, for an athletic celebration and adopts the custom of an olive victory crown. Or, in an alternate version, the games are meant to imitate or commemorate the cosmic power struggle between Zeus and his father.[43] Of course these versions from Pausanias were more obscure than those of Pindar's *Olympian Ode* 10. More important, Greek literary and mythographic traditions evidence the desire to attach the games and even specific competitions to the cosmic power-struggles of gods and heroes.

Perhaps the best known association of contests with power struggle in the Olympic foundation myths is the myth of Pelops. The Lydian Pelops competes with and causes the death of King Oenomaus in a chariot race to win his daughter as bride discussed earlier in chapter 4.[44] The Pelops-Oenomaus contest was the subject of the most prominent pedimental sculpture on the exterior of the Temple of Zeus at Olympia, placed on the east side facing the stadium and hippodrome.[45] The placement of Zeus between the two contestants served as a constant reminder of who was the final arbitrator of human affairs. Pelops, in one version of the myth, held games of thanksgiving to Zeus to celebrate his succession to the kingship.[46] The mythic contest of Pelops thus communicates in poetry and in visual arts the associations between athletic contests and their metaphorical application to establishing merit and status in nonathletic endeavors.

Myths of the other Panhellenic games make similar points about the establishment of divine hegemony in their foundation. The origins of the Pythian Games at Delphi are associated with Apollo's legendary slaying of the monster Pytho (*Homeric Hymn to Apollo* 355–87), and the earliest contests were musical, reflecting both the destructive and peaceful aspects of the divinity (Paus. 10.7.2).[47] A ritual cleansing at Delphi, reenacting the god's own purification after the murder of Pytho, involved the symbolic exile of a young boy, who returned after a period with the boughs of laurel from which the Pythian victor's crown was made.[48] As at Olympia, the foundation stories at Delphi indicate the destructive power of competition, and its ability to establish a new, productive order.

The foundation myth of the Isthmian Games sacred to Poseidon tell of the death of the young Melicertes and his apotheosis as the sea-god Palaemon, in whose honor the festival was established.[49] The death of the boy and his mother was caused by Melicertes' father, King Athamas, who went mad, in one version, because of (un-justified) suspicions of a conspiracy.[50] There is also for Isthmia a rationalized, later version that explains that the first games were held jointly by Poseidon and Helios, who had been rivals for patronage of the city; again, a series of gods and heroes are listed as the victors in that first festival, which included a full program of gymnic, hippic, musical, and even boating contests.[51] As in the other foundation myths, a struggle arises from the desire to establish a social order, with the result of a death or murder, which in turn leads to the foundation of a festival.

The foundation of the Nemean Games follows a similar pattern and also has alternative myths. According to one, when the famous Seven Heroes travel through

Nemea on their expedition against Thebes, Opheltes, the infant son of Lycurgus, the local king and priest of Zeus, is accidentally killed by a snake. The Seven hold funeral games in honor of the infant, whom they call "Archemoros," or "beginning of doom," since his death bodes ill for the expedition.[52] Each of the Seven is victor in a different event. The other, probably late myth connects the foundation with Heracles' wrestling with the Nemean lion. After that labor, the hero either founded the games or else managed and reorganized them, dedicating them to Zeus.[53] While the Archemoros myth is not directly associated with power struggles and the restoration of order, the Heracles myth does concern the power of humans over nature and ties the games through Heracles to the prestigious Olympic foundation myth. The Archemoros myth is, however, indirectly and importantly associated with the military expedition of the Seven Heroes to restore proper leadership to Thebes. Since the infant was the "beginning" (archē) or harbinger of "death" (moros) in the power struggle to follow, the myth ties the death of the infant to the political and military strife that occasioned the misfortune.[54]

The four great Panhellenic games are discussed here to characterize them according to their foundation myths, the spirit of which persisted in the regular celebrations of the festivals themselves. The many local games each had their own cults and foundation stories, and all sought to demonstrate in the spirit of their foundation, their divine patronage, and their competition, the positive character of their polis. The divine patron was a powerful benefactor of the state, and usually of Greece generally. The local hero with whom the games were often associated served as an intermediary between mortals and immortals and also served as a public representative of the order and power of the state. So the Panathenaic festival at Athens was first held by the local hero Erichthonius to commemorate Athena's part in the war against the Giants, but, in the "political version," the festival was founded by Theseus to celebrate the new civic unity.[55] Even games founded in the historical period are demonstrations of civic strength and find validation by association with divine patrons. The Eleutheria held at Larisa, Thessaly, for example, was instituted in 196 B.C. to commemorate the freeing of Greece by Flaminius from Philip V of Macedon, and Zeus Eleutherius, god of freedom, was divine patron.[56]

Female Athletic Performance and Its Cultic Contexts

Details of the foundation myths and cult contexts of the female games, which are discussed in more detail in chapters 4 to 6, contrast with men's games most obviously in the silence of all but a few sources on their very existence. The silence of testimonia is of course entirely in keeping with the traditional "goal" or telos of females as stated earlier, to strengthen the order of the Greek private domain by preparing for the roles of wife and mother. Women's roles are then private in character and in object.[57] Though the communal celebration of women's roles was no doubt taken very seriously, the fame of their festivals was more restricted than that of the men's—due to restrictions on either attendance or published reports of the phenomena.

Women apparently did attend at least some of the men's athletic festivals, though precisely how many and where is uncertain.[58] If practice varied at the men's games, there is even more uncertainty about the composition of the audience at female athletic performances. We do know that only unmarried women actually participated in all known contests. It seems likely that, in a festival devoted to the celebration of women's status, free-born women of all age groups attended.[59] But it is more difficult to assess whether men attended any or all of the women's athletic festivals. The Heraia festival at Olympia, if a Panhellenic festival and so open to a wider audience, probably would have admitted both women and men of all ages. Yet why is Pausanias the only source in all ancient literature to record this event? The girls' public competitions at Sparta, by contrast, were apparently watched by men, including those young enough to assess the girls as potential wives.[60] The notorious public exposure, literal and figurative, of Spartan girls in athletic events is reported widely and early on in testimonia. Yet this tells of a whole social movement—the exception to the rule. The only known athletic festival of Spartan girls in honor of a specific deity or hero was the footrace of the Dionysiades at Sparta. This Spartan race and that of the Arkteia festivals of Attica were, however, more local than the Olympian Heraia, and thus perhaps restricted to an audience of females of all ages. The Arkteia in particular, since it is referred to as a "mystery" ritual (μυστήριον) in some sources,[61] was very probably confined to a female audience. The ideal whereby women were restricted to the private domain is probably then reflected in some known local female contests.

That very ideal of public silence about women suggests that there may have been many more local contests for girls, about which ancient male authors and artists kept silent.[62] We have, for instance, the tantalizing report, preserved as a marginal comment in a Renaissance manuscript of Pausanias, of an inscription on a column at Patras: "Nikophilos here dedicated a portrait-statue of Parian marble of Nikegoras, his dearest sister, winner in the race for young women [τὸν τῶν παρθένων δρόμον]."[63] One would expect the Heraia to be named if that were the race in question. More likely the fortuitously preserved evidence points to another local contest, perhaps part of the festival in Patras for Artemis Laphria or for Artemis Triklaria.[64]

The cult contexts and foundation myths for the festivals for women discussed earlier share certain features. The contests are restricted to maidens, that is, they are prenuptial, they are in the form of a race (the Arkteia chase being a type of race), and they are held in honor of divinities and heroes associated with the transitional status of the young girls. First let us consider some direct and indirect associations of the girls' footraces with worship of Dionysus. Dionysus is, among his myriad attributes, a god of release through expressions of sexuality, drunkenness, and ecstatic communion with him in the wild space of the mountain sides; he is also "the women's Zeus," the mythical partner of Ariadne, and husband of "Basilinna" in a *hieros gamos* ritual at the Athenian festival of the Anthesteria.[65] As a divinity of release and freedom, particularly for women, Dionysus embodied a carnival spirit also reflected in the Athenian dramatic festivals sacred to him. A Dionysian Theoria for men appears to have been held at the same time as the Arkteia at Brauron, and there men indulged in drunkenness and sexual licence with prostitutes. At Sparta in the race of the Dionysiades, Dionysus was honored along with the nameless "hero" who introduced him. The god was also, as discussed in chapter 4, honored at Elis by the Sixteen Women who organized the Heraian footrace for local girls. The parallel with the Spartan ritual is striking, since at Elis Dionysus is honored along with his other legendary mate, Physcoa, and their offspring, Narcaeus, both of whom introduced his worship to in that area. The Elean Dionysus is mysteriously addressed as a "Hero," which may allude to his mortal mother or tales of his being "twice born." Might the "Hero" Dionysus be somehow parallel to the Spartan Dionysus honored in the local festival together with a nameless "Hero" who introduced his worship? Were the two figures originally one, another "Hero" Dionysus, at Sparta? Or was the Elean Dionysus a conflation of two original figures, the god and the local hero (later named Narcaeus) who introduced his worship? We can note that the parallel contexts are striking and testify at least to similar functions in the two cities concerned with proper honors for a nonautochthonous deity with direct or indirect ties to prenuptial rites for girls.

The Elean Dionysus is also summoned to come "running on a bull's foot," which recalls the associations of bulls with athletics. The girls' footraces of the Arkteia, the race of the Dionysiades, and the Heraia occur in direct or indirect association with cults for Dionysus. The presence of the god is, in one respect, not surprising and may be coincidental: Dionysus had widespread special importance for women and was likely to figure somewhere among their local festivals. To this extent, the occurrence of the association in at least three distinct competitions suggests that Dionysus' direct or indirect ties to girls' races marking the transition to adult womanhood is more a function of his general importance to Greek women than of coincidence.

There is in these girls' festivals and their cultic contexts a pattern in which appropriate deities function as patrons or patronesses of the transition. The ritual evokes particular characteristics of the deities through the foundation myths to communicate, through the performance of the competition, the ambivalence and the tensions accompanying change of status which are both natural and social. At the Attic Arkteia, the polar tensions communicate the ambiguous status of being on the margin between maiden and woman, wild and civilized, free and tamed. The Arkteia race imitates the legendary girl's flight from a bear, which is both wild and tame. The race is also a ritual performance required by Artemis of girls before marriage; so the prenuptial status is protected and the transition to marriage is assisted.

Moreover, the Dionysian Theoria of Brauron complements the Arkteia in its social function, and serves as a public reminder of the fact that the girls will ultimately be "abducted" by men.[66]

The Heraian race at Olympia celebrates the marriage of Pelops and Hippodameia—the heroine who was won in a chariot race itself illustrating the tension between father and suitors/husband, between death in defeat and flourishing in victory. Hippodameia appropriately instituted a race in thanksgiving, which, though a footrace, recalls the race men ran to win her. There is also an aspect of marginality or ambiguity in the dress of the Heraia racers, adopted from a lightweight workman's garment, appropriated by young females in a "leisure" ritual, and very much displaying, in part exposing, the female body in action. As at the Arkteia, a contrast between wild and tame is conveyed, and the whole ritual looks forward to the goal of marriage for the participants. The ambivalence is also manifest in the women's public celebration of Dionysus, his "bride" Physcoa, and their son Narcaeus organized by the women who oversee the footrace. The triad honored in the Dionysian worship in some sense complements in function the triad of the Heraia: Hera, Hippodameia, and Pelops. Although Hera and her athletics are clear counterparts of Zeus and the Olympics, the Hera-Dionysus pairing communicates in ritual symbolism the major aspects of female life.

The Spartan race of the Dionysiades celebrates in ritual the Dionysian orientation of the young maidens to adulthood but oddly lacks any explicit affiliation with a female deity. Yet the pervasive worship of Artemis Orthia and of Helen at Sparta were an important part of the life of Spartan maidens.[67] In these cults and in the possible expression of devotion to female deities in connection with the pervasive physical education of Spartan females, there may be seen a complementarity of cults (Dionysus-Artemis-Helen?) similar to that found at Olympia and Attica. Plutarch's allusion to "the public contests" (τὰς ἀγῶνας) in which girls competed before boys suggests that the Dionysiades race was not the only regular such competition, and that others took place at other festival occasions such as the Heleneia for Helen or the Issoria for Artemis, both of which were probably held at or near "the Race-course" (Dromos).[68] Inscriptions name several agōnothetai or contest organizers of the festival of Artemis Limnatis, on the border between Sparta and Messenia.[69] Artemis Limnatis was clearly a fertility deity, reminiscent of Dionysus Limnaios, in whose honor Spartan maidens gathered for a regular festival.[70] The literary sources suggest that in the second half of the eighth century B.C. girls attended the festival without men, or with only a nominal male escort; the inscriptions (of the Roman period) indicate that some contests were held there for Artemis Limnatis. It is therefore possible that the later contests (footraces?) were exclusively for girls, and of prenuptial importance. It has been suggested that the festival included a prenuptial, orgiastic dance, also typical of the cults of Artemis.[71] If the festival did include girls' races, the parallels with the Arkteia at Brauron are striking: a setting in the wilds, at the geographical margin of the territory, and stories of the rape of female participants.

The Dionysian element is then slightly different in each of the women's festivals surveyed here, but in general each conveys the notion of release, fertility, and strength associated with the adult women's traditional worship of the god best known from Euripides' *Bacchae*.[72] This character is simultaneously complemented by the presence of female deities or heroines who embody the ambiguities in the transitional status of girl participants. The character of the female athletic events, like that of men, must be analyzed in its total cultic context, and in the precise symbolism of the forms of competition. Full appreciation of the female rituals can only be understood with a view beyond the stadium and the competition, to the complex relations of patron gods and goddesses to the heroes and heroines of the foundation myths and, in both of these mythical groups, to the women who organized or participated in the races.

Dionysus and Athletics

In a wider sense, one can see a Dionysiac spirit of different sort associated with men's athletics and athletic festivals. Festivals in honor of Dionysus which include competitions for men are rare compared with the larger numbers for the other major Olympians. The Anthesteria of Athens seems to have had at least a torch race, but the numerous depictions of other events on the small choes vases for children at that festival are better understood as images to exhort young males to aspire to athletic ideals than as prize vases similar to those given at the Panathenaia.[73] The name of the festival which is connected with the root meaning "to blossom" and the clear function of fostering children's transitions to youth and adulthood indicates that Dionysus here functions as a divinity overseeing the general prosperity of the city in both economic and social aspects.[74] The footrace of the Oschophoria of Athens began at a sanctuary of Dionysus and involved the symbolism of carrying grapevines in the race itself, again characterizing the race as a communal ritual of fertility and prosperity.[75] An Anthesteria at Teos in Ionia apparently had a full gymnic program accompanying the local wine festival, and an odd festival for Dionysus Melanaigis at Hermione had aquatic events emphasizing Dionysus' various nautical adventures in his myths.[76] The festivals, then, showcase men's athletic contests that celebrate and promote civic prosperity particularly in relation to the powerful forces of fertility in nature.

Turning to the archaeological evidence, we find a number of vases of the Classical period on which Dionysiac scenes are juxtaposed with athletic ones, such as a cup depicting in the interior a scene with a boy athlete holding a strigil and standing near a turning post, and on the exterior maenads and satyrs with Dionysus in a scene of revelry.[77] Two stamnoi vases in the National Museum in Athens also show athletes on one side and Dionysiac maenads and satyrs reveling on the other.[78] Two other stamnoi at the Villa Giulia show Dionysus with revelers in a natural setting on one side, and a naked athlete with a peplos-clad admiring female on the other.[79] A kylix in the Getty Museum shows athletes in scenes of cleaning up with strigils on the exterior, in the center of which is molded a large face of a satyr (fig. 9-1).[80] Most athletic-Dionysiac vases, then, depict, in separate scenes, athletes at rest with strigils, after the contest or exercise, and maenads and satyrs in active revelry. I have found no scenes in which the athletes and revelers are shown together or directly interacting, which is not surprising since the athletes belong to the realm of daily life, the revelers generally to that of myth. An exception that may prove the exclusivity of the two realms is the case of athletics frequently represented in the satyr plays; these plays consistently mix real-life activities with the fabulous and notorious behavior of satyr characters.[81]

The juxtaposition of scenes of revelry with athletics may arguably be coincidental and poses a greater question of the reasons why an artist or patron juxtaposed any scenes together on the same vase. The complex socio-aesthetic motives cannot be fully discussed here, but it seems reasonable to assume that scenes put together on one object were thought to be complementary or harmonious in theme or spirit. If this assumption is correct, the spirit of rest, release from toil, and perhaps celebration of prosperity may link the two themes of Dionysus and athletics. The fact that the athletes on these vases are all male also suggests that the Dionysiac

Figure 9-1. Attic red-figure mask kantharos, ca. 480 B.C., The J. Paul Getty Museum, Los Angeles 85.AE.263, Foundry Painter and possibly Euphronios (potter). Courtesy of The J. Paul Getty Museum, Los Angeles, California.

cult's associations with male athletics are essentially different from its connections with the female ritual contests discussed earlier. The "ecstasy," loss of individuality, and union with the god which characterizes the communal and dramatic festivals of Dionysus may share some aspects with athletic festivals.[82] But since the association of Dionysus with actual men's athletic festivals is neither widespread nor prominent, and the artistic associations only indirect and suggestive, the link between Dionysus and male athletics is probably secondary. The connection found its fullest expression in the scenes of Nonnus' late (fifth century A.D.?) epic fantasy, *Dionysiaca*, in which the god himself indulges in athletic competition.[83] Greek drama, whatever its origins, overlapped considerably with athletics in its reverence for Dionysus and the powers that he represented in the polis.

Desire in Greek Athletics

Thus far, we have observed that athletic events are in many senses performances or displays of social values, that mythic and cult contexts define the character and the social function of both male and female athletic competitions, and that the contests have similar functions for each gender in reinforcing the societal roles of men and women. Greek athletics is, in one aspect, an artificially constructed performance of male or female values and ideals, normally in the context of myths and rituals of a festival that validate the fundamental ideals.

Let us now turn to two other aspects of the athletic performance which largely cut across lines of gender, namely, the themes of desire and death, *erōs* and *thanatos*. Both of these are communicated through athletics, and both complement the distinct male and female values in subtle and complex ways. The fact that the majority of examples in the following discussion refer to male athletes is more an indication of the much greater focus on male competition in the sources than an indication of exclusively male athletic phenomena. Although *erōs* has been treated earlier in a discussion of the explicit associations of sexual desire with Greek athletics (ch. 8), here the topic of *erōs* will be investigated in its wider sense of "desire," "yearning for status or role," or "emulation in view of a shared goal." Sexual *erōs* and the cult of Eros as they relate to athletics are here understood as a part of the phenomenon of desire in the wider sense. Sexual desire of audiences, habitués of the gymnasium, or other athletes for an athlete may be a manifestation of high valuation of the beloved's beauty, personal qualities, social status, or some complex combination of all of these. In other words, the erotic attraction can evidence a type of yearning on the part of the potential lover to share or somehow participate in the high esteem paid to a successful or beautiful athlete. It can be a type of yearning for personal advancement to a similar status. Since in the Greek construction of sexuality the beloved is normally younger than and socially subordinate to the lover, fulfillment of sexual desire with a successful athlete does imply a kind of erotic victory over the athletic victor. The "success" of athletic victory is symbolic of success in nonathletic aspects of life, and so the lover of an athlete has, in a sense, enjoyed real-life victory while his beloved has taken the symbolic one.

The general concept of desire is paired here with the antiphonal human phenomenon of death, also in its widest sense to include the proximity to death or risk in competition, the 'delight' in risk, the fear of death, and attitudes toward death and fame as demonstrated in athletic performance. Just as athletic desire corresponds to analogous yearnings for success in nonathletic aspects of life, so death and its related concepts in the athletic sphere correspond to similar aspects of life outside the stadium and gymnasium. Death is "antiphonal" to desire since the two principles respond to one another in a kind of dialogue or dynamic in the athlete, in the audience, and in society as it reflects upon and reacts to athletic displays. Death and desire are apparently in polar tension, more accurately complementary, and frequently at play in athletic performance. Their simultaneous presence in athletics lends richness and meaning to the 'drama' of the performance for both athletes and audience. The precise ways in which the two phenomena interact will be discussed later.

First, then, the phenomenon of athletic desire. It is not the intention here to pursue a doctrinal analysis, Platonic, Freudian, Foucaultian, or other, of how such a general notion of Eros or "desire" functions in Greek society, but merely to offer some observation on how it did work within Greek athletics, with some broader suggestions on what this might all mean for us in our attempts to understand "sport" and society generally. After a general discussion of goals of athletic desire, we will consider the phenomena of collective desire, the desire of the audience and trainers, and the self-centered desire of the athlete.

The *agōn* by definition establishes a hierarchy among competitors, each of whom strives to outperform the opponents, "always to excel and to be superior to others" (Homer, *Iliad* 6.208, 11.784).[84] That is the goal, the *telos* of the Greek contest, to achieve *aretē*," excellence," in one's chosen field of competition and in a particular festival. As Homer expresses it in the words inviting Odysseus to compete in the games on Phaeacia:

No greater fame [*kleos*] is there for a man so long as he lives
than whatever he might accomplish with his own feet and hands.
(Odyssey 8.147–48)

"Excellence" and "fame" of course differ for Greek men and women, but the principle is the same in their respective contests, to excel in one's own respective virtues to establish a reputation. For this reason the story of Cynisca, first female to win at Olympia in the chariot race, is a remarkable for the ambiguity of *aretē* in a male arena in which a woman dominates.[85] The Greek stadium is not so much a field of dreams as one of desire in which each participant yearns to excel.

The desire to win, to be superior, to dominate, and to attain fame is led on by essentially two aims, to establish individual self-sufficiency and to strengthen relations with others. These two principles of self-reliance and friendship with others, respectively *autarkeia* and *philia* in Greek, appear to be mutually antagonistic, though Aristotle and other philosophers attempt to reconcile them or explain the delicate balance in various ways.[86] In the realm of athletics, family, friends, and self most obviously benefit from an athlete's successful performance. Victory redounds on the reputation of the victor's kin, fellow citizens, and self. Since athletic events were normally competitions of individuals, public contests afforded many opportunities for a citizen to rise to instant fame and often financial self-sufficiency with prizes of great value; honor and wealth brought influence and independence within one's community. Prizes of great economic and honorary value were meted out in athletic contests in Homer, and cash prizes were given to victors by their home cities for victories in prestigious crown games from at least the sixth century onward.[87] The desire for such rewards was strong and widespread. Numerous anecdotes about the behavior of athletes testify to the power of athletic desire to build or ruin reputations. The stories of famous (and infamous) athletes recount acts both of self-sufficiency and of friendship: selling one's athletic talents to another state (Astylos of Croton); hybristically entering more events than one can win (Theogenes of Thasos); having a victory statue in one's home city with beneficial powers (Theogenes); boxing a ghost who menaced a community (Euthymus of Locri); using one's strength to hold up (or pull down) a roof in order to save (or kill) fellow citizens (Milo of Croton; Polydamas of Scotoussa; Cleomedes of Astypalaea).[88]

Tales of real-life heroes such as Theogenes with some fourteen hundred victories set impossibly high standards for the average competitor. Yet the desire of the would-be Theogenes was not dampened. Records of the "first-" or "only-one-to" sort advertised the unique achievements of individuals who won two or three different events in the same day. Over the centuries, competitive desire was not dampened but sharpened to obtain some unique victory by which an athlete might win distinction.[89] Ancients were not concerned with quantitative absolutes such as "fastest man on earth," "longest jump," and the like partly due to the limits of technology, but also due to a greater concern with the quality or distinction of achievement relative to the festival: "[Theogenes was proclaimed at the Isthmian Games] first man on earth to win in a single day both boxing and pankration."[90] So individuals in training set forth a goal for achievement measured against themselves ("personal best") and others. For the Greeks, the degree to which personal performance is improved is irrelevant unless victory is attained. Even with victory, there looms a greater challenge of additional victories or a total career record. With the achievement of each plateau, a new goal looms on the horizon. Success need not dampen desire but may stimulate it ceaselessly toward new objects, new *agōnes*, increasingly impossible standards of higher excellence. Athletic competition among the Greeks (and among modern athletes) grants a type of glory that risks vanishing unless the level of performance is maintained or improved, or unless the fame is preserved in more permanent media, which were, for the Greeks, primarily victory odes, statues, or inscriptions.

The desire inherent in competition has been termed by René Girard "mimetic desire," applied by him to social rivalry in general, but relevant to the present discussion of athletic rivalry and desire. It is worth quoting Girard at some length to explain the principle:

> Rivalry does not arise because of the fortuitous convergence of two desires on a single object; rather *the subject desires the object because the rival desires it*. In desiring an object the rival alerts the subject to the desirability of the object. . . . [The subject] desires *being* something he himself lacks and which some other person seems to possess. The subject thus looks to that other person to inform him of what he should desire in order to acquire that being. If the model, who is apparently already endowed with superior being, desires some object, that object must be capable of conferring an even greater plenitude of being. . . . [D]esire is essentially mimetic, toward an object desired by the model. . . . The adult likes to assert his independence and to offer himself as a model to others; he invariably falls back on the formula, "Imitate me!" in order to conceal his own lack of originality. Two desires converging on the same object are bound to clash. Thus mimesis coupled with desire leads automatically to conflict.[91]

Girard believes that rivals elect violence as a shortcut to a supremely desired goal, and that violence and desire are hence linked in the subject's mind: "Violent opposition, then, is the signifier of ultimate desire, of divine self-sufficiency, of that 'beautiful totality' whose beauty depends on its being inaccessible and impenetrable."[92]

Though Girard's views address neither athletic rivalry nor ancient society specifically, his assessment can be used, with some qualifications, for clarifying the phenomenon of athletic desire among the Greeks. Athletic desire is not an absolute, but an intersubjective construction of society dependent upon the values commonly invested in symbolic objects and actions of competition. Girard's 'model' individual is of course analogous to the victor, or to the legendary athletic hero or even a patron deity whom rival athletes emulate. The adult who seeks to assert self-sufficiency, who desires a quasi-divine independence, has parallels among athletes, but the desire for self-sufficiency, *autarkeia*, is ideally balanced, or in the structuralist term of Levi-Strauss, "mediated" by a desire for friendship, *philia*, well-being of family and fellow citizens who share in his victory. Thus the rivalry bridges or mediates both egotistic and altruistic aims. And we can soften Girard's expression "violent opposition" to "competition involving an expenditure of physical energy." Violence and risk to personal health were certainly part of some Greek athletics, particularly the "combat sports," but all athletics demanded pain and effort. This will be discussed more fully later when I consider "death" in athletics.

The athletic phenomenon, then, involves a complex interaction of antagonists seeking a common object that is given value by participants, organizers, and audience. The emergence of a victor whose desire is at least momentarily fulfilled puts that individual into the position of a 'model' who is imitated by others against whom reputation must be defended in future matches. One dominates, and all others are dominated. The dominant individual shares most fully in the character of previous victors, whose ranks he or she joins, and of heroes and gods associated with the festival. The dominant individual has symbolically achieved the goal, the *telos*, whose values are upheld by that particular construction of a competition, be it for males or females with their respective, unique goals. With a subsequent loss, or with the inevitable succession of new victors who take up the dominant position in later competitions, the roles of "dominant" and "dominating" shift. While the individuals who assume the "personae" are constantly shifting, the high valuation of the positions and titles, for example, *Olympionikēs*, *Periodonikēs* (Olympic victor, circuit victor), remain fairly constant. Athletic inscriptions recording athletic victories show extreme care, not only in making clear the name and patronymic of the victor, but also the number and frequency of the more important victories that are usually listed according to an order of relative importance, namely Olympia, Pythia, Isthmia, Nemea, followed by local festivals in less fixed sequences.[93] Victories in local festivals were given priority to honor the victor's birthplace;[94] political considerations also determined the order to some extent. But the need to display successful performance in the major contests remained constant from classical Greece to the Roman period.

So athletic desire drove the competitor to work for victory in an ever-shifting series of 'actors' who took on constant 'roles' in the performance. Unlike dramatic actors, however, athletes had greater freedom in delineating their own character and in staging their own actions.[95] And unlike actors, athletes could not be sure of their ultimate 'persona' ("victor" or "defeated," "first one to . . . ," etc.) until the end of the performance. It is, in fact, the very indeterminacy of action and roles that spurs on athletic desire with hope of success.

The athletic phenomenon also arouses a desire in the audience, who, in supporting particular competitors, can express the emotion in various ways. As noted earlier, Pindar describes women and girls who admire Telesicrates, the victor at Games for Athena, hoping that he could be their son or husband. Obviously the desire is to possess the young man in some way, or to possess someone else of his caliber. Men in the audience might also wish to have a son of this sort, or to have their son emulate the victor. Qualities of high virtue are implied in successful performance that inspires desire in the audience: emotions ranging from sexual lust to admiration of spiritual strength to yearning to have the victor or someone like him in the family. The image desired is that of the victor in his moment of triumph, after the pain of the struggle and before an inevitable deterioration in strength and status in the stadium. Again we recall Lucian's report, noted in the Introduction, that through witnessing competition those in the audience were led to "immoderate desire for excellence and hard work" (*Anacharsis* 36), but they were also inspired to outdo one another in the contest system of society. The victors and their idealized images more likely encouraged social hierarchies and provoked envy than they mitigated tensions or enchanted citizens with their erotic and quasi-numinous power.[96]

Victor statues are also images of the acme of performance, bodies idealized in their classical physique, and, in the case of the majority of these preserved today, images of the male nude. Nudity was of course the style in which men's athletics was performed for most of the historical period, with most recent studies suggesting that the custom was more widely adopted early in the sixth century.[97] Homer's athletes wear the *perizōma*, a loincloth, though no athletic statues preserve this early style. Whatever the historical development of the practice, the setting up of nude victory statues evokes similar artistic conventions at the same time for statues of male gods. This has led at least one scholar to claim that athletic nudity, in art and in practice in society, was meant to evoke the beauty, purity, and self-sufficiency of the gods.[98] It is inevitable that the nude statues also evoked erotic reactions or attraction to an ideal physique; as Kenneth Clark remarks: "No nude, however abstract, should fail to arouse in the spectator some vestige of erotic feeling, even though it be only the faintest shadow—and if it does not do so, it is bad art and false morals."[99] Aside from arousing erotic desire, these statues inspire and encourage others to emulate excellence. Some of the tales about the wrestler Milo's strength probably derive from admirers standing around his statue and topping one another's stories: the great man stood on a greased discus, burst the fillet around his head, and firmly grasped a pomegranate without squashing it. The anecdotes probably correspond to misinterpreted details of the conventional victory statue: a circular base, a crown, and a prize of fruit held in the hand. The details, moreover, are related by Pausanias, perhaps informed by local guides, in a context in which he also describes Milo's statue at Olympia (6.14.5–9). The statues, then, had a life of their own and inspired onlookers with lust, wonder, or other strong emotions that may have had little basis in the reality of the victor or victory commemorated.

While those acting as coach or trainer—*gymnastēs*, *paidotribēs*, or *aleiptēs* in Greek terminology—share with the audience the same desires of encouraging the athlete in the quest for victory, and in some ways of possessing him or her if successful, they do so with different affective methods.[100] The admirer in the audience feels overcome with enthusiasm and anxiety over the outcome in the course of competition but can only shout encouragement without much clear or direct control over the outcome. The trainer is in a stronger position to incite the athlete's desire, as we are informed by a series of *exempla* from Philostratus (*Gymn.* 18–24). Most of the anecdotes show that intimate knowledge of a trainee's personal character can be used to arouse an extraordinary display of strength. The famous boxer Glaucus was in midmatch at Olympia when his *gymnastēs* reminded him of the strength he once used in straightening out a crooked plough with a blow from his fist (20). One coaching tale is a particularly good example of erotic desire combined with athletic desire, the one inducing the other. The trainer of Promachus the pankratiast, sensing that the young man was in love with a "girlie" (γυναίῳ), pretended to bring back a message from her that "she would not at all reject him as her darling if he should win at Olympia" (22). He not only won, he beat Polydamas, the biggest and fiercest opponent of his day (Paus. 6.5.4–7). Three other coaching anecdotes all play upon the willingness to risk death for the sake of victory. The *gymnastēs* of the pankratiast Arrhichion spurred him on by telling him as he fought at Olympia: "What a beautiful epitaph! 'He never gave in at Olympia.'" (21). Here we see the desire for fame, even if he lost, inspiring a victorious effort. The coach of Mandrogenes, a young pankratiast, sent a letter to the boy's mother saying: "If you should hear that your son has died [in competition] believe it. If you hear he's defeated, don't believe it!" (23). He fulfilled the coach's prediction to avoid making the coach a liar and misleading his mother with a lie. Strong affective ties to coach and family thus led Mandrogenes on to success. The coach of the runner Opiatos staked his life in bond that his athlete would win the race at Plataea (24). The trainer-trainee bond is shown to be stronger than fear of death on the part of both the coach and the athlete.

The role of the coaches illustrates how desire of the athlete is mediated, aroused, and subject to affective manipulation with a view to personal fame among family, a beloved, and posterity generally. When a significant victory has been achieved, satisfaction of the desire comes at least temporarily:

> [T]here time stands still, the record is written in eternity, the athlete is metamorphosed by the excelling of standard human boundaries, in world records, in a new nature, and with induction into the "eternal victors' list" of Olympia, metamorphosed into an immortal.[101]

The metamorphosis is, of course, temporary; true "immortality" is elusive. The immortal fame of a Heracles or a Theogenes, much less of the immortals themselves, is always out of reach, the desire is destined to be frustrated. Still the pull of athletic desire is felt, albeit against the opposing pull of more mortal inclinations. The athlete, while alive, remains subject to the limitations of mortality, and the decision to risk one's life or, more ordinarily, to undergo physical hardship and pain, at the instigation of the coach or others, is not taken easily. The athlete's desire for fame and excellence is in permanent tension with the lure of a less risky, and less glorious, existence.

Death in Greek Athletics

Death is neither a usual nor a desirable outcome of "sporting" competitions as constructed in most societies.[102] Some scholars have sought to find the origin of Greek athletics in duels to the death held on the occasions of funerals for heroes, duels intended to detect and punish an individual supposedly responsible for the death of the honored hero. Yet this thesis does not adequately explain the origin of many of the more peaceful competitions not requiring physical contact between opponents, and of those that take place outside of funeral contexts.[103] The practice of funeral games is significant both as a display of quasi-heroic activity to honor the deceased and as an effective contrast between fame achieved by the living and already achieved by the dead, but the practice of human sacrifice through funeral-game combat is at best a remote possibility for the origins of Greek athletics.

It seems more productive, then, to explore the associations of "death" and athletics in known historical contexts, with reference to contemporary attitudes to the connections. So the consideration of "death" in this context concerns rather a general principle, as noted earlier, taken in a wide sense to include the proximity to actual death or the risk to well-being in competition, the 'delight' in risk, the fear of human mortality, and attitudes toward death and fame as demonstrated in athletic performance. Earlier I termed death "antiphonal" and not "antithetical" to athletic desire, since the two are complementary principles and not clear opposites like death and life or desire and hatred. Athletic *erōs* and athletic *thanatos* are two extremes that give meaning to the contest. The ideal athlete combines a strong desire to demonstrate excellent achievement and attain fame with disdain for physical risk; the real athlete struggles with his or her own need to find self-motivation and overcome fear of or aversion to pain or injury.

Though death is normally not a part of athletic competition, its presence is pervasive indirectly through risk of serious injury and through myths connecting death with contests. Death is then the line that distinguishes athletic from nonathletic conflict. The locus classicus for the distinction is Homer's description of Achilles chasing Hector around the walls of Troy:

> [T]here they ran, one fleeing, the other pursuing;
> it was a good man who fled in front, but a much better one chased him
> swiftly, since the two strove not for
> a sacrificial beast nor an oxhide, which are the prizes for men in a
>   footrace,
> but they ran for the life of horse-taming Hector.
> As when prize-winning, single-hoofed horses run at full speed
> around the turning posts. A great prize is laid up for them,
> either a tripod or a woman, when funeral games are held at a man's death.

So the two whirled three times round the city of Priam
with their swift feet.

(*Il.* 22.156–66)

Two different metaphors, the footrace and the horse race, are used to describe with
ironic formulae the sharp distinctions between athletics and warfare. The metaphorical description of Hector's life (*psuchē*) as a prize (*aethlion*) is striking, as is the
simile of a chariot race at a funeral game in juxtaposition to the death to follow the
present 'race.' Homer has chosen athletics as the strongest analogue at a dramatic
high point of the poem, since it underscores the mortal seriousness of the chase.[104]

Later Greek thought continued to play on the comparison of life in contest with
death in combat. A third or second century B.C. inscription for a boxer and pankratiast,
Athanichos of Thebes, combines a victory epigram with a warrior's epitaph:[105]

[Πάμμα]χος ἐν Νεμ[έ]αι νικῶ καὶ τρὶς Βασίλεια
 [π]αῖς καὶ ἀνήρ· καὶ πὺξ τὸν τ[ρίτ]ον [ἀ]μ[φ]εθ[έ]μην·
[θν]ήισκω δ᾽ [ἐ]μ [π]ρομάχοις ῎Αρεως δορὸς ἡγεμονεύων
[κλ]εινὸς ᾽Αθάνιχος, ὃν θοῦρος ῎Αρης δ[ά]μ[α]σεν.

(*IG* 7.4247)

I won once in pankration at Nemea, and three times at the Basileia
    Games [at Lebadeia]
both in the boys' and men's categories. And the third time I was
    crowned in boxing!
I died leading the spearmen in the front lines of Ares,
I, the famous Athanichos, whom impetuous Ares subdued.

There is a real sense of irony here, as in the famous scene of Hector and Achilles,
which relies upon the juxtaposition of death-dealing battle with strenuous but
much safer athletics. But unlike the Homeric episode, Athanichos' inscription
takes great pride in the victories in contest that ultimately made him famous; there
he was not easily subdued in the two most brutal competitions. The language
hearkens back to the epic and to the martial lyrics of Tyrtaeus, with particular
allusion to the death of Sarpedon, the only Homeric hero of whom the expression
"Ares subdued" is used (δάμασ᾽ . . . ῎Αρης, *Il.* 16.543, cf. ῎Αρης δάμασεν, the last
words of the inscription).[106] Also in this context should be mentioned the close parallel of Tyrtaeus' poem 12, extolling the man who remains "in the front lines,"[107]
whose "prize" is *aretē*, not athletics, and who has the "impetuous" might of a
warrior. Later historical practice, then, reflects and preserves earlier analogies and
contrasts in the myths.

A life is often at stake with death the prescribed punishment for the loser in a
mythical *agōn*. Here athletics connects with drama in describing a "struggle of life

and death." *Agōn* is often applied to a serious struggle for life and death in dramatic confrontations, frequently in the form of a duel, for example, between Ajax and Odysseus, Eteocles and Polyneices, Orestes and Aegisthus, Heracles and Acheloos, and even Heracles and Thanatos (Death) wrestling over Alcestis.[108] It is of course a typical motif of the myths of many cultures that a hero arrives as the last in a line of challengers, all of whom have met their deaths at the antagonist's hands, and puts an end to the contest and the killings. Many of these in Greek culture take the form of an athletic contest, each with its own rich tradition of narratives and with a variety of themes, including notably the contest for the bride and the contest of the civilized Greek over the barbarian.[109] Most important here is one element of the myths, the fatal consequences of the contest. We have discussed earlier the stories of Atalanta's murder of her would-be suitors after an unsuccessful footrace, and Oenomaus' killing of Hippodameia's suitors when he beat them in a chariot race. A variation on the marriage contest motif is at the basis of the contest of the axes in the Odyssey, since there Penelope's suitors abuse the custom of guest-friendship until the hero beats them in archery and takes vengeance on them. Heracles wrestled and killed Antaeus, who had killed strangers passing through Libya; a similar plot underlies Theseus' wrestling match with Cercyon and Polydeuces' boxing match with Amycus.[110] Death comes to all of those defeated in these contests (with the exception of Atalanta herself), as myth is used to distort the norm by overstatement to make a point about excessive cruelty and the balance of violence in society. Death is normally present in contests only in a symbolic sense.

A few myths introduce death directly as the focal issue of the contest; here the fragility of human mortality is the central concern. Heracles' wrestling with Thanatos was mentioned earlier. So in another legendary match of Heracles, his very immortality is wagered as prize when he wrestles, defeats, and kills Eryx, who challenged the hero for possession of his cattle. And in a match with Menoetes, herdsman of the underworld, Heracles is restrained in the end only by the intercession of Persephone.[111] In these myths, the contests themselves are highly realistic wrestling bouts, yet death, life, and immortality become the stakes. Our awareness of mortality is heightened in the unusual context of an athletic struggle. The real athlete with these mythical matches in mind participates indirectly in, and even measures him or herself against, heroes in legendary contests.

Let us turn now from myth generally to Homeric legend and later historical sources. Apart from the dead hero honored by funeral games[112] and the rare death of an athlete in the course of competition, death is not directly and explicitly associated with Greek athletics. Contests are played with an extreme seriousness that can and sometimes does lead to an accidental fatality, but true excellence is demonstrated as much in the exercise of restraint as in the show of strength. As discussed earlier, excessive violence or *hybris* was discouraged in the ethics of competition, and restraint or *aidōs* was praised, for example, in the case of a boxer who "walks straight on the path hostile to insolent violence" (Pind., *Ol.* 7.90–91).[113] In the funeral games for Patroclus, Homer illustrates several examples of death or injury closely avoided in competition. In the chariot race, Menelaus deliberately holds back his horses to avoid a collision with the reckless Antilochus, and Menelaus' *aretē* is duly acknowledged in the end when the prize of Antilochus, who finished ahead of him, is yielded to him (Il. 23. 426–37). In the boxing match, the victor Epeius helps his opponent to his feet (694–97), and Achilles ends the wrestling so that the two heroes "not wear themselves out with injuries" (μηδὲ τρίβεσθε κακοῖσι, 735).

Homer's "combat in armor" or *hoplomachia*, virtually without parallel in later contests,[114] called for two men to face off with shields and spears; the victor who "first pierces the fair skin and reaches the entrails through the armor and dark blood" would get a Thracian sword; the loser, presumed to survive, was also awarded a valuable prize. Yet the epic version of this contest shows an aversion to violence on the part of the spectators, who call for the duel to be stopped when Diomedes threatens to wound Ajax in the neck (Il. 23.822–23). The armed combat may well be grounded on the practices of Mycenaean funeral games, as evidenced by a recently discovered thirteenth century B.C. *larnax* (sarcophagus) from Tanagra on which are depicted a funeral, armed combat, and bull-leaping.[115] A late-eighth-century kantharos shows, in a funerary context, armed combat on two sides (fig. 9-2).[116] This important and fascinating piece may be the best contemporary evidence supporting the inclusion of armed combat as an authentic contest of funeral games. Two sorts of *hoplomachia* are depicted: on one side (B) with spears and shields, as in Homer's version, and, on the other side (A), with swords alone and no apparent armor of any sort. Moreover, the duels take place in the presence of other festival activities, boxing and possibly jumping or dancing next to the spear duel, and a lyre player (and singer?) with the sword duel. A curious scene (side A) of a man with a spear being eaten alive by two huge, wolflike beasts, also next to the sword duel, may depict hunting or perhaps some otherwise unknown Greek version of the Roman *venatio* (hunting spectacle). In any case, the presence of both male and female spectators (the competitors are all male) and the similarity of the vessel to other Geometric pots found in grave contexts in the Athenian Kerameikos suggest that the kantharos illustrates funeral games. It is unclear whether the funeral games were historical or legendary, whether they depict eighth-century practices or scenes from some lost epic reflecting even earlier practices. A sixth-century sarcophagus from Clazomenae also shows pairs of armed combatants accompanied by flute-players often seen on athletic vases, and flanked by depictions of chariot-racers and prizes.[117] This later piece, like the one from Tanagra and the Geometric kantharos, also appears to be in the context of a funeral with a figure of the dead hero looking on. The armed combat in Homer may, therefore, be a reminiscence of a Bronze Age practice that vanished during the Dark Age.[118] The evidence for actual armed dueling contests in Mycenaean Greece is, however, slim, and it is safer to speculate on reactions to such a contest by later Greeks as presented in Homer. The poet honors by inclusion the event preserved by earlier tradition but avoids a noxious outcome by dramatiz-

Figure 9-2 a (top, side A) and b (bottom, side B). Geometric kantharos, late 8th c. B.C. The National Museum of Denmark, Copenhagen, 727. Courtesy of the Department of Classical and Near Eastern Antiquities, National Museum of Denmark.

ing the fear and concern of the onlookers in the story. The notion of a deliberately injurious contest would have repulsed Homer's audience five centuries later.

As with much in Greek culture, Homer defines the ethos of the *agōn*, the restrained but vigorous spirit of later athletic competition in which opponents suffer and skirt serious injury or death, but ultimately avoid it. Lucian's Solon, if he does reflect sixth century B.C. realities on this topic, rejects the suggestion of the foreigner that armed combat would be a better mode of training for war than athletics: "With regard to testing men in arms, and watching them get wounded—forget it! It is animal-like and terribly wrongheaded, and, even more so, unprofitable to slaughter off the best men who would be put to better use against the enemy" (*Anach.* 37).

A later form of *hoplomachia*, popular particular among Athenians of the fourth century B.C. and later, is attested in literary and epigraphic sources. Little is known about the exact way in which this was practiced, but all evidence indicates that it was a nonviolent, yet strenuous paramilitary event. According to Plato's account in the *Laws* (833d–834a), it probably resembled the modern sport of fencing in avoiding real wounds and in giving victory to the competitor with the best qualitative performance. Plato recommends that the competition be for both men and women, and that it be adopted in place of any "heavy events," that is, the combat sports of boxing, wrestling, and so on. Plato favors *hoplomachia*, then, because it is more utilitarian as training for soldiers than ordinary athletics.[119] Three centuries later Galen assessed the value of *hoplomachia* as exercise.[120] The competition became a formal part of the agonistic program of the Theseia games in Athens at least by the mid second century B.C., according to extant inscriptions of victor lists.[121] The inscriptions list two sorts of combat in arms, namely "with small shield and spear" (ἐν ἀσπιδίῳ καὶ δόρατι; in the manner of hoplites and of the Homeric combatants), and "with large shield and sword" (ἐν θυρεῷ καὶ μαχαίρᾳ; in the manner of light-armed soldiers). They also list as many as four age divisions: three for boys, and one for older youths, the ephebes; men seem not to have competed. There is probably one other form of military duel known only from Plato's *Laws* (830e), *sphairomachia*, literally "ball fighting," which seems to allude to the practice of training-bouts in the gymnasium in which spears or swords were tipped with small balls, like the button at the end of a modern fencing foil.[122] These later phenomena, in short, are much milder versions of the vicious armed contest related in Homer. Yet in spirit the armed combat as contest is the clearest reminder to participants and onlookers that athletic competition is violent only to a point, while nonathletic conflicts of physical force often do aim at killing one's opponent.

Since the "heavy events," as the Greeks called them, namely boxing, wrestling, and pankration (which combines the techniques of the former two) were the most violent of the gymnic contests, it is no surprise that the accidental deaths of athletes are most often reported in these events. A total of eight such deaths are preserved in ancient sources, four in boxing, two in wrestling, and two in pankration.[123] The ideal attitude of the athlete facing a life or death struggle is conveyed by an inscription of the boxer Agathos Daimon of Alexandria, nicknamed "the Camel," who died at Olympia at age 35:

ἐνθάδε πυκτεύων ἐν τῷ σταδίῳ ἐτελεύτα,
   εὐξάμενος Ζηνὶ ἢ στέφος ἢ θάνατον....[124]

Boxing here in the stadium I died,
   praying to Zeus for either the wreath or death. . . .

This ethos is an extension of the ideals of athletic virtue discussed earlier, particularly in the formulations of Pindar on the need for risk to achieve excellence:[125]

Work and expense always in the company of excellent accomplishments
[ἀρεταῖσι] struggle for a deed, wrapped in risk [κινδύνῳ κεκαλυμμένον].
                                                            (Ol. 5.16)

The ancient Scholiast comments on this passage: "[Pindar] says 'wrapped in risk' here not only because victory at Olympia is uncertain in relation to its expense, but also since many of those who compete die in the stadium" (Sch. ad Pind., Ol. 5.34a Drachmann). Since the athletic fatalities known to us all involve victors, the Scholiast provides a sober reminder that there may have been scores of athletes who died in defeat.[126] One such victim may have been Polemarchos, whose funeral monument calls him "hapless" (δύσμορος) since "the struggle over a victory in pankration destroyed me."[127] The epitaph retrieves for the athlete at least the honor of having died "in action," for the sake of glorious victory. We should also recall here the stories mentioned above of the two pankration coaches who spurred on their charges, Arrhichion and Mandrogenes, respectively, by shouting encouragement, "What a beautiful epitaph! 'He never gave in at Olympia,'" or by this letter to the boy's mother: "If you should hear that your son has died [in competition], believe it. If you hear he's defeated, don't believe it!"[128]

   The former of these two coaches, the gymnastēs of Arrhichion of Phigalia, literally "instilled in him a desire for death" (εἰς ἔρωτα θανάτου κατέστησεν, Gymn. 21).[129] Arrhichion apparently took the encouragement to heart, died while in a painful hold in a contest at Olympia, and was crowned posthumously as his opponent had signaled defeat at the last moment (Paus. 8.40.1–2). One account preserves the reaction of the audience:

He seems to have overpowered not only his opponent but his audience as
well. At any rate, they have jumped from their seats and are shouting,
some of them waving their hands, some flapping their garments, some
are leaping from the ground, while others are wrestling good-spiritedly
with those nearby. For the spectators are not able to control themselves

at the truly amazing turn of events. Who is so without feeling as not to
cry out for the athlete? Although his two previous victories at Olympia
were a great achievement, the present one is greater since having won
this victory at the cost of his life he is being sent down to the land of the
blessed with this dust still on him. Don't consider this an accident. Very
cleverly it was thought out before the victory [σοφώτατα γὰρ προυνοήθη
τῆς νίκης]. (Philostr., *Imagines* 2.6)

The deliberateness of Arrhichion's decision to die seems to be at odds with the earlier mention of his coach's inspirational mention of the glory of death at Olympia.
But the two stories can be reconciled if the pankratiast's resolve before the match
was merely strengthened by his trainer. Whatever the truth of this report, the author presents a scene that is plausible to his audience and reflects contemporary
ideals. He suggests that the victor (and victim) not only tolerated death in victory;
he sought it out with the strategy that this would bring the greatest fame. The reaction of those in the audience is also noteworthy. They have taken the lesson from
the event. They are inspired, ecstatic with delight, and probably filled with desire
to emulate such excellence. Arrhichion's premeditated desire for simultaneous victory (at least according to Philostratus' account) has ignited the audience with similar courage and aspirations that will, presumably, be exercised outside the stadium.

The common ethos in the stories of Polemarchos, Mandrogenes, and Arrhichion
is that the extreme effort expended in victory must ideally show an utter disregard,
even a desire, for death. Some restraint was called for, however, as two other stories of fatalities illustrate. A boxer, Creugas of Epidamnus, was killed by a vicious
and illegal stab of the hand by which he was eviscerated; Creugas was awarded
the victory posthumously (Paus. 8.40.3–5). Another boxer, Diognetus of Crete,
killed his opponent and was denied a victory by the judges at Olympia in 488 B.C.,
but he was, nevertheless, honored as a hero by his countrymen.[130] Cleomedes of
Astypalaea killed his opponent in boxing at Olympia in 484 B.C., was denied a victory by the umpires, and went mad (Paus. 6.9.6–8). Like Diognetus, Cleomedes was
ultimately honored as a hero by his fellow citizens, this according to an oracle from
the Pythia and despite his having killed sixty schoolchildren after his return from
Olympia. The death resulting from excessive violence, *hybris*, was not tolerated,
though the killing of one's opponent was not in itself censured. And in some cases,
the killing of an opponent even lends heroic stature to the athlete. Hence a late myth
was attached to the stories of Theogenes, wherein he is said to have killed an opponent at Olympia.[131] How could such a great, heroic athlete not have matched others even in their morbid distinctions?

The inscription on the famous Daochus monument at Delphi, dated ca. 338–
332 B.C., boasts of a wrestling victory by Telemachus of Pharsalus in which the
opponent, the strongest man in his region, died. The text of the inscription is incomplete, and so there is controversy over whether both opponents willingly en-

tered a contest to the death, whether the victor declared that the death was accidental (as seems likely), and whether this took place even in a regular Greek festival, or at some specially held demonstration match between two great strongmen
of the day.[132] In the case of Telemachus' match, there was sufficient pride in his
victory and sufficient confidence that the public would not censure Telemachus,
despite the attendant death, that the victory and the fatality were recorded on a very
conspicuous monument. The wrestler capitalizes on a distinction that associates
him with other heroic athletes.

Athenian law classified unintentional killing in an athletic contest as similar
to accidental killing of a fellow soldier in war. Both acts were violent but involuntary. In both cases, to confirm that the death was "lawful," a trial was held in a
special location, the temple of Apollo Delphinius, where the killer could be purified
according to the Delphic rule.[133] While death in the *agōn* was tolerated so long as it
was accidental, the killer still had to be relieved of blood guilt.

"Excellent achievements without risk [ἀκίνδυνοι δ' ἀρεταὶ] are honored neither among men, nor in hollow ships; many remember if something fine is accomplished with toil" (Pind., *Ol.* 6.9). Risk of violence is, as implied by the finely wrought
expression of Pindar, a legacy of the heroic ethos in athletics and warfare. But the
risk is balanced by the promise of success. In praising a victorious pankratiast,
Pindar explains that victory alleviates the pain and toil of competition:

> As a healing remedy
> for the wearying blows received at deep-plained Nemea,
> he carries off a glorious victory.
>
> (N. 3.17–19)

The Scholiast comments on this: "He considers victory to be a drug for the blows
[φάρμακον ... τῶν πληγῶν]. Those who win even if they receive wounds do not
feel it on account of their pleasure [διὰ τὸ ἥδεσθαι]" (Schol. *ad* Pind., *Nem.* 3.29
Drachmann). The athlete is drawn on by pleasure, by a desire that, at its most intense, aims even at death.

Though all of the above examples of death and violence in sport have been
drawn from the realm of the "heavy events," the combat sports of boxing, wrestling,
and pankration, other contests shared in the mystique of the risk of death. The comparison of Achilles' chasing of Hector to athletic races serves as a universal, mythical image of the parallels between contests for life and death, and those for prizes.
The risk of life by mythical contenders is seen, for instance, in the horse race of
Pelops, and the footrace of Atalanta. The type of contest is less important than the
fact that the tale illustrates a struggle of life and death. Myths may overstate the
risks and inflate the degree of violence found in actual competition, but they illustrate some of the fundamental principles upon which all athletic contests were
based. Athletic performances result in either the 'life' of immortal acclaim or the

'death' of ignominious silence and therein serve as metaphors for the greater struggles of life beyond the stadium.

Lucian, in his *Anacharsis*, does not distinguish sports that can inspire the spectators with courage. The inspirational benefits are universal. By analogy with an audience at a cock-fighting event, he notes that the souls of those who watch "adopt a certain subtle eagerness for dangers, so that they not seem less noble or less bold than the cocks, nor give up early because of wounds, weariness, or some other discomfort" (*Anach.* 37). Though cock-fighting is notoriously violent, the implication of Lucian's argument is that Greeks can become inspired to undergo risks from watching even less violent contests; the very form of performance in the *agōn* instills courage in the audience.

Let us now add to this survey of the associations of death with athletics some examples of noncombat sports to illustrate the breadth of the theme. Myth has preserved several instances of fatalities from discus-throwing. The most famous mishap is that of Hyacinthus, who died when struck by a discus thrown by Apollo.[134] But there are also the following tales of death-by-discus, some accidental, some deliberate: Hermes' killing of Crocus, Oxylus' killing of Thermius (or Alcidocus), Perseus' killing of Acrisius, and Peleus' killing of Phocus.[135] Plutarch tells of a man accidentally killed by a javelin in competition at the time of Pericles (*Per.* 36); and Antiphon's *Second Tetralogy* treats the hypothetical case of a boy accidentally killed by a javelin in a gymnasium (Antiph. 2.2.7).

Even running events are directly and indirectly associated with the theme of risk and mortality. The myth of Hippomenes and Atalanta certainly provides the strongest example of running for the ultimate stakes, and it has resonances therein with the Achilles-Hector pursuit. There was apparently a custom for the *hoplito-dromos* or "race in armor" held every four years at Plataea that "a victor, if he competes another time, must put his life at stake. If defeated, he is condemned to death" (Philostr., *Gymn.* 8). This extreme and unparalleled penalty for defeat in a contest may be due to the ominous symbolism of a 'victor' becoming the 'defeated' in the Eleutheria or "Freedom Festival," which celebrates the Greek victory over the Persians at Plataea in 479 B.C.[136] At the Plataean race, the victor was hailed as "best" (ἄριστος) among the Greeks, and "very great prizes" were awarded to him. In other words, the race was meant to distinguish an individual who represented all Greeks, and whose honor was to be protected even at the cost of his own life. This is as close as the Greeks came to ritualized human sacrifice in historic times. The symbolic importance of the contest for the community outweighs the well-being of the individual and suggests that other competitions also operated on a symbolic, communal level in less extreme ways.

In a wholly different aspect of footraces, the hazard of wearing the *perizōma* or loincloth is sometimes connected with the stories about the introduction of nudity as a custom in athletics. Orsippus of Megara, the victor in the Olympic stade race of 720 B.C., was "tripped up by his *perizōma* during the race, fell and died or, according to some, was simply defeated. Whence it was ordained that these athletes were to compete in the nude."[137] An alternate version of the origin tells of the Athenian archon, Hippomenes, who decreed that athletes were to compete naked after one fell over his *perizōma* during a competition.[138] Like his legendary namesake, the happy victor over Atalanta in the footrace, this Hippomenes also heralded the end of the fatal footrace. It would be quite unusual, a freak accident, for an athlete to die from falling down in a race, and the death, unmentioned by earlier and better sources, may be "an aetiological story to account for a custom which could not easily be explained."[139] Still, the *perizōma* seems to have been precariously held up, a simple cloth tied up much like a diaper, apparently without a pin, cincture, or other extraneous fastening.[140] In short, it probably did and could occasionally fall down and entangle a runner's feet. This does not, however, argue that the *perizōma* was a serious risk. The fact that the hazards of falling during the footrace play an important role in the stories of Ajax, Orsippus, and Hippomenes merely suggests that even the most risk-free of contests has its downfalls. I personally learned of the hazards of the footrace in the Greek stadium when, some years ago during an impromptu race with colleagues in the stadium at Olympia, I slipped on some pebbles in midcourse and badly hurt both knees— a painful memory of my 'death' at Olympia.

Flight and pursuit in the footrace, then, do not always symbolize the "erotic pursuit" as acted out in the rituals of girls' transition to adulthood, where roles of hunter and hunted are implied. The act of racing can also symbolize a "fatal pursuit" in which the loser also loses his life or his reputation. "Fatal pursuit" has its mythological counterpart, particularly in stories in which a mortal amorously pursues or is pursued by an immortal, for example, Eos and Tithonus, Hades and Persephone, and Peleus and Thetis.[141] The rapes and seductions do not always take the form of a race, but flight and pursuit are often implied, and erotic and fatal motifs are combined. Since the footrace and the chase are such simple, even primitive forms of contest, the "performance" symbolism can be broadly applied to any of the major *termini* in life—preeminently among which are life and love. One's success in the course and the outcome are easily understood by the footrace metaphor.

Of the noncombat events in which fatalities are attested, horse- and chariot-racing seem to have been the most dangerous. Equestrian events and the breeding of horses were primarily for the wealthy, who even competed at times as charioteers in search of thrills. So the rich young Athenian character, Pheidippides, dreaming of a race in his sleep, shouts out his opening lines of Aristophanes' *Clouds*: "Philon! You're cheating! Stay in your own lane!" (*Cl.* 25).[142] The famous report in Sophocles' *Electra* of Orestes' supposed death in a chariot wreck at Delphi no doubt reflects a common occurrence in Greek chariot racing:

> Then the Aenean man's hard-mouthed
> colts became violent. From the turn,
> finishing the sixth lap and starting the seventh,

they crashed headlong into the Barcaean team.
After that, from this one accident, each
shattered and overturned another. All the plain
of Crisa was filled with the hippic shipwreck.

(Soph., El. 724–30)

The very structure of the track without a central dividing strip greatly increased
the risk of head-on collisions.[143] In the four-horse chariot race at Delphi in 462
B.C., only the chariot of Arcesilas of Cyrene crossed the finish line without dam-
age (Pind., P. 5.49–51). Pindar's phrase about "the deed wrapped in risk" and his
disdain for "excellent deeds without risk" both occur in victory odes for the mule-
cart race.

But it is in the Homeric and Olympic traditions of chariot racing that the symbolic importance of this competition is made clearest. The chariot-race of Homer's
funeral games for Patroclus, in which Menelaus avoids a dangerous collision in the
narrow part of the straightaway, was mentioned briefly earlier. But the most notoriously dangerous part of any hippodrome was the turning post (terma, or nussa) at
which a 180-degree turn was required; there it was particularly perilous in the first
turn of the race when the field had not thinned out. And so prior to the chariot race
Nestor advises the young Antilochus to drive slowly and near the terma at the turn
to take a winning lead (Il. 23.322–45). Most interesting is Nestor's description of
the terma in this race:

σῆμα δέ τοι ἐρέω μάλ' ἀριφραδές, οὐδέ σε λήσει.
ἕστηκε ξύλον αὗον ὅσον τ' ὄργυι' ὑπὲρ αἴης
ἢ δρυὸς ἢ πεύκης· τὸ μὲν οὐ καταπύθεται ὄμβρῳ,
λᾶε δὲ τοῦ ἑκάτερθεν ἐρηρέδαται δύο λευκὼ
ἐν ξυνοχῇσιν ὁδοῦ, λεῖος δ' ἱππόδρομος ἀμφίς·
ἤ τευ σῆμα βροτοῖο πάλαι κατατεθνηῶτος,
ἢ τό γε νύσσα τέτυκτο ἐπὶ προτέρων ἀνθρώπων,
καὶ νῦν τέρματ' ἔθηκε ποδάρκης δῖος 'Αχιλλεύς.

I will tell you a clear sign [sēma] and you cannot miss it.
There stands a seasoned post six-feet above the earth.
either oak or pine. It has not been rotted by rain,
and two white stones lean against it on either side
at the intersection of the course, and the racetrack is smooth round about.
Either it is the grave [sēma] of some man who died long ago,
or it was set up as a turning post [nussa] by people in earlier times.
Now swift-footed brilliant Achilles has designated this as the goal [termat'].

(Il. 23.326–33)

The boundary then is clearly designated as a *sēma*, a "sign" or "symbol" of something else, namely the crucial place for implementing a victorious strategy. The "sign" may at the same time be either a *sēma* in another common sense of the Greek word, a "tomb-marker," or a *nussa*, the specific word for the "turning post" of a racecourse. The following equation thus results: *sēma*—"sign" = *sēma*—"old tomb" or *nussa*—former "goal" = *terma*—present "goal." The description of the object as a "seasoned post," standing at about the height of a man and not rotted by the elements, reflects contradictory physical properties (dead, yet prominent and sturdy).[144] The physical description thus echoes the functional ambiguity of the sign (death-marker, or goal for lively contest). The ambiguity is never resolved, and the *terma* is mentioned only once more in the narrative, in the empty speculations of the spectator Idomeneus about Eumelus and his chariot possibly "coming to harm" (*eblaben*, 461):

I saw those horses going first around the turn [*terma*]. . . .
Either the driver lost the reins, or he was not able
to hold the horses properly around the turn [*terma*] and happened not to
    wheel around.
There I think he fell out and wrecked his chariot.
The horses swerved from the course, when a spiritedness seized their
    minds.

(Il. 23.462, 465–68)

Though Eumelus comes in last, Achilles, perhaps believing that he had suffered an accident, awards him second prize out of sympathy (532–46). The turning post again becomes an ambiguous phantom, imagined by members of the audience to be the site of harm to the man with the best reputation in horse racing (289, 536, 546). And it is the place where a sudden "spiritedness" or "wildness" (*menos*) seizes the horses. We never learn if Eumelos crashed there, since he did drop inexplicably from first place to last, and yet he and his chariot were not apparently harmed. Not the turning post, but the ravine where Antilochus nearly crashed with Menelaus was the real site of danger in the contest.

Why then is so much attention given to the turning post? There are, to be sure, good narrative reasons for Homer's inclusion of it. Among other things, it illustrates the advice of the wise counsellor, ignored by the impetuous youth at his own peril, and it gives reason to Achilles' manipulation of the prizes out of sympathy and perceived status. But the inherent ambiguity in the object, in the threatening space around it, and in the fate of one who passes through it (first becomes last), calls attention to the symbolic importance of the *terma*. Athletic heroes in all sorts of contests, as we have seen, frequently risk death or injury and sometimes even die during the contest. They win honor and glory, whether or not they win the contest. In Homer the turning post, located exactly at the midpoint of the course, symbolizes the crossroads of events; it is the point at which one's fortune can change for the better or worse, depending on one's skill and on conditions beyond control ("chance," *tuchē*; cf. 466 ἐτύχησεν). It is a point that can be crossed more easily if one properly prays to the gods for assistance (546–47). It is, in short, the critical juncture of an athletic *agōn* which is analogous to the crucial moment in the life of the nonathletic hero, or of any individual.

The details about a possible tomb at the turning post, and the wildness of the horses at that point are amplified by reference to later racing traditions. At the far turn of the Olympic hippodrome, on the spectators' mound opposite the turning post, Pausanias tells us, there stood

... τὸ τῶν ἵππων δεῖμα ὁ Ταράξιππος. σχῆμα μὲν βωμοῦ περιφεροῦς ἐστι, παραθέοντας δὲ κατὰ τοῦτο τοὺς ἵππους φόβος τε αὐτίκα ἰσχυρὸς ἀπ' οὐδεμιᾶς προφάσεως φανερᾶς καὶ ἀπὸ τοῦ φόβου λαμβάνει ταραχή, τά τε δὴ ἅρματα καταγνύουσιν ὡς ἐπίπαν καὶ οἱ ἡνίοχοι τιτρώσκονται· καὶ τοῦδε ἡνίοχοι ἕνεκα θυσίας θύουσι καὶ γενέσθαι σφίσιν ἵλεων εὔχονται τὸν Ταράξιππον.

... Taraxippus, the terror of horses. It is in the shape of a round altar and there the horses are seized by a strong and sudden fear for no apparent reason, and from the fear comes a disturbance. The chariots generally crash and the charioteers are injured. Therefore the drivers offer sacrifices and pray to Taraxippus to be propitious to them. (Paus. 6.20.15)

Pausanias then offers several stories of the origin of Taraxippus, whose very name means "disturber of horses" (6.20.16–18). The altar marks the possible spot of the tomb of a famous Elean charioteer of former times, Olenius; or it is the burial place both of Dameon, an ally of Heracles against Augeas, and of his horse; or it is a cenotaph for Pelops' charioteer, Myrtilus, whose spirit frightens horses on the Olympic course as he had frightened Oenomaus' horses earlier; or it is the spirit of Oenomaus himself, harming Olympic drivers as he had killed the suitors of Hippodameia; or it is the hostile spirit (οὐκ εὐμενῆ δαίμονα) of Alcathus, one of those unsuccessful suitors; or it is some magical object buried by Pelops and obtained from Amphion of Thebes. Another source even claims that Taraxippos was another name for Pelops (Hesychius, s.v. *Taraxippos*). Pausanias also notes the parallel custom of a Taraxippus at the Isthmian hippodrome, said to have originated from the spirit of Glaucus, son of Sisyphus, who was killed by his horses at the funeral games for his father (Paus. 6.20.19). All of these obviously attribute the animals' disturbance to the tomb of the restless spirit of a mortal, and all explain why the *terma* in the Homeric race might have been the site of a hero's burial. Though the explanations in Pausanias apparently contradict one another, there is no decisive evidence or consensus to privilege one over another. All are listed by the author since each is plausible. And, taken together, they all reveal a folktale association of the hero's tomb with the crucial point of success or disaster.

Pausanias also remarks on the absence of any such malicious hero at the Isthmian racecourse, though the flash of color from a fire-red rock near the turn frightens horses (6.20.19). He also notes the absence of any such spirit at Delphi:

> The hippodrome of Apollo perhaps might also seem to trouble some of
> the competitors in the hippic events since some *daimōn* allots to men
> equally good and bad to every deed. But this course does not present a
> disturbance for horses, and as an explanation neither is a hero said to be
> at work nor does it happen for some other excuse. (10.37.4)

Much as a modern observer might agree with Pausanias' rationalization of folk aetiologies behind chariot crashes, the tales evidence a pattern pervasive enough that its absence calls for comment. The tomb near the *terma* was an entrenched part of popular belief.

Pausanias gives one final and very different aetiology of Taraxippus, an origin which he himself finds "most convincing," and with which Dio Chrysostom later agrees: the name is an epithet of the god Poseidon "of the Horses" (*Hippios*, 6.20.18).[145] There was also a sanctuary of Poseidon Hippios near the hippodrome and stadium at Mantinea (Paus. 8.10.2), and one of Poseidon Earthshaker at the hippodrome in Sparta (Xen., *Hell.* 6.5.30). And in the agora at Corinth, near the horse-race course, there was a cult of Helotis, a hero connected with Poseidon Hippios and Athena Hippia.[146] To this close connection has been compared the Roman cult of Consus, a deity identified with Poseidon/Neptune, who had a cult located underground and near the turning post of the Circus Maximus. The Roman custom of using three cones at the turning post has been seen as possibly influenced by the shape of some Etruscan funerary monuments, or, in view of egg-shaped tips, an allusion to the cult of Castor and Polydeukes, the Dioscuri, twins hatched from an egg and also strongly associated with horses and with death-and-resurrection cults.[147]

Both the Homeric and the later historical associations of the turning-post area with death probably arose from the many accidents that did occur at the point where the chariots had to wheel around, literally sliding behind the team of horses, to reverse course as sharply as possible. The "terror of the horses" would naturally have been attributed to one of the restless spirits who died at that very place, given the very literally descriptive name "Taraxippus." No one could agree upon exactly which of the many eligible spirits this could be at Olympia. Or could it even be the god of horses himself, Poseidon? Similar myths and cults might then have arisen elsewhere in Greece, and perhaps even at Rome, either on direct analogy with Olympic custom, or because of a similar need to find a spirit (or, in the case of Nemea, a rock) to which charioteers could make offerings to avert calamity before the big race. This rationalization of the origin of the Taraxippus does not, however, deny that turning-post cults or tombs were very real to the people of the day, and that cults frequently invest tangible objects with symbolic meaning.

Though the combat events were the most hazardous "gymnic" events (the Greek name for nonequestrian contests), horse- and chariot-racing, and even foot-races, afforded a closer analogy to running the 'course' of life, in which the space on the track stood for the span of time until death. By this analogy, those who met misfortune at the *terma* had their lives cut short and died an inglorious death. Those, on the other hand, who made it to the finish could be said to have led happy, virtuous, or even heroic lives. The metaphor is frequent in classical literature, both Greek and Roman: "to make the last turn in the course of life."[148] Thus the poem of the third-century B.C. author Herodas links the racing image to that of the chariot-borne sun god:

> ἐπὴν τὸν ἑξηκοστὸν ἥλιον κάμψηις,
> ὦ Γρύλλε, Γρύλλε, θνῆισκε καὶ τέφρη γίνευ·
> ὡς τυφλὸς οὐπέκεινα τοῦ βίου καμπτήρ·
> ἤδη γὰρ αὐγή τῆς ζοῆς ἀπήμβλυνται.

> When you will make the sixtieth turn in the sun's cycles,
> O Grullus, Grullus, die and turn to ashes.
> How blind is the turning-post of life thereafter,
> for already the sunbeam of existence is dimmed.

> (*Mime* 10)

The single complete cycle of a person's life is composed, in this version of the metaphor, of yearly "circuits" made by the sun. This may be the reason that the Roman sun god, Sol, was, along with Poseidon/Neptune, closely associated with chariot racing.

The depictions of chariot races on Roman sarcophagi and a funerary urn also offer a neat example of the connection of chariot racing generally with death in that society.[149] Most interesting for the present discussion is the Romans' frequent use of figures of Eros (Cupido, Amor) as drivers on the sarcophagi races, exclusively on the sarcophagi of children, as seen on this example from Mainz (fig. 9-3).[150] Interpretation of this iconography varies. Since many of these scenes include a wreck, some have taken this hapless figure to represent the child who died an untimely death. Who, then, by this analogy, is represented by the omnipresent figure of the victor? Is the deceased perhaps in some sense a "victor"? It is less problematic to see the entire race as a metaphor of the infant's life, or of any person's life, since adult human charioteers are depicted on many adult sarcophagi.[151] The Roman iconography thus complements the

Figure 9-3. Sarcophagus, ca. A.D. 300, Mainz Römanisch-Germanisches Zentralmuseum. Courtesy of the Römanisch-Germanisches Zentralmuseum, Mainz, Germany.

earlier Greek literary metaphor but embellishes it with the addition of Erotes in lieu of human charioteers. The tradition of associating children with Erotes has long been acknowledged and perhaps depends upon the natural assimilation of the playful divinity with the spirit of children, an assimilation that had its roots in Classical and Hellenistic Greek iconography. Thus a late fifth century B.C. *chous* vase depicts a chariot drawn by fawns and driven by one youthful Eros while another assists (fig. 9-4); Hellenistic art and literature transformed the youthful Eros first into a mischievous child, then an infant.[152] Art of the Classical period associates the youthful Eros with various games such as dice, hoop-bowling, and ball-playing. One vase showing the youth with a ball in his hand next to the palace of Hades combines the motifs of desire, death, and play.[153] Another motif of vases showing Eros with a torch held downward has commonly been taken to indicate a connection of the god with death. The association of Eros with the torch race in Athens, discussed in the chapter 8, would make this interpretation attractive, but, in a recent study, the significance of the upside-down torch has been justly taken as an ambiguous symbol.[154] The association of death with chariot races and particularly the turning posts also begins with earlier Greek traditions, as we have seen, and it is noteworthy that the turning posts

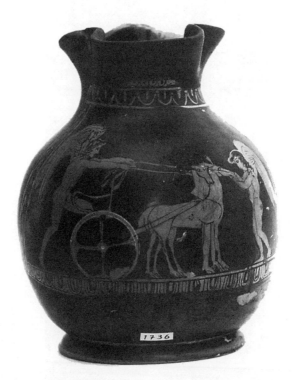

Figure 9-4. Miniature oinochoe (shape 3), ca. 420 B.C., Hobart Painter, Athens Nat. Mus. 1736; Beazley, *ARV²* 1258. Courtesy of the National Archeological Museum and the Archeolgical Receipts Fund, Athens, Greece.

are the one architectural adornment that is always present on the sarcophagi, usually framing the two ends of the object. Normally there are also wrecks and unfortunate participants being trampled in the scenes.

The presence of Erotes racing chariots on funerary objects is, I suggest, a complex synthesis of several Greco-Roman traditions, in part the immense popularity
in Roman times of infant Amores shown performing any number of activities from
daily life, but also a specific expression of the spirit of playful desire in competition
that flaunts or defies death. The iconography of Erotes wrestling, boxing, or participating in other contests, as discussed earlier, goes back at least to fifth century
B.C. Greece.[155] The metaphor comparing Eros, the human phenomenon of desire,
with the tension, the struggle, and the agonistic spirit of the contest is thus married explicitly on the Roman sarcophagi with the theme of death, risk, and hazard
present in the life of any person who acts on his or her desires. A series of Roman
glass cups depicting chariot races, the most famous of which is the Colchester cup,
illustrate the attitudes toward the participants more simply: next to the name of each
of the losing charioteers is inscribed VA[LE], "farewell," and next to the victor is
AV[E], "hail!"[156] The majority "die" in ignominy, the exceptional one prospers. The
fact that this synthesis of death, desire, and contest finds its ultimate expression on
the monuments of children's deaths is singularly appropriate, since it represents well
the (perhaps idealized) condition and character of the children at the point of death:
full of desire and potential, full of an antagonistic spirit, and faced with an untimely
fall at the hands of fate. Though the medium is Roman, the ideas that inform it derive
from, or at least are in harmony with, Greek concepts of athletic death and desire.

Those who die at the turning post in the Greek hippodrome are not the great
heroes. Most of those mortals whose spirits Pausanias tentatively identifies with
Taraxippus are secondary figures or even losers in their respective legends. The true
heroes praised in the tales of contest are those who, like Pelops, finish the course of
life by winning the race. The 'victory' is found, according to popular Greek values,
not in the length of life, nor in the amount of wealth or power amassed, but in dying
"happy," *eudaimōn*, that is, having flourished in one's personal health, familial circumstances, and relation to fellow citizens.[157]

The topography of the Olympic hippodrome, and of the sanctuary generally,
encourages athletic desire against the risk of death. The figure of Taraxippus is
balanced by "a bronze statue of Hippodameia on one turning post , holding a ribbon and about to tie it on Pelops for his victory" (Paus. 6.20.19). Hippodameia,
whose name means literally "subduer of horses," serves as the exact counterpart of
Taraxippos, in the architecture and in the spirit of the competition. Her presence at
Olympia in the hippodrome and in her sanctuary, probably located just west of that
course, is a symbolic reminder of the rewards of success in contests and in life (Paus.
6.20.7). The sanctuary of Pelops still farther west in the sanctuary also reminds
competitors of the glory and happiness that can come to the victor; the chthonic
sacrifices to the hero, mentioned at the beginning of this chapter, encourage others

to seek fame after death (Paus. 5.13). The altars of the hippodrome also inform us about the divine powers thought to wield influence in the dynamics of the race:

> As you approach the starting-gate for the horse-races, there is an altar inscribed "Bringer of Fate" (*Moirageta*). This is clearly an epithet of Zeus who knows the affairs of humans, whatever the Fates give them, and what is not allotted to them. Near there is an oblong altar of the Fates, and after it one of Hermes and the two next are for Zeus Most High. At the starting point for the horses and out in the open, just about in the middle of the gates, are altars of Poseidon Hippios and Hera Hippia and near the pillar an altar of the Dioscuri. (Paus. 5.15.5)

This group constitutes the primary divinities associated with horses and with the abstract power of the "Fates" (*Moirai*), which would be of greatest concern to participants and spectators in the hippic events. Hermes is here primarily a god of transitions and doorways, hence generally of the starting gates both in stadia and hippodromes,[158] but he is also appropriate in view of his associations with good luck and with death, since he is "Conductor of Souls." These divinities underline the symbolic importance of the race as the "course of life," since that is also their domain. Poseidon is commonly associated with horses, but the altar of Hera Hippios, a less common epithet of the goddess, calls for comment.[159] Hera must here represent one of the early and primary forms of a fertility goddess, a type of "Mistress of the Beasts," who had power over humans and animals. This aspect of her may be reflected most clearly in the story of Cleobis and Biton, the Argive heroes who died while heroically pulling their mother on a cart to the Argive Heraion (Herodotus 1.31). Hera's presence here is also appropriate, it has been suggested, as goddess of fulfillment, Hera Teleia, in view of the *telos* or "completion" of the race.[160]

There are also at Olympia the altars of Ares Hippios, and Athena Hippia, naturally also in view of their hippic connections; and of Good Fortune, Pan, Aphrodite, and the Flourishing Nymphs, all of these latter being connected with the expected fertility or flourishing of the participants (Paus. 5.15.6). The presence here of Aphrodite and not Eros, and the proximity to the gods of wild nature, Pan and the Nymphs, suggest that Aphrodite's functions include both civilized and wild forms of procreation, among animals and humans. In any case the presence of these cults reinforces the impression that more was at stake here than simple victory in one race. The performance had a symbolic value with implications for life generally.

Concluding Remarks

Death and desire in Greek athletics, then, function antiphonally, in a kind of tension. Stopping short of death in all earnest competition is a principle common to both humans and animals to preserve one's species and yet establish a hierarchy.[161] Athletic desire of some commonly sought goal supplies athletes, audience, and even coaches with the incentive to succeed at any cost, and preferably with some visible cost by which their victory will be distinguished. When a contest is interrupted by death, the event suddenly breaks through the normal limits of the athletic, and all must stop for judges, audience, and the participants to determine whether the contest has lost its symbolic significance and taken on the real meaning of mundane affairs—whether the death of an opponent was by accident or chance, rather than the result of deliberately excessive force. Part of the interest in the Arrhichion story is that he was praised despite having deliberately planned his own death to garner the greatest glory. This was within the norms of the contest since Arrhichion, like each athlete, ultimately competed against himself and was within the bound of justice to embrace rather than fear his own death in the contest.

So Arrhichion died at the climax of a pankration match, and the audience literally leaped with ecstasy at such a dramatic end. Arrhichion's famous death recalls both later and earlier images of athletes achieving the high honor as a result of this sort of self-sacrifice. On Crete was found the grave of an athlete whose skull had a first century A.D. coin in its mouth, a golden victor's crown on its top, and a bronze aryballos nearby (fig. 9-5).[162] We do not know whether he died in a contest, but we can assume that the deceased placed great value in the trappings of his vic-

Figure 9-5. Skull of an athletic victor with gold crown, found with first-century A.D. silver coin of Polyrrhenia. Hagios Nikolaos Museum 7355-56. Courtesy of the Archeological Museum of Hagios Nikolaos, Crete, and the Archeological Receipts Fund, Athens, Greece.

tory, and that he wished to be honored chiefly as an athletic victor after his death. A second image reminiscent of Arrhichion's moment of glory is that of the bull-leaper gored on the horns of a charging bull on the visual center of the Minoan Hagia Triada rhyton (fig. 9-6).[163] It cannot be known whether the figure in the Bronze Age artifact was a victor, but he lends a dramatic point to the piece and shows that the audience in that period was as fascinated by and attracted to violence and death in competition as are later cultures. In a modern parallel, the bull fighter José Cubero, "El Yiyo," was killed by the dying thrust of a bull that he had in turn mortally wounded; the toreador was lauded by the audience and buried with great celebration. In connection with this incident, a modern commentator remarks:

> [The bullfight] establishes a crisis point which can only be resolved by
> the shedding of blood; in it is related a sacrifice. . . . The decision,
> associated with power and domination, became purely symbolic. . . .
> The death of the toreador and bull has an element of the necessary,
> perhaps even somewhat conciliatory. A ritual has been fulfilled.[164]

The elements of reaching a crisis, risking violent injury, and resolving events by establishing a hierarchy are of course part of Greek athletics. But if the coincidence of victory in death has resonances with a sacrificial ritual, that aspect is not marked in Greek culture. What impressed the Greeks was rather the traditionally heroic spirit of the individual willing to undergo such a risk for the sake of fame, and the dramatic quality of risk-filled competition.

Yet death in Greek athletics in the historical periods was of prime interest because of its absence from normal competition. After the Bronze Age, there were rarely staged contests of men versus beasts in Greece. No longer the hunt, but other forms of daily competition between humans, notably warfare, supplied the closest analogy with athletic events. The governing metaphor behind the *agōn* was not so much a 'sacrifice' either of human life or even, *pace* Sansone, of energy, but a performance of antagonists in which desire for the same goal leads on each competitor, and in which the special character of the contest is given meaning by a complex social context. It is not at all clear nor provable that some subconscious or primitive motivation, be it bloodlust, bloodguilt, or the residual practices of our hunting ancestors, gave rise to athletic competition among the Greeks (or, in my view, to the 'sports' of any other culture). More can be learned by studying the immediate and largely conscious values attached by social contexts to actions in themselves of little intrinsic meaning.

An athletic performance was characterized by local myths, cults, tales of previous heroes and heroic athletes, the civic function of particular festivals and events, and the status or gender of the participants, to list only some of the aspects surveyed in the chapters of this book and a few of the many other aspects it does not cover. This performative quality is inherent in the very terminology of contests: *agōn* sig-

Figure 9-6. Hagia Triada "Boxer Rhyton," including death of bull-leaper on horns of charging bull. Archeological Museum, Herakleion, Crete. Courtesy of the Archeological Museum of Herakleion, Crete, and the Archeolgical Receipts Fund, Athens, Greece.

nifying "the place where competition for dominance" takes place, and *aethlos* meaning "competitive toil." The ethic of the martial hero in performance is communicated through the use of athletics in military training, and martial-cum-athletic images in literature. The direct association of athletics with warfare clearly plays upon the awareness that the two phenomena are very close in agonal spirit, but ordinarily differentiated by the absence or presence of death. The civic function of athletics, underlined in the imagery of Pericles' Funeral Oration, is to inspire citizens with desire for the 'prize' of fame in warfare and in all service of the state.

10

CONCLUSIONS—

THE NEXUS OF ATHLETICS,

RELIGION, GENDER, AND EROS

The individual chapters of this work have examined some ways in which Greek athletics was connected with religion and cults, with the shaping of male and female youth in their transition to adulthood, and with homo- and hetero-erotic phenomena. I begin my conclusions with a chronological overview of these phenomena, and some suggestions regarding their broader interrelationship over time. I then proceed to general observations on the ways in which athletics, religion, *paideia,* and *erōs* both link us to and distance us from the ancient Greeks, affording us some insights into our own culture.

Chronological Overview

Homer's epic heroes were also athletes, and so the epics give us a glimpse of how an eighth-century poet portrayed athletics in an idealized past. Homer's athletes and their contests, either impromptu or occasioned by funerals for important individuals, comprise and attest to an athletic culture that was much less formal than the one known from later, institutionalized festivals held at regular intervals. Post-Homeric legends extend the origin of the earliest regular athletic festival, the Olympics, back into the Bronze Age, and Homer even alludes to games held near Olympia at Elis in Nestor's time. But archeological finds at Olympia suggest that no festivals of any magnitude were held there prior to the eighth century.[1] Homer's heroic athletes seem to reflect an era in which athletic contests were not yet formally tied to regular cult festivals, nor does athletics especially function as an initiation to adulthood. Rather, Homer's athletes are mostly adult heroes, and there were no special games for boys or youth. The games in Homer certainly reflect the popular belief that the gods took a vested interest in athletics by helping or harming mortal participants. If this belief was vaguely formulated prior to Homer's poems, the epic narratives doubtless formulated images of divine patronage of athletes which was a transitional step in the process by which the gods became patrons of contests incorporated into their festivals.

In the eighth and seventh centuries, interest in the Homeric epics may have contributed to interest in the newly formalized Olympics, the Olympics may have boosted the epics, or, most likely, both phenomena simultaneously fed enthusiasm for each other by encouraging the common cultural heritage of all Greeks. In any case, the eighth-century Olympic beginnings mark the earliest significant, institutional linking of religious festivals to athletics. Of course, funeral games for heroes or kings may well have a pedigree going back to the Bronze Age, and these embodied religious aspects. We also set aside here the foundation myths of the other Panhellenic Games, all of which lack early testimony and archeological evidence, and which may well have arisen to match the antiquity of the Olympics. Our survey of the archeology and myths connected with Olympia finds that cults may possibly have been present at Olympia in the Bronze Age, in view of buildings including a hero shrine for 'Pelops.' Yet there is no cult continuity until the tenth century, and some have suggested that occasional games in nearby Elis or at Olympia itself may have been held in the 'Dark Age' (1100–800) prior to the eighth-century reorganization of the Olympics. But prior to that reorganization, there was apparently no festival periodically celebrated with athletic contests and held primarily in honor of a divinity. If contests were held in the Dark Age at Olympia, they were likely to have been less regular, more informal, and on a smaller scale, perhaps secular contests for fun among the mostly élite pilgrims attending festivals for Zeus or other gods and heroes. Hesiod (*Theogony* 435–43; ca. 700 B.C.) posits Hecate as a primary goddess of athletes, though Hecate probably functioned as a bringer of luck through magic, a role later usurped mainly by Hermes, rather than the patron goddess of an athletic festival, a role for which she is not otherwise known. The early seventh century *Homeric Hymn to Apollo* (146–50) is our earliest text celebrating games in honor of a god. Thus, with the seventh century, the trend to combine religious festivals with athletic competitions, following the Olympic model, begin to spread.

Our survey of the Olympics in the Roman era, 146 B.C. to the fourth century A.D., illustrates the resilience of the institution of the athletic festival during the five centuries preceding Christian emperors. In short, the festival to Zeus and the games remained very strongly popular and flexible despite the huge political, economic, and cultural changes of that era. The élite ideology of the contest system was taken up by people from all ranks in the social hierarchy, and, somewhat ironically, what began as the contests of the aristocracy in Homer became a 'ritual of conviviality' among all who took part as athletes or audience for the contest festivals. Both athletes and audience expanded to include individuals from Asia Minor, Egypt, and Roman Italy, while the games, their ideology, their religious basis, and gymnasium culture with its focus on the body remained more or less the same as it had been during the Classical period. The broadening of participation in this period was part of a larger cultural phenomenon that included most other athletic festivals, local and Panhellenic, a survey of which is beyond our present scope. One noteworthy non-Olympic manifestation of the phenomenon was the occasional participation of women in the male world of athletics, as competitors in contests held in conjunction with some non-Olympic Panhellenic and local games, and as sponsors of games (*agonothetai*) (see Introduction). In sum, the Olympics gained momentum as a truly ecumenical model of Greek culture which attracted participants from all over the Mediterranean, while preserving and even fostering the cults of the Olympian gods despite periodic attempts by yet another elite, the Romans, to usurp or even move the festival to Italy.

Given this model of Olympic continuity, and having established that the traditional Greek athletic festival was based upon and remained centered around the core of a religious festival, we turn to a chronological survey of the relation between athletics, religion, gender, and sexuality in various city-states during the thousand years of the ancient Olympics. Evidence points not to a 'prehistoric' or Indo-European origin for pederastic and athletic *paideia*, but for gradual evolution of these practices since the eighth century B.C. The lack of athletic age categories, and indeed the existence instead of competitions almost exclusively for adult males, both in Homer's texts and in the earliest Olympics argues against the linking of the earliest athletics with initiation rituals in Greece. Both Crete and Sparta institutionalized, or more precisely reorganized, educational systems in the seventh or sixth centuries B.C. in forms that introduced young males both to athletic training and to formalized pederasty. Both of these systems of *paideia* also had religious elements that, along with pederasty and athletic contests, helped mark the progress of the boys to adulthood. Cretans and Spartans have both been credited with introducing nudity to athletics, and with fostering the practice of pederasty. Both of these customs seem to have spread to other Greek city-states beginning in the seventh century, though without the structured educational systems of Crete and Sparta which formally required those practices. The pederastic inscriptions in the vicinity of a gymnasium on the island of Thera begin in the sixth century B.C., appearing to echo the Doric customs of Sparta, though we have no clear evidence of a Spartan-like *agōgē* on Thera. Though Athenian education of its males was far less structured than Sparta's or Crete's, there is evidence that pederasty and a gymnasium-athletic culture were flourishing by the beginning of the sixth century, that is, from the time of Solon's reforms (594/3 B.C.). By 527 B.C. Peisistratus had set up a statue of Eros in the Academy at the starting point of the Panathenaic torch race, further institutionalizing the erotic dimension of Athenian athletics. In the central Greek city of Thebes, the tomb of an Olympic victor of 728 B.C., the beloved of a legendary Theban lawgiver, became the site of a male kissing contest and may evidence the beginnings of pederastic *erōs* joined to gymnasium culture there by the late eight or early seventh century. In the fourth century B.C., the Theban "Sacred Company" of soldiers consisting of homosexual couples attests to the continued high valuation of pederasty in that state's institutions.

The seventh century B.C. marked a virtual revolution in athletic body culture with the widespread adoption of nudity for athletes between 650 and 600 B.C. coincident with the broad acceptance of the pederastic ethos in individual Greek city-states during that same period. As we have seen, the two phenomena were complementary, and likely gradual processes, which fostered one another and became more widely evidenced by the end of the seventh century and the beginning of the sixth. Chronologically, Crete, Sparta, and Thera, that is, Dorian states, seem to have led the way with more formal institutions of male upbringing which included pederasty, athletic training, and athletic nudity. The establishment of a circuit of Panhellenic 'Crown' games at Delphi, Isthmia, and Nemea within the first thirty years of the sixth century both reflected strong civic interest in athletic festivals and no doubt also encouraged the spread of gymnasium culture, including pederastic liaisons. The gymnasium in each polis became the more or less formal focus of male *paideia*, a model that persisted for centuries to come.

Athletic activities were even rare for Greek women in the Archaic and Classical periods, but the few historical and mythical examples of them can tell us much about the lines drawn between the genders. The best attested historical athletic events for females, the Heraia festival at Olympia, the girls' education system at Sparta, and the Arkteia festival in Attica comprise a meager collection of events next to the myriad of men's games. And the female games were exclusively for unmarried girl participants, events which served to usher the girls into adulthood in their respective communities. At Olympia, quadrennial footraces were held for girls in three age divisions in honor of Hera, patron goddess of wives, and the mortal Hippodameia, legendary wife of the hero Pelops, a founder of the men's Olympics. The Heraia was probably founded or reorganized about 580 B.C., though some form of the festival, with or without contests, may go back to the eighth century founding of the men's Olympics held at the same site. If the Heraia first incorporated footraces in the early sixth century, the practice may well have been influenced by the very famous custom of athletic training for girls at Sparta, though we can only speculate on the specific influence. It is likely that girls' athletic training at Sparta began in the second half of the seventh century, with participants organized into "herds" (*agelai*) like Spartan boys, and taking part in running, wrestling, discus-throwing, and other physical exercises. Most notably, we find female alongside male pederasty as part of that upbringing. The fact that female homosexuality is absent from the other female contests examined here suggests that the phenomenon most conventionally occurred in contexts where collective, sexually segregated education took place. As with male pederasty, the woman-girl relations were based on an important pedagogical function alongside the sexual aspect. A special ritual footrace to Dionysus "of the Hill" (*Colonatas*) and the hero who led him to Sparta was part of their program, though its foundation period is uncertain; it seems to have been a ritual of communal solidarity. The running rituals of the Arkteia at Brauron and Munichion in Attica, quadrennial festivals held for girls in honor of Artemis, certainly date at least to the first half of the fifth century but may have begun in the late sixth century. The Arkteia apparently included a chase in which the maidens imitated the foundation myth of a girl running from the bear sacred to the sanctuary, and therefore also served as a prenuptial initiation to adulthood.

Apart from these few athletic events for girls in the Classical period, there are a smattering of attested contests for girls from the Roman period in which female events were grafted onto the men's festivals, and a few instances of women sponsoring (though likely not driving) chariots in the Hellenistic and Roman periods.[2] These later contests and sponsorships attest only to the occasional influence of the daughters of the elite and say little about the conventional gender roles of women in athletics. The Heraia, the Arkteia, and the Spartan girls' contests, on the other hand, indicate a reuse of conventional men's athletics for far different purpose, namely the subjecting of maidens to events normally alien to their gender prior to their assumption of normal adult female roles. Though we can only surmise about the audiences at these rituals, it is likely that the Arkteia festivals were attended by women only. At Sparta and Olympia, however, girls may have competed before male spectators who could view them as potential spouses, and so the events there had a potentially erotic and socializing function. In any case, the ritual running of girls (and, in Sparta, their fuller training in athletics) did not generally include any of the open, institutionalized homoeroticism that was connected with men's athletics, though there probably were same-sex female relations in conjunction with girls' physical and cultural education at least in Sparta and on Sappho's Lesbos (Plutarch *Lycurgus* 18.4).

The myth of Atalanta only further reinforces the impressions gained from the historical festivals about the relation of women to athletic activities. Hesiod's epithet for her, "swift-footed," indicates that she was portrayed as athletic remarkably by about 700 B.C.; Theognis' poem may confirm that the tale of her rejecting marriage was in circulation as early as the sixth century. Vases from 550–500 B.C. show Atalanta as a wrestler, and one of 500 B.C. shows her in the footrace. Thus, the story that directly discourages girls from unladylike athleticism and goads them to the proper gender roles, culminating in marriage, has eighth-century roots and was widespread by the sixth century. The disassociation of females from athletics is therefore contemporaneous with the growth in popularity of the male athletic festivals from the eighth to sixth centuries. This gender distinction makes the Spartan institution of games for all citizen girls all the more remarkable vis-à-vis other Greek states, leading to the scorn of muscular Spartan women by Athenians and others as documented for the Classical period. In this context we can perhaps understand why the contests at the Heraia were limited to footraces: unlike the wrestler Atalanta, the Heraia girls did not require the more masculine upper-body strength, and, like the footracer Atalanta, they could race with the hopes of winning a husband.

Eros both as the god and the phenomenon of sexual desire plays a major role in the Atalanta myth; some vases even show the divinity hovering near the heroine (figs. 7-1, 7-3). By extension eros was at work in the girls' athletic rituals that marked their transition to adulthood. At Sparta, young men were meant to be attracted to the nude girls in the process of competing or training. The seminude girl racers at the Heraia no doubt caused a sensation among any male viewers, if they were present. Even if the entire audience there was female, as it probably was for the Arkteia in Attica, the girls were celebrating their transition to the goal of marriage and sexual activity. The boys' *paideia* also varied in formality of ritual from place to place, but by the sixth century pederastic aspects were attached to their upbringing in many Greek city-states. Male conventions of *paideia* thus directly incorporated sexual activity alongside athletics. And boys' athletic eroticism, like that of girls, was overseen by the patronage of divine cults, particular gods for each local festival for boys, and Eros himself omnipresent with a statue or a shrine in gymnasia since the late sixth century. The practice of nudity that probably spread from 650 to 600 B.C. fostered pederasty in the gymnasium, and the nudity of young and adult males in public competition aroused the desire of both male and female onlookers, sources tell us.

But the process of the 'eroticization' of Greek athletics was gradual and complex, spanning the eighth to the sixth centuries before it settled into the forms described in earlier chapters and maintained them as relatively constant for centuries thereafter. Sexuality, like religion and rites of passage for youth, is not commonly associated with athletics in the eighth century. The texts of Homer and Hesiod avoid any explicit mention of pederastic relationships in any contexts, so it is unlikely that homoeroticism was openly connected with athletics in the eighth century. Certainly homosexual or pederastic relationships with athletes did occur, as that between the Olympic stade victor of 728 B.C., Diocles, and Philolaus, lawgiver of Thebes, mentioned in chapter 3. But this is attested no earlier than the fourth century B.C., and only in the sixth century do literature and art openly celebrate the homosexual or heterosexual aspects of athletics. Certainly the adoption of athletic nudity and the establishment of local gymnasia, both public and private, by about 600 B.C. contributed to the erotic atmosphere. When male and female prostitution and female hetaerae become common by the fifth century, athletes are found enjoying the favors of them all to various degrees, as numerous anecdotes and some vase paintings (e.g., fig. 8-8) indicate. Vase paintings of both hetero- and homosexual scenes, and scenes with Eros himself near the athlete, virtually inviting the viewer to yield to the desire inspired by such beauty, abound in the sixth, fifth, and fourth centuries. The later tailing-off of the theme on vases indicates merely that artists and their clientele sought new subjects, not that the erotic fervor of athletics was itself on the wane.

Indulgence by some athletes was, of course, balanced by the abstinence of others, notably beginning in the fifth century. Whether those showing restraint in that early period did so out of personal inclination or because of the encouragement of a trainer or the sermon of a stern philosopher, I cannot say for certain; no doubt the truth included instances of each motivation. In any case, philosophers from Plato onward praised the victory over pleasure by these chaste athletes. The implication is that restraint was exceptional, and by the Hellenistic and Roman periods the sexual appetite of athletes was matched only by their legendary gluttony in the lampoons of the epigrammatists.

Sculptures of Eros, often accompanied by Hermes or Heracles, began to appear in the late sixth century and remained common accoutrements of gymnasia for centuries after the fourth century, when vase paintings of the god in athletic contexts disappeared. Most striking are the images of Eros wrestling Anteros, "Reciprocal Love," notably in the (possibly fifth century B.C.) version in the gymnasium at Elis, where athletes trained before the Olympics. More subtle but just as important was the Eros statue at the entrance to the Academy in Athens, counterbalanced by the statue of Anteros at the foot of the Acropolis, shrines precisely at the beginning and end of the Panathenaic torch race. The inherent tension in an individual's struggle with Eros, most vivid in the Eros-Anteros images, can be seen as symbolic of the Greek contest system in general. Desire was a struggle, whether its object was a beloved or another source of status (such as an Olympic crown) in the display of rank-demonstration within society.

The rare athletic festival to Eros, the Erotidaea at Thespiae in Boeotia, was established at least by the second century B.C., showing the robust interest in the cult and its athletic associations by that time. The cult at Thespiae was old, with a nonathletic festival likely existing long before the games were attached. The Erotidaea was still thriving by Pausanias' time (ca. A.D. 150). An even older Eros festival with athletics, the Eleutheria at Samos, was founded sometime between the sixth and fourth centuries B.C., possibly to celebrate the fall of Polycrates in 522. Here we return to the theme of the association of athletics with religion, but now with direct connection to sexuality as well. The rarity of games for Eros helps us situate erotic phenomena in relation to athletics, since the Erotidaea shows a relatively late grafting of games onto a venerable old festival to the god as happened with many other festivals in that period, and the Eleutheria points up the function of Eros as one who promoted social and political bonding (*philia*) that could oppose tyranny (ch. 8). Neither festival was directly connected with institutionalized pederasty or *paideia*, even though the god played a crucial role in fostering these phenomena. Eros was not himself a god of initiation to adulthood, though the force he represented was essential in both male and female institutionalized upbringing.

Athletics, sexuality, gender-formation, and religion are all linked to the Greek contest system. Some links begin with Homer; by 600 B.C. a mature system is evident in athletic contests and is concerned with rank-demonstration and glory through the exercise of manly virtue (*aretē*). The gods, as constructed by the Greeks, gave metaphysical authority to the honor of individuals. Since the contest system was from the first dependent on displays of prowess by the body and the very beauty of the body, both athletic and sexual success became obvious indexes of one's hierarchy in the culture. Thus, it is no surprise that by the sixth century in many cities, athletics and sexuality became directly associated, and both were institutionalized in the upbringing of youths under the aegis of religious cults and festivals. But pervasive and fierce competition was mitigated by "rituals of conviviality," group expressions of communal solidarity which mitigated and balanced agonic tensions. These rituals took different forms over time in different cities but generally included male and female *paideia*, religious rituals, socialization in the gymnasium and in athletic festivals, and the friendship (*philia*) of which Eros is a symbol. Of course these potential forces for social union are ambivalent; *paideia*, athletics, religion, and Eros can also be instruments or expressions of social division. Hence Peisistratus celebrated pederastic love in vogue among the élite of sixth-century Athens by setting up the first Athenian shrine to Eros at the Academy gymnasium, but later his son was assassinated by a pederastic couple, Harmodius and Aristogeiton. And Athenaeus (13.602d) tells us that another sixth-century tyrant, Polycrates of Samos, demolished the palaestras since they were seen as a threat to his power; the *philia* of pederastic couples could lead to a threatening conspiracy. But with the broadening of "rituals of conviviality" away from aristocrats and to the people at large in the fifth century, these cultural phenomena became less threatening and more instrumental in forming cultural solidarity or, as at Samos, expressing freedom.

"Sports," *Paideia*, Gender, and Sexuality, Ancient and Modern

If one examines carefully the social context, Greek athletics differs radically in form and substance from any other similar cultural pursuits before or since. Thus, we have avoided referring to them as "sports" and attempted to trace several manifestations of the phenomena with certain thematic threads throughout. The complex and unique historical circumstances that converged to produce Greek athletics ensure that the "sports" of later societies which appear to be similar in fact carry with them a host of values and ideals alien to the Greeks. By way of contrast to modern "sports," we may cite one perceptive critic of the current scene who is attempting to account for the great popularity of (American) football, the most violent of major spectator sports:

> All sports serve as some kind of release but the rhythm of football is
> geared particularly to the violence and the peculiar combination of
> order and disorder of modern life. Baseball is too slow, too dependable,
> too much like a regional drawl. Basketball is too nervous and too tight;
> hockey too frenzied; boxing too chaotic, too folksy. Only football
> provides a genuine catharsis. [3]

In view of the pervasiveness of violence in many aspects of American life, these observations may point to a frightening, deep-seated attraction to violence in the popular culture of this society. The full implications of this cannot be treated here, but we may comment on the contention that sports serve as a "release." Surely this perceived "release" is not simply a purgation of pent-up emotions, but, as in drama, a way vicariously to act through one's view of society and self. As with Greek athletics, the effect is more often conservative of popular values than revisionary. The ideals behind the competition reinforce societal norms since the contests are a product of normative social institutions.

Team sports are the most popular athletic category in the United States and generally in the modern world, whether measured by participation at school, attendance, or television audience.[4] Do team sports represent a high valuation of community while individual sports value the individual? How can we reconcile the American tradition of praise for the individual and the loner with the love of team sports? One commentator attributes this to our modern notions of freedom, which often include elements of both autonomous effort and of cooperation toward common goals.[5] Although Greek athletics consisted almost entirely of individual competitions, there were, by most measures and in most city-states, fewer individual freedoms and a higher priority of the well-being of the polity than is the case in most modern states. The Greeks also confronted the ambiguities or tensions in the competing notions of freedom of the individual and of the state, which are also manifest in their athletics in displays of self-sufficiency and of social affiliations, in Greek terms, *autarkeia* and *philia*.[6]

In short, the form of competition, team or individual, is neither a necessary nor a sufficient indication of a society's dominant values. Cultural phenomena that bear a superficial resemblance, or are even formally identical to one another, take on significance and are interpreted by members of the culture who collectively participate in or interact with those phenomena. The phenomena are, in other words, largely culturally constructed, though that construction obviously does not have free reign but must take account of a society's established customs and traditions and the given factors of human physiology. The Greeks relied upon foundation myths, epic descriptions, artistic depictions, religious contexts, and many other formal and informal signs that led them to place certain values upon their athletic activities. Nor were these activities, the associated values, and the social contexts in which they were found entirely static. There were thematic aspects, some of which have been traced earlier, more of which could be investigated, carried over the years in the essentially conservative milieu of athletic festivals. But there were also significant individual, local, and historical deviations, some of which were noted in the earlier discussion of the "Ecumenical Olympics" of the Roman era (ch. 2). Comparable modern phenomena offer certain analogous "myths" of sports heroes and representations of sports in art, but the parallels between these and ancient "analogues" are more apparent than real.

The erosion of an eros integrated into Greek society was a gradual but pervasive process of late antiquity and the early Middle Ages, a process driven, of course, by the widespread conversion to Christianity. "In Christian circles," Peter Brown informs us, "the body was stripped of its ancient, civic associations; it was stripped by means of an increased emphasis on its intrinsic sexuality." The civic associations are those we have seen linking the eros of sexual desire with that of communal *philia*. Brown continues: "Nudity also ceased to be a form of civic dress. The ease with which the great ladies of Antioch would strip down in the baths . . . this must cease. So must the public nudity of the games."[7] Human sexuality continued to find less direct expression in the games of the Mediterranean Christian world, for example, in the chivalric heroism of the medieval tournament attended by lords and ladies, and in the fencing and folk-football of Renaissance communities which affirmed masculine gender roles. Though erotic athleticism was largely submerged in the seventeenth and eighteenth centuries, still erotic sensibilities can be detected in the folk contests and pugilistic bouts, whose values varied according to class and gender affiliations. The greater leisure for some classes in the nineteenth and early twentieth centuries afforded ample opportunity for the construction of regular sporting events familiar today, including soccer, American football, baseball, basketball, and the full panoply of events found in the modern Olympics. Women's participation in some of these began in earnest only in the 1920s, and so modern sports were ushered in with a strongly male character that still largely persists in the professional arena.[8]

The decades following World War II in developed nations have seen a swiftly changing valuation of gender roles and sexual mores which cannot be covered in a brief summary. Major factors that are complexly related include the wide availability of new measures for birth control, the sharp increase of women in the work force, the re-evaluation of the role of religion generally and Christianity in particular with regard to sex and gender issues, and the much greater idealization of a 'body culture' in contemporary media and popular culture. The new 'body culture' with its ever more public display of male and female physique and ever more central placement of sports in daily life suggests that we have more in common with the Greeks in those areas than with any other culture since ancient times.

The ancient and modern similarities, however, are more formal than substantial, when we consider some of the pointed differences in areas of thematic importance to this study. The centrality of athletic contests today is almost entirely secular, and hence lacking in the validation of a religious hierarchy essential to most ancient Greek thought. Our modern categories of sexuality differ widely from those of the 'bisexual' Greeks, most significantly in the practice of (more or less formally) institutionalized pederasty. Notably, Greek pederasty was firmly attached to the gymnasium and the 'contest system' of ancient culture, to which there is nothing directly comparable today. This brings us to the final substantive difference, the construction of the upbringing of adolescents to adulthood. We have in this study questioned the theories that pederasty and athletics arose, separately or in tandem, from primitive rites of passage. Instead, we have posited the historical institutionalization of *paideia*, most elaborately on Crete and at Sparta but also in the gymnasia and ephebeia of Athens and elsewhere, as the media for transmitting sexual and cultural values, inter alia through athletic training. The Athenian Academy and other gymnasia that were the loci of the civic formation of youth may be seen as the spiritual ancestors of modern academe and our schools ("school" comes from Greek *scholē*, "leisure"). Yet historically the path between ancient and modern Western education is not at all direct, since the modern phenomenon derives more immediately from the medieval monastic schools and the universities of the Renaissance.[9] Physical education became attached to the modern curriculum only in the nineteenth century, and public schools today are of course rigorously separated from the business of communicating sexual mores (leaving aside the pragmatic courses in sex education). In short, the openly institutionalized Greek nexus of upbringing, athletics, religion, and Eros is alien to modern culture, even though scholars of today's phenomena can usefully uncover less explicit and less formalized interconnections.[10]

We can gain from ancient athletics an insight into the functions of that phenomenon in ancient culture, into the values that informed it, and, through the distance of that perspective, into crucial ways in which our own cultural construction is different. The scholarship of recent decades has turned openly to questions of how gender and sexuality are defined by our own and other cultures. Contemporary social scientific studies have looked at the ways in which women athletes are perceived by men and by themselves.[11] Feminism and gay studies arising from contemporary cultural movements have studied women's history and the history of sexuality. Better understandings of human sexuality have led scholars to examine the place of sex in cultural history. And a new 'body culture' expressed more freely in many forms of culture has opened up discussion of how phenomena like sports are connected with sexuality in ways that Western culture has not seen since the Greco-Roman era.

Among other functions, Greek athletics reinforced the Greeks' interpretations of the past, ethos of the present, and visions of the future. Athletic myths and the historical stories of ancestral athletes, which were not so clearly separate as they are today, could be reflected upon, revised, or embellished; they could inspire action, enhance fame and prestige, and validate normative values. The ancient athlete could aspire to equal or improve upon the achievements of the past, while attaining in one sphere of public activity his or her own form of athletic fame. The athlete became, in turn, a source of inspiration to subsequent generations. Both athlete and audience stood Janus-like with one face toward past performances, one toward the future, each viewing a goal with the mixed but productive feelings of desire for renewal and fear of literal or figurative death. The ideal was to defeat death by desire in the neatly constructed agonal struggle of athletics, which offered some strength and strategy for the even more complex stadium of Greek life.

ABBREVIATIONS

The abbreviations used in the notes and bibliography follow those used by the standard reference tools for classical studies. For journal abbreviations, I have used those of *L'Année Philologique*; for ancient authors and their works, I followed the usage in Lidell and Scott's *Greek-English Lexicon* (1968) and in the *Oxford Latin Dictionary* (1985). For the spelling and transliteration of ancient names I have used the conventions followed by *The Oxford Classical Dictionary* (1996). Here is a select list of abbreviations for reference works used frequently:

ARV² = J. D. Beazley, *Attic Red-figure Vase-painters* (Oxford: Clarendon, 1963²).

CVA = *Corpus Vasorum Antiquorum* (various publishers and dates).

IG = *Inscriptiones Graecae*. Numerous volumes and fascicules by various publishers over the past century.

I.Ol. = W. Dittenberger and K. Purgold, *Die Inschriften von Olympia*, E. Curtius and F. Adler, eds., *Olympia*, vol. V (Amsterdam: Hakkert, 1966 reprint of Berlin: A. Asher & co., 1896).

FGH = F. Jacoby, ed. *Die Fragmente der griechischen Historiker* (Berlin: Weidmann, 1923–58).

LIMC = L. Kahil, ed. *Lexicon Iconographicum Mythologiae Classicae*, 8 vols. each in 2 pts. Zurich: Artemis, 1981–; vols. Cited in this work: vol. II. Zurich: Artemis, 1984. vol. III.1. Zurich: Artemis, 1986. vol. IV.1. Zurich: Artemis, 1988.

LSJ² = H. G. Lidell, R. Scott, and H. S. Jones, eds. *Liddell and Scott Greek English Lexicon with a Supplement* (Oxford: Clarendon, 1968).

Paralipomena = J. D. Beazley, *Paralipomena. Additions to Attic Black-figure Vase-painters and Attic Red-figure Vase painters* (Oxford: Clarendon, 1971).

RE = A. F. von Pauly. *Paulys Real-Encyclopädie der classischen Altertumswissenschaft.* Georg Wissowa, Wilhelm Kroll and Karl Mittelhaus et al. Ed. Konrat Ziegler et al. 34 vols. (Stuttgart: J.B. Metzler, 1856–1980).

NOTES

Introduction

1. Most noteworthy are the series of studies by H. W. Pleket: "Zur Soziologie des antiken Sports," *Mededelingen Nederlands Historisch Instituut te Rome* 36 (1974) 57–87; id., "Games, Prizes, Athletes and Ideology: Some Aspects of the History of Sport in the Greco-Roman World," *Arena* (= *Stadion*) 1 (1975) 49–89; id., "Some Aspects of the History of Athletic Guilds," *ZPE* 10 (1973) 197–227; id., "Olympic Benefactors," *ZPE* 20 (1976) 1–20; and M. I. Finley and H. W. Pleket, *The Olympic Games: The First Thousand Years* (New York: Viking Press, 1976). See also the very balanced survey of scholarship on the history of Greek and Roman sports by I. Weiler, *Der Sport bei den Völkern der alten Welt. Eine Einführung*, rev. ed. (Darmstadt: Wissenschaftliche Buchgesellschaft, 1988).

2. See, for example, the excellent studies by M. Poliakoff, *Combat Sports in the Ancient World: Competition, Violence, and Culture* (New Haven: Yale University Press, 1987), and D. Kyle, *Athletics in Ancient Athens* (Leiden: E. J. Brill, 1987). Other technical studies of athletic practices can be found in the older but still valuable works of broader scope by E. N. Gardiner, *Greek Athletic Sports and Festivals* (London: Macmillan, 1910), and id., *Athletics of the Ancient World* (Oxford: Clarendon, 1930; reprint Chicago: Ares, 1980); H. A. Harris, *Greek Athletes and Athletics* (London: Hutchinson, 1964) and id., *Sport in Greece and Rome* (Ithaca, N.Y.: Cornell University Press, 1972); J. Jüthner, *Die athletischen Leibesübungen der Griechen*, ed. F. Brein, 2 vols. (Graz: Hermann Böhlaus, 1965 and 1968). Studies of local athletic festivals: Irene C. Ringwood Arnold, *Agonistic Features of Local Greek Festivals Chiefly from Inscriptional Evidence* (Ph. D. diss., Columbia University, 1927) and id., "Agonistic Festivals in Italy and Sicily," *AJA* 64 (1960) 245–51; id., "Festivals of Ephesus," *AJA* 69 (1965) 17–22; id., "Festivals of Rhodes," *AJA* 40 (1936) 432–36; id., "Local Festivals at Delos," *AJA* 37 (1933) 452–58; id., "Local Festivals at Euboea, Chiefly from Inscriptional Evidence," *AJA* 33 (1929) 385–92; id., "The Shield of Argos," *AJA* 41 (1937) 436–40; Onno Van Nijf, "Athletics, Festivals, and Greek Identity in the Roman East," *PCPS* 45 (1999) 176–200. See other references to specialized studies on various aspects of Greek and Roman sports in the bibliographies by N. Crowther, "Studies in Greek Athletics," *CW* 78 (1984) 497–558 and 79 (1985) 73–135, and by me, *Greek and Roman Athletics: A Bibliography* (Chicago: Ares, 1984) 70–73; see also the periodic reviews of bibliography in the journal *Nikephoros*.

3. I take "social function" here in both its "organicist" sense, in which an institution has a function or role in a social aggregate, and in its "logistic" or "symbolic" sense in which, for example, mythology is seen to have a symbolic sense in the structuring of social relations. See P. Vidal-Naquet, *The Black Hunter: Forms of Thought and Forms of Society in the Greek World*, trans. A. Szegedy-Maszak (Baltimore: Johns Hopkins University Press, 1986) 135–36.

4. See the informative discussion of this issue in S.R.F. Price, *Rituals and Power: The Roman Imperial Cult in Asia Minor* (Cambridge: Cambridge University Press, 1984) 234–48.

5. See H. Siska, *De Mercurio ceterisque deis ad artem gymnicam pertinentibus* (Ph.D. diss., University of Halle, 1933) for a catalogue of epigraphic and literary sources on these and other cults related to Greek athletics.

6. For rhetorical and philosophical education in the gymnasium, see H. Marrou, *A History of Education in Antiquity*, trans. G. Lamb (London: Sheed and Ward, 1956); L. Grasberger, *Erziehung und Unterricht im klassischen Altertum*, 3 vols. (Aalen: Scientia, 1971 reprint of Würzburg, 1864–81); R. E. Wycherley, "Peripatos: The Athenian Philosophical Scene—II," *G&R* 9 (1962) 2–21. For cultural and political views of *paideia*, see P. Schmitt-Pantel, "Collective Activities and The Political in the Greek City," in *The Greek City: From Homer to Alexander*, ed. O. Murray and S. Price (Oxford: Oxford University Press, 1990) 199–213, esp. 206; R. Sallares, *The Ecology of the Ancient Greek World* (London: Duckworth, 1991) 265. For Hermes as patron of ephebes and initiation, see G. Costa, "Hermes dio delle iniziazioni," *Civiltà classica e cristiana* 3 (1982) 277–95.

7. See D. Halperin, *One Hundred Years of Homosexuality* (New York: Routledge, 1990) 15–53, for a similar argument denying that there can be a history of sexuality since sexuality is a cultural construct that by definition varies with each society. For a good overview of the different philosophies of sport in various cultures, see E. Segal, "To Win or Die of Shame, A Taxonomy of Sporting Attitudes," *Journal of Sport History* 11 (1984) 25–31.

8. Bernd Wirkus, "'Werden wie die Griechen': Implikationen, Intentionen und Widersprüche im Olympismus Pierre de Coubertins," *Stadion* 16.1 (1990) 103–28.

9. E. Mähl, *Gymnastik und Athletik im Denken der Römer*, Heuremata 2 (Amsterdam: B. R. Grüner, 1974).

10. The definitions quoted are those of *The American Heritage Dictionary of the English Language, New College Edition* (Boston: Houghton Mifflin, 1979). *The Compact Edition of The Oxford English Dictionary* (Oxford: Oxford University Press, 1971) gives 1594 as the earliest occurrence of "sport" in the sense of "a series of athletic contests," then in reference to ancient Greek games; and only in 1892 is it applied to contemporary athletic events.

11. For a discussion of modern terminology of sports, see D. Sansone, *Greek Athletics and the Genesis of Sport* (Berkeley and Los Angeles: University of California Press, 1988) 3–6; for one view on the differences between sports, games, play, and competition, see A. Guttmann, *From Ritual to Record: The Nature of Modern Sports* (New York: Columbia University Press, 1978) 1–16; for discussion of Guttmann's influential thesis, see J. Marshall Carter and A. Krüger, *Ritual and Record: Sports Records and Quantification in Pre-Modern Societies* (New York: Greenwood Press, 1990). I use the collective plural term "sports" at times to designate the same concept as "sport," except

that the plural connotes that various distinct activities constitute the general concept; at other times, according to context, I will use the term "sports" to designate several specific contests considered together.

12. J. Huizinga, *Homo Ludens: A Study of the Play Element in Culture*, trans. R.F.C. Hull (Boston: Beacon, 1955), from the original *Homo ludens: Proeve eener bepaling van het spel-element der cultuur* (Haarlem : H. D. Tjeenk Willink, 1940).

13. "Spontane motorische Aktivität aus spielerischem Antrieb, die nach messbarer Leistung und geregeltem Wettkampf strebt"; *Lexikon der Pädagogik* (Freiburg: Herder, 1971) 4.144, quoted by Weiler (1988) xi. "Measurable" may be misleading here, if one takes it to mean that the resulting performances must be quantified, as contests were not until recently. "Measurable," as I understand it in Bernett's definition, indicates that one competitor (or team) can be "measured' or judged to be the winner relative to the other competitors. Another working definition of "sport" has been proposed by Guttmann (1978) 7: "'playful' physical contests . . . non-utilitarian contests which include an important measure of physical as well as intellectual skill," although this omits the important aspects of judging victors and regulating competitors. Guttmann is also, in my view, in error in denying to sport an essential function of communication (11–13). Although most activities termed "sport" do not necessarily call for an "allegorical" or symbolic interpretation, there is inevitably a level at which such phenomena convey lessons or values, if only implicitly.

14. Guttmann (1978) 11–13.

15. Ibid., 16–55. See also the stimulating analysis of the rise of modern sport by Richard Mandell, *Sport: A Cultural History* (New York: Columbia University Press, 1984).

16. Guttmann (1978) admits that all of the modern characteristics except quantification and records were present in ancient Greece. Purely 'secular' athletic contests are found in *Odyssey* 8.97–384; equality of admission as contestant and conditions of competition were enforced among participants at Olympia and other festivals; Greek athletes in fact became more specialized as time went; Greek athletics was extremely "rationalized" according to notions of ancient justice and fairness; Greeks had a "nascent form of sports bureaucracy" (45) in their athletic guilds and in their mechanisms of sponsorship. Achievements were admittedly not "quantified" with tape-measures and timing devices, but they were measured relative to one another in speed, distance, and strength; records of achievement in events, particularly of a qualitative sort to designate "firsts" and "onlys," were a facet of both Greek and Roman sports. See M. N. Tod, "Greek Record-Keeping and Record-Breaking," *CO* 43 (1949) 106–12; D. Young, "First with the Most: Greek Athletic Records and 'Specialization,'" *Nikephoros* 9 (1996) 175–97.

17. Sansone (1988) 6. See the cautious criticisms in reviews of this book by I. Weiler in *Gnomon* 62 (1990) 218–22 and by D. Kyle and A. Guttmann (separately) in *Journal of Sport History* 15 (1988) 356–61 and 361–63.

18. Sansone (1988) 15–24 provides a useful review of other "monocausal" theories, including the Marxist view of scholars from the former East Germany and Carl Meuli's peculiar attempt to link all sports to duels performed at funerals. For a criticism of the latter, see also the excellent discussion by Poliakoff (1987) 149–57.

19. For other surveys of scholarship on the origin of sports, see I. Weiler, "Langzeitperspektiven zur Genese des Sports," *Nikephoros* 2 (1989) 7–26; C. Ulf,

"Die Frage nach dem Ursprung des Sports, oder: weshalb und wie menschliches Verhalten anfängt, Sport zu sein," *Nikephoros* 4 (1991) 13–30.

20. See, as one excellent example of the ancient-modern contrast, D. Young, *The Olympic Myth of Greek Amateur Athletics* (Chicago: Ares, 1984), on many of the historical misapprehensions of those who organized the International Olympic Committee in the late nineteenth century. M. I. Finley and H. W. Pleket (1976) also outline many ways in which the ancient and modern Olympics differ.

21. Poliakoff (1987) 178–79, note 49 gives a fair critique of Burckhardt's argument in the light of later scholarship.

22. A. W. Gouldner, *Enter Plato: Classical Greece and the Origins of Social Theory* (New York: Basic Books, 1965) 41–77. For a restatement of the agonistic system, see D. Cohen, *Law, Violence and Community in Classical Athens* (Cambridge: Cambridge University Press, 1995) 61–70. For a broader, economic and historical overview of the social tensions in the "contest system," see C. G. Starr, *The Cambridge Ancient History*, vol. 3, pt. 3, 431–41, eds. J. Boardman and N. G. L. Hammond (Cambridge: Cambridge University Press, 1982).

23. Pleket (1975) 75, further distinguishing two forms of idealized beauty, the slender, noble, and beardless "ephebe"-type, and the bull-neck and bearded "Herakles"-type.

24. For the estimate of *kouroi*, see A. Snodgrass, in *Trade in the Ancient Economy*, ed. P. Garnsey et al. (Berkeley: University of California Press, 1983) 21; for *kouroi* as evidence of an "overriding preoccupation" with the youthful male nude, see J. Bremmer, "Adolescents, Symposion, and Pederasty," *Sympotica: A Symposium on the Symposium*, ed. O. Murray (Oxford: Oxford University Press, 1990) 143; A. Stewart, *Art, Desire, and the Body in Ancient Greece* (Cambridge: Cambridge University Press, 1997) 63–70 also explores the youthful-citizen ideology of the *kouros*, successfully challenging the arguments of C. Sourvinou-Inwood, *'Reading' Greek Death* (Oxford: Oxford University Press, 1995) 147–97 that they represent athletes.

25. D. Konstan, "Greeks, Persians, and Empire," *Arethusa* 20.1–2 (1987) 59–73 points out the consistent association of non-Greeks with quantified wealth, and Greeks with qualitative excellence in Herodotus' narrative.

26. Euripides, *Autolycus* fr. 282 (Nauck *TGF* 441) *ap.* Ath. 10.413c–f (ca. 420 B.C.), a good translation of which is found in S. Miller, *Arete: Greek Sports from Ancient Sources* (Berkeley: University of California Press, 1991) 185, number 168. It is likely that the criticisms of athletes' excessive self-indulgence by Euripides, Xenophanes, Aristophanes, the "Old Oligarch," and others are overstatements that reflect various prejudices more than realities; in general, on criticism of athletes, see Kyle (1987) 124–54; Stefan Müller, *Das Volk der Athleten: Untersuchungen zur Ideologie und Kritik des Sports in der griechisch-römischen Antike* (Trier: Wissenschaftlicher Verlag Trier, 1995) 72–82, 88–108, and 115–23; H. W. Pleket, "Sport and Ideology in the Greco-Roman World," *Klio* 80 (1998) 315–24. On the general discouragement of self-sufficiency, see G. W. Most, "Self-Disclosure and Self-Sufficiency in Greek Culture," *JHS* 109 (1989) 114–33; A. J. Festugière, "Autarky and Community in Ancient Greece," in *Freedom and Civilization among the Greeks*, trans. P. T. Brannan (Allison Park, Pa.: Pickwick, 1987, from the original, *Liberté et civilisation chez les Grecs* (Paris: Revue des jeunes, 1947).

27. For the use of *sōma* as "person," see R. Hirzel, *Die Person: Begriff und Name Derselben im Altertum* (Munich: Verlag der Königlich Bayerischen Akademie der Wissenschaften, 1914; reprint, New York: Arno, 1976); H. Pelliccia, *Mind, Body, and Speech in Pindar and Homer*. Hypomnemata, 107 (Goettingen: Vandenhoeck & Ruprecht, 1995) studies the poetic tradition in which bodily organs can act or exist separately from the "self." Thus, the unified body has a complex and almost schizophrenic relation to its individual parts.

28. See also Thucydides 2.41.1, in which Pericles, echoing Herodotus' Solon, claims that Athenians have attained a great degree of personal self-sufficiency, yet one ultimately in accordance with civic obligations, and Thuc. 2.51.3, where *sōma* refers to the bodies of Athenian plague victims which are *not* self-sufficient in the face of the epidemic; T. Scanlon, "Echoes of Herodotus in Thucydides: Self-sufficiency, Admiration, and Law," *Historia* 43.2 (1994) 143–76.

29. We should be careful to see the "zero-sum" aspect of honor not as a rigid absolute, but as a generally true, yet flexible characteristic of the contest system: see D. Cohen, "Sexuality, Violence, and the Athenian Law of Hybris," *GRBS* 38 (1991) 183, note 30; id. (1995) 63, note 6; and id., *Law, Sexuality, and Society. The Enforcement of Morals in Classical Athens* (Cambridge: Cambridge University Press, 1991) 183–86.

30. For two excellent studies on these concepts, see D. L. Cairns, *Aidōs: The Psychology and Ethics of Honour and Shame in Ancient Greek Literature* (Oxford: Oxford University Press, 1993) and N.R.E. Fisher, *Hybris: A Study in the Values of Honour and Shame in Ancient Greece* (Warminster, England: Aris & Phillips, 1992). Cairns, p. 94, note 141, rightly cautions that "The zero-sum view . . . can be taken too far; . . . to dishonour another is not always to require his honour for oneself. . . ." See also, on *hybris*, Cohen (1995) 143–50 and id., (1991a) 176–80. On the *kudos* of the athlete, see L. Kurke, "The Economy of *kudos*," in Carole Dougherty and Leslie Kurke, *Cultural Poetics in Archaic Greece: Cult, Performance, Politics* (Cambridge: Cambridge University Press, 1993), who identifies *kudos* as "an active negotiation between the aristocracy and the community at large over the forms of charismatic power" (155); that is, *kudos* is an almost talismanic attribute bestowed by the community upon the individual athlete, warrior, or exceptional citizen. See also D. Steiner, "Moving Images: Fifth-Century Victory Monuments and the Athlete's Allure," *Classical Antiquity* 17 (1998) 133–34 on the power of *kudos* in athletes and the coyness of *aidos*, which can be a sexual lure.

31. Pleket (1975) 79.

32. Philostratus, *Gymn.* 23; cf. M. Poliakoff (1987) 63.

33. On the modern ideals, see, e.g., J. A. Michener, *Sports in America* (Greenwich, Conn.: Fawcett, 1976) 15–32, who cites health, entertainment, and "fun" as the three guiding criteria for modern sports. Although Michener criticizes the erosion of character-building notions like "sportsmanship," he actually illustrates the strength of this as an ideal, however far short of it U.S. culture falls in reality.

34. For an elaboration on some of these characteristics, see Poliakoff (1987) 105–7; E. Segal, "To Win or Die of Shame, A Taxonomy of Values," *Journal of Sport History* 11 (1984) 25–31; Young (1984) 171–76; Pleket (1975); Finley and Pleket (1976) 14–25.

35. Isocrates, *De Biga* 16.33; Kyle (1987) 136; M. Golden, *Sport and Society in Ancient Greece* (Cambridge: Cambridge University Press, 1998) 123, 170. Golden gen-

erally suggests that equestrian events were one way in which the elite could generally avoid being dishonored in defeat by lower classes. So also Alexander the Great is
said to have avoided taking part in competitions since kings should compete only
against kings: Plutarch, *Alexander* 4.5; Xenophon, *Hiero* 4.6; Harris (1964) 40, and
Golden (1998) 160–61.

36. Xenophanes, fr. 2 (Diels) *apud* Ath. 10.413f–414c; C. M. Bowra, "Xenophanes
and the Olympic Games," *AJP* 59 (1938) 257–79; Müller (1995) 88–99.

37. Schmitt-Pantel (this ch., note 6, 1990) 205–6. L. Burckhardt, "Von Agon'
zur 'Nullsummenkonkurrenz': Bemerkungen zu einigen Versuchen, die kompetitive
Mentalität der Griechen zu erfassen," *Nikephoros* 12 (1999) 71–93 and 309, also argues that the zero-sum agonal culture should not be overstated, but "antagonism
. . . was weakened by various structures and mechanisms" (309). For discussions
of theories of whether sport in classical and Hellenistic Greece generally functioned as a stabilizing safety-valve or as a tool to teach social competiton, see
Pleket (1998) 321–22, discussing Müller (1995) 126–41. As Pleket indicates, both
functions of sport co-existed. The 'safety-valve' never radically pacified internal
social conflict nor did it eliminate inter-polis rivalries.

38. See Plato *Leges* 1.643e–644a: [*Paideia* is] "that training in excellence (*aretē*)
from childhood which makes one into an adherent and a lover (*erastēs*) of becoming
a perfect citizen, knowing both how to rule and how to obey in accord with justice
. . . whereas an upbringing that aims at money or physical strength or some other
cleverness without reason and justice is workmanlike, slavish, and entirely unwor-
thy of being called *paideia*."

While Plato's criticism of wealth or bodily beauty as ends in themselves are con-
sonant with values of the contest system generally, he elsewhere criticizes contemporary athletic training more strongly than most Athenians would have. H. Hutter,
*Politics as Friendship. The Origins of the Classical Notions of Politics in the Theory and
Practice of Friendship* (Waterloo, Ontario, Canada: Wilfrid Laurier University Press,
1978) 82–90, following Gouldner in many aspects, sees *eros* as an ambiguous force
of friendship or conflict, a force which is most productive with the restraint recommended by Plato. See also Kyle (1987) 137–40. Steiner (1988) 144–46 notes the ambiguous responses of spectators to "the victorious body," especially in artistic images; the body may be either envied or desired as a lover while the victory image has
a numinous power.

39. One might also mention here the following important studies in symposia
and choruses as forms of group activities: O. Murray (this ch., note 24, 1990); id.,
"The Symposium as Social Organisation," in *The Greek Renaissance of the Eighth Century B.C.: Tradition and Innovation*, ed. R. Hägg (Stockholm: Svenska institutet i Athen,
1983) 195–99; F. Lissarrague, *The Aesthetics of the Greek Banquet*, trans. A. Szegedy-
Maszak (Princeton: Princeton University Press, 1990 from the original *Un flot
d'images: Une ésthetique du banquet grec* (Paris: A. Biro, 1987); Steven H. Lonsdale,
Dance and Ritual Play in Greek Religion (Baltimore: Johns Hopkins University Press,
1993); C. Calame, *Choruses of Young Women in Ancient Greece: Their Morphology,
Religious Role, and Social Functions*, trans. D. Collins and J. Orion (Lanham, Md.:
Rowman & Littlefield, 1997, from the original *Les choeurs de jeunes filles en Grèce
archaïque, vol. I: Morphologie, fonction religieuse et sociale* [Rome: Ateneo & Bizzarri,
1977]). Yet in these activities the contest system, while clearly traceable, is not so

clearly exemplified as in athletics. L. Foxhall, "Pandora Unbound: A Feminist Critique of Foucault's *History of Sexuality*," in *Rethinking Sexuality: Foucault and Classical Antiquity*, ed. D.H.J. Larmour, P. A. Miller, and C. Platter (Princeton: Princeton University Press, 1998) 136, writes: "In summary, the gymnasium, like other institutions of male social reproduction, pulled young men away from the dominions of their households, thus encouraging their development as sexual and political individuals. . . . [I]t is these masculine institutions of social reproduction which are monumentalized and celebrated in art and literature, to the near exclusion of female roles in social reproduction."

40. On the presence of dance at games in Homer, see Lonsdale (1993) 250–52; on music to accompany exercise and competition since the archaic age, see W. Raschke, "Aulos and Athlete: The Function of the Flute Player in Greek Athletics," *Arete* 2 (1985) 177–200.

41. H. W. Pleket, "The Participants in the Ancient Olympic Games: Social Background and Mentality," in *Proceedings of an International Symposium on the Olympic Games, 5–7 September 1988*, ed. W. Coulson and H. Kyrieleis (Athens: Luci Braggiotti Publications for the Deutsches Archäologisches Institut Athen, 1992) 147–52; see Pleket (1974 and 1975). D. Young (1984) argues that non-nobles participated in athletics, possibly often, prior to the fifth century. Despite the open possibility and a few cases of probable participation by non-nobles, it seems likely that aristocrats dominated the athletic field in the sixth century and earlier; see reviews of Young's book by M. B. Poliakoff in *AJP* 110 (1989) 166–71 and by D. G. Kyle in *Echos du Monde Classique. Classical Views* 29 (= N.S. 4) 134–44. Golden (1998) 141–45 argues generally along the lines of Pleket, though he admits that the scarcity of evidence means that we will probably never know for sure the class divisions of athletes in any age. See also Leslie Kurke, *The Traffic in Praise: Pindar and the Poetics of Social Economy* (Ithaca, N.Y.: Cornell University Press, 1991) 1–12 on the continuity of aristocratic ideology in the sphere of fifth-century athletics.

42. O. Murray, *Early Greece*, 2nd ed. (Cambridge, Mass.: Harvard University Press, 1993) 202; cf. 329–30; D. Young, *Pindar Isthmian 7: Myth and Exempla* (Leiden: E. J. Brill, 1971) 43; N.G.L. Hammond, in Boardman and Hammond (this ch., note 22, 1982) 340–41. On warfare and Greek sport, Golden (1998) 23–28. On the social position of hoplites, see P.A.L. Greenhalgh, *Early Greek Warfare: Horsemen and Chariots in the Homeric and Archaic Ages* (Cambridge: Cambridge University Press, 1973) 150–55; V. Davis Hanson, *The Western Way of War: Infantry Battle in Classical Greece* (Oxford: Oxford University Press, 1989) 27–39. More generally on the topic, *id.*, ed., *Hoplites: The Classical Greek Battle Experience* (London: Routledge, 1991).

43. See Kyle (1987) 127–29; Poliakoff (1987) 94–103; Golden (1998) 26–27 argues that the élite provided the impetus for new gymnasia and games, though in my view an impulse for the movement solely or mainly by an élite class is not so clear. See Tyrtaeus' élitist critique of athletes (fr. 12 West) and Pleket (1998) 319–20. If the élite subsidized athletics, this did not prevent others from competing with and even besting them.

44. Murray (1993) 218; Müller (1995) 133–34, 137–41, notes Pindar's technique of ascribing élite Homeric values to athletes, and he suggests that in the fifth century these values, especially the love of honor (*philotimia*), came to be practiced by individuals more for the polis than for themselves.

45. Cairns (this ch., note 30, 1993) 389–91; Müller (1995) 141–61.

46. Lucian's Syrian perspective: Poliakoff (1987) 175, note 15. The dialectal humor of Lucian's *Anacharsis*: R. Bracht Branham, *Unruly Eloquence: Lucian and the Comedy of Traditions* (Cambridge, Mass.: Harvard University Press, 1989) 81–104, according to which the characters represent "the tacit assumptions and ego-ideals of aging ideologies" and the work serves "to create comically unorthodox perspectives from which to interrogate [the ideologies'] traditional meanings" (102).

47. See *Iliad* 2.774–75; *Odyssey* 8.131, 17.168, 17.174, 18.37; cf. *Il.* 1.747 and 9.186; *Od.* 1.107, where cognates of *terpomai* are used of musical performance and dice games; Pindar, *Olympian* 13.115 speaks of "a brief delight" (βραχύ τι τερπνόν) for those who win in athletics without a song to commemorate the occasion, and *id. Pythian* 10.19 of the victor who "takes delight" (τέρπνων) in running. See also, on *terpsis* and athletics, J. Puhvel, "Hittite Athletics as Prefigurations of Ancient Greek Games," in *The Archaeology of the Olympics: The Olympics and Other Festivals in Antiquity*, ed. W. J. Raschke, (Madison: University of Wisconsin Press, 1988) 30; J. Latacz, *Zum Wortfeld "Freude" in der Sprache Homers* (Heidelberg: Carl Winter, 1966) 174–219; S. Laser, *Sport und Spiel, Archaeologia Homerica*, vol. 3, ch. T (Göttingen: Vandenhoeck & Ruprecht, 1987) 5–6. Prodicus *test.* 19 DK *ap.* Aristot. *Top.* B 6. 112b 22 defines *terpsis* as "audial pleasure," one type of the more general term *hēdonē*, "pleasure"; it may in contexts of athletic enjoyment refer to the more general experience of pleasure through any of the senses. See ch. 1, note 8 of this volume for athletic "delight" in the *Homeric Hymn to Apollo* 146–50.

48. Graham Anderson, *Lucian: Theme and Variation in the Second Sophistic* (Leiden: E. J. Brill, 1976) 115 notes that Lucian elsewhere condemns "the favor of the crowd and public recognition" as the height of arrogance in works such as *Rhetorum praeceptor* and *Peregrinus*. Yet Solon's argument recognizes an actual phenomenon of audience learning, a point valid in itself and somewhat different from the Cynic disdain of popular favor: see Müller (1995) 137 and Pleket (1998) 321 on the "achievement-seeking" (*Leistungsmotiv*) theory of spectatorship.

49. Cairns (1993) 217–18. Homer, who also contributes much to our understanding of the importance of athletics in Greek life, will be discussed briefly in ch. 1. Pindar is perhaps more useful in the present overview since his victory odes were a direct product of athletic culture and were written during the acme of the classical period, ca. 500–446 B.C. For a general study of Pindar as a source of historical information on victors and contests, see K. Kramer, *Studien zur griechischen Agonistik nach den Epinikien Pindars* (Ph.D. diss., University of Cologne, 1970).

50. H. Lee, "Athletic Arete in Pindar," *AncW* 7.1–2 (1983) 31–37.

51. See W.K.C. Guthrie, *The Sophists* (Cambridge: Cambridge University Press, 1971) 251–52 on this passage and generally on Pindar's view of *arete*.

52. Laser (1987) 13–16; T. Irwin, *Classical Thought* (Oxford: Oxford University Press, 1989) 6–19; A.W.H. Adkins, *Moral Values and Political Behaviour in Ancient Greece* (London: Chatto and Windus, 1972); K. J. Dover, *Greek Popular Morality in the Time of Plato and Aristotle* (Oxford: Blackwell, 1974).

53. Pleket (1975).

54. E. N. Gardiner (1930) 68–71 discusses "The Athletic Ideal in Pindar" but misleadingly includes in his citations of Pindar some taken from mythological contexts that do not necessarily characterize athletic values. The examples discussed

here are taken from exclusively athletic contexts. For noteworthy uses of *aidōs* in Pindar, see Cairns (this ch., note 30, 1993) 176–77.

55. On the association of athletics with "delight" (τέρψις), see note 47.

56. Though this statement most obviously applies to the citizens of Etna mentioned in lines 28–33 in Pindar's poem (*N. 9*), it also applies to the victor himself, Kromios, in lines 34–35.

57. Pausanias 5.21.12–14. Paus. 5.21. 2–17 tells of numerous athletes from the fourth century B.C. onward who received fines at Olympia for attempting to secure victories by bribes. This may also be evidence of "love of gain," since the Olympic victor often received great value prizes from his home town (Young [1984] 128–33).

58. Young (1984) 134–62 illustrates a number of instances in which athletes of the fifth century or earlier were attracted to athletics at least in part by the possibility of accumulating great wealth. For the theme of profit (κέρδος and cognates) taken in greed, see Pindar, *P.* 1.92, 2.78, 3.54, 4.140; *N.* 7.18; *I.* 2.6; but note that profit itself, if taken from one who freely gives it, is not reprehensible (*P.* 8.13). On the ancient negative view of wage-labor and on value prizes in later contests, see Golden (1998) 146–66.

59. Fisher (this ch., note 30, 1992) 242–43 concludes in his analysis of the term *hybris* in Pindar and Bacchylides that it denotes "intentional behaviour that causes dishonour or the disposition to indulge in such behaviour. . . . [P]redominantly it denotes humans who unjustly and deliberately infringe the obligations of *xenia* [friendship], *charis* [favor], and *aidōs* towards others, and endanger the peace and stability of harmonious social relations and settings inside a community, or threaten the freedom of independent states. . . . Hence in eulogies it will be appropriate to observe that the honourand and his family or city have avoided, or have chastised, *hybris*, and will continue so to do."

60. On Diagoras' family, see M. Poliakoff (1987) 119–21. On the passage quoted here, see D. Young, *Three Odes of Pindar: A Literary Study of Pythian 11, Pythian 3, and Olympian 7* (Leiden: E. J. Brill, 1968) 94; Fisher (this ch., note 30, 1992) 218–19.

61. For more on the paradox and on Athenian laws against violence, see M. Poliakoff (1987) 92, 175, note 14, and 181–82, note 80. The importance of the attitude of the actor is marked in one definition of *hybris* as "self-indulgent egotism" quoted by Poliakoff (92). See also Cohen (1991a) 171–88.

62. J. Gould, "Law, Custom, and Myth: Aspects of the Social Position of Women in Classical Athens," *JHS* 100 (1980) 38–59; R. Just, *Women in Athenian Law and Life* (London: Routledge, 1989).

63. For a sensitive interpretation of this statement and all its ambiguities, see J. S. Rusten, *Thucydides, The Peloponnesian War Book II* (Cambridge: Cambridge University Press, 1989) 175–76.

64. See Xen., *Oeconomicus* 7.26–27; for a general discussion of the complex topic of female virtues, see E. Cantarella, *Pandora's Daughters: The Role and Status of Women in Greek and Roman Antiquity*, trans. M. B. Fant (Baltimore: Johns Hopkins University Press, 1987) 55–57.

65. Cairns (this ch., note 30, 1993) 305–40, esp. 305–7.

66. L. Moretti, *Olympionikai, I Vincitori negli Antichi Agoni Olimpici, MemLinc* ser. 8.8.2 (Rome: Accademia Nazionale dei Lincei, 1957) 114–15; id., *Iscrizioni Agonistiche Greche* (Rome: Angelo Signorelli, 1953) 40–44; G. Arrigoni, "Donne e

sport nel mondo greco: Religione e società," 55–201, esp. 100–101, in *Le donne in Grecia*, ed. G. Arrigoni (Rome: Laterza, 1985). K. Mantas, "Women and Athletics in the Roman East," *Nikephoros* 8 (1995) 128–29 lists a total of fifteen female victors in chariot races, beginning with Cynisca in the fourth century and continuing to the first century B.C.; see also Golden (1998) 133–34.

67. Xen., *Agesilaus* 9.6–7; Plut., *Agesilaus* 20.1 and *Apophthegmata Laconica* 212B; Paus. 3.8.1–2, 3.15.1, 15.12.5, 6.1.6–7; *Anth. Pal.* 13.16 = W. Dittenberger and K. Purgold, *Die Inschriften von Olympia* [hereafter cited as *I.Ol.*], ed. E. Curtius and F. Adler, *Olympia*, vol. 5 (Berlin, 1896; reprint Amsterdam: Hakkert, 1966) no. 160 = *IG* V.1564 a.

68. Tod (1949); Young (1996).

69. See Moretti (1953 and 1957); M. R. Lefkowitz and M. B. Fant, *Women's Life in Greece and Rome. A Sourcebook in Translation* (Baltimore: Johns Hopkins University Press, 1982) 23–24. For women chariot victors at other Greek festivals, see Arrigoni (1985) 108 (Eleutheria at Larisa); 108–9 (Amphiaraia at Oropus); Mantas (1995) 131–32 cites female chariot victors in the Romaia at Xanthos, Lycia (L. Robert, "Catalogue Agonistique des Romaia de Xanthos," *Rev. Archéol.* [1978] 277–79, lines 42–44) and at the Olympics (*I.Ol.* no. 233, 340, 2–3 c. A.D.). See also the report of Athenaeus concerning races in chariots driven by Spartan maidens at the annual Spartan festival of Hyakinthia: Ath. 4.139f; cf. Xen., *Ages.* 8.7; Plut., *Ages.* 19.5; *IG* 4.586 and 587.

70. Plutarch is more explicit on Agesilaus' motivation for persuading his sister and the occasion of victory:

> When [King Agesilaus] saw that some citizens esteemed themselves highly and were overly proud of themselves because of their accomplishments in horse-breeding, he persuaded his sister Cynisca to prepare a chariot team and to enter it in the Olympics, since he wished to show the Greeks that her victory was not a matter of excellence [*aretēs*], but of wealth and expense. (Plut., *Ages.* 20.1)

Note that Xenophon, whose version is probably more accurate since he was a close confidant of Agesilaus, uses a term for excellence meaning "manly valor," *andragathia*, which is even more marked by connotations of gender than Plutarch's *aretē*. For Agesilaus' general disdain of chariot racing, see Xen., *Ages.* 9.7 and P. Cartledge, *Agesilaos and the Crisis of Sparta* (London: Duckworth, 1987) 149–50.

71. Chariot (or horse) racing is a particularly problematic competition, since there is an inherent ambiguity in assigning credit for the victory. Should it go to the owner/breeder, or to the driver/jockey? The ancient answer, somewhat like the modern one, is to credit the victory first to the owner, but to share it to some extent with the driver or rider. Modern practice clearly differs from ancient Greece by giving today much more credit to the horses themselves.

72. Lefkowitz and Fant (1982) 23–24.

73. *IG* V (i) 235.

74. For girls "at the race-course . . . longing for Helen," see Theocritus *Idyll* 18.39–42 and in chapter 5 here; for Helen as an initiatory divinity at Sparta, see G. Charachidzé, "The Cult of Helen and the Tribal Initiation of Women in Greece," in *Mythologies*, vol. 1, ed. Y. Bonnefoy and W. Doniger (Chicago: University of Chicago Press, 1991) 174–78.

75. Arrigoni (1985) 115 and 199 n.232; L. Robert, "Sur des inscriptions de Chios," *BCH* 59 (1935) 462 = *Opera Minora Selecta*, vol. 1 (Amsterdam: A. M. Hakkert, 1969) 521; *Die Inscriften von Kyme* (Bonn, 1976) 113 no. 46; Mantas (1995) 133.

76. See chapters 4, 5, and 6. For general treatments of the topic, see K. Mantas (1995) 125–44; P. Angeli Bernardini, "Aspects ludiques, rituels et sportifs de la course feminine dans la Grèce antique," *Stadion* 12–13 (1986–87) 17–26; G. Arrigoni (1985); M Lämmer, "Women and Sport in Ancient Greece. A Plea for a Critical and Objective Approach," in *Women and Sport. An Historical, Biological, Physiological and Sportsmedical Approach, Sports Medicine* vol. 14, ed. J. Borms, M. Hebbelinck, and A. Venerando Basel (New York: S. Karger, 1981) 17–24. Golden (1998) 131–32 notes a possible "discourse (conscious or not) of male supremacy" in both the modern Olympics and the ancient Heraia and Olympics, whereby women are admitted only to contests where they will do less well than men; this reinforces a stereotype of women failing to measure up to men.

77. We know from Paus. (5.6.7–8) that married women were excluded from even attending the Olympic Festival at Olympia as spectators on pain of execution by being cast off some local cliffs. Unmarried girls, on the other hand, were not barred from attending (ibid. 6.20.9). The bias against married women here seems to reflect the general, conservative view that married women were not to appear in public. This prohibition is known only for Olympia, and, given the conservatism of that sanctuary, it may not have been in force elsewhere. At games in honor of Athena at the Theran colony of Cyrene in North Africa, both married women and maidens were present as early as the fifth century B.C. (Pindar, *P.* 9.98–103, dated 478 B.C.). And one article leans in favor of judging that women did attend dramatic performances in Athens: A. Podlecki, "Could Women Attend the Theater in Ancient Athens? A Collection of Testimonia," *AncW* 21 (1990) 27–43.

78. For the analogous, symbolic understanding of footraces as transitions, see Philostratus, *Gymn.* 4–8.

79. H. Lee, "SIG 802: Did Women Compete against Men in Greek Athletic Festivals?" *Nikephoros* 1 (1988) 103–17, reviews the evidence of an A.D. 45 inscription recording the athletic victories of girls in Panhellenic festivals and concludes that the field was probably restricted to girls for the events named (stade race and chariot race in armor). See also the Corinth inscription of A.D. 25 mentioning the establishment of a *virginum certamen* at the Tiberea Caesarea Sebastea at Isthmia in 23 (?) A.D.: J. H. Kent, *The Inscriptions 1926–1950. Corinth, Results of the Excavations*, vol. 8, pt. 3, *The Inscriptions* (Princeton: Princeton University Press, 1966), no. 153, pp. 28–29 and 70–73; an Italian inscription of ca. A.D. 154 commemorating the victory of a girl in a race for the daughters of the members of the council at Pithicussa (στάδιον βουλευτῶν θυγατέραις), Italy (H. W. Pleket, *Epigraphica II: Texts in the Social History of the Greek World* [Leiden: E. J. Brill, 1969] no. 17; G. Buchner, "Epigrapfe da Ischia. 154 d. C.," *Parola del Pasato* 7 [1952] 408).

80. See *SIG³* 802 = *IGRom.* IV 257, discussed in H. A. Harris (1964) 41; Moretti (1953) 168–69, and Lefkowitz and Fant (1982) 160 for a monument for three daughters of Hermesianax of Tralles, dated A.D. 47, recording their total of nine victories in the Isthmian, Pythian, and Nemean Games in footraces and a chariot race, though it is uncertain whether the footraces were mixed or for girls only; M. Lämmer (1981) 16–23 posits, plausibly, that the father managed to get permission to allow his daughters

to participate in the men's games since he lacked a son. See also J. Kent (1966) no. 153 on a girls' footrace at Isthmia; *IG* XIV. 755, Add. G (p. 691) mentions a race for daughters of magistrates at the Sebastea festival in Naples during the imperial period; Suetonius, *Domitian* 4.4 and Dio Cassius 67.8.1 both mention the races for women instituted by Domitian at the Capitoline Games in Rome in A.D. 86; and Malalas, *Chronographia* 12, p. 288.10–11 Dindorf mentions footraces and wrestling, as well as the cultural contests of philosophy, singing, and tragedy for girls at the Olympic Games in Antioch ca. A.D. 180–92. Mantas (1995) gives a general survey of the evidence, adding notably a list of 26 women who served as *agonothetai* or "producers of games" in Asian Minor and the Aegean region in the Roman era. The title was not only a great honor, it carried with it serious organizational responsibilities. Mantas also cites the following inscriptions or texts of the Roman period which record the participation of women and girls in gymnasium-related activities: *CIG* 3185.15–20 re supervisors of girls in the gymnasium; Menander Rhetor, III.364 (3 c. A.D.) on regulations for the *agōgē* of girls; a series of inscriptions from Stratonikeia in Caria re distribution of oil to and supervision of women in the gymnasium: I.Stratonikeia II.2, Bonn, 1990, nos. 1325A, 1325B.18–20, 698, 760.4–8, 181, 201.30–31, 120.18–20, 245.5–248.7–8, 256.8, 311.20–21; *IGRom.* IV 522 from Doryleum, Phrygia re a gymnasiarch of women. The Stratonikeia sources, Mantas notes (131), do not mean that the older women competed or trained in athletics, or enjoyed public education, but merely that they received oil at the gymnasium, which seems to have become a distribution center for the commodity widely used in the home. The wording of the inscriptions confirms this interpretation: they consistently refer to "women" (*gunaikes*) getting oil, not "maidens" (*parthenoi*). The gymnasium was still the male-civic domain in these cities in the Roman era, though no longer exclusively: occasionally girls, under women's supervision, may have used the facility for socializing, leisure activity, or possibly for physical or cultural education.

Chapter 1

1. On the etymology of "sport," see J. Sofer, "Kurze Bemerkungen zur Vorgeschichte des Worte 'Sport,'" *Leibesübungen—Leibeserziehung* 14 (1960) 13–14; E. Mehl, "'Sport' kommt nicht von *dis-portare*, sondern von *de-portare*," *Die Leibeserziehung* 15 (1966) 232–33. On ancient athletics and religion, see M. Golden, *Sport and Society in Ancient Greece* (Cambridge: Cambridge University Press, 1998) 10–23; S. Laser, *Sport und Spiel, Archaeologia Homerica*, vol. 3, ch. T (Göttingen: Vandenhoeck & Ruprecht, 1987) 86–88 for a discussion of gods and athletics in early epic literature; see E. Reisch, "Agones," *RE* I.1 coll. 836–66, for a general discussion of athletic festivals and their history, and J. Sakellarakis, "Games and Religion," in N. Yalouris, *The Eternal Olympics: The Art and History of Sport* (New Rochelle, N.Y.: Caratzas, 1979) 36–37; H. Siska, *De Mercurio ceterisque deis ad artem gymnicam pertinentibus* (Ph.D. diss., University of Halle, 1933) provides a convenient and extensive, though not exhaustive, catalogue of epigraphical and literary sources of cults related to Greek athletics and the gymnasium.

2. I. Weiler, " ΑΙΕΝ ΑΡΙΧΤΕΥΕΙΝ: Ideologiekritische Bemerkungen zu einem vielzitierten Homerwort," *Stadion* 1 (1976) 199–227.

3. For the use of athletic festivals to celebrate funeral games for both legendary and historical persons, see L. Roller, "Funeral Games in Greek Art," *AJA* 85 (1981a) 107–19; *id.*, "Funeral Games for Historical Persons," *Stadion* 7 (1981b) 1–18; *id.*, *Funeral Games in Greek Literature, Art, and Life* (Ph.D. diss., University of Pennsylvania, 1977).

4. The games of *Iliad* 23 comprise, of course, the earliest and most extensive description of athletics in extant Greek literature. Within that narrative, we find the reminiscences of Nestor concerning his victories in the funeral games of an earlier day (*Il.* 23.630–42). Golden (1998) 88–95 has a general discussion of Homeric games in Greek culture.

5. Also on the games for Patroclus, see chapter 9, notes 114 and 144.

6. James F. McGlew, *Tyranny and Political Culture in Ancient Greece* (Ithaca: Cornell University Press, 1993) 35–51 examines the rhetoric by which the epinician poetry of Pindar and Bacchylides asserted the divine source of victory for athletes: "Victory, the poet asserts, is the source of praise, and praise is the source of honor, the public acknowledgment that victory comes from the gods" (47). See also generally on the civic context of the epinician genre L. Kurke, *The Traffic in Praise: Pindar and the Poetics of Social Economy* (Ithaca: Cornell University Press, 1991). For another clear example of the belief in divine intervention in contests, see the discussion of magical spells use to invoke divine aid in preventing an athlete from winning a contest in C. Faraone, "The Agonistic Context of Greek Binding Spells," in *Magika Hiera: Ancient Greek Magic and Religion*, ed. C. A. Faraone and D. Obbink (New York: Oxford University Press, 1991), 3–32. The earliest literary mention of this practice in Greece, which is documented in numerous later inscribed curse tablets against athletes and charioteers, is Pelops' curse against Oenomaus in Pindar, *Olympian* 1.75–78. See further examples in D. Jordan, "Inscribed Lead Tablets from the Games in the Sanctuary of Poseidon," *Hesperia* 63.1 (1994) 111–26.

7. See R. Janko, *Homer, Hesiod, and the Hymns: Diachronic Development in Epic Diction* (Cambridge: Cambridge University Press, 1982) 200, table 4, argues plausibly for the approximate date of 675–60 B.C.; cf. W. Burkert, "Kynaithos, Polykrates, and the Homeric Hymn to Apollo," in *Arktouros: Hellenic Studies Presented to Bernard M. W. Knox on the Occasion of his 65th Birthday*, ed. G. W. Bowersock et al. (Berlin and New York: Walter de Gruyter, 1979) 53–62.

8. See the discussion of *terpsis* in relation to delight in athletics in the introduction, note 47.

9. See M. Golden (1998) 93; I. Weiler, *Der Sport bei den Völkern der alten Welt: Eine Einführung*, 2nd ed. (Darmstadt: Wissenschaftliche Buchgesellschaft, 1988) 77–80 for discussion and bibliography. Cf. J. Sakellarakis, in Yalouris (1972) 24–25, who opines that chariot racing, wrestling, boxing, and running probably reflect Mycenaean practice, while archery, javelin, and the long jump belong to a later period. T.B.L. Webster, *From Mycenae to Homer: A Study in Early Greek Literature and Art* (London: Methuen, 1964) 174 cites examples of geometric pots showing the following events also in the Patroclus games: four-horse chariot racing, boxing, wrestling, footrace, and armed combat. See also chapter 9, notes 43–53 for discussion of funeral games.

10. See Roller (1981a); *id.* (1981b). Thomas Yiannakis, "The Relationship between the Underground-Chthonian World and the Sacred Panhellenic Games,"

Nikephoros 3 (1990) 23–30, stresses the funereal aspects of the Panhellenic Games, arguing that such games served as a medium of communication between the living and chthonian spirits or divinities.

11. See chapter 4 here and Pausanias 5.16 on Hippodameia's games for Hera in thanks for her marriage to Pelops; I. Weiler, *Der Agon im Mythos: Zur Einstellung der Griechen zum Wettkampf*, Impulse der Forschung vol. 16 (Darmstadt: Wissenschaftliche Buchgesellschaft, 1974) 256–58.

12. Weiler (1974) 247–53.

13. For a dated but still somewhat useful overview of the varieties in different periods, see P. J. Meier, "Agones," *RE* 1.1, cols. 852–62.

14. Panhellenic Games: Golden (1998) 10–11; games in Pindar: K. Kramer, *Studien zur griechischen Agonistik nach den Epinikien Pindars* (Ph.D. diss., University of Cologne, 1970).

15. See the studies by Irene C. Ringwood Arnold listed in introduction, note 2. More recently on the Roman-era games: O. Van Nijf, "Athletics, Festivals, and Greek Identity in the Roman East," *PCPS* 45 (1999) 176–200 (especially on contests in Lycian Oenoanda); W. Orth, "Kaiserliche Agonistik und althistoriche Forschung," *Stadion* 24.1 (1998) 1–12; A. Farrington, "Olympic Victors and the Popularity of the Olympic Games in the Imperial Period," *Tyche* 12 (1997) 15–46; A.J.S. Spawforth, "Agonistic Festivals in Roman Greece," in *The Greek Renaissance in the Roman Empire. Papers from the Tenth British Museum Classical Colloquium*, ed. S. Walker and A. Cameron (London: University of London, Institute of Classical Studies, 1989) 193–97 (on the genres of games and their social importance). See other references to specialized studies on various aspects of Greek and Roman sports in the bibliographies by N. Crowther, "Studies in Greek Athletics," *CW* 78 (1984) 497–558 and 79 (1985a) 73–135 and by myself, *Greek and Roman Athletics: A Bibliography* (Chicago: Ares, 1984) 70–73.

16. H. A. Harris, *Greek Athletes and Athletics* (London: Hutchinson, 1964) 44–47; 226–27 with map 4 listing cities and numbers of known athletic festivals at each. M. I. Finley and H. W. Pleket, *The Olympic Games: The First Thousand Years* (New York: Viking, 1976) 24, estimate that there were eventually over three hundred athletic festivals. Since the numbers are cumulative of evidence over the thousand-year history of Greek athletics and do not reckon synchronically for any given period, they may be slightly high. A conservative estimate is that at least two hundred athletic festivals were held, at various intervals of one, two, or four years, during the more prosperous economic periods of the Roman Empire in the first two centuries A.D. A careful cataloguing of the evidence for local festivals should be high on the agenda for research on ancient athletics.

17. See J. Fontenrose, "The Cult of Apollo and the Games at Delphi," and Stella Miller, "Excavations at the Panhellenic Site of Nemea: Cults, Politics, and Games," in *The Archaeology of the Olympics: the Olympics and Other Festivals in Antiquity*, ed. W. Raschke (Madison: University of Wisconsin Press, 1988) 121–40 and 141–51, respectively; Stephen G. Miller, ed., *Nemea: A Guide to the Site and Museum* (Berkeley: University of California Press, 1990) 1–8. For competition among members of the "circuit," see C. Morgan, *Athletes and Oracles: The Transformation of Olympia and Delphi in the Eighth Century* B.C. (Cambridge: Cambridge University Press, 1990) 212–23.

18. O. Broneer, "Isthmia and the Sanctuary of Poseidon," *Greek Heritage* 4 (1964) 42–49; W. R. Biers and D. J. Geagan, "A New List of Victors in the Caesarea at Isthmia," *Hesperia* 39 (1970) 79–93; D. J. Geagan, "Notes on the Agonistic Institutions of Roman Corinth," *GRBS* 9 (1968) 69–80; K. Schneider, "Isthmia," in *RE* 9.2 cols. 2251–53.

19. See M. P. Nilsson, *Griechische Feste von religiöser Bedeutung mit Ausschluss der Attischen* (Leipzig: B. G. Teubner, 1906; reprint, Darmstadt: Wissenschaftliche Buchgesellschaft, 1957) 123.

20. See E. Kadletz, "The Race and Procession of the Athenian *Oschophoroi*," *GRBS* 21(1980) 363–71; L. Deubner, *Attische Feste* (Berlin: Heinrich Keller, 1932; reprint, Darmstadt: Wissenschaftliche Buchgesellschaft, 1956) 142–47; H. W. Parke, *Festivals of the Athenians* (London: Thames and Hudson, 1977; reprint, Ithaca: Cornell University Press, 1986) 77–80.

21. E. N. Gardiner, *Olympia: Its History and Remains* (Oxford: The Clarendon Press, 1925; reprint, Washington, D.C.: McGrath, 1973) 59–63, 79–103. See C. Ulf and I. Weiler, "Der Ursprung der antiken Olympischen Spiele in der Forschung," *Stadion* 6 (1981) 1–38 for a systematic overview of the myriad scholarly theories regarding the founding of the Olympic Games, concluding with the view that no theory wins out in view of the unreliability of textual testimonia and the inconclusiveness of archeological evidence. Golden (1998) 12–14, 21–23 surveys some of the evidence about Olympic origins, with mostly negative results.

22. Ancient chronology is noted here merely to give a sense of a relative sequence of celebrations at the site as conveyed by legend.

23. R. S. Robinson, *Sources for the History of Greek Athletics* (Cincinnati: Robinson, 1955; reprint Chicago: Ares, 1979) 35–39.

24. Ibid. 39–43.

25. L. Lacroix, "La Légende de Pélops et son Iconographie," *BCH* 100 (1976) 327–41; Weiler (1974) 209–17.

26. See the chariot race depicted on the Late Helladic III C amphora from Tiryns, in Nauplion, Arch. Mus.: Laser (1987) fig. 2; also the chariots present at what appears to be an armed combat in the context of funeral games on a larnax (terracotta coffin) from Tanagra: W. Decker, "Die mykenische Herkunft des griechischen Totenagons," *Stadion* 8–9 (1982–83) 6–15 and figs. 1–2; see chapter 9, note 119, this volume.

27. A. Mallwitz, "Cult and Competition Locations at Olympia," in Raschke (1988) 79–109, argues against the earlier date, but see my discussion in chapter 4, note 72, of this volume, and also the arguments of A. Hönle against Mallwitz's dating in *Gnomon* 62 (1990) 223.

28. H. Lee, "The 'First' Olympic Games of 776 B.C.," in Raschke (1988) 110–18.

29. Morgan (1990) 1–25, 223–34.

30. H.-V. Herrmann, "Zur ältesten Geschichte von Olympia," *MDAI(A)* 77 (1962): 3–34; id., "Olympia und seine Spiele im Wandel der Zeiten," *Gymnasium* 80 (1973) 172–205; id., "Prähistorisches Olympia," in *Ägaische Bronzezeit*, ed. H. G. von Buchholz (Darmstadt: Wissenschaftliche Buchgesellschaft, 1987) 426–36.

31. A. Mallwitz, *Olympia und seine Bauten* (Athens: S. Kasas, 1981) 235–40.

32. V. R. d'A. Desborough, *The Last Mycenaeans and Their Successors; An Archaeological Survey, c. 1200–c. 1000 B.C.* (Oxford: Clarendon Press, 1964); V. Des-

borough and M. Hammond, in *The Cambridge Ancient History*, 2nd ed., vol. 2, part. 2 (Cambridge: Cambridge University Press, 1975) 658ff.; A. M. Snodgrass, *The Dark Age of Greece* (Edinburgh: Edinburgh University Press, 1971) 311–12 allows for an 'invasion' ca. 1200 but has substantive differences with Desborough.

33. Lee (1988); Morgan (1990) 22, 41–43, 47–49 cautiously denies any cult continuity before the tenth century B.C. on the basis of votive deposits and is skeptical of the existence of any games prior to the eighth century B.C., but does admit the possibility of some cult of Zeus prior to the eighth century. The presence of the earlier apsidal houses on the site does allow the possibility that Olympia was an important local cult site in the late Mycenaean period.

34. V. Mitsopoulos-Leon, "Zur Verehrung des Dionysos in Elis nochmals: AΞIE TAYPE und die Sechzehn heiligen Frauen," *MDAI(A)* 99 (1984) 281–84.

35. Morgan (1990) 42–43; Herrmann (1962) 3–34.

36. U. Sinn, "Olympia. Die Stellung der Wettkämpfe im Kult des Zeus Olympios," *Nikephoros* 4 (1991) 31–54.

37. A. Hönle, *Olympia in der Politik der griechischen Staatenwelt von 776 bis zum ende des 5. Jahrhunderts* (Bebenhausen, Germany: Lothar Rotsch, 1972) 7–13, discusses the historicity of the truce.

38. C. Renfrew, "The Minoan-Mycenaean Origins of the Panhellenic Games," in Raschke (1988) 13–25 points up the uniqueness of the contribution of "peer-polity interaction" in the foundation of the Olympics.

39. Altar not at finish line: A. Mallwitz, in Raschke (1988) 94–95, followed by Golden (1998) 22–23.

40. J. Puhvel, "Hittite Athletics as Prefigurations of Ancient Greek Games," in Raschke (1988) 26–31 illustrates how the combination of religious ritual and athletic competition functioned similarly in Hittite culture of the second millennium B.C.; W. Decker, *Sport und Spiel im Alten Ägypten* (Munich: C. H. Beck, 1987) = id., *Sport and Games in Ancient Egypt*, trans. A. Guttmann (New Haven: Yale University Press, 1992), gives many examples of similar athletic-religious rituals in Egyptian practice as early as the third millennium B.C. I repeat, however, the cautions expressed in the introduction that the cultural constructions of other peoples can offer only very rough parallels in form and function to the Greek experience.

41. I do not find convincing the arguments of Golden (1998) 40–45, seeking, against Hippias' supposedly antiaristocratic victor list, to backdate equestrian events into the Olympic program from the beginning, since the evidence is either from silence or from myths that mention chariot racing in games prior to 776 B.C. Golden's thesis does not explain the absence from the first historical games of combat sports and other field events, all as anti-elitist as footraces, and all mentioned in Pindar's mythical earliest games (*Ol.* 10.60–73).

42. Mallwitz (1988) 80–94; Eric L. Brulotte, "The 'Pillar of Oinomaos' and the Location of Stadium I at Olympia," *AJA* 98 (1994) 53–64, argues that the so-called "Pillar of Oenomaus" at Olympia, discussed by Pausanias (5.20.7), was actually the original turning post of the first stadium, located between the altar and the Temple of Zeus; against this, see Golden (1998) 23 and note 17.

43. R. Patrucco, *Lo stadio di Epidauro* (Florence: L. O. Olschki, 1976) figs. XXI.1 and XXV.1; re Nemea, see Miller (1990) 184–91. For additional comments on the location of Archaic and Classical stadia near the altar of the divinity in whose honor

the games were held, see D. G. Romano, *Stadia of the Peloponnese* (Ph.D. diss., University of Pennsylvania, 1981) 186; id., "An Early Stadium at Nemea," *Hesperia* 46 (1977) 27–31; and S. G. Miller, "The Stadium at Nemea and the Nemean Games," in *Proceedings of an International Symposium on the Olympic Games*, ed. W. Coulson and H. Kyrieleis (Athens: Luci Braggiotti Publications for the Deutsches Archäologisches Institut Athen, 1992) 82.

44. Hugh M. Lee, "Some Changes in the Olympic Program and Schedule," in W. Coulson and H. Kyrieleis (1992) 105–11 argues convincingly, along the lines of L. Weniger's earlier thesis, that the program at some later point expanded to six days.

45. Stephen G. Miller, "The Date of Olympic Festivals," *MDAI(A)* 90 (1975) 215–31.

46. J. Swaddling, *The Ancient Olympic Games* (London: British Museum Publications, 1980) 36–39; L. Weniger, "Das Hochfest des Zeus in Olympia I: Die Ordnung der Agone," *Klio* 4 (1904) 125–51. See especially H. M. Lee, "Some Changes in the Olympic Program and Schedule," in W. Coulson and H. Kyrieleis (1992) 105–11, where the probable changes in the order of events and length of the festival (eventually extending to six days) are outlined.

47. W. Burkert, *Homo Necans: The Anthropology of Ancient Greek Sacrificial Ritual and Myth*, trans. P. Bing (Berkeley: University of California Press, 1983) 97–98; see also the discussion of this passage at chapter 9, note 1, this volume.

48. M. Lämmer, "Der Sogenante Olympische Friede in der Griechischen Antike," *Stadion* 8–9 (1982–83) 47–83; L. Drees, *Olympia: Gods, Artists and Athletes*, trans. G. Onn (New York: Praeger, 1968) 36–37, 154–55.

49. Drees (1968) 43–45.

50. C. Forbes, "Crime and Punishment in Greek Athletics," *CJ* 47 (1952) 169–74; Drees (1968) 52–54.

51. Drees (1968) 85–86.

52. A. Brelich, *Paides e Parthenoi*, vol. 1, Incunabula Greca vol. 36 (Rome: Edizione dell'Ateneo, 1969) 29–31; see also chapter 4 of this volume, re male-female segregation at Olympia, and chapter 3 re the lack of evidence for the origin of athletic festivals from initiation rituals.

53. Drees (1968) 13–14.

54. E. Simon, *Die Götter der Griechen*, 2nd ed. (Munich: Hirmer, 1980) 38–39; W. Burkert, *Greek Religion*, trans. J. Raffan (Cambridge, Mass.: Harvard University Press, 1985) 87–92, 131–35 (= *Griechische Religion der archäischen und klassischen Epoche* [Stuttgart: W. Kohlhammer, 1977] 146–54, 208–9).

Chapter 2

1. E. N. Gardiner, *Olympia: Its History and Remains* (Oxford: Clarendon, 1925; reprint Washington, D.C.: McGrath, 1973) 165, 166, and 174; J. Jüthner, *Die athletischen Leibesübungen der Griechen*, ed. F. Brein, vol. 1, SB Wien 249 (Graz: Hermann Böhlaus, 1965) 135; H.-V. Herrmann, *Olympia: Heiligtum und Wettkampfstätte* (Munich: Hirmer, 1972) 185; F. Brein, "Die Leibesübungen in alten Griechenland," in *Geschichte der Leibesübungen*, ed. H. Überhorst, vol. 2 (Berlin: Bartels & Wernitz KG, 1978) 88–89. More reliable recent studies: U. Sinn, "Das Auftreten der Athleten in Olympia in Nachklassischer Zeit," in *Proceedings of an In-*

ternational Symposium on the Olympic Games, ed. W. Coulson and H. Kyrieleis (Athens: Luci Braggiotti Publications for the Deutsches Archäologisches Institut Athen, 1992) 45–49, which sees a continuity of positive images of athletes in the Roman era; A. Farrington, "Olympic Victors and the Popularity of the Olympic Games in the Imperial Period," *Tyche* 12 (1997) 15–46, which gives a reliable and nuanced analysis showing a general decline in interest in the games in the middle of the Hellenistic period, with a resuscitation among participants in Asia Minor in the Roman Imperial period; W. Orth, "Kaiserzeitliche Agonistik und althistorische Forschung," *Stadion* 24.1 (1998) 1–12 criticizes the deficits of past scholarship on this topic and suggests useful new approaches. Farrington's study, which postdates but does not cite a version of this chapter published earlier (1986), is the best overview and essentially complements this study with different emphases of interest using the statistics from known victors. Notably, he estimates that the recorded victories known to us today likely constitute 22 percent to 25 percent of all Olympic victories, "a comparatively large volume of the evidence" (24).

2. J. Ebert et al., *Olympia von den Anfängen bis zu Coubertin* (Leipzig: Koehler & Amelang, 1980) esp. 109–14, "Das Wirken Roms—zwischen Farce und Restauration."

3. Polybius 28.13; W. Dittenberger and K. Purgold, *Die Inschriften von Olympia* [hereafter cited as *I.Ol.*], ed. E. Curtius and F. Adler, *Olympia*, vol. 5 (Berlin, 1896; reprint Amsterdam: Hakkert, 1966) no. 318.

4. Polyb. 39.5.1–6; *I.Ol.* no. 302.

5. Plutarch, *Sulla* 12; Sextus Julius Africanus, *Olympionikai* 175; Appian, *Bellum Civile* 1.99; id., *Bellum Mithridaticum* 54; Jüthner and Brein (1965) 135; Gardiner (1925) 152–53.

6. Gardiner (1925) 153.

7. *I.Ol.* no. 330 (Fufius); *I.Ol.* no. 365 (Caesar).

8. Gardiner (1925) 153.

9. Ibid. 154.

10. *I.Ol.* no. 184 = L. Moretti, *Olympionikai, i Vincitori negli Antichi Agoni Olimpici*, *MemLincei* ser. 8.8.2 (Rome: Accademia Nazionale dei Lincei, 1957) no. 590 (Akestorides); *I.Ol* . 329 = ibid. no. 895 (ca. A.D. 193 victor).

11. P. J. Meier, "*Agōnes*," in *Paulys Real-encyclopädie der classischen Altertumswissenschaft* [hereafter *RE*], ed. A. F. von Pauly and G. Wissowa, vol. 1, part 1 (Stuttgart: A. Druckenmüller, 1894), esp. cols. 866–67, on *agōnes* in Rome.

12. *I.Ol.* no. 913, and pp. 696ff.

13. Josephus, *Bellum Judaicum* 1.427; M. Lämmer, "Die Kaiserspiele von Caesarea im Dienst der Politik des Koenigs Herodes," *Kölner Beiträge zur Sportwissenschaft* 3 (1974) 95–163.

14. Moretti (1957) nos. 512, 539, 555, 569, 575, and 586. On Egypt's development of gymnasia as civic institutions in the Hellenistic and Roman periods: H. I. Marrou, *A History of Education in Antiquity*, trans. G. Lamb (London: Sheed and Ward, 1956) 104.

15. Moretti (1957) nos. 349, 434, 439, 445, 463, 527, 533, 549, and 552.

16. L. Moretti, *Iscrizioni agonistiche greche* (Rome: Angelo Signorelli, 1953) nos. 58, 62, 67, 68, 69, 70, 71, 75, 77, 78, 79, 80, 81, 82, 84, 85, 87, 88, 90.

17. E. Reisch, "Aktia," in *RE* vol. I, part 1, cols. 1213–14.

18. *RE* supplement vol. 5, col. 630. The full name of the Augustalia at Naples was "Italica Romaia Sebasta Isolympica," or "the Italian and Roman Games of

Augustus based on the Olympic Program." They were quinquennial, reckoned by an era of "Italids," had a mandatory, thirty-day training period, boys' (12–17 years old) and men's classes of competitors, and an athletic and equestrian program identical to that of Olympia. All of this we are fortunate to learn from the lengthy inscription (*I.Ol.* no. 56) of the first century A.D. See N. Crowther, "The Age Category of Boys at Olympia," *Phoenix* 42 (1988) 304–8; Gardiner (1925) 159. Farrington (1997) 35–43 lists thirty-six known festivals that were not only isolympic but called "Olympian."

19. According to the index in Moretti (1953).

20. S.R.F. Price, *Rituals and Power: The Roman Imperial Cult in Asia Minor* (Cambridge: Cambridge University Press, 1984) authoritatively discusses the process whereby Augustus incorporated himself into the religious and political institutions and beliefs of Greek cities. Though this is a more artificial process than is usually meant by the term "syncretism," it did require the same modes of incorporation of new beliefs within old.

21. *I.Ol.* pp. 135–234, nos. 58–141.

22. Herrmann (1972) 184 and 259, note 703.

23. *I.Ol.* no. 218 = Moretti (1957) no. 738 (Tiberius); Sextus Julius Africanus, *Olympionicarum fasti*, Olympiad 99 (Germanicus).

24. Two (*I.Ol.* nos. 369, 371) and possibly three (including 370) inscriptions honor Tiberius as patron and benefactor of the city of Elis, and presumably its sponsorship of the Olympics, but nothing else is known of the nature of his subsidy to the games.

25. Dio Cassius 59.28.3–4; Josephus, *Antiquitates Judaicae* 19.8–10; Suetonius, *Caligula* 57.1.

26. Africanus; Eusebius, *Chronicles* II.273 Aucheri; Paus. 10.36.4; Suet. *Nero* 23.1; Philostratus, *Life of Apollonius of Tyana* 5.7.

27. Gardiner (1925) 158, 168.

28. See Moretti (1957) nos. 641 (= 144 B.C. victory), 681–83 (triple victor of 72 B.C.); early imperial victories: nos. 726, 729, and 731 (by one victor); 728, 735, and 749; L. Moretti, "Nuovo Supplemento al Catalogo degli Olympionikai," *Miscellanea Greca e Romana* 12 (Rome, 1987) 87, "Thaliarchos"; this supplement, reprinted in W. Coulson and H. Kyrieleis (1992) 119–28, incorporates his earlier supplement in *Klio* 52 (1970) 295–303.

29. Nikophon: Moretti (1957) no. 735; *Anthologia Greca* 6.256. Demosthenes: Moretti (1957) no. 726, 729, and 731; *Anthologia Greca* 6.350.

30. S. A. Cook, F. E. Adcock, and M. P. Charlesworth, eds., *The Cambridge Ancient History. Volume X: The Augustan Empire, 44 B.C.–A.D. 70* (Cambridge: Cambridge University Press, 1952) 497, 563.

31. J. Delorme, *Gymnasion: Étude sur les monuments consacrées a l'éducation en Grèce (des origines à l'Empire romain)* (Paris: De Boccard, 1960) 137–39. C. Forbes, *Greek Physical Education* (New York: Century, 1929) 251–57 observes how "the gymnasium people" (*hoi apo gumnasiou*) formed a "privileged class in the cities" of Roman Egypt; see *Papyrus Oxyrhynchus* IX.1202.

32. *Papyrus London.* 1912.53ff. See Forbes (1929) 254. N. B. Crowther, "Slaves and Greek Athletics," *Quaderni Urbinati di Cultura Classica* (1992) 35–42, points out that, while only free citizens could become ephebes and generally only they could use gymnasia, some exceptions allowed them to practice in gymnasia and even to compete at some local festivals.

33. On "Successor of Heracles": Paus. 5.21.10; Dio Cassius 79.10; Gardiner (1925) 166. On Tiberius Claudius Rufus, later seen as an activist for athetes' unions: U. Sinn et al., "Bericht über das Forschungsprojekt 'Olympia während der römischen Kaiserzeit und in der Spätantike' III. Die Arbeit im Jahr 1994," *Nikephoros* 7 (1994) 236, 239.

34. Against Africanus' mention of the long discontinuation of horse races prior to A.D. 17, there is the evidence of eight inscriptions recording hippic victors at Olympia between 60 B.C. and A.D. 1 (Moretti (1957) nos. 705, 707, 711, 714, 720, 740, 741, and 750). We might better place this hiatus between ca. A.D. 17 and A.D. 53, for which period no hippic victories are recorded in the sources. Africanus may have incorrectly listed the hiatus under Germanicus' victory; the author's reliability in this entry has already been questioned by the omission of Germanicus' name from the text as we have it. See H. Gelzer, *Sextus Julius Africanus und die byzantanische Chronographie* (Leipzig: B. G. Teubner, 1880–85) part 1, 169).

35. U. Sinn (1992) 45–46.

36. S. Specht, in U. Sinn et al., "Bericht über das Forschungsprojekt 'Olympia während der römischen Kaiserzeit und in der Spätantike' V. Die Arbeit im Jahr 1995 Teil 2," *Nikephoros* 9 (1996) 203–15; U. Sinn et al., "Bericht über das Forschungsprojekt 'Olympia während der römischen Kaiserzeit und in der Spätantike' IV. Die Arbeit im Jahr 1995 Teil 1," *Nikephoros* 8 (1995) 162–71.

37. Philostr., *Life of Apollonius of Tyana* 4.31; Gardiner (1925) 168.

38. M. Lämmer, *Olympien und Hadrianeen im Antiken Ephesos* (Cologne: W. Kleikamp, 1967) 11.

39. Herrmann (1972) 190.

40. Ibid. 189–90.

41. Ibid. 191–92; Gardiner (1925) 168 and 173.

42. Suet., *Domitian*, 4.4; Dio Cassius 67.8.1. There seems to have been some vogue for female competitions in Greek games of the Imperial period. One inscription honors a benefactor of games at Isthmia, Lucius Castricius Regulus, who "introduced [poetry contests in honor of] the divine Julia Augusta, and [a contest (*certamen*)] for girls" at the Tiberea Kaisareia Sebasteia early in A.D. 23(?): See J. Kent, *Corinth*, vol. 8, pt. 3 (Princeton: Princeton University Press, 1966) 70–73, no. 153). Another inscription (*SIG*³ 802, A.D. 47) commemorates the victories of three daughters of Hermesianax of Tralles in the stade races at the Pythian, Isthmian, and Nemean Panhellenic games, as well as victories in local games in various events. A third inscription from the Imperial period records races for daughters of magistrates in the Sebasta festival at Naples (*IG* 14.755, Add. G (p. 691). It is difficult to say whether liberalized rules allowing girls to compete in Greek contests were influenced by the practices of female gladiators at Rome (Juvenal, *Satire* 6.246–267), or, as is more likely, that both phenomena simply manifested a larger and wealthier leisure class in Greece, Rome, and elsewhere during the Empire.

43. See Moretti (1953) index.

44. B. Bilinski, "Il fisico e l'intelletto: equilibrio o supremazia nell'epoca ellenistica e greco-romana," in *Agoni Ginnici: Componenti Artistiche ed Intellectuali nell'Antica Agonistica Greca* (Wroclaw: Zaklad Narodowy im. Ossolinskich, 1979) 111–12.

45. *I.Ol.* no. 547, 2nd. c. A.D.; *I.Ol.* no. 482, A.D. 233; Bilinski (1979) 113.

46. J. Ebert, "Zu griechischen agonistischen Inschriften," *Wissenschaftliche Zeitschrift der Universität Halle, Geistliche-sprachwissenschaftliche Reihe*, 15 (1966) 383ff.; id. et al. (1980) 112.

47. Moretti (1957) nos. 414, 431, 438 = 368, 356, and 352 B.C.

48. Moretti (1957) nos. 848, 850–52, 856 (all by Aelius) and 858 = A.D. 133[?], 137[?], 141[?], and 145[?].

49. Moretti (1957) nos. 846 (*I.Ol.* no. 236, = A.D. 129); 866 (*I.Ol.* 233 = A.D. 153 (?). On the dearth of Hippic events at Olympia in the Roman era: Farrington (1997) 22.

50. Herrmann (1972) 193.

51. Moretti (1953) nos. 203 and 267.

52. Bilinski (1979) 112.

53. Herrmann (1972) 192.

54. A. Mallwitz, *Olympia und seine Bauten* (Athens: S. Kasas, 1981) 113–14.

55. Herrmann (1972) 196.

56. Ibid. 194.

57. M. Poliakoff, *Studies in the Terminology of the Greek Combat Sports* Bieträge zurklassischen Philologie, vol. 146 (Königstein/Ts.: Anton Hain, 1982) 143–47.

58. *I.Ol.* no. 239 and *IG* II-III².3767 = Moretti (1953) 89; id. (1957) no. 932.

59. Varazdates, a Persian Arsacid from Armenia who won in boxing in A.D. 369: Moretti (1957) no. 944; also in 369 was Moretti (1957) no. 943; 277 victory = Moretti (1957) no. 942. For a recently discovered inscription commemorating the Olympic victories of two Athenian brothers in A.D. 381 and 385 (Ol. 290 and 291), see J. Ebert, in Sinn et al. (1994) 238–41.

60. Farrington (1997) 35.

Chapter 3

1. Bernard Sergent, *Homosexuality in Greek Myth*, trans. Arthur Goldhammer, pref. by George Dumezil (Boston: Beacon Press, 1986a; from the original *L'homosexualité dans la mythologie grecque* [Paris: Payot, 1984]); id., *L'homosexualité initiatique dans l'Europe ancienne* (Paris: Payot, 1986b); id., "Paederasty and Political Life in Archaic Greek Culture," *Journal of Homosexuality* 25 (1993) 147–64; J. Bremmer, "An Enigmatic Indo-European Rite: Paederasty," *Arethusa* 13 (1980) 279–98; id., "Adolescents, Symposion, and Pederasty," in O. Murray, ed., *Sympotica: A Symposion on the Symposium* (Oxford: Clarendon, 1990) 135–48; H. Patzer, *Die Griechische Knabenliebe* (Wiesbaden: F. Steiner, 1982).

2. P. Cartledge, "The Politics of Spartan Pederasty," in *Sexualität und Erotik in der Antike*, Wege der Forschung, vol. 605, ed. A. Karsten Siems (Darmstadt: Wissenschaftliche Buchgesellschaft, 1988) 383–415, esp. 407 (= *Proceedings of the Cambridge Philological Society* 207, N.S. 27 [1981] 17–36); K. J. Dover, *Greek Homosexuality*, 2nd ed. (Cambridge, Mass.: Harvard University Press, 1989) 54–57; Carola Reinsberg, *Ehe, Hetärentum und Knabenliebe im antiken Griechenland* (Munich: C. H. Beck, 1989) 179–80; D. G. Kyle, *Athletics in Ancient Athens* (Leiden: E. J. Brill, 1987) 65, 133. See ch. 8 of this volume.

3. H. Jeanmaire, *Couroi et Couretes. Essai sur l'éducation spartiate et sur les rites d'adolescence dans l'antiquité hellénique* (Lille: Bibliothèque universitaire, 1939; reprint

New York: Arno Press, 1974); A. Brelich, *Le Iniziazioni: Parte II. Sviluppi storici nelle civiltà superiori, in particolare nella Grecia antica* (Rome: Ateneo, 1962); id., *Paides et Parthenoi*, vol. 1, Incunabula Greca, vol. 36 (Rome: Ateneo, 1969).

4. M. Eliade, *Rites and Symbols of Initiation: The Mysteries of Birth and Rebirth*, trans. W. R. Trask (New York: Harper & Row, 1958; reprint, 1965) 7. The scheme was originally defined by A. van Gennep, *Les rites de passage* (Paris: É. Nourry, 1909) = id., *The Rites of Passage*, trans. M. B. Vizedom and G. L. Caffe (Chicago: University of Chicago Press, 1960); see discussion in P. Vidal-Naquet, *The Black Hunter: Forms of Thought and Forms of Society in the Greek World*, trans. A. Szegedy-Maszak and forward by B. Knox (Baltimore: Johns Hopkins University Press, 1986) 137. V. Turner, *The Forrest of Symbols. Aspects of Ndembu Ritual* (Ithaca: Cornell University Press, 1967) defines a "liminal" period that corresponds roughly to the marginal period in Van Gennep's schema; the theoretical differences are not crucial to the present thesis.

5. M. Eliade (this ch., note 4, 1958) 2. This threefold division is a somewhat artificial but convenient one for the sake of this study. Overlap is common, especially concerning "tribal" initiation and "mystery" religion initiation.

6. V. Popp, *Initiation, Zeremonien der Statusänderung und des Rollenswechsels. Eine Anthologie* (Frankfurt: Suhrkamp, 1969) 7–8; W. Burkert, *Greek Religion*, trans. J. Raffan (Cambridge, Mass.: Harvard University Press, 1985) 260–61, from the original *Grieschische Religion der Archaïschen und Klassichen Epoche* (Stuttgart: W. Kohlhammer, 1977) 391.

7. A. Brelich, "The Historical Development of the Institution of Initiation in the Classical Ages," *AAntHung* 9 (1961) 269.

8. W. Burkert, "Kekropidensage und Arrhephoria," *Hermes* 94 (1966) 13.

9. A. Brelich, "Initiation et Histoire," in *Initiation: Contributions to the Theme of the Study-Conference of the International Association for the History of Religions Held at Strasburg, Sept. 17th–22nd, 1964*, ed. C. J. Bleeker, Studies in the History of Religion, Numen Supplement vol. 10 (Leiden: E. J. Brill, 1965) 228. The tribes of non-state societies are here to be distinguished from the 'tribes' or 'clans' (*phylai*; *phratriai*) of the Greek cities which were artificially created subdivisions of the citizen body, varying in size and function from state to state, and therefore not a reliable index of initiatory groups as commonly defined: see L. Bruit Zaidman and P. Schmitt Pantel, *Religion in the Ancient Greek City*, trans. P. Cartledge (Cambridge: Cambridge University Press, 1994) 85–86; D. Roussel, *Tribu et cité: Études sur les groupes sociaux dans les cités grecques aux époques archaïque et classique* (Paris: "Les Belles Lettres," 1976); N. Robertson, *Festivals and Legends: The Formation of Greek Cities in the Light of Public Ritual* (Toronto: University of Toronto Press, 1992) 58–64 (on Athenian groups).

10. Brelich (this ch., note 9, 1965) 229; Bruit Zaidman and Schmitt Pantel (1994) 65–67.

11. Vidal-Naquet (1986) 143.

12. See Jan Bremmer, *Greek Religion*, Greece and Rome, New Surveys in the Classics, no. 24 (Oxford: Oxford University Press, 1994) 54–68; K. Dowden, *The Uses of Greek Mythology* (London: Routledge, 1992) 102–18.

13. M. I. Finley, *The Use and Abuse of History* (New York: Viking, 1975) 117, re the application of anthropological parallels to ancient Spartan institutions; see Nigel

M. Kennell, *The Gymnasium of Virtue: Education and Culture in Ancient Sparta* (Chapel Hill: University of North Carolina Press, 1995) 143–44.

14. Vidal-Naquet (1986) 140.

15. M. I. Finley, "Sparta and Spartan Society," in *Economy and Society in Ancient Greece*, ed. B. D. Shaw and R. P. Saller (New York: Chatto & Windus, 1982) 38; Jeanmaire (1939) 463–65.

16. K. J. Dover, "Greek Homosexuality and Initiation," ch. 12 of *The Greeks and Their Legacy: Collected Papers, Volume II: Prose, Literature, History, Society, Transmission, Influence* (Oxford: Blackwell, 1988) 119.

17. Sergent (1986a and b, and 1993); Bremmer (1980 and 1990).

18. Dover (1988) 116–19.

19. Ibid. 131–32 (his emphasis).

20. Cartledge (1988) 407; Bremmer (1980) 291.

21. Robert Sallares, *The Ecology of the Ancient Greek World* (London: Duckworth, 1991) 160–92. M. Golden, *Sport and Society in Ancient Greece* (Cambridge: Cambridge University Press, 1998) 104–16, 139–40, discusses age-classes and suggests a likely motive for their establishment, "the avoidance of intergenerational rivalry," especially between fathers and sons.

22. Brelich (1969) 449–56 (appendix 3, "L'agonistica"); Jeanmaire (1939) 413–18 (appendix to ch. 5, "The Origins of the Olympic Games").

23. Brelich (1969) 453.

24. A. Hönle, *Olympia in der Politik der griechischen Staatenwelt von 776 bis zum ende des 5. Jahrhunderts* (Bebenhausen, Germany: Lothar Rotsch, 1972) 5–13; I. Weiler, *Der Sport bei den Völkern der alten Welt: Eine Einführung*, 2nd ed. (Darmstadt: Wissen schaftliche Buchgesellschaft, Germany, 1988) 105–7; H. Lee, "The 'First' Olympic Games of 776 B.C." in *The Archaeology of the Olympics: the Olympics and Other Festivals in Antiquity*, ed. W. J. Raschke (Madison: University of Wisconsin Press, 1988) 110–18; B. J. Peiser, *Das Dunkel Zeitalter Olympias* (Frankfurt: Peter Lang Gmbh, 1993) 222–39.

25. Philostr. (*Gymn.* 13), Paus. (5.8.9), and Africanus note the introduction of the first boys' events in the 37th Olympics. N. Crowther, "The Age Category of Boys at Olympia," *Phoenix* 42 (1988) 304–8, M. Golden, *Children and Childhood in Classical Athens* (Baltimore: Johns Hopkins University Press, 1990) 68–69, and A. J. Papalas, "Boy Athletes in Ancient Greece," *Stadion* 17.2 (1991) 165–92, discuss age limits and boys' participation at various athletic contests. Classes of "boys" (*paides*) athletes were included at the other Panhellenic Games, the Pythia, Isthmia, and Nemea, from their foundation between 586 and 573 B.C., though none of these Panhellenic Games ever included a third age-class of "youths" (*ageneioi*), as did some (later) local games. If initiation rituals were the source of athletic festivals, one would expect to find both "boys" and "youths" grades established from the start as they are in initiatory institutions.

26. Weiler (1988) 93–94.

27. *Iliad* 11.698ff. mentions a chariot race in Elis and may allude to the Olympic tradition.

28. Plut., *Pelopidas* 19.1–2 (287–88).

29. Plut., *Pelop.* 18.1 (287); Dover (1989) 192. For a neutral overview of some of the educational functions of pederasty, see Reinsberg (1989) 170–78.

30. Sallares (1991) 164–92; the quote is cited by Sallares (169) from B. Bernardi, *Age-Class Systems: Social Institutions and Polities Based on Age* (Cambridge: Cambridge University Press, 1985) 170; see also D. Cohen, *Law, Sexuality, and Society. The Enforcement of Morals in Classical Athens* (Cambridge: Cambridge University Press, 1991) 193–94, re pederasty as a solution to late marriage, with anthropological parallels.

31. William Armstrong Percy, *Pederasty and Pedagogy in Archaic Greece* (Urbana: University of Illinois Press, 1996) 62–72. Though Percy's general time-frame and ascription of the origins of institutionalized pederasty to Crete are plausible, his precise assignment of the 'reforms' to the Cretan Onomacritus is much more speculative, as are some of his other suggestions for the details for likely diffusion of the custom to the mainland. We lack evidence to trace this in any detail.

32. Dover (1989) 167–68; 185–86; generally on the connection of pederasty with institutionalized *paideia*, see H. I. Marrou, *A History of Education in Antiquity*, trans. G. Lamb (London: Sheed and Ward, 1956) 25–35 (though not reliable on the phenomenon of pederasty per se).

33. Sergent (1986b) 136 characterizes as "polycentrique" Greek homophilia in its local manifestations in Ionia and northwestern Greece, but he nonetheless maintains that they all evidence traces of an Indo-European pattern. See also Cohen (1991a) 174 on the different views of homosexuality among city-states, and even the complex ambiguities of the practices within Athens and Sparta.

34. Sergent (1986a) 59–67.

35. Dover (1988) 126–29.

36. Dover (1988) 128–29, and id., (1989) 198.

37. Apollodorus, *Bibliotheca* 3.5.5; Sergent (1986a) 67–70.

38. Hyginus, *Fabula* 9.

39. Sergent (1986b) 81–90 sees an Indo-European initiatory pattern of homosexual lover:beloved::tutor:initiate in this myth.

40. Sallares (1991) 166, 169–70.

41. Ibid. 172.

42. Ephorus *ap.* Strabo, *Geographica* 10.4.21 (483); Sergent (1986a) 7–8, 35.

43. Ephorus *ap.* Strabo, *Geog.* 10.4.20 (482); Plato, *Leges* 636 c–d (generally about Cretan custom of athletics and pederasty); Aristotle fr. 611.15; Dosiades, *FGH* 485 F 2; Nicolaus, *FGH* 90 F 103.

44. Dover (1988) 123.

45. Gortyn Code col. VII. 35ff.; Ar. Byz. *ap.* Eustathius 1592.58; R. F. Willetts, *Aristocratic Society in Ancient Crete* (London: Routledge and Paul, 1955) 11–12; re the age of the *dromeus*, see Percy (1996) 67. C. A. Forbes, *Greek Physical Education* (New York: Century, 1929) 44–53 gives a (mostly outdated) overview of Cretan physical education.

46. *IC* I.9.1 (Dreros); *IC* I.19.1.18 (Mallia); see W. Burkert (1985) 261 (= 1977, 392). On *ekdramein*, see D. D. Leitao, "The Perils of Leukippos: Initiatory Transvestism and Male Gender Ideology in the Ekdusia at Phaistos," *Classical Antiquity* 14 (1995) 134.

47. Ephorus *FGH* 70 F 149 *ap.* Strabo 10.482; see R. F. Willetts (1955) 8.

48. A. Stewart, *Art, Desire, and the Body in Ancient Greece* (Cambridge: Cambridge University Press, 1997) 240; see 28–29, where he suggests that the Dorians

may have introduced the custom of stripping for initiatory rituals on Crete, but this relies on the questionable theses of Bremmer, Sergent, and others. On the Ekdysia: Antoninus Liberalis 17; cf. Ovid, *Metamorphoses* 9.666–797; see M. P. Nilsson, *Griechische Feste von religiöser Bedeutung mit Ausschluss der Attischen* (Leipzig: B. G. Teubner, 1906; reprint, Darmstadt: Wissenschaftliche Buchgesellschaft, 1957) 370–71; W. Burkert (1985) 261 (= 1977, 392). Recently Leitao (1995) 130–63, has cited an eighth-century pederastic grafitto from Phaistos which may indicate an intiatory origin for this ritual in that era. And a find of bronzes from Kato Simi dated ca. 1000 B.C. depicting a boy and man together with erections and other male figures with a cup and hunting paraphernalia may allude to rituals of the type described by Ephorus: A. Lembesis, "A Sanctuary or Hermes and Aphrodite in Crete," *Expedition* 18 (1976) 2–13; A. Byrne, "The Greek Geometric Warrior Figure," *Archeologia Transatlantica* 10 (Louvain: Institut Superieuer d'Archeologie et d'Histoire de l'Art College Erasmus, 1991) 81–83. Even earlier evidence for male initiations on Crete has been seen in the famous "Chieftain Cup," dated ca. 1650–1500 B.C., from the palace at Ayia Triada: R. B. Koehl, "The Chieftain Cup and a Minoan Rite of Passage," *Journal of Hellenic Studies* 106 (1986) 99–110. Koehl suggests that the Cretan custom of communal men's dining, found also in Sparta, might have originated on Minoan Crete and was only later widely adopted by mainland Dorians. If this is correct, two observations can be made: a) an Indo-European origin of the custom of pederastic initiation is even less likely, and b) no archeological or other evidence from Crete indicates a continuity of athletic contests attached to these rituals. On the latter point Koehl (109–10, note 66) sees a possible connection of the bull-leaping and 'boxing' (if that is indeed what is depicted) on the Boxer Rhyton as part of the rituals associated with the initiation of a particular class of Minoan young men into adulthood," which "would form the background to the post-Bronze Age institution of athletic events as initiation rites." See my article, "Women, Bull Sports, Cults and Initiation in Minoan Crete," *Nikephoros* 12 (1999) 33–70. Percy (1996) 24–25 rightly questions Koehl's thesis of the continuity of Minoan with later Dorian rites of pederasty since the evidence (including the Chieftain Cup and the bronzes from Kato Simi) is too slim and ambiguous to be certain of institutionalized pederasty; the Dorian occupation and the devastation of the Dark Age make the continuity less likely. There are several other difficulties with a thesis of Minoan–later Cretan continuity in athletics: a) the assumption that later Greek athletic festivals have their origins in prehistoric initiation rites (argued against in this chapter), b) the fact that bull-leaping and the sort of boxing seen on the Boxer Rhyton and elsewhere in Minoan art seems to have disappeared after ca. 1300 B.C., and c) the fact that young women participated alongside young men in Minoan bull-leaping events whereas later Greek athletics was strictly segregated.

49. L. Moretti, *Olympionikai, i Vincitori negli Antichi Agoni Olimpici, MemLincei* ser. 8.8.2 (Rome: Accademia Nazionale dei Lincei, 1957) no. 590; (Akestorides) nos. 158, 181, 274, 296, 367b, 390/398; (same victor) nos. 752, and 906.

50. Mabel Lang, *Graffiti in the Athenian Agora* (Princeton: American School of Classical Studies at Athens, 1974) fig. 20. For the use of *katapugōn* as a common term of insult for the passive male homosexual, see E. Cantarella, *Bisexuality in the Ancient World*, trans. C. Ó Cuilleanáin (New Haven: Yale University Press, 1992) 46–48; J. Winkler, in *Before Sexuality: The Construction of Erotic Experience in the Ancient*

Greek World, ed. D. Halperin, J. J. Winkler, and F. I. Zeitlin (Princeton: Princeton University Press, 1990) 195 n. 73.

51. The Isthmian victor is a certain Alkon, mentioned in Simonides fr. 158 Bergk; see T. Klee, *Zur Geschichte der Gymnischen Agone an Griechischen Festen* (Leipzig: B. G. Teubner, 1918; reprint, Chicago: Ares, 1980) p. 95, no. 216.

52. Apart from a festival competition at Gortyn sponsored by the *koina Kretēs*, in which a herald and dramatic victor took part in the mid second century A.D., sources mention no other contest festivals, athletic or otherwise, on Crete. See L. Moretti, *Iscrizioni agonistiche greche* (Rome: Angelo Signorelli Editore, 1953) no. 74.

53. P. Brulé, *La Piraterie crétoise hellénistique* (Paris: Les Belles Lettres, 1978).

54. Finley (1982) 38. For an overview of Spartan education, see Marrou (1956) 14–25, though this dated treatment must be used cautiously; for a more recent and more reliable, scholarly treatment, see Kennell (1995). On Spartan athletics: S. Hodkinson, "An Agonistic Culture," in S. Hodkinson and A. Powell, eds., *Sparta: New Perspectives* (London: Duckworth, 1999) ch. 6, pp. 147–87.

55. Cartledge (1988) 404; see id., *Agesilaos and the Crisis of Sparta* (London: Duckworth, 1987) 25: the *agōgē* was "a mainly secular educational cycle with important religious elements."

56. Kennell (1995) 146; Cartledge (1988) 404 asserts that the Spartan social reorganization into hoplites was probably in the first half of the seventh century B.C. The *agōgē* subsequently underwent two revivals, one relatively short one under Cleomenes II in the 220s B.C., and a second one after 146 B.C. lasting to the fourth century A.D., and these archaizing renaissances of 'Lycurgan' tradition make it all the more difficult to discern which practices actually follow faithfully those of the sixth century; see P. A. Cartledge and A.J.S. Spawforth, *Hellenistic and Roman Sparta: A Tale of Two Cities* (London: Routledge, 1989) 207; Kennell (1995) 5–27. Vidal-Naquet (1986) 147 argues that the "sixth century revolution" of some accounts was "a complex process of innovation, transformation, and revival of features and institutions apparently transmitted from remote prehistory," without cogent evidence of the prehistoric elements. Percy (1996) 69–72, accepting too literally the claims of ancient sources, argues for a Cretan diffusion that resulted in the Spartan *agōgē*.

57. Kennell (1995) 135.

58. Xenophon, *Respublica Lacedaemoniorum* 2.12–14; Cartledge (1988) 405; C. Calame, *Choruses of Young Women in Ancient Greece: Their Morphology, Religious Role, and Social Functions*, trans. D. Collins and J. Orion (Lanham, Md.: Rowman & Littlefield, 1997) 7–8, 244–55, from the original *Les choeurs de jeunes filles en Grèce archaïque, I: Morphologie, fonction religieuse et sociale* [Rome: Ateneo & Bizzarri, 1977] 26–27, 420–36); Dover (1989) 179–82. Alcman and female homoeroticism: Cantarella (1992) 81–82; Alcman and female athletics: below, ch. 5, note 13.

59. Cartledge (1988) 406–7.

60. Kennell (1995) 125.

61. Kennell (1995) 125–30.

62. Plut., *Lycurgus* 17.1.

63. Plut., *Lyc.* 14.1–3; 15.1, 9–10; Aristotle, *Politics* 1270b1–7; see discussion of girls' parades in ch. 5. Kennell (1995) 134 discusses other remedies to the population problem involving the enrollment of noncitizens into the ephebic system.

64. Based on victories listed in Moretti (1957). Hodkinson (1999) 161–65, regarding the sharp decline in Spartan athletic victories between 600 and 580 B.C., attributes the decline mainly to increased participation by other states, notably western Greeks, in this period. While Hodkinson notes that the demands of the Spartan lifestyle may not have actually curbed the opportunities for participation, he does not consider the possiblity that Spartans may have deliberately shifted their time and energies more to local contests as part of their cultural 'revolution.'

65. See the story of the chariot victory of the Spartan woman, Cynisca, at Olympia in ca. 390 B.C., an achievement thought to exemplify wealth and not valor (*andragathia, aretē*), and Agesilaus' general disdain for hippic events (introduction to this volume); Xen., *Agesilaus* 9.6; Plut., *Agesilaus* 20.1; Cartledge (1987) 149–50.

66. Philostr., *De gymnastica* 9, see also 58; Plut., *Lyc.* 19.4, Plut., *Moralia* 189E, 228D (ca. A.D. 100); Seneca, *De beneficiis* 5.3.1 (first c. A.D.); M. Poliakoff, *Combat Sports in the Ancient World: Competition, Violence and Culture* (New Haven: Yale University Press, 1987) 100–2; Hodkinson (1999) 157–60. If the prohibition was indeed real rather than legendary, it was either not strictly enforced or it was rescinded in the early third century A.D., when we know of boxing and pankratiom as part of the program of the Euryclea festival at Sparta: Moretti (1953) nos. 79 and 84.

67. Moretti (1953) nos. 9, 16, and 18. Moretti's list is of course far from exhaustive, but a representative selection of the more substantial victor monuments available at the time of its publication. A more complete collection or database is badly needed, but Moretti's authoritative study is a useful cross-section of the better known local victors.

68. On the Parparonia, see Robertson (1992) 179–207. The Damonon inscription: Hodkinson (1999) 152–53.

69. Moretti (1953) no. 18; see Kennell (1995) 51–55, re the "Boys' Contests," though he argues that these events as later described were invented in the late second century B.C. If this hypothesis is correct, the nature of Arexippos' contest is uncertain.

70. Klee (1980) 76–108, depending on both literary and inscriptional sources. Hodkinson (1999) 161 notes that there are tens of fragments from Panathenaic amphorae dedications from Spartan sanctuaries, but of the few of these pubished, only equestrian events are in evidence.

71. Klee (1980) 117–20; the six lists are *IG* VII 414 (fourth c. Amphiaraia, Oropus); *IG* V 2.549ff. (fourth c. Lykaia); the Coan victor list (ca. 198 B.C., edited by Klee 1980); *IG* II 2.966ff. (the Panathenaia, second c. B.C.); *IG* IX 2.525ff (second–1st c. B.C. Eleutheria, Larissa); *IG* VII.416 (first c. B.C. Amphiaraia, Oropus).

72. Cartledge and Spawforth (1989) 232–33. Kennell (1995) 84–87 documents non-Spartans' cultural attraction to Sparta, including the *agōgē* and festivals during the Roman Empire.

73. Burkert (1985) 262–63 (= 1977, 393); W. G. Forrest, *A History of Sparta, 950–192 B.C.* (London: Hutchinson, 1980) 51–55.

74. Arist. fr. 611.10; Plut., *Lyc.* 28; *Cleomenes* 28; Kennell (1995) 74 notes that the isolation is also called the "fox time" (Hesychius, s.v *phouaxir*) and he describes it as " a liminal period in a rite of passage contained within the *agōgē*."

75. Paus. 3.16.10; Plut., *Lyc.* 18, *Aristides* 17; Statius, *Thebaid* 4.233; Xen., *Lac.* 2.9; Cic., *Tusc. Disp.* 2.34; see Kennell (1995) 77–78; H. J. Rose, "The Cult of Artemis

Orthia at Sparta," in *The Sanctuary of Artemis Orthia at Sparta, JHS Suppl.* 5, ed. R. M. Dawkins (London: Council of the British School at Athens, with Macmillan, 1929) 404ff.; S. Wide, *Lakonische Kulte* (Leipzig: B. G. Teubner, 1893) 99–100.

76. Kennell (1995) 79.

77. Nilsson (1957) 118–29; S. Wide (1893) 63–66, 73–87. Though the festival is considered by most to have been founded in the twenty-sixth Olympiad (Kennell [1995] 65), Robertson (1992) 164–65 argues that it is much older and was artificially attached to the floruit of the poet Terpander, allegedly the first victor at the Carneia. I see no reason not to accept the traditional dating.

78. *CIG* 1446; cf. Apollo Dromaios worshiped on Crete, Plut., *Quaestiones conviviales* 724C.

79. Kennell (1995) 56.

80. Sosibius, *Peri Charon, ap.* Ath. 14.635E; Africanus, *ap.* Euseb. I.198 Sch.; Kennell (1995) 67 argues that the *Staphylodromoi* had "no direct structural connection with the *agōgē* in the Roman period," yet the strict exclusion of married men suggests that, in broader terms at least, it symbolically associated the men of prenuptial status with the welfare of the state.

81. "Carneia of Zeus," Theopompus *ap.* Scholia in Theocritum 5.83; "Zeus Agetor," Xen., *Lac.* 13.2; see M. P. Nilsson (1957) 123.

82. M. P. Nilsson (1957) 406–7; Kennell (1995) 55–59.

83. M. P. Nilsson (1957) 407.

84. Many commentators take the name to mean "naked boys." Robertson (1992) 158 observes that the participants were not strictly "boys" (*paides*), however, but ephebes or youths; he therefore interprets the name to mean "naked sports," alluding to the Greek term *paidia*, a general term for children's leisure play or, generally, jesting in fun. The difficulty with the translation "naked sports" is that *paidia* never referred to "sports" or "athletics" in Greek vocabulary; that term was covered by *a(e)thla* or *agōnes*. Hence, the preference here for "naked playfulness," which describes the (strictly speaking) noncompetitive dances and performances of the youths at the festival.

85. Ath. 14.630C, 631B; 15.687C.

86. Robertson (1992) 148–49. As with the Carneia, Robertson seeks to place the foundation date of the Gymnopaedia much earlier than the traditional, historical date (in this case, 668/7): "The early dates were excogitated because the festivals had already been traced back to the remotest times, as a matter of local pride" (164–65). Again I find the argument unconvincing.

87. See Paus. 3.14.6 and *IG* 5.674–79; E. N. Gardiner, *Greek Athletic Sports and Festivals* (London: Macmillan, 1910) 185; id., *Athletics of the Ancient World* (Oxford: Clarendon Press, 1930; reprint, Chicago: Ares, 1980) 231; Forbes (1929) 21; M. N. Tod, "Teams of Ball-Players at Sparta," *ABSA* 10 (1903–1904) 63–77; id., "Three New *Sphaireïs*-Inscriptions," *ABSA* 13 (1906–1907) 212–18; A. M. Woodward, "Some Notes on the Spartan Sphaireis," *ABSA* 46 (1951) 191–99; Kennell (1995) 59–64.

88. Pollux 9.104–95; Luc., *Anach.* 38; M. Poliakoff, *Studies in the Terminology of Greek Combat Sports*, Beiträge zur Klassischen Philologie, vol. 146 (Königstein/Ts.: Anton Hain, 1982) 94.

89. Kennell (1995) 61–62.

90. *IG* 12, pt. 3.536–601 (esp. 536–49 with texts including possible pederastic expressions or epithets; the rest are simply names or dedications to divinities, esp. "[Apollo] Lykeios"); discussions in Sergent (1986b) 29–39; Calame (1997) 247 (= 1977, vol. I, 424–25); Y. Garlan and O. Masson, "Les acclamations pédérastiques de Kalami (Thasos)," *BCH* 106 (1982) 17, note 25; Félix Buffière, *Eros adolescent: La pédérastie dans la Grèce antique* (Paris: Les Belles Lettres. 1980) 57–59; Percy (1996) 31–32. Dover (1989) 195 says that the graffiti may go well back into the seventh century, "but the paucity of relevant evidence leaves much room for disagreement on their date."

91. Hiller von Gaertringen and P. Wilski, *Thera. Untersuchungen, Vermessungen und Ausgrabungen in den Jahren 1895–1902*, vol. 3, *Stadtgeschichte von Thera* (Berlin: G. Reimer, 1904) 66–70; Hiller von Gaertringen, *Thera. Untersuchungen, Vermessungen und Ausgrabungen in den Jahren 1895–1898*, vol. I, *Die Insel Thera in Altertum und Gegenwart mit Ausschluss der Nekroplen* (Berlin: G. Reimer, 1899) 289–96 (gymnasium).

92. Sergent (1986b) 35; see 29–39 generally on the graffiti; Bremmer (1980) 283.

93. David Bain, "Six Verbs of Sexual Congress (*binō, kinō, pugizō, lēkō, oiphō, laikazō*)," *CQ* 41 (1991) 72–74.

94. Dover (1988) 125–26. Cantarella (1992) 7–8 is not convincing in her argument that the inscriptions are "designed to celebrate completion of initiation ceremonies" on the basis of their sacred location, references to gods possibly in charge of education, and the precision of personal references.

95. Garlan and Masson (1982) 3–22.

96. Bain (1991) 73, notes 173–74.

97. Stephen G. Miller, *Nemea: A Guide to the Site and the Museum* (Berkeley: University of California Press, 1990) 36–37, 186–89.

98. J. Delorme, *Gymnasion: Étude sur les Monuments consacrés a l'Éducation en Grèce (des origines à l'Empire romain)* (Paris: de Boccard, 1960) 192, 326, and index, s.v. *graffiti*; Gardiner (1910) 494–96 (Priene).

99. Delorme (1960) 84, 395, note I. Contra the association of the Theran inscriptions both with sacred initiation and with athletics (though his arguments are not compelling): Marrou (1956) 367, note 10.

100. S. L. Glass, "The Greek Gymnasium: Some Problems," in W. Raschke (1988) 155–73.

101. Boasts of "first" were common in agonistic inscriptions: Moretti (1953) p. 151, no. 59, line 5, *prōton pantōn* (ca. 20 B.C.); J. Ebert, *Griechische Epigramme auf Sieger an Gymnischen und Hippischen Agonen* (Berlin: Akademie, 1972) p. 138, no. 43, line I, *prōtos . . . nikais* (beginning of fifth c. B.C.), and p. 188, no. 64, line 5, *pratistos* (third c. B.C.).

102. Dover (1988) 126, takes *Konialos* as a term for "penis," though this is more conjectural and loses the connection with dances found in Hesychius and in the inscriptions themselves. He also suggests that "dance" may be sexual slang, though this seems unlikely. The only parallel I can find is the distant one from Aristophanes' *Lysistrata* 409, *orchoumenēs*, "dancing/fornicating(?)," which may pun on *orcheis* (testicles): J. Henderson, *The Maculate Muse: Obscene Language in Attic Comedy* (New Haven: Yale University Press, 1975) 125.

103. Plato the Comedian, fr. *Phaon* 2.31; Strabo, *Geographica* 13.1.12.

104. Galen 12.283; Eustathius 590.10–14. See D. Sansone, *Greek Athletics and the Genesis of Sport* (Berkeley: University of California Press, 1988) 122–28 on the magical properties of scrapings from athletes using strigil-instruments after exercise; the mixtures were felt to contain the essence of the athlete's expenditure of energy.

105. D. F. Sutton, "Athletics in the Greek Satyr Play," *RSC* 23 (1975) 203–9.

106. It is noteworthy that in the Comic Plato, Konisalos is invoked "with his two comrades" (*parastatai*), reminiscent of the term *parastathentes* "comrades," used for the beloved in the Cretan practice of pederastic initiation and *paideia*, who were also honored guests at athletic contests (Ephorus *ap.* Strabo, *Geographica* 10.4.21; see note 42 of this ch.). Might the god originally have been a patron of pederastic relationships?

107. Burkert (1985) 263 (= 1977, 394); O. W. Reinmuth, *The Ephebic Inscriptions of the Fourth Century* B.C., Mnemosyne Suppl. 14 (Leiden: Brill, 1971), and review by D. Lewis, *CR* (1973) 254; id., "The Genesis of the Athenian Ephebia," *TAPA* 83 (1952) 34–50; C. Pélékidis, *Histoire de l'Ephébie Attique des Origines à 31 avant Jésus-Christ*, École Française d'Athènes, Travaux et Mémoires, vol. 13 (Paris: de Boccard, 1962). Generally on the role of the Athenian ephebe, see Vidal-Naquet (1986) 106–22.

108. C. Pélékidis (1962) 79.

109. See Poll. 8.105 and Stobaeus, *Florilegium* 43.48, who quote the oath.

110. Forbes (1929) 155–59.

111. Vidal-Naquet (1986) 98.

112. Two older, but still to some extent useful, surveys of the topic are Marrou (1956) 36–45 and Forbes (1929) 54–92.

113. Golden (1990) 62.

114. Kyle (1987) 64–77.

115. Sallares (1991) 176, quoting B. Bernardi, *Age Class Systems: Social Institutions and Polities Based on Age* (Cambridge: Cambridge University Press, 1985) 28; see Sallares 175 re Solon.

116. Re Arrephorai, cf. Burkert (this ch., note 8, 1966) 1–25; Brelich (1962) 105. Re the Panathenaic *lampadēdromia*, cf. H. J. Rose, "The Greek Agones," *Aberystwyth Studies* 3 (1922) 12–13; Brelich (1969) 104–5. N. Robertson, in *Worshipping Athena: Panathenaia and Parthenon*, ed. J. Neils (Madison: University of Wisconsin Press, 1996) 56–65 does not find initiatory origins but sees a likely Bronze Age origin for the unusual military events (a *pyrrichē* dance and the *apobatēs* race of a rider dismounting his chariot) of the Panathenaia and a later, sixth-century date for the addition of the torch race to the festival program. Robertson (60–63) also argues against the initiatory character of the Arrephoria.

117. Kyle (1987) 42.

118. D. Kyle, "Solon and Athletics," *Ancient World* 9 (1984) 99–102.

119. Sergent (1993) 154.

120. Dover (1989) 54–55; Kyle (1987) 65, note 51; Golden (1990) 56–72.

121. Alain Schnapp, "Eros the Hunter," in *A City of Images: Iconography and Society in Ancient Greece*, ed. C. Bérard et al., trans. D. Lyons (Princeton: Princeton University Press, 1990) 71–87 (orig. *La cité des images* [Paris: F. Nathan, 1984]).

122. Vidal-Naquet (1986) 119.

123. This universal influence of hunting practices on sports do not, however, require that we accept the thesis of Sansone (1988), who sees the origin of most Greek customs in primitive hunting ritual. Even if Sansone is correct, the 'traces' that he posits are not shown to be conscious reflections of hunting in Greek historical culture, which is our concern here.

124. J. K. Anderson, *Hunting in the Ancient World* (Berkeley: University of California Press, 1985); "Perhaps the establishment of Athenian democracy after the expulsion of Hippias, son of Peisistratus, in 510 B.C., had something to do with the disappearance of an aristocratic sport [sc., hunting], but the end seems to come gradually, since at least one of these hunting sketches should probably be dated to the early years of the democratic government."

125. H. A. Shapiro, "Courtship Scenes in Attic Vase-Painting" *AJA* 85.2 (1981) 133–43; see also Bremmer (1980).

126. Shapiro (1981) 142.

127. Plut., *Solon* 1.7; Paus. 1.30.1; Ath. 609d; Sergent (1986b) 116–19; Robertson (1992) 105–8; Robertson, in Neils (1996) 64–65.

128. Aristodemus *FGH* 383 F 9; Demon *FGH* 327 F 6; Proclus *Chrestomathia, ap.* Photius *Bibliotheca* Cod. 239 (p.322a; V 165–166 Henry); Schol. Nicander *Alexipharmaca* 109a (pp.65f. Geymonat); Hsch., s.v. *Oschophoria* (IV.333 Scmidt); *Anecdota Bekker* 285 and 318. See E. Kadletz, "The Race and Procession of the Athenian *Oschophoroi*," *GRBS* 21(1980) 363–71; L. Deubner, *Attische Feste* (Berlin: Heinrich Keller, 1932; reprint, Darmstadt: Wissenschaftliche Buchgesellschaft, 1956) 142–47; H. W. Parke, *Festivals of the Athenians* (London: Thames and Hudson, 1977; reprint, Ithaca: Cornell University Press, 1986) 77–80; E. Simon, in Neils (1996) 19–21, re the associations with Theseus; Jeanmaire (1939) 347 briefly mentions the initiatory character of the Oschophoria. Robertson (1992) 120–33 sees the race as an event separate from, though ritually connected with the Oschophoria, since both relate ritually to the legend of Theseus' departure for and return from Crete. If he is correct, he does not contradict my thesis under discussion, which requires only that both events are rituals connected through Theseus. See Kyle (1987) 47–48.

129. A. Walde and J. Pokorny, *Vergleichendes Wörterbuch der Indogermanischen Sprachen*, vol. I (Berlin and Leipzig: W. de Gruyter, 1930; reprint, Berlin: W. de Gruyter, 1973) 185.

130. Henderson (1975) 125. See Nicander, *Alexi.* 109, where the two words are played upon.

131. Kadletz (1980) 370.

132. Henry J. Walker, *Theseus and Athens* (Oxford: Oxford University Press, 1995) 98–101 points out the strongly initiatory aspects of the Oschophoria and attendant race, namely its progression from sexual ambiguity of the transvestites to the ritual at the 'marginal' locus of Phaleron, and finally a return of the youths to become adults; he concludes, "[T]he Oschophoria is clearly a festival of initiation." See also Leitao (1995) 148–49.

133. Aeschin. [*In Tim.*] 9–12; Plato, *Lysis* 206d–e with Schol.; *IG* II² 2980 (early second c. B.C., torch race), 2971(? late fourth c., chariot race); Deubner (1956) 217.

134. Kyle (1984) 101–102.

135. G. Costa, "Hermes dio delle iniziazione," *Civiltà classical e cristiana* 3 (1982) 277–95.

136. Kyle (1987) 32–48.

137. Ibid. 226, appendix B P109.

138. Kyle (1987) appendix A nos. 1, 2, 7, 9, 12, 17, 18, 23, 41, 48, 50, 52, 54, 61, 67, 72, 75; all of these fall within the dates of 468–338 B.C.

139. Based on Klee (1980); the victor is Menodorus, no. 218.

140. The Athenian Panhellenic victories pre-322 B.C. are found in Kyle (1987) appendix A, nos. 1, 3, 4, 15, 17, 18, 29, 30, 42, 43, 45, 57, 58, 64, 71, 74, 78, 86, 96; later ones are noted in Moretti (1957) no. 826 for Athenaios (?), a victor in the Pythian, Nemean, and Isthmian Games ca. A.D. 93 and in Klee (1980) nos. 218, 219, 220 for Menodorus, a victor at Nemea three times ca. 150 B.C., once in boy's wrestling, once in men's wrestling, and once in men's pankratiom.

141. *IG* 8 414; Klee (1980) 117. Oropus was under the control of Athens from 338 to 322, i.e., the period after Philip II's defeat of Thebes until the period after the Lamian War.

142. Date of *IG* 8 414: Klee (1980) 29–32. Date of Ephebeia: Reinmuth (1971) and Pélékidis (1962). Athenian victors are notable by their absence in the first century B.C. victor inscriptions from the Amphiaraia festival: *IG* VII 416, 417, and 420, dating from ca. 80–60 B.C. In these lists, the strong presence of Boeotian and Spartan victors, entirely absent from the fourth-century list but now comprising respectively fifteen and eight of the fifty-two total victors, reminds us that politics was also a determinant in the representation of particular city-states in local festivals.

143. Kyle (1987) 215 no. A77, citing Xen., *Hellenica* 4.1.40 and Plut., *Ages.* 13.3.

144. Sergent (1986a) 67–70, 143–73; id., (1986b) 139; Percy (1996) 133–35. For the poorly attested athletic education at Thebes, see the (somewhat outdated) overview of Forbes (1929) 182–85; for the Erotidaea, a (Hellenistic?) athletic festival at Thebes in honor of Eros, see ch. 8, note 209.

145. Paus. 9.23.1; see Calame (1997) 246–47 (= 1977, vol. 1, 423–24).

146. Iolaus as squire and beloved: Plut., *Amatorius* 761D; id., *Pelopidas* 18.5. Pindar on tomb: *Ol.* 9.98–99. See Sergent (1986a) 143.

147. Palaimonion: Paus. 2.2.1; E. R. Gebhard, "The Early Stadium at Isthmia and the Founding of the Isthmian Games," in *Proceedings of an International Symposium on the Olympic Games, 5–9 September 1988,* ed. W. Coulson and H. Kyrieleis (Athens: Luci Braggiotti Publications for the Deutsches Archäologisches Institut Athen, 1992) 73–79; id., in *Greek Sanctuaries: New Approaches,* ed. N. Marinatos and R. Hägg (London and New York: Routledge, 1993) 154–77. Pelopion: Paus. 5.13; A. Mallwitz, *Olympia und seine Bauten* (Athens: S. Kasas, 1981) 133–37. Generally: Jorge Jose Bravo, *The Hero Cults of the Panhellenic Sanctuaries: The State of the Archaeological Evidence at Olympia, Delphi, Isthmia, and Nemea* (Ph.D. diss., University of California, Berkeley, 1996).

148. T. Gantz, *Early Greek Myth: A Guide to Literary and Artistic Sources* (Baltimore: Johns Hopkins University Press, 1993) 192–93.

149. A. Schachter, *Cults of Boiotia,* vol. 1, Acheloos to Hera, University of London, Institute of Classical Studies Bulletin Supplement no. 38.1 (London: University of London, Institute of Classical Studies, 1981 [1994]) 2.17–18, 64–65; Gantz (1993) 464–65.

150. Plut., *Mor.* 761D; id., *Pelop.* 18.4 (= Arist. fr. 97 [Rose]).

151. Sergent (1986a) 151 compares the Theran graffiti to the oaths to Iolaus by describing both not as "oaths of loyalty" but declarations to the gods that the homosexual "ritual" was completed—in my view too serious an interpretation of the informal Theran texts.

152. Nilsson (1957) 446–47; Percy (1996) 134.

153. Diodorus 4.24.4–6 (trans. A. Goldhammer, Loeb); see Sergent (1986b) 62–63.

154. Arist., *Pol.* 2.9.6 (1274a); Sergent (1986a) 167–73, who improbably identifies Diocles as an 'alter ego' of Heracles and takes the name Philolaus to mean "army of friends" (it is more likely "lover of the people"), both supposedly associated with "a very ancient collection of Theban legends associated with initiation ritual of a military and homosexual character."

155. Theocritus 12.27–38.

156. Moretti (1957) no. 13.

157. Homeric epic as a reflection of contemporary culture: M. I. Finley, *The World of Odysseus*, 2nd ed. (New York: Viking, 1978); C. Renfrew, "Minoan-Mycenaean Origins of the Panhellenic Games," in W. Raschke (1988) 13–25. Homeric pederasty and initiation: Dover (1988) 128–31. Homeric education: Marrou (1956) 1–13. The 'world of Homer' generally: see the recent overview in R. Osborne, *Greece in the Making: 1200–479 B.C.* (London: Routledge, 1996) 137–60 and 367–68.

158. L. Roller, "Funeral Games in Greek Art," *AJA* 85 (1981a) 107–19; id., "Funeral Games for Historical Persons," *Stadion* 7 (1981b) 1–18. For a recent, general survey of seventh-century Greek culture, see Osborne (1996) 161–214.

159. Hoplites, polis, and athletics: H. W. Pleket, "Zur Soziologie des antiken Sports," *Mededelingen Nederlands Historisch Instituut te Rome* 36 (1974) 57–87; Delorme (1960) *passim*; Golden, (1998) 25–27.

160. M. McDonnell, "The Introduction of Athletic Nudity: Thucydides, Plato, and the Vases," *JHS* 111 (1991) 182–93.

Chapter 4

This chapter is a revised and updated version of an article originally published as "The Footrace of the Heraia at Olympia," *Ancient World* 9 (1984) 77–90.

1. The most important studies are G. Arrigoni, "Correre per Hera," in G. Arregoni, ed., *Le donne in Grecia* (Rome: Laterza, 1985) 95–100; Angeli Bernardini, "Aspects ludiques, rituels et sportifs de la course feminine dans la Grèce antique," *Stadion* 12–13 (1986–87) 17–26, esp. 20–21; N. Serwint, "The Iconography of the Ancient Female Runner," *AJA* 97 (1993) 403–22.

2. E. Mehl, "Mutterliche Reste in der Olympischen Festordnung," in *Festschrift Carl Diem*, ed. W. Körbs, H. Mies, and K. C. Wildt (Frankfurt: W. Limpert, 1962) 71–81; O. von Vacano, Über Mädchensport in Griechenland" in *Das Problem des alten Zeustempels in Olympia* (Naumburg [Salle]: Lippert, 1937) suppl. "51–58; K. Zeigler, s.v. "Heraia," *RE* 8, 407–18; L. Weniger, "Das Hochfest des Zeus in Olympia II," *Klio* 5 (1905) 1–38, esp. 22–28; id., "Vom Ursprunge der olympischen Spiele," *RM* 72 (1917–18) 4–5.

3. H. Jeanmaire, *Dionysos: Histoire du culte de Bacchus* (Paris: Payot, 1951) 216.

4. For Dionysus cults linked to girls' contests in Sparta and Elis, see ch. 9, note 65.

5. Weniger (1905) 30.

6. M. P. Nilsson, *Grieschische Feste von religiöser Bedeutung mit Ausschluß der attischen* (Leipzig and Berlin: B. G. Teubner, 1906; reprint, Darmstadt: Wissenschaftliche Buchgesellschaft, 1957) 62–63.

7. Hesychius s.v. "Ergastinai": Suda χαλχεῖα 35; *Etymologicum Magnum* 805 .43; W. Dittenberger, *Sylloge inscriptionym Graecarum*[3] (Leipzig: S. Hirzel, 1915–24) 718; see H. W. Parke, *Festivals of the Athenians* (London: Thames and Hudson, 1977; reprint, Ithaca: Cornell University Press, 1986) 38.

8. C. Sourvinou-Inwood, *'Reading' Greek Culture: Texts and Images, Rituals and Myths* (Oxford: Oxford University Press, 1991) 168; Arrigoni (1985) 97 and 192, note 162.

9. If the Heraia occurred on the same year and within one month of the Olympics, as Weniger argues, the mandatory ten-month training period for Olympic contestants would have occurred about the same time as the weaving of the *peplos* (Paus. 5.24.9). Cf. Weniger (1905) 25; L. Drees, *Olympia: Gods, Artists, and Athletes*, trans. G. Onn (New York: Praeger, 1968) 43 (training period).

10. Parke, (1977) 33 and note 9. E. N. Gardiner, *Olympia: Its History and Remains* (Oxford: Clarendon, 1925; reprint, Washington, D.C.: McGrath, 1973) 215, improbably suggests that the *peplos* custom may have been instituted on analogy with the Panathenaia in 420 B.C. when Athens, Argos, and Elis formed an alliance, but he admits that there is no evidence for this supposition.

11. M. P. Nilsson, *The Minoan-Mycenaean Religion and Its Survival in Greek Religion*, 2nd ed. (Lund: C.W.K. Gleerup, 1968) 311; Elizabeth W. Barber, *Women's Work, The First Thousand Years: Women, Cloth, and Society in Early Times* (New York: Norton, 1994) 110–17, 283.

12. B. Lavagnini, *Aglaia. Nuova antologia della lirica Greca da Callino a Bacchilide* (Torino: G. B. Paravia, 1938) 126.

13. The interpretations of the crucial words φάρος, taken as "robe" or "plough," and Ὀρθρίαι, which most scholars take as a reference to "Orthia," are disputed. D. Page, *Alcman: The Parthenion* (Oxford: Clarendon, 1951) 71–79; C. Calame, *Les choeurs de jeunes filles en Grèce archaïque, vol. II: Alcman* (Rome: Ateneo & Bizzarri, 1977) 120–33. The footrace of the Dionysiades is discussed further in ch. 5 below.

14. Weniger (1905) 30, argues for the priority of the Heraian stade, since the later lengthening eastward displaced the temenos of Chamynaia—an unprovable test. D. Romano, "The Ancient Stadium: Athletes and Arete," *Ancient World* (1983) 13–14 suggests that the difference in length corresponds to the difference between 600 shorter "Temple of Hera" feet and 600 "Temple of Zeus" feet. This thesis does not help us decide on the priority of one or the other.

15. See ch. 6 on the Arkteia. On age classes at Sparta: H. Michell, *Sparta* (Cambridge: Cambridge University Press, 1952).

16. See ch. 5.

17. London, British Museum 208, from Prisrend (?), Albania (ancient Epirus), ancient Greek bronze statuette, left leg restored, dated to ca. 580 B.C.; Arrigoni (1985) tab. 3 and commentary and bibliography, 157.

18. Rome, Vatican City, Vatican Museum Galleria dei Candellabri, XXXIV.36.1, inv. no. 2784. N. Serwint (1993) very convincingly argues the dating on the basis of parallels with the so-called "Charioteer of Motya"; see also A. S. Giammellaro, "Eine Marmorstatue aus Mozia (Sizilien)," *Antike Welt* 16 (1985) 16–22. Former opinion had been that the piece was a classicizing work of the South Italian School of Pasiteles (first century B.C.): see G. Lippold, *Die Skulpturen des vaticanischen Museum*, 3.2 (Berlin: Walter De Gruyter, 1956) 370–74, no. 3, pls. 161–62; W. Helbig, *Führer durch die öffentlichen Sammlungen klassischer Altertümer in Rom*, ed. H. Speier, 4 vols. (Tübingen: E. Wasmuth, 1963–72⁴) 2:558; E. Q. Visconti, *Musée Pie-Clementin* III (Milan: I. P. Giegler, 1818) pl. 27; B. Schröder, "Die vaticanische Wettläuferin," *RM* 24 (1909) 109–20, figs. 1–3; B. Ridgway, *The Severe Style in Greek Sculpture* (Princeton: Princeton University Press, 1970), 136, note 8 and 143, note 3. Serwint also convincingly argues that the victor statue did authentically derive from the Heraia at Olympia on its close correspondence with Pausanias' description. See also Arrigoni (1985) table 6 and pp. 159–60 with commentary and bibliography.

19. Athens, National Museum, Collection Carapanos no. 24, bronze statuette from Dodona (ancient Epirus), Greece; Arrigoni (1985) table 2 and p. 156; E. Langlotz, *Frühgriechische Bilderhauerschulen* (Nuernberg: E. Frommann, 1927; reprint, Rome: "L'Erma" di Bretschneider, 1967) 48a (London, BM 208) and pl. 48b.

20. Sparta Museum 3305; C. Chrestou, *Archaia Spartē: syntomos hodēgos gia tēn historia, ta mnēmia kai tou mouseiou tēs* (Sparta: n.p., 1960) 112 fig. 33r; Arrigoni (1985) 158, on table 4 (b), but without photograph, and I have not seen a photo of this object.

21. Palermo, Museo Nazionale, inv. no. 8265 (42), of unknown provenance, possibly from Tarantum or Paestum, Italian bronze statuette. See for Silaris comparison, P. Zancani Montuoro and U. Zanotti-Bianco, ch. 31, "Leucippidi," in *Heraion alla Foce del Sele*, vol. 2 (Rome: Libreria dello Stato, 1964) 341–48, fig. 86; Arrigoni (1985) table 5 and pp. 158–59, suggests that the piece is of Italian workmanship and reflects a local interest in the customs of Spartan girl athletes.

22. See ch. 5. Yet another bronze figurine, now in the Delphi museum, preserves only the upper half of a girl dressed in Spartan costume and, according to commentators, apparently in a running pose. This does not seem convincing to me, largely in view of the position of the arms akimbo at the sides and the hands held in fists slightly in front of the waist. I know of no other runner so depicted. The Delphi girl rather appears to be in a dance position.

23. See ch. 7.

24. Gardiner (1973) 48–51 sees clear parallels between the cults of Olympia and Dodona, possibly due to very early migrations from Epirus to Elis.

25. The possibility of other festivals with footraces for girls should not be dismissed; the Heraia and Dionysiades, for instance, are known by chance preservation in only one source each. There might have been, for instance, girls' footraces among the competitions at the Naïa festival at Dodona in honor of both Zeus and Dione: see Nilsson (1957) 32 and note 1. The sites of Paestum and Tarentum were Dorian in origin and might also have copied (or simply admired) the Spartan custom of physical education or athletic contests for girls. In South Italy, Sybaris also had games for Hera, but no contests for girls are mentioned: Aelian, *Varia Historia* 3.43; Nilsson (1957) 64.

26. See especially the imagery of the Arkteia of Attica, discussed in ch. 6.

27. The gesture is not on the Vatican statue, but this may be due to the difficulties of carving in marble such a fragile arc of a left hand lifting the hem of the garment.

28. Attic white-figure lekythos, Cleveland Museum 66.114, ca. 500–490 B.C. showing Atalanta surrounded by three Erotes; Attic red-figure kylix, Paris, Louvre, CA 2259, from Kertsch, ca. 470–450 B.C. See A. Ley, "Atalante—Von der Athletin zu Liebhaberin: Ein Beitrag zum Rezeptionswandel eines mythologischen Themas auf Vasen des 6.–4. Jhs. v. Chr.," *Nikephoros* 3 (1990) 46–49 and fig. 13.

29. Plut., *Lyc.* 14–15 (Sparta); L. G. Kahil, "Autour de l'Artémis attique," *AntK* 8 (1965) 20–33 and pls. 7–10, esp. pls. 7.3, 5; 8.7 (Brauron); see chs. 5 and 6 of this volume.

30. W. Burkert, *Greek Religion*, trans. J. Raffan (Cambridge, Mass.: Harvard University Press, 1985) 261 (from the original *Griechische Religion der Archaïschen und Klassichen Epoche* [Stuttgart: W. Kohlhammer, 1977] 392) on the Cretan feast of *Ekdysia*, the "undressing."

31. See ch. 6 and Kahil (1965), pls. 7.2, 7.4, 7.6, 8.1–3; and id., "L' Artémis de Brauron: rites et mystère," *AntK* 20 (1977) fig. A., pl. 18.

32. Serwint (1993); see also N. Serwint, Greek *Athletic Sculpture from the Fifth and Fourth Centuries* B.C.: *An Iconographic Study* (Ph.D. diss., Princeton University, 1987) 420–62.

33. P. E. Arias (text and notes), M. Hirmer (photos), and B. B. Shefton (translation and revision), *A History of Greek Vase Painting* (London: Thames and Hudson, 1962), pl. 230: *krater* showing Artemis with Dionysus, maenads, and satyr ca. 410 B.C. Tarentum. On the Brauron costume, see ch. 6.

34. D. von Bothmer, *Amazons in Greek Art* (Oxford: Clarendon, 1957) pp. 122–23, nos. 8–9, Athens 6589, 6622, 6624, and 13230.

35. Ibid. 216–22, pl. 89; B. Ridgway, "A Story of Five Amazons," *AJA* 78 (1974) 1–17, pls. 1–4. Although the Lansdowne has its left, and not the right, breast exposed, it might still have been inspired by the "spirit" of the Heraia costume, with alterations for aesthetic reasons.

36. A. Brelich, *Paides et Parthenoi*, vol. 1, Incunabula Greca vol. 36 (Rome: Ateneo, 1969) 31, 72, note 60; Burkert (1985) 260–64 (= 1977, 390–95).

37. P. Vidal-Naquet, *The Black Hunter*, trans. A. Szegedy-Maszak (Baltimore: Johns Hopkins University Press, 1986) 116–17; M. Eliade, *Rites and Symbols of Initiation*, trans. W. R. Trask (New York: Harper, 1975) 26. See discussion of the questions of transvestism in D. D. Leitao, "The Perils of Leukippos: Initiatory Transvestism and Male Gender Ideology in the Ekdusia at Phaistos," *Classical Antiquity* 14 (1995) 130–63, esp. 136–42. Leitao (162–63) notes that marriage ceremonies were often an occasion for gender differentiation and transvestism, and the custom of Spartan brides in male clothing may serve as a device to ease the anxiety of the bridegroom who was more accustomed to the company of males. The evidence of the prenuptial transvestism in the Heraia suggests rather that the Heraian and Spartan customs were meant to introduce girls to the "other" and perhaps ease their anxieties as well as those of the boys.

38. See the discussion of athletic nudity in ch. 8, note 27.

39. Re the earliest stadium at Olympia, see A. Mallwitz, "Cult and Competition Locations at Olympia," in *The Archaeology of the Olympics: The Olympics and Other*

Festivals in Antiquity, ed. W. Raschke (Madison: University of Wisconsin, 1988) 79–109, who places it closer than later stadia to the probable location of the Altar or Zeus. See also earlier discussions by H.-V. Herrmann, *Olympia: Heiligtum und Wettkampfstatte* (Munich: Hirmer, 1972) 106 and notes 418, 419 with bibliography; Drees, (1968) 88.

40. Weniger (1905).

41. Ibid. 5–6.

42. See ch. 6 and Kahil, (1965) pls. 7.2, 7.4, 7.6, 8.1–3, 10.6–7.

43. Paus. 5.14.8, 5.8.1; W. Dörpfeld, *Alt-Olympia*, vol. 1 (Berlin: E. S. Mitter, 1935) 186–87; Herrmann, (1972) 67–68 and note 237.

44. Bull for Zeus: Dio Chrysostom, *Or.* 12.51; Ath. 412–13a (Milo's bull); Phylarchos, *FGH* 81 F 3. Cf. W. Burkert, *Homo Necans: The Anthropology of Ancient Greek Sacrificial Ritual and Myth* (Berkeley: University of California Press, 1983) 141 and note 22; Gardiner, *Greek Athletic Sports and Festivals* (London: Macmillan, 1910) 194–207; Paus. 5.9.3. Prizes on the last (16th) day: Schol. Pind., *Ol.* 5.8. Meal: Paus. 5.15.12.

45. Paus. 5.15.3; Phlegon, *FGH* II B257 F1, 10–11; Theophrastus, *Historia Plantarum* 4.13.2; Herrmann (1972) 32–35 and note 108.

46. Herrmann, (1972) 34 and note 113.

47. Ibid. 35.

48. Burkert (1985) 39–41; 85–86 (= 1977, 76–78; 144–45). See, however, the thesis of Joan V. O'Brien, *The Transformation of Hera: A Study of Ritual, Hero, and the Goddess in the Iliad* (Boston: Rowman & Littlefield, 1993), esp. ch. 6 and appendix. O'Brien suggests that the custom of putting portraits of victors on the columns of the temple of Hera at Olympia goes back to the same original "tree cult" evidenced by the statuette of nymphs dancing in a circle. The thesis is original and attempts to reconcile much disparate evidence on Hera the literary figure and divinity of cults; the results vary in cogency.

49. Herrmann (1972) 95, fig. 62; Dörpfeld, (1935), vol. 1, 170–71, fig. 40–41.

50. Arrigoni (1985) 98 and 192, note 170 cites the case of the Spartan woman, Euryleonis, whose portrait (εἰκών) was set up on the Spartan acropolis, yet this was not done at the sanctuary where the race was held.

51. L. Moretti, *Iscrizioni Agonistiche Greche* (Rome: Angelo Signorelli, 1953) 40–44 and note 17.

52. Paus. 6.18.7; see Drees (1968) 104–5.

53. I. Weiler, *Der Agon im Mythos: Zur Einstellung der Griechen zum Wettkampf*, Impulse der Forschung, vol. 16 (Darmstadt: Wissenschaftliche Buchgesellschaft, 1974) 202–3.

54. Bethe, *RE* III (1899) 2348–49.

55. Paus 2.21.9; J. G. Frazer, *Pausanias's Description of Greece*, vol. 3 (London: Macmillan, 1913) 200–201 with further bibliography.

56. Strabo 8.4.4; Paus. 6.21.18; 10.5.7; N. Kaldis-Henderson, *A Study of Women in Ancient Elis* (Ph.D. diss., University of Minnesota, 1979) 328–30.

57. See also the discussion by Arrigoni (1985) 157.

58. See Paus. 3.13.7 and ch. 5.

59. Weniger, (1917–18) 4–5; id., (1905) 25–28.

60. S. Miller, "The Date of Olympic Festivals," *MDAI(A)* 90 (1965) 215–31.

61. C. Ulf and I. Weiler, "Der Ursprung der antiken Olympischen Spiele in der Forschung," *Stadion* 6 (1981) 1–38, presents a fair and open-ended treatment of scholarship on the origins of the Olympics with full bibliography.

62. H. A. Harris, *Greek Athletes and Athletics* (London: Hutchinson, 1964) 179–80.

63. Phleg., *FGH* 2.B.257.1; Paus. 5.8.2; Eus., *Chron.* I. col. 192 [Shoene].

64. Herrmann, (1972) 70 and note 254; cf. L. Weniger, "Der Artemisdienst in Olympia und Umgebung," *N.Jb.Kl.Alt.* 19 (1907) 96ff.

65. See ch. 6 and C. Calame, *Choruses of Young Women in Ancient Greece: Their Morphology, Religious Role, and Social Functions*, trans. D. Collins and J. Orion (Lanham, Md.: Rowman & Littlefield, 1997) 115–16, from the original *Les choeurs de jeunes filles en Grèce archaïque, vol. I: Morphologie, fonction religieuse et sociale* [Rome: Ateneo & Bizzarri, 1977a], 212–14). For a speculative interpretation of the races as part of a fertility ritual leading to a *hieros gamos*, see L. Drees, *Der Ursprung der olympischen Spiele* (Stuttgart: K. Hofmann, 1962) 86–92. Drees identifies Hera as a "Magna Mater" who displaced an earlier form of Hippodomeia ca. 1200–900 B.C. with the advent of the Indo-Europeans.

66. Tenth century for earliest Olympia cults: C. Morgan, *Athletes and Oracles: The Transformation of Olympia and Delphi in the Eighth Century* B.C. (Cambridge: Cambridge University Press, 1990) 22, 41–43, 47–49; eleventh-century foundation of cults at Olympia: H.-V. Herrmann, "Zur ältesten Geschichte von Olympia," *MDAI(A)* 77 (1962) 3–34; id., "Olympia und seine Spiele im Wandel der Zeiten," *Gymnasium* 80 (1973) 180; id. (1972) 36 and 69. H. Lee, "The 'First' Olympic Games of 776 B.C.," in Raschke (1988) 111, notes that some of the numerous tripods found at Olympia and dating 1000 B.C. to the seventh century B.C. may have been votive offerings by victors in athletic contests held at Olympia before 776 B.C.

67. A. Mallwitz, *Olympia und seine Bauten* (Athens: S. Kasas, 1981) 138.

68. O'Brien (1993) 192–201. Cf. the same identification made (with less justification) by Drees (1968) 15. O'Brien notes the paucity of Mycenaean remains at Olympia, the absence of any mention of Olympia in the Homeric epics, and the tradition of chariot races at Bouprasion in Elis as mentioned in *Iliad* 11.697–701, 758–59, and 23.629–42. From these observations and from the apparent associations of Hera with horses and four-horse chariots in the *Iliad*, O'Brien postulates the existence of festival races in honor of Hera at Bouprasion which were the model for the later Olympic festival for Zeus. Some of these associations are problematic, for instance the fact that Poseidon and even Athena were much more associated with horses than was Hera, and that the Bouprasion Games were not cyclical, but funeral games for an Epeian king. Yet the suggestions that Hera's worship was important in the Mycenaean era and that the Bouprasion Games may have inspired the later ones at Olympia are worth serious consideration. Funeral games are frequently associated with the origins of games that were formalized and made cyclical. Hippodameia is to be closely associated with Hera, if not totally identified with her. Her tomb and cult were at Midea in the Argolid, territory associated with both Hera and Pelops (Paus. 2.25.9). On Hera as a Mycenaean goddess whose epithet "Hippodameia," literally "Horse-tamer," was later transferred to a local heroine, see O'Brien (192–201) for further discussion of Hera's role as Hera Teleia, "the fulfiller," in bringing to completion the life-cycles of young women, *and* young men, in marriage or in death.

69. Herrmann, (1972) 69 and note 241.

70. Mallwitz in Raschke (1988) 86 puts the earliest temple of Hera at 600 B.C. with some earlier slab installation beneath it dating to the first half of the seventh century.

71. Herrmann, (1972) 62–65.

72. Mallwitz (1981) 133–37 denies, on good archaeological evidence, that a "mound" of any height was ever built within the circle. Yet a sacred area for earlier heroes need not contain a "mound," nor even a real grave. Nor do I find compelling Mallwitz's total dismissal of Dörpfeld's stone circle, which constituted the supposed Pelopion I. The clear curve of the excavated section and its close correspondence to the area of the fourth-century B.C. Pelopion argue for its identity as a true "sacred area." H. V. Herrmann, "Pelops in Olympia," in: *Stēlē: Tomos eis Mnēmēn tou Nikolaou Kontoleōnos* (Athens: Sōmateio Hoi Philoi tou Nikolaou Kontoleōntos, 1980) 59–74 argues for an earlier Pelops cult.

73. On Lerna: N.G.L. Hammond, *A History of Greece to 322 B.C.*, 3rd ed. (Oxford: Clarendon, and New York: Oxford University Press, 1986) 38. On grave circles: W. Taylour, *The Mycenaeans* (London: Thames and Hudson, 1983) 65–69.

74. Gardiner (1973) 27–28; A. Snodgrass, *Archaic Greece: The Age of Experiment* (London: J. M. Dent, 1980) 59–60.

75. Gardiner (1973) 273; Mallwitz (1981) 235–40.

76. Gardiner (1973) 28–34.

77. Drees (1962) 13–16.

78. Ibid. 124; Mallwitz (1981) 79, 199, and 298, note 100. On the presence of prehistoric female cults, and an oracle of Gaia, see ch. 1, notes 33–35.

79. ὕστερον δὲ καὶ τὸν ἀγῶνα ἐπετράπησαν ὑπ' αὐτῶν θεῖναι τὰ Ἡραῖα καὶ ὑφήνασθαι τῇ Ἥρᾳ τὸν πέπλον (Paus. 5.16.6). Τίθημι is the verb regularly used as the verb meaning either to "institute" or "manage" games (ἀγῶνας). "Management" seems a more likely translation, since Pausanias used a more precise phrase (διαθεῖναι πρώτην) earlier to describe the inauguration of the games by Hippodameia, and since he states that the alternate story of origin refers specifically to the institution of the Sixteen Women and not to the games themselves, which may have had an earlier origin. (*LSJ*, 2nd ed., s.v. τίθημι VI. citing Aeschylus, *Agamemnon* 845; Xen., *Anabasis* 1.2.10; *Fouilles de Delphes*, vol. 3, *Epigraphie* fascicle 3, ed. G. Daux and A. Salac (Paris: de Boccard, 1932) no. 120, line 17 (second cent. B.C.); Pind., *Ol.* 3.21).

80. Strabo, *Geographica* 8.355; E. Meyer, "Pisa," *RE* XII.1747–51; Swoboda, "Elis," *RE* XII.2390–91; N.G.L. Hammond, in *The Cambridge Ancient History* vol. 3, pt. 3 (Cambridge: Cambridge University Press, 1982) 353.

81. Cf. the Pythian Games reorganized in 582 B.C., the Isthmian Games in 581, and the Nemean in 573.

82. J. Fontenrose, "The Cult of Apollo and the Games at Delphi," in Raschke (1988) 124–25; Gardiner (1910) 62–64; C. Gasper and E. Pottier, "Pythia," in C. Daremberg and E. Saglio, eds., *Dictionnaire des antiquités grecques et romaines*, vol. 4.1 (Paris: Hachette, 1907) 484–794; B. Bilinski, *Agoni Ginnici: Componenti artistiche ed intellectuali nell'antica Agonistica Greca* (Wroclaw: Zaklad Narodowy im. Ossolinskich, 1979) 73–74.

83. Paus. 2.17.1; Hsch., s.v. *Heresides*; Et. Mag., s.v. *Heresides*; Dionys. Hal., *Ant. Rom.* 1.21.; Nota Kaldis-Henderson (1979) 190–91.

84. Gardiner (1973) 214; W. Dittenberger and K. Purgold, *Die Inschriften von Olympia*, ed. E. Curtius and F. Adler, *Olympia*, vol. 5 (Berlin, 1896; reprint, Amsterdam: Hakkert, 1966) nos. 429, 435, 438.

85. G. Treu, *Die bildwerke von Olympia in Stein und Thon*, ed. E. Curtius and F. Adler, *Olympia*, vol. 3 (Berlin, 1894–97; reprint, Amsterdam: Hakkert, 1966) 252–54; N. Kaldis-Henderson, (1979) 203–12.

86. But see Paus. 5.6.7 which refers to "women" (γυναῖκας) being disbarred without mention of maidens attending.

87. J. A. Turner, "Greek Priesthoods," in *Civilization of the Ancient Mediterranean: Greece and Rome*, ed. M. Grant and R. Kitzinger, vol. 2 (New York: Scribner's, 1988) 925–31; id., *Hiereiai: Acquisition of Feminine Priesthoods in Ancient Greece* (Ph.D. diss., University of California, Santa Barbara, 1983).

88. Herrmann, (1972) 69 and note 241, cf. 41–42 on Pelops; see note 68 in this chapter for O'Brien's theory of the introduction of the Hera-Hippodameia cult to Olympia.

89. Herrmann, (1972) 65, note 176.

90. Ibid. 45–67 and note 147 for Bronze Age cults at Olympia; Mallwitz, in Raschke (1988) 86–87 and Mallwitz (1981) 134–37 convincingly demonstrates that archaeological evidence for the sanctuary of Pelops at Olympia is not earlier than the Archaic period. C. Renfrew, in Raschke (1988) 13–25, argues, contrary to his chapter title, "Minoan-Mycenaean Origins of the Panhellenic Games," that the later Olympics did not derive, directly at least, from Minoan-Mycenaean traditions.

91. See Lee, in Raschke (1988) 110–18; Herrmann (1972) 45–67 and note 147.

92. Paus. 5.4.5–6; Phleg., *Olympiades*, FGH 2B 257, 1160F; Mallwitz, in Raschke (1988) 93–94, on the controversy of the Aetolian (= Dorian) vs. the Achaean origin of the cult of Zeus at Olympia.

93. Drees (1962) 31–32.

94. L. Weniger, *Das Kollegium der Sechzehn Frauen und der Dionysosdienst in Elis* (Weimar, 1883); Nilsson (1957) 291–93; on a possible distinction between the Thyia and a "Wine Festival" and the location of the two, see V. Mitsopoulos-Leon, "Zur Verehrung des Dionysos in Elis nochmals: ΑΞΙΕ ΤΑΥΡΕ und die Sechzehn heiligen Frauen," *MDAI(A)* 99 (1984) 275–90.

95. The identity of the women who officiate as priestesses at the Thyia for Dionysus is usually assumed, on the basis of Plut., *Mul.vir.* 251e, to be the same as the Sixteen Women who organize the Heraia, and choral dances in honor of Physcoa and Hippodameia. For further discussion, with some controversy over the apparently corrupt reading of ἥρω in the text of the hymn of invocation, see C. Brown, "Dionysus and the Women of Elis: *PMG* 871," *GRBS* 23 (1982) 305–14.

96. Nilsson (1957) 291; Calame (1977) vol. 1, 61 and 211, note 23.

97. Weniger, (1905) 9.

98. Ibid. 8–10.

99. Nilsson, (1957) 271–74.

100. See esp. ch. 6 and, chiefly in iconography, C. Sourvinou-Inwood (1991) 58–98.

101. Zancani Montuoro and Zanotti-Bianco (1964) vol. 2, 339–49, pls. 49.2 and 97–100; Calame (1997) 185–91 = id. (1977a) vol. 1, 323–33. See the discussion of the Silaris metope, above, note 21.

102. A. Brelich (1969) vol. 1, 241–90; id., *Le Iniziazioni: Parte II. Sviluppi storici nelle civiltà superiori, in particolare nella Grecia antica* (Rome: Ateneo, 1962) 83–106. Cf. H. Jeanmaire, *Couroi et Courètes. Essai sur l'éducation spartiate et sur les rites d'adolescence dans l'antiquité hellénique* (Lille: Bibliotheque universitaire, 1939; reprint, New York: Arno, 1974) 413–18. On initiation in ancient Greece in general, see Burkert (1985) 260–64 (= 1977, 390–95) with further bibliography. The typical initiatory characteristics of women's footraces include segregation of the sexes, prenuptial status of participants, and special clothing.

Chapter 5

1. The following give general surveys of women's role in Greek athletics: J. Krause, *Die Gymnastik und Agonistik der Hellenen* (Leipzig, 1841; reprint, Wiesbaden: Dr. Martin Sändig, 1971) vol. 1, 31–33; L. Grasberger, *Erziehung und Unterricht im klassischen Altertum*, vol. 3 (Würzburg, 1881; reprint, Aalen: Scientia, 1971) 498–508; L. Meyer, *De virginum exercitationibus gymnicis apud veteres* (Klausthal, 1872); B. Schröder, *Der Sport im Altertum* (Leipzig: Spamerschen Buchdruckerei, 1927) 162–66; O. von Vacano, *Das Problem des alten Zeustempels in Olympia* (Naumburg [Salle]: Lippert, 1937) esp. "Über Mädchensport in Griechenland," 51–58; J. Jüthner, *Die athletischen Leibesübungen der Griechen*, ed. F. Brein, vol. 1, SB Vienna 249 (Graz: Hermann Böhlaus, 1965) 100–102; H. A. Harris, *Greek Athletes and Athletics* (London: Hutchinson, 1964) 179–86. Specifically on Spartan female (and male) athletics: S. Hodkinson, "An Agonistic Culture," in *Sparta: New Perspectives*, ed. S. Hodkinson and A. Powell (London: Duckworth, 1999) ch. 6, 147–87. For interpretations of women's sport as part of initiatory ritual, see H. Jeanmaire, *Couroi et Courètes. Essai sur l'éducation spartiate et sur les rites d'adolescence dans l'antiquité hellénique* (Lille: Bibliotheque universitaire, 1939; reprint, New York: Arno, 1974) 413–18; A. Brelich, *Le Iniziazioni: Parte II. Sviluppi storici nelle civiltà superiori, in particolare nella Grecia antica* (Rome: Ateneo, 1962) 72–74, 83–105 and 127–46; id., *Paides e Parthenoi*, vol. 1, Incunabula Greca, vol. 36 (Rome: Ateneo, 1969) 449–56; W. Burkert, *Greek Religion*, trans. J. Raffan (Cambridge, Mass.: Harvard University Press, 1985) 260–64 (from the original *Griechische Religion der Archaïschen und Klassichen Epoche* [Stuttgart: W. Kohlhammer, 1977] 390–95); C. Calame, *Choruses of Young Women in Ancient Greece: Their Morphology, Religious Role, and Social Functions*, trans. D. Collins and J. Orion (Lanham, Md.: Rowman & Littlefield, 1997) esp. 186–87, 202–6 (from the original *Les choeurs de jeunes filles en Grèce archaïque, I: Morphologie, fonction religieuse et sociale* [Rome: Ateneo & Bizzarri, 1977] 324–26, 350–57); L. Kahil, "L'Artémis de Brauron: rites et mystère," *AntK* 20 (1977) 86–98; P. Perlman, "Plato *Laws* 833C–834D and the Bears of Brauron," *GRBS* 24 (1983) 115–30. I wish to thank John Mansfield for sharing with me the text of a lecture he delivered at the University of California, Berkeley, in February 1981, "Women in Greek Athletics: A Man's View" and the very useful collection of sources appended to it, "Women in Greek Athletics: Sources and Materials" (unpublished). Also of interest is the consideration of boys' and girls' complementary roles in rites of passage to adulthood as discussed by P. Vidal-Naquet, *The Black Hunter: Forms of Thought and Forms of Society in the Greek World*, trans. A. Szegedy-Maszak (Baltimore: Johns Hopkins University Press, 1986) 129–56, esp. 145–52 (ch. 6 was orig.

publ. as "Le cru, l'enfant grec et le cuit," in *Faire de l'histoire: nouveaux objets*, ed. J.le Goff and P. Nora [Paris: Gallimard, 1974] 137–68, esp. 156–62).

2. Mansfield (this ch., 1981, note 1).

3. H. Jeanmaire, *REG* 26 (1913) 134–35; M. P. Nilsson, "Die Grundlagen des spartanischen Lebens," *Klio* 12 (1912) 308–40, reprinted in *Opuscula Selecta* (Lund 1951–60), vol. 2, 826–69 at p. 848; Vidal-Naquet (1986) 147 (1974) 160; P. Cartledge, "Spartan Wives: Liberation or Licence?" *CQ* 31 (1981) 84–105, esp. 91–93.

4. See generally F. Ollier, *Le mirage spartiate* (Paris: Les Belles lettres, 1933; reprint, New York: Arno Press, 1973); A. Andrewes, *The Greek Tyrants* (London: Hutchinson University Library, 1956; reprint, New York: Harper & Row, 1963) 66–77; E. N. Tigerstedt, *The Legend of Sparta in Classical Antiquity* (Stockholm: Almquist & Wiksell, 1965) vol. 1, 70–78; W. G. Forrest, *A History of Sparta: 950–192 B.C.* (London: Hutchinson, 1968; reprint, London: Duckworth, 1980) 35–60; Pavel Oliva, *Sparta and Her Social Problems* (Amsterdam: Hakkert, 1971) 63–70. See also A. Szegedy-Maszak, "Legends of the Greek Lawgivers," *GRBS* 19 (1978) 199–209.

5. Nigel M. Kennell, *The Gymnasium of Virtue: Education and Culture in Ancient Sparta* (Chapel Hill: University of North Carolina Press, 1995) 146; see ch. 3 of this volume, note 56; Tigerstedt (1965) vol. 1, 38, 68–69, places the intensification of the *agōgē* in the mid seventh century, since it would have been called for after the serious Spartan defeat at Hysiae (699/8? B.C.) and after the Second Messenian War. Brelich (1962) esp. 48–74, discusses initiatory characteristics and function of Sparta (and Cretan) *agōgē* and festivals. Regarding the *agōgē*, he concludes (57–58):

> The summary illustration of the Spartan *agoge* given above seems to answer most perfectly to the social institution of the primitive type hinged on initiation at most stages: after the first years of infancy, the individual is separated from the family and entrusted to the community; he lives with his *coetanei* ("age equals") under the control of male adults; he is subject to deprivations, vigorous discipline, and to an especially harsh test, while at the same time he is placed outside the normal laws which are enforced in society; he passes from year to year . . . into a new category of age where he can strengthen himself by means of agonistic combats with his peers. Only at a relatively late age (corresponding to Spartan gerontocratic ideals) does he acquire the normal status of an adult.

6. D. Page, *Alcman: The Parthenion* (Oxford: Clarendon, 1951) 67–68; C. Calame, *Les choeurs de jeunes filles en Grèce archaïque, vol II: Alcman* (Rome, 1977) 84–85 re: *anepsiai* in Alcman, and id. (1977) vol. 1, 372–85 on "*L'agélé* spartiate" and "Les choeurs de jeunes filles lacédémoniennes." In other terms associated with Spartan education and on the *agōgē* in general, see Grasberger, vol. 3 (1881) 57–60; C. Forbes, *Greek Physical Education* (New York: Century, 1929) 12–43; H. Michell, *Sparta* (Cambridge: Cambridge University Press, 1952) 165–204; K.M.T. Chrimes (Atkinson), *Ancient Sparta: A Re-examination of the Evidence* (Manchester: Manchester University Press, 1952) 84–136; H. I. Marrou, *A History of Education in Antiquity*, trans. G. Lamb (London: Sheed and Ward, 1956) 14–25; J. T. Hooker, *The Ancient Spartans* (London: J. M. Dent, 1980) 132–44.

7. Plutarch, *Philopoemen* 16; Chrimes (1952) 97ff., 221ff., and 442ff.; Forbes (1929) 38.

8. *Hymn* 5. 33–34; see Schol. *ad loc.*: ἴλα· ἡ τῶν νυμφῶν φρατρία καὶ ἄθροισις, "*ila*: the clan-division and collection of maidens."

9. C. Wehrli, "Les gynéconomes," *MH* 19 (1962) 33–38.

10. On equestrian metaphors for girls' organization, see Calame (1977) vol. 2, 67–72 and Page (1951) 89–90. Neither of these notices the metaphor in Aristophanes, *Lysistrata* 1308–13.

11. *SEG* XI (1954) no. 610; P. A. Cartledge and A.J.S. Spawforth, *Hellenistic and Roman Sparta: A Tale of Two Cities* (London: Routledge, 1989) 205–6; Kennell (1992) 45–46.

12. On Spartan women's education in philosophy and speaking, see Cartledge (1981) 92 and id., "Literacy in Spartan Oligarchy" (apophthegms) *JHS* 98 (1978) 25–37. On apophthegms illustrating the free speech of Spartan women, see Tigerstedt (1965) vol. 2, 16–30. Contrast male Athenian attitudes to women's free speech in public: Sophocles, *Ajax* 293; Euripdes, *Her.* 476–77, and fr. 61; Thucydides 2.45.2–46.1.

13. On female homoeroticism in Alcman's poetry and Spartan society, see Calame (1997) vol. 1, 7–8, 244–55 (= 1977, vol. 1, 25–27, 420–36); K. J. Dover, *Greek Homosexuality*, updated and with a new postscript (Cambridge, Mass.: Harvard University Press, 1989) 179–82; Elaine Fantham, Helene Peet Foley, et al., eds., *Women in the Classical World: Image and Text* (Oxford: Oxford University Press, 1994) 57–59; Plutarch, *Lycurgus* 18.4. On the male beauty contests, see ch. 8, note 24 of this volume.

14. Sappho fr. 1 (Lobel-Page), 71 (Bergk). Harris (1964) 182. On Sapphic homoeroticism and education, see Calame (1997) vol. 1, 249–53 (= 1977, vol. 1, 427–33); Dover (1989) 173–79; M. Williamson, *Sappho's Immortal Daughters* (Cambridge, Mass.: Harvard University Press, 1995); Jane Mcintosh Snyder, "Public Occasion and Private Passion in the Lyrics of Sappho of Lesbos," in *Women's History & Ancient History*, ed. Sarah B. Pomeroy (Chapel Hill: University of North Carolina Press, 1991) 1–19.

15. On Spartan women's music and gymnastics, see Plato, *Leg.* 806A where, however, it is suggested that slave girls did the weaving. But their weaving skills are alluded to by Paus. 3.16.2, where they are said to weave a *chiton* for Apollo of Amyclae each year. Re their freedom from other sedentary domestic tasks, see Cartledge (1981) 91 and n. 40, which cites Heracleides Lembus, 373.13 (Dilts) (baking) and the discussion in P. Herfst, *Le travail de la femme dans la Grèce ancienne* (Utrecht: A. Oosterhoek, 1922). 18–24 (weaving), 24–32 (cooking), and 112–13 (Spartan women's exemption).

16. J.-P. Vernant, *Problèmes de la guerre en Grèce ancienne* (Paris: La Haye, Mouton, 1968) 15, cited by P. Vidal-Naquet (1986) 146 (= id. 1974) 149. See Vidal-Naquet's further comments on pages 151–52, where he concludes his discussion of the similarity between boys' and girls' education: "At any rate the impression given by the few ancient texts is not so much of a parallelism between the education of girls and that of boys as of a direct reproduction. . . . The Spartiate girl was in a real sense a boy *manqué*." See Cartledge (1981) 94.

17. Cicero, *Tusculanae Disputationes* 2.15.36; Propentius 3.14.1ff. Cartledge (1981) 87–88.

18. J. Jüthner, *Philostratus über Gymnastik* (Leipzig: B. G. Teubner, 1909; reprint, Stuttgart: Teubner, 1969) 242 *ad. loc.*

19. J. H. Krause, *Die Gymnastik und Agonistik der Hellenen*, vol. 2 (Leipzig, 1841; reprint, Wiesbaden: Dr. Martin Sändig, 1971) 682–86 argues for total nudity but allows that they may have later worn the short chiton for certain exercises. W. A. Becker, *Charicles*, trans. F. Metcalfe, 6th ed. (London, 1882; reprint, London: Longmans, Green, 1906) 297–300, also maintains that Spartan girls exercised in total nudity, but G.M.A. Richter, "An Archaic Greek Mirror," *AJA* 42 (1938) 337–44, esp. 342 no. 4 wants *gumnos* to mean "lightly clad" with reference to Spartan girls. The archaeological evidence from the sixth century, examined later, shows girls totally naked, wearing trunks only, and wearing the Doric *chiton*. For discussion of the latter form of dress, see M. Johnson, *Ancient Greek Dress* (Chicago: Argonaut, 1964) 52–53.

20. Ibycus fr. 58 Page; see Eur., *Hecuba* 933 f.; Pollux, *Onomastikon* 2. 187, 7.54f.; Clement, *Paedagogus* 2.10.114.1. Cartledge (1981) 92 no. 46, cites Ath. 13.602E for thighs as an erotogenic feature and proposes that "thighs" may have also been a conventional euphemism for female *pudenda*. This would leave unresolved the ambiguity between being literally naked and scantily clad and would, in any case, not contradict the evidence of bronze statuettes to be examined below.

21. Cf. Plut., *Comp Lycurgi et Numae* 3.3.4 citing Sophocles, fr. 788 Nauck.

22. Dionysius of Halicarnassus 7.72. 3–4.

23. F. Pfister, s.v. "Nacktheit," *RE* 16.2 (1935) 1541–49; A. Brelich (1969) 157–58; 171–73; 200–201.

24. Xen., *Hellenica* 6.4–16; Plut., *Agesilaus* 29; Plat., *Leg.* 633 b–c; Ath. 678C. Bölte, "Zu Lakonischen Festen," *RhM* 78 (1929) 124–43; H. T. Wade-Gery, "A Note on the Origin of the Spartan Gymnopaidiai," *CQ* 43 (1949) 79–81; M. P. Nilsson, *Griechische Feste von religiöser Bedeutung mit Ausschluß der attischen* (Leipzig: B. G. Teubner, 1906; reprint, Darmstadt: Wissenschaftliche Buchgesellschaft, 1957) 140–42. See also discussion in ch. 3.

25. Antoninus Liberalis 17. Nilsson (1957) 370–71; R. F. Willetts, *Cretan Cults and Festivals* (London: Routledge and Paul, 1962) 173–79; Burkert (1985) 261 = (1977) 392.

26. L. Kahil (1977); P. Perlman (1983) esp. 125–27; see ch. 6 of this volume.

27. Aristoph., *Lys.* 1308–13; Theocr. 18–39; Cic., *Tusc.* 2.15–16; Paus. 3.14–6.

28. See Cartledge (1981) 93–96, who discusses beauty as an important, and possibly an essential, ingredient in Spartan matrimony as suggested by Alcman's poems and by an anecdote in Plutarch (*Mor.* 1D). The anecdote relates the story of King Archidamus II (reigned c. 469–427) who was fined for marrying an ugly (or small—see Plut., *Ages.* 2.6) woman. Cartledge (94–95) estimates the marriage age of girls as between 18 and 20.

29. C. Praschniker, "Bronzene Spiegelstütze im Wiener Hofmuseum," *Österreichisches Archäologisches Institut, Wien*, vol. 15 (1912) 219–52 presents the first extensive treatment of the bronzes and, largely on the basis of their youthful physique, identifies them with the Spartan girls of Plut., *Lyc.* 14 (esp. pp. 250–51). See W. A. Mueller, *Nacktheit und Entblössung* (Leipzig: B. G. Teubner, 1906) 142; S. Heckenbach, *De nuditate sacra, Religionsgeshichtliche Untersuchungen und Vorarbeiten* (Giessen: Alfred Töpelmann, 1911) vol. 9, pt. 3, 15f. cited by Praschniker, 250 notes 72–73. Lists of bronze girl handles are also given in U. Jantzen, *Griechischen Griff-Phialen*, Winckelmannsprogramm 114 (Berlin: De Gruyter, 1958) 7 and

P. Oberländer, *Griechische Handspiegel* (Ph.D. diss, Universität Hamburg, 1967) 211, 275–76, note 147. K. Schefold, "Griechische Spiegel," *Die Antike* 16 (1940) 24ff. and id., *Orient, Hellas und Rom* (Bern: A. Francke, 1949) sees the bronze mirror handles as representations of handmaidens or attendants of Artemis. L.O.K. Congdon, in a thorough and important study, *Caryatid Mirrors of Ancient Greece. Technical, Stylistic and Historical Considerations of an Archaic and Early Classical Bronze Series* (Mainz: von Zabern, 1981) 13ff., sees the girls as maidens related to cult practices, but not as goddesses themselves. Congdon, who studies the naked-maiden-with-trunks type on pp. 136–37, no. 14, pl. 10 and pp. 211–12, no. 16, pl. 95, identifies female handle forms from Laconian workshops as the earliest and most enduring type. H. Jucker, "Der archaische griechische Standspiegel in Cincinnati," in *In Memoriam O. J. Brendel: Essays in Archaeology and the Humanities*, ed. L. Bonfante, H. von Heintze and C. Lord (Mainz: von Zabern, 1976) 25–35 discusses a naked female bronze handle in Cincinnati which may be added to the items discussed in this study; most important, the Cincinnati piece is, according to Jucker, the earliest Greek mirror handle and from a Laconian workshop.

    30. Those from Laconia: App. 1 (this ch.) nos. 3, 6, 7 , 14, 20, 21, 22, 26. From the Peloponnese outside Laconia: app. 1, nos. 5, 25. From Greece above the Peloponnese: app. 1, nos. 2, 4, 8. From Ionia: 12, 15. From Italy: 10, 23. Of unknown provenance: 1, 9, 11, 13, 16, 17, 18, 19, 24. For a discussion of app. 1, no. 16, see G.M.A. Richter, *Greek, Etruscan and Roman Bronzes* (New York: Gilliss, 1915).

    31. E. Langlotz, *Frühgriechischen Bildhauerschulen* (Nürnburg: E. Frommann, 1927; reprint, Rome: "L'Erma" di Bretschneider, 1967) vol. 1, 86–98 and vol. 2, plates 44b and c, 45b, 46, 48a and b.

    32. Richter (1938) and id., "Another Archaic Greek Mirror," *AJA* 46 (1942) 319–24.

    33. Richter (1938) 343.

    34. U. Häfner, *Das Kunstschaffen Lakoniens in archaischer Zeit* (Ph.D. diss., University of Munich, 1965) 88–89, no. 20.

    35. U. Jantzen, *Bronzewerkstätten in Grossgriechenland und Sizilien* (Berlin: W. de Gruyter, 1937), *JDAI Erganzungsheft* 13, 9–10 and 66, appendix 1: mirror handles A and C. The eleven female mirror handles mentioned by Jantzen include app. 5.1 (to this chapter) nos. 3, 9, 10, 15, 25 (all Spartan) and 8, 12, 14. The votive statuette is app. 5.1, no. 13.

    36. Häfner (1965) 12–38.

    37. Cf. L. Jeffery, *Archaic Greece: The City States c. 700–500 B.C.* (London: Ernest Benn, 1976) 213, 217.

    38. L. E. Roller, "Funeral Games in Greek Art," *AJA* 85.2 (1981a) 107–19, pls. 19–20, esp. 111–12. Vases from the second half of the sixth century show scenes of Peleus and Atalanta wrestling in similar poses. Fifth- to fourth-century vases show the pair in a more relaxed palaestra setting.

    39. Cartledge (1981) at 92 no. 47 has cited eleven bronzes as confirmation of Spartan girls' public nudity; the bronzes he mentions are those in app. 5.1, nos. 6, 7, 8, 9, 16, 17, 19, 25, and 26. He also cites Sparta 594 and 3302, with further bibliography. It is beyond the scope of this study to trace the ultimate origins of nude female figurines and mirror handles from possible Near Eastern or Egyptian proto-

382   NOTES TO PAGE 129

types. J. Boardman, *The Greeks Overseas* (Harmondsworth: Penguin, 1964) 81–82, pl. 1a and fig. 12d, discusses five nude female figures in ivory found in a grave in Athens dated to the third quarter of the eighth century, but these "clearly imitate the eastern 'Astarte' type of the nude fertility goddess" known from Nimrud, Assyria, and do not otherwise resemble the later bronzes in question. Boardman, pp. 163–64 and figs. 44 a and b, in reference to the Greek girl bronzes and certain Egyptian counterparts, concludes that the motif is ultimately Egyptian, possibly transmitted in part via the Near East. But "[t]he number of Egyptian traits in sixth-century Spartan art," Boardman notes, "may be due to her close relations with Cyrene in North Africa" as well as other individual instances of Spartan trade with Egypt in this period. Even if Egypt initially inspired Sparta to produce the statuettes and mirrors, the public nudity of girls at Sparta seems to have further encouraged manufacture of the images otherwise generally absent from Greek sculpture of this period.

40. Cartledge (1981) 92 note 47 and 93 note 54 observes that "from the late seventh century onwards we have *ex voto*'s from Sparta inscribed with the name of a dedicatrix. Since the recipient deities were also female and a fair proportion of the uninscribed offerings have feminine associations, many of the dedications were probably offered by women." See P. Cartledge, "Literacy in the Spartan Oligarchy," *JHS* 98 (1978) 25–37.

41. Plut., *Lyc.* 14.2. Cf. Theocritus 18. 26–37, alluding to Helen's musical talent and Pl., *Leg.* 771e–772a, where he proposes public dances for youths and maidens for the new city so that they could view one another "each of them naked, within the limits of sober modesty." In general, on the make-up and activity of Spartan girls' choruses, see Calame (1997) 219–21 = (1977) vol. I, esp. 381–85 and id. (1977) vol. 2 *passim* on the chorus in Alcman's *Parthenion*.

42. Girl flautist from Sparta: Athens NM 15900, c. 520 B.C.; Mirror handle from Amyclaeon: Athens NM 7548, c. 530–520 B.C. The shoulder strap is also seen in app. 5.1, nos. 8, 15 (fig. 5-1), 17 (fig. 5-2), 21, 25. To the strap are usually attached small objects (amulets?), and one larger crescent-shaped object (seen in app. 5.1, nos. 15 (fig. 5-1), 17 (fig. 5-2), 25) to be discussed later. The "amulets" on a shoulder strap are identified by Häfner as the usual accoutrements of children: (1965) 88 note 18, citing a terracotta statuette of a child from Paestum; see a bronze statuette of a boy in Kassel, M. Bieber, ed., *Die antiken Skulpturen und Bronzen des Konigl. Museum Fridericianum in Cassel* (Marburg: N. G. Elwertsche Verlagsbuchhandlung, 1915) no. 214, pl. 44. The strap thus argues against identifying the bronze girls as *hetairai* and in favor of seeing in them representations of young Spartan maidens at some stage before marriage.

43. Plut., *Lyc.* 15.3 relates the cutting of Spartan girl's hair on her wedding night. Cartledge (1981) 101 cites the following additional literary evidence for the fact that Spartan females have their hair long only while *parthenai* or *korai* but had it shorn at marriage and kept it short thereafter: [Aristotle], *Respublica Lacedaemoniorum ap.* Heracleides Lembus 373.13 (Dilts); Lucian, *Fugitivi* 27; Xenophon of Ephesus 5.1.7. For short hair on Spartan boys and long on their men, see Cartledge *JHS* 97 (1977) 11–27, esp. 15, no. 39; Plut., *Lyc.* 16.6: "As they grew in age, their bodily exercise was increased and their heads were close-clipped . . ."; and Plut., *Lyc.* 22.1: "They [sc., the boys] wore their hair long as soon as they ceased to be youths."

44. Brelich (1969) 71–72 note 59 and 80–81 note 88 re other cultures; 115, 129, 358, 447, 464 re Greek custom of tonsure in ritual contexts. In Athens young boys about to become members of the Phratria during the Apaturia dedicated their hair to the god: H. W. Parke, *Festivals of the Athenians* (London: Thames and Hudson, 1977; reprint, Ithaca: Cornell University Press, 1986) 89 and no. 101; Burkert (1985) 255 and 447, note 18 = (1977) 384, note 18; J. Labarbe, *Bull. Acad. R. de Belgique* 39 (1953) 358–94. In general on the significance of hair in ritual: Burkert (1985) 70 and 373–74, note 29 = (1977) 120–21 and note 29. G. Thomson, *Aeschylus and Athens*, 2nd ed. (London: Lawrence & Wishart, 1966; reprint, New York: Haskell House, 1967) 107–8 and 438 no. 19 remarks that in Greece and elsewhere "hair was cut on two distinct occasions—the attainment of puberty by a boy or the marriage of a girl and the death of a relative." These crises, or cruces, of life require some outward manifestation of commemoration of loss, but also a sense of renewed identity by those cutting their hair.

45. Figure 5-1, from Curium: New York Met. no. 74.51.5680, c. 530 B.C. (= app. 1, no. 15) The best attested type of cap was known as the *amphōtides* or *apōtides* (ear guards), which J. H. Krause (1971) vol. 2, 517–18 discusses as a late innovation for the palaestra, but E. N. Gardiner, *Greek Athletic Sports and Festivals* (London: Macmillan, 1910) 433 no. 2, adds: "The evidence for these lappets is all late, but the caps belong to the fifth century B.C." See ibid., figs. 17, 149, and 150, but note that only in fig. 149, a Roman imperial sculpture, are the ears covered by the device. In the other illustrations, sixth- and fifth-century vases London BM 326 and Munich 795 as well as in numerous sculptures, notably the famous stone base from Athens with pentathletes (late sixth c. B.C.), the athletes wear caps of hair nets that do not cover the ears but do keep the hair in place. On the stone relief base with athletes, see S. Casson, "The New Athenian Statue Bases," *JHS* 45 (1925) 164–79. The cap or net worn on the heads of male athletes from the sixth to fifth centuries is probably reflected also in the bronzes of girls from the same period.

46. App. 5.1, nos. 6, 7, 11 (fig. 5-4b), 13, 15 (fig. 5-1), 17 (fig. 5-2), 22, 25, 26.

47. *AG* 6.280; *IG* V.1, 225–26. Perlman (1983) 125 note 52 and 126 note 57 notes other prenuptial dedications in Archilochus, fr. 18 Bergk (veil to Hera), *AG* 6.276 (snood to Artemis), Paus. 2.33.1 (girdles of Troezenian maidens to Athena Apatouria *pro gamou*), and *IG* II², 1514, lines 60–62; 1516, lines 35–38 (saffron-colored robe to Artemis Brauronia in fourth century).

48. For sickles as prizes in the *paidikos* agon, see Chrimes, (1952) 1 and 87–88, 94, 98–99. See also Nik. D. Papachatze, *Pausaniou Ellados Periēgesis Biblio 2. kai 3.: Korinthiaka kai Lakōnia* (Athens: Ekdotikē Athenōn, 1976) vol. 2, 372, pls. 386 and 387.

49. Juvenal, *Satire* 3.67–68: *rusticus ille tuus sumit trechedipna, Quirine,/ et ceromatico fert niceteria collo*. (O Romulus, that country bumpkin now wears the parasite's dinner outfit and carries his athletic prizes around his neck anointed for wrestling.)

50. See note 42.

51. Mirror handle with crescent on shoulder strap (fig. 5-2): New York Met. 38.11.3, ca. 550 B.C. Statuettes with an oil flask (*lekythos* or *aryballos*): Sparta Mus. 27, N.Y. Met. 38.11. 3; Dresden H⁴ 44/16. See Jantzen (1937) pl. 4, nos. 18–19, showing a male athlete holding an oil flask. On the use of oil by athletes, see H. A.

Harris (1964) 158–59; E. N. Gardiner (1910) 476–78 and figs. 175, 176, and 177; id., *Athletics of the Ancient World* (Oxford: Oxford University Press, 1930; reprint, Chicago: Ares, 1980); and C. Ulf, "Die Einreibung der griechischen Athleten mit Öl. Zweck und Ursprung," *Stadion* 5 (1979) 220–38. A naked woman is shown anointing herself with the aryballos amid other women swimming (*hetairai?*) on Paris, Louvre F203, a red-figure amphora of ca. 530–515 B.C.; see N. Yalouris, ed., *The Eternal Olympics: The Art and History of Sport* (New York: Caratzas, 1979) 261, pl. 151. For depictions of male athletes using the aryballos fastened to the wrist with a looped strap, see ibid. 119, pl. 48; R. Patrucco, *Lo Sport nella Grecia antica* (Florence: L. S. Olschki, 1972) figs. 161, 162, and 163a (= Berlin, terracotta figure; Leiden XVe 28 (PC 63) black-figure hydria; Berlin 2180, red-figure krater); and Schröder (1927) pls. 104 (alabastron and aryballoi) and 106a (Berlin 2180).

52. Mirror handle from Cerveteri: Dresden Skulpturensammlung Inv. H⁴ 44/16, c. 500 B.C. The flower is in the hand of nude female bronze figures Vienna VI 4979; Sparta Mus. 27; Paris, Louvre (J. Charbonneaux, *Les bronzes grecs* [Paris: Presses Universitaires de France, 1958]). Munich, Museum d. antike Kunst, 3482; N.Y. Met. 38.11.2; N.Y. Met. 06.11.04; and Dresden H⁴ 44/16. We may note that the lotus is also seen in the lotus palmette frieze from Amyclaeon, Sparta Mus., M. N. Tod and A.J.B. Wace, *A Catalogue of the Sparta Museum* (Oxford: Clarendon, 1906) 206 no. 731a, b, 732. If the flower is a lotus in the girls' hands, the blossom may have had a special (sacred?) local significance in Sparta.

53. Athletes "losing their bloom": Philostr., *Gymn.* 48. Votive statuette from Sparta: Vienna KM VI 4979, ca. 500; mirror handle from Hermione: Munich, Museum Antiker Kleinkunst 3482, ca. 510; peplos-clad Spartan maiden: Berlin, Staatliche Museum 7933, ca. 500.

54. Munich amphora ca. 550–520: Munich 584J. See Roller (1981), 111, note 31, whence E. Gerhard, *Auserlesene Vasen* (Berlin: W. Moser und Kühn, 1847) pl. 177; Yalouris (1979) fig. 13. For three of the bronzes under consideration (app. 5.1, nos. 2, 5, and 8), I could not determine whether there is a *diazōma* or not, due to the absence of photos or mention of the fact in publications I surveyed.

55. Mirror handle in New York (fig. 5-3): New York Met. 41.11.5, ca. 540 B.C.; in Trent (fig. 5-4): Museo Provinciale d'Arte inv. no. 3061, sixth c. B.C.; in Hamburg (fig. 5-4): Museum für Kunst und Gewerbe, inv. no. 1917. 362 (fig. 5-4b, here) nude female bronze figurine, Roman, of Spartan type. Schröder (1927) pls. 110a and b, and p. 196. Schröder cites the parallel to the Hamburg statuette of a Lucanian calyx-krater (c. 380–360? B.C.) from Epizephyrian Locri, Reggio Calabria 5014, *NSc* (1917) 110 fig. 12: A. D. Trendall, *The Red-figured Vases of Lucania, Campania, and Sicily* (Oxford: Clarendon, 1967) 76/386, Locri Group showing a girl wearing trunks and holding a strigil in a palaestra setting with a naked young man. Although the Hamburg figure has been identified as a Roman statuette, it bears comparison with the Spartan girl mirror handles from which it may have been directly or indirectly derived. See A. Kossatz-Diessmann, "Zur Herkunft des Perizoma im Satyrspiel," *JDAI* 97 (1982) 79 and note 50, and pl. 17 on p. 80 discusses the Hamburg girl in this connection and generally sees the *perizōma* (= *diazōma* of my discussion) as "anfangs eine weibliche Sportracht" (90), which was later adapted for female dancers and acrobats in secular contexts and then for male actors, including satyrs. For earlier publications of the Hamburg girl, see E. von Mercklin, "Antiken im

Hamburgischen Museum für Kunst und Gewerbe," *AA* (1928) 434–35 and fig. 147,
and H. Hoffmann, *Kunst des Altertums im Hamburg* (Mainz: P. von Zabern, 1961)
fig. 49. For publications of the Trent girl, see E. Walde Psenner, *I bronzetti bigurati*
antichi del Trentino (Trent: Provincia autonoma di Trento, 1983) 122, 123, note 103;
and G. Cuirletti, ed., *Divinità e uomini dell'antico Trentino*, Quaderni della Sezione
Archeologica, Museo Provinciale d'Arte 3 (Trent: Museo Provinciale d'Arte, 1986) 61.
I wish to express my appreciation to Dr. Hornbostel of the Hamburg Museum and to
Sr. Cuirletti of the Trent Museum for their generous assistance and helpful references.

56. Charbonneaux (1958) pl. 22 no. 2 and p. 144.

57. Burkert (1985) 260 = (1977) 391 with further references; Brelich (1969)
29–30 and *passim*, see index under "segregazione."

58. Laconian figure from Cyprus: New York Met. 74.51.5680 (fig. 5-1), c. 530
B.C. (= app. 1, no. 15).

59. Paus. 3.14.6; J. Delorme, *Gymnasion* (Paris: De Boccard, 1960) 72–74; W.
Zschietzschmann, *Wettkampf und Übungsstätten in Griechenland, II.Palaestra—*
Gymnasion (Stuttgart: K. Hofmann, 1961) 37–39. Xenophon, Euripides, Aristophanes,
and Theocritus omit any mention of palaestrae or gymnasia in their discussion of
Spartan exercise. Delorme discounts Plutarch's report (*Cimon* 16.5) of a gymnasium building in 464 B.C. The two buildings seen by Pausanias (3.14.6) are dated
by Delorme to the first centuries B.C. and A.D., while the *dromos* is considered to be a
simple *campus* in its earlier form.

60. Aristoph., *Lys.* 1308–13; Theocr. 18.39; Cic., *Tusc.* 2.15.16; Paus. 3.14.6.

61. The five bronze statuettes of female runners are (1) Athens N.M. Carapanos
24, female runner from Dodona, ca. 600 B.C. (fig. 4-3): see Langlotz (1967) 88 and 93;
Häfner (1965) 127–28; Jantzen (1937) 39, 70, and 71. (2) Delphi Inv. no. 3072.
(3) London BM 208, female runner from Albania (?) (fig. 4-1). The short chiton
with one breast exposed is reminiscent of the girl runners in the Olympian Heraia
mentioned in Pausanias 5.16.3. See Häfner (1965) 144–45, who believes that the
piece is not Laconian since the modeling is too lively; Langlotz (1967) 94 dates the
piece to c. 560 B.C. (4) Palermo, Museo Nazionale, "maenad" from Collection
Salnitrano (fig. 4-4). See Jantzen (1937) 27, 39, and 70–71, who sees the piece as
a decorative figure on a vessel and judges it to be from a south Italian workshop
(Tarentum?) but with Peloponnesian influences; P. Marconi, *Il Museo Nazionale di*
Palermo (Rome: La Libreria dello stato, 1932) 48. (5) Sparta, Mus. Inv. no. 3305,
female runner from Sparta. The figures of running girls have been called "maenads"
by Jantzen (1937) 70–71. Cf. four known figures of running Amazons clearly distinguished by their dress and headdress: Athens NM 6589, 6622, 6624 (all from the
Acropolis), and 13230 (from Thessaly); D. von Bothmer, *Amazons in Greek Art* (Oxford: Clarendon, 1957) 122–123 nos. 8 and 9; A. de Ridder, *Catalogue des bronzes de*
la Société archéologique d'Athènes (Paris: Thorin, 1894) 327–29 nos. 815–17, fig.
321; H. A. Shapiro, "Amazons, Thracians, and Scythians," *GRBS* 24 (1983) 105–
15, pls. 3 and 4.

62. See Hesychius, s.v. "Dionysiades." 1) 323–33; Nilsson (1957) 298; S. Wide,
Lakonische Kulte (Leipzig: B. G. Teubner, 1893) 160–61. Hesychius, s.v. *"en Drionas"*
(E 2823 Latte), merely mentions "a race of girls in Sparta," apparently in honor of the
Driodones, divinities worshiped in Sparta; id., s.v. *triōlax* (IV, p. 197 Schmidt): "a
running contest for maidens" seems to have been a race of three stades length

(cf. the *diaulos* of two stades), but its location is uncertain. An inscription (*SEG* XI [1950–54] 610) records twelve Dionysiades running, not eleven as in Pausanias, and notes that they were supervised by the *biduoi*, magistrates who also supervised boys' education.

63. Paus. 3.16.1–2.

64. P. Zancani Montuoro and U. Zanotti-Bianco, *Heraion alla Foce del Sele*, vol. 2, *Il Primo Thesauros* (Rome: Libreria dello Stato, 1964) ch. 31. "Leucippidi," ibid., 339–349 and pls. 49.2 and 97–100.

65. Calame (1997) vol. 1, 185–91 = (1977) vol. 1, 323–33; see also E. Kuhnert in Roscher, s.v. "Leukippiden," col. 1992.

66. Nilsson (1957) 298.

67. Calame (1997) vol. 1, 190–91 = (1977) vol. 1, 330–33.

68. Paus. 5.16.2–3. On the Heraia, see Nilsson (1957) 62; and Calame (1997) 28, 114–16 = (1977) vol. 1, 67 and 211–14.

69. The Sixteen Women of Elis who organize the Heraia also organize a chorus for Physcoa, a local heroine who gave birth by Dionysus to a child Narcaeus and who introduced his worship into Elis (Paus. 5.16.6). The Sixteen also hold a special Thyia or rite for Dionysus where they invoke him as a bull (Plut., *Quaestiones Graecae* 299 and *Isis et Osiris* 364F). Compare the sacrifice and footrace staged by the Dionysiades and Leucippides at Sparta (Paus. 3.13.7).

70. Calame (1997) 191, note 315 = (1977) vol. 1, 332, note 315 cites references to the Dioscuri as *leukippoi* or *leukopoloi*: Pindar, *Pythian* 1.66; Eur., *Helen* 638, *Ant.* fr. 223 (Suppl. C55 Nauck); Hsch., s.v. *Dioskouroi* (D1929 Latte).

71. Paus. 5.16.4. L. Drees, *Der Ursprung der olympischen Spiele* (Stuttgart: K. Hofmann, 1962) 28, note 62.

72. Besides wrestling by Spartan women, there is evidence that it was practiced by Etruscan women in the fourth century B.C. (Theopompus, *ap.* Ath. 13.517D), by Roman women at the Floralia festival (Juv., *Sat.* 6.246–52), and by women in Antioch at the Olympic festival held there (Malalas, *Chronographia* 12, p. 288; 10–13 Dindorf). Wrestling between girls and boys seemed to have been practiced occasionally but was regarded as a curiosity: Schol. Juv. 4.53 mentions that "Palfurius Sura, the son of a man of consular rank, during the reign of Nero once wrestled with a Lacedaemonian maiden in an athletic contest"; Ath., *Deipnosophistae* 12.566E (200 A.D.) reports with lascivious interest the fact that boys and girls wrestle together in the gymnasium on Chios. L. B. Warren, "The Women of Etruria," *Arethusa* 6 (1973) 91–101, on 92–93 attributes, without good reason, the report on Etruscan women's wrestling to Theopompus' imagination. There is, for instance, a 330–300 B.C. Etruscan strigil with a handle in the shape of a naked girl in turn holding a strigil and crowning herself: London BM Catalogue of Bronzes 665.89R; see H. A. Harris, *Sport in Greece and Rome* (Ithaca: Cornell University Press, 1972) fig. 43; H. Walters, *Catalogue of the Bronzes, Greek, Roman, and Etruscan, in the Department of Greek and Roman Antiquities, British Museum* (London: Trustees of the British Museum, 1899) 110, no. 665; see 104–5, no. 640 showing a female wrestler on the handle of an Etruscan cista. On *bibasis*, see Pollux, *Onom.* 4.102, I, p. 231 (Bethe) (third quarter of second c. A.D.):

The *bibasis* was a kind of Laconian dance. Contests were held in it not only for boys, but also for young women. You had to jump up and touch your buttocks with your feet and they counted the number of leaps, which is the explanation for the epigram of one girl, who '. . . once did the *bibasis* a thousand times, the most of anyone ever!'

For Spartan female dances, see Michell (1952) 188, who mentions five cult dances for girls.

73. See appendix 5.2, where sources and events are listed chronologically. It is beyond the purview of this study to examine the two Spartan female chariot victors who are known to have won Olympic crowns in the fourth century, since the women only sponsored the chariots, which were driven by men: Cynisca won in 396 and 392 b.c. and Euryleonis in 368 (?). See L. Moretti, *Olympionikai, i Vincitori negli Antichi Agoni Olimpici, MemLincei* ser. 8.8.2 (Rome: Accademia Nazionale dei Lincei, 1957) 114–15, 121. There appears to have been a female victor in the *diaulos* footrace of the Livian games organized under either Tiberius or Claudius: SEG XI (1950–54) no. 819; B. D. Meritt, "The Epigraphic Notes of Francis Vernon," *Hesperia Suppl.* (1949) 215, second century A.D.; K. Mantas, "Women and Athletics in the Roman East," *Nikephoros* 8 (1995) 134.

Chapter 6

1. L. G.-Kahil, "Quelques vases du sanctuaire d'Artemis à Brauron," *Antike Kunst*, suppl. 1 (1963) 5–29; id., "Autour de l'Artémis attique," *Antike Kunst* 8 (1965) 20–33; id., "Artémis attique," *CRAI* (1976) 126–30; id., "L'Artémis de Brauron: rites et mystère," *Antike Kunst* 20 (1977) 86–98; id., "La déesse Artémis: mythologie et iconographie," in *Greece and Italy in the Classical World*. Acta of the xi International Congress of Classical Archaeology, London 3–9 September 1978, ed. J. N. Coldstream and M.A.R. Colledge (London: National Organizing Committee, XI International Congress of Classical Archeology, 1979) 73–87; id., "Le 'craterisque' d'Artémis et le Brauronion de l'Acropole," *Hesperia* 1 (1981) 253–63; id., "The Mythological Repertoire of Brauron," in *Ancient Greek Art and Iconography*, ed. W. Moon (Madison: University of Wisconsin Press, 1983) 231–44; Richard Hamilton, "Alcman and the Athenian Arkteia," *Hesperia* 58.4 (1989) 449–72 and pls. 83–86; Ellen D. Reeder, *Pandora: Women in Classical Greece* (Princeton: Trustees of the Walters Art Gallery in association with Princeton University Press, 1995) 321–28 ("Little Bears"), cat. nos. 98–100.

2. C. Montepaone, "L'arkteia a Brauron," *Studi storico-religiosi* 3 (1979) 363 claims without citing specific evidence that dance is a recurrent iconographic motif, but the motif of running is rarely found depicted. Yet the present study shows that running scenes far outnumber those of dance in cases where either can be identified with some certainty.

3. Kahil (1965) 30 and n. 76.

4. For the Heraia, see ch. 4; for the Dionysiades, see ch. 5, and C. Calame, *Choruses of Young Women in Ancient Greece: I: Their Morphology, Religious Role, and Social Functions*, trans. D. Collins and J. Orion (Lanham, Md.: Rowman & Littlefield, 1997) 185–91, from the original *Les choeurs de jeunes filles en Grèce archaïque, I: Morphologie, fonction religieuse et sociale* (Rome: Ateneo & Bizzarri, 1977) 323–33.

5. Kahil (1965) 23–24 notes the provenance of many of the unusually shaped *krateriskoi*.

6. L. Palaiokrassa, *To hiero tēs Artemidos Mounichias* (Ph.D. diss., Aristotelian University, Salonica, 1983); Christiane Sourvinou-Inwood, *Studies in Girls' Transitions: Aspects of the Arkteia and Age Representation in Attic Iconography* (Athens: Kardamitsa, 1988). I wish to thank Dr. Palaiokrassa for sending me a copy of her dissertation, which had been otherwise difficult to obtain for this study. Munichion Kk55, a *kratēriskos* fragment (= Palaiokrassa, pl. 52a, reproduced in Sourvinou-Inwood, pl. 5, and = fig. 6–8 in this chapter) shows two naked girls, one wearing her hair bound up, and holding a wreath in one hand in a manner very similar to appendix 6-1, no. 9. But unlike the latter fragment, the arms of the Munichian figure are held straight out in back and front like the runners in app. 6.1, nos. 2 and 5 (= fig. 6-1 here), indicating a more animated pace of running. On the basis of the similarities of style and iconography to the other *kratēriskoi* dated to the first half of the fifth century, I place the Munichion vase in that period. See discussion by Palaiokrassa, 76–77.

7. For a typical example of several male sprinters in the stade race, see N.Y. Met. 14.130.12, black-figure. Panathenaic amphora, ca. 525 B.C., showing five runners in a group, some with fingers splayed, but most held together (= E. N. Gardiner, *Athletics of the Ancient World* [Oxford: Clarendon, 1930; reprint, Chicago: Ares, 1980] fig. 89; N. Yalouris, *The Eternal Olympics: The Art and History of Sport* (Athens: Caratzas, 1979) fig. 70; J. Jüthner, *Die athletischen Leibesübungen der Griechen*, ed. F. Brein, vol. 2, SB Vienna 249 (Graz: Hermann Böhlaus, 1968) table 5. Another vase, Athens NM 761, frag. of black-figure Panathenaic amphora, ca. 550 B.C., shows runners in the diaulos, again with fingers tight together (= Gardiner, fig. 90; Yalouris, fig. 73). Compare the depiction of long-distance runners with hands in a fist in British Museum B.609 black-figure Panathenaic amphora of 333 B.C. (= Gardiner, fig. 93; Yalouris, fig. 75). Other sprinters are illustrated in Yalouris, figs. 69–72 and Jüthner table IIIb, IX, Xa, and b).

8. Kahil (1965) 27–30.

9. E. Simon, *Festivals of Attica: An Archaeological Commentary* (Madison: University of Wisconsin Press, 1983) 87–88.

10. Only one piece in fact shows girls running with splayed fingers, app. 6.1, no. 16. Although the girls wear short chitons and run away from an altar with a flame, the piece is in many other aspects unusual and may not, in fact, represent the same ritual or Arkteia festival as the other piece under consideration here. app. 6.1, no. 16 is from Salamis, the only lekythos with girl runners, and the background decoration of branches or trailing vines is otherwise unknown for the Arkteia iconography. Kahil suggests that the vase may have come from the sanctuary of Artemis on Salamis (1965) 30 and note 79, cf. Paus. 1.36.1 and A. Mommsen, *Feste der Stadt Athen im Altertum* (Leipzig: B. G. Teubner, 1898) 462–63. Might there have been a girls' race on Salamis somewhat different from the courses of the Arkteia?

11. Kahil (1977) 97 identified the *krokōtos* with the *chitōniskos*. Although I use here the reading *kai cheousa* proposed by T.C.W. Stinton, "Iphigeneia and the Bears of Brauron," *CQ* N.S. 26 (1976) 11–12, the *katacheousa* of the Ravennas defended by C. Sourvinou-Inwood, "Aristophanes, *Lysistrata*, 641–647," *CQ* N.S. 21 (1971) 339–42 would also convey the notion of shedding the robe as a part of the ritual and would associate the text with the ritual nudity depicted on the vases. The reading *kat'echousa* of the modern texts, while not supporting this particular association,

would also not disallow the general identification of the activity on the vases as part of the Brauronian ritual.

12. Kahil (1979) 79–80, and Montepaone (above, note 2, 1979) 361 propose that the *krokōtos* resembled a bear's coat; T. Linders, *Studies in the Treasure Records of Artemis Brauronia Found in Athens* (Lund: P. Äström, 1972) 45 records the *krokotos* dedications; Sourvinou-Inwood (above, note 6, 1988) 121–22 sees it as some type of short or long chiton that was not necessarily portrayed on the vases for reasons of ritual secrecy.

13. Aristoph., *Lys.* 44 speaks disparagingly of women lounging around "wearing their saffron robes" (*krokōtophorousai*); cf. also id., *Thesmophoriazousae* 138 and *Ecclesiazousae* 879 re women, and Araros, fr. 4 Koch. In the Iliad, *krokopeplos* is a consistent epithet of Eos (8.1, 19.1, etc.). On the female associations of saffron with women and possibly with their initiation to adulthood, see Reeder (1995) 239–40.

14. Linders (1972) 9, 12, 26, 59–62 records dedications of *chitōniskoi*; H. Lloyd-Jones, "Artemis and Iphigeneia," *JHS* 103 (1983) 94 identifies the *krokōtos* rather with long robes of certain statues from Brauron.

15. Kahil (1965) 30–31 and note 80 cites the Amphidromia; Sourvinou-Inwood (1971) 339–42 and Kahil (1977) 97 discuss the sequence of clothed-nude in the ritual. P. Perlman, "Plato *Laws* 833C–834D and the Bears of Brauron," *GRBS* 24 (1983) 115–30, esp. 123, note 42 disputes Kahil's determination of ages for girls on the vases. Sourvinou-Inwood (1988) *passim*.

16. Kahil (1979) 81 draws the Iphigeneia parallel; R. Osborne, *Demos: The Discovery of Classical Attika* (Cambridge: Cambridge University Press, 1985) 164 and W. Sale, "The Temple Legends of the Arkteia," *RhM* 118 (1975) 265–84, esp. 282–83, discuss the relation of the Iphigeneia sacrifice at Brauron to the Arkteia ritual. Lloyd-Jones (1983) more precisely defines Artemis' relation with Iphigeneia at Brauron and elsewhere with regard to "ritual slaying."

17. P. Vidal-Naquet, *The Black Hunter: Forms of Thought and Forms of Society in the Greek World*, trans. A. Szegedy-Maszak (Baltimore: Johns Hopkins University Press, 1986) 145–46 (ch. 6 = orig. publ. as "Le cru, l'enfant grec et le cuit," in *Faire de l'histoire: nouveaux objets*, ed. J. le Goff and P. Nora [Paris: Gallimard, 1974] 156–57).

18. Torch races at the Panathenaia and elsewhere in Attica are discussed by H. W. Parke, *Festivals of the Athenians* (London: Thames and Hudson, 1977; reprint, Ithaca: Cornell University Press, 1986) 45–46, 171, and 200, note 1, and by D. Kyle, *Athletics in Ancient Athens* (Leiden: E. J. Brill, 1987) 190–93. Neither author includes a discussion of the Arkteia as a torch race.

19. On men's torch racing generally, see J. Jüthner (1968) vol. 2, 134–56, and tables XXXVIIa, XXXVIIIa and b, and XLa for illustrations of racing in this team-relay contest. It is noteworthy that for these bona fide races, normally over long distances, the running style is that of other long-distance runners and does not resemble the sprintlike running of the Brauronian girl torch carriers. For the epithet *Phosphoros*, see Kahil (1979) 83–84; see also Kahil (1965) 31 and id. (1963) 28–29 for additional discussion of Artemis and torches in ritual. M. P. Nilsson, *Geschichte der griechischen Religion*, 2nd ed., vol. 1 (Munich: C. H. Beck, 1955) 495, note 2 cites Sophocles, *Oedipus Tyrannus* 206ff. for the epithet *Purphoros* in the context of Artemis in Lycia.

20. E. Kadletz, "The Race and Procession of the Athenian Oschophoroi," *GRBS* 21 (1980) 363–71 has convincingly argued that the procession of the Oschophoria

and the race of the Scira are part of the same Attic festival. See also L. Deubner, *Attische Feste* (Berlin: Heinrich Keller, 1932; reprint, Darmstadt: Wissenschaftliche Buchgesellschaft, 1956) 142–47; Parke (1977) 77–80.

21. Coincidentally, our word *punch* comes from Sanskrit *pança*, that is, "[the drink with] five [ingredients]" originally used in a religious ritual.

22. M. P. Nilsson, *Grieschische Feste von religiöser Bedeutung mit Ausschluß der Attischen* (Leipzig: B. G. Teubner, 1906; reprint, Darmstadt: Wissenschaftliche Buchgesellschaft, 1957) 121.

23. Sourvinou-Inwood, "Altars with Palm-Trees, Palm-Trees and *Parthenoi*," *BICS* 32 (1985) 125–46 and pls. 7–8, concludes that in fifth-century Attic iconography an altar combined with a palm tree is connected with the role of Artemis as protector of marriageable *parthenoi*.

24. H. F. Miller, *The Iconography of the Palm Tree in Greek Art* (Ph.D. diss., University of California, Berkeley, 1979).

25. Philostratus' reliability has been questioned with regard to unique factual details of athletic events, but there seems little reason to suspect bias or bald invention in the report of a simple ritual at such a widely popular festival. M. Poliakoff, *Studies in the Terminology of the Greek Combat Sports*, Beiträge zur Klassischen Philologie, vol. 146 (Königstein/Ts.: Anton Hain, 1982), app. 4, pp. 143–48, presents a firm case for suspecting Philostratus of misinformation due to ideological preoccupations arising from the Second Sophistic movement and "limited interest in the realities of Greek sport." The most egregious of such errors are, however, those of interpretation serving his philosophical bias, and I can see no reason for such distortion in the report of the position of the altar vis-à-vis the footraces at Olympia.

26. W. Burkert, *Homo Necans: The Anthropology of Ancient Greek Sacrificial Ritual and Myth* (Berkeley: University of California Press, 1983) 93–103, accepts Philostratus' account of the torch ritual associated with the stade race at Olympia and interprets the finish at the altar as a symbolic acknowledgment of Zeus as the god of daylight who purifies the victor through the sacrificial fire.

27. Black-figure Panathenaic Amphora, Berlin Painter, Castle Ashby *ABV* 408.1, ca. 470 B.C. (= Gardiner [1930] pl. 92; Jüthner [above, note 7, 1968] vol. 2, table 4b; J. D. Beazley, *The Development of Attic Black-Figure* (Berkeley: University of California Press, 1964) 95 and pl. 44.2; Yalouris [1976] pl. 74); black-figure Panathenaic amphora, N.Y. Met. Mus. 14.130.12, ca. 525 B.C. (= Gardiner [1930] pl. 89).

28. Kahil (1979) 80–81 suggested that faces A and B of app. (6.1) no. 17 represent, respectively, the preparations for the girls' race ("les preparatifs de la course sacrée des petites filles") and the race itself ("la course elle-même"). The branches somewhat resemble the one seen on app. 6.1, no. 11, where it stands beside a *kratēriskos* in front of an altar. In the latter scene, it has been suggested that the branch was used for aspersions sprinkled from some liquid in the *kratēriskos*. See Kahil (1979) 80, and Simon (1983) 83.

29. H.-G. Buchholz, "Zum Bären in Syrien und Griechenland," *Acta Praehistorica et Archaeologica* 5/6 (1974/5) 175–85.

30. Osborne (1985) 69 discusses the status of the *arktoi* as tamed and untamed in the foundation myths of the Arkteia ritual but does not cite the specific iconography of this vase, app. 6.1, no. 18 (= fig. 6-6).

31. The following comment on the "human" characteristics of the bear noted by Aristotle and others: Reeder (1995) 301–2; Simon, (1983) 85; S. Cole, "The Social Function of Rituals of Maturation: The Koureion and the Arkteia," *Zeitschrift für Papyrologie und Epigraphik* 55 (1984) 241, and Osborne (1985) 167). J. K. Anderson, *Hunting in the Ancient World* (Berkeley: University of California Press, 1985) 15 comments on the Greek reluctance to hunt bears; K. Meuli, "Griechische Opferbräuche," in *Phylobolia für Peter von der Mühll*, ed. Olof Gigon, Karl Meuli, Willy Theiler, Fritz Wehrli, and Bernhard Wyss (Basel: B. Schwabe, 1946) 232 and *passim* [= in K. Meuli, with T. Gelzer, eds., *Gesammelte Schriften*, vol. 2 (Basel and Stuttgart: Schwabe, 1975) 956 and *passim*] discusses the taboos associated with bear-hunting in numerous cultures in view of the animal's human qualities.

32. Anderson (1985) 49–50 discusses the Greek practices of hunting fawns with hounds as related in Xenophon, *Cynēgetica* 9.1–7. In commenting on the hunting of fawns in the spring, the season of their birth, Anderson writes, "we should nowadays deplore the destruction of the breeding stock." The particular brutality of this aspect of Greek hunting may be one reason that it was chosen for the vase: it illustrates an especially savage side of humans.

33. See Kahil (1963) 14 and pls. 6.3, 6.4; p. 19, pl. 10.3; p. 20, pl. 11.2; p. 22, pl. 13.2, for Brauronian vases with hunting motifs, including Artemis with bow, arrow, and quiver, and Actaeon being attacked by his hounds. E. Simon, *Die Götter der Griechen*, 2nd ed. (Munich: Hirmer, 1980) 149 speculates that hunting may be the oldest of Artemis' functions, perhaps the remnant of elitist leisure activity of aristocrats in the Minoan/Mycenaean era.

34. I. D. Kondis, "Artemis Brauronia," *AD* 22 (1967) 187–88 first argued for the identification. Linders (1972) 13, note 46 writes, without citing reasons, that the phrase may refer either to the Brauronion on the Acropolis, or to a ceremony enacted at Brauron. Kahil (1977) 93 relates the phrase to *hieron kunēgesion* to the Arkteia ritual depicted in pl. 20 [= app. (6.1) no. 19, fig. 6-7], but does not mention the hound hunt in app. (6.1) no. 18 (fig. 6-6). Cole (1984) takes Kahil's observations more loosely, equating the *mustērion* as a whole depicted on app. (6.1) nos. 17, 18, and 19 to "the sacred hunt," but she also neglects the particularly relevant iconography on app. (6.1) no. 18 (fig. 6-6). Osborne (1985) 160–61 does not attempt to identify the *kunēgesion* more precisely than as a ritual under the control of a priestess of Artemis; he thus distinguishes it from the major penteteric festival of the Brauronia which was controlled by the *hieropoioi kat' eniauton* appointed by the *Boulē* (Aristotle, *Athenaion Politeia* 54.7). There is, however, no reason to believe that the *hieropoioi* actually officiated at the ritual, and so the priestess mentioned in *Hypothesis ad Demosthenes* 25 may in fact be a priestess of the Brauronia. This identification is supported further by the mention of *himatia* mentioned in Hyp. Dem. 25 as being required for the ritual. *Himatia* are portrayed on several of the Brauronian vases, and they may also be the *krokōtoi*, "the saffron robes," characteristic of the Arkteia festival.

35. Artemis is also depicted with a quiver on another vase fragment from Brauron: Kahil (1963) 9 and pl. 10.3.

36. Kahil (1977) 93 and (1979) 81, Cole (1984) 241, and G. Arrigoni, "Donne e Sport nel Mondo Greco," in *La donne in Grecia*, ed. G. Arrigoni (Bari, Italy: Laterza,

1985) 103 discuss the bear-headed figures as the masked priest and priestess of Artemis. Simon (1983) 88 convincingly argues that the two are Callisto and Arcas, based on parallels with other scenes of metamorphosis in vase painting.

37. For the flautist and dancers on a Brauron fragment, see Kahil (1963) pl. 1.4. Sirens (or possibly sphinxes) are also evident in ibid. pl. 1.3.

38. W. Burkert, *Structure and History in Greek Mythology and Ritual* (Berkeley: University of California Press, 1979) 57.

39. W. Sale (1975) 265–84 presents a full analysis of the Brauronian and Munichian sources and suggests some common ancestry or contamination, the precise nature of which cannot be determined. The sources are also discussed at length by A. Brelich, *Paides e Parthenoi*, vol. 1, Incunabula Graeca vol. 36 (Rome: Ateneo, 1969) 230–79.

40. Discussions are also found in Osborne (1985) 163–69; Montepaone (1979) 351–52; A. Henrichs, "Human Sacrifice in Greek Religion: Three Case Studies," in *Le Sacrifice dans L'Antiquité*, ed. J. Rudhardt and O. Reverdin, Entretiens sur l'antiquité classique vol. 27, Fondation Hardt (Geneva: Fondation Hardt, 1981) 198–208; Arrigoni (1985) 103; Vidal-Naquet (1986) 145–46 = (1974) 155; Cole (1984) 242; Lloyd-Jones (1983) 94.

41. Brelich (1969) 230–79 offers the most literal interpretation of Aristoph., *Lys.* 641–45 as a kind of initiatory *cursus honorum* in four stages for girls in Attica, including duties in turn as *arrēphoros*, *aletris*, *arktos*, and *kanēphoros*. The very limited participation of girls in some of these positions makes it unlikely that the duties were meant as a kind of fixed *cursus*, especially in a comic context where women directly challenge men in their service of the *polis*. This is not to deny that a prenuptial, initiatory function may underlie at least the Arkteia, as some scholars have noted: Kahil (1977) 87 and Parke (1977) 137–40. Cole (1984) 233–44 views "playing the bear" as a form of "wild" behavior antithetical to and preparatory for the prescribed behavior of girls and women; it corresponds to the *koureion* for boys. Arrigoni (1985) 103 essentially follows Cole.

42. P. Vidal-Naquet (1986) 129–56 = (1974) 137–68 sees the required period of ritual "savagery" in the Arkteia as a compensation for the death of wild animals. Simon (1983) 86 and Lloyd-Jones (1983) 94 hold similar views. Henrichs (1981) 197–235, esp. 198–208 compares the Arkteia myths (with Brauron and Munichion combined) to those of Iphigeneia, Iphimede, and Callisto; the Arkteia, he concludes, is "a ritualized struggle for physical survival, with emphasis on the reconciliation of such fundamental opposites as life and death, man and animal, as well as male and female" through the figure of Artemis (207).

43. Osborne (1985): "The girls put on and put off the bear, they relate as bears to men and men to bears. They are and are not bears at every stage of the ritual . . . [like Iphigeneia] they must strip for sacrifice, but what they sacrifice is precisely what they have stripped off, the wild . . ." (169); "None of this [iconographic or literary] information allows us to reconstruct a day in the life of the Brauron sanctuary but all of it together does enable a certain comprehension of the place of the cult in Athenian society" (164–65).

44. Montepaone (1979) 364: "Ritengo, infatti, che proprio perché il mito era la drammatizzazione del passaggio dal selvaggio alla civilizzazione, l'ordine dovesse essere questo: mimesi–(*himation krokōton*)–nudità–vestizione degli abiti civil . . . Questo doveva essere il momento significativo del rito."

45. Lloyd-Jones (1983) 94 argues that the *krokōtos*, which is not to be identified with the short chiton of the vases, was shed as part of the ritual in rites de passage.

46. Sourvinou-Inwood (1971) has emended to *katacheousa*; Stinton (1976) followed by Osborne (1985) 164, proposed *kai cheousa*. These readings are supported by the parallel with Aeschylus, *Ag.* 239, in which Iphigeneia is described as "shedding her garment died with saffron" and the participle *cheousa* is used. Given the importance of the Iphigeneia cult at Brauron, and, in the Leyden Scholion to Aristoph., *Lys.* 645, the claim that Iphigeneia was sacrificed at Brauron, not Aulis, Sourvinou-Inwood or Stinson's reading seems preferable to the more traditional *kat' echousa*. But even Lloyd-Jones (1983), who adheres to the latter reading, admits that the shedding of the *krokotos* was a part of the ritual. See also Sourvinou-Inwood (1988) 127–42 for a further defense of the *-cheousa* reading and for additional arguments on the shedding of the *krokōtos* as evidenced by the iconography on the vases.

47. Sourvinou-Inwood (1988) 119–26, where it is also suggested that Athens Agora P 128 (here app. 6.1, no. 13) shows a running girl dressed in a longer chiton tucked into or arranged to resemble the athletic "trunks" associated with Atalanta on other vases. Certainly short chitons, like trunks, were functionally useful garments worn by active girls. But I see little formal resemblance between the mini-culottes (?) type of dress of Agora P 128 and the tight, skimpy bikini briefs worn, for instance, by the girl athletes in some early bronze statuettes: see Arrigoni (1985) pls. 9–11, cited as parallels by Sourvinou-Inwood (1988) 125, note 12. The unusual skirt style of Agora P 128 may in fact argue against an overly literal interpretation of a hem that happens to ride up high on the raised left leg. Compare the even sketchier Appendix 6.1 no. 5 (fig. 6-1) (Brauron *kratēriskos* fr. 6), in which the *chitōniskos* rises so high as to reveal the runner's groin area, apparently without trunks.

48. The clearest documents for relative ages of the *chitōniskoi*-clad girls vs. those in the nude are Appendix 6-1, nos. 17 and 18 (figs. 6-5 and 6-6), discussed earlier.

49. Osborne (1985) 163 argues that the major difference is that the Piraeus myth seeks to explain the problematic substitution of a goat for the still more problematic killing of a bear, whereas the Brauron version "exploits the way in which bears are like men as part of a structure where men appear like bears."

50. The sources, including Bekker; Suidas, *Embaros eimi*; Pausanias in Eustathius, *Iliad* 2.732; Apostol. 7.10; and *Append. prov.* 2.54, are quoted in full in Brelich (1969) 248–49.

51. L. Deubner (1956) 206–7.

52. Osborne (1985) 163.

53. Henrichs (1981) 206–7 notes that Artemis was indifferent as to which animal she received as a favorite prey—deer, bear, or goat—as ritual surrogates for a young girl.

54. Palaiokrassa (1983).

55. Simon (1983) 86.

56. Brelich (1969) 264–65 posits that all freeborn girls participated at first, then later only the daughters of the élite. Osborne (1985) 159–60 notes that there was at least some aristocratic interest in the cult in view of the presence of some identifiable names in the Brauronian inscriptions. Lloyd-Jones (1983) agrees with the notion of a representative group as participants. Cole (1984) 242 argues on the basis of *dekateuein* as a gloss for *arkteuein* in Harpokration that only one in ten participated in later times. Vidal-Naquet (1986) 145–46 = (1974) 155–56 suggests that only a small

number of representative girls participated in view of the small size of the sanctuary. Arrigoni (1985) 103 suggests that the offering of *kratēriskoi* may signify a symbolic and indirect participation for some girls, although one would expect to find many more *kratēriskoi* if this were the case. Sourvinou-Inwood (1988) 111–18 argues cogently for a representative selection of *arktoi* on the basis of tribes, perhaps instituted as part of the Cleisthenic reorganization of the *polis*.

57. Sourvinou-Inwood (1988) 15–105 presents the most thorough and exacting survey of iconographic and literary evidence, with the conclusion that all evidence points to an age range of 5 to 10 years. Brelich (1969) 266–70 relates the age-limits to the fact that the festival was celebrated with special pomp every four years, at which time new *arktoi* were inaugurated. See Arist., *Ath. Pol.* 54.7, which names the Brauronia as a penteteric festival. Lloyd-Jones (1983) 93 infers from Aristoph., *Lys.* 645 that the age was originally over 10, that is, closer to puberty but was later, at the time of the scholia on that passage, changed to the lower limits of 5 to 10.

58. T. Klee, *Zur Geschichte der Gymnischen Agone an Griechischen Festen* (Leipzig: B. G. Teubner, 1918; reprint, Chicago: Ares, 1980) 43–51; M. Poliakoff, *Combat Sports in the Ancient World: Competition, Violence, and Culture* (New Haven: Yale University Press, 1987) 20 and 168, note 29; L. Drees, *Olympia: Gods, Artists, and Athletes*, trans. G. Onn (New York: Praeger, 1968) 50–51.

59. Deubner (1956) 208 with quotation of sources; Kahil (1963) 19–20 and pl. 11.1; id. (1965) 26–27; Brelich (1969) 276–77; and Arrigoni (1985) 103–4.

60. Lloyd-Jones (1983) 92, note 31.

61. Kahil (1963) pl. 11.1 shows a red-figure fragment of a plate, Brauron A 40, ca. 500 B.C., on which a maenad dances in a diaphanous chiton, and pl. 12, red-figure plate A 43, ca. 430–420 B.C., shows two hetairai, one in a bikini and playing *krotala* (castanets), the other in a chiton and himation about to disrobe. On the bikini trunks are depicted two figures in silhouette, apparently either nude or bikini-clad, and either performing a dance or running. Kahil does not relate these to the Theoria, but such plates might well have commemorated the festival or even been used at a Dionysiac feast at the site. Kahil (1965) 26–27 elsewhere accepts the Theoria as historical but states that it may well not have coincided with the Arkteia.

62. Brelich (1969) 278 cites the parallel of Menander's *Epitrepontes* in which there is an assault on girls at an Attic festival, probably the Tauropolia for Artemis held near Brauron; and he notes the affinities between the Theoria and the historical rape by Pelasgian or Tyrrhenian men of Attic women during a festival at Brauron as reported in Herodotus 6.138. Brelich concludes that the Brauronian Theoria was a similar, ritualized rape of the kind known from these related reports.

63. Deubner (1956) 208; Arrigoni (1985) 103–4. The Spartan festivals are somewhat the inverse of the Brauronian ones, in that the girls worship Dionysus and the boys, Artemis. Yet both may be seen to have initiatory functions in introducing youths to adulthood. For the race of the Dionysiades, see Calame (1997) 186–87 = (1977) vol. 1, 325–26 and ch. 5 of this study.

64. See chapter 4 on the Heraia at Olympia, and Nilsson (1957) 291–93 on the Thyia at Elis.

65. W. Burkert, *Greek Religion*, trans. J. Raffan (Cambridge, Mass.: Harvard University Press, 1985) 132–33, 223, from the original *Griechische Religion der Archaïschen und Klassichen Epoche* (Stuttgart: W. Kohlhammer, 1977) 210–12,

340–41; Calame (1997) 113–23 = (1977) vol. 1, 209–24 on Hera, 134–38 = (1977) vol. 1, 241–45 on Dionysus.

66. For the etymology of Artemis from the Indo-European root for "bear," see Simon (1980) 148–49 and 331, note 3; J. Puhvel, *Comparative Mythology* (Baltimore: Johns Hopkins University Press, 1988) 136. The same root is evident in the dialectal cognate *Arkas*, son of Artemis' follower Callisto. Nilsson (1955) 485–86 argues that the tales of bears associated with Artemis at least show her close connection with the animal world. Kahil (1977) 94 notes that bears were sometimes associated with chthonic deities, and the presence of the bear at Brauron may point to Iphigeneia's original identity as a chthonic deity later syncretized with Artemis.

67. J.-P. Vernant, "Etude comparée des religions antiques," *ACF* (1980–81) 402.

68. The sources for Atalanta are outlined in W. H. Roscher, *Ausfürliches Lexikon der griechischen und römischen Mythologie*, s.v. (Schirmer). The fullest version, including the nursing by a bear, is mentioned by Apollodorus, *Bibliotheca* 3.102–9.

69. Metamorphosis into lions: Apollod. *Bibl.* 3.108–9. Lions do not copulate: Servius Ver. *Aen.* 3.113; *Mythographi Vaticani* 1.39; Palaephatus 14.

70. Schol. Theocr. 3.40; Serv., Verg. *Aen.* 3.113 and *Eclogae* 6.61.

71. Pseudo-Eratosthenes, *Catasterismi* I.I.1–11.

72. Apollod. 3. 101: ὅτι τὴν παρθενίαν οὐκ ἐφύλαξεν. Cf. the scene on App. (6-1), no. 19 (= fig. 6-7), a Brauron-type, fifth-century krateriskos that shows Artemis shooting Callisto.

73. Ovid, *Metamorphoses* 409–530, id., *Fasti* 155–92. Other sources in Roscher s.v. "Callisto" (Reinhold Franz).

74. Roscher, *Ausfürliches Lexikon der griechischen und römischen Mythologie*, s.v. "Polyphonte" (Höfer) discusses Polyphonte and the primary source, Anton. Lib. 21.

75. Arrigoni (1985) 103.

76. For Callisto as a hypostasis of Artemis, see Kahil (1976) 130.

77. φεύγων … ἀπεσσύμεναι … 'αδμάτοι, Bacchylides, *Epinicion* 11.50–63, cf. φεύγων ll. 84 and 94. Apollodorus similarly emphasizes the wild abandon of their flight: ἐπλάνοντο … ἐτρόχαζον … μετ' ἀκοσμίας ἀπάσης.

Chapter 7

1. Important bibliography on Atalanta as an athlete includes: Ellen D. Reeder, *Pandora: Women in Classical Greece* (Princeton: Princeton University Press, 1995) 363–71, cat. nos. 117–19; A. Ley, "Atalante—Von der Athletin zur Liebhaberin: Ein Beitrag zum Rezeptionswandel eines mythologischen Themas auf Vasen des 6–4 Jhs. V Chr.," *Nikephoros* 3 (1990) 31–72; ead., *Atalante—Darstellungen auf Vasen des 6.–4. Jhs. v.u.Z.* (M.A. thesis, University of Hamburg, 1987; I am most grateful to Ms. Ley for letting me see a copy of this); J. Boardman, with advice from G. Arrigoni, "Atalante," in *Lexicon Iconographicum Mythologiae Classicae* (hereafter *LIMC*) (Zurich: Artemis Verlag, 1984) II.1, 940–50 with pls. II.2, 687–700; G. Arrigoni, "Donne e sport nel mondo greco: Religione e società," in *Le donne in Grecia*, ed. G. Arrigoni (Rome: Laterza, 1985) 167–68 and 171–72 with pls. 14 and 20; G. Arrigoni, "Atalanta e il Cinghiale Bianco," *Scripta Philologica* 1 (1977) 9–47; "Atalante," in *Ausführliches Lexikon der griechischen und römischen Mythologie*, (Schirmer); R. A. Howell and M. L. Howell, "The Atalanta Leg-

end in Art and Literature," *Journal of Sport History* 16 (1989) 127–39; J. Escher, *s.v.*
"Atalante," cols. 1892–98, in *RE* II.2 (Stuttgart, 1896).

2. See Boardman and Arrigoni II.1, (1984) 940 for the literary sources.

3. Though most consider Theognis to have flourished in the mid-sixth century,
there is much controversy over the dating of the body of poems (*Theognidea*) which
are in his corpus, possibly ranging in date from the late seventh century to the Hellenistic period: B. Knox, in P. E. Easterling and B.M.W. Knox, *The Cambridge History of
Classical Literature: I. Greek Literature* (Cambridge: Cambridge University Press,
1985) 136–46; T. J. Figueira and G. Nagy, eds., *Theognis of Megara* (Baltimore:
Johns Hopkins University Press, 1985); M. L. West, 1503, s.v. "Theognis," in S. Horn-
blower and A. Spawforth, eds., *The Oxford Classical Dictionary*, (Oxford: Oxford University Press, 1996).

4. Ley (1987) 19–20.

5. See P. Vidal-Naquet, *The Black Hunter: Forms of Thought and Forms of Society
in the Greek World*, trans. A. Szegedy-Maszak (Baltimore: Johns Hopkins University
Press, 1986) 119–20.

6. See the fourth century A.D. author, Libanius, *Progymnasma* 2.33–34: "On
account of this clever trick [σοφίσματος] Atalanta had the apples, but Hippomenes
had Atalanta . . . by skill rather than strength [τέχνῃ μᾶλλον ἢ ῥώμῃ] he obtained
the marriage of Atalanta. Vidal-Naquet (1986) *passim* elucidates the cunning character of the ephebe; see also M. Detienne and J.-P. Vernant, *Cunning Intelligence in
Greek Culture and Society*, trans. J. Lloyd (Sussex: Humanities Press, 1978).

7. D. Fasciano, "La Pomme dans la Mythologie Greco-romaine," in *Mélanges
d'études anciennes offerts à Maurice Lebel*, ed. J-B Caron et al., (St-Jean-Chrysostôme,
Quebec: Sphinx, 1980) 45–55.

8. W. S. Anderson, *Ovid's Metamorphoses, Books 6–10* (Norman, Okla.: University of Oklahoma Press, 1977) 527 on lines 629–30.

9. See Plato, *Republic* 5.452a–b and comments on it by S. Halliwell, ed., *Plato:
Republic 5* (Warminster, U.K.: Aris & Phillips, 1993) 141–43. S. Halliwell, in his
commentary on the book 10 passage, notes that Atalanta's choice is evidence of
her *philotimia*, "ambition for honor": *Plato, Republic 10* (Warminster, U.K.: Aris &
Phillips, 1988) 191.

10. See the other ancient sources that refer to an affair between Meleager and
Atalanta: Eustathius *ad Il.* 2.786.18; Paus. 8.45.2, 6; Hyginus, *Fab.* 173; Palaiphatos
14; Apollod., *Bibliotheca* 3.9.2; Propertius. 1.9–16; Ov., *Ars Amatoria* 2.188; id.,
Amores 2.29–30.

11. T.B.L. Webster, *The Tragedies of Euripides* (London: Methuen, 1967) 233–36,
on Euripides' *Meleager*. Ley (1987) 14–35 and 115–28 nos. K1–K23, catalogues and
discusses twenty-three representations of Atalanta as a hunter on 6th–4th c. vases,
noting that only the vases done after Euripides' *Meleager* of ca. 416 B.C. (i.e., nos.
K18–23) consistently reflect the love theme. See also LIMC, vol. II.1, 940–43, citing
eleven additional Greek or Etruscan depictions of Atalanta as huntress in sculpture,
reliefs, and mirrors from the third century or earlier. For references in the dramatists, see Soph., *TGF* IV fr. 401–6 Nauck²; Eur., *TGF* fr. 525–39 Nauck²; Eur., *TGF* II
fr. 632? Nauck²; and extensive discussion in Arrigoni (1977).

12. Apollod., *Bib.* 3.106, 164; Hyg., *Fab.* 273.10 ; cf. Ibycus, *SLG* S 176 [Page];
Tzetzes, *Chiliades* 12.937.

13. Stesichorus, Page *PMG* fr. 178–80; Ibycus, Page *SLG* S 176, mentioning Peleus as a wrestler.

14. Ley (1990) 37–46, nos. K1–K14, respectively = Boardman and Arrigoni in *LIMC* II.1 (1984) nos. 62, 65, 63, 64, 66, 67, 74, 72, (K9 omitted) 68, 69, *sub* 69, 71, 70. Boardman and Arrigoni in *LIMC* II.1 (1984) 946 nos. 75–80, also cite seven objects other than vases on which the match is depicted, dating from the sixth to the third century B.C.

15. Ley (1990) 46–49, nos. K15–K16, dated 500–490 and 450 B.C.

16. Attic white ground lekythos, Cleveland Mus. of Art 1966.114, 500–490 B.C. = Ley (1990) 67 no. K15; Boardman and Arrigoni in *LIMC* II.1 (1984), 947 and II.2, 699, no. 90. Ley notes that this romanticized portrait seems to resemble those in the later literary versions of Theocritus and Ovid.

17. Attic red-figure hydria, Madrid, Mus. Arqueológico Nac. 11130, from Cyreanaika; ca. 450 = Ley (1990) 68 no. K16. For a possible parallel to the goddess figure, see the Roman clay relief, late second–third c. A.D. showing, with names inscribed, Schoeneus, Atalanta, Hippomedon (a variant on Hippomenes), and Palaistra holding a palm branch: Gallo-Roman jug, fr. Orange, N.Y. Met. Mus. 17.194.870 = Boardman and Arrigoni in *LIMC* II.1 (1984), 946 no. 82 with fig. For Aphrodite depicted with Hippomenes, see the calyx-krater from Bologna, Mus. Civ. 300, discussed later.

18. Attic red-figure calyx-krater, from Bologna, Dinos Painter, ca. 420 B.C., Bologna, Mus. Civ. inv. no. 300 = Ley (1990) 70–71 no. K 23; Boardman and Arrigoni in *LIMC* II.1 (1984), 946 no. 81; Reeder (1995) 365–68, cat. no. 117.

19. For the headgear worn by athletes in combat sports mainly to protect the ears, see M. Poliakoff, *Combat Sports in the Ancient World: Competition, Violence, and Culture* (New Haven: Yale University Press, 1987) 14 and fig. 4. For depictions of Atalanta in a cap wrestling Peleus or in his presence, see Ley (1990) nos. K8, K18, K22 = Boardman and Arrigoni in *LIMC* II.1 (1984), 945 no. 72, 947 no. 86, 946 no. 73.

20. See note 36 of this chapter.

21. Ley (1990) 61–67, nos. K 1–14 and 70, no. K22. There are also at least two gems (early fifth century), a clay relief (discussed later), a shield band relief (sixth century), an Etruscan mirror (late fifth century), and Etruscan cista handles (third century B.C.), all depicting the Peleus and Atalanta match; except for the clay relief, these are without significant deviation from the iconography of the vases: see Boardman and Arrigoni in *LIMC* II.1 (1984), 946 nos. 75–80.

22. Ley (1990) 44–45.

23. Black-figure hydria, ca. 550 Adolfseck, Schloss Fasanerie 6 = Ley (1990) 62–63, no. K4; Boardman and Arrigoni *LIMC* II.1 (1984), 945, no. 64.

24. Black-figure neck amphora, ca. 500 B.C., Munich Staatl. Antikensamml. 1541 (J584) = Ley (1990) 65–66, no. K10; Boardman and Arrigoni in *LIMC* II.1 (1984), 945, no. 68. On the *perizōma*, see Reeder (1995) 364.

25. Clay relief, "Melian," fr. Attica, ca. 460–450, Berlin, Staatl. Mus. 8308 = Boardman and Arrigoni in *LIMC* II.1 (1984), 946, no. 77.

26. D. Young, *The Olympic Myth of Greek Amateur Athletics* (Chicago: Ares, 1984) 114–15; Ley (1990) 41; C. Morgan, *Athletes and Oracles: The Transformation of Olympia and Delphi in the Eighth Century* B.C. (Cambridge: Cambridge University Press, 1990) 43–47; H. Lee, "The 'First' Olympic Games of 776 B.C.," in *The Archaeol-*

ogy of the Olympics: The Olympics and Other Festivals in Antiquity, ed. W. Raschke (Madison: University of Wisconsin Press, 1988) 111.

27. Attic red-figure hydria, ca. 520–510, Psyax, now in Tessin, private collection, and an Attic black-figure neck amphora, early fifth c., Diosphos Painter, Berlin, Staatl. Mus. F. 1837 = Ley (1990) 41, 65, 67, nos. K9 and K13; Boardman and Arrigoni in *LIMC* II.1 (1984), 945, no. 71 (Berlin amphora).

28. Black-figure hydria, Chalcidican, Munich, Staatl. Antikenslg. 596 (J125) from Vulci, ca. 540 B.C. = Ley (1990) 41–42, 64 no. K7; Boardman and Arrigoni in *LIMC* II.1 (1984), 946, no. 74.

29. Scaraboid, plasma, Cypriot, N.Y. Met. Mus. 74.51.4152 = Boardman and Arrigoni in *LIMC* II.1 (1984), 946, no. 75.

30. See note 27 to this chapter for citation of the vase (= Ley [1990] 65 no. K9); see also B. Jeske and C. Stein, "Eine frührotfigure Hydria des Psyax," *Hefte des Archäologischen Institutes der Univ. Bern* 8 (1982) 5–20 and pls. 1–7.

31. I. Weiler, *Der Agon im Mythos: Zur Einstellung der Griechen zum Wettkampf*, Impulse der Forschung, vol. 16 (Darmstadt: Wissenschaftliche Buchgesellschaft, 1974) 129–52; H. Siska, *De Mercurio ceterisque deis ad artem gymnicam pertinentibus* (Ph.D. diss., University of Halle, 1933) 38–43; Ley (1990) 40. It should, however, be noted that in Pausanias' version of the wrestling contest the match is between Peleus and Jason, and Atalanta does not participate.

32. This is in accordance with Ley's careful study of the question in (1990) 42–45.

33. Apollod., *Bib.* 3.9.2 ; Hyg., *Fab.* 273.10 ; Ley (1990) 35; see note 12 to this chapter. Hyginus does not, however, name Peleus' opponent, who is, in at least one variant version, Jason (Paus. 5.17.10).

34. Bronze statuette, Vienna, Kunsthistorisches Mus. VI.2757, fr. Elbassan (Albania) = Boardman and Arrigoni in *LIMC* II.1 (1984), 948, no. 99. For other possible iconographic parallels to the Amazons or Artemis, see Ley (1990) 45.

35. E.g., Xen., *Symposium* 7. On the *perizōma*, see A. Kossatz-Deissmann, "Zur Herkunft des Perizoma im Satyrspiel," *JdI* 97 (1982) 64–90; L. Bonfante-Warren, *Etruscan Dress* (Baltimore: Johns Hopkins University Press, 1975) 20–21. I am not convinced by Kossatz-Deissmann's argument that the *perizōma* should be derived primarily from the realm of Peloponnesian-Dorian female athletes, which, though certainly one source of the costume, need not define it. I do agree, however, with the notion that the costume in vase painting generally defines the "other" in opposition to the civilized Greek.

36. Fragment of an Attic red-figure volute krater, fr. Spina, ca. 440, Peleus Painter, Ferrara, Mus. Naz. di Spina T 404 = Ley (1990) 51–53 (discussing the wrestling hold), 70 no. K22; Boardman and Arrigoni in *LIMC* II.1 (1984), 946, no. 73; J. D. Beazley, *Attic Red-Figure Vase Painters*, 2nd ed., vol. II (Oxford: Clarendon Press, 1968) 1039.9.

37. Amycus may also be mistaken for "Mopsos son of Ampyx," whom Pausanias names as a competitor in the boxing match at the Games for Pelias (5.17.10).

38. Ley (1990) 17–21, 23–26 = respectively, with omissions as indicated, Boardman and Arrigoni in *LIMC* II.1 (1984), 945, no. 60, 947 no. 86, (K19 omitted), 947 no. 85; (K21 omitted); 946 no. 81; (K24 omitted); 947 no. 87; 947 no. 89. To these nine, add Arrigoni (1985) 171–72 with table 20.

39. I use the terms "palaestra" (literally, "wrestling school") and "gymnasium" interchangeably here since they were often interchangeable for the ancients in the

classical period. See S. Glass, "The Greek Gymnasium: Some Problems," in Raschke (1988) 155–73.

40. C. Bérard, "L'Impossibile Femme Athlete," *Annali Archeologia e Storia Antica* (Naples) 8 (1986) 195–202 and figs. 58–62; K. J. Dover, *Greek Homosexuality*, 2nd ed. (Cambridge, Mass.: Harvard University Press, 1989) 54–57; F. Cantarella, *Bisexuality in the Ancient World*, trans., C. Ó Cuilleanáin (New Haven: Yale University Press, 1992) 27–34; F. Buffière, *Eros adolescent: la pédérastie dans la Grèce antique* (Paris: "Les Belles Lettres," 1980) 561–73.

41. Red-figure Attic column-krater, manner of the Göttingen Painter, 500–490 B.C., fr. Rutigliano (Bari), Bari, Mus. Civ. 4979 = Bérard (1986) fig. 59.1, and Arrigoni (1985) 166–67, table 13. Red-figure column-krater, Painter of Tarquinia 707, ca. 450 B.C., from Cortona (formerly Raccolta Obizzi), Vienna, Kunsthistorisches Museum AS IV 2166 = Bérard (1986) fig. 59.2, and Arrigoni (1985) 168–69, table 15. Red-figure Attic column-krater, fr. Conversano (Bari), ca. 430 B.C., Painter of Monaco 2335, Havanna, Collection Conde de Lagunillas = Arrigoni (1985) 169, table 16. For the fourth vase, see note 42 (= fig. 7–9).

42. Red-figure stamnos, ca. 480 B.C., Siren Painter, private collection; formerly in the Nelson Bunker Hunt Collection = Bérard (1986) fig. 61.1; see J. Frel and F. Causey-Frel, eds., *Stamnoi: An Exhibition at the J. Paul Getty Museum* (Malibu: Getty Museum, 1980) no. 15; A. Greifenhagen, "Odysseus in Malibu," *Pantheon* 40 (1982) 211–17; no. 13 in the catalogue, *The Nelson Bunker Hunt Collection, Highly Important Greek Vases* (New York: Sotheby's, 1990). A red-figure stamnos, Boston 95.21, by a member of the group of Polygnotos, shows two nude women at a basin with a strigil, and, to one side, a nude young man with a strigil disinterestedly turning to a clothed servant girl: R. Sutton, "Pornography and Persuasian on Attic Pottery," in *Pornography and Representation in Greece and Rome*, ed. Amy Richlin (Oxford: Oxford University Press, 1992) 23.

43. F.-H. Massa-Pairault, "Strigiles féminins et idéologie funéraire (IVᵉ-IIIᵉ siècles av. n. è.)," *Nikephoros* 4 (1991) 197–201; Arrigoni (1985) 161–62, table 8 and 164–65, table 11; P. Bruneau, "Tombes d'Argos," *BCH* 94 (1970) 530.

44. For girls swimming, see the red-figure amphora, Rome, Villa Giulia (no inv. no.), from Cerveteri, ca. 515 B.C., Painter of Priam = Arrigoni (1985) 173–74, table 22; Bérard (1986) 200 and fig. 60.1; also see the red-figure amphora, Paris, Louvre F 203 (unknown provenience), ca. 530 B.C., Andocides Painter = Arrigoni (1985) 172–72, table 21.

45. P. Ducrey and H. van Effenterre, "Un règlement d'époque romaine sur les bains d'Arcadès," *Kreta Chronika* 25 (1973) 281ff. See also introduction in this volume, note 80.

46. Naked young women bathing under public fountains (in a gymnasium?): red-figure amphora, Berlin Staatliche Museen, Antiken-Sammlung 1843 = Bérard (1986) 200 and fig. 60.2. Naked young women bathing at a basin with folded garments, boots, comb, and perfume bottle: stamnos, fr. Vulci, Polygnotan group, Munich 2411; *ARV* 1051.18; J. Boardman, *Athenian Red Figure Vases: The Classical Period* (London: Thames and Hudson, 1989) fig. 156. Unlike the other scenes near the basin, the Berlin amphora (see note 27) and the Munich stamnos show the folded garments of the girls hanging in the background, a clearer indication that the bathing does not follow athletic exercise.

47. Red-figure pelike, Washing Painter, Paris, Louvre G 550 = *ARV*² 1129.108; CV France 12. Pl. 47.8.

48. Red-figure oinochoe, the Brown-Egg Painter, Ferra, T. 347 B VP, from Spina; *ARV*² 1353.

49. Faliscan red-figure stamnos, fourth century B.C., Rome, Villa Giulia 43794 = *CV* Italy, Villa Giulia vol. I, IV B. fig. 1, 3–5 with commentary.

50. For the Göttingen Painter vase, see note 41, for the Siren Painter vase, see note 42. The two earliest vases with Atalanta or Atalanta and Peleus in a gymnasium are Paris Louvre CA 2259, dated 475–450 B.C. (= Ley [1990] 68 K17; Boardman and Arrigoni in *LIMC* II.1 (1984), 945, no. 60), and Ferrara T 991, dated 475–450 B.C. (= Ley [1990] 69 K18; Boardman and Arrigoni in *LIMC* II.1 (1984), 947, no. 86).

51. Tondeau of a red-figure kylix, fr. Kerch, 475–450 B.C., the Euaion Painter, Paris, Louvre CA 2259 (= Ley [1990] 68–69 K 17; Boardman and Arrigoni in *LIMC* II.1 (1984), 945, no. 60).

52. Basin: Ley (1990) nos. K19–21, 23, and 25–26. Atalanta standing, Peleus seated: ibid. K 24–25; Peleus standing, Atalanta seated: ibid. K 19–21; both standing: ibid. K 18 and 23; both sitting: ibid. K 26.

53. Attic red-figure kylix, fr. Spina, ca. 475–450 B.C., Aberdeen Painter (tondeau with Peleus and Thetis), Ferrara, Mus. Arch. Naz. T.991 inv. no. 1340 (VL³ 316: B5) = Ley (1990) nos. K18 (positing a strigil in the missing fragment), Boardman and Arrigoni in *LIMC* II.1 (1984), 947, no. 86; Lucanian red-figure calyx-krater, Locri Painter, 380–360 B.C., fr. Locri Epizephyrii T. 1119, Reggio Calabria Mus. Naz. 5014 = Arrigoni (1985) 171–72, table 20.

54. Ley (1990) nos. K18–21 and Arrigoni (1985) 171–72, table 20. Attic red-figure bell-krater, fragment, ca. 400 B.C. fr. Perachora, near the Pronomos Painter, Athens, Nat. Mus. (= *ARV*² 1337.7; Ley [1990] no. K 24) is fragmentary and is missing the head of Atalanta, but the poses suggest the depiction of a mutual gaze.

55. See the Bologna krater, note 18, and Attic red-figure kylix, ca. 400–370 B.C., fr. Vulci, tondeau by Jena Painter (Peleus and Atalanta), Paris, Cab. des Médailles 818 = Ley (1990) 71 no. K24; Boardman and Arrigoni in *LIMC* II.1 (1984), 947, no. 87; *ARV*² 1512, 23.

56. Attic red-figure bell-krater, ca. 400–390 B.C., fr. Al Mina, Oxford, Ashmolean Museum 1954.270 = Ley (1990) 72 no. K26; Boardman and Arrigoni in *LIMC* II.1 (1984), 947, no. 89.

57. Ley (1990) 68–72, nos. K18–21 and 25; K26 has on the other side three youths who may be athletes; K23 has on the other side three bearded men in long cloaks (in a gymnasium?); Ley (1990) K17 has only the Atalanta scene; ibid. K 24 possibly has a Dionysian scene on the other side (see Postscript to ch. 7, on Dionysus and athletics).

58. Arrigoni (1985) 171–72, table 20.

59. See P. Veyne, *Did the Greeks Believe in Their Myths? An Essay on the Constitutive Imagination*, trans. P. Wissing (Chicago: University of Chicago Press, 1988).

Chapter 8

1. U. Dix, *Sport und Sexualität: Eine Kritik der Sport-Sexualpädagogik aus psychoanalytischer Sicht* (Frankfurt-am-Main: März, 1972). See also Brian Pronger, *The Arena of Masculinity: Sports, Homosexuality, and the Meaning of Sex* (New York: St. Martin's, 1990), which sees the modern category of homosexuality as a fluid mode of

understanding and action, including sports, a mode that can be variously appropriated by individuals but is not the fixed identity of an individual.

2. Wilfred Fiedler, "Sexuelle Enthaltsamkeit griechischer Athleten und ihre medizinische Begründung," *Stadion* 11 (1985) 137–38 and 164, note 5. See also April Carlin, "Athletic Performance and Sexuality," *Modern Athlete and Coach* 32(3) (1994) 34–36. Condoms at the 2000 Olympic Games: *Riverside Press Enterprise*, September 28, 2000, page H-2. During a lull due to bad weather, which delayed the ski-jumping, broadcasters of the 1992 Winter Olympics in Banff, Canada, interviewed Dr. Ruth Westheimer, the popular sex counsellor, who criticized some of the myths about athletic performance and sexual abstinence. I thank Prof. Don Kyle for this reference.

3. The conviction of the superstar boxer Mike Tyson on rape charges would, one hopes, discourage sexual aggression against women. But here the case is, I suspect, less clear in the public perception since the boxer still vehemently maintains his innocence, and many of his fans may, in believing him and seeing him as a victim of a court system, may not be dissuaded from similar "macho" aggressiveness toward women.

4. S. Freud, *Three Essays*, 2nd ed. (1910) [= *Werkausgabe: Drei Abhandlungen zur Sexualtheorie*, ed. Anna Freud and Ilse Grubrich-Simitis (Frankfurt: Fischer, 1978), vol. 1, 289, note.], cited by A. Guttmann in his essay, "Eros and Sport," in *Essays on Sport History and Sport Mythology*, ed. D. G. Kyle and G. D. Stark (College Station, Tex.: Texas A & M University Press, 1990), 153, note 32. See also A. Guttmann, *The Erotic in Sports* (New York: Columbia University Press, 1996), which is a much broader treatment of his earlier essay. I decided to work on the present topic before any of Professor Guttmann's work was known to me. His stimulating and convincing treatment differs significantly from my own in that he gives good evidence for the interrelation of sport and eros through the history of Western sport, and his thesis is more concerned with acknowledging the universal and diachronic existence of an erotic element in sport, both for athletes and spectators. Along the way, he voices reasonable skepticism about the theoretical rationalizing of eros' relation with sport by Freud and other modern observers. My approach is more synchronic, with a focus on ancient Greece, mostly of the Classical and later periods. My aim is to uncover the *ancient* view of the relation between eros and sport, thereby better to understand both ancient society and sexuality in general.

5. P. Coubertin, originally writing in 1913 cited and translated by Richard Mandell, *The First Modern Olympics* (Berkeley: University of California, 1976) 68–69.

6. T. Irwin, *Classical Thought, A History of Western Philosophy*, vol. 1 (Oxford: Oxford University Press, 1989) 8–10.

7. On the transmission of the ideology of *aretē* in sports, see the introduction to this book; H. W. Pleket, "Games, Prizes, Atheltes and Ideology. Some Aspects of the History of Sport in the Greco-Roman World," *Arena* (= *Stadion*) 1 (1975) 49–89; H. Lee, "Athletic Arete in Pindar," *Ancient World* 7.1–2 (1983) 32–37; on the pervasively agonistic culture of ancient Greece, see M. Poliakoff, *Combat Sports in the Ancient World: Competition, Violence, and Culture* (New Haven: Yale University Press, 1987) 104–15.

8. See discussion in chapter 9 and in Poliakoff (1987) 89–93.

9. Though of course the lowercase word "eros," not italicized and without a macron, has its own specialized modern uses and connotations, I intend it here to be taken as closely as possible in the ancient Greek senses of the term.

10. Félix Buffière, *Eros adolescent: la pédérastie dans la Grèce antique* (Paris: "Les Belles Lettres," 1980) 142 notes that the clients for the vases with *kalos* scenes are probably aristocratic. K. J. Dover, *Greek Homosexuality* 2nd ed. (Cambridge, Mass.: Harvard University Press, 1989) 4–9, voices reasonable caution about the use of visual evidence in determining social attitudes or trends, while admitting that vase paintings together with literary evidence can support an interpretation. See J. Henderson, "Greek Attitudes toward Sex," in *Civilization of the Ancient Mediterranean: Greece and Rome* ed. M. Grant and R. Kitzinger (New York: Scribners, 1988) vol. 2, 1249–63 for a good general survey of sexual attitudes, social status, and primary evidence.

11. On the composition of the audience of Greek drama, see K. J. Dover, *Aristophanic Comedy* (Berkeley: University of California, 1972) 16–17; V. Ehrenberg, *The People of Aristophanes: A Sociology of Old Attic Comedy* (New York: Schocken, 1962) 20–37.

12. See the discussion of terminology in D. Halperin, *One Hundred Years of Homosexuality* (New York: Routledge, 1990) 15–40, which follows a Foucaultian perspective. See also D.H.J. Larmour, P. A. Miller, and C. Platter, eds., *Rethinking Sexuality: Foucault and Classical Antiquity* (Princeton: Princeton University Press, 1998), which presents critiques of Foucaultian approaches to antiquity.

13. Among studies from a variety of perspectives, see James N. Davidson, *Courtesans and Fishcakes: The Consuming Passions of Classical Athens* (London: St. Martin's, 1997) 167–82; D. Cohen, *Law, Sexuality, and Society. The Enforcement of Morals in Classical Athens* (Cambridge: Cambridge University Press, 1991), esp. 171–202; E. Cantarella, *Bisexuality in the Ancient World*, trans. C. Ó Cuilleanáin (New Haven: Yale University Press, 1992); J. J. Winkler, *The Constraints of Desire: The Anthropology of Sex and Gender in Ancient Greece* (New York: Routledge, 1990); D. Halperin, J. J. Winkler, and F. I. Zeitlin, eds., *Before Sexuality: the Construction of Erotic Experience in the Ancient Greek World* (Princeton: Princeton University Press, 1990); Carola Reinsberg, *Ehe, Hetärentum und Knabenliebe im antiken Griechenland* (Munich: C. H. Beck, 1989); Henderson (1988); A. K. Siems, ed., *Sexualität und Erotik in der Antike, Wege der Forschung* vol. 605 (Darmstadt: Wissenschaftliche Buchgesellschaft, 1988); A. Rouselle, *Porneia: On Desire and the Body in Antiquity*, trans. F. Pheasant (New York: Oxford University Press, 1988); C. Calame, ed., *L'Amore in Grecia* (Rome: Laterza, 1983; reprint, 1988; esp. the editor's introduction, "Eros Inventore e Organizzatore della Società Greca Antica," ix–xl; K. J. Dover, "Classical Greek Attitudes to Sexual Behavior," *Arethusa* 6 (1973) 59–73 (= 264–81 in Siems 1988 = id. *Women in the Ancient World: The Arethusa Papers*, ed. J. Peradotto and J. P. Sullivan (Albany: State University of New York Press, 1984) 143–57; H. I. Marrou, *A History of Education in Antiquity*, trans. G. Lamb (London: Sheed and Ward, 1956) 26–35 ("Pederasty in Classical Education") for the connections with *paideia*, though much of this is out of date.

14. I agree, in essence, with the terminological disclaimer voiced by Dover (1989) vii–viii and 206.

15. See Athenaeus 13.561; S. Fasce, *Eros: la Figura e il Culto* (Genoa: Universita di Genova, Facoltá di lettere Istituo di filologia classica e medievale, 1977) esp. 39–

43; H. Siska, *De Mercurio ceterisque deis ad artem gymnicam pertinentibus* (Ph.D. diss., University of Halle, 1933) esp. 32 and 38–43, including both literary and epigraphical testimonia; Calame (1988) xxxiii–xxxviii.

16. Attic red-figure kantharoid skyphos, ca. 420 B.C., attributed to Aison, Los Angeles, Getty Museum 86.AE.269. The "friendship" scene probably does not depict lovers, since both athletes are young boys, but seems to illustrate a general spiritual affiliation that ideally balanced the physical desire depicted on the other side. For the notion of bathing with a strigil before turning to erotic pursuits, see Aristophanes' *Birds* 139–42, where a character sees the opportunity for seducing a boy after he has "left the gymnasium, after a bath," cited by Dover (1989) 55.

17. A. Fürtwangler, "Eros," in *RE* I.1 col. 1339. Calame (1988) xxviii–xxxiii.

18. C. Sourvinou-Inwood, "A Series of Erotic Pursuits: Images and Meanings," *JHS* 107 (1987) 131–53; for a literal extension of the concept in Greek iconography, see A. Schnapp, "Eros the Hunter," in *A City of Images: Iconography and Society in Ancient Greece*, trans. D. Lyons, ed. C. Bérard et al. (Princeton: Princeton University Press, 1990) 71–87 (orig. *La cité des images* [Paris: F. Nathan, 1984]).

19. Henderson (1988) 1256–57; Dover (1989) 49–54 discusses the complex relation between *philia* and *erōs* in various sexual contexts.

20. Halperin (1990) 29–38; Dover (1989) 100–109. Davidson (1997) 169–82 disputes the theories of Dover, Halperin, et al., which he calls the "power-penetration theory" of Greek sexuality, whereby the sexual penetrator is understood as the dominator, the penetrated as the subordinate. Davidson argues that this theory ignores the primary Greek concern with self-control or lack of it in sexual relations. Indeed, we might further ask, if *erōs* is commonly characterized in Greek poetry as a disease (this chapter, note 206), how can even the active partner be characterized as 'dominant'? While a "power-penetration theory" risks being overschematized, it does clearly correspond to the parallel between Greek social relations and sexual roles, and the theory may be seen as a complementary schema to the one of self-control. Though all mortals (and all gods including Zeus) can be 'dominated' by Eros, yet there is a hierarchy among sexual participants with penetrators being in power. Moderation is valued at all ranks within the socio-sexual hierarchy, but the women- or boy-mad men were much less criticized than nymphomaniac women or buggered men (*katapugōnes*), as Davidson himself admits (161). Cohen, (1991a) 171–202, also convincingly complicates the overly schematized view of a 'penetrator-penetrated' homosexual hierarchy. He reveals tensions between social norms allowing licit homosexual affairs and the legal protection of boys against suffering dishonor. Davidson's and Cohen's nuancing critiques are useful, but neither negates the preponderance of evidence (including widespread, anthropological parallels) connecting sexual with social dominance: for further examples, see Eva C. Keuls, *The Reign of the Phallus: Sexual Politics in Ancient Athens* (New York: Harper & Row, 1985) and Amy Richlin, ed., *Pornography and Representation in Greece and Rome* (Oxford: Oxford University Press, 1992) on the inequality of partners and the objectification of women in particular in the views of the Greeks. In sum, there is in the "power-penetration" view of Greek erotic relations a valid parallel with the competitive aspects of athletics which was widely exploited in Greek culture.

21. D. G. Kyle, *Athletics in Ancient Athens* (Leiden: E. J. Brill, 1987) 71–92.

22. Ibid. 115 and 225 no. P 107.

23. I. Weiler, *Der Sport bei den Völkern der alten Welt: Eine Einführung*, 2nd ed. (Darmstadt: Wissenschaftliche Buchgesellschaft, 1988) 94–95.

24. Ath. 13.565f–566a and C. Gulick, trans., vol. 1 (*Athenaeus Deipnisophistai*, vol. 6 (Cambridge, Mass.: Harvard University Press, 1950) 56, note a. See J. H. Krause, *Die Gymnastik und Agonistik der Hellenen*, Leipzig: Johann Ambrosius Barth, 1841; reprint, Wiesbaden: Dr. Martin Sändig, 1971) 33–38 with sources; N. Reed, "The Panathenaic Euandria Reconsidered," *AW* 15 (1987) 59–64, who views the contest as more than "merely a beauty contest, a 'Mr. Athens' competition," but a competition involving skill in handling shields and in armed combat. D. Kyle disputes this view in "The Panathenaic Games: Sacred and Civic Athletics," in J. Neils, ed., *Goddess and the Polis: The Panathenaic Festival in Ancient Athens* (Hanover, N.H.: Hood Museum of Art, Dartmouth College, co-published with Princeton: Princeton University Press, 1992) 95–96 and 206–7, notes, where he argues that *euandria* suggests a contest rather in moral and physical beauty, with the tone of a pageant or procession. Kyle thus agrees with N. Crowther, "Male 'Beauty' Contests in Greece: The Euandria and the Euexia," *AC* 54 (1985) 285–91; id., "Euexia, Eutaxia, Philoponia: Three Contests of the Greek Gymnasium," *ZPE* 85 (1991) 301–4. These other unusual contests in moral and physical excellence also illustrate the Greek ethos in which both qualities were to be fostered. Essentially, Crowther defines *euexia* as a kind of physique competition where "symmetry, definition, tone and bearing and especially a general fit and healthy appearance" were the criteria; the *eutaxia* seems to have been a contest for "the best behaved, most disciplined of those in the gymnasium"; and the *philoponia* was for "the most diligent or industrious in the gymnasium" over the course of a year. Most of these events date to the third to first centuries B.C. and are thus a product of the increasingly regulated gymnasia of the Hellenistic period. I find less convincing the argument by A. L. Boegehold, in *Worshipping Athena: Panathenaia and Parthenon*, ed. J. Neils (Madison: University of Wisconsin Press, 1996) 95–105, that the *Euandria* was a choral and not an individual competition, though it makes little difference to my argument if his suggestion is correct.

25. Red-figure calyx-krater, from Capua, ca. 510–500 B.C., Berlin Antikenmuseum F 2180. For discussion of the historical Leagros and his athletic associations, see Kyle (1987) 222–23, no. P100. A wine cooler vase (psykter) in the Getty Museum (fig. 8–6, ca. 510 B.C.) shows a gymnasium scene with labels of couples including the vase painter Euphronius embracing Leagros: see R. Sutton, in Richlin (1992) 15; D. Steiner, "Moving Images: Fifth-Century Victory Monuments and the Athlete's Allure," *Classical Antiquity* 17 (1998) 127 and figs. 1 and 2. For a recent discussion of kalos inscriptions and homosexuality, see Buffière (1980) 131–43. For the *kalos* inscription on other athletic scenes of Euphronius, see *ARV²* 13–14, calyx-krater, Berlin 2180; *ARV²* 15, neck-amphora, Louvre C 11071; *ARV²* 16, hydria, Dresden 295. One must, however, be careful not to draw too much from the *kalos* inscriptions which, by their ubiquity, may have become something of a cliché.

26. Stephen G. Miller , ed., *Nemea. A Guide to the Site and Museum* (Berkeley: University of California Press, 1990) 188; id., "Tunnel Vision: The Nemean Games," *Archaeology* 33 (1980) 54–56; the above translation is essentially that of Miller. For other views, see F. D. Harvey, " A Nemean Metagraffito," *AJA* 86 (1982) 586, and id.,

"Second Thoughts on the Nemean Metagraffito," *AJA* 88 (1984) 70; L. Pearson, "The Fair Akrotatos from Nemea," *AJA* 88(1984) 69–70; I. Worthington, "The Nemean 'The Good Akrotatos' Again," *AJA* 90 (1986) 41.

27. Discussions on this widely researched topic include, most recently, M. Golden, *Sport and Society in Ancient Greece* (Cambridge: Cambridge University Press, 1998) 65–69; Steiner (1998) 123–49; A. Stewart, *Art, Desire, and the Body in Ancient Greece* (Cambridge: Cambridge University Press, 1997) 24–42; M. McDonnell, "The Introduction of Athletic Nudity: Thucydides, Plato, and the Vases," *JHS* 111 (1991) 182–93; A. J. Papalas, "Boy Athletes in Ancient Greece," *Stadion* 17.2 (1991) 169–72; L. Bonfante, "Nudity as a Costume in Classical Art," *AJA* 93.4 (1989) 543–70, esp. 552–58; id., "The Naked Greek," *Archaeology* (Sept.–Oct. 1990) 28–35; N. Himmelmann, *Ideale Nacktheit in der griechischen Kunst, Jahrbuch des deutschen archäologischen Instituts*, vol. 26 (Berlin: Walter De Greuter, 1990) 38, 43, 68–69, 106, 113; J.-P. Thuillier, "La nudité athlétique (Grèce, Etrurie, Rome)," *Nikephoros* 1 (1988) 29–48; H. P. Duerr, *Nacktheit und Scham*, 2nd ed. (Frankfurt-am-Main: Suhrkamp, 1988) 13–23; J. Mouratidis, "The Origin of Nudity in Greek Athletics," *Journal of Sport History* 12 (1985) 213–32; N. Crowther, "Athletic Dress and Nudity in Greek Athletics," *Eranos* 80 (1982) 163–68; id., "Nudity and Morality: Athletics in Italy," *CJ* 76.2 (1980–81) 119–23; J. Arieti, "Nudity in Greek Athletics," *CW* 68 (1975) 431–36; W. W. Hyde, "Nudity of Victor Statues," in *Olympic Victor Monuments and Greek Athletic Art* (Washington: Carnegie Institution of Washington, 1921) 47–50. Stewart (25) prefers the terms "naked" and "nakedness" since, he argues, they are more neutral, and "nude" and "nudity" connote the quality of being on display. I follow the convention of most literature on this topic, however, and use these terms interchangeably since they seem to be rarely so marked in practice.

28. Bonfante (1989) 556. The attribution of the original artistic nudity to ideal types of gods goes back at least to the eighteenth century views of J. J. Winckelmann: see Stewart (1997) 25.

29. O. Murray, *Early Greece* (Stanford: Stanford University Press, 1980) 205–6, cited by Bonfante (1989) 554.

30. Discussed in Bonfante (1989) 557–58; see also E. Kornexl, *Leibesübungen bei Homer und Platon*, Studientexte zur Leibeserziehung, vol. 5 (Frankfurt-am-M.: Limpert, 1969) 64–66.

31. Cf. W. G. Thalmann, "Thersites: Comedy, Scapegoats, and Heroic ideology in the Iliad," TAPA 118 (1988) 16–28; M. Dillon, "Tragic Laughter," *CW* 84.5 (1991) 345–55: "In approximately 70 of the 80 extant examples from tragedy, laughter may be characterized as malevolent in the extreme" (345).

32. Thucydides 1.6; Pl., *Rep.* 452c; Dionysius of Halicarnassus, *Antiquitates Romanae* 7.72.2–3; Plutarch, *Moralia* 274D–E; translations and discussion in W. Sweet, *Sport and Recreation in Ancient Greece. A Sourcebook with Translations* (New York: Oxford University Press, 1987) 124–33.

33. Bonfante (1989) 562–69; Crowther (1980–81) 119–23.

34. "Perizoma Group": *ABV* 343–46; T.B.L. Webster, *Potter and Patron in Classical Athens* (London: Methuen & Co., 1972) 197, 270–72, 292.

35. Bonfante (1989) 564; *contra* Crowther (1982).

36. Pleket (1975) 49–89.

37. R. Hirzel, *Die Person: Begriff und Name derselben im Altertum* (Munich: Koniglich Bayerische Akademie der Wissenschaften, 1914; reprint, New York: Arno, 1976) esp. the *Nachtrag* on p. 54 re Thuc. 2.41.1.

38. Dover (1989) 156–57; S. Monoson, "Citizen as *Erastēs*: Erotic Imagery and the Idea of Reciprocity in the Periclean Funeral Oration," *Political Theory* 22.2 (1994) 1–27.

39. J. Mouratidis, "The Origin of Nudity in Greek Athletics," *Journal of Sport History* 12 (1985) 213–32.

40. Bonfante (1989) 569: "In Greece, the remarkable innovation of athletic male nudity, which surely originated in a ritual, religious context, developed a special social and civic meaning. It became a costume, a uniform: exercising together in the *gymnasia* marked men's status as citizens of the polis and as Greeks."

41. Bonfante (1989) 569. On the "scopic regime" in which audience and the representation are engaged, see generally the fine work of Steiner (1998).

42. N. Serwint, *Greek Athletic Sculpture from the Fifth and Fourth Centuries B.C.: An Iconographic Study* (Ph. D. diss., Princeton University, 1987). Generally on the construction of aesthetic ideals, see A. Stewart (1997) 3–23.

43. On the date, see ch. 7, note 3, and Dover (1989) 10; J. Delorme, *Gymnasion: Étude sur les Monuments consacrés a l'Éducation en Grèce (des origines à l'Empire romain)* (Paris: E. De Boccard, 1960) 19.

44. Delorme (1960) 19, note 6; S. Glass, "The Greek Gymnasium," in *The Archaeology of the Olympics: The Olympics and Other Festivals in Antiquity*, ed. W. Raschke (Madison: University of Wisconsin Press, 1988) 159–60; Kyle (1987) 65.

45. Re the theory of nudity's gradual adoption ca. 650–600 B.C., see McDonnell (1991). Note that the date for the popularization of athletic nudity may lag considerably behind that of its origin, which several sources ascribe to ca. 720 B.C. through the agency of either Orsippus of Megara or Akanthos of Sparta: for sources, see W. Sweet (1987) 124–29; Stewart (1997) 33 suggests that the adoption of nudity at Olympia may indeed have been by accident, as Orsippus' legend has it, rather than design, given the lack of any such tradition in Greek states other than Sparta. It is equally plausible that the custom was introduced by a Spartan, to whose society Thucydides (1.6) and Plato (*Rep.* 452c) attribute its introduction on the mainland, with the practice widely adopted later. Significantly, no sources ever say that the Olympic organizers instituted or required nudity, which is what one would expect if it had explicit religious or ritual significance.

46. On the early popularity of homosexuality, see Dover (1989) 196; on the sixth-century gymnasium, see Delorme (1960) 26–30; Kyle (1987) 65; Glass (1988) 155–73.

47. Dover (1989) 54–55.

48. For the *paidotribēs*, whose name contains the root -*trib*-, "to rub," "to anoint," see J. Jüthner, *Die athletischen Leibesübungen der Griechen*, ed. F. Brein, vol. 1, SB Vienna 249 (Graz: Hermann Böhlaus, 1965) 161–82. For the action of *agkalizein* as a term for a neck-hold, see Plut., *Mor.* 638f. (*Quaestiones conviviales* 2.4) and M. Poliakoff, *Studies in the Terminology of the Greek Combat Sports*, Beiträge zur klassischen Philologie, vol. 146 (Königstein/Ts.: Anton Hain, 1982) 12, note 1.

49. D. G. Kyle, "Solon and Athletics," *Ancient World* 9 (1984) 99–102, accepting a date ca. 580 B.C. for the reforms that may encompass athletics and pederasty;

id., (1987) 21–22. Kyle's conclusions are persuasive and preferable to the skepticism of Percy on the authenticity of these as authentic reforms of Solon: William Armstrong Percy, *Pederasty and Pedagogy in Archaic Greece* (Urbana; University of Illinois Press, 1996) 177 and 213–14, note 17, following the older studies of Ruschenbusch and Drerup.

50. See also on this law Solon fr. 74b Ruschenbusch = Plut., *Solon.* 1.6; fr. 74c Ruschenbusch = Plut., *Mor.* 152d (*Septem sapientium convivium*); fr. 74d = Plut., *Mor.* 751b (*Amatorius*); fr. 74a Ruschenbusch = Hermias Alex. in Pl., *Phdr.* 231e. Cf. the conservative views of Aristotle, *Politics* 1336a.6, which advocates restriction by tutors (*paidonomoi*) on children's association with slaves; 1331a.2 proposes gymnasia for men separate from those for boys, each in the presence of magistrates (*archontes*) to engender true "shame" or "modesty" (*aidōs*). M. Golden, "Slavery and Homosexuality at Athens," *Phoenix* 38 (1984) 308–24, elucidates the reason for excluding boys from having sexual relations with slaves, whereas no such prohibition existed for men. A boy (*pais*) as beloved (*erōmenos*) was subordinate to an adult male citizen lover (*erastēs*); slaves were also subordinate to adult citizens. The sexual relationship between two individuals with, albeit different, subordinate status, may give rise to ambiguity regarding who is dominant. When the boy becomes an adult male, he becomes master of slaves and of a household, erasing any possible ambiguity.

51. Percy (1996) 178.

52. Cantarella (1992) 28–31; Percy (1996) 179.

53. Cantarella (1992) 34–36; Kyle (1984) 101.

54. *SEG* 27.261, side B, lines 26–29; translation of whole inscription in English by S. Miller, *Arete: Greek Sports from Ancient Sources* (Berkeley: University of California Press, 1991) 126–38; for full commentary, see Philippe Gauthier and M. B. Hatzopoulos, *La loi gymnasiarchique de Beroia*, Meletēmata (Kentron Hellenikēs kai Romaikēs Archaiotētos), vol. 16 (Athens: Centre de recherches de l'antiquité grecque et romaine, and Paris: Diffusion de Boccard, 1993) 78–87; see discussion in Cantarella (1992) 28–32. L. Moretti, "Sulla legge ginnasiarchica di Berea," *RIFC* 110 (1982) 52, incorrectly takes *hetaireukotēs* as referring to a general exclusion of homosexuals; Miller, 134, incorrectly translates *hetaireukotēs* as "homosexuals." For the general disenfranchisement of male prostitutes in Athens, see Halperin (1990) 88–112.

55. *SEG* 27.261, side B, lines 13ff.

56. Cantarella (1992) 32; see also Dover (1989) 85–87 on the ambiguity of Athenian youths classified as *neaniskoi*.

57. See the commentary by Poliakoff (1982) 129–33.

58. Ibid. 133–35.

59. [Lucian], *The Ass*, trans. J. P. Sullivan, in *Collected Ancient Greek Novels*, ed. B. P. Reardon (Berkeley: University of California Press, 1989) 596; see commentary by Poliakoff (1982) 101–27. For a similar metaphor, see Aristophanes, *Acharnians* 271–75 (produced 425 B.C.), where Dikaiopolis exclaims: "O god Phales, I know nothing more pleasant than when I discover a beautiful girl stealing wood. . . . [P]ut a waist-lock on her, lift her up, throw her for a fall, and then deflower her"; see Fernando García Romero, ""Ερως ἀθλητής: les métaphores érotico-sportives dans les comédies d' Aristophane," *Nikephoros* 8 (1995) 59; Poliakoff (1982) 41. See also Aristoph., *Ecclesiazusae* 256–61 (dated ca. 391 B.C.) for another instance of the wrestling metaphor used erotically, with commentary by Romero, 60–66.

60. See K. J. Dover, ed. and comm., *Plato, Symposium* (Cambridge: Cambridge University Press, 1980) 168–69 *ad loc.*

61. Dover (1989) 56.

62. See the very similar sentiment in Aristoph., *Wasps* 1023–28; Dover (1989) 138.

63. Other references in Dover (1989) 54–55; Kyle (1987) 133; Stella Miller, "Eros and the Arms of Achilles," *AJA* 90 (1986) 166 and note 56.

64. Theophr. *ap.* Ath. 13.609f–610a.

65. Hilaire-Germain-Edgar Degas (1834–1917), *Young Spartans Exercising.*

66. On the widespread ancient notion of eros as an involuntary compulsion, see Winkler (1990) 82–91; Dover (1989) 60–68.

67. S. Halliwell, ed., *Plato: Republic 5* (Warminster, England: Aris & Phillips, 1993) 159 *ad loc.*

68. See G. Arrigoni, "Donne e sport nel mondo greco: Religione e società," in *Le donne in Grecia*, ed. G. Arrigoni (Rome: Laterza, 1985) 117–18 and 200, notes 239–42 for discussion of the festival at Cyrene. B. Zweig in Richlin (1992) 76, discusses the likelihood of some women choosing to attend dramatic festivals in classical Athens. In the Roman era, women in the Eastern Mediterranean regularly attended the theater and games, though mostly in the upper seats only (K. Mantas, "Women and Athletics in the Roman East," *Nikephoros* 8 [1995] 140–41). I. N. Perysinakis, "The Athlete as Warrior: Pindar's *P.* 9.97–103 and *P.* 10.55–59," *BICS* 37 (1990) 43–49, suggests that both Telesicrates and the athlete Hippocleas of *Pythian* 10, discussed later, were admired by maidens much like returning warriors; further, he suggests that some of the admiration may have taken place not just at the games themselves but publicly in their own communities at ceremonies, at festivals, or in victory processions. Also on Pind., *P.* 9: A. Carson, "Wedding at Noon in Pindar's *Ninth Pythian*," *GRBS* 23 (1982) 121–28 and Steiner (1998) 141, who calls Telesicrates "an omni-erotic being, alluring to all alike."

69. See T. Klee, *Zur Geschichte der Gymnischen Agone an Griechischen Festen* (Leipzig: B. G. Teubner, 1918 reprint, Chicago: Ares, 1980) 79–80.

70. L. Moretti, *Olympionikai, I Vincitori negli Antichi Agoni Olimpici, MemLincei,* ser. 8.8.2 (Rome: Accademia Nazionale dei Lincei, 1957) 10 no. 5 = *IG* I² 472, line 5, dated ca. 550–545 B.C.: ’Aθάναις Παλ(λ)άδος πανέ[γυρις].

71. M. P. Nilsson, *Griechische Feste von religiöser Bedeutung mit Ausschluß der attischen* (Leipzig: B. G. Teubner, 1906; reprint, Darmstadt: Wissenschaftliche Buchgesellschaft, 1957) 279 and 426.

72. S. Instone, "Love and Sex in Pindar: Some Practical Thrusts," *BICS* 37 (1990) 39. Also on this poem: Steiner (1998) 126–27 and 137–43.

73. Attic red-figure squat lekythos, the Eretria Painter, Nicosia C 756, from Marion = *ARV²* 1248, 7; J. D. Beazley, *Proceedings of the British Academy* 33 (1947) 239 mistakenly takes Eros as a jumper. For Eros here at the starting post of a footrace, see also *LIMC* III.1.912 no. 717 and another squat lekythos, Prague, Univ. E 61, not by the Eretria Painter, noted in *ARV²*, *loc. cit.*.

74. Klee (1980) 43 and 46–48

75. Instone (1990) 32.

76. Ibid. 35–39; Percy (1996) 135–38, focuses on the pederastic aspect of Pindar's epinician odes (e.g., *Ol.* 10.97–105), and possibly of the poet's own life, as in

his *skolion* (drinking song) praising the attractiveness of the young Theoxenus (Ath. 601d). Steiner (1998) 137–43 discusses the erotic elements in Pindar, focusing on the parallels between physical monuments and the odes: both poetry and sculpture emphasize an eroticized beauty and the attraction of both male and female viewers to it; the male audience responds not only with voyeuristic pleasure, but narcissistic identification, though full identification with the idealized athlete is ultimately impossible.

77. Xenophon of Ephesus, *An Ephesian Tale* 1.2 (trans. Graham Anderson, in Reardon [1989] 129).

78. Nilsson (1957) 244–45; S.F.R. Price, *Rituals and Power: The Roman Imperial Cult in Asia Minor* (Cambridge: Cambridge University Press, 1984) 110.

79. L. Moretti, *Iscrizioni agonistiche greche* (Rome: Angelo Signorelli, 1953) nos. 73 (boxer), 75 (pentathlete), and 76 (runner), records victories by athletes in the Artemis Festival at Ephesus from the second century A.D.

80. Pl., *Rep.* 468c suggests that a victor in battle should get the beloved of his choice—male or female.

81. Moretti (1957) 106 no. 329; Fiedler (1985) 146; Aristroph., *Ecclesiazusae* 22 (with Scholia); Cratinus frr. 15 and 256 (Koch). See also Tertullian, *De pallio* 4.4, echoing the testimony of Strabo.

82. Winkler (1990) 45–54 = Halperin, Winkler, and Zeitlin (1990) 171–86; Davidson (1997) 167–82.

83. Moretti (1957) 125–26 no. 458; Fiedler (1985) 146.

84. On the ambiguities and complexities of prostitution and *hetairai*, see Halperin (1990) 88–112, esp. 107–112; Reinsberg (1989) 80–162; Davidson (1997) 73–136, esp. 92 on *hetairai* at festivals. Leontiscus and Mania: Machon, fr. 15.218–25 Gow, *ap.* Ath. 13.578f; Leontiscus, Olympic pancration victor in 304 B.C., and Antenor, Olympic pancration victor in 308 B.C.: respectively, Moretti (1957) 132 no. 495 and 131 no. 488.

85. Attic red-figure column-krater, ca. 500–490 B.C., attributed to Myson, Getty Mus. 73.AE.135.

86. Ath. 4.128b–130d, esp. 129a, 129d, 130c; Xen., *Symposium* 2 and 9 for an acrobatic woman entertainer inspiring courage and a ballet of dancers (portraying Dionysus and Ariadne) inspiring Eros in the male spectators at a symposium.

87. W. Sweet, "Protection of the Genitals in Greek Athletics," *AncW* 11 (1985) 43–52 notes that modern coaches counsel against or even prohibit sex for athletes in training. Athletes and coaches with whom I have talked confirm the existence of such a rule, but the advice seems to exist more by an informal, oral tradition than in coaching manuals, where I have not been able to find it. See also Fiedler (1985) 137–75 and A. Guttmann (1996). My debt to Fiedler's careful survey of athletic abstinence and its medical basis will be evident in this section, though my interpretation of the sources differs on many points.

88. Oribasius, *Medicae Collectiones* 6.37–38, cited and with a brief discussion by A. Rousselle, (1988) 17–18. On the use of oil and dust, see D. Sansone, *Greek Athletics and the Genesis of Sport* (Berkeley: University of California Press, 1988) 95–103, 122–25; and C. Ulf, "Die Einreibung der griechischen Athleten mit Öl," *Stadion* 5 (1979) 220–38.

89. Fiedler (1985) 159–63.

90. E. J. Dingwall, *Male Infibulation* (London: John Bole, Sons & Danielsson, Ltd., 1925) 39–40, discusses the passage.

91. Cf. Galen, *In Hippocratis librum primum epidemiarum commentarii iii*, 17 A 521; E. Wenkebach, ed., *Galeni in Hippocratis epidemiarum librum i commentaria iii* (*Corpus medicorum Graecorum*, vol. 5.10.1 [Leipzig: B. G. Teubner, 1934]), also alluding to athletes who abstain from sexual relations.

92. See Introduction, note 30.

93. See Fiedler (1985) 144–45 and 166–67, notes 25–28; Moretti (1957) 141 no. 584.

94. Dion Chrysostomus, *Orationes* 28.10, 12; 29.18. See Fiedler (1985) 145–46 and 168, note 31.

95. Fiedler (above, note 2, 1985) 141–142 with 165–166 n. 18 re Laïs generally, and Eubatas' story.

96. On Eubatas (Eubotas) see Moretti (1957) 110 no. 347.

97. M. P. Nilsson, *Geschichte der Griechischen Religion*, 2nd ed., vol. 1 (Munich: C. H. Beck, 1955) 94.

98. Fiedler (1985) 169, note 44.

99. Ibid. 150–55; see D. C. Young, *The Olympic Myth of Greek Amateur Athletics* (Chicago: Ares, 1984) 134–45 on Pythagoras and athletics.

100. Dingwall (1925) 39–41, noting also J. Cassian, *Opera* (Corp. Script. Eccl. Lat., 17) (Prague, 1888), *De institutis coenobiorum* 6, ch. 7, p. 119, in reference to the custom of using leaden plates.

101. Phrynichus, *Praeparatio Sophistica* (epitome), ed. J. de Borries (*Phrynichi sophistae praeparatio sophistica* [Leipzig: B. G. Teubner, 1911]) 85B: "*kunodesmai*: the cords with which the inhabitants of Attica roll back and tie up the penis. They call the penis a *kuōn* and the word *desmos* means a leash" (Sweet [1985] 46); cf. also Pollux, *Onomasticon* 2.4.171: "The cord with which they tie up the foreskin they call the *kunodesmē*" (Sweet [1985]). Also on infibulation, see ibid. 43–52; Keuls (1985) 68–73; J.-P. Thuillier, *Les jeux athlétique dans la civilisation Étrusque*, Bibliothèque des Écoles Françaises d'Athène et de Rome, fasc. 256 (Rome: École Française de Rome, 1985) 394–401; Dingwall (1925), esp. 67–123, the most extensive review of the subject.

102. Sansone (1988) 120.

103. Sweet (1985) 43–49.

104. Cf. O. Taplin, "Phallology, *Phylakes*, Iconography and Aristophanes," *PCPS* 213 (N.S. 33) (1987) 102, note 17: "Its [*kunodesmē's*] prime purpose was evidently to protect the organ during violent athletics, and it may also have warded off sexual approaches as it would inhibit erection (cf. Aesch, *Theoroi* or *Isthmiai* fr. 78a line 29 [Radt])." Dingwall (1925) 78 cites a passage of Celsus, *De medecina* 7.15, headed "For the purpose of covering the head of the penis, if it is uncovered" (*Ad tegendam glandem colis, si est nuda*), in which it is considered a deformity of an individual if his foreskin does not completely cover the *glans penis*.

105. Arieti (1975). Stewart (1997) 31 questions the motive of athletic nakedness adopted to show conspicuous self-control: "Yet if so, it is odd that we know of no contestant who failed in this unwelcome task, and a 100 percent success rate is difficult to credit if it were indeed a serious problem."

106. Dover (1989) 205–25 provides a "List of Vases" discussed as evidence in his book; the catalogue does not claim to be a complete list of Greek vases with ho-

moerotic scenes, nor are *all* the vases listed restricted to such scenes. But it does provide a useful and readily available compendium of iconographic sources on this topic. I refer in my text only to those vases for which Dover has provided illustrations. M. F. Kilmer, *Greek Erotica on Attic Red-figured Vases* (London: Duckworth, 1993) supplements Dover's list of vases and offers a caveat regarding the identification of palaestra scenes simply by the presence of oil-flasks: see his index, s.v. *palaestra*. Kilmer suggests plausibly that olive oil may have been used as a lubricant for hetero- and homosexual activities.

107. Attic red-figure psykter, ca. 510 B.C., attr. to Smikros, Los Angeles, Getty Mus. 82.AE.53.

108. Attic red-figure kylix, Peithinos Painter, Berlin, Stiftung Staatliche Kulturbesitz F 2279; Dover (1989) R 196 (a); C. Johns, *Sex or Symbol* (Austin, Tx.: University of Texas Press, 1982) fig. 82; O. Brendal, in *Studies in Erotic Art*, ed. T. Bowie and C. V. Christenson (New York: Basic Books, 1970) figs. 15–16.

109. Black-figure skyphos cup, Paris, Louvre A479 (MNB 1746), Amasis Painter, third quarter of the sixth century B.C., from Camiros, Rhodes; *ABV* 156, 688 (Amasis Ptr. no. 80); *Paralipomena* 65; see D. von Bothmer, *The Amasis Painter and His World: Vase-Painting in Sixth-Century Athens* (Malibu, Calif.: J. Paul Getty Museum, 1985) 200–203 no. 54; Dover (1989) no. B 84.

110. Dover (1989) section II.B.5; for a vase scene with a bearded man giving a hare to a boy holding a strigil and standing next to a *terma*, see the tondeau of the Attic red-figure kylix *ARV*² 874.4 = *CVA* France 20, pl. 47.5

111. See, e.g., a red-figure skyphos, attributed to the C Painter, Paris, Louvre, MNC 676 = von Bothmer (1985) 202 fig. 105; a fourth c. B.C. red-figure stamnos, *CVA* Italy, Villa Giulia, vol. 1, IVB.I, pl.1, 3–5, showing on side B a nude athlete with a strigil gazing at a young woman in a peplos opposite with a basin in between them.

112. Attic red-figure kylix, Getty Museum 85.AE.25, Athens 510–500 B.C., attributed to the Carpenter Painter.

113. Attic red-figure kylix, 500–475 B.C., Brygos Painter, Oxford, Ashmolean Mus. 1967.304; Johns (1982) fig 81.

114. Attic red-figure kylix, first third of the fifth century B.C., attributed to Douris, Berlin, Pergamon Mus. 3168; *ARV*² 428.13; Beazley, *Paralipomena* 374; E. Olshausen, "Eros mit dem Barbiermesser," *AA* (1979) 17–24; A. Hermary, H. Cassimatis and Vollkommer, s.v. "Eros," 902, no. 600 in L. Kahil, ed., *Lexicon Iconographicum Mythologiae Classicae* III.1 (Zurich: Artemis, 1986).

115. Lucanian red-figure bell-krater, ca. 440–430 B.C., Pisticii Painter, London, British Mus. GR 1824.5–1.38 (vase F. 39) = Hermary, Cassimatis and Vollkommer, in *LIMC* III. 1 (1986), 903 no. 606; see a similar scene on an Apulian red-figure bell-krater, ca. 425–400 B.C., Berlin, Staatl. Mus. F 3181 = Hermary, Cassimatis and Vollkommer, in *LIMC* III.1 (1986), 903 no. 606.

116. Attic red-figure aryballos, ca. 470–460 B.C., Douris, Athens NM 15375; showing Eros and Anteros pursuing in flight a draped youth = *ARV*² 447, 274 (210) = Greek Ministry of Culture, *Eros Grec: Amour des Dieux et des Hommes* (Athens: Éditions du Ministère de la culture de Grèce, Direction des antiquités, 1989) 51 no.1.

117. The Veii Painter vases: *ARV*² 904, 71, red-figure kylix, 475–450 B.C., once Munich, Preyss; *ARV*² 904, 72 red-figure kylix, Bologna 420, from Bologna.

118. Attic red-figure kylix, 475–450 B.C., the Clinic Painter, Boston 08.478, fr., from Orvieto; *ARV*² 809, 6.

119. Attic red-figure kylix, 475–450 B.C., Orvieto, Faina, from Orvieto (?), the Painter of Würzburg 487; *ARV*² 836, 2.

120. Attic red-figure kylix, 475–450 B.C., the Painter of Heidelberg 211, Montauban 6; *ARV*² 948, 4.

121. Attic red-figure pelike, the Washing Painter, Brussels R 340; *ARV*² 1129, 110; *CVA*. d pl. 11, 12. On the painter and his period, see G.M.A. Richter, *Attic Red-Figured Vases: A Survey*, rev. ed. (New Haven: Yale University Press, 1958) 136–37.

122. Attic red-figure kylix, the Washing Painter, Heidelberg; *ARV*² 1133, 198.

123. *ARV*² 1410, 16; *ARV*² 1410, 18; *ARV*² 1411, 34; *ARV*² 1411, 35. On the painter and his period, see Richter (this chapter, note 121, 1958) 157.

124. Attic red-figure oinochoe, first third of the fourth century B.C., the F. B. Group, Ferrara, T.863, from Spina = *ARV*² 1489, 138; Attic red-figure oinochoe, first third of the fourth century B.C., the F. B. Group, Ferrara, T.597, from Spina = *ARV*² 1489, 137. On the rarity of ugly athletes in vase painting: Steiner (1998) 128, note 26.

125. For athletic victor and Nike, see the nineteen pieces cited by A. Goulaki-Voutira, and U. Grote, s.v. "Nike," in *LIMC* VI.1 (1992), 876–78, nos. 315–33; to which add *ARV*² 450, 18 = kylix, Berlin inv. 3389, fr. = *CVA* Deutschland 6, Taf. 99.3. Lyre-victors with Nike, e.g. *ARV*² 835, 1 = *CVA* Italy 13 fig. 1, cf. *ARV*² 853, 1 = *CVA* Deutschland 6, fig. 76.1–2 showing a lyre-player with Eros.

126. Attic red-figure skyphos, ca. 475–450 B.C., Zephyros Painter, Cambridge, Fitzwilliam Mus. GR 13.1955; *ARV*² 976.

127. Attic red-figure pelike, 440–430 B.C., Bathers' Painter, Brussels, Mus. Roy. 340 = *ARV*² 1129, 110; = Hermary, Cassimatis and Vollkommer in *LIMC* III.1 (1986), 903 no. 611.

128. Attic red-figure kylix, first third of the fourth century B.C., Painter of Vienna 155, Frankfurt, Museum für Kunsthandwerk, WM 06 *CVA* pl. 68, 3–6; *Paralipomena* 501, 12*bis*.

129. Attic red-figure pelike (small), 450–420 B.C., Manner of the Washing Painter, Naples Market (Barone); *ARV*² 1134, 13; here the athlete has a sprig in his right hand, perhaps a token of his victory. Attic red-figure pelike (small), Manner of the Washing Painter, London Market; *ARV*² 1134, 14.

130. Attic red-figure pelike, the Painter of London E 395, Gela V lxvii, from assallagi; *ARV*² 1140, 4. Attic red-figure pelike, the Painter of London E 395, Paris Market (Mikas); *ARV*² 1141, 27; Eros flies toward the athlete who accepts from him a fillet.

131. Red-figure kylix, 460–450 B.C., Wurzburg, Wagner Mus. L 487 = Hermary, Cassimatis and Vollkommer in *LIMC* III.1 (1986), 903 no. 609 and in *LIMC* III.2, (1986) 644 pl. 609; for the "flower" held by a trainer with a stick on the sideline, see Attic red-figure amphora, ca. 530 B.C., Andocides Painter, Berlin, Staatl. Mus. 2159, F.R. 133.

132. Attic red-figure bell krater, early fourth century B.C., Athens, Nat. Mus. 10959.

133. Attic red-figure bell krater, early fourth century B.C., Athens, Nat. Mus. 1662.

134. Oxford, Miss.; *ARV²* 177 (the Kiss Painter, no. 3); *Paralipomena* 339; Dover (1989) no. R305. H. A. Shapiro, in Richlin (1992) 71 discusses parallel portrayals of Eros attracted to a youth holding a lyre, probably an indication of victory in a musical competition that has enhanced the beloved's attractiveness.

135. For the vases, see Hermary, Cassimatis and Vollkommer in *LIMC* III.1 (1986), 901, nos. 587, 587a, 587b, 587c, 589, 589a, 589b, 589c, 589d.

136. Apulian red-figure pelike, ca. 310–290 B.C., Paris, Louvre K 96 = Hermary, Cassimatis and Vollkommer in *LIMC* III.1 (1986), no. 587c.

137. See Hermary, Cassimatis and Vollkommer in *LIMC* III.1 (1986), nos. 588, 588a, 588b (the latter two mislabeled in the plates, respectively as 588b and 588c).

138. Dover (1989) 153, 196.

139. See the Attic red-figure stemless kylix, Painter of Athens 13908, late fifth century, Athens, Nat. Mus. 13908 = *ARV²* 1404; Attic red-figure stemless kylix, late fifth century, Athens, Nat. Mus. 1408. See also the Attic red-figure pelike, from Corinth, Athens Nat. Mus. 16025; on side A a naked youth with a discus holds his hand out to a seated woman who holds a strigil; on side B a seminude youth holds a strigil over a turning post. Steiner (1998) 128, note 33 notes the motif on a Protolucanian pelike from the fifth century (A. Cambitoglou and A. D. Trendall, *Apulian Red-figured Vase-painters of the Plain Style* [n.p.: Archaeological Institute of America,, 1961] 467).

140. Attic red-figure krater, Thesalloniki Museum 5206; cf. a similar scene of a jumper and a woman on the interior of an Attic red-figure kylix, the Washing Painter, Heidelberg = *ARV²* 1133, 198 with two exterior scenes of a jumper and two Erotes.

141. Lucanian red-figure bell-krater, 440–430 B.C., Cyclops Painter, Tarentum, Mus. Naz. De Rutigliano = Hermary, Cassimatis and Vollkommer in *LIMC* III.1 (1986), 912 no. 719; Lucanian red-figure bell-krater, 430–420 B.C., Pisticii Painter, Pilsen, Mus. of W. Bohemia 8327 = Hermary, Cassimatis and Vollkommer in *LIMC* III.1 (1986), 912 no. 719a (with pl. in vol. III.2; Eros offers a strigil to the woman!); Lucanian red-figure bell-krater, 430–420 B.C., Amykos Painter, Naples, Mus. Naz. 82898 = Hermary, Cassimatis and Vollkommer in *LIMC* III.1 (1986), 912 no. 719b (Eros stands before a woman at one terma); Lucanian red-figure bell-krater, 430–420 B.C., Amykos Painter, Brindisii, private collection = Hermary, Cassimatis and Vollkommer in *LIMC* III.1 (1986), 912 no. 719c.

142. Athlete with woman: *ARV²* 1518, 6; *ARV²* 1520, 38; *ARV²* 1520, 39; *ARV²* 1520, 40; *ARV²* 1520, 41; *ARV²* 1520, 42; *ARV²* 1520, 43; *ARV²* 1521, 44; *ARV²* 1521, 45 (?). Eros with youth and athlete with youth: *ARV²* 1518, 3. Eros with woman and athlete with woman: *ARV²* 1520, 38.

143. Attic red-figure kylix, Group YZ (iii), Vienna 91 = *ARV²* 1524, 1 = *CVA* pl. 29.

144. *Paralipomena* 489,2; id., 5; id., 6; id., 7; id., 8; id., 9.

145. Woman with athlete(s): *ARV²* 1413, 62; *ARV²* 1413, 64; *ARV²* 1413, 66; *ARV²* 1413, 67; *ARV²* 1413, 68; *ARV²* 1413, 69; *ARV²* 1413, 70; *ARV²* 1413, 71; *ARV²* 1413, 73; *ARV²2* 1413, 79 (?);*ARV²* 1413, 80; *ARV²* 1413, 81; *ARV²* 1413, 82 (?);*ARV²* 1413, 84. Woman with athlete(s) and Eros in the same scene: *ARV²* 1412, 57; *ARV²* 1412, 58; *ARV²* 1414, 93. Woman with athlete(s) and Eros in a separate scene: *ARV²* 1412, 59; *ARV²* 1412, 60; *ARV²* 1413, 61; *ARV²* 1413, 63. Woman with Eros (interior), and athletes with Nike on the exterior: *ARV²* 1414, 86.

146. *ARV*² 1411, 39 neck amphora, Athens, NM 15113, ca. 400 B.C.
J. Boardman, with advice from G. Arrigoni, "Atalante," in L. Kahil, ed., *Lexicon Iconographicum Mythologiae Classicae* (Zurich: Artemis Verlag, 1984) vol. II.1, 944 no 41b; A. Ley, *Atalante—Darstellungen auf Vasen des 6.–4. Jhs. v.u.Z* (M.A. thesis, University of Hamburg, 1987) no. 19; Atalanta (seated) and Meleager (standing) facing one another, holding hunting spears, and surrounded by other young men (3) and women (2). See also *ARV*² 1411, 40 neck amphora, Toronto, Royal Ont. Mus. 919.5.35, purchased in Palermo, provenance unknown, ca. 400; Boardman and Arrigoni in *LIMC* II.1 (1984), 944 no 40; Ley (1987), no. 21; face A: Atalanta, standing with one leg resting on the top of a *terma*, is in the center of six young men, to the right of which is Meleager, returning her gaze and in a similar pose. And see *ARV*² 1412, 49 hydria, Ruvo, Mus. Jatta 1418, from Ruvo, ca. 400; Boardman and Arrigoni in *LIMC* II.1 (1984), 944 no 41; Ley (1987), no. 22; hunting scene with youths on horses on body of vase, and Atalanta (seated) and Meleager (standing) on the neck, leaning on one another and looking at each other. We may compare here a kylix by the Jena Workshop, *ARV*² 1512, 12, which on one side depicts a woman with athletes; that painter was also known for his portrayal (inscribed) of Peleus and Atalanta on *ARV*² 1512, 23; see ch. 7, note 55.

147. On the *ephebia*, see O.W.R. Reinmuth, *The Ephebic Inscriptions of the Fourth Century* B.C., Mnemosyne Suppl. 14 (Leiden: E. J. Brill, 1971); C. Pélekidis, *Histoire de l'Éphébie Attique des Origines à 31 avant Jésus-Christ*, École Française d'Athènes, Travaux et Mémoires, Fasc. 13 (Paris: E. de Boccard, 1962).

148. See N. Blanc and F. Gury, in *LIMC* III.1 (1986), 988 nos. 267–70.

149. D. Halperin, "Plato and Erotic Reciprocity," *CA* 5 (1986) 60–80.

150. Bronze statue of Eros, ca. 130 B.C., Boethus of Calcedonia, found in the sea near Mahdia, Tunis, Bardo Mus. F 106; see Hermary, Cassimatis and Vollkommer in *LIMC* III.1 (1986), 911 no. 712. Bronze statue of a herm, end of the second century B.C., Boethus of Calcedonia (?), Los Angeles, Getty Museum 79.AB138; see A. Stewart, *Greek Sculpture: An Exploration* (New Haven: Yale University Press, 1990) 229, figs. 849–50.

151. See youth at a terma on side B, Eros bestowing a fillet on face A of *ARV*² 1141, 27; Meleager and Atalanta, each resting a foot on a terma on face A of *ARV*² 1411, 40.

152. Neither of the two calyx-krateres are attributed to an artist and hence are not listed in *ARV*², *Paralipomena*, or *Beazley Addenda: Additional References to ABV, ARV*² *& Paralipomena*, ed. T. H. Carpenter, 2nd ed. (Oxford: Oxford Univ. Press for the British Academy, 1989). Both appear to be by the same artist, with two very sketchily drawn figures in cloaks, perhaps discussants in a palaestra, on the other face of each vase, and seem stylistically to be from the first half of the fourth century. For further discussion of satyrs in athletic contexts, see ch. 9 and fig. 9-1.

153. See N. Blanc and F. Gury in *LIMC* III.1 (1986), 988 nos. 271 (a Pompeian painting) and 272–74 (citing six gem carvings).

154. D. F. Sutton, "Athletics in the Greek Satyr Play," *RSC* 23 (1975) 203–9.

155. Hermes *enagōnios*: Simon. 50.1 (West), Pind., *P.* 2.10; id., *I.* 1.60; Aesch., *fr.* 738 (Mette); Aristoph., *Plutus* 1161; *IG* 2².3023 (338/7 B.C.); *IG* 2².3089 (200–150 B.C.); *IG* 2².4572 (mid-fourth c. B.C.); *SEG* 21.540. Hermes *palaistritēs*: Callimachus *fr.* 191 Schneider; *IG* 12(5). 911.22 (Tenos). See generally on Hermes and the gymna-

sium: L. Grasberger, *Erziehung und Unterricht im klassischen Altertum* (Würzburg, 1864–81; reprint, Aalen: Scientia, 1971) vol. I, 255–59.

156. For Hermes' function, especially as a god of transitions and boundaries, see W. Burkert, *Greek Religion*, trans. J. Raffan (Cambridge, Mass.: Harvard University Press, 1985) 156–59 (= *Griechische Religion der archaïschen und klassichen Epoche* [Stuttgart: W. Kohlhammer, 1977] 243–47).

157. Hermes as teacher of wrestling: Hyg., *Fab.* 227.3; cf. Lucian, *Dialogus Deorum* 26.2. Daughter Palaestra: Philosti., *Imagines* 2.32.1.

158. See I. Weiler, *Der Agon im Mythos: Zur Einstellung der Griechen zum Wettkampf*, Impulse der Forschung, vol. 16 (Darmstadt: Wissenschaftliche Buchgesellschaft, 1974) 156–57.

159. So argues Weiler (1974) 156.

160. For Eros with Hermes' caduceus, see *ARV*² 676, 14 = Hermary, Cassimatis and Vollkommer in *LIMC* III.1 (1986), 928 no. 949. For the god with Zeus' thunderbolts, see *LIMC* III.1 nos. 944–45, cf. 946–47; for the famous image on Alcibiades' shield: Plut., *Alc.* 16.1; Ath. 12.534e; P. H. von Blanckenhagen, in *Essays in Memorial of Karl Lehmann*, ed. Lucy Freeman Sandler (Locust Valley, N.Y.: distributed by J. J. Augustin, published by [New York] Institute of Fine Arts, New York University, 1964) 38–42.

161. Heracles as founder of the Olympics: Pind., *Ol.* 2.3–4; 3.10–22; 6.67–69; 10.43–59. Heracles and the Olympic olive crown: Pind., *Ol.* 3.13–16; Paus. 5.7.7; [Arist.], *Mirabilium auscultationes* 834 a 18; Pliny, *Naturalis Historia* 16.240. Heracles as competitor in wrestling and pancration: Paus. 5.8.4; Hyg., *Fab.* 273.5; Dio Cassius 79.10; Ptolemaeus Chennos *ap.* Photius, *Bibliotheca* 151 a 35; *Scholia in Lycophrontem* 41. Diodorus 4.14.2 has Heracles as winner in all of the contests of the first Olympics. For fuller literary and artistic sources, see J. Boardman, "Heracles and athletics," in *Lexicon Iconographicum Mythologiae Classicae* IV.1, ed. L. Kahil (Zurich: Artemis Verlag, 1988) 796–97; Siska (1933) 38–43.

162. *Schol.* Lucian, *Bis acc.* 2, id., *Dial. deor.* 7; Probius in Vergil, *Georg.* 3.19.

163. Boardman in *LIMC* IV.1 (1988), 796–97, nos. 1316–21 with commentary.

164. W. Raschke, "Images of Victory: Some New Considerations of Athletic Monuments," in Raschke (1988) 38–54.

165. Boardman in *LIMC* IV.1 (1988), 797.

166. Pind., N. 10.52; Cicero, *Ad Atticum* 1.6.2. For Heracles' cult in the gymnasium, see the sources collected by Siska (1933) 41–42.

167. S. Woodford, "Herakles' Attributes and Their Appropriation by Eros," *JHS* 109 (1989) 200–204. See also an Etruscan, carnelian scarab gem, first half of the fourth century B.C., Paris, Cab. Méd. 17772 = I. Kraukopf, "Eros (in Etruria)," in *LIMC* IV.1 (1988) 5, number 55, showing a young Eros crowning Heracles who, however, retains his club and lion skin, and has no athletic accoutrements.

168. *GA* 16.103 and 104; Lucian, *Herodotus and Aetion* 4-6 describing Aetion's painting; Woodford (1989) 202.

169. A. Jacquemin, "Notes sur Quelques Offrandes du Gymnase de Délos," *BCH* 105 (1981) 158.

170. Woodford (1989) 203–4.

171. Hermary, Cassimatis and Vollkommer in *LIMC* III.1 (1986), 927 no. 924; N. Blanc and F. Gury in *LIMC* III.1 (1986), 984–85 no. 239–43.

172. Kyle (1987) 192; N. Robertson, "The Origin of the Panathenaia," *RhM* N.S. 120 (1985) 281–88; L. Deubner, *Attische Feste* (Berlin: Heinrich Keller, 1932; reprint, Darmstadt: Wissenschaftliche Buchgesellschaft, 1956) 211; H. W. Parke, *Festivals of the Athenians* (London: Thames and Hudson, 1977; reprint, Ithaca: Cornell University Press, 1986) 171–73.

173. There were also torch races in the Classical period at festivals for Hephaestus, for Pan, and (on horseback) for Bendis, the Thracian equivalent of Artemis. In the Hellenistic period, torch races were part of the Theseia and the Epitaphia. See Kyle (1987) 193. I omit discussion of these other races here, since their routes were either unknown or do not, so far as we know, relate to the altar of Eros.

174. Ibid. 191 notes the importance of the ritual and athletic aspects of the contest in the Panathenaia, and (193) distinguishes the athletic torch races of that festival, the Theseia, and the Epitaphia, from the nonathletic, ritual torch races of the Prometheia, Hephaestia, Bendidia, and a festival for Pan; H. A. Harris, *Greek Athletes and Athletics* (London: Hutchinson, 1964) 33 and E. N. Gardiner, *Athletics of the Ancient World* (Oxford: Oxford University Press, 1930; reprint, Chicago: Ares, 1980) 143 deny that the event was ever truly "athletic." Perhaps the greater popularity of the Panathenaia, Theseia, and Epitaphia would have inevitably heightened the competitive fervor, but in my view nothing suggests that any one of the known torch races at Athens was inherently less "athletic" and more "ritual" than any other. Except perhaps for the Bendidia, they were probably all conducted according to the same rules for determining victory and thus all demanded similar skills and degrees of fitness.

175. See Aristoph., *Frogs* 1087–98 for a general criticism of the puffing and panting torch race. See also Arist., *Ethica Nicomachea* 1114a 23–25, suggesting that being unfit was, then as today, a cause for public censure: "No one blames those who are ugly [αἰσχροῖς] by nature, but we do find fault with those ugly because of lack of exercise [ἀγυμνασίαν) and care."

176. J. Travlos, *Pictorial Dictionary of Ancient Athens* (London: Thames and Hudson, 1971) 42.

177. Kyle (1987) 73.

178. See Delorme (1960) 37–38, 40; Travlos (1971) 42. On "Eros with many devices," see Eur., *Hippolytus* 1270 (poikilopteros Erōs), and Ibyc., fr. 6 (Page).

179. See *LSJ²*, s.v. τέρμα I.1 and II.1

180. Kyle (1987) 191; Deubner (1956) 211–12; Parke (1977) 45–46.

181. Plat., *Symp.* 189c; Eur., *Hipp.* 538ff.

182. O. Broneer, "Eros and Aphrodite on the North Slope of the Acropolis," *Hesperia* 1 (1932) 31–55, 2 (1933) 31–55; Fasce (1977) 32–39. Broneer convincingly identifies the Acropolis shrine as that of "Aphrodite in the Gardens" (*en Kēpois*) mentioned by Pausanias (1.19), yet Eros is not named by Pausanias in conjunction with this site, and the identification of it with the Anteros cult at the foot of a cliff is still an open possibility.

183. Robertson (1985) 283.

184. See the plan of Travlos (this chapter, note 176, 1971) 71, fig. 91; Robertson (1985) 283 objects, unconvincingly, that "the torch-racers would hardly dash up to the Acropolis and into Athena's precinct." Such a climb, while taxing on the athletes, was not unthinkable and may have provided a dramatically grueling finish.

185. Parke (1977) 46.

186. I omit from consideration here the many instances of Eros holding a torch reversed, which first appears in the fourth century, perhaps symbolizing one who has lost the race, but is later established as a funerary image, particularly wide-spread in art of the Roman period: Hermary, Cassimatis and Vollkommer in *LIMC* III.1 (1986), 882 nos. 369, 370, 984–93. The earliest use of this motif may be the gold ring, second quarter of the fourth century B.C., from the Peloponnese, Evans Collection = Hermary, Cassimatis and Vollkommer in *LIMC* III.1 (1986), 882 no. 372, on which is depicted a seated Eros, with torch held down, sitting on a plat-form with his back to a column, on top of which is a statue-sized Eros running with a torch. Might the statue be a representation of the Peisistratid Eros in the Academy?

187. Attic red-figure amphora, ca. 460–450 B.C., Charmides Painter, London, BM 96.7–23.1 = *ARV*² 654, 12 = Hermary, Cassimatis and Vollkommer in *LIMC* III.1 (1986), 881 no. 366.

188. Apulian, red-figure lekane, ca. 330–320 B.C., attributed to the Three Ro-sette Painter, *The Summa Galleries Inc., Catalogue 4: Ancient Vases* (Beverly Hills, Ca-lif.: The Summa Galleries, 1978) no. 25; Marit Jentoft Nilsen, *Getty Museum Journal* 6/7 (1978–79) 207, fig. 7–8; Trendall *RVAp* II, p. 690, no. 22/526.

189. Apulian red-figure bell-krater, Gnathian style, Naples, Mus. Nat. Stg. 613 = Hermary, Cassimatis and Vollkommer in *LIMC* III.1 (1986), 881 no. 367a; cf. no. 367, a Sicilian red-figure lekane cover, ca. 350 B.C., Palermo, Mus. Naz. De Selinonte T. 51, showing a kneeling Eros holding a torch.

190. Bronze Eros with a torch: Tunis, Bardo Mus. F 106; see Hermary, Cassimatis and Vollkommer, in *LIMC* III.1 (1986), 911 no. 714. Terracotta Eros with a torch: Hermary, Cassimatis and Vollkommer in *LIMC* III.1 (1986), 911 *sub* no. 714.

191. Marble relief of Eros with a torch, late second to early first c. B.C., Delos, Mus. A 4018, from the "Maison de Fourni"; J. Macardé, in *Études déliennes: publiées à l'occasion du centième anniversaire du début des fouilles de l'École française d'Athènes à Délos*. BCH Supplement 1 (Athens: École française d'Athènes; Paris: E. de Boccard, 1973) 349, fig. 28; Hermary, Cassimatis and Vollkommer in *LIMC* III.1 (1986), 911 no. 713.

192. *ID* 1417 face A, 119–120A. Jacquemin (1981) 159–63.

193. Eros with torch graffito on a marble stele from the Granite Palaestra, Delos, Mus. Δ 585, second to early first century B.C. This figure is taken as a torch runner, *pace* Jacquemin (1981) 159 and notes 21 and 23, who, despite noting the evidence of the relief and the gymnasium seats, argues unconvincingly that "l'attitude évoque ici plus les représentations de ce dieu dans le cercle d'Aphrodite qu'un épreuve sportive" (the attitude here is more evocative of representations of this god in the circle of Aphrodite than an ordeal of sports).

194. *IG* 9.4. 1157, 1159–62.

195. "Éros s'il fait l'objet d'invocations privées, comme l'attestent de nombreux graffites, n'est jamais honoré manifestment au gymnase de Délos, où il apparaît plus comme le protecteur de la *philia* éphebique que comme une divinité agônistique." Jacquemin (1981) 160–61.

196. See N. Blanc and F. Gury in *LIMC* III.1 (1986), 974–77, nos. 146–71 with 32 other representations *passim*, nos. cited on 977.

197. See J. G. Frazer, *Pausanias' Description of Athens*, vol. 4 (London: Macmillan, 1913) 103, s.v. 6.23.5; see also Fürtwangler in W. H. Roscher, ed.,

Ausführliches Lexikon der griechischen und römischen Mythologie, vol. I.1, (Leipzig: B. G. Teubner, 1884–86) col. 1368 for a Roman relief of Eros and Anteros contending for a palm branch.

198. Terracotta altar, mid fifth century B.C. (?), Sicilian, Oxford, Ashmolean Mus. 1966.1163 = Hermary, Cassimatis and Vollkommer in *LIMC* III.1 (1986), 883 no. 392.

199. Percy (1996) 125–27.

200. Attic red-figure pyxis, ca. 430 B.C., Washing Painter, Würzburg, Wagner-Mus. L 541 (H4455) = *ARV²* 1133, 196; see A. Greifenhagen, *Griechische Eroten* (Berlin: De Gruyter, 1957) 42–45 with Abb. 31-33; Hermary, Cassimatis and Vollkommer in *LIMC* III.1 (1986), 882 no. 388.

201. Cf. the youth acting as umpire to the left of the wrestlers on the Attic red-figure amphora of about 530–525 B.C., Berlin, Staatliche Mus. 2159 = Gardiner (1980) 186, fig. 154.

202. Attic red-figure lebes gamikos fragments, ca. 430 B.C., Washing Painter, Munich, Antikensammlung 8926 = *ARV²* 1127, 6 (bis); Greifenhagen (1957) 44–45, Abb.34; Hermary, Cassimatis and Vollkommer in *LIMC* III.1 (1986), 882–83 no. 389.

203. For Harmonia's associations with marriage and Aphrodite, see E. Simon, *Die Götter der Griechen*, 2nd ed. (Munich: Hirmer, 1980) 259–61 and Keuls (1985) 253–56; for Peitho's associations with Aphrodite, see Simon (1980) 251–53.

204. Apulian red-figure pelike, first half of the fourth century B.C., Louvain-la-Neuve, Univ. Mus. = Hermary, Cassimatis and Vollkommer in *LIMC* III.1 (1986), 883 no. 390. Cf. the other early Greek images of Eros wrestling Anteros: *LIMC*, 883 nos. 393 (fourth century B.C. bronze mirror cover) and 394 (iron ring, fourth to third century B.C.). Later Roman-era images from Greece may have been influenced by the great popularity of the theme in Roman iconography: see Hermary et al. in *LIMC* III.1 (1986), 883 nos. 391 (Thasos mosaic, second to third c. A.D.), and 395 (terracotta figurines from Delos, first c. A.D.), to which add the terracotta medallion from Archane, Crete, second to first century B.C., Heracleion Mus. 3262.

205. See N. Blanc and F. Gury in *LIMC* III.1 (1986), 985–86, nos. 247–53. There are thirteen Amores, depicted as wrestlers, judges, and victors, on one sarcophagus (no. 248); eleven on another including wrestlers, boxers, judges, and victors (no. 249). In these scenes, at least the focus is on the whole of the athletic festival, and not the phenomenon of the single match by itself, perhaps celebrating the lively atmosphere at a festival in contrast to the somber funeral for which the sarcophagi were made.

206. Dover (1989) 52–53; Halperin (1986) 66, note 14. On Anacreon's erotic themes, see Percy (1996) 157–60. On the Anacreon fragment and the use of sports metaphors for Eros, see B. S. Thornton, *Eros: The Myth of Ancient Greek Sexuality* (Boulder, Colo: Westview Press, 1997) 43–44.

207. On the *Acharnians* passage, see Romero (this ch., note 59, 1995) 59. Cf. metaphors for Eros' superiority in Eur., fr. 271 and 132. Note Eros as the driver for the wedding chariot of Zeus and Hera in Aristoph., *Birds* 1737; as umpire in the music contest in Nonnus, *Dionysiaca* 19.237; other references to Eros as a symbol of harmony in Fürtwangler in Roscher (1884–86) I.1, 1350; ibid., 1352 for Eros driving Aphrodite's chariot, on an Aeginetan terracotta.

208. See Dover (1989), sections II.B.4–5 and E. Cantarella (1992) 17–22.

209. Paus. 9.31.3; see, for full bibliography and citation of the many ancient sources, A. Schachter, *Cults of Boiotia*, vol. 1, Acheloos to Hera, University of London, Institute of Classical Studies Bulletin Supplement no. 38.1 (London: University of London, Institute of Classical Studies, 1981, reprint, 1994) 216–19; Fasce (1977) 45–50; Nilsson (1957) 423–24; Klee (1980) 35–37.

210. Schachter (1981) 219, note 1, catalogues all probable victor-list inscriptions for the Erotidaea, among which *BCH* 95 (1971) 921 and *SEG* 22.385, the only ones with headings preserved, can certainly be associated with the festival; the others, found at Thespiae, very likely also record victors and events of the festival: *IG* 7. 1764–73.

211. Schachter (1981) 218, note 5; but see Fasce (1977) 50, who argues unconvincingly that the athletic nature of dance caused it to be listed here, though it was later subsumed under the category of musical competitions.

212. Paus. 1.20.1; *Greek Anth.* 16. 56 and 57 (Menander), 16.165 (Antipater of Sidon), 16.203 (Julian of Egypt), 16.204 ([Simonides]), 16.205 (Tullius Geminus), 16.206 (Leonidas, the earliest source, fourth–third c. B.C.), 16.260 (Tullius Geminus).

213. Paus. 9.31.3; Plut., *Amat.* 748f.; Schachter (1981) 219.

214. Fasce (1977) 47; Plut., *Amat.* 549c mentions that those attending the festivals conversed "in the palaestrae and theaters" before fleeing the turmoil of the gathering for the more peaceful setting of Mount Helicon.

215. Schachter (1981)

216. Plut., *Amat.* 749b–c, describing Plutarch's own visit to the festival with his new wife; Nilsson (1957) 424, note 2.

217. *IG* 7.1764, lines 7–8, second to first century B.C. The absence of the torch race on other inscriptions seems to be due to accidents of preservation. Note, by comparison, that the torch race is listed near or at the end of the Panathenaic program, also a place of prominence: *IG* II². 2311, lines 77–81.

218. For the age estimates, see Klee (1980) 48.

219. Cantarella (1992) 43–44; Buffière (1980) 605–17; Dover (1989) 85–87.

220. Other local festivals with three divisions other than men, according to Klee (1980) 43–44, are those at Cos, Chios, Chalchis, and possibly Plataea.

221. The reason why a festival for Eros was called the Eleutheria is not clear from Ath. 13.561f–562a, but it may be related to the overthrow of the Peisistratids from the *erotikē xuntuchia* (love affair) of Harmodius and Aristogeiton (Thucydides 6.54). On the Samian gymnasium, see Delorme (1960) 122; C. Forbes, *Greek Physical Education* (New York: Century, 1929) 205–6.

222. Fasce (1977) 71.

223. K. J. Gallis, "The Games in Ancient Larisa," in Raschke (1988) 217–35.

224. Nilsson (1957) 34.

225. Fasce (1977) 66–70 proposes the ties with Polycrates' fall. On Polycrates' fall and the rise of a "freedom" cult, see James F. McGlew, *Tyranny and Political Culture in Ancient Greece* (Ithaca: Cornell University Press, 1993) 124–30.

226. See C. Meier, *The Greek Discovery of Politics*, trans. D. McLintock (Cambridge, Mass.: Harvard University Press, 1990, from the original *Entstehung des Politischen bei den Griechen* [Frankfurt am Main: Suhrkamp, 1980]) 169–70; K. Raaflaub, *Die Entdeckung der Freiheit: zur historischen Semantik und Gesellschaftsgeschichte eines politischen Grundbegriffes der Griechen* (Munich: C. H. Beck, 1985).

227. W.K.C. Guthrie, *A History of Greek Philosophy, Vol. III: The Fifth-Century Enlightenment* (Cambridge: Cambridge University Press, 1969) 149–50.

228. See Thuc. 6.52–59; Herodotus 55. For the connection of pederasty with liberty generally in Greek thought, see Marrou (1956) 29.

229. Dionysius of Halicarnasus, *Roman Antiquities* 7.9.3–4; Percy (1996) 166.

230. W. Arrowsmith, "Aristophanes' Birds: The Fantasy Politics of Eros," *Arion* N.S. 1.1 (1973) 119–67. For Alcibiades as an embodiment of the interplay of politics and erotics, see V. Wohl, "The Eros of Alcibiades," *CA* 18.2 (1999) 349–85.

231. For the personification of Theoria, see Deubner (1956) 250–51. For the use of 'horse-riding' as a sexual position, see J. Henderson, *The Maculate Muse: Obscene Language in Attic Comedy* (New Haven: Yale University Press, 1975) 165 §§ 276–77; Davidson (1997) 196–97, with further examples from Hellenistic epigrams: Machon 11.308 and 362 (Gow) and Asclepiades, *Palatine Anthology* 5.203. For analyses of the athletic metaphors and vocabulary in Aristophanes *Peace* 894–905, see Poliakoff (1982) 118–19 and 126–27, and Romero (1995) 67–76.

232. In Nonnus, *Dionysiaca* 48.90–182, Dionysus wrestles Pallene to win her in marriage (cf. Poliakoff [1982] 168–69); cf. 48.258–644, in which Dionysus overpowers and rapes Aura, a devotee of Artemis, and 10.321–77, in which Dionysus and Apollo, *athlēteres Erōtōn*, "athletes of Love," wrestle one another in a match in which "mad Eros" stands in the middle (336–37).

233. See, e.g., Poliakoff (1987) illustrations 1, 7, 8, 9, 10, 11, 15, 16, 17, 18, 24, 41, 48, 49, 50, 51, 64, and 69 of Egyptian, Sumerian, and Mesopotamian wrestlers.

234. Kyle (1987) 73.

Chapter 9

1. W. Burkert, *Homo Necans: The Anthropology of Ancient Greek Sacrificial Ritual and Myth* trans. P. Bing (Berkeley: University of California Press, 1983) 97–98; see also the discussion of this passage above, ch. 1, note 45.

2. My thinking in this chapter was inspired in part by the stimulating essays of Gunther Gebauer in *Sport—Eros—Tod*, new series, vol. 335, ed. G. Gebauer and G. Hortleder (Frankfurt/M: Suhrkamp, 1986) 7–21, 113–43, and 167–87, although my ideas differ fundamentally from his and he refers only in passing to Greek athletics.

3. A. Guttmann, *From Ritual to Record: The Nature of Modern Sports* (New York: Columbia University Press, 1978) 11–12; also Gebauer (1986) 15: "Sport . . . possesses no individual aesthetic and follows only formal goals of description (high achievement of performance, generation of tension and emotion), ("Der Sport . . . besitzt keine eigene Ästhetik und folgt keine andere als formale Darstellungszeile [höchste Leistungen, Spannungs- und Emotionserzeugung]").

4. This notion of modern sports as analogues of drama is discussed by S. Kleinman, "The Athlete as Performing Artist: The Embodiment of Sport Literature and Philosophy," in *Coroebus Triumphs: The Alliance of Sport and the Arts*, ed. S. J. Bandy (San Diego: San Diego State University Press, 1988) 47–56; K. Kerrane, "Plays about Play," *Contemporary Literary Scene*, ed. F. Magill (Englewood Cliffs, N.J.: Salem Press, 1979) 137. By "drama" in my discussion, I mean mainly "tragedy": see D. H. J. Larmour, *The Interrelationship of Drama and Athletics in Classical Greece* (Ph.D. diss., University of Illinois at Champaign-Urbana, 1987), 116–17. See also id.,

Stage and Stadium: Drama and Athletics in Ancient Greece, Nikephoros suppl. vol. 4 (Hildesheim: Weidmann, 1999), which expands upon and refines his dissertation. The present study complements Larmour's studies by focusing on two central themes by which the drama of athletics is produced.

5. Larmour (1999) 37–41.

6. M. Poliakoff, *Combat Sports in the Ancient World: Competition, Violence, and Culture* (New Haven: Yale University Press, 1987) 104–7, on ancient Greece as a pervasively agonistic culture, with further bibliography on this generally accepted characterization. See also I. Weiler, *Der Agon im Mythos: Zur Einstellung der Griechen zum Wettkampf*, Impulse der Forschung, vol. 16 (Darmstadt: Wissenschaftliche Buchgesellschaft, 1974) 23–36 for a general discussion of the meaning of the Greek *agōn*.

7. *Anacharsis* 15, 36; see Introduction to this volume.

8. The traditional date for Thespis' first dramatic performance at Athens is 534 B.C., the traditional date for the founding of the Olympics is 776 B.C., and that for the founding (or reorganization) of the games at the Greater Panathenaia at Athens is 566 B.C., although the much disputed "origins" of tragedy probably lie earlier in the sixth century (R. P. Winnington-Ingram, in *The Cambridge History of Classical Literature, I. Greek Literature*, ed. P. E. Easterling and B.M.W. Knox [Cambridge: Cambridge University Press, 1985]) 258–63, and A. Mallwitz has argued for a founding date of the games at ca. 700 B.C. on the basis of archaeological remains of the first stadium at Olympia ("Cult and Competition Locations at Olympia," *The Archaeology of the Olympics: The Olympics and Other Festivals in Antiquity*, ed. W. Raschke [Madison: University of Wisconsin Press, 1988]) 79–109. I leave aside here consideration of the even earlier evidence for athletic-type contests in Minoan Crete due to the even greater geographical and chronological problems in continuity. Minoan contests in bull-leaping and combat sports probably did, however, have the same "dramatic" aspects as had later Greek athletics.

9. See Larmour (1999) for a general study of the topic.

10. C. J. Herington, *Poetry into Drama: Early Greek Tragedy and Poetic Tradition* (Berkeley: University of California Press, 1985) 9; Larmour (1999) 56–67.

11. I have read in interviews with the actor, Jack Nicholson, that he in part is such a great fan of sports like basketball and boxing because of the authentic 'drama' of those sports, heightened by the fact that the pain and the delight experienced by the athletes are not artificially adopted, but real expressions of emotion. Michael Douglas and numerous other modern actors, especially males, are sports fans, perhaps for the same reasons. Some modern athletes, on the other hand, such as Johnny Weismuller and Arnold Schwarzenegger, have so admired the acting profession that they changed over into that profession after their sports careers had waned.

12. F. Bohringer, "Cultes d'athlètes en Grèce classique: Propos politiques, discours mythiques," *REA* 81 (1979) 5–18; J. Fontenrose, "The Hero as Athlete," *CSCA* 1 (1968) 73–104; A. Hönle, *Olympia in der Politik der griechischen Staatenwelt von 776 bis zum ende des 5. Jahrhunderts* (Bebenhausen, Germany: Lothar Rotsch, 1972) 98–106.

13. J. Pouilloux, *Recherches sur l'histoire et les cultes de Thasos*, vol. 1 (Paris: E. de Boccard, 1954) 62–105; M. Launey, "L'athlète Théogene et le hieros gamos d'Héraklès Thasien," *RA* 18 (1941) 22–49. Although D. Young, *The Olympic Myth of Greek Amateur Athletics* (Chicago: Ares, 1984) 151–52, note 49 correctly questions

Launey and Pouilloux on the possible nobility of Theogenes, their observations about his heroic status remain of interest.

14. See Larmour (1999) 36–37.

15. See ibid. 56–67 for a more extended comparison of athletic and dramatic heroes, most interestingly (63) the athletic imagery applied to Orestes in Sophocles' *Electra* 684–94 and Euripides' *Electra* 528 and 854–89.

16. A salient reminder of this association is the relief sculpture of a winged boy personifying "Agon" on the throne of the priest of Dionysus Eleuthereus, front and center at the Theater of Dionysus in Athens: M. Bieber, *The History of the Greek and Roman Theater* (Princeton: Princeton University Press, 1961) 70–71 and fig. 269. Cf. also the Pompeian paintings of stages on which Greek athletes are depicted as part of the normal decorations of the stage backdrop: ibid. 232–33, fig. 777; though Roman, this painting shows a continuation of the Greek spirit of *agōn*. On the distinctions between the three senses of agōn, "athletic competition," "dramatic competition," and "dramatic conflict," see Larmour (1999) 28.

17. Larmour (1999) 170–92, documenting ninety-five festivals of which sixteen or fewer combined athletics and drama, another twenty-four had both musical and athletic competitions, with the balance being festivals with exclusively musical, dramatic, or athletic competitions.

18. T. F. Scanlon, "The Vocabulary of Competition: *Agōn* and *Aethlos*, Greek Terms for Contest," *Arete* (now *Aethlon*) 1.1 (1983) 185–216.

19. Larmour (1999) 29–34, 74–82.

20. Ibid. 161–70.

21. Xenophon, *Hellenica* 7.4 uses *theatron*, referring to the spectators' area of the stadium. H. A. Harris, *Greek Athletes and Athletics* (London: Hutchinson, 1964) 152 also notes the common athletic and dramatic usage of the term.

22. See Mallwitz in Raschke (1988) 79–109 for the date of 700; H. Lee, "The 'First' Olympic Games of 776 B.C.," in Raschke (1988) 110–18 for the earlier date.

23. See L. Drees, *Olympia: Gods, Artists, and Athletes*, trans. G. Onn (New York: Praeger, 1968) gives the figure of 40,000 capacity. I estimate a maximum capacity of about 28,500 people for Stadium III (Hellenistic-Roman), based on one square meter of space occupied by each spectator, although a standing-room-only crowd, with each individual occupying only ca. .71 m², would reach 40,000. On a study of the capacity of the Athenian Pnyx, H. A. Thompson, "The Pnyx in Models," *Hesperia* Suppl. 19 (1982) 135, assumes that .40 m² per person would have sufficed; this figure applied to the Olympic stadium would yield a capacity crowd of 71, 250! Generally on the stadium, see A. Mallwitz, *Olympia und seine Bauten* (Athens: S. Kasas, 1981) 180–86; Drees (1968) 87–100.

24. Bieber (1961) 54–73; Larmour (1999) 3–4.

25. Mallwitz (1981) 180–86 (Olympic stadium); Stephen G. Miller, ed., *Nemea: A Guide to the Site and Museum* (Berkeley: University of California, 1990) 172–84 and Stella Miller, "Excavations at the Panhellenic Site of Nemea: Cults, Politics, and Games," in Raschke (1988) 145–46 (Nemean stadium); O. Broneer, "The Later Stadium at Isthmia," *AJA* 69 (1965) 166 (Isthmian stadium); D. Romano, "The Panathenaic Stadium and the Theater of Lykourgos: A Re-examination of the Facilities on the Pnyx Hill," *AJA* 89 (1985) 441–54 (Athenian stadium); R. Patrucco, *Lo stadio di Epidauro* (Florence: Olschki, 1976) and E. N. Gardiner, *Athletics of the Ancient*

World (Oxford: Clarendon Press, 1930; reprint, Chicago: Ares, 1980) 128–29 (Epidauros stadium).

26. For fourth-century and Hellenistic theater construction generally, see Bieber (1961) 108–28. For the theater at Isthmia, see E. R. Gebhard, *The Theater at Isthmia* (Chicago: University of Chicago Press, 1973) 16–17; for Lycurgus' stone theater at Athens and Polycleitus' at Epidauros, see Bieber (1961) 70–73.

27. On Lycurgus' program, see Bieber (1961) 70–71; Romano (this ch., note 25, 1985); and F. W. Mitchel, "Lykourgan Athens 338–322," *University of Cincinnati Classical Studies* 2 (1973) 163–214. Cf. Herodes Atticus, the famous Athenian benefactor of the second century A.D., who built a new Panathenaic stadium and a famous odeon at Athens, refurbished the stadium at Delphi, and built an exedra shaped water-fountain at Olympia: see Philostr., *Vitae Sophistarum* 2.1; Paus. 1.19.6; C. Gasparri, "Lo stadio Panatenaico," *ASAtene* 52–53, n.s. 36–37 (1974–75) 313–92; P. Graindor, *Hérode Atticus et sa famille* (Cairo: Faculté des Lettres, Université Égyptienne, 1930) 182–202, 218–24. On the growth of "civic athletics" in Athens, see D. Kyle, *Athletics in Ancient Athens* (Leiden: E. J. Brill, 1987) 32–55.

28. C. R. Beye, *Ancient Greek Literature and Society* (Garden City, N.Y.: Anchor/Doubleday, 1975) 243–46.

29. For the distinction, see Larmour (1999) 36–41.

30. See, for example, a discussion of the tactics and rules for Greek combat sports in Poliakoff (1987) *passim*.

31. Larmour (1999) 37, 137–44 makes a similar point. On athletic nudity as a costume, see ch. 8, note 27; on use of oil and powder, see ch. 8, note 88; on infibulation, see above, ch. 8, note 101.

32. Paus. 5.24.9–10 (oath to Zeus Horikos at Olympia); Ps.-Andocides 4.29 (sacrifices to Zeus at Olympia); Pind., *Ol.* 10. 72–77 (victor's hymn to Zeus).

33. On Hecate and athletics, see ch. 1, quoting the Hesiod passage.

34. C. Faraone, "The Agonistic Context of Early Greek Binding Spells," in *MAGICA HIERA: Ancient Greek Magic and Religion*, ed. C. A. Faraone and D. Obbink (New York: Oxford University Press, 1991) 3–32. See also Stephen Miller (1990) 38–39 for a catalogue of equipment from a pentathlon contest evidently left as votive offerings to Zeus by successful athletes at Nemea.

35. See *LSJ*², s.v. τέλος III.2 and 3.

36. The clearest example of this is the famous family of Diagoras of Rhodes: see discussion in Poliakoff (1987) 119–20; H. A. Harris (1964) 123–24; S. Miller, *Arete: Greek Sports from Ancient Sources* (Berkeley: University of California Press, 1991) 109–10, 195–96.

37. Cylon's aborted attempt to seize power in Athens largely on the strength of his status as Olympic victor is perhaps the best illustration of a people's unwillingness to translate athletic prowess literally into political ability. Alcibiades also claimed the right to command the Athenian expedition to Sicily partly on the basis of his breeding of horses which won an Olympic victory (Thuc. 6.16.1–2), but his actual base of power depended on much more than that. For discussion of athletics and political power generally in Athens, see the excellent survey by Kyle (1987) 155–68.

38. See H. W. Pleket, "Games, Prizes, Athletes and Ideology. Some Aspects of the History of Sport in the Greco-Roman World," *Arena* (= *Stadion*) 1 (1975) 49–89.

39. See ch. 5 for a discussion of the Spartan girls' athletic regimen.

40. W. J. Raschke, "Images of Victory: Some New Considerations of Athletic Monuments," in Raschke (1988) 43–44.

41. τῶν ὑπὲρ τῆς ἀθανασίας ἄθλων, Diod. 3.30.4; see Diod. 4.9.5–4.59.6 for the consistent use of ἄθλοι for Heracles' labors.

42. Weiler (1974) 199–201.

43. Ibid. 173–74, 201.

44. Ibid. 209–17; the earliest versions of the Pelops-Oenomaus agōn are found in the pseudo-Hesiodic *Megalai Ehoiai* fr. 259a (Merkelbach), and most famously in Pind., *Ol.* 1. G. Howie, "Pindar's Account of Pelops' Contest with Oenomaus," *Nikephoros* 4 (1991) 55–120 argues that Pindar's account and the Olympia pediment enhance the grim side of chariot racing generally, reflecting the terror and superstition surrounding it.

45. Raschke (1988) 42.

46. Paus. 5.8.2.

47. See J. Fontenrose, "The Cult of Apollo and the Games at Delphi," in Raschke (1988) 121–40; E. N. Gardiner, *Greek Athletic Sports and Festivals* (London: Macmillan, 1910) 208–14; J. H. Krause, *Die Pythien, Nemeen und Isthmien aus den Schrift- und Bildwerken des Altertums*, with an essay by J. Ebert (Leipzig, 1841; reprint, Hildesheim: Georg Olms, 1975) 1–106. Delphi, like Olympia, also preserves a late, rationalizing version of the first contests played there by the gods: Apollo presided, Castor won in the stade footrace, Polydeuces in boxing, Kalaïs in the long-distance footrace, Zetes in armed combat, Peleus in discus-throwing, Telamon in wrestling, and Heracles in pankration (Hyginus, *Fabulae* 273; Schol. *ad* Pind., *Hypoth. Pyth.* p. 297 Böckh).

48. J. Fontenrose, *Python: A Study of Delphic Myth and Its Origins* (Berkeley: University of California Press, 1959; reprint, 1980) 453–56.

49. Schol. in Pind., *Hypoth. Isth.* Drachmann, vol. 3, p. 193; Ovid, *Metamorphoses* 4. 512–42.; Paus. 1.44.11, 2.2.1; Krause (1975) 171; Gardiner (1910) 214–23.

50. Paus. 1.44.11.

51. Dio Chrysostom, *Oratio* 20.11–15.

52. Apollodorus, *Bibliotheca* 3.64–66; Schol. in Pind., *Hypoth.Nem.* a–e, Drachmann, vol. 3, pp. 1–5; E. Simon, "Archemoros," *AA* (1979) 31–45; W. Pülhorn, "Archemoros," in *LIMC* II.1 (1984), 472–75; Stella Miller in Raschke (1988) 142–43.

53. Schol. in Pind., *Hypoth. Nem.* a, d, e, Drachmann, vol. 3; Stephen Miller (1990) 24–30.

54. In the narrative of the Scholia, the Seven directly associate the founding of the Nemean Games with an admission that their arrival was "the cause of the infant's death" (Schol. *in* Pind., *Hypoth. Nem.* d, e Drachmann vol. 3, pp. 4–5).

55. Kyle (1987) 24; J. A. Davison, "Notes on the Panathenaea," *JHS* 78 (1958) 24–25.

56. K. J. Gallis, "The Games in Ancient Larisa," in Raschke (1988) 218; I. C. Ringwood, *Agonistic Features of Local Greek Festivals Chiefly from Inscriptional Evidence* (Ph.D. diss., Columbia University, 1927) 15–16.

57. F. Zeitlin, "Cultic Models of the Female: Rites of Dionysus and Demeter," *Arethusa* 15 (1982) 143–44.

58. See above, ch. 8, note 68.

59. Cf. the Thesmophoria, which admitted adult and young women (but not children) and rigorously excluded men from attending: W. Burkert, *Greek Religion*, trans. J. Raffan (Cambridge, Mass.: Harvard University Press, 1985) 242–46, from the original *Grieschische Religion der archaïschen und klassichen Epoche* [Stuttgart: W. Kohlhammer, 1977] 365–70. Other Athenian festivals for women, the Skira and the Adoneia, were similarly exclusive, though different in character: ibid. 176–77, 230 (= [1977] 274–75, 350).

60. See Plut., *Lyc.* 15.1.

61. A. Brelich, *Paides e Parthenoi*, vol. 1, Incunabula Graeca vol. 36 (Rome: Ateneo, 1969) 261–62.

62. For numerous other possible instances of girl's athletic contests in the Hellenistic and Roman-era Greek world, in addition to the earlier ones discussed at greater length in chapters 4 to 6, see introduction, notes 79–80; G. Arrigoni, "Donne e sport nel mondo greco: Religione e società," in *Le donne in Grecia*, ed. G. Arrigoni (Rome: Laterza, 1985) esp. 107–19. Excluding the hippic events, which are a special case (see introduction, notes 66–71), the evidence for these is either much slimmer (Aegina, Patras [see notes 63 to 64 this chapter], Chios, Lesbos, Kyme [see Introduction, note 75]), or the events are later Roman insertions into older programs (Pythia, Isthmia, Nemea, Sicyon, Epidauros) than that of the cases already discussed.

63. The gloss may have been written by the fifteenth-century author Michael Souliardos, or by a ninth-tenth century native of Patras, Areta di Cesarea: F. Spiro, "Ein Leser des Pausanias," *Festschrift Johannes Vahlen zum 70. Geburtstag* (Berlin, 1900) 135–38; Arrigoni (1985) 109–10 and 197–98, notes 220–21.

64. Arrigoni (1985) 109 and 197–98, notes 220–21; Harris (1964) 181 and 217, note 3.

65. Burkert (1985) 164 (= [1977] 255); E. Simon, *Die Götter der Griechen*, 2nd ed. (Munich: Hirmer, 1980) 279–80.

66. Brelich (1969) 276–79.

67. M. P. Nilsson, *Griechische Feste von religiöser Bedeutung mit Ausschluß der attischen* (Leipzig: B. G. Teubner, 1906; reprint, Darmstadt: Wissenschaftliche Buchgesellschaft, 1957) 190–96 (Artemis Orthia), 426–27 (Helen).

68. Paus. 3.14.2, 3.14.6, 3.15.3; Nilsson (1957) 213–14, 427. At 214, Nilsson notes that the association of the Issoria with the athletic *agōn* in Pitane is not clear.

69. *IG* 5.1 1375, line 2; 1376 face A, lines 1 and 2, face B line 4 (possibly a female agonothete, Ἑλιξώ); 1377, line 1. The inscriptions are all from the Roman period (Nilsson [1957] 211).

70. Paus. 4.4.2–3; Strabo 8.4.9.

71. Nilsson (1957) 211–12.

72. Zeitlin (1982) 129–38.

73. Kyle (1987) 45–46; L. Deubner, *Attische Feste* (Berlin: Heinrich Keller, 1932; reprint, Darmstadt: Wissenschaftliche Buchgesellschaft, 1956) 116; R. Hamilton, *Choes and Anthesteria: Athenian Iconography and Ritual* (Ann Arbor, Mich.: University of Michigan Press, 1992).

74. Deubner (1956) 114–15; Nilsson (1957) 267, note 5.

75. See above, ch. 3, note 128.

76. On the Anthesteria of Teos, see Nilsson (1957) 267–68; cf. L Moretti, *Iscrizioni agonistiche greche* (Rome: Angelo Signorelli, 1953) 156–58, no. 60, where

the inscription refers to the Tean festival as the "Dionysia." Hermione's annual festival included a musical contest, boat-races and a swimming (or diving) contest: μουσικῆς ἀγῶνα ... καὶ ἀμίλλης κολύμβου καὶ πλοίων ... ἆθλα, Paus. 2.35.1; cf. D.H.J. Larmour, "Boat-Races and Swimming Contests at Hermione," *Aethlon* 7 (1990)128–38.

77. *ARV*² 874, 4, red-figure cup, Laon (France) 37.1056, from Vulci, by the Ancona Painter; the young athlete on the interior is approached by an older man who courts him by offering him a hare.

78. Red-figure Attic stamnoi, Athens, Nat. Mus., inv. nos. 12255 and 1399.

79. Faliscan red-figure stamnoi, fourth century B.C., Rome, Villa Giulia 26017 = *CVA* Italy, Villa Giulia vol. 1, IV B. fig. 1, 1–2; the commentary in *CVA* suggests that the naked youth may be a satyr with a sistrum, but the circular object he holds is most likely a wreath given to the victor: see H. Lee, "Athletics and the Bikini Girls from Piazza Armerina," *Stadion* 10 (1984) 59 with pls. 6 and 10; the Pompeian fresco of a victorious athlete crowned with such a wreath, first century A.D., Naples, Mus. Naz. = catalogue no. II.97, fig. 15 in Ministerio della Pubblica Istruzione Direzione Gen. Antichita' e Belle Arti, eds., *Lo Sport nella Storia e nell' Arte* (Rome: Tipografia Artistica, 1960) (catalogue for an exhibit held in conjunction with the 17th Olympic games, Rome). For stamnos Villa Giulia 43794 = *CVA* Italy, Villa Giulia, vol. 1, IV B. fig. 1, 3–5, see ch. 7, note 49.

80. Attic red-figure mask kantharos, J. Paul Getty Museum, 85.AE.263.

81. D. F. Sutton, "Athletics in the Greek Satyr Play," *RSC* 23 (1975) 203–9.

82. Burkert (1985) 161–62 (= [1977] 251–52).

83. See ch. 8, note 232.

84. See I. Weiler, "ΑΕΙΝ ΑΡΙΣΤΕΥΕΙΝ: Ideologiekritische Bemerkungen zu einem vielzitierten Homerwort," *Stadion* 1 (1976) 199–227.

85. See introduction, note 71.

86. Arist., Politics 1253a 25–29; 1261b 11–15; 1291a10. See G. W. Most, "Self-disclosure and Self-sufficiency in Greek Culture," *JHS* 109 (1989) 114–33; A. J. Festugière, "Autarky and Community in Ancient Greece," in *Freedom and Civilization among the Greeks*, trans. P. T. Brannan (Allison Park, Pa.: Pickwick, 1987; orig., *Liberté et civilisation chez les Grecs* (Paris: Revue des jeunes, 1947) 68–70; A. Mannzmann, s.v. Αὐταρκία (!) *Kleine Pauly*, vol. 1, 777–79.

87. See Young (1984) 111–33.

88. On Astylus, see ibid. 141–45. On other athlete heroes, see Poliakoff (1987) 117–24; Harris (1964) 110–19; Fontenrose (1968). For Polydamas, see Paus. 6.5.4–7.

89. See M. N. Tod, "Greek Record-Keeping and Record-Breaking," *CQ* 43 (1949) 106–12; D. C. Young, "First with the Most: Greek Athletic Records and 'Specialization,'" *Nikephoros* 9 (1996) 175–97; introduction, note 15.

90. J. Ebert, *Griechische Epigramme auf Sieger an gymnischen und hippischen Agonen* (Berlin: Akademie, 1972) 118, #37; see Young (1984) 96, note 95.

91. René Girard, *Violence and the Sacred*, trans. P. Gregory (Baltimore: Johns Hopkins University Press, 1977) 145–46 (with original emphases).

92. Ibid. 148.

93. E. J. Morrissey, *Studies in Inscriptions Listing the Agonistic Festivals* (Ph.D. diss., Harvard University, 1973).

94. Moretti (1953) 126–27, nos. 49 and 51; see discussion in Morrissey (1973).

95. Certain athletes adopted characteristic strategies of competition and hence were known by appropriate nicknames (as happens widely in the sports of various cultures): a boxer, Apollonius *Rhantēs*, "the Sprinkler" (Paus. 5.21.12); Polycles, a chariot victor, called *Polychalcus*, "Rich in Bronze" (Paus. 6.1.7) ; Sostratus a pankratiast, surnamed *Acrocheristēs*, "the Finger-Breaker" (Paus. 6.4.2); Hermogenes, a runner, called *Hippos*, "the Horse" (Paus. 6.13.3); and a Cilician athlete called "the Dumb-bell" (Philostr., *Heroicus* 53–54).

96. Telesicrates: Pind., *P.* 9.97–100, quoted in ch. 8, note 68. D. Steiner, "Moving Images: Fifth-Century Victory Monuments and the Athlete's Allure," *Classical Antiquity* 17 (1998) usefully distinguishes the ambivalent male-audience responses of attraction to and emulation of (or voyeurism and narcissism in response to) the victor presented in poetry or in the visual arts, but, in my view, reads too much into a connection beween "the representations' erotic allure and talismanic powers" (146).

97. See ch. 8, note 27.

98. L. Bonfante, "Nudity as a Costume in Classical Art," *AJA* 93 (1989) 556.

99. K. Clark, *The Nude* (New York: Pantheon, 1956) 8, cited by A. Guttmann, "Eros and Sport," in *Essays on Sport History and Sport Mythology*, ed. D. G. Kyle and G. D. Stark (College Station, Texas: Texas A & M Press, 1990) 146. Cf. the anecdote about the emperor Tiberius, who is said to have lusted so much after Lysippus' statue of the Apoxyomenos (Youth with a Strigil) that he had it removed to his bedroom (Pliny, *Naturalis Historia* 34.61–62).

100. Gebauer (1986) 177–78. Re Greek trainers, see Harris (1964) 170–78; Poliakoff (1987) 11–18; Gardiner (1910) 503–5; J. Jüthner, *Die athletischen Leibesübungen der Griechen*, ed. F. Brein, vol. 1, SB Vienna 249 (Graz: Hermann Böhlaus, 1965) 161–97.

101. Gebauer (1986) 184: "[D]ie Zeit bleibt stehen; die Marke des Records schreibt sich in die Ewigkeit ein; der Athlet verwandelt sich beim Überschreiten der gültigen menschlichen Grenzen, beim Weltrekord, in eine neue Natur und bei der Eintragung in die 'ewige Siegerliste' Olympias in einen Unsterblichen."

102. The radical difference in social constructions of sport is evident particularly in the quotient of violence or even life-threatening action permitted. For discussions of the Roman construction, where death was not only tolerated but even widely approved as an outcome, see K. Hopkins, *Death and Renewal* (Cambridge: Cambridge University Press, 1983); R. Auguet, *Cruelty and Civilization: The Roman Games* (London: Allen & Unwin, 1972); J.-C. Golvin and C. Landes, *Amphitheatres & Gladiateurs* (Paris: CNRS, 1990); P. Plass, *The Game of Death in Ancient Rome: Arena Sport and Political Suicide* (Madison: University of Wisconsin Press, 1995); A. Futrell, *Blood in the Arena* (Austin: University of Texas Press, 1997); C. A. Barton, *The Sorrows of the Ancient Romans: The Gladiator and the Monster* (Princeton: Princeton University Press, 1993); D. Kyle, *Spectacles of Death in Ancient Rome* (London: Routledge, 1998). Cf. also the mysterious Etruscan contest *Phersu*, which resembled the later Roman *venatio*: J.-P. Thuillier, *Les jeux athlétiques dans la civilisation Étrusque*, Bibliothèque des Écoles Françaises d'Athène et de Rome, fasc. 256 (Rome: École Française de Rome, 1985) 586–93. A useful cross-cultural comparison can also be made to the Mesoamerican ballgame, where death of some participants was expected and desired: V. L. Scarborough and D. R. Wilcox, eds., *The Mesoamerican Ballgame* (Tucson: University of Arizona Press, 1991).

103. See the thesis enunciated by K. Meuli, *Der griechische Agon: Kampf und Kampfspiel im Totenbrauch, Totentanz, Totenklage, und Totenlob* (Cologne: Historisches Seminar der Deutsche Sporthochschule Köln, 1968, publ. of University of Basel, Habilitationsschrift, 1926) and id., "Der Ursprung der Olympischen Spielen," *Die Antike* 17 (1941) 189–208, and the excellent critique of it in Poliakoff (1987) 149–57 ("Appendix: Combat Sport, Funeral Cult, and Human Sacrifice").

104. For the Homeric representation of death and its relation to heroic fame, see J. Griffin, *Homer on Life and Death* (Oxford: Oxford University Press, 1980) 95–102.

105. Ebert (1972) 209–11, no. 70.

106. Not noted by Ebert (1972) no. 70, who does, however, mention the parallels of "impetuous Ares" (θοῦρος "Αρης) found in Homer, *Il.* 5. 507 and 24.498, and in Tyrtaeus 9.43 Diehl.

107. ἐν προμάχοισι = l. 16 of Tyrtaeus and l. 3 of the inscription.

108. Weiler (1974) 30–31, citing here examples of *agōn* as used by Sophocles and Euripides.

109. Ibid. 129–243.

110. Ibid. 129–39, 153–56, 174–81; Poliakoff (1987) 136–37.

111. Weiler (1974) 145–49; Poliakoff (1987) 138–39.

112. On the tradition of funeral games, both legendary and historical, see L. Roller, "Funeral Games in Greek Art," *AJA* 85 (1981a) 107–19; id., "Funeral Games for Historical Persons," *Stadion* 7 (1981b) 1–18. An exceptional association of death with funeral games is Achilles' live sacrifice of Trojan youths on the pyre of Patroclus (*Il.* 23.20–23, 175–77); this unusual practice is better explained by the particular circumstances of the epic and is without historical parallel in Greek funeral games.

113. See Introduction, notes 59–60.

114. Athenaeus (4.41) refers to the practice of a paramilitary duel in armor (*hoplomachia*) founded by the Mantineans and copied by the Cyreneans, but this appears to be military training rather than athletics proper. Plutarch (*Moralia* 675c–d) relates a dubious anecdote, told in a drunken stupor, of the contest of a duel to the death (μονομαχίας ἀγὼν ... μέχρι φόνου καὶ σφαγῆς) which supposedly took place at Pisa, in the environs of Olympia, "in former days" (πάλαι).

115. W. Decker, "Die mykenische Herkunft des griechischen Totenagons," *Stadion* 8–9 (1982–83) 1–24.

116. Geometric kantharos, late eighth c. B.C., Copenhagen, National Museum of Denmark, 727; T.B.L. Webster, *From Mycenae to Homer: A Study in Early Greek Literature and Art* (London: Methuen, 1964) 174 and pls. 24a–b; V. Olivová, *Sports and Games in the Ancient World* (New York: St. Martin's Press, 1984) 86 with pl. and figs.

117. Gardiner (1910) 21 and fig. 2; Rudolph Malten, "Lichenspiel und Totenkult," *MDAI (R)* 38–39 (1923–24) 313–14. The fact that more than one pair of combatants are shown suggests that the piece was not meant to depict the Homeric games but was rather a reminiscence of some other funeral game tradition. Poliakoff (1987) 155 argues that the dueling on the Clazomenae sarcophagus could represent a battle scene since flutes are also used for military occasions. Yet all such uses of the flute are, to my knowledge, to accompany marching and not combat. See also W. Raschke, "Aulos and Athlete: The Function of the Flute Player in Greek Athletics," *Arete* 2 (1985) 177–200; Thuillier (1985) 231–54; Larmour (1999) 67–74.

118. The evidence of the Tanagra sarcophagus ultimately leads me to see the Homeric duel as a reminiscence of an actual earlier contest rather than, *pace* Poliakoff, a reworking of an original tale of conflict between two heroes within the Greek camp.

119. See also Plato, *Leg.* 813e and *Euthydemus* 299c.

120. Galen, *De sanitate tuenda* 6.6.153–54 and 157–58.

121. *IG* II². 957, col. 2, 47–61; 958, col. 2, 67–73; 960, col. 2, 32–35; 962, fr. b, 1–7. These four inscriptions are dated ca. 158–140 B.C. See Gardiner (1910) 248; A. Wilhelm, "Siegerlist aus Athen," *MDAI (A)* 30 (1905) 213–19.

122. See the convincing analysis of this difficult passage by Poliakoff (1987) 91–95. For an example of javelins tipped with rounded ends, see the use of σφαιρομαχία to denote ἀκόντια ἐσφαιρομένα (or σφαιρωτά) not noted by Poliakoff, but discussed by E.K. Borthwick, "The Gymnasium of Bromius. A Note on Dionysius Chalcus, fr. 3," *JHS* 84 (1964) 53, note 25, and H. Frère, *Mélanges Ernout* (Paris: C. Klincksieck, 1940) 151.

123. See the discussions by M. Poliakoff, "Deaths in the Panhellenic Games: Addenda et Corrigenda," *AJP* 107 (1986) 400–403; id. (1987) 175, note 12; R. and M. Brophy, "Death in the Panhellenic Games II: All Combative Sports," *AJP* 106 (1985) 171–98; id., "Deaths in the Panhellenic Games. Arrachion and Creugas" *AJP* 99 (1978) 363–90; Thuillier (1985) 639–46; C. A. Forbes, "Accidents and Fatalities in Greek Athletics," in *Classical Studies in Honor of W. A. Oldfather*, presented by a committee of his former students and colleagues (Urbana, Ill.: University of Illinois Press, 1943) 50–59.

124. Olympic Museum inv. no. 848; G.J.M.J. te Riele, "Inscriptions conservées au Musée d'Olympie," *BCH* 88 (1964) 186–87; Ebert (1972) 143; J. and L. Robert, "Bulletin épigraphique," *REG* 78 (1965) 182; Poliakoff (1987) 90.

125. See introduction, note 54.

126. Moretti (1953) 73 cites, for instance, the report of an international sports organization that from 1945 to 1952 over one hundred boxers died in competition or from injuries that ultimately proved fatal.

127. *IK* Ephesos 7.1, 3445 = W. Peek, *Griechische Versinschriften* I (Berlin: Akademie, 1955) 680; Poliakoff (1986) 400.

128. Philostr., *Gymn.* 21, 23.

129. J. Jüthner, *Philostratus über Gymnastik* (Leipzig: B. G. Teubner, 1909; reprint, Stuttgart, 1969) 233 *ad loc.* notes that the phrase "desire for death" occurs in other writings of Philostratus (but not the *Imagines*); see also W. Schmid, *Der Atticismus* (Stuttgart: B. G. Teubner, 1897; reprint, Hildesheim: Georg Olms, 1964) vol. 4, 186–87 with references. The fact that the author may have had a philosophical interest in this theme does not distract from the appropriateness of the observation with regard to Arrhichion.

130. Photius 190. 151 a; Hönle (1972) 100; L. Moretti, *Olympionikai, I Vincitori negli Antichi Agoni Olimpici, MemLincei* ser. 8.8.2 (Rome: Accademia Nazionale dei Lincei, 1957) 84 no. 181; Poliakoff (1987) 175, note 12.

131. Athenagoras, *Supplicatio pro Christianis* 14.62 (Otto); Poliakoff (1987) 175, note 12.

132. Thuillier (1985) 639–46.

133. Dem. 23.53; Arist., *Athenaion Politeia* 57.3; Pl., *Leg.* 865 a. See Poliakoff (1987) 175, note 12 and 402; D. M. MacDowell, *The Law in Classical Athens* (Ithaca: Cornell University Press, 1978) 117.

134. Apollodorus 1.3.3, 3.10.3; Ovid, *Metamorphoses* 10.174ff. See M. Lavrencic et al., *Diskos, Quellendokumentation zur Gymnastik und Agonistik im Altertum* 1 (Vienna: Böhlau, 1991) 142 for additional sources.

135. Galen, *De compositione medicamentorum secundum locos libri x* 9 (Hermes-Crocus); Paus. 5.3.7 (Oxylus-Thermius/Alcidocus); Paus. 2.16.2 and Apollonius Rhodius 4.1091 (Perseus-Acrisius); Paus. 2.29.7 (Peleus-Phocus). See for further bibliography: Lavrencic (1991) 142; Forbes (1943); Weiler (1974) 227–28; J. Jüthner, *Die athletischen Leibesübungen der Griechen*, ed. F. Brein, vol. 2, SB Vienna 249 (Graz: Hermann Böhlaus, 1968) 251, note 75.

136. Jüthner (1909) 201 *ad Gymn.* 8, text on p. 128, line 24; id. and F. Brein, vol. 2 (1968) 114, note 250. See Philostr., *Gymn.* 24, the only other reference to the severe regulation, where, however, the competitor himself does not risk the death penalty, but his coach pledges his own life as surety and encourages the athlete on to a second victory. The fact that anyone could place his life as surety in lieu of the competitor suggests that any willing individual could serve as communal scapegoat, so long as someone was sacrificed in compensation.

137. Eustath. 4.316 (Stallbaum), *ad* Hom., *Il.* 23.683; *Etymologicum Magnum* s.v. γυμνάσια; Moretti (1957) 61–62, no. 16.

138. Isidor., *Origines* 18.17.2; Schol. Venetus A *ad Il.* 23.638; Moretti (1957) 62.

139. N. Crowther, "Athletic Dress and Nudity in Greek Athletics," *Eranos* 80 (1982) 168; cf. the other sources on Orsippus, Paus. 1.44.1; *IG* 7.52 = *CIG* 1.1050 = G. Kaibel, *Epigrammata Graeca ex lapidibus conlecta* (Berlin: Reimer, 1878; repr. Hildesheim: Olms, 1965) 843.

140. A. Kossatz-Diessmann, "Zur Herkunft des Perizoma im Satyrspiel," *JDAI* 97 (1982) 75.

141. D. Williams, "The Brygos Tomb Reassembled," *AJA* 96 (1992) 634.

142. See Young (1984) 111, note 6; Kyle (1987) 131, note 31.

143. H. A. Harris, *Sport in Greece and Rome* (Ithaca: Cornell University Press, 1976) 162.

144. I translate ξύλον αὗον as "seasoned post" in spite of the nearly universal tradition of English translations taking it as a "dry stump": cf. translations of R. Fagles, M. Hammond, R. Lattimore, S. Miller, E. Rees, E. V. Rieu, and W. Sweet. Only *LSJ*² s.v. II takes ξύλον, a *hapax legomenon* in Homer, as "piece of wood, log, beam, post"; cf. "dry pole" in ibid., s.v. αὗος 1. Dried timber is of course seasoned and stronger, and the two stones flanking the wood are presumably there to hold it upright in the post hole.

145. See Dio Chr., *Orationes* 15.76 (Arnim), which also agrees with Pausanias' censure of attributing accidents to a *daimōn*. See also J. G. Frazer, *Pausanias's Description of Greece*, vol. 4 (London: Macmillan, 1913) 84–85, *ad* 6.20.15, citing Lycophron, *Cassandra* 42–43, and Tzetzes, *Schol. ad Lyc. Cass.*, *ad loc.*, which offers still another identification of Taraxippus, namely with a certain "earth-born Ischenus" whose tomb was at the hill of Cronus, and who may have been a local nobleman who agreed to obey an oracle and die in order to end a famine.

146. O. Broneer, "Hero Cults in the Corinthian Agora," *Hesperia* 11 (1942) 128–61.

147. J. H. Humphrey, *Roman Circuses: Arenas for Chariot Racing* (Berkeley: University of California Press, 1986) 11, 255–59. The suggestion that Homer's *sēma* and

the Circus Maximus turning posts both reflect a gateway or *dokana* of the Dioscuri, however, relies upon an incorrect analogy: W. K. Quinn-Schofield, "The Metae of the Circus Maximus as a Homeric Landmark; *Iliad* 23.327–333," *Latomus* 27 (1968) 142–46; *contra*, Humphrey (1986) 256 and notes 155–56. E. P. McGowan, "Tomb Marker and Turning Post: Funerary Columns in the Archaic Period," *AJA* 99 1995) 615–32, studies actual Archaic funerary column monuments placed near or on racecourses, apparently to gain prestige by association with the age of Homeric heroes.

148. See κάμψειν τὸν ταλαίπωρον βίον, Soph. *Oedipus Coloneus* 91; τέλος δὲ κάμψαιμ᾽ ὥσπερ ἠρξάμην βίου, Euripides, *Hippolytus* 87; τέλος κάμψη βίου, id., *Electra* 956; ὅταν δὲ κάμψῃς καὶ τελευτήσῃς βίον, id., *Helen* 1666. Cf. the Latin expression *meta vitae*: Vergil *Aeneid* 10.472; Ov., *Tristia* 1.9.1; Valerius Flaccus 6.310; Silius Italicus 5.406; Apuleius, *Metamorphoses* 4.20. The "turning-post" and "course-of-life" metaphors are, of course, equally applicable to footraces, and the same Greek and Latin terms (καμπτήρ, κάμπτω, νύσσα, τέρμα, *meta*) apply to both equestrian contests and footraces.

149. Humphrey (1986) 196–207; M. Turcan-Deléani, "Contribution à l'étude des amours dans l'art funéraire romaine: les sarcophages à courses de chars," *MEFR* 76 (1964) 43–49; N. Blanc and F. Gury, in *LIMC* III.1 (1986), 952–1001, nos. 380 (cinerary urn) and 381–84 (sarcophagi).

150. Sarcophagus, Mainz Römisch-Germanisches Zentralmuseum = Humphrey (1986) 199 pl. 100.

151. Humphrey (1986) 196–97 and 655, note 49. Thirty-seven of the sarcophagi, all A.D. mid-second century to ca. 300, are children's' with Erotes; only six are adults' with real charioteers, dating from ca. A.D. 200 into the fourth century. See also the seven representations of Erotes/Cupids racing in *LIMC* III.1, s.v. "Eros/Amor, Cupido," 1000–1001, nos. 380–386; four of these, nos. 381–84, are on children's sarcophagi.

152. Miniature oinochoe (shape 3), Athens Nat. Mus. 1736; *ARV*² 1258. Two Erotes, one mounting chariot, second holding fawns, with a fawn biga: Deubner (1956) 245 and pl. 32.2. On the changing morphology of Eros/Amor, see Blanc and Gury in *LIMC* III.1 (1986), 1043–44. The famous scene of the child Eros playing games in Apollonius' *Argonautica* 3.114–66 may have been instrumental in popularizing the transformation.

153. K. Schauenburg, "Erotenspiele, 2. Teil," *Antike Welt* 7.7 (1976b) 30–31, citing the krater, Leningrad 424.

154. A. Hermary, H. Cassimatis, and R. Vollkommer, in *LIMC* III.1 (1986) 939.

155. See ch. 8 and A. Hermary, H. Cassimatis, and R. Vollkommer, in *LIMC* III.1 (1986) 882–83, nos. 388–95 and 911–12, nos. 712–22; K. Schauenburg, "Erotenspiele, 1. Teil," *Antike Welt* 7.3 (1976a) 39–52; Schauenburg (1976b) 28–35.

156. Humphrey (1986) 188–93.

157. See especially Solon's discussion with Croesus in Herodotus (1.30–33), and, for general treatments, A.W.H. Adkins, *Moral Values and Political Behaviour in Ancient Greece* (London: Chatto and Windus, 1972) and K. J. Dover, *Greek Popular Morality in the Time of Plato and Aristotle* (Berkeley: University of California Press, 1974).

158. Humphrey (1986) 135–36.

159. Burkert (1985) 64–65 (= [1977] 113–14); Simon (1980) 79–84 (Poseidon Hippios); 43–44, 49–50 (Hera Hippia).

160. Joan V. O'Brien, *The Transformation of Hera: A Study of Ritual, Hero, and the Goddess in the Iliad* (Lanham, Md.: Rowman and Littlefield, 1993) 192–201. Yet I would not go as far as O'Brien does in assigning Hera primary symbolic powers over the race, nor in analogizing between the untimely death of heroes like Achilles and the tomb of heroes at the turning post, that is, prior to the end of the race. The chronological length of life is not tied to success, which is the operative metaphor here for "victory" in the race. On Hera Teleia: Burkert (1985) 133, 135 (= [1977] 210–11, 214).

161. Girard (1977) 145.

162. Skull of an athletic victor with gold crown and first century A.D. silver coin of Polyrrhenia, Hagios Nikolaos Museum 7355–56; bronze aryballos (from same tomb), 3709.

163. Hagia Triada "Boxer Rhyton," including death of bull-leaper on horns of charging bull. Archeological Museum, Herakleion, Crete. Cf. T. Scanlon, "Women, Bull Sports, Cults, and Initiation in Minoan Crete," *Nikephoros* 12 (1999) 33–70.

164. Gebauer (1986) 272.

Chapter 10

1. Contests in Elis: *Il.* 11.698–702. Games prior to the eighth century at Olympia: H. Lee, "The 'First' Olympic Games of 776 B.C.," in *The Archaeology of the Olympics: The Olympics and Other Festivals in Antiquity*, ed. W. Raschke (Madison: University of Wisconsin Press, 1988) 110–18.

2. See above, introduction, notes 79–80.

3. W. Phillips, "A Season in the Stands," *Commentary* 48 (1969) 66, quoted in A. Guttmann, *From Ritual to Record: The Nature of Modern Sports* (New York: Columbia University Press, 1978) 118.

4. Guttmann (1978) 139–52, who notes, however, that American youth prefer team sports to individual ones, while the preferences of European and Japanese youth are the reverse (151).

5. Guttmann (1978) 157–61.

6. See above, Introduction, notes 27 and 38; ch. 9, note 86.

7. Peter Brown, "Bodies and Minds: Sexuality and Renunciation in Early Christianity," in *Before Sexuality: The Construction of Erotic Experience in the Ancient Greek World*, ed. D. Halperin, J. J. Winkler, and F. I. Zeitlin (Princeton: Princeton University Press, 1990) 488.

8. A. Guttmann, *The Erotic in Sports* (New York: Columbia University Press, 1996) 37–72; A. Guttmann, *Women's Sports: A History* (New York: Columbia University Press, 1991).

9. H. Marrou, *A History of Education in Antiquity*, trans. G. Lamb (London: Sheed and Ward, 1956) 330–50.

10. For some recent studies of sexuality and gender in modern sports (without ancient comparisons), see Aaron Baker and Todd Boyd, eds., *Out of Bounds: Sports, Media, and the Politics of Identity* (Bloomington: Indiana University Press, 1997); chapter 8: "Zero-Sum Contests," in Ray Raphael, *The Men from the Boys: Rites of Pas-*

sage in Male America (Lincoln: University of Nebraska Press, 1988) 129–43;
J. A. Mangan and Roberta J. Park, eds., *From 'Fair Sex' to Feminism: Sport and the Socialization of Women in the Industrial and Post-industrial Eras* (London: F. Cass, 1987); Helen Lenskyj, *Out of Bounds: Women, Sport and Sexuality* (Toronto: Women's Press, 1986); Pamela J. Creedon, ed., *Women, Media and Sport: Challenging Gender Values* (Thousand Oaks, Calif.: Sage, 1994); Mariah Burton Nelson, *The Stronger Women Get, the More Men Love Football: Sexism and the American Culture of Sports* (New York: Harcourt Brace, 1994); Eric Dunning, "Sport as a Male Preserve: Notes on the Social Sources of Masculine Identity and Its Transformations," in *Quest for Excitement: Sport and Leisure in the Civilizing Process*, ed. Norbert Elias and Eric Dunning (Oxford: Oxford University Press, 1986).

11. Steven Houseworth, Kenneth Peplow, and Joel Thirer, "Influence of Sport Participation upon Sex Role Orientation of Caucasian Males and their Attitudes toward Women," *Sex Roles* 20.5/6 (1989) 317–25; Janice E. Butcher, "Adolescent Girls' Sex Role Development: Relationship with Sports Participation, Self-Esteem, and Age at Menarche," *Sex Roles* 20.9/10 (1989) 575–93; M. Messner, "The Meaning of Success: The Athletic Experience and the Development of Male Identity," in *The Making of Masculinities: The New Men's Studies*, ed. Harry Brod (Boston: Allen & Unwin, 1987) 193–209. These studies show that the image of the athlete is more strongly masculine than feminine, but we may posit that the image of a female athlete may well lose its oxymoronic character over time with the wider popular interest in and encouragement of women's sports.

SELECT BIBLIOGRAPHY

Anderson, J. K. *Hunting in the Ancient World*. Berkeley: University of California Press, 1985.

Arias, P. E., M. Hirmer, and B. B. Shefton. *A History of Greek Vase Painting*. London: Thames and Hudson, 1962.

Arieti, J. "Nudity in Greek Athletics." *CW* 68 (1975) 431–36.

Arrigoni, G. "Donne e Sport nel Mondo Greco Religione e Società." In *Le donne in Grecia*, ed. G. Arrigoni, 55–201. Rome: Laterza, 1985.

Arrowsmith, W. "Aristophanes' Birds: The Fantasy Politics of Eros." *Arion* N.S. 1.1 (1973) 119–67.

Bain, D. "Six Verbs of Sexual Congress (*binō, kinō, pugizō, lēkō, oiphō, laikazō*)." *CO* 41 (1991) 72–74.

Beazley, D. *The Development of the Attic Black-Figure*. Berkeley: University of California Press, 1964.

———. *Attic Red-Figure Vase Painters*. 2nd ed. Vol. II. Oxford: Clarendon, 1968.

Becker, W. A. *Charicles*, Trans. F. Metcalfe. London: Longmans, Green, 1882. Reprint, London: Longmans, Green, 1906.

Bérard, C. "L'Impossibile Femme Athlete." *Annali Archeologia e Storia Antica* (Naples) 8 (1986) 195–202.

Bérard, C., et al., eds. *A City of Images: Iconography and Society in Ancient Greece*. Trans. D. Lyons. Princeton: Princeton University Press, 1990. From the original *La cité des images* (Paris: F. Nathan, 1984).

Bernardi, B. *Age-Class Systems: social institutions and polities based on age*. Cambridge: Cambridge University Press, 1985.

Bernardini, A. " Aspects ludiques, rituels et sportifs de la course féminine dans la Grèce antique." *Stadion* 12–13 (1986–87) 17–26.

Bieber, M. *Die antiken Skulpturen und Bronzen des Königl. Museum Fridericianum in Cassel*. Marburg: N. G. Elwertsche Verlagsbuchhandlung, 1915.

———. *The History of the Greek and Roman Theater*. Princeton: Princeton University Press, 1961.

Bilinski, B. *Agoni Ginnici: Componenti Artistiche ed Intellectuali nell'Antica Agonistica Greca*. Wroclaw: Zaklad Narodowy Narodowy im. Ossolinskich, 1979.

Blanc, N. and F. Gury, "(Eros) / Amor, Cupido," in *LIMC* III.1 (1986), 952–1049 and III 2, 678–727.

Boardman, J. *Athenian Red Figure Vases: The Classical Period*. London: Thames and Hudson, 1989.

Boardman, J., with advice from G. Arrigoni. "Atalante." In *LIMC* vol. II, pts. 1 and 2. ed. L. Kahil, 940–950. Zurich: Artemis, 1984.

Bonfante, L. "Nudity as A Costume in Classical Art." *AJA* 93.4 (1989) 543–70.

Bothmer, D.-V. *Amazons in Greek Art.* Oxford: Clarendon, 1957.

Bowie, T., and C. V. Christenson, eds., *Studies in Erotic Art.* New York: Basic Books, 1970.

Bowra, C. M. "Xenophanes and the Olympic Games." *AJP* 59 (1938) 257–79.

Brelich, A. *Le Iniziazioni: Parte II.* Rome: Ateneo, 1962.

———. *Paides e Parthenoi.* vol. 1. Incunabula Graeca, vol. 36. Rome: Anteneo, 1969.

Bremmer, J. "An enigmatic Indo-European Rite: Paederasty." *Arethusa* 13 (1980) 279–98.

———. "Adolescents, *Symposion,* and Pederasty." In *Sympotica: A Symposium on the Symposium,* ed. O. Murray, 135–48. Oxford: Clarendon, 1990.

———. *Greek Religion.* Greece and Rome, New Surveys in the Classics No. 24. Oxford: Oxford University Press, 1994.

Broneer, O. "Eros and Aphrodite on the North Slope of the Acropolis." *Hesperia* 1 (1932) 31–55, 2 (1933) 31–55.

———. "Hero Cults in the Corinthian Agora." *Hesperia* 11 (1942) 128–61.

Brophy, R. and M. "Deaths in the Panhellenic Games. Arrachion and Creugas." *AJP* 99 (1978) 363–90.

———. "Death in the Panhellenic Games II: All Combative Sports." *AJP* 106 (1985) 171–98.

Bruit Zaidman, L., and P. Schmitt Pantel. *Religion in the Ancient Greek City.* Trans. P. Cartledge. Cambridge: Cambridge University Press, 1994.

Brulotte, E. L. "The 'Pillar of Oinomaos' and the Location of Stadium I at Olympia." *AJA* 98 (1994) 53–64.

Buffière, F. *Eros adolescent: la pédérastie dans la Grèce antique.* Paris: Société d'Edition "Les Belles Lettres," 1980.

Burkert, W. *Structure and History in Greek Mythology and Ritual.* Berkeley and Los Angeles: University of California Press, 1979.

———. *Homo Necans: The Anthropology of Ancient Greek Sacrificial Ritual and Myth.* Trans. P. Bing. Berkeley: University of California Press, 1983.

———. *Greek Religion.* Trans. J. Raffan. Cambridge, Massachusetts: Harvard University Press, 1985. From the orig. *Griechische Religion der archaischen und klassischen Epoche* (Stuttgart: W. Kohlhammer, 1977).

Calame, C. ed. *L'Amore in Grecia.* Rome: Laterza, 1983. Reprint, 1988.

———. *Les choeurs de jeunes filles en Grèce archaïque, Vol. II: Alcman.* Rome: Ateneo & Bizzarri, 1977b).

———. *Choruses of Young Women in Ancient Greece: I: Their Morphology, Religious. Role, and Social Functions.* Trans. D. Collins and J. Orion. Lanham, Md.: Rowman & Littlefield, 1997. From the original *Les choeurs de jeunes filles en Grèce archaïque Vol. I: Morphologie, fonction religieuse et sociale. Vol. II: Alcman.* (Rome: Ateneo & Bizzarri, 1977a).

Cantarella, E. *Pandora's Daughters: The Role and Status of Women in Greek and Roman Antiquity.* Trans. M. B. Fant. Baltimore: Johns Hopkins University Press, 1987.

————. *Bisexuality in the Ancient World*. Trans. C. Ó. Cuilleanáin. New Haven: Yale University Press, 1992.

Carson, A. "Wedding at Noon in Pindar's *Ninth Pythian*." *GRBS* 23 (1982) 121–28.

Cartledge, P. "Literacy in the Spartan Oligarchy." *JHS* 98 (1978) 25–37.

————. *Agesilaos and the Crisis of Sparta*. London: Duckworth, 1987.

————. "The Politics of Spartan Pederasty." In *Sexualität und Erotik in der Antike*, Wege der Forschung. vol. 605, ed. A. Karsten Siems, 383–415. Darmstadt: Wissenschaftliche Buchgesellschaft, 1988.

Cartledge, P., and A.J.S. Spawforth. *Hellenistic and Roman Sparta: A Tale of Two Cities*. London: Routledge, 1989.

Charbonneaux, J. *Les bronzes grecs*. Paris: Presses Universitaires de France, 1958.

Cohen, D. *Law, Sexuality, and Society. The Enforcement of Morals in Classical Athens*. Cambridge: Cambridge University Press, 1991a.

————. "Sexuality, Violence, and the Athenian Law of Hybris." *GRBS* 38 (1991b) 171–88.

————. *Law, Violence and Community in Classical Athens*. Cambridge: Cambridge University Press, 1995.

Cole, S. "The Social Function of Rituals of Maturation: The Koureion and the Arkteia." *Zeitschrift für Papyrologie und Epigraphik* 55 (1984) 233–44.

Congdon, L.O.K. *Caryatid Mirrors of Ancient Greece. Technical, Stylistic and Historical Considerations of an Archaic and Early Classical Bronze Series*. Mainz: von Zabern, 1981.

Coulsen, W., and H. Kyrieleis, eds. *Proceedings of an International Symposium on the Olympic Games. 5–9 September 1988*. Athens: Luci Braggiotti Publications for the Deutsches Archäologisches Institut Athen, 1992.

Crowther, N. "Nudity and Morality: Athletics in Italy." *CJ* 76.2 (1980–81) 119–23.

————. "Athletic Dress and Nudity in Greek Athletics." *Eranos* 80 (1982) 163–8.

————. "Studies in Greek Athletics." *CW* 78 (1984) 497–558 and 79 (1985a) 73–135.

————. "Male 'Beauty' Contests in Greece: The Euandria and the Euexia." *AC* 54 (1985b) 285–91.

————. "The Age Category of Boys at Olympia." *Phoenix* 42 (1988) 304–8.

————. "Euxia, Eutaxia, Philoponia: Three Contest of the Greek Gymnasium." *ZPE* 85 (1991) 301–4.

Davidson, J. N. *Courtesans and Fishcakes: The Consuming Passions of Classical Athens*. London: St. Martin's, 1997.

Decker, W. "Die mykenische Herkunft des griechischen Totenagons." *Stadion* 8–9 (1982–83) 1–24 and Abb. 1–2.

Delorme, J. *Gymnasion: Étude sur les Monuments consacrés à l'Éducation en Grèce (des origines à l'Empire romain)*. Paris: De Boccard, 1960.

Deubner, L. *Attische Feste*. Berlin: Heinrich Keller, 1932. Reprint, Darmstadt: Wissenschaftliche Buchgesellschaft, 1956.

Dingwall, E. J. *Male Infibulation*. London: John Bole, Sons & Danielsson, Ltd., 1925.

Dittenberger, W., and K. Purgold, eds. *Die Inschriften von Olympia. Olympia*. Vol. 5, ed. E. Curtius and F. Adler. Berlin: A. Asher & co., 1896. Reprint, Amsterdam: Hakkert, 1966.

Dix, U. *Sport und Sexualität: eine Kritik der Sport-Sexualpädagogik aus Psychoanalytischer Sicht*. Frankfurt/M: März, 1972.

Dörpfeld, W. *Alt-Olympia*. Vol. 1. Berlin: E. S. Mitter, 1935.

Dougherty, C., and L. Kurke. *Cultural Poetics in Archaic Greece: Cult, Performance, Politics*. Cambridge: Cambridge University Press, 1993.

Dover, K. J. *Aristophanic Comedy*. Berkeley: University of California Press, 1972.

———. "Classical Greek Attitudes to Sexual Behavior." *Arethusa* 6 (1973) 59–73.

———. *The Greeks and Their Legacy: Collected Papers, Volume II: Prose, Literature, History, Society, Transmission, Influence*. Oxford: Blackwell, 1988.

———. *Greek Homosexuality*. 2nd ed. Cambridge, Mass.: Harvard University Press, 1989.

Dowden, K. *The Uses of Greek Mythology*. London: Routledge, 1992.

Drachmann, A. B., ed. *Scholia vetera in Pindari carmina*. 3 volumes. Leipzig: Teubner, 1903–27. Reprint, Amsterdam: Hakkert, 1966–69.

Drees, L. *Der Ursprung der olympischen Spiele*. Stuttgart: K. Hofmann, 1962.

———. *Olympia: Gods, Artists, and Athletes*. Trans. G. Onn. New York: Praeger, 1968.

Duerr, H. P. *Nacktheit und Scham*. 2nd ed. Frankfurt/M: Suhrkamp, 1988.

Easterling, P. E., and B.M.W. Knox, eds. *The Cambridge History of Classical Literature: I. Greek Literature*. Cambridge: Cambridge University Press, 1985.

Ebert, J. *Griechische Epigramme auf Sieger an gymnischen und hippischen Agonen*. Berlin: Akademie, 1972.

Ebert, J., et al. *Olympia von den Anfängen bis zu Coubertin*. Leipzig: Koehler & Amelang, 1980.

Faraone, C. A., and D. Obbink, eds. *Magika Hiera: Ancient Greek Magic and Religion*. New York: Oxford University Press, 1991.

Farrington, A. "Olympic Victors and the Popularity of the Olympic Games in the Imperial Period." *Tyche* 12 (1997) 15–46.

Fasce, S. *Eros: la Figura e il Culto*. Genoa: Universita di Genova, Facoltá di lettere Istituo di filologia classica e medievale, 1977.

Fiedler, W. "Sexuelle Enthaltsamkeit griechischer Athleten und ihre medizinische Begründung." *Stadion* 11 (1985) 137–75.

Figueira, T. J., and G. Nagy, eds. *Theognis of Megara*. Baltimore: Johns Hopkins Uninversity Press, 1985.

Finley, M. I. *The World of Odysseus*. 2nd ed. New York: Viking, 1978.

———. "Sparta and Spartan Society." In *Economy and Society in Ancient Greece*, ed. B. D. Shaw and R. P. Saller, 24–40. New York: Chatto & Windus, 1982.

Finley, M. I., and H. W. Pleket. *The Olympic Games: The First Thousand Years*. New York: Viking, 1976.

Fontenrose, J. *Python: A Study of Delphic Myth and its Origins*. Berkeley: University of California Press, 1959. Reprint, 1980.

Forbes, C. A. *Greek Physical Education*. New York: Century, 1929.

———. "Accidents and Fatalities in Greek Athletics." In *Classical Studies in Honor of W. A. Oldfather*, presented by a committee of his former students and colleagues, 50–59. Urbana, Ill.: University of Illinois Press, 1943.

Forrest, W. G. *A History of Sparta. 950–192 B.C.* London: Hutchinson, 1968. Reprint, London: Duckworth, 1980.

Frazer, J. G. *Pausanias's Description of Greece*. Vols 3 and 4. London: Macmillan, 1913.

Fürtwangler, A. "Eros." In *RE* I.1. 1339.

Gaertringen, H. von. *Thera. Untersuchungen, Vermessungen und Ausgrabungen in den Jahren 1895–1898.* Vol. 1, *Die Insel Thera in Altertum und Gegenwart mit Ausschluss der Nekroplen.* Berlin: G. Reimer, 1899.

Gaertringen, H. von, and P. Wilski. *Thera. Untersuchungen, Vermessungen und Ausgrabungen in den Jahren 1895–1902.* Vol. 3, *Stadtgeschichte von Thera.* Berlin: G. Reimer, 1904.

Gantz, T. *Early Greek Myth: A Guide to Literary and Artistic Sources.* Baltimore: Johns Hopkins University Press, 1993.

Gardiner, E. N. *Greek Athletic Sports and Festivals.* London: Macmillan, 1910.

———. *Olympia: Its History and Remains.* Oxford: Clarendon, 1925. Reprint, Washington, D.C.: McGrath, 1973.

———. *Athletics of the Ancient World.* Oxford: Clarendon, 1930. Reprint, Chicago: Ares, 1980.

Garlan, Y., and O. Masson. "Les acclamations pederastiques de Kalami (Thasos)." *BCH* 106 (1982) 3–22.

Gauthier, P., and M. B. Hatzopoulos. *La loi gymnasiarchique de Beroia, Meletēmata* (Kentron Hellenikēs kai Romaikēs Archaiotētos), vol. 16. Athens: Centre de recherches de l'antiquité grecque et romaine, and Paris: Diffusion de Boccard, 1993.

Gebauer, G. *Sport—Eros—Tod.* New Series, vol. 335, ed. G. Gebauer and G. Hortleder. Frankfurt: Suhrkamp, 1986.

Golden, M. "Slavery and Sexuality in Athens." *Phoenix* 38 (1984) 308–24.

———. *Children and Childhood in Classical Athens.* Baltimore: Johns Hopkins University Press, 1990.

———. *Sport and Society in Ancient Greece.* Cambridge: Cambridge University Press, 1998.

Gouldner, A. W. *Enter Plato: Classical Greece and the Origins of Social Theory.* New York: Basic Books, 1965.

Graindor, P. *Hérode Atticus et sa famille.* Cairo: Faculté des Lettres, Université Égyptienne, 1930.

Grant, M., and R. Kitzinger, eds. *Civilization of the Ancient Mediterranean: Greece and Rome.* 3 vols. New York: Scribners, 1988.

Grasberger, L. *Erziehung und Unterricht im klassischen Altertum.* 3 vols. Würzburg, 1864–81. Reprint, Aalen: Scientia, 1971.

Greek Ministry of Culture. *Eros Grec: Amour des Dieux et des Hommes.* Athens: Ministère de la culture de Grèce, Direction des antiquités, 1989.

Greifenhagen, A. *Griechische Eroten.* Berlin: De Gruyter, 1957.

Guthrie, W. K. C. *A History of Greek Philosophy. Vol. III: The Fifth-Century Enlightenment.* Cambridge: Cambridge University Press, 1969.

Guttmann, A. *From Ritual to Record: The Nature of Modern Sports.* New York: Columbia University Press, 1978.

———. "Eros and Sport." In *Essays on Sport History and Sport Mythology,* ed. D. G. Kyle and G. D. Stark, 139–154. College Station, Texas: Texas A & M University Press, 1990.

———. *Women's Sports: A History.* New York: Columbia University Press, 1991.

———. *The Erotic in Sports.* New York: Columbia University Press, 1996.

Häfner, U. *Das Kunstschaffen Lakoniens in archaischer Zeit.* Ph.D. diss., University of Munich, 1965.

Halliwell, S., ed. *Plato: Republic 10.* Warminster, U.K.: Aris & Phillips, 1988.

―――. ed. *Plato: Republic 5.* Warminster, U.K.: Aris & Phillips, 1993.

Halperin, D. "Plato and Erotic Reciprocity." *CA* 5 (1986) 60–80.

―――. *One Hundred Years of Homosexuality.* New York: Routledge, 1990.

Halperin, D., J. J. Winkler, and F. I. Zeitlin, eds. *Before Sexuality: The Construction of Erotic Experience in the Ancient Greek World.* Princeton: Princeton University Press, 1990.

Hamilton, R. "Alcman and the Athenian Arkteia." *Hesperia* 58.4 (1989) 449–72.

―――. *Choes and Anthesteria: Athenian Iconography and Ritual.* Ann Arbor, Mich.: University of Michigan Press, 1992.

Harris, H. A. *Greek Athletes and Athletics.* London: Hutchinson, 1964.

―――. *Sport in Greece and Rome.* Ithaca: Cornell University Press, 1976.

Henderson, J. *The Masculate Muse: Obscene Language in Attic Comedy.* New Haven: Yale University Press, 1975.

―――. "Greek Attitudes Toward Sex." In Grant and Kitzinger (1988) vol. 2, 1249–63.

Henrichs, A. "Human Sacrifice in Greek Religion: Three Case Studies." *Le Sacrifice dans L'Antiquité.* Entretiens sur l'antiquité classique, vol. 27, ed. J. Rudhardt and O. Reverdin, 197–235. Geneva: Fondation Hardt, 1981.

Hermary, A., H. Cassimatis and R. Vollkommer, s.v. "Eros," in *LIMC* III.1 (1986) 850–942 and III.2, 609–668.

Herrmann, H.-V. "Zur ältesten Geschichte von Olympia." *MDAI(A)* 77 (1962) 3–34.

―――. *Olympia: Heiligtum und Wettkampfstätte.* Munich: Hirmer, 1972.

―――. "Olympia und seine Spiele im Wandel der Zeiten." *Gymnasium* 80 (1973) 172–205.

Himmelmann, N. *Ideale Nacktheit in der griechischen Kunst, Jahrbuch des deutschen archäologischen Instituts, Jahrbuch des deutschen archäologischen Instituts,* Supplement 26. Berlin: Walter De Greuter, 1990.

Hodkinson, S. "An Agonistic Culture." In *Sparta: New Perspectives,* ed. S. Hodkinson and A. Powell, 147–87. London: Duckworth, 1999.

Hönle, A. *Olympia in der Politik der griechischen Staatenwelt von 776 bis zum ende des 5. Jahrhunderts.* Bebenhausen, Germany: Lothar Rotsch, 1972.

Howie, G. "Pindar's Account of Pelops' Contest with Oenomaus." *Nikephoros* 4 (1991) 55–120.

Huizinga, J. *Homo Ludens: A Study of the Play Element in Culture.* Trans. R.F.C. Hull. Boston: Beacon, 1955. From the original *Homo ludens: proeve eener bepaling van het spel-element der cultuur.* Haarlem : H. D. Tjeenk Willink, 1940.

Humphrey, J. H. *Roman Circuses: Arenas for Chariot Racing.* Berkeley: University of California Press, 1986.

Hyde, W. W. *Olympic Victor Monuments and Greek Athletic Art.* Washington: Carnegie Institution of Washington, 1921.

Instone, S. "Love and Sex in Pindar: Some Practical Thrusts." *BICS* 37 (1990) 39.

Jacquemin, A. "Notes sur quelques offrandes du gymnase de Délos." *BCH* 105 (1981) 155–69.

Jantzen, U. *Bronzewerkstätten in Grossgriechenland und Sizilien.* Berlin: W. de Gruyter, 1937.

―――. *Griechischen Griff-Phialen.* Winckelmannsprogramm 114. Berlin: De Gruyter, 1958.

Jeanmaire, H. *Couroi et Couretes. Essai sur l'éducation spartiate et sur les rites d'adole-scence dans l'antiquité hellénique.* Lille: Bibliothèque universitaire, 1939. Reprint, New York: Arno, 1974.

Johns, C. *Sex or Symbol.* Austin, Tx.: University of Texas Press, 1982.

Jüthner, J. *Philostratus über Gymnastik.* Leipzig: B. G. Teubner, 1909. Reprint, Stuttgart: Teubner, 1969.

———. *Die Athletischen Leibesübungen der Griechen.* Ed. F. Brein. 2 vols. SB Vienna 249. Graz: Herman Böhlaus, 1965 (vol. 1) and 1968 (vol. 2).

Kadletz, E. "The Race and Procession of the Athenian *Oschophoroi.*" *GRBS* 21 (1980) 363–71.

Kahil, L. "Quelques vases du sanctuaire d'Artemis à Brauron." *Antike Kunst,* Suppl. 1 (1963) 5–29.

———. "Autour de l'Artémis attique." *AntK* 8 (1965) 20–33.

———. "L'Artémis de Brauron: rites et mystère." *AntK* 20 (1977) 86–98.

———. "Le 'craterisque' d'Artémis et le Brauronion de l' Acropole." *Hesperia* 1 (1981) 253–63.

———. "The Mythological Repertoire of Brauron." In *Ancient Greek Art and Iconography,* ed. W. Moon, 231–44. Madison: University of Wisconsin Press, 1983.

Kaldis-Henderson, N. *A Study of Women in Ancient Elis.* Ph.D. thesis, University of Minnesota, 1979.

Kennell, N. M. *The Gymnasium of Virtue: Education and Culture in Ancient Sparta.* Chapel Hill: University of North Carolina Press, 1995.

Keuls, E. C. *The Reign of the Phallus: Sexual Politics in Ancient Athens.* New York: Harper & Row, 1985.

Kilmer, M. F. *Greek Erotica on Attic Red-figured Vases.* London: Duckworth, 1993.

Klee, T. *Zur Geschichte der Gymnischen Agone an Griechischen Festen.* Leipzig: B. G. Teubner, 1918. Reprint, Chicago: Ares, 1980.

Kleinman, S. "The Athlete as Performing Artist: The Embodiment of Sport Literature And Philosophy." *Coroebus Triumphs: The Alliance of Sport and the Arts,* ed. S. J. Bandy, 47–56. San Diego: San Diego State University Press, 1988.

Koehl, R. B. "The Chieftan Cup and a Minoan Rite of Passage." *Journal of Hellenic Studies* 106 (1986) 99–110.

Kondis, I. D. "Artemis Brauronia." *AD* 22 (1967) 187–88.

Kornexl, E. *Leibesübungen bei Homer und Platon.* Studientexte zur Leibeserziehung, vol. 5. Frankfurt/M: Limpert, 1969.

Kossatz-Diessmann, A. "Zur Herkunft des Perizoma in Satyrspiel." *JDAI* 97 (1982) 65–90.

Kramer, K. *Studien zur griechischen Agonistik nach den Epinikien Pindars.* Ph.D. diss., University of Cologne, 1970.

Krause, J. H. *Die Pythien, Nemeen und Isthmien aus den Schrift- und Bildwerken des Altertums.* With an essay by J. Ebert. Leipzig, 1841. Reprint, Hildesheim: Georg Olms, 1975.

———. *Die Gymnastik und Agonistik der Hellenen.* Vols. 1 and 2. Leipzig, 1841. Reprint, Wiesbaden: Dr. Martin Sändig, 1971.

Kurke, L. *The Traffic in Praise: Pindar and the Poetics of Social Economy.* Ithaca: Cornell University Press, 1991.

Kyle, D. G. "Solon and Athletics." *Ancient World* 9 (1984) 91–105.

———. *Athletics in Ancient Athens*. Leiden: E. J. Brill, 1987.

Lämmer, M. "Women and Sport in Ancient Greece. A Plea for a Critical and Objective Approach." In *Women and Sport in Historical, Biological, Physiological and Sports Medical Approach. Sports Medicine* vol. 14, ed. J. Borms, M. Hebbelinck, and A. Venerando Basel, 17–24. New York: S. Karger, 1981.

Langlotz, E. *Frühgriechischen Bildhauerschulen*. 2 vols. Nürnburg: E. Frommann, 1927. Reprint, Rome: "L'Erma" di Bretschneider, 1967.

Larmour, D.H.J. "Boat-Races and Swimming Contests at Hermione." *Aethlon* 7 (1990) 128–38.

———. *Stage and Stadium: Drama and Athletics in Ancient Greece*. Nikephoros suppl. vol. 4. Hildesheim: Weidmann, 1999.

Larmour, D.H.J., P. A. Miller, and C. Platter, eds. *Rethinking Sexuality: Foucault and Classical Antiquity*. Princeton: Princeton University Press, 1998.

Laser, S. *Sport und Spiel. Archaeologia Homerica*. Vol. 3, ch. T. Göttingen: Vandenhoeck & Ruprecht, 1987.

Lavrencic, M., et al. *Diskos, Quellendokumentation zur Gymnastik und Agonistik im Altertum* 1. Vienna: Bohlau, 1991.

Lee, H. "Athletic Arete in Pindar." *Ancient World* 7.1–2 (1983) 31–37.

———. "Athletics and the Bikini Girls from Piazza Armerina." *Stadion* 10 (1984) 45–76.

———. "SIG 802: Did Women Compete against Men in Greek Athletic Festivals?" *Nikephoros* 1 (1988) 103–17.

Leitao, D. D. "The Perils of Leukippos: Initiatory Transvestism and Male Gender Ideology in the Ekdusia at Phaistos." *Classical Antiquity* 14 (1995) 130–63.

Ley, A. *Atalante—Darstellungen auf Vasen des 6.–4. Jhs. V.u.Z.* M.A. thesis, University of Hamburg, 1987.

———. "Atlante—Von der Athletin zur Liebhaberin: ein Beitrag zum Rezeptionswandel eines mythologischen themas auf Vasen des 6–4 Jhs. v Chr.," *Nikephoros* 3 (1990) 31–72.

Linders, T. *Studies in the Treasure Records of Artemis Brauronia Found in Athens*. Lund: P. Äström, 1972.

Lloyd-Jones, H. "Artemis and Iphigeneia." *JHS* 103 (1983) 87–102.

Lonsdale, Steven H. *Dance and Ritual Play in Greek Religion*. Baltimore: Johns Hopkins University Press, 1993.

MacDowell, D. M. *The Law in Classical Athens*. Ithaca: Cornell University Press, 1978.

Mähl, E. *Gymnastik und Athletik im Denken der Römer*, Heuremata 2. Amsterdam: B. R. Grüner, 1974.

Mallwitz, A. *Olympia und seine Bauten*. Athens: S. Kasas, 1981.

Malten, Rudolph. "Lichenspiel und Totenkult." *MDAI(R)* 38–39 (1923–24) 313–14.

Mantas, K. "Woman and Athletics in the Roman East." *Nikephoros* 8 (1995) 125–44.

Marinatos, N., and R. Hägg, eds. *Greek Sanctuaries: New Approaches*. London: Routledge, 1993.

Marrou, H. I. *A History of Education in Antiquity*. Trans. G. Lamb. London: Sheed and Ward, 1956.

Massa-Pairault, F.-H. "Strigiles féminins et idéologie funéraire (IVe–IIIe siècles av. n. è.)." *Nikephoros* 4 (1991) 197–209.

McDonnell, M. "The Introduction of Athletic Nudity: Thucydides, Plato, and the Vases." *JHS* 111 (1991) 182–93.

McGlew, J. F. *Tyranny and Political Culture in Ancient Greece*. Ithaca: Cornell University Press, 1993.

Meier, C. *The Greek Discovery of Politics*. Trans. D. McLintock. Cambridge, Massachusetts: Harvard University Press, 1990, from the orig. *Entstehung des Politischen bei den Griechen*. Frankfurt am Main, Suhrkamp.

Meuli, K. "Griechische Opferbräuche." In *Phyllobolia für Peter von der Mühll zum 60. geburtstag am. 1 August 1945*, ed. Olof Gigon, Karl Meuli, Willy Theiler, Fritz Wehrli, and Bernhard Wyss, 185–297. Basel: B. Schwabe, 1946. Reprinted in *Gesammelte Schriften*, vol. 2, ed. K. Meuli and T. Geizer, 907–1018. Basel: B. Schwabe, 1975.

Michell, H. *Sparta*. Cambridge: Cambridge University Press, 1952.

Miller, S. G. "The Date of Olympic Festivals." *MDAI(A)* 90 (1965) 215–31.

———. "Tunnel Vision: The Nemean Games." *Archaeology* 33 (1980) 54–56.

———. ed. *Nemea: A Guide to the Site and Museum*. Berkeley: University of California Press, 1990.

———. *Arete: Greek Sports from Ancient Sources*. Berkeley: University of California Press, 1991.

Mitsopoulos-Leon, V. "Zur Verehrung des Dionysos in Elis nochmals: AΞIE TAϒPE und die Sechzehn heiligen Frauen." *MDAI(A)* 99 (1984) 275–90.

Mommsen, A. *Feste der Stadt Athen im Altertum*. Leipzig: B. G. Teubner, 1898.

Montepaone, C. "L'arkteia a Brauron." *Studi storico-religiosi* 3 (1979) 343–64.

Montuoro, P. Zancani, and U. Zanotti-Bianco. *Heraion alla Foce del Sele*. Vol. 2, *Il Primo Thesauros*. Rome: Libreria dello Stato, 1964.

Moretti, L. *Iscrizioni Agonistiche Greche*. Rome: Angelo Signorelli, 1953.

———. *Olympionikai, I Vincitori negli Antichi Agoni Olimpici*. MemLincei ser. 8.8.2. Rome: Accademia Nazionale dei Lincei, 1957.

———. "Sulla legge ginnasiarchica di Berea." *RIFC* 110 (1982) 45–63.

———. "Nuovo Supplemento al Catalogo degli Olympionikai." *Miscellanea Greca e Romana* XII (Rome, 1987) 67–91.

Morgan, C. *Athletes and Oracles: The Transformation of Olympia and Delphi in the Eighth Century B.C.* Cambridge: Cambridge University Press, 1990.

Morrissey, E. J. *Studies in Inscriptions Listing the Agonistic Festivals*. Ph.D. diss., Harvard University, 1973.

Mouratidis, J. "The Origin of Nudity in Greek Athletics." *Journal of Sport History* 12 (1985) 213–32.

Müller, S. *Das Volk der Athleten: Untersuchungen zur Ideologie und Kritik des Sports in der griechisch-römischen Antike*. Trier: Wissenschaftlicher Verlag Trier, 1995.

Murray, O. *Early Greece*. 2nd ed. Stanford, Calif.: Stanford University Press, 1993.

Neils, J., ed. *Goddess and the Polis: The Panathenaic Festival in Ancient Athens*. Hanover, N.H.: Hood Museum of Art, Dartmouth College, co-published with Princeton: Princeton University Press, 1992.

———, ed. *Worshipping Athena: Panathenaia and Parthenon*. Madison: University of Wisconsin Press, 1996.

Nijf, Onno Van. "Athletics, Festivals, and Greek Identity in the Roman East." *PCPS* 45 (1999) 176–200.

Nilsson, M. P. *Geschichte der Griechen Religion*. 2nd ed. Vol. 1. Munich: C. H. Beck, 1955.

———. *Grieschische Feste von religiöser Bedeutung mit Ausschluss der Attischen.* Leipzig: B. G. Teubner, 1906. Reprint, Darmstadt: Wissenschaftliche Buchgesellschaft, 1957.

———. *The Minoan-Mycenaean Religion and Its Survival in Greek Religion.* 2nd ed. Lund: C.W.K. Gleerup, 1968.

O'Brien, Joan V. *The Transformation of Hera: A Study of Ritual, Hero, and the Goddess in the Iliad.* Lanham, Md.: Rowman and Littlefield, 1993.

Olivová, V. *Sports and Games in the Ancient World.* New York: St. Martin's Press, 1984.

Osborne, R. *Demos: The Discovery of Classical Attika.* Cambridge: Cambridge University Press, 1985.

———. *Greece in the Making: 1200–479 B.C.* London: Routledge, 1996.

Palaiokrassa, L. *To hiero tēs Artemidos Mounichias.* Ph.D. diss., Aristotelian University, Salonica, 1983.

Papachatze, N. D. *Pausaniou Ellados Periēgesis Biblio 2. kai 3.: Korinthiaka kai Lakōnia.* Athens: Ekdotikē Athenōn, 1976.

Papalas, A. J. "Boy Athletes in Ancient Greece." *Stadion* 17.2 (1991) 169–72.

Parke, H. W. *Festivals of the Athenians.* London: Thames & Hudson, 1977. Reprint, Ithaca, New York: Cornell University Press, 1986.

Patrucco, R. *Lo sport nella Grecia antica.* Florence: L. S. Olschki, 1972.

———. *Lo stadio di Epidauro.* Florence: Olschki, 1976.

Patzer, H. *Die Griechische Knabenliebe.* Wiesbaden: F. Steiner, 1982.

Peiser, B. J. *Das Dunkel Zeitalter Olympias.* Frankfurt: Peter Lang Gmbh, 1993.

Pélekidis, C. *Histoire de l'Éphébie Attique des Origines à 31 avant Jésus-Christ.* École Française d'Athènes, Travaux et Mémoires, vol. 13. Paris: E. de Boccard, 1962.

Percy, W. Armstrong. *Pederasty and Pedagogy in Archaic Greece.* Urbana: University of Illinois Press, 1996.

Perlman, P. "Plato *Laws* 833C-834D and the Bears of Brauron." *GRBS* 24 (1983) 115–30.

Perysinakis, I. N. "The Athlete as Warrior: Pindar's P. 9.97–103 and P. 10.55–59." *BICS* 37 (1990) 43–49.

Pleket, H. W. "Some Aspects of the History of Athletic Guilds." *ZPE* 10 (1973) 197–227.

———. "Zur Soziologie des antiken Sports." *Mededelingen Nederlands Historisch Instituut te Rome* 36 (1974) 57–87.

———. "Games, Prizes, Athletes and Ideology. Some Aspects of the History of Sport in the Greco-Roman World." *Arena* (= *Stadion*) 1 (1975) 49–89.

———. "Olympic Benefactors." *ZPE* 20 (1976) 1–20.

———. "The Participants in the Ancient Olympic Games: Social Background and Mentality." In *Proceedings of an International Symposium on the Olympic Games, 5–7 September 1988,* ed. W. Coulson and H. Kyrieleis, 147–52. Athens: Luci Braggiotti Publications for the Deutsches Archäologisches Institut Athen, 1992.

———. "Sport and Ideology in the Greco-Roman World." *Klio* 80 (1998) 315–24.

Poliakoff, M. *Studies in the Terminology of the Greek Combat Sports.* Beiträge zur Klassischen Philologie, vol. 146. Königstein /Ts.: Anton Hain, 1982.

———. "Deaths in the Panhellenic Games: Addenda et Corrigenda." *AJP* 107 (1986) 400–403.

———. *Combat Sports in the Ancient World: Competition, Violence, and Culture.* New Haven: Yale University Press, 1987.

Pouilloux. J. *Recherches sur l'histoire et les cultes de Thasos*. Vol. 1. Paris: E. de Boccard, 1954.

Praschniker, C. "Bronzene Spiegelstütze im Wiener Hofmuseum." *Österreichisches Archäologisches Institut, Wien*, vol. 15 (1912) 219–52.

Price, S.F.R. *Rituals and Power: The Roman Imperial Cult in Asia Minor*. Cambridge: Cambridge University Press, 1984.

Pronger, B. *The Arena of Masculinity: Sports, Homosexuality, and the Meaning of Sex*. New York: St. Martin's Press, 1990.

Raaflaub, K. *Die Entdeckung der Freiheit: zur historischen Semantik und Gesellschafts-geschichte eines politischen Grundbegriffes der Griechen*. Munich: C. H. Beck, 1985.

Raschke, W. "Aulos and Athlete: The Function of the Flute Player in Greek Athletics." *Arete* 2 (1985) 177–200.

———, ed. *The Archaeology of the Olympics: The Olympics and Other Festivals in Antiquity*. Madison: University of Wisconsin Press, 1988.

Reed, N. "The Panathenaic Euandria Reconsidered." *AW* 15 (1987) 59–64.

Reeder, E. D. *Pandora: Women in Classical Greece*. Princeton: Trustees of the Walters Art Gallery in Association with Princeton University Press, 1985.

Reinmuth, O.W.R. " The Genesis of the Athenian Ephebia." *TAPA* 83 (1952) 34–50.

———. *The Ephebic Inscriptions of the Fourth Century* B.C. Mnemosyne Suppl. 14. Leiden: E. J. Brill, 1971.

Reinsberg, C. *Ehe, Hetärentum und Knabenliebe im antiken Griechenland*. Munich: C. H. Beck, 1989.

Richlin, A., ed. *Pornography and Representation in Greece and Rome*. Oxford: Oxford University Press, 1992.

Richter, G.M.A. *Greek, Etruscan and Roman Bronzes*. New York: Gilliss, 1915.

———. "An Archaic Greek Mirror." *AJA* 42 (1938) 337–44.

———. "Another Archaic Greek Mirror." *AJA* 46 (1942) 319–24.

Ringwood Arnold, I. C. *Agonistic Features of Local Greek Festivals Chiefly from Inscriptional Evidence*. Ph.D. diss., Columbia University, 1927.

Robertson, N. "The Origin of the Panathenaia." *RhM* N.S. 120 (1985) 231–95.

———. *Festivals and Legends: The Formation of Greek Cities in the Light of Public Ritual*. Toronto: University of Toronto Press, 1992.

Robinson, R. S. *Sources for the History of Greek Athletics*. Cincinnati: Robinson, 1955. Reprint, Chicago: Ares, 1979.

Roller, L. " Funeral Games in Greek Art." *AJA* 85 (1981a) 107–19.

———. "Funeral Games for Historical Persons." *Stadion* 7 (1981b) 1–18.

Romano, D. G. "An Early Stadium at Nemea." *Hesperia* 46 (1977) 27–31.

Roscher, W. H., ed. *Ausfürliches Lexikon der griechischen und römischen Mythologie*. Vols. 1–6. Leipzig: B. G. Teubner, 1884–1937.

Rose, H. J. "The Greek Agones." *Aberystwyth Studies* 3 (1922) 1–24.

———. "The Cult of Artemis Orthia at Sparta." In *The Sanctuary of Artemis Orthia at Sparta*. JHS Suppl. 5, ed. R. M. Dawkins, 404ff. London: Council of the British School at Athens, with Macmillan, 1929.

Roussel, D. *Tribu et cité: études sur les groupes sociaux dans les cités grecques aux époques archaïque et classique*. Paris: "Les Belles Lettres," 1976.

Rousselle, A. *Porneia: On Desire and the Body in Antiquity*. Trans. F. Pheasant. New York: Oxford University Press, 1988.

Sale, W. "The Temple Legends of the Arkteia." *RhM* 118 (1975) 265–84.

Sallares, R. *The Ecology of the Ancient Greek World*. London: Duckworth, 1991.

Sansone, D. *Greek Athletics and the Genesis of Sport*. Berkeley: University of California Press, 1988.

Scanlon, T. F. "The Vocabulary of Competition: *Agōn* and *Aethlos*, Greek Terms for Contest." *Arete* (now *Aethlon*) 1.1 (1983) 185–216.

———. "Women, Bull Sports, Cults and Initiation in Minoan Crete." *Nikephoros* 12 (1999) 33–70.

Schachter, A. *Cults of Boiotia*. Vol. 1, Acheloos to Hera. University of London, Institute of Classical Studies Bulletin Suppl. no. 38.1. London: University of London, Institute of Classical Studies, 1981.

Schauenburg, K. " Erotenspiele, 1. Teil." *Antike Welt* 7.3 (1976a) 39–52.

———. "Erotenspiele, 2. Teil." *Antike Welt* 7.7 (1976b) 28–35.

Schröder, B. *Der Sport im Altertum*. Leipzig: Spamerschen Buchdruckerei, 1927.

Segal, E. "To Win or Die of Shame, A Taxonomy of Values." *Journal of Sport History* 11 (1984) 25–31.

Sergent, B. *Homosexuality in Greek Myth*. Trans. Arthur Goldhammer, pref. by George Dumezil. Boston: Beacon, 1986a. (From the original *L'homosexualité dans la mythologie grecque*. Paris: Payot, 1984).

———. *L'homosexualité initiatique dans l'Europe ancienne*. Paris: Payot, 1986b.

———. " Paederasty and Political Life in Archaic Greek Culture." *Journal of Homosexuality* 25 (1993) 147–64.

Serwint, N. *Greek Athletic Sculpture from the Fifth and Fourth Centuries B.C.: An Iconographic Study*. Ph.D. diss., Princeton University, 1987.

———. "The Iconography of the Ancient Female Runner." *AJA* 97 (1993) 403–22.

Shapiro, H. A. "Courtship Scenes in Attic Vase-Painting." *AJA* 85.2 (1981) 133–43.

———. "Amazons, Thracians, and Scythians." *GRBS* 24 (1983) 105–15.

Siems, A. K., ed. *Sexualität und Erotik in der Antike, Wege der Forschung*, vol. 605. Darmstadt: Wissenschaftliche Buchgesellschaft, 1988.

Simon, E. *Die Götter der Griechen*. 2nd ed. Munich: Hirmer, 1980.

———. *Festivals of Attica: An Archaeological Commentary*. Madison: University of Wisconsin Press, 1983.

Sinn, U. "Olympia. Die Stellung der Wettkämpfe im Kult des Zeus Olympios." *Nikephoros* 4 (1991) 31–54.

Sinn, U., et al. "Bericht über das Forschungsprojekt 'Olympia während der römischen Kaiserzeit und in der Spätantike' III. Die Arbeit im Jahr 1994." *Nikephoros* 7 (1994) 229–50.

——— et al. "Bericht über das Forschungsprojekt 'Olympia während der römischen Kaiserzeit und in der Spätantike' IV. Die Arbeit im Jahr 1995 Teil 1." *Nikephoros* 8 (1995) 161–82.

——— et al. "Bericht über das Forschungsprojekt 'Olympia während der römischen Kaiserzeit und in der Spätantike' V. Die Arbeit im Jahr 1995 Teil 2." *Nikephoros* 9 (1996) 199–228.

Siska, H. *De Mercurio ceterisque deis ad artem gymnicam pertinentibus*. Ph.D. diss., University of Halle, 1933.

Snodgrass, A. *Archaic Greece: The Age of Experiment*. London: J. M. Dent, 1980.

Sourvinou-Inwood, C. "A Series of Erotic Pursuits: Images and Meanings." *JHS* 107 (1987) 131–53.

———. *Studies in Girls' Transitions: Aspects of the Arkteia and Age Representation in Attic Iconography.* Athens: Kardamitsa, 1988.

———. *'Reading' Greek Culture: Texts and Images, Rituals and Myths.* Oxford: Oxford University Press, 1991.

Steiner, D. "Moving Images: Fifth-Century Victory Monuments and the Athlete's Allure." *Classical Antiquity* 17 (1998) 123–49.

Stewart, A. *Greek Sculpture: An Exploration.* New Haven: Yale University Press, 1990.

———. *Art, Desire, and the Body in Ancient Greece.* Cambridge: Cambridge University Press, 1997.

Sutton, D. F. " Athletics in the Greek Satyr Play." *RSC* 23 (1975) 203–9.

Swaddling, J. *The Ancient Olympic Games.* London: British Museum Publications, 1980.

Sweet, W. "Protection of the Genitals in Greek Athletics." *AncW* 11 (1985) 43–52.

———. *Sport and Recreation in Ancient Greece. A Sourcebook with Translations.* New York: Oxford University Press, 1987.

Taplin, O. "Phallology, *Phylakes*, Iconography and Aristophanes." *PCPS* 213, N.S. 33 (1987) 92–104.

Thomson, G. *Aeschylus and Athens.* 2nd ed. London, Lawrence & Wishart, 1966. Reprint, New York: Haskell House, 1967.

Thornton, B. S. *Eros: The Myth of Ancient Greek Sexuality.* Boulder, Colo.: Westview, 1997.

Thuillier, J.-P. *Les jeux athlétiques dans la civilisation Étrusque.* Bibliothèque des Écoles Françaises d'Athène et de Rome, vol. 256. Rome: École Française de Rome, 1985.

———. "La nudité athlétique (Grèce, Etrurie, Rome)." *Nikephoros* 1 (1988) 29–48.

Tod, M. N. " Teams of Ball-Players at Sparta." *ABSA* 10 (1903–4) 63–77.

———. "Three New *Sphaireîs*-Inscriptions." *ABSA* 13 (1906–7) 212–18.

———. "Greek Record-Keeping and Record-Breaking." *CQ* 43 (1949) 106–12.

Turner, J. A. *Hiereiai: Acquisition of Feminine Priesthoods in Ancient Greece.* Ph.D. diss., University of California, Santa Barbara, 1983.

Uberhorst, H, ed. *Geschichte der Leibesübungen.* Vol. 2. Berlin: Bartels & Wernitz KG, 1978.

Ulf, C. "Die Einreibung der griechischen Athleten mit Öl." *Stadion* 5 (1979) 220–38.

———. "Die Frage nach dem Ursprung des Sports, oder: weshalb und wie menschliches Verhalten anfängt, Sport zu sein." *Nikephoros* 4 (1991) 13–30.

Ulf, C., and I. Weiler. "Der Ursprung der antiken olympischen Spiele in der Forschung." *Stadion* 6 (1981) 1–38.

Vidal-Naquet, P. *The Black Hunter: Forms of Thought and Forms of Society in the Greek World.* Trans. A. Szegedy-Maszak. Baltimore: Johns Hopkins University Press, 1986.

Walker, H. J. *Theseus and Athens.* Oxford: Oxford University Press, 1995.

Webster, T.B.L. *From Mycenae to Homer: A Study in Early Greek Literature and Art.* London: Methuen, 1964.

Weiler, I. *Der Agon im Mythos: Zur Einstellung der Griechen zum Wettkampf.* Impulse der Forschung, vol. 16. Darmstadt: Wissenschaftliche Buchgesellschaft, 1974.

———. "ΑΕΙΝ ΑΡΙΣΤΕΥΕΙΝ: Ideologiekritische Bemerkungen zu einem vielzitierten Homerwort." *Stadion* 1 (1976) 199–227.

———. *Der Sport bei den Völkern der alten Welt. Eine Einführung.* 2nd ed. Darmstadt: Wissenschaftliche Buchgesellschaft, 1988.

———. "Langzeitperspektiven zur Genese des Sports." *Nikephoros* 2 (1989) 7–26.

Weniger, L. *Das Kollegium der Sechzehn Frauen und der Dionysosdienst in Elis.* Weimar: Hof-Buchdruckerei, 1883.

———. "Das Hochfest des Zeus in Olympia I: Die Ordnung der Agone." *Klio* 4 (1904) 125–51.

———. "Das Hochfest des Zeus in Olympia II." *Klio* 5 (1905) 1–38.

———. "Vom Ursprunge der olympischen Spiele." *RM* 72 (1917–18) 1–13.

Wide, S. *Lakonische Kulte.* Leipzig: B. G. Teubner, 1893.

Willetts, R. F. *Aristocratic Society in Ancient Crete.* London: Routledge and Paul, 1955.

Winkler, J. J. *The Constraints of Desire: The Anthropology of Sex and Gender in Ancient Greece.* New York: Routledge, 1990.

Woodford, S. "Herakles' Attributes and Their Appropriation by Eros." *JHS* 109 (1989) 200–204.

Yalouris, N. *The Eternal Olympics: The Art and History of Sport.* New Rochelle, N.Y.: Caratzas, 1979.

Young, D. C. *The Olympic Myth of Greek Amateur Athletics.* Chicago: Ares, 1984.

———. "First with the Most: Greek Athletic Records and 'Specialization.'" *Nikephoros* 9 (1996) 175–97.

Zeitlin, F. "Cultic Models of the Female: Rites of Dionysus and Demeter." *Arethusa* 15 (1982) 129–157.

Zschietzschmann, W. *Wettkampf und Übungsstätten in Griechenland, vol. II. Palaestra—Gymnasion.* Stuttgart: K. Hofmann, 1961.

INDEX

abduction of beloved, 73, 75
abstinence, sexual, 227–36, 328–29, 407n87. *See also* celibacy; chastity
Academy, 87, 89, 95, 204, 218, 255, 256, 259, 273, 325, 329, 330, 333
Acanthus of Sparta, 125
Achaea, Roman province of, 48
Achaean League, 41–42, 46, 54
Acheloos, 301
Achilles, 26, 28, 82, 179, 299–300, 302, 307, 310, 311
Achilles Tatius, 224
Acropolis, Athenian, 107, 140, 142, 166, 171, 273
Actian Games (Aktaia), 45–46
actors, 277, 296
Adonis, 210
Aegisthus, 301
Aelian, 231
Aemilius Paulus, Lucius, 42
Aeschines, 91, 218
Aeschylus, 149, 175
aethlos, 279, 281
Africanus, Sextus Julius, 52
Agamemnon, 156
Agathos Daimon (Olympic boxer), 305
age categories of athletes, 68–69, 92, 98–99, 101, 107, 111, 159, 165, 264, 266, 276, 357n25
age-class hierarchy, 67–68, 70–71, 75, 77–78, 81, 87, 93, 122, 149, 159, 357n21
agelē (pl. *agelai*; herd; youth group), 74–75, 122, 135, 213, 326

ageneioi, 264, 266, 357n25
Agesilaus, 22–23, 93
agōgē (Spartan education system), 77–83, 95, 121–38, 325, 360n56, 376n5
agōn (pl. *agōnes*; contest), 9–10, 98, 111, 120, 260, 264, 275, 278, 279, 293, 300, 304, 308, 320
    and *Agōn* (the god), 6, 420n16
    definition of, 9–10
    and hoplite warfare, 14
    as sacred festival, 27
    system, 9–13
agonistics of desire, 269
agonothete (*agōnothetēs*, pl. *agōnothetai*; producer of games), 265, 345–46n80, 423n69
Agora, Athenian, 140, 149, 151, 165, 166, 168, 169
Agrionia festival, 119
Agrippa, Marcus, 43
Agyrion, 94
aidōs. See shame
Aiglatas (Spartan runner), 79
Ajax, 300, 302, 309
Akestorides (Olympic victor), 43
Akrotatos (Nemean athlete), 206
Alcaeus, 123
Alcestis, 301
Alcibiades, 12, 217, 238, 239, 268, 421n37
Alcman's *Parthenion*, 78, 100, 122, 123, 127, 135, 165, 197

Alexandria, 45, 51–52, 56
Alpheus, 118
altar, 111, 141, 143, 151
Altis (Olympic grove), 32, 36, 49, 54,
    109, 110, 118
Amasis Painter, 237
Amazons, 105, 107, 108, 133, 177, 189
Amor, 240, 259, 314, 416n205
Amphiaraia Games (Oropus, Boeotia),
    80, 92, 366n142
Amphidromia, 148, 149, 151
Amphion of Thebes, 110, 312
Amphissos, 222
Amyclae, 100
Amycus, 189, 301
Anacharsis, 208
Anacreon, 260
andreia. See courage
Antaeus, 301
antagonist, 281
Antenor (pankration victor), 227
anterastēs (rival), 263
Anteros (god), 239, 249, 255–64, 269,
    275, 329
    altar of, 256
    shrine of, 257
anterōs (reciprocal desire), 6, 89, 222
Anthesteria, 288
    of Athens, 290
    at Teos, 290
Antilochos, 302, 308, 310, 311
Antoninus Liberalis, 222
Antoninus Pius, Emperor, 54–55
apalaistroi (infirm), 214
Apelles, 22
Aphrodisias, 56
Aphrodite, 70, 156, 161, 163, 175, 176,
    178, 179, 180, 181, 182, 184, 210,
    219, 260, 270, 318
apodromos (minor), 75
Apollo, 27, 29–30, 82, 94, 100, 116, 126,
    154, 158, 171, 253, 284, 285, 308
    Amyclae, 134
    Carneius, 31, 81, 83–84
    Delphius, 307
    and Hyacinthus, 73–74
    at Thera, 83

Apollodorus, 74, 164, 175, 180, 182,
    187
Apollonius of Tyana, 53
Appian, 42
apples of Aphrodite, 162, 179, 180
Aratus (poet), 206
Arcadia, 175, 177
Arcas, 144, 154, 171
Arcesilos of Cyrene (chariot victor), 310
Archemoros, 286
Ares, 284, 300
    Hippios, 318
Aretaius, 229
aretē (excellence), 11, 14, 17–20, 24,
    121, 125, 178, 181, 201, 239, 246,
    253, 283, 293, 300, 302, 329,
    340n38
    of women, 21–24
Arethusa, 224
Arexippos (Spartan boy victor), 79
Argolid, 117
Argonauts, 175, 189, 279
Argos, 30
Ariadne, 232, 288
Aristodemus of Cyrene, 268
Aristophanes, 10, 122, 128, 132, 133,
    135, 145, 159, 215, 218, 226, 255,
    262, 269, 309
    Lysistrata, 127
Aristotle, 11, 124, 204, 278, 280
Aristotle of Cyrene (athlete), 232, 233
Arkteia festival, 31, 100, 101, 107, 112,
    120, 121, 126, 130, 132, 139–74,
    287, 288, 289, 326, 327
arktos (pl. arktoi; girl-bear), 148–49, 153,
    154, 156, 159, 162
Arrēphoria, 87
arrēphoroi, 99
Arrhichion of Phigalia, 276, 298, 305–
    306, 319
Arrigoni, G., 163, 171, 191
art, 277, 285
Artemis, 24, 31, 82, 99, 107, 108, 109,
    113, 115, 120, 126, 175, 177, 178,
    180, 181, 189, 289, 327
    Aristoboule, 168
    Arkteia, 112, 139–74

of Ephesus,
   festival of, 225
   Laphria, 287
   Limnatis, 130, 289
   at Olympia, 33–34
   Orthia at Sparta, 81, 83, 100, 130, 133
   Phosphorus, 149
   Purphoros, 149
   the Tamer, 164
   Triklaria, 287
Asclepieia (festival of Asclepius), 30
Asclepius, 30, 36
Asia Minor, 43, 49, 324
Astylos of Croton (footrace victor), 223, 230, 232, 233, 234, 294
Atalanta, 6, 29, 98, 105, 106, 129, 130, 161–63, 175–98, 199, 225, 236, 248, 254, 301, 307, 308, 327, 328
   as hunter, 394n11
Athamas, 285
Athanichos of Thebes (heavy-event victor), 300
Athena, 26, 29, 99, 118, 273, 286
   altar to, 255, 257
   Hippia, 313, 318
   Sciras, 31, 90
   shrine to, 258
Athenaeus, 5, 13, 127, 210, 219, 249, 251, 254, 256, 258, 259, 266, 267, 268, 330
Athens, 30, 87–93, 95, 96–97, 147, 209, 213, 217, 218, 219, 244, 249, 268, 271, 273, 280, 281, 286, 325, 329
athletics, definition of, 9, 330
Atlas, 210
Attica, 86, 87, 98, 101, 105, 121, 139
audience, 277–78, 281, 282, 287, 297, 305–306, 327, 342n48, 425n96
Augustalia festival, 46
Augustine, 236
Augustus, 41, 43, 45–49, 51–52, 80
Aulis, 156
Automedon (poet), 214

Bacchylides, 164
ball games, 79, 82–83
baseball, 200, 332

Basileia Games, 300
basketball, 332
bathing, 190, 191, 192, 237, 397n46
bears, 139–74, 327, 389n31, 393n66
beauty 126–127, 191, 198, 201, 212, 218, 220, 224, 242, 249, 256, 266, 273, 330, 378n28
   in athletes, 10, 15, 205
   contests, 123, 259
   of female athletes, 21
   manly, 205, 338n23
   Plato's critique of, 340n38
Bedlam Painter, 169
bed-wrestling, 216
beloved. *See erōmenos*
Bérard, C., 191, 192
Beroea, Macedonia, 214, 219
bibasis (jumping exercise), 136, 384–85n72
birth control, 71, 74, 96
bisexuality, 203, 239, 246, 332
blossom, 130, 237, 382n52
boat races, 87, 285
body, 5, 209, 273
   as locus of Greek culture, 9–12, 332
   in modern culture, 332–33
Boeotia, 71, 175, 251
bōmonikas (victor at the altar), 81
Bouleuterion (at Olympia), 33, 38, 114
Bouprasion Games, 372n68
boxing, 17, 27, 32, 56, 79, 201, 226, 269–70, 284, 294, 298, 301, 302, 304, 305, 307
   modern, 332
Boys' Contests (*paidikoi agōnes*), 79–80
Brauron, 31, 101, 107, 109, 111, 120, 126, 139–74, 288, 327
   altar at, 150, 152, 155, 168, 169, 170, 172, 173
Brauronia festival, 139–74. *See also* Arkteia festival
bravery. *See* courage
Brelich, A., 64–66, 68–69, 95, 160
Bremmer, Jan, 67, 93, 95
bride, 135, 147
British Museum, 239
Brown, Peter, 332

bullfight, Spanish, 320
bull-leaping, 320
Burckhardt, Jacob, 10
Burkert, Walter, 274–75

Caesar, Julius, 42, 49
Cahn, Herbert A., 165, 169–71
Calame, C., 135
Caligula, Emperor, 48, 51
Callimachus, 107, 122
Callisto, 144, 153, 154, 161, 162–63,
    171, 390n42
Calydonian boar hunt, 162, 175, 181
Campania, 192
cap, athletic, 184, 381n45, 395n19
Capitolia festival, Roman, 55
Carinus, Emperor, 56
Carneia festival, Spartan, 31, 37, 81–82,
    83, 135, 150
  contests at, 82
Cartledge, Paul, 77–78, 129
castanets, 173
Castor and Polydeukes, 313
celebration, 291
celibacy, 68, 178, 231, 232. See also
    abstinence; chastity
Cercyon, 301
Cerveteri, 130
Chamynaion, 109
chance, 312
chariot, 110
  with fawns, 314
chariot-racing, 279, 301, 302, 309–18
  ten-horse, of Nero, 48
  by women, 343–44n66, 344n69,
    385n73
  see also hippic events
charis, 249, 343n59
Charites (Graces), 118
Charmus (Athenian general), 89, 256,
    273
chase, 154, 163, 164, 165. See also flight
    and pursuit
chastity, 230, 231, 233, 234, 235. See
    also abstinence; celibacy
childbirth, 157, 284
Chios, 219, 222, 384n72

chitōn, 99, 101, 105, 107, 109, 111, 125,
    141, 154, 155, 172, 173, 174
  exōmis, 108, 125
  short (chitōniskos), 143, 145, 148, 149,
    151, 152, 157, 158, 167, 168, 169,
    173, 184, 378n19, 383n61, 391n47
Chloris, 99, 110, 111, 116
choes, 290
choruses, 13, 123, 165, 264, 278,
    380n41
Chrison (celibate athlete), 230, 233,
    234
Christianity, 201, 324, 332
Chrysippus, 73
Cicero, 49, 133, 199, 211, 254, 277
cinaedus, 226
Circuit Games. See Periodic Games
Circus Maximus, 313
civil strife, 71–72, 251, 267
Cladeus Thermae (baths at Olympia),
    54
Clark, Kenneth, 297
class and athletics, 13–14, 283, 324,
    339–40n35
Claudius, Emperor, 47–48, 52
Cleisthenes, 87
Cleitomachus of Thebes (pankration
    victor), 231–32, 234, 273
Clement of Alexandria, 232, 233
Cleobis and Biton, 318
Cleomachus of Magnesia (boxing
    victor), 226, 227
Cleomedes of Astypalaea, 294, 306
Cleosthenes of Pisa, 34
cleverness, 252, 253
Clinias of Crete (character in Plato's
    Laws), 230
Clymenus of Crete (legendary patron of
    Hera), 109
Cohen, D., 401n20
Cole, S., 171
Comaneci, Nadia, 128
combat sports, 13, 52, 56, 284, 304, 307
Commodus, Emperor, 41
communal meals. See phitidia; syssitia
concord, 258, 267, 269
condoms, 200

Consus (Roman god), 313

contest system, Greek, 9–13, 89, 292–98, 332

  and drama, 281–82

  and Eros-Anteros images, 329

  and pederasty, 70

  and women, 20–24

  in Sparta

Corinth, 29, 49, 51, 94, 95, 120

Cos, 30

costume, 282

Coubertin, Baron Pierre, 200

courage (andreia), 14, 71, 79, 81, 124

Cratinus (comic poet), 226

Crete, 73, 74–77, 80, 86, 87, 90, 95, 96, 125, 126, 207, 213, 268, 319, 325, 326, 333, 358n31

Creugas of Epidamnus (boxing victor), 306

Crisa (city near Delphi), 116

Crison of Himera, 232

Critias, 124, 218

Croesus, king of Lydia, 129

Cronus, 34, 114, 284, 285

  Hill of, 33–34

crown games. See stephanitic games

crowns, 99, 109, 218, 227–28, 231, 239, 243, 244, 245, 249, 251, 252, 284, 285

Crowther, N., 402n24

Cupid, 199, 249, 259, 314

Curetes, 284

Curium, 130

curse tablets, 282

Cybele, 175

Cylon (Athenian Olympic victor), 421n37

cymbals, 128, 129, 130

Cynics, 11, 204

Cynisca (chariot victor), 6, 21–23, 110, 293, 344n70

Cynosarges, 204

Cyprus, 132

Cyrene (city), 223, 233

  and Sparta, 379–80n39

Cyrene (legendary maiden), 223–24, 246

Damodica (chariot victor), 23

Damonon (Spartan runner and chariot racer), 79

Damophon, 99, 112, 115

Danaids, 223–24

Danaus, 223

dance, 13, 83, 85–86, 99, 119, 127, 130, 136, 140–41, 143, 155, 167, 168, 171, 172, 173, 174, 264, 289, 363n102, 369n22

Daochus monument at Delphi, 306–307

Davidson, J. N., 401n20

death, 4, 67, 73–74, 88, 94, 88, 94, 178, 214, 274–322, 333, 428n136

Decker Slaney, Mary, 128

Degas, H.-G.-E., 220–221

Delian Festival, 27, 225

delight. See pleasure

Delos, 225, 258, 259

  Granite Palaestra, 258

  gymnasium at, 254

Delphi, 29–30, 33, 42, 116, 118, 130, 133, 134, 271, 284, 285, 309, 310, 326. See also Pythian Games

Delphic Oracle, 35, 38, 110, 306

demes, 87

Demeter, 30, 109, 116, 275

  Chamyne (at Olympia), 55

Demetrius Scepsius (grammarian), 82

Demosthenes of Miletus (Olympic trumpeter), 51

Descent of Misē, festival of, 227

desire, 4, 6, 272, 274–322, 333

  of the athletes, 16

  for death, 427n129

  mimetic, 295–96

  of the spectators, 16, 328

Deubner, L., 160

Diagoras of Rhodes (boxer), 19–20

diaulos (two-stade footrace), 26, 36, 140, 151, 264

diazōma (trunks), 130, 382n54, 382–83n55

diet of athletes, 38, 65, 68–69, 75, 328

Dio Cassius, 48–49

Dio Chrysostom, 30–31, 56, 232

Diocles of Corinth (Olympic stade
    victor), 94, 95, 97, 328, 367n154
Diogenes Laertius, 226
Diogenes of Crete (boxer), 306
Diogenes the Cynic, 226
Diognetos (Olympic boxer), 76
Diomedes (Homeric hero), 302
Dionysiades (Spartan cult of Dionysus),
    100, 104, 105, 116, 119, 122, 134,
    135, 139, 160, 287, 288, 289, 383–
    84n62
Dionysus, 90, 99, 111, 112, 116, 118,
    119, 120, 135, 150, 159, 160, 287–
    88, 289
    in Athens, 31
    and athletics, 290–92, 418n232
    Colonatas, 31, 100, 134, 326
    and female contests, 24
    Melanaigis, 290
    theater of, at Athens, 280, 281
Diopompus, 230, 233
Dioscuri, 313. See also Castor and
    Polydeukes
Dioxippus of Athens (pankration victor),
    226
discus-throwing, 13, 32, 56, 124, 136,
    201, 227, 236, 308
Dodona, 105, 133
doe, 143, 171, 172
dolichos (long footrace), 36, 264
Domitian, 47, 53, 55, 216
Dorian migration, 33–34
Dorians, 33–34, 326
Dover, K. J., 67–68, 71, 73–75, 83, 236
drama, 268, 274–322. See also
    performance
dress, 65, 68, 75, 81, 107, 108, 191, 289
    ritual, 145–149
    see also nudity
Dromaios (divinity), 81
dromeus (runner), 75–76
dromos (pl. dromoi; track), 70, 126, 132,
    184, 271
    at Sparta, 81, 289
    see also stadium
duel, 301, 302, 427n118. See also
    hoplomachia

dust. See konis
Dryope, 222

ecstasy, 292
education
    Greek (see paideia)
    modern, 333
Egypt, 43, 51–52, 56, 324
    and Sparta, 379–80n39
    sports in, 350n40
Eileithyia, 34, 38, 116, 358–59n48
Ekdysia festival, 75, 126, 370n37
ekecheiria. See Olympic Armistice
Eleusinian festival (Eleusinia), 30,
    92
Eleusis, 30
eleutheria (freedom), 267
Eleutheria festival
    Larissa, 80, 286
    Plataea, 267, 308
    Samos, 266–68, 269, 273, 329,
    417n221
Eliade, M., 65, 166
Elis, 34, 41–45, 68–69, 99, 112, 115,
    116, 117, 120, 135, 160, 259, 260,
    275, 288, 323–24, 329
Embaros (legendary hero in Artemis
    cult), 158, 159
en Drionas (Spartan female footrace),
    100
endurance (karteria), 14, 83, 229
Ennius, 211
Enyalios (god), 82
Enymakratidas (Spartan runner), 79
Eos, 309
Epeius, 302
ephebe (pl. ephebes; young men), 14, 52,
    82–83, 87, 88, 89, 90, 94, 178, 249,
    252, 256, 259, 266, 304
ephēbeia, 87, 92, 93, 97
Ephesus, 56, 107
Ephorus, 75, 358–59n48
Epictetus, 53
Epidaurus, 30, 36, 280
Epirus, 101, 102, 105, 111
Epitaphia, 92
equestrian contests. See hippic events

erastēs (lover), 75, 78, 203, 209, 210, 292–93, 340n38

erection, 235

Eretria, 114

Ergastinai (group of Athenian women weavers), 99

Erichthonius, 286

erōmenos (beloved), 75, 78, 84, 203, 210, 249, 292–93

erōs (desire), 94, 95, 199–273, 276, 292, 299, 328

Eros (god), 3, 4, 6, 9, 12, 24, 70, 85, 89, 90, 93, 95, 180, 182, 184, 193, 194, 196, 199–273, 275, 314, 323, 325, 328, 329, 330
  altar to, 255–57, 273
  as boxer, 260
  as charioteer, 316, 416n207
  as disease, 262
  Games for (Erotidaia), 40
  statue of, 256
  as torch bearer, 258–59, 316
  as umpire, 416n207
  wrestling Anteros, 259–60, 262–64

Eros and Aphrodite, sanctuary of, 257

Erotes, 182, 316–17, 429n151, 429n152

Erotidaea festival, 264–66, 273, 329

Erxias, 266

Eryx, 301

Eteocles, 301

Etruria, 192

Etruscans, 209, 235
  and female athletes, 384n72

Eualkes, 93

euandria (beauty contest), 205, 210, 255, 402n24

Eubatas of Cyrene (footrace victor), 233

euexia (fitness contest), 205, 402n24

eugenics, 124–125

Eumelus, 311

Euripides, 94, 125, 126, 156, 175, 181, 189, 257, 290
  Autolycus, 10, 14
  Helen, 74

Eurotas River, 132, 133

Eustathius, 159, 234

eutaxia (discipline contest), 402n24

Euthymus of Locri (boxing victor), 226, 294

exercise, 229

fame, 10–12, 273, 277, 283, 293, 294, 298, 320
  of athletes, 10, 17, 28, 231
  of women, 21

fatalities in athletics, 304–14

Fat Boy Group (vases), 242

Fates (*Moirai*), 318

fawn, 153, 155, 171, 172, 389n32

feasts within festivals, 25, 99

female athletes, 6, 69, 97, 98–120, 121–38, 139–74, 175–98, 276, 283–84, 286–304, 345n79, 345–46n80
  modern, 333
  in the Roman era, 354n42
  see also women

fencing, Renaissance, 332

festivals, 6, 10–11, 25, 278, 325
  number of athletic, 348n16
  sacred character of, 27, 29–39

fillets, 167, 168, 218, 237, 238, 243, 245, 246, 249, 258

finish line. *See telos, terma*

fire, 256–57

flame, 167, 168, 172, 273
  on an altar, 143

Flamininus, Titus Quinctius (Roman consul), 30, 41, 286

flight and pursuit, 105, 152, 154, 163, 164, 242, 263, 309

flower, 244, 382n52

flute playing, 56, 70, 129, 143, 154, 155, 171, 302, 426n117

football, 200
  American, 330–31
  Renaissance, 332

footrace, 13, 56, 75, 76, 98, 100, 102, 109, 111, 112, 121, 124, 133, 135, 161, 197, 201, 222, 230, 275, 279, 284, 289, 308, 309, 327
  for females, 23, 55, 160, 175–98, 369n25, 383n61, 385n73
  victor, 223

fornication, 230

freedom, 10, 48–49, 249, 251, 267–68, 272, 286, 330, 331
  sacred character of, 27, 29–39
  see also eleutheria
Freud, Sigmund, 200
friendship, 5, 123, 199, 203, 258, 267, 268, 273, 294
funeral, 93, 96, 129
funeral games, 28, 299, 302, 323, 324, 426n117
  at Bouprasion, 372n68
  for Patroclus, 26, 28, 301–302, 310, 347n9
  for Pelias, 175, 225
  for Sisyphus, 312
Funeral Oration, 209

Gaia (at Olympia), 33–34, 114, 115
Galba, Emperor, 48
Galen, 15, 229,230
Games of Pallas, 222, 223
Ganymede, 225
Gardiner, E. N., 42–43, 49, 52, 114
Ge Chthonia festival, 223
gender roles, 6, 275, 323–33, 340–41n39, 431n11
Genesia, 87, 92
genitals, male, 230, 234–36, 238, 241
Getty Museum, 227, 241
Girard, René, 295
girls. *See* maidens
gladiators, 43
  female, 354n42
Glaucus (boxing victor), 298
gloios (salve from sweat), 85
glory, 329
goal. *See* telos; *terma*
Gorgidas of Thebes, 70
Gorgo, 125
Gouldner, Alvin, 10–11
graffiti, 84, 86, 94, 96
  Eros sketches, 258–59
  at Phaistos, 358–59n48
  for Roman gladiator, 249
  at stadium, 206
  at Thera, 367n151
Griffith-Joyner, Florence (Flo-Jo), 200

Group YZ (iii) (vases), 246
gumnos, 271
gunaikonomoi, 122
Guttmann, A., 8, 399n4
gymnasiarch, 91
gymnasium, 11, 12, 14, 88, 89, 90, 121, 182, 187, 190–96, 201, 205, 207, 211–19, 236, 237, 239, 243, 250, 251, 252, 253, 254, 256, 258, 266, 267, 268, 271, 272, 273, 275, 293, 325, 326, 328, 329, 330, 332, 333, 346n80
  and homosexuality, 64, 71–72, 78
  and initiation, 66–68, 70
  Maltho at Elis, 259
  at Olympia, 54
  at Thera, 83–84
gymnic events, 92, 94, 201, 225, 264, 285, 290, 314
  and social class, 13
Gymnopaedia festival, Spartan, 82–83, 86, 126, 362n84, 362n86

Hades, 277, 309
Hadrian, 53–55
Hafner, U., 128, 129
Hagia Triada rhyton, 320, 358–59n48, 430n163
hair, 99, 168, 173, 268
  of Athenian youths, 381n44
  and initiation, 129–30
  of Spartan youths, 380n43
Halieia festival, 264
Hamburg Museum, 130
Hamilton, Richard, 165–73
Hamm, Mia, 199
Harmodius and Aristogeiton, 268, 330, 417n221
Harmonia (goddess), 70, 260
harmony, 70–71. *See also* rituals of conviviality
health, 191, 256
  and athletics, 15–16, 219, 220, 229
Health of the Emperor, Games for, 46
heavy events. *See* combat sports
hēbōntes (age-group), 78
Hecate, 27–28, 282, 324
Hecatombaea festival, 30, 82

Hector, 179, 299–300, 307

Heleneia, 289

Helen of Sparta, 23, 124, 125, 126, 210, 289

Helios, 285

Hellanodikai (Greek Judges), 38, 48, 54

Helotis, cult of, 313

Henrichs, A., 157

Hephaestus, 253

Hera, 98–120, 99, 109, 156, 160, 171, 289, 326, 372n68, 430n160
  and female contests, 24
  Hippia, 318
  at Olympia, 33–34, 39
  Teleia, 318, 372n68
  temple of, 110

Heracleia, 92, 94

Heracleidae, 33

Heracles, 5, 7, 9, 12, 24, 32, 83, 85, 91, 93, 94, 110, 187, 210, 225, 250–55, 267, 273, 275, 279, 286, 301, 329
  altar to, 255
  Idaean, 109, 275, 284
  labors of, 254, 284

Heraia (Games to Hera at Olympia), 38, 40, 98–120, 121, 130, 133, 135, 139, 160, 197, 287, 289, 326, 327, 328

Heraion, Argive, 318

heralds contest, 56

Hermaia (Contests of Hermes), 91, 92, 97, 213, 214

hermaphrodite, 239

Hermes, 5–6, 9, 12, 24, 83, 85, 91, 250–55, 259, 267, 273, 275, 284, 308, 318, 324, 329
  altar to, 255
  enagōnios, 252
  herm statue of, 251
  palaistritēs, 252

Hermione, 130

hero, 93, 94, 96, 134, 135, 210, 232, 254, 276, 283, 284–86, 288, 294, 312, 317, 323, 324, 326

Herod I, king of Judea, 43

Herodas (poet), 227, 314

Herodes Atticus, 54–55

Herodotus, 10, 15, 129

Heroön of Iphigeneia, 167

Hesiod, 27–28, 73–74, 164, 175, 176, 179, 197, 282, 324, 328

Hestia, 114

hetairai (courtesans), 128, 226–27, 246, 265, 266, 270, 328, 392n61, 407n84

heterosexuality, 200, 202, 203, 222, 225, 236, 237, 242, 246, 260, 263, 266, 271

Hiero, 225

himatia, 143, 169, 171

himeros, 203

Hippias, 256, 257, 273, 365n124

hippic events, 92, 94, 201, 264, 270, 285, 309–18
  and gender, 344n70
  at Olympia, 52, 76, 79, 350n41, 354n34
  in the Roman era, 43, 48
  and social class, 13

Hippocleas of Thessaly (footrace victor), 26–27, 35, 224–25

Hippodameia, 32, 38, 73, 99, 110, 111, 112, 113, 114, 115, 116, 118, 119, 120, 135, 160, 289, 301, 312, 317, 326, 372n68

Hippodameion, 109, 117

hippodrome, 93, 285
  at Corinth, 313
  at Delphi, 313
  at Isthmia, 312–313
  at Mantinea, 313
  at Olympia, 312, 317
  at Sparta, 313

Hippolytus, 156, 177, 179

Hippomenes (Athenian archon), 309

Hippomenes (legendary hero), 106, 161, 163, 175–98, 308

Hippothales (Platonic character), 217

HIV virus, 200

Holloway, R. R., 172

Homer, 14, 17, 25, 26, 28, 67–69, 86, 96, 114, 127, 179, 201, 294, 297, 299–300, 302, 304, 310, 311, 323–24, 325, 328
  Iliad, 205
  Odyssey, 126

Homeric Hymn to Apollo, 27, 324

homoeroticism, 123, 206, 219, 225, 236, 239, 260, 263, 266, 327, 328

homosexuality, 200, 202, 203, 211–219, 222, 246, 249
  female, 78, 97, 326
  male, 64–97, 328

honor, 5, 10, 14, 283, 311, 329, 339n29
  from the gods, 28s

hoplite race, 264, 308

hoplites, 14, 89, 96, 189, 223, 304

hoplomachia (combat in armor), 87, 302–305, 426n114

horse imagery for marriage, 135

horse racing, 269, 309

hostility, 267

hunting, 88, 89, 162, 164, 170, 177, 178, 181, 186, 189, 309, 320, 365n123, 389n32
  and Artemis, 153, 154, 157, 163, 389n33, 389n34
  in Spartan ritual, 81–82

hunting spectacle, 302

Hyacinthia festival, 83

Hyacinthus, 73–74, 94, 308

hybris, 11, 19–20, 23, 283, 301, 306, 339n30, 343n59

Hyginus, 28, 175, 177, 178, 180, 182, 187

Ibycus, 125, 127, 182, 197, 270

Iccus of Tarentum (pentathlon victor), 230–31, 234

Idomeneus, 311

Ikadion (Olympic runner), 76

ila (company), 122

Indo-European ritual, 64, 67, 70, 72, 75, 88, 89, 95

infibulation (*kunodesmē*), 202, 234–36, 241, 282, 408n101, 408n104

initiation, 5–6, 31–32, 64–97, 217, 275, 276, 290, 332–33
  prenuptial, 121–38, 327, 390n41
  tribal, 65

inscriptions, 295, 296, 304, 305, 325

Iphigeneia, 149, 156, 390n42

Iphitus, king of Pisa, 34, 109, 110, 116

Iolaeia, 94

Iolaus, 93, 94

Ionia, 127

isolympian games, 46

Issoria, 289

Isthmia (sanctuary), 42, 48–49, 92, 93, 271, 280, 284, 296, 326

Isthmian Games (Isthmia), 29–30, 41, 51, 76, 96, 269, 285, 294

Istros, 233

Italy, 105, 127, 192, 324–25

Jason, 232, 279

javelin, 245

javelin-throwing, 3, 13, 32, 56, 87, 124, 136, 201, 308

Jeanmaire, H., 64, 68–69, 83, 95

Jews, 52

Johnson, Magic, 200

Jordan, Michael, 199

judges at Olympia. *See* Hellanodikai

jumping, 56

jump, long, 201

Kahil, Lily, 139, 140, 148, 165–73

Kaisareia festival, 46

kaloikagathoi, 207

kalokagathia, 205, 217

kalos (beautiful), 205, 206, 217, 218

Karneiatai (Spartan tribes), 81–82

Kennell, Nigel, 77, 83

Kerameikos, 302

Keuls, E., 401n20

kissing, 95, 238

Klee, T., 80, 92

Kleomolpos, 189

kleos. See fame

Koni(s)alos (dance; salve; god), 85–86

konis (dust), 86, 229, 282, 306

kouroi statues, 10, 207, 338n24

kratēriskoi, 139–74, 166–74

krokōtos (saffron garment), 147, 149, 157, 158, 166

krypteia (ritual seclusion), 81, 87

kudos (glory, fame), 339n30

kunodesmē. See infibulation

Kyle, Donald, 92

Kyle, J. W., 169

Laconia, 127, 129
Lactantius, 199, 211, 271
Lais (hetaira), 232–33
Laius of Thebes, 70, 73, 93
Lampito, 127, 128
Langlotz, E., 127–28
Larisa, Thessaly, 267
Lato Phytia, 126
laughter. *See* ridicule
law, 88, 91, 92, 96, 307
leaden plates, 234
Leagros, 205
Lee, Hugh, 33
legislation on gymnasia, 211–19
Leonidaion (building at Olympia),
    53
Leontiscus (pankration victor), 227
Lerna, 114
Lesbos, 327
Leto, 82, 110, 154, 171
Leucippides, 100, 104, 105, 111, 116,
    119, 120, 134, 135
Leucippus, 126
Libanius, 74
libations within festivals, 25
Libys, 223
Livy, 30, 51
local games. *See* thematic games
Locri Epizephyrii, 99
London, British Museum, 133
long-jumping, 246
loutērion (washbasin), 184, 191
lover. *See* erastēs
love-wrestling, 269
Lucian, 342n46
    Anarcharsis, 6, 10, 12, 14, 208, 278,
        282, 297, 308
    and athletic values, 15–17, 20
    On the Death of Peregrinus, 55
    Dialogus deorum, 74
Lucillius (Greek poet), 269
Lycaia Games (Arcadia), 80
Lyceum, 204, 218
Lycurgus (Athenian), 281
Lycurgus (father of Opheltes), 286
Lycurgus (Spartan lawgiver), 13, 34,
    78, 101, 122, 124, 125, 220

lyre-player, 243, 411n134
Lysis, 91, 217

Macedonia, 267
Macedonian wars, 41, 45
Madonna, 210
maenads, 290–91
magic and contests, 347n6
maidens, 21, 66, 75, 84, 87, 90, 270,
    272, 287, 327
    as spectators, 38, 222–26, 248,
        345n77, 406n68
    in contests, 23, 31, 38, 78, 98–198,
        219–220, 423n62
    in gymnasium, 190–96, 237, 346n80
Mallwitz, Alfred, 35
Mandrogenes (pankration victor), 298,
    306
Marcus Aurelius, Emperor, 41, 55
Marius (Roman consul), 42
marriage, 71, 75, 78, 98, 101, 105, 106,
    112, 113, 119, 124, 125, 135, 149,
    156, 157, 158, 159, 160, 164, 219–
    26, 233, 260, 266, 272, 273, 289,
    328
    age at Sparta, 378n28
marriage (bride) contests, 28–29, 73,
    178–85, 223–26, 301, 327
McDonald, M., 211
Medea, 232
medieval tournament, 332
Mehl, E., 98
Meilanion. *See* Hippomenes
Melampus, 164
Melancomas of Caria (boxing victor), 52,
    232, 234
Melanion, 106, 161–62, 163
Meleager, 178, 181, 189, 248
Meleager Painter, 246, 248
Menelaus, 302, 310, 311
Menoetes, 301
Messenia, 115
metagraffito, 206
Metroön (Temple of the Mother Goddess
    at Olympia), 46
Metropolitan Museum, New York, 130
Middle Ages, 332

Midea, 117
Miletus, 51, 71, 251
military training, 66–67, 77, 82, 87, 208, 209, 304, 322
Milo of Croton, 294, 297
mimesis, 279
Minos, 90
mirror handles, 127–37
mirror held by Eros, 195
Mithridates Painter, 246
moderation, 52–53, 71–72, 180, 202
modesty, 235, 236
Monroe, Marilyn, 210
Montepaone, C., 157
Moretti, L., 76, 79–80
Mount Helicon, 265
Mummius, Lucius, 42
Munichia festival, 139, 155, 158
Munichion, 31, 126, 139, 140, 151, 158, 159, 165, 166, 172, 173, 174, 327
murder, 285
Musaea festival, 265
Muses, 265
musical contests, 46, 48, 55, 225, 264, 265, 273, 278, 285
Mycenaean Age, 32–33
Myrtilus, 312
myth, 26, 28–29, 30, 32–33, 36, 47, 60, 73–75, 153, 171, 178, 181, 190, 197, 212, 223, 225–26, 232, 246, 254, 279, 284–86, 300–304, 307, 308, 320, 324, 326, 331, 422n47
  of Artemis, 155, 161–66
  of Er, 181
  as historical evidence, 66, 74

Narcaeus, 118, 288, 289
neaniskoi, 213, 214, 217, 218, 266
necessity, natural (anagkē), 220, 248
Neleus, 110
Nemea (sanctuary), 29, 33, 36–37, 206, 271, 280, 284, 285, 295, 300, 314, 326
Nemean Games (Nemea), 29, 73, 76, 96, 253, 269, 285–86
Nemean lion, 286
neoi (youths), 213, 214, 218

Nero, Emperor, 30, 41, 46, 48, 52–53
Neroneia festival, 46
Nerva, Emperor, 53
Nestor, 310
Nicholson, Jack, 419n11
Nikander (poet), 74
Nike, 243
Nikegoras (female footrace victor), 287
Nikophon (Olympic boxer), 51
Nilsson, M. P., 82, 135, 150
nocturnal emission, 229, 234
Nonnus (poet), 177, 179, 180, 269, 292
nudity, 71, 75, 96, 101, 106–107, 108, 124, 129, 130, 201, 205, 211, 212, 220, 271, 272, 273, 282, 297, 308, 326, 328, 332
  athletic adoption of, 211–12, 404n45
  female, 78, 143, 145, 147, 148, 149, 151, 157, 163, 167, 168, 169, 184, 207–8, 378n19, 379–80n39
  male, 83
  terminology, 403n27
Nymphaeum of Regilla, 54
nymphs, 109–110

O'Brien, Joan, 113
odes, 295
Odysseus, 17, 26, 29, 126, 225, 301
Oenomaus, king of Elis, 28–29, 32, 118, 119, 285, 301, 312
oikos (household), 283
oil, 229, 282
oil flask, 130, 191, 193, 236, 238, 245, 381–82n51
Olympia, 21–22, 32–39, 40–63, 76, 93, 96, 98–120, 114, 121, 135, 160, 197, 224, 234, 253, 259, 260, 279, 284, 296, 298, 305, 306, 327
  cult officials at, 47
  Sacred Way to, 42
Olympics (Olympic Games), 21, 26, 29, 40–63, 73, 92, 96, 98, 100, 112, 116, 117, 118, 125, 151, 200, 222, 223, 224, 226, 231, 253, 259, 264, 269, 284, 289
  armistice for, 37–38

foundation myths for, 28, 32–34,
    284–85, 349n21
historical foundation of, 29, 34–39
modern, 332
Nero and, 47–49
oath, 38
Sparta and, 79–80
Olympic stadium, 99, 280
capacity of, 420n23
Olympic victors (*Olympionikai*), 51, 76,
    95, 274, 296, 325
Spartan, 79–80
ōphein (to copulate), 83–84
Opheltes (legendary Nemean infant),
    286
Opiatos (footrace victor), 298
Orchomenos, 119
Orestes, 301, 309
orgia, 118, 135
orgy, 269
Oribasius, 229
Oropus, 92
Orsippus of Megara (footrace victor),
    125, 308, 309
Orthia (deme of Elis), 99, 118
Osborne, R., 149, 157
Oschophoria (Athenian festival), 31, 36,
    66, 90, 97, 150, 290, 365n128,
    365n132
Ovid, 126, 153, 171, 175, 178, 180, 181
Oxylus (Dorian leader), 33–34, 308

Paestum, 134
paideia, 6, 12–13, 17, 86, 87, 88, 92, 93,
    94, 95, 97, 98, 123, 139, 217, 275,
    277, 323, 325, 326, 328, 329, 330,
    333
    and initiation, 67, 69–73, 75–76, 79–
    80, 84
paides (boys' age-group), 78, 213, 214,
    217, 218, 266
paidiskoi (youths' age-group), 78
paidonomoi (supervisors of young men),
    122
paidotribēs (trainer), 212, 213, 216
Palaemon (divinity at Isthmia), 285
Palaestra (goddess), 182, 252

palaestra (pl. palaestrae; wrestling
    school), 70, 72, 88, 91, 95, 96, 97,
    126, 129, 207, 212, 219, 236, 252,
    254, 266, 268, 271, 330
of Taureas, 218
Palaimonion (shrine to Palaemon), 93
Palaiokrassa, L., 140
Palermo, 102, 104, 105, 133, 134
Palestrina, 192
palm branch, 130, 249, 251, 259
palm tree, 143, 150, 153, 166, 167, 170
Pan, 254, 318
Panathenaic games (Panathenaia), 29–
    30, 37, 56, 87, 89, 92, 149, 205,
    223, 255, 259, 264, 271, 286, 325,
    364n116
Panathenaic stadium, 281
pankration, 11, 56, 79, 82, 231, 254,
    259, 269, 279, 294, 304, 305–306,
    307, 319
Pantarkes of Elis (wrestling victor), 260
Patrae (Patras), 49, 287
Pausanias, 21, 32, 34, 38, 49, 55, 82, 98,
    109, 112, 113, 114, 115, 117, 118, 119,
    133, 187, 224, 225, 256, 257, 259,
    265, 285, 287, 297, 312, 313, 329
value as a source, 55
pederasty, 64–97, 88, 89, 92, 93, 95, 96,
    123, 199, 211–219, 260, 268, 271,
    325, 326, 328, 329, 330, 332
Peisistratids, 256, 268
Peisistratus, 213, 256, 257, 268, 273,
    325, 330
Peitho, 260
Peleus, 29, 129, 130, 175, 182, 187, 189,
    190, 193, 194, 195, 196, 197, 199,
    225, 236, 308, 309
Pelias, 94, 189
games of, 187
Pelopion (shrine for Pelops), 32–34, 93,
    274, 324, 373n72
Peloponnese, 127
Pelops, 18, 28–29, 32–34, 36–38, 73, 112,
    113, 114, 117, 160, 225, 275, 279,
    285, 289, 307, 312, 317, 324, 326
"Mound of," 117, 118
on Olympia pediment, 422n44

Penelope, 254, 301

penis, *See* genitals, male

pentaploa, 90

pentathlon, 13, 36, 56, 130, 201, 225, 238, 239, 264, 279

peplos, 98, 99, 100, 112, 115, 368n9, 368n10, 377n15

Percy, William, 71, 75

performance (drama) in athletic contests, 23, 28, 269, 273, 274–322

Pericles, 16, 21, 25, 87, 209

Periodic Games (Circuit Games; *periodos*), 30, 46, 55–56, 326

periodic occurrence (of ritual), 68–69

periodonikeis (circuit victors), 46, 296

perizōma (trunks; loincloths), 186, 189, 209, 297, 308, 309, 396n35. *See also* trunks

Perizōma Group (vases), 209

Perlman, P., 148

Persephone, 99, 309

Perseus, 308

persona, 296

personal best (of an athlete), 294

perspiration (*gloios*), 229

Phaestus, 126

Phaleron, 150

Pheidippides, 309

Phidias, 42, 48, 53–54, 260

philia, 249, 250, 259, 294, 295, 329, 330, 331, 332. *See also* friendship

Philip V, king of Macedon, 267

Philocles of Argos, 206

Philolaus (Theban lawgiver), 94, 97, 328, 367n154

Philostratus, 14, 35–36, 74, 79–80, 125, 136, 140, 151, 210, 227, 229, 252, 274, 298, 305–306, 388n25

phitidia (communal meals), 78, 80–81

Phlegon, 32, 32, 34

Photius, 236

phratries, 87

Phryne (hetaira), 265, 266

Physcoa (heroine from Elis), 99, 110, 112, 116, 118, 119, 120, 160, 288, 289

Pindar, 6, 11, 12, 14, 25, 29, 93, 107, 122, 253, 254, 272, 277, 283, 284, 285, 296, 305, 307, 310, 342n49

on athletes and gods, 26–27

and athletic values, 17–20, 341n44

on the Olympic origins, 32, 34, 73

and sexuality, 73, 222–26, 406–407n76

Piraeus, 31, 158

Pisa, 69–69, 99, 111, 115, 116, 117, 277

plague, 158

Plataea, 267, 298, 308

Platanistas (Spartan ritual), 79, 82

Plato, 11, 14, 71–72, 82, 91, 101, 122, 124, 126, 135, 148, 181, 198, 203, 205, 207, 208, 211, 217, 220, 222, 230, 231, 232, 248, 250, 251, 256, 258, 263, 264, 267, 283, 304, 329

Lysis, 204

on *paideia*, 340n38

Phaedrus, 204

Symposium, 204

pleasure (*terpsis*) in competition, 15, 25, 27, 342n47

Pleket, H. W., 14

Plutarch, 21, 70–72, 78, 94, 118, 119, 122, 124, 125, 126, 129, 210, 212, 213, 220, 222, 232, 248, 256, 265, 271, 289, 308

Polemarchos (pankratiast), 305, 306

polis, 96, 122, 269, 286, 326, 331

Polybius, 42

Polycrates of Samos (tyrant), 267, 268, 329–30

Polydamas of Scotoussa, 294, 298

Polydeuces (heroic boxer), 301

Polyneices, 301

Polyphonte, 161, 163–64

pornai (prostitute), 226–27

Poseidon, 29–30, 73, 225, 285, 313

Earthshaker, 313

Hippios, 313, 318

pothos, 203

Praeneste, 192

Praschniker, C., 127–28

Praxidamas, 110

Praxiteles, 111, 264, 266

prenuptial ritual, 126, 286–90

prize games. *See* thematic games
prizes, 16, 28, 209, 243, 244, 246, 249,
    255, 263, 282–83, 290, 294, 300,
    308, 311, 381n48
Proetids, 163, 164
Proetus, 163, 164
professionalism in Greek athletics, 29,
    40–41
Promachus (pankration victor), 298
Prometheia festival, 255, 257
Prometheus, 273
    altar to, 255
Propertius, 121, 126, 161
prostitutes and prostitution, 203, 226–
    27, 249, 272, 328
    female, 246
    male, 214
prostitution, 328
Prytaneion at Olympia, 54, 114
Pseudo-Lucian's *The Ass*, 216
Pythagoras, 51, 271
Pythagoreans, 234
Pythian Games (Pythia), 17, 26–27, 29–30,
    76, 96, 116, 223, 224, 231, 285, 296

Q Painter, 246
Quintilian, 53

rank-demonstration, 329–30. *See also*
    contest system, Greek
Reconciliation (*Diallagē*) 262–63
records, 8, 363n101
Reeder, E. D., 171
Regilla, wife of Herodes Atticus, 55
release, 291
    of emotions, 331, 324, 325, 331, 332
religion, 5, 9, 25–39
    and Spartan education, 77
revolution, Greek athletic, 271, 326
Richter, G. M. A., 128
ridicule, 207–209
risk, 18–19, 23, 273, 275, 293, 305, 307,
    310, 320
rites of passage, 4–5, 65, 73, 77, 165. *See
    also* initiation
ritual(s), 5, 8, 155, 255
    of conviviality, 12, 20, 324, 330

Rodman, Dennis, 199
Roman Games (Rhomaia), 46
Romans, 209, 267
    and their sports, 425n102
Rome, 249, 265
    site of Greek athletics, 43
    site of Olympics (80 B.C.), 42
rule, 282
running, 165, 173

Sacred Battalion (Sacred Company), 70,
    93, 268, 325–26
sacrifice, 25, 37, 111, 164, 165, 217,
    274, 308, 320
    to Athena, 256
Salamis vase with girl runners, 109,
    140, 151, 169, 386n10
Sallares, Robert, 71
Samos, 129, 266, 268, 273, 330
Sansone, David, 8–9
Sappho, 100, 123, 266, 327
sarcophagi, 314, 317
satyrs, 235, 251, 290–91
Schmitt-Pantel, Pauline, 12
Schnapp, Alain, 88
Schoeneus, 175, 177, 178, 179,
    184
Schwarzenegger, Arnold, 210,
    419n11
Scira, 150
sculpture, 13, 22, 110, 127, 202, 210,
    328. *See also* statues; statuettes
segregation, initiatory, 69–70, 73, 75,
    95, 107, 122, 123, 157, 289, 376n5.
    See also krypteia
self-control, 227–36, 276, 408n105. *See
    also* moderation
self-sufficiency, 10–11, 12, 209, 272,
    294, 295, 297, 331, 339n28
sēma (sign, marker), 310–11
semen, 229, 234
Sergent, Bernard, 67, 70, 83, 93, 95
Serwint, Nancy, 107, 108
Seven Heroes, 285–86
sex, 178–79 199–273. *See also*
    Aphrodite; *erōs*
sex symbols, 210

shame (*aidōs*), 11, 18–21, 208, 236, 301, 343n59
Shapiro, Alan, 89
shield of Alcibiades, 253
Sicilian Expedition, 268
Sicily, 94
sickle, 130
Sikyon, 45, 56
Silaris Treasury, 102, 134
Simon, E., 168, 171
Simonides, 205
siren, 143, 155, 171, 172
Sixteen Women, 99, 100, 112, 115, 116, 117, 118, 119, 120, 160, 288, 373n79, 374n95, 384n69
separation, 87
slaves and slavery, 88, 212–213, 214, 216, 353n32, 405n50
soccer, 332
Socrates, 91, 217, 218, 238
Solon, 87, 88, 89, 91, 96, 272, 325
    in Lucian's *Anacharsis*, 10, 15–17, 20, 24, 208, 304
    in Herodotus, 10, 429n157
Solonian legislation, 212–214, 218, 257
sōma. See body
Sophocles, 92, 175, 261, 309–10
sōphrosunē. See moderation
Sosipolis (cult at Olympia), 38–39, 114, 116
Sourvinou-Inwood, C., 140, 148, 157, 166
Sparta, 77–83, 87, 92, 93, 95, 96, 98, 99, 100, 101, 102, 105, 107, 111, 115, 116, 119, 121–38, 160, 189, 193, 207, 213, 220, 222, 268, 276, 284, 287, 288, 325, 326, 327, 328, 333
    and education, 74, 86
    local festivals at, 79–80
spectators, 278, 280, 302, 423n59
sphaireis (ballplayers), 83
sphairomachia (ball-fighting), 304, 427n122
spondophoroi (truce-bearing messengers), 37
sport(s), 7–9, 25
    definition of, 337n13
    modern, 330–333, 430–31n10

stade race (one-stade footrace), 32, 56, 100, 140, 223, 264, 274–322
    at the Heraia, 368n14
    at Olympia, 35–36, 69, 76
stadium, 93, 109, 182, 190, 206, 243, 269, 272, 280–81, 285, 294, 304
    at Olympia, 35–37, 54
    at Thera, 84–85
stage, 280–81
Stallone, Sylvester, 210
Staphylodromoi (*Staphylodromia*) (Spartan footrace), 31, 36, 82, 90, 135, 150, 362n80
statues, 49, 116, 251, 295, 297, 325, 328, 329
    of Augustus at Olympia, 46
    see also sculpture
statuettes, bronze, of girl athletes 127–37, 378–79n29. *See also* mirror handles
stephanitic games (crown games), 29
Stesichorus, 182, 197
Stewart, Andrew, 75
Stobaeus, 126
Strabo, 32–33, 127
Strato (poet), 216, 219, 249
Street, Picabo, 199
strength, 198, 229, 252, 253, 266, 273
    in athletes, 10, 12, 28, 232
    and cult, 5
    initiatory test of, 65, 69, 81–82, 111, 112, 121, 122, 165, 225, 376n5
strigil, 130, 184, 191, 192, 193, 194, 236, 237, 239, 241, 245, 290, 291
Suetonius, 216
Sulla, 42
sweat. *See* perspiration
symposia, 13, 189, 213, 231–32, 239, 261
syncretism, religious and athletic, 46, 353n20
Synesius, 85
syssitia (communal meals), 71, 75

tameness, 153, 154, 156, 161, 162, 163, 164, 170, 181, 283, 288
Tanagra larnax, 302

Tantalus, 73

Taraxippus (Olympic divinity), 312–14

Tarentum, 258

team contests, 79, 331

Telemachus of Pharsalus (wrestling victor), 306–307

Telesicrates of Cyrene, 222, 223, 296

telos (goal), 23, 177, 179, 198, 224, 272, 282–83, 293, 296, 318

Temessa, Italy, 226

terma, 184, 194, 243, 246, 256, 310, 311, 313, 314

terpsis. See pleasure

thanatos, 292, 299

Thanatos (god), 301

theater, 28–81, 281

Thebes, 70–71, 93–95, 97, 111, 268, 325

thematic games (prize or local games), 29

Themis, 34

Theocritus, 95, 124, 132, 133, 179

Theodosius I, Emperor, 41

Theogenes of Thasos, 279, 294, 306

Theognetus of Aegina (wrestler), 205

Theognis of Megara, 176, 197, 211, 271, 327

Theokoleon (priest's house) at Olympia, 54

Theopompus (historian), 384n72

Theoria, 159, 160, 269, 288, 289, 392n62

Thera, 83–86, 95, 96, 325, 326, 367n151

Thermon, 114

Thersites, 205

Theseia, 92, 205
  games in Athens, 304

Theseus, 66, 90, 126, 232, 279, 286, 301, 365n128

Thespiae (Boeotia), 40, 264–66, 268, 273, 329

Thessaly, 107

Thetis, 309

Thucydides, 16, 21, 25, 209, 225, 268

Thurii, 71, 250

Thyia, 118, 160, 374n95

thyiades, 119

Tiberius Claudius Rufus (Olympic pankratiast), 52

Tiberius, Emperor, 47

timē. See fame

Timocles, 86

Titas (Olympic victor), 76

Tithonus, 309

Titus, Emperor, 47, 53

toil (*ponos*), 14, 18, 218–19, 291, 307, 322

tomb, 93, 94, 95

torch, 89, 141, 149, 151, 167, 169, 173, 415n186, 415n193

torch-races, 87, 149, 264, 266, 279, 290, 325, 414n173, 414n174
  Eros as runner in, 258–59
  at the Panathenaia, 255, 273, 329, 364n116
  at the Prometheia, 255

track. *See dromos*

trainer, 214–16, 234, 245, 249, 271, 297–98, 305

training, 229, 234, 255, 256, 259, 271, 326

Trajan, Emperor, 53

transvestism, 66, 90, 108, 370n37

Trent Museum, 130

tribes, 65–67, 81, 90
  of Attica, 255
  in Greek cities, 356n9

tripod, 186, 372n66

Truce of Iphitus, 34

truce, messengers of. *See spondophoroi*

truces during festivals, 81

trumpeters contest, 56

trunks (loincloths), 194, 209, 391n47.
  See also perizôma

Tunic (*Chitôn*; weaving house at Amyclae), 100

Tunis Eros statue, 258

tunnel, as entrance to stadia
  at Epidaurus, 36
  at Nemea, 36–37, 206
  at Olympia, 36–37

turning posts, 256, 290, 310–18, 429n148

Tyndaridai, 134, 135

tyranny, 199, 211, 250, 329
tyrants, 89, 267, 268, 269
Tyrtaeus, 14, 300
Tyson, Mike, 399n3
Tzetzes (scholiast), 182

value prizes, 10
Vatican Museums, 101
Veii Painter, 241
Vespasian, Emperor, 41, 53
victor, 280
    female, 110
    statues, 110, 205
victory, 243, 244, 245, 246, 251, 256,
    258, 268, 273, 276, 293, 294, 297,
    305, 306, 307, 317
Vidal-Naquet, P., 66, 87, 89, 149
violence, 295–96, 307, 330–31
virgins. See maidens
von Vacano, O., 98

walk-over victory (akoniti), 11
warfare, 124, 201, 277, 300, 304, 307,
    320, 322, 276, 282. See also military
    training
Washing Painter, 242
wealth, 10, 343n58
Weismuller, Johnny, 419n11
Weniger, L., 109
whipping ritual, 81, 83, 88, 182, 213,
    275
wildness, 105, 132, 149, 153, 156, 157,
    161, 162, 163, 164, 170, 181, 283,
    288, 289
wine, 261
Winkler, Jack, 220
woman-and-athlete vase motif, 193
women
    in the Arkteia, 139–74
    attending the Olympics, 38–39, 234
    in the Heraia, 38
    and initiation, 64
    see also female athletes
World Wrestling Federation, 7
wreath, 149, 150, 166, 168, 169, 172,
    173, 424n79
wrestling, 32, 36, 56, 69, 82, 92, 124,
    136, 182, 184, 185, 193, 197, 201,
    216, 217, 219, 230, 236, 249,
    252, 253, 254, 259, 260, 262,
    264, 269, 277, 279, 284, 286,
    304, 307, 327
    of Atalanta, 185–90

Xenocrates (poet), 252
Xenophanes (philosopher), 12
Xenophon of Athens (historian) , 13, 21,
    78, 124, 177, 178
Xenophon of Ephesus (novelist), 225

Young, David, 40–41

Zanes (statues of Zeus), 38
Zephyrus (god), 74
zero-sum contest, 11, 71, 339n29,
    339n30, 340n37
Zeus, 29, 32, 109, 110, 112, 114, 115,
    120, 161, 171, 175, 225, 253, 268,
    275, 285, 289, 324
    Altar of, at Olympia, 34–37, 39, 114,
    151, 274
    Bringer of Fate, 318
    cult at Olympia, 350n33
    Eleutherios (of Freedom), 267, 286
    Horkios (of Oaths), 38
    Most High, 318
    statue in Olympic Bouleuterion, 38
    statue in temple at Olympia, 42, 48,
    53–54, 260
    Stoa of, 169
    Temple of, at Olympia, 32, 53–54, 253,
    284–85

Date Due